A Special Issue of
Visual Cognition

Neural Binding of Space and Time: Spatial and Temporal Mechanisms of Feature–Object Binding

Edited by

Hermann J. Müller and Mark A. Elliott
University of Munich, Germany

Christoph Herrmann and Axel Mecklinger
Max-Planck Institute of Cognitive Neuroscience, Germany

PSYCHOLOGY PRESS
Taylor & Francis Group

Published in 2001 by Psychology Press Ltd
27 Church Road, Hove, East Sussex BN3 2FA

www.psypress.co.uk

Simultaneously published in the USA and Canada
by Taylor & Francis Inc
29 West 35th Street, New York, NY 10001

Psychology Press is part of the Taylor & Francis Group

British Library Cataloguing in Publication Data
A catalogue record for this book is available from the British Library

ISBN 1–84169–913–6
ISSN 1350-6285

Cover design by Joyce Chester
Typeset in the UK by Quorum Technical Services Ltd, Cheltenham
Printed in the UK by Henry Ling Ltd, Dorchester
Bound in the UK by TJ International Ltd, Padstow

Contents*

---

* This book is also a special issue of the journal *Visual Cognition* and forms Issues 3, 4 and 5 of Volume 8 (2001). The page numbers are taken from the journal and so begin with p. 273.

VISUAL COGNITION, 2001, *8* (3/4/5), 273–285

Neural binding of space and time: An introduction

Hermann J. Müller and Mark A. Elliott
Institute of Psychology, General and Experimental Psychology, University of Munich, Germany

Christoph S. Herrmann
Max Planck Institute of Cognitive Neuroscience, Leipzig, Germany

Axel Mecklinger
Max Planck Institute of Cognitive Neuroscience, Leipzig, and Department of Psychology, Saarland University, Saarbrücken, Germany

Some of the central problems to be solved by the brain, such as figure–ground coding and object recognition, concern the binding of separately coded feature elements into coherent object representations. The binding problem has recently been approached by a variety of disciplines, notably psychophysics and experimental psychology, electrophysiology and neurophysiology, and computational modelling. This Special Issue brings together 21 of papers, mainly all from psychology and computational modelling, that address issues in Gestalt formation, the relation of the grouping and binding processes to visual attention, the role of temporal factors for grouping and binding, the neuronal correlates of binding mechanisms, the development of binding operations in infants, and the breakdown of these processes following brain damage.

Some of the central problems to be solved by the brain—such as figure–ground coding, object recognition, and the formation of object memories—concern the binding of separable elements into coherent structures. The binding problem has recently been approached by investigators in a variety of disciplines,

---

Please address all correspondence to H.J. Müller, Allgemeine und Experimentelle Psychologie, Institut für Psychologie, Ludwig-Maximilians-Universität München, Leopoldstraße 13, D-80802 München, Germany. Email: mueller@psy.uni-muenchen.de

The authors express gratitude to the Deutsche Forschungsgemeinschaft (DFG, German National Research Council) for supporting the symposium "Neural binding of space and time" out of which this Special Issue developed. Preparation of this editorial was supported by DFG grant Schr 375/8-1 (3), and it benefited from insightful comments by Hans-Georg Geissler and Glyn W. Humphreys.

http://www.tandf.co.uk/journals/pp/13506285.html DOI:10.1080/13506280143000007

notably psychology (psychophysics and experimental psychology), physiology (electrophysiology and neurophysiology), and computational modelling (neurocomputing). Within psychology, researchers have been concerned with the Gestalt principles of perceptual grouping, the relation of the grouping and binding processes to visual attention, the role of binding processes in memory formation, and with how these principles and processes are implemented in the feature–object coding system. One recent strand of the psychological work has examined the role of temporal factors for grouping and binding using psychophysical means. This work has been inspired by prominent studies in neurophysiology, which found that, when feature elements were presented simultaneously and their arrangement accorded to some Gestalt principle, visuo-cortical cells responding to those elements adjusted their firing pattern and oscillated in synchrony, with zero phase lag. These findings have been taken to suggest that the critical neurophysiological correlates of perceptual grouping and binding are synchronous and oscillatory patterns of activity that are phase-locked across feature-coding neurones. Last but not least, investigators in computational modelling have studied how synchronization and phase-locking may be realized in networks of oscillating neurons, what constraints must be implemented to achieve elementary grouping and binding operations, how such networks give rise to fully assembled object representations that may be compared with object descriptions stored in visual memory, and how contextual memories are formed.

What follows is a brief overview of important issues and developments within the three disciplines of psychology, neurophysiology, and computational modelling, relating to the theme of this Special Issue.

PSYCHOLOGY

In the first decades of this century, the Gestalt psychologists (Wertheimer, 1912, 1923; Köhler, 1924; Koffka, 1935) were concerned with the principles governing perceptual organization or grouping and figure–ground perception (e.g., Rubin, 1915). Amongst the "laws" of perceptual organization that have been described, are grouping based on proximity, continuation (e.g., collinearity), similarity, and common-fate motion. More recently, psychologists working within the Gestalt tradition have postulated further laws, such as uniform connectedness and common region (Palmer, 1992; Palmer & Rock, 1994). Furthermore, there have been attempts to re-address the issue of figure–ground coding. Using reversible patterns such as Rubin's face–vase pictures, this work showed that the dividing edge is assigned to just one of the patterns: That which is perceived as the figure (e.g., Baylis & Driver, 1995). There have also been early attempts to explain the brain mechanisms underlying perceptual grouping (e.g., Köhler, Held, & O'Connell, 1952), which were, however, limited by the knowledge available at the time concerning the functioning of the (visual) brain. Importantly, however, the Gestalt psychologists proposed that perceptual organization and figure–ground coding is based on hard-wired brain mechanisms that operate preattentively.

By contrast, subsequent theories in information processing psychology have proposed that (correct) feature–object bindings require attention (e.g., Treisman & Gelade, 1980). According to the notion of *attentional* binding, the initial parallel (or simultaneous) coding of feature elements across the visual scene is followed by a serial traversal of the display by a focal-attentional mechanism. As attention is focused on a cluster of features, they are transiently "bound" into a coherent object representation (see also Crick, 1984). In contrast, alternative theories of *preattentive* feature conjunction (e.g., Duncan & Humphreys, 1989) have proposed that at least some types of feature bindings can occur during the parallel stage of visual coding, and the resulting feature assemblies compete for access to the limited-capacity object recognition stage. Evidence in favour of the latter theories was provided by visual search experiments which showed that Kanizsa figures defined by good-continuation illusory contours were detected in parallel (e.g., Davis & Driver, 1994), as were breaches of collinearity within single Kanizsa-type figures (Donnelly, Humphreys, & Riddoch, 1991).

Other recent research in psychology have been inspired by findings from single-cell recordings (see later) pointing to a role of synchronized visuo-cortical cell oscillations for feature-object binding (temporal binding). There have been several attempts to examine the temporal-binding hypothesis psychophysically, by testing whether synchronized target element presentation, asynchronized relative to background element presentation, promotes efficient target coding at particular stimulus presentation frequencies (e.g., Blake & Yang, 1997; Fahle, 1993; Fahle & Koch, 1995; Kiper, Gegenfurtner, & Movshon, 1991, 1996; Leonards, Singer, & Fahle, 1996). Although the results tended to be inconsistent, several novel paradigms have been developed recently supporting the notion that feature–object binding involves temporal coding (e.g., Elliott & Müller, 1998; Usher & Donnelly, 1998). Thus, the emerging psychological evidence is that perceptual organization operates at early, preattentive levels of visual processing and that temporal coding might play a role in these processes.

NEUROPHYSIOLOGY

Single cell studies have long been informative about the nature of neural coding (e.g., Hubel & Wiesel, 1968). Much of the early work on low-level coding in vision indicated that there was considerable separation of the neural pathways for different properties of the image: For shape, motion, colour, depth, and so forth (see Zeki, 1993, for a summary). Within each of these streams, there may be some degree of "binding" based on local Gestalt properties; for instance, collinearity between edges coded in V1 can lead to selective firing of cells in V2 (Peterhans & von der Heydt, 1989; von der Heydt & Peterhans, 1989). More recently, though, studies of neural responses at higher levels of vision (e.g., in inferior-temporal cortex) indicate that cells can respond not only to complex shapes (which must presumably be "bound" from their parts) but also to conjunctions of shape and colour (e.g., Tanaka, 1993). Thus, there is physiological evidence for neural coding of "bound" objects. However, cells in higher levels of cortex also tend to have large receptive fields, which introduces another constraint on binding, namely, that inputs to such cells may need to be modulated such that the cells are not driven by appropriate stimulus attributes in separate objects. In this context, modulation of cells in the ventral visual stream by cells in the dorsal stream linked to attention and action may offer one solution (e.g., Moran & Desimone, 1985).

The role of temporal coding within the nervous system during feature–object binding was originally highlighted by the work of Gray, Engel, and colleagues. Gray, König, Engel, and Singer (1989) reported that, when the receptive fields of visuo-cortical cells were stimulated by separate bars of light moving in opposite directions, oscillatory neural activity showed low cross-correlation. However, when bars were passed across the receptive fields in the same direction, a correlative relationship was observed between oscillatory activity within the 20–80 Hz frequency range. The strongest cross-correlations were obtained when a single bar, formed by the addition of a bar element connecting the previously unconnected elements, stimulated the two neurons. Thus, correlated neuronal activity was only obtained when cells responded to different aspects of the same "Gestalt". Subsequent to this work, "binding" of neural oscillatory activity has been discovered between cells in various parts of the visual cortex (e.g., Engel, König, Kreiter, & Singer, 1991), subcortical structures such as the lateral geniculate nucleus (e.g., Sillito, Jones, Gerstein, & West, 1994), and the pulvinar complex (e.g., Shumikhina & Molotchnikoff, 1995). In each case, oscillations were found specific to neurons that coded different aspects of the same visual stimulus.

In addition to the single-cell recordings of inter-neural oscillatory binding, studies recording EEG from the human scalp have also shown that oscillations in the mid-gamma (or 25–50-Hz) waveband reveal stimulus-specific activity. Mid-gamma band activity that is both evoked and induced by stimulus presentation (e.g., Galambos, 1992), has been found to accompany the presentation of stimuli that group preattentively (e.g., Tallon-Baudry & Bertrand, 1999), and stimuli that "bind" following a cued shift of focal attention (e.g., Müller, Teder-Sälejärvi, & Hillyard, 1998). Gamma-band activity has been found to accompany both N100 (Herrmann, Mecklinger, & Pfeifer, 1999) and P300 (Başar, Başar-Eroglu, Demiralp, & Schürmann, 1993) ERP components. In addition, these and other studies have revealed that stimulus-specific gamma-band activity is not confined to the visual brain areas, but may be found across a wide region of cortex. Thus, stimulus-specific gamma-band oscillations have been recorded at electrode sites above the frontal lobes (Başar-Eroglu, Strüber, Kruse, Başar, & Stadler, 1996; Herrmann et al., 1999) and the premotor cortex (Tallon-Baudry, Bertrand, Delpeuch, & Pernier, 1996). More recent work employing coherence analysis techniques (e.g., Miltner, Braun, Arnold, Witte, & Taub, 1999) has demonstrated coherence between mid-gamma-band activity at occipito-parietal and occipito-central electrodes during an associative learning task. These findings raise the issue of the role of both stimulus and task specificity during generation of the cortical 40-Hz potential. EEG coherence between different cortical areas has also been reported for lower frequency ranges such as the beta1 range (von Stein, Rappelsberger, Sarntheim, & Petsche, 1999) or the theta band (Sarntheim, Petsche, Rappelsberger, Shaw, & von Stein, 1998), suggesting that these lower frequencies play an important role in synchronizing cortical ensembles across larger distances.

COMPUTATIONAL MODELLING

Attempts to understand how the "binding process" may operate have also been made by computational modelling. In models developed within the connectionist framework, "binding" presents a serious problem. Stored knowledge may be "bound" by being represented within local units. However, there arises then a problem of scale, since the number of units required becomes equal to the number of individual elements of knowledge to be stored, something even beyond the capacity of the brain (a problem that had been noted before the rise of neo-connectionism; e.g., Weisstein, 1970). Alternatively, knowledge may be represented by distributed patterns of activation across multiple units. But this approach introduces problems concerning how the individual representations are linked in appropriate spatial and/or temporal relations. These are, of course, similar problems to those encountered by real neural systems. Explorations of how the binding problem may be solved in artificial networks can thus be helpful for attempting to understand how it is solved in the brain (e.g., Grossberg & Grunewald, 1997). In addition, artificial networks can make a valuable contribution to examining theories of neural binding. For example, simulations can be used to test the role in memory of learning "updates" provided by the hippocampus for cortical representations (e.g., McClelland, McNaughton, & O'Reilly, 1995), which have been suggested by "consolidation" theories of human learning. Such updates can help to prevent learned information from being overwritten by new items, and similar procedures can also be used, conversely, to prevent effects such as "catastrophic forgetting" in networks. We are now at an exciting stage in which direct collaborations between modellers and neuroscientists can lead to real advances in our understanding of behaviour within neural systems, gained by means of detailed model simulations.

THE SPECIAL ISSUE

This Special Issue brings together 21 papers mostly from psychology and computational modelling, which are based, in the main, on invited presentations delivered at the interdisciplinary symposium "Neural binding of space and time", held in Leipzig on 16–18 March 2000 (supported by the Deutsche Fortschungsgemeinschaft—German National Research Council). The call for Special Issue contributions stated that papers should be theoretically focused on the theme of the symposium and that they should make a novel theoretical and/or empirical contribution to the study of binding. Following an extensive process of peer review, the collection of 21 papers included in this Special Issue provides such a contribution. The following sections provide a précis of the individual papers.

From the perspective of Gestalt psychology, the problem of binding involves the problem of the relationship between wholes and their constituent parts. One fundamental point of controversy concerning the general concept of feature binding is the extent to which object and Gestalt perception relies upon the construction of wholes from basic, featurally separable constituent parts. Both Chen, and Marković and Gvozdenović raise this issue in their contributions. Chen argues strongly against this local-to-global assumption, maintaining that the "problem" of feature binding arises essentially as a consequence of this particular perspective. According to Chen, "local-to-global" suggests a fundamentally inaccurate description of the hierarchy of processing stages through which a given Gestalt grouping or stimulus object would proceed. Instead, Chen attempts to show that, through the analysis of perceptual invariants across transformations, the nature and rules of perceptual organization may be precisely expressed in terms of topological invariants that describe the geometrical potentiality of the entire stimulus configuration. Chen's position is in part (although not entirely) supported by that of Marković and Gvozdenović, who show that the perceptual system will adopt processing strategies on the basis of the relative simplicity or complexity of the entire stimulus configuration. This approach emphasizes that fine-scaled (or feature) analysis will be more effective when stimulus configurations are relatively simple, and as such reverses the hard assumption of the feature-binding approach that stimulus analysis proceeds exclusively from local-to-global levels of processing. The role of figural specification as a determining factor for elementary perceptual operations, such as figure–ground segmentation, is also illustrated by Peterson and Kim. They show, by means of a priming paradigm, that object memories are accessed for regions initially seen as ground when their outline contours correspond to the silhouette of an object, but not when ground outline contours do not form object silhouettes. Finally, Aksentijević, Elliott, and Barber suggest a "force field" theory, based on a differential-geometric interpretation of perceptual space, can provide a promising starting point for a systematic exploration of the subjective properties of certain classes of visual and auditory grouping phenomena, such as apparent motion, grouping within static two-dimensional displays and auditory streaming.

The issue of binding between brain regions and, by extension, binding between different attributes of the same object and between different objects is addressed in the contributions by Baylis, Gore, Rodriguez, and Shisler, Humphreys, and Davis. For some time, it has been suggested that there is a division of the visual system into a dorsal and a ventral stream (e.g., Ungerleider & Mishkin, 1982). The dorsal stream, running from the occipital lobe into the parietal lobe, is concerned with scene-based properties such as location and movement; the ventral stream, running from occipital areas into the inferior part of the temporal lobe, analyses object-based properties such as shape and colour. The correct binding of the dorsal "where" system to the ventral "what" system would seem essential for unified awareness of objects within a scene. In support of this, Baylis et al. present new neuropsychological evidence that visual extinction may be greatest when information about object location cannot be bound to information about object identity. Similarly, Humphreys reviews neuropsychological data from patients with lesions to different visual areas (in the ventral and dorsal streams) that result in impairments of separable binding processes. Binding from elements to contours, contours to shapes, and shapes to surfaces can be differentially impaired, suggesting a hierarchy of binding processes at different stages of the visual system. Finally, Davis reviews his recent work on differences in performance between within-object and between-object comparisons. His findings lead him to suggest that the visual system binds together features between different objects, just as it binds features within an object. He argues that the information stored about relationships between different objects should be considered as a form of binding, similar to the combination of information within an object representation. The within-object links and between-object links are stored in different brain regions, ventral stream vs. dorsal stream, and they serve different functions, object recognition vs. guidance of actions.

Taken together, the papers just mentioned suggest that the problem of "binding" extends beyond a simple description of feature integration and Gestalt formation. Rather, there are likely to be different forms of binding subserved by different types of mechanism. This raises the question as to the precise system states and processes by which the various types of binding are generated—an issue that has lain at the core of the binding problem since it was first posed.

Perceptual binding and selective attention have been extensively studied with human and animal experiments, both behaviourally and electrophysiologically, but also by the development of computational models that incorporate physiological principles and architectures of connectivity to account for psychophysical data. Raizada and Grossberg offer such an approach. In their model, they show basic perceptual operations such as orientation contrast, perceptual grouping, and visuo-spatial attention can be accounted for by the activity of interlaminar circuits in early visual areas V1 and V2. In order to account for visual selection, Cave considers two means of achieving feature-object binding (besides binding by conjunction units): Attentional binding and temporal binding. He argues that a location-based attention mechanism, as implemented in his "FeatureGate" computational model, can initiate selection (and binding) processes very quickly, and that the visual system employs location selection and attentional binding whenever possible because of their reliability. However, temporal binding can potentially enhance selection in complex scenes, to (1) allow a target object to be selected without also selecting a superimposed distractor, (2) maintain representations of objects after attention has moved to another object, and (3) permit multiple parts of an object to be selected, segmented, and analysed simultaneously. Hummel proceeds from behavioural, neural, and computational considerations, which suggest that the visual system may use at least two approaches to binding an object's features and/or parts into a coherent representation of shape: Dynamically bound (e.g., by synchrony of firing) representations of part attributes and spatial relations form a structural description of an object's shape, while units representing shape attributes at specific locations (i.e., a static binding of attributes to locations) form an analogue (image-like) representation of that shape. Hummel presents a computational model of object recognition based on this proposal and empirical tests of the model.

One central topic in this Special Issue, also related to the nature of the states and processes by which binding is realized, concerns the tendency for neurons to synchronize their firing following presentation of stimulus elements that group according to one or another Gestalt principle. These findings have resulted in the "temporal-correlation hypothesis", which, in its simplest form, states that binding occurs through the temporal correlation of neuronal firing (Singer, 1993; von der Malsburg, 1981). A more specific formulation of this hypothesis refers to the tendency for neurons that synchronize to stimulus Gestalten to do so within a relatively broad range of frequencies referred to as the "gamma band". The gamma band extends, at the most liberal estimate, from around 20 to 120 Hz, although activity in the 30–60 Hz region, and more specifically in a narrower bandwidth at around 40 Hz, appears to be of particular importance.

Synchronous firing has so far mostly been demonstrated using cross-correlation of the firing rates of two neurons (e.g., Gray et al., 1989). Eckhorn, Bruns, Saam, Gail, Gabriel, and Brinksmeyer present an extension of the binding-by-synchronization hypothesis by showing how elementary perceptual processes such as figure–ground segmentation, object continuity, and feature binding are reflected in temporal and spatial aspects of gamma activity recorded in single units of monkey brain. A new aspect of this model is the idea that long distance coupling of neuronal activation patterns between different brain regions is accomplished by transmitting the strength of local gamma activities, that is, "gamma envelopes". Intracellular recordings often display a wide variation in the precise frequency of synchronization. In order to address this issue, Panzeri, Golledge, Zheng, Tovée, and Young discuss a new method for differentiating the functionally significant patterns of neuronal activity and neuronal synchrony, based on Information Theory. In her contribution, Giersch presents psychopharmacological manipulations of visual integration processes, which show that the benzodiazepine lorazepam, and, by extension, a very specific subset of receptors within the GABAergic interneural system, is specifically involved in the processing of primitive feature elements such as luminance discontinuities. These physiological and psychophysiological findings point to much greater sophistication in our understanding of how visual information processing may be specified in terms of particular properties of dynamic and anatomical cortical structures.

Johnson addresses developmental aspects in visual perception that provide insights into mechanisms underlying visual binding. In a comprehensive review of developmental studies that use the habituation paradigm in infants between birth and 4 months of age, he shows that (infants') veridical surface segregation relies on a variety of subprocesses, such as "depth placement" and "contour ownership", that develop in this early period of life. Johnson addresses computational and neurophysiological issues in visual development and stresses the importance of the interplay of experience-independent (figure–ground segregation, attention towards motion and contour) and experience-dependent (changes in synaptic strength and neuronal firing patters) mechanisms for visual development in early childhood.

The findings of bandwidth-specific neuronal responses in the animal cortex have encouraged investigations of the patterning of the human EEG response, which offer interpretations of brain activity according to psychophysical and psychological models of perceptual processes. Müller and Gruber review a number of these studies, showing that power in the frequency range at around 40 Hz is indeed enhanced during experimental tasks requiring the deployment of focal-attentional mechanisms. However, whether an attentional account provides a sufficiently general description for the role of 40-Hz brain activity during perceptual processing is brought into question by the findings of Herrmann and Mecklinger, who show that the strength of a 40-Hz response is closely related to a memory-based feature comparison process (related to Gestalt classification), and that this response occurs in a time period before full deployment of focal attention. Perceptual binding and "unbinding" are needed when ambiguous figures (e.g., the Necker cube or Rubin's vase) are sequentially perceived with one or the alternative interpretation. Here, Strüber, Başar-Eroglu, Miener, and Stadler report that subjects who quickly change from one to the other of two alternative percepts exhibit more gamma activity in their EEG as compared to subjects who switch more slowly. The fact that this gamma activity was measured over frontal electrodes is taken as another indication that attentional, top-down mechanisms influence perceptual reversals.

The development of the temporal-binding hypothesis has also encouraged the development of psychophysical paradigms designed to probe the temporal dynamics of the binding process, normally associated with physiological research. Herzog, Koch, and Fahle present two new visual illusions: "feature inheritance" and "shine-through", which involve the attribution of stimulus properties such as the tilt, spatial offset, or apparent motion of a very briefly presented stimulus to subsequently presented stimuli. The experiments presented by Herzog et al. contribute to our understanding of the role of attention for binding and the spatial limitations of binding in terms of a few neighbouring stimuli, with the transfer of feature attributes from a first to a subsequent stimulus promising an indication of the temporal development of global configuration influences on the percept. Recently, Usher and Donnelly (1998) presented psychophysical evidence that external temporal modulation can influence the visual grouping of dots in a symmetric (ambiguous) grid into either rows or columns of elements, and Elliott and Müller (1998) demonstrated that synchronized prime stimulus presentation resulted in the generation of a pattern of prime activity that expedited detection of a Kanizsa-type figure in a subsequently presented target display, even though the prime stimulus was non-detectable. Parton, Donnelly, and Usher take their work further in three experiments designed to rule out possible problems with the Usher and Donnelly findings and to examine the interaction between temporal (external temporal modulation) and spatial cues in the perceptual organization of the dot grids. The results strengthen and extend upon the grouping account, according to which spatial cues dominate over temporal cues. Elliott and Müller examine another issue concerning the theoretical significance of figural bindings evoked by flickering stimulus presentation, namely, to which extent perceptual (figural) correlations might result from correlations ordinarily computed within systems sensitive to the motion signals generated by the flickering stimuli. Elliott and Müller show that this explanation is not sufficient to account for the priming effects in their paradigm, suggesting that the use of spatially static, flickering displays offers a paradigmatic means of manipulating the binding processes in operation.

Finally, research on binding has long been concerned with apparent motion phenomena and associated stimulus groupings, such as in "beta motion". Geissler and Kompass ask whether a relationship can be established between psychophysically determined temporal characteristics of apparent motion and critical temporal parameters of spatio-temporal binding. In particular, they examined at what inter-stimulus intervals (ISIs) between periodically presented stimuli at separate locations apparent motion transforms into the perception of simultaneous (at their respective locations) flickering stimuli, that is, at what ISIs one state of binding transforms into another. They found that such transitions are likely to occur only at ISIs that are multiples of a smallest quantum time interval. Such discrete time quantum-like structurings, which are also manifest in other perceptual phenomena (such as in the paradigm of Elliott and Müller; see this issue), raise the question of the physiological correlate of very fast periodic processes, the physiological basis of the high temporal precision observed, and the physiological implementation of "single-shot" periods, which the authors discuss.

REFERENCES

Başar, E., Başar-Eroglu, C., Demiralp, T., & Schürmann, M. (1993). The compound P300-40 Hz response of the human brain. *Electroencephalography and Clinical Neurophysiology, 87,* 14.

Başar-Eroglu, C., Strüber, D., Kruse, P., Başar, E., & Stadler, M. (1996). Frontal gamma-band enhancement during multistable visual perception. *International Journal of Psychophysiology, 24,* 113–125.

Baylis, G.C., & Driver, J. (1995). One-sided edge assignment in vision: 1. Figure–ground segmentation and attention to objects. *Current Directions in Psychological Science, 4,* 140–146.

Blake, R., & Yang, Y. (1997). Spatial and temporal coherence in perceptual binding. *Proceedings of the National Academy of Sciences USA, 94,* 7115–7119.

Crick, F. (1984). Function of the thalamic reticular complex: The searchlight hypothesis. *Proceedings of the National Academy of Sciences USA, 81,* 4586–4590.

Davis, G., & Driver, J. (1994). Parallel detection of Kanizsa subjective figures in the human visual system. *Nature, 371,* 791–793.

Donnelly, N., Humphreys, G.W., & Riddoch, M.J. (1991). Parallel computation of primitive shape descriptions. *Journal of Experimental Psychology: Human Perception and Performance, 17,* 561–570.

Duncan, J., & Humphreys, G.W. (1989). Visual search and stimulus similarity. *Psychological Review, 96,* 433–458.

Elliott, M.A., & Müller, H.J. (1998). Synchronous information presented in 40-Hz flicker enhances visual feature binding. *Psychological Science, 9,* 277–283.

Engel, A.K., König, P., Kreiter, A.K., & Singer, W. (1991). Interhemispheric synchronization of oscillatory neuronal responses in cat visual cortex. *Science, 252,* 1177–1179.

Fahle, M. (1993). Figure–ground discrimination from temporal information. *Proceedings of the Royal Society of London, Series B,* 254, 199–203.

Fahle, M., & Koch, C. (1995). Spatial displacement, but not temporal asynchrony, destroys figural binding. *Vision Research, 35,* 491–494.

Galambos, R. (1992). A comparison of certain gamma band (40-Hz) brain rhythms in cat and man. In E. Başar & T.M. Bullock (Eds.), *Induced rhythms in the brain* (pp. 201–216). Boston: Birkhäuser .

Gray, C.M., König, P., Engel, A.K., & Singer, W. (1989). Oscillatory responses in cat visual cortex exhibit intercolumnar synchronization which reflects global stimulus properties. *Nature, 338,* 334–337.

Grossberg, S., & Grunewald, A. (1997). Cortical synchronization and perceptual framing. *Journal of Cognitive Neuroscience, 9,* 117–132.

Herrmann, C.S., Mecklinger, A., & Pfeifer, E. (1999). Gamma responses and ERPs in a visual classification task. *Clinical Neurophysiology, 110,* 636–642.

Hubel, D., & Wiesel, T. (1968). Receptive fields and functional architecture of monkey striate cortex. *Journal of Physiology, 195,* 215–243.

Kiper, D.C., Gegenfurtner, K.R., & Movshon, J.A. (1991). The effect of 40 Hertz flicker on the perception of global stimulus properties. *Society of Neuroscience Abstracts, 17,* 1209.

Kiper, D.C., Gegenfurtner, K.R., & Movshon, A. (1996). Cortical oscillatory responses do not affect visual segmentation. *Vision Research, 36,* 539–544.

Köhler, W. (1924). *Physische Gestalten in Ruhe und im stationären Zustand.* Erlangen, Germany: Verlag der philosophischen Akademie.

Köhler, W., Held, R., & O'Connell, D.N. (1952). An investigation of cortical currents. *Proceedings of the American Philosophical Society, 96,* 290–330.

Koffka, K. (1935). *Principles of Gestalt psychology.* New York: Harcourt & Brace.

Leonards, U., Singer, W., & Fahle, M. (1996). The influence of temporal phase differences on texture segmentation. *Vision Research, 36,* 2689–2697.

McClelland, J.L., McNaughton, B., & O'Reilly, R. (1995). Why there are complimentary learning systems in the hippocampus and neocortex. *Psychological Review, 102,* 419–457.

Miltner, W.H.R., Braun, C., Arnold, N., Witte, H., & Traub, E. (1999). Coherence of gamma-band EEG activity as a basis for associative learning. *Nature, 397,* 434–436.

Moran, S., & Desimone, R. (1985). Selective attention gates visual processing in the extrastriate cortex. *Science, 229,* 782–784.

Müller, M.M., Teder-Sälejärvi, W., & Hillyard, S.A. (1998). The time course of cortical facilitation during cued shifts of spatial attention. *Nature Neuroscience, 1,* 631–634.

Palmer, S. (1992). Common region: A new principle of perceptual grouping. *Cognitive Psychology, 24,* 436–447.

Palmer, S., & Rock, I. (1994). Rethinking perceptual organization: The role of uniform connectedness. *Psychological Bulletin and Review, 1,* 29–55.

Peterhans, E., & von der Heydt, R. (1989). Mechanisms of contour perception in monkey visual perception. II. Contours bridging gaps. *Journal of Neuroscience, 9,* 1749–1763.

Rubin, E. (1915). *Synoplevde Figurer.* Copenhagen, Denmark: Gyldendalske.

Sarntheim, J., Petsche, H., Rappelsberger, P., Shaw, G.L., & von Stein, A. (1998). Synchronization between prefrontal and posterior association cortex during human working memory. *Proceedings of the National Academy of Science, 95,* 7092–7096.

Sekuler, R., Armstrong, R., & Weisstein, N. (1970). Neural symbolic activity. *Science, 170,* 1226–1228.

Shumikhina, S., & Molotchnikoff, S. (1995). Visually-triggered oscillations in the cat lateral posterior-pulvinar complex. *Neuroreport, 6,* 2341–2347.

Sillito, A.M., Jones, H.E., Gerstein, G.L., & West, D.C. (1994). Feature-linked synchronization of thalamic relay cell firing induced by feedback from the visual cortex. *Nature, 369,* 479–482.

Singer, W. (1993). Synchronization of cortical activity and its putative role in information processing and learning. *Annual Review of Physiology, 55,* 349–374.

Tallon-Baudry, C., & Bertrand, O. (1999). Oscillatory gamma activity in humans and its role in object representation. *Trends in Cognitive Sciences, 3,* 151–159.

Tallon-Baudry, C., Bertrand, O., Delpeuch, C., & Pernier, J. (1996). Stimulus specificity of phase-locked and non-phase-locked 40 Hz visual responses in human. *Journal of Neuroscience, 16,* 4240–4249.

Tanaka, K. (1993). Neuronal mechanisms of object recognition. *Science, 262,* 685–688.

Treisman, A., & Gelade, G. (1980). A feature-integration theory of attention. *Cognitive Psychology, 12,* 97–136.

Ungerleider, L.G., & Mishkin, M. (1982). Two cortical visual systems. In D.J. Ingle, M.A. Goodale, & R.J.W. Mansfield (Eds.), *Analysis of visual behavior* (pp. 549–586). Cambridge, MA: MIT Press.

Usher, M., & Donnelly, N. (1998). Visual synchrony affects binding and segmentation in perception. *Nature, 394,* 179–182.

von der Heydt, R., & Peterhans, E. (1989). Mechanisms of contour perception in monkey visual cortex: I. Lines of pattern discontinuity. *Journal of Neuroscience, 9,* 1731–1748.

von der Malsburg, C. (1981). *The correlation theory of brain function* (Internal Rep. 81-2). Göttingen, Germany: Department of Neurobiology, Max-Planck-Institute for Biophysical Chemistry.

von Stein, A., Rappelsberger, P., Sarntheim, J., & Petsche, H. (1999). Synchronization between temporal and parietal cortex during multimodal object processing in man. *Cerebral Cortex, 9,* 137–150.

Wertheimer, M. (1912). Experimentelle Studien über das Sehen von Bewegung. *Zeitschrift für Psychologie, 61,* 161–265.

Wertheimer, M. (1923). Untersuchungen zur Lehre von der Gestalt: II. *Psychologische Forschung, 4,* 301–350.

Zeki, S. (1993). *A vision of the brain.* Oxford, UK: Blackwell Scientific Publications.

VISUAL COGNITION, 2001, *8* (3/4/5), 287–303

Perceptual organization: To reverse back the inverted (upside-down) question of feature binding

Lin Chen

Beijing Laboratory of Cognitive Science, and School of Life Science, University of Science and Technology of China

In addressing the most fundamental question of "Where visual processing begins", all theories of perception can be segregated into two contrasting lines of thinking: "early feature-analysis" (i.e., from local to global processing) and "early holistic registration" (i.e., from global to local processing). The problem of feature binding is then essentially a consequence of the particular local-to-global assumption. However, from the global-to-local perspective, the problem of feature binding may be a wrong question to ask to begin with, while the Gestalt concept of perceptual organization serves to reverse this inverted position. Inspired by the analysis of invariants over transformations, particularly shape-changing transformations, a topological approach has been proposed to describe precisely the nature and rules of perceptual organization. Evidence supporting topological perception will be illustrated in topics of visual sensitivity, apparent motion, illusory conjunctions, and the relative salience of different geometric invariants.

A GREAT DIVIDE

As a Chinese proverb says: Everything is difficult at its very beginning. Divergence in the main schools of vision begins with their answers to the question of "Where visual processing begins" (Pomerantz, 1981) or, put another way: "What are the primitives of visual perception" (Chen, 1982). The question is so fundamental and also so controversial as to serve as a watershed, a Great Divide, separating two most basic and sharply contrasting lines of thinking in

Please address all correspondence to Prof. Lin Chen, Beijing Laboratory of Cognitive Science, University of Science & Technology of China, PO Box 3908, 100039 Beijing, China. Email: lchen@public2.bta.net.cn

This study was supported by National Nature Science Foundation of China (Grant number: 69790080), Chinese State Commission of Science and Technology (Grant number: 1998030503), and the Human Frontiers Science Program. I thank Sheng He and Jun Zhang for careful review of the drafts, and three anonymous reviewers for helpful comments on the manuscript.

http://www.tandf.co.uk/journals/pp/13506285.html DOI:10.1080/13506280143000016

the study of perception: specifically, the general line of the "Early feature-analysis" approach and the general line of the "Early holistic registration" approach. In addressing the most fundamental question of "Where to begin", all theories of perception fall on one or the other side of this Great Divide (Chen, 1999).

On one side, the early feature-analytic viewpoint holds that perceptual processing is *from local to global*: Objects are initially decomposed into separable properties and components, and only in subsequent processes are objects recognized, on the basis of extracted features. As is well known, a representative theory of the "early feature-analysis" viewpoint is the computational approach to vision by Marr (1982). As is commonly accepted, the computational approach claims the primitives, or "primal sketch", of visual-information representation are local geometric properties of simple form components, such as, line-segments with slopes.

On the other side, the early holistic registration approach claims that perceptual processing is *from global to local*: Wholes are organized prior to perceptual analysis of their separable properties or parts, as indicated by the conception of perceptual organization in Gestalt psychology. The major principle of Gestalt psychology is that "whole is more than the simple sum of it parts". As we will see in the following discussion, with respect to the fundamental question of "Where to begin", the core contribution of Gestalt idea goes far beyond the notion that "whole is more than the simple sum of it parts"; rather it is that "holistic registration is prior to local analysis".

Supporters of early feature analysis have been quite successful in collecting physiological, anatomical, behavioural, and other evidence (for an overall review, see Treisman, 1986b). Thus, the idea of early feature analysis has gained wide acceptance among scientists from various fields, such as psychology, physiology, and computer science, and has dominated the current study of visual cognition.

In contrast, the early holistic registration approach remains outside of the main stream of contemporary visual sciences. Gestalt psychology, the representative of the general line of early holistic registration, always seems to fall somewhat short of current standards for the scientific establishment.

Problem of feature binding: The other side of the coin

Although the idea of feature analysis has been supported by many experimental findings, not much attention has been paid to the other side of the coin until recently. Specifically, regardless of how an object is decomposed into properties and components, the decomposed features themselves are unlikely to be sufficient for achieving object recognition. The question then remains, how does feature analysis lead to object recognition? Given that separate features from different dimensions are initially extracted, and yet we do not normally perceive isolated features such as brightness, colours, and orientations free from an object, there must be a further process that binds them together and as a result gives an integrated percept of object. The problem of feature binding presents a central problem in current vision research. Questions such as "How are separable features, having been teased apart in the primary analysis of an image, put *back* together to make coherent objects?" (Hurlbert & Poggio, 1985; emphasis added) raises a fundamental problem in psychology and in artificial intelligence of vision.

However, despite the centrality of feature binding in the current study of visual perception and selective attention, and despite the fact that feature binding looks like a straightforward question, no breakthrough has been made in the study of this question after decades of extensive research. Various theoretical treatments and experimental approaches have been applied to address the question. Possible featural factors, particularly space and time, are considered to provide the most likely cues for binding features together. It seems to be natural and reasonable to relate the function of feature binding to either spatial location or temporal occurrence, because space and time are commonly considered intrinsic to visual processing and the medium within which vision operates. Nevertheless, principles for feature binding based on either space or time are neither always obeyed nor exclusive. The problem of feature binding turns out to be much more difficult than it appeared to be. Such difficulties faced by the study of feature binding forced one to trace back the very starting point of early feature analysis.

Feature binding and perceptual organization

Feature binding and perceptual organization appear to be very similar problems (Duncan, 1989) in the sense that both of them are dealing with the same questions, such as "what goes with what" and grouping, and with similar concepts, such as belongingness and assignment. It turns out that, even though early feature analysis emphasizes the fundamental importance of the initially parallel and modular processing, the problems faced by perceptual organization are still indispensable to any early feature analytic theory. After decades of effort to establish early feature analytic theories, it is interesting to observe that problems related to perceptual organization have neither been resolved nor sidestepped, despite the apparent success and domination of early feature analytic theories over early holistic registration theories. As Kubovy and Pomerantz (1981) pointed out: "In analyzing these themes, we have found that the main problems facing us today are quite similar to those faced by the Gestalt psychologists in the first half of this century." After half a century, as is indicated by the very problem of feature binding, the study of visual perception appears, in some sense, to be back to square one.

The concepts of "perceptual organization" and "feature binding", however, involve very different underlying issues. As was already emphasized, the concept of perceptual organization, which was synonymous with Gestalt psychology, is rooted in the general theory of Early holistic registration. In contrast, the problem of feature binding essentially comes from the assumption of early feature-analysis: Features are supposed to be analysed at early stages of visual processing; it is, therefore, logically necessary that such features be, in one way or another, bound together later in order to achieve holistic object recognition. Thus, with respect to the fundamental question of "Where to begin", perceptual organization and feature binding are essentially contrary concepts, going in opposite directions.

Feature binding: an inverted (upside-down) question

The issues of perceptual organization, originally raised by the Gestaltists, continue to present themselves in the inconsistent patterns of results of feature-binding experiments currently at the centre of debate. This situation leads us to wonder whether the problems facing us in the study of feature binding are due to, instead of technical issues, difficulties in the fundamental underlying principles. An analysis such as this drives one to reconsider the most fundamental question of "Where to begin", the Great Divide, and the significance of which side of the Great Divide one chooses. Is there something problematic with the original assumptions about feature binding?

In terms of our understanding of objects in the real word, there may be little disagreement that the real features of an object, whatever geometrical or physical properties they are, exist together as a coherent whole of a physical entity in the outside world. It is true that the relations between real objects and their corresponding perceptual objects may not be simple or direct. It is also true that the question of "How on earth does the perceptual system achieve the perceptual objects as the fundamental units of conscious perceptual experience?" has either given rise to much controversy when considered, or has not been considered at all. There may be, however, not much doubt about the truism that real features of a real object, at a given time, originally coexist together rather than being separated. A real object is an integral stimulus, a single thing. This truth is a fundamental property of a real-world object. There is not any doubt of accepting the direct perception of various featural properties such as brightness, colour, line-orientation, and so on. Why, then, is only this fundamental property, the property of "belonging together as a whole", excluded from the membership of primitives in our perceptual world?

It appears that there is, in principal, no necessary reason for rejecting the ability of the perceptual system to perceive this fundamental property of "belonging together as a whole". With respect to a real object, there is no problem about "which feature goes with which feature": Features of a real object go with each other in the first place. In this sense, the problem of feature binding is an artificial one. It is the consequence of a particular assumption of early feature analysis, and a sort of prejudice about what perceptual primitives should be. From the point of view of early feature analysis, features, except for the property of being one single object, are supposed to be separated at early stage. Thus there comes a need to bind them back together. However, the assumption that the visual system cannot directly perceive a real integral object as a perceptually integral one has not yet been proven or disproven. Indeed, the continuing challenges to issues raised by feature binding suggest that this question deserves closer scrutiny.

From the perspective of early holistic registration, the feature-binding problem is an ill-posed question: Not just a question of getting off on a wrong foot but even a question of "standing upside down". In this sense, the feature-binding problem might be a wrong, inverted question.

Where does the previous analysis leave us? It leaves us an impression that the line of thinking of early holistic registration, by its very nature, may provide a way to avoid the feature-binding problem altogether by focusing instead on issues of perceptual organization. In other words, we may apply the concept of perceptual organization to reverse back the inverted (upside-down) question of feature binding.

TOPOLOGICAL APPROACH TO PERCEPTUAL ORGANIZATION: WHY AND HOW?

Despite its deep and rational core in the idea of early holistic registration, the conception of perceptual organization has its own problem. Like other traditional Gestalt concepts, it has suffered from a lack of proper theoretical treatment. This weakness is responsible for early holistic registration remaining outside the mainstream of contemporary theories. Gestalt evidence has often been criticized for being mainly phenomenological and relying mainly on conscious experience. Explanations from theories of perceptual organization usually rely on intuitive or mentalistic concepts that are somewhat vague and elusive. To modern information-processing psychologists, Gestalt-inspired explanations always appear to display a tendency of circularity. These problems with Gestalt ideas caused more than just damage to the acceptance or scientific respectability of Gestalt psychology. They were also responsible for much confusion over the fundamental question of "Where does visual processing begin?"

What is needed is a proper formal analysis of perceptual organization that goes beyond intuitive approaches, and which may provide a theoretical basis for describing or defining precisely the core concepts in the study of perceptual organization, such as "objects", "global" vs. "local", "grouping", and so on.

Until the intuitive notions of these Gestalt-inspired concepts become properly and precisely defined, the proposed principles of perceptual organization would not be entirely testable and would, to some extent, retain the tendency of circular explanation.

Precisely what kind of mathematical concepts may be proper for the formal analysis of the nature and rules of perceptual organization, including "what goes with what", grouping, belonging, assignment, figure–background segregation, and so on? To address this question, let us examine a typical case that demands in-depth consideration in perceptual organization.

What are correspondence tokens in apparent motion with shape-changing transformations?

It is commonly accepted that at the core of understanding apparent motion lies the correspondence problem, that is, "identifying a portion of the changing visual array as representing a single object in motion or in change" (Ullman, 1979, p. 27). In the process of perceiving apparent motion one has to establish, at some level, a correspondence that identifies which parts of successively presented, complex stimuli represent the same object. So, one of the most fundamental questions for understanding apparent motion is: What are the constituents of stimuli that are matched by correspondence processes? With respect to the question of "What is the input representation in apparent motion?", Ullman (1979), in his well-known theory (driven by his theoretical stance towards the side of the early feature analysis of the Great Divide), concluded that some simple features, such as edge, line segments, bars, and blobs, are taken to be correspondence tokens to be matched in perceiving apparent motion, and there is no indication that structural figures are part of the basic elements.

Important phenomenon of shape-changing transformations. One distinguishing aspect of apparent motion is that when one perceives apparent motion, one perceives not only translation and rotation of rigid shapes but also intriguing "plastic deformations", occurring when apparent motion is produced by dissimilar pairs. In this type of apparent motion, there are shape-changing transformations from one stimulus pattern to another, for example, a square moves and changes its shape simultaneously to become a triangle or vice versa.

Enlightenment. This phenomenon of plastic deformation has raised the following stimulating question: What kinds of properties still remain invariant and are matched by the correspondence process under this kind of transformation of plastic deformations? With translation or rotation of a rigid shape, simple objects such as line segments may still keep their identity and, thus, possibly serve as correspondence tokens. With plastic deformation, however, it is difficult to imagine how simple rigid objects such as line segments can ever act as correspondence tokens. This is because, as a shape changes (e.g., a triangle transforms to a circle) line segments making up the shape (e.g., the triangle) lose their identity and their qualification for correspondence tokens. This forces us to understand the concept of correspondence tokens in apparent motion in terms of transformations and invariants that survive form deformations. This notion of identity preserving over transformations is in the core of the intuition of perceptual object; and the phenomenal impression of identity preservation over transformations could provide a starting point for a more formal analysis.

Further question. In light of the previous analysis of correspondence tokens in apparent motion, the next essential question is: What kinds of invariant under the transformation of plastic deformation does the visual system depend upon to determine that the two figures, however different in shape or other featural properties, nevertheless represent the same object and thus produce apparent motion?

Based on the previous analysis, it becomes clear that the critical treatment needed is to find a mathematical language to describe precisely the essence of the holistic identity of an object preserved under this kind of plastic deformation or the shape-changing transformation. This is true for establishing a formal analysis of correspondence problem in apparent motion in particular, and for turning intuitive approaches to a formal approach to the holistic concepts such as perceptual object in general.

Invariants over shape-changing transformations and invariance perception

Even though the earlier discussion has mainly focused on the phenomenon of apparent motion, many other phenomenological observations of perceptual organization also leave us with an impression that they are all, in one way or another, intrinsically related to the concepts of shape-changing transformations and the holistic identity preserving over shape-changing transformations. For example, consider figure–ground perception, a typical kind of phenomena in perceptual organization. As a classical observation reported, when a stimulus display is presented under impoverished visual conditions, figure and background achieve some measure of differentiation, although the detailed structure of the stimulus remains vague and amorphous. That the precise shape could not be perceived means that the discrimination of figure from background does not depend on the details of featural properties, such as orientation, location, size, etc., which are commonly considered as primitives in early feature analysis. In other words, a stimulus was separated into different global wholes (a figure and a ground), dependent only on global properties, which remain invariant under local changes to featural properties. It also appears necessary to understand the nature of figure–ground problem, a seemingly static problem, from the perspective of changes, particularly shape changes, and identity preserving over shape changes.

These analyses converge on one common underlying principle: The perception of invariants over transformations. This principle leads us to realize that our theoretical treatment of perceptual organization needs not be restricted to the static or stationary approaches. Rather, as our analyses suggest, in order to grasp the nature of perceptual organization, it is necessary to understand it from the perspective of transformations and invariants over transformations, particularly the shape-changing ones.

The central question. Thus, the central question for establishing a formal framework for perceptual organization turns out to be: What branch of mathematics is good at describing precisely the unified principle underlying various expressions of transformations and invariants over transformations, particularly shape-changing transformations?

A strong conclusion. The previous analyses about the shape-changing transformation lead to a strong conclusion, that is, for such properties that are entailed in describing principles of perceptual organization, some fundamental and common mathematical concepts, particularly distance, or metrics, used for describing featural properties, may not be relevant. This implies that any mathematics constructed on the basis of distance, or metrics, such as all mathematical branches of calculus we are familiar with, will not be suitable mathematical frameworks for describing perceptual organization.

Instead and as discussed next, topology is just the mathematical language we need.

Topological invariants and topological approach to perceptual organization

Topology is considered as a promising framework for formal description of perceptual organization. The shape-changing transformation observed in phenomenal world may be precisely described as the topological transformation, i.e., the "one-to-one" and "continuous" transformation. Invariants over the shape-changing transformation are termed topological properties, namely (mathematically) invariants over the topological transformation. Intuitively, the one-to-one and continuous transformation can be imagined as an arbitrary "rubber-sheet" distortion without breaking or fusion, whatever the changes in shape the "rubber-sheet" may undergo. Under this kind of "rubber-sheet" distortion, for example, connectivity, the number of holes, and the inside/outside relationship remain invariant, so they are topological properties. In contrast, local geometric properties, such as orientation, size, and symmetry, are not topological properties.

From the perspective of topological perception, let us briefly return to the starting questions discussed earlier, and further illustrate why and how a topological approach has been applied. With respect to the figure–ground discrimination, it appears to be straightforward that the Gestalt principle of figure–ground organization may be described formally in terms of the topological invariant of connectivity. When we speak of "figures" or "objects", we usually imply that they are connected entities. With respect to apparent motion, the shape-changing transformation observed in apparent motion appears to be, phenomenologically, very similar to the "rubber-sheet" distortion. So, we are led to consider topological transformations as a formal description of shape-changing transformations observed in motion, and hence, to consider topological properties as candidates for correspondence tokens in apparent motion. In general, identity preserving over shape-changing transformations, the core of intuitive notion of perceptual object, may be precisely described as topological invariants such as connectivity or connected components, which remain invariant over transformations such as "rubber-sheet" distortion through time.

Evidence supporting the topological approach to perceptual organization

The observations and analyses, discussed previously, are very helpful for the formulation of the hypothesis of topological perception. However, in order to establish a scientific theory of the topological approach to perceptual organization, which is faced with a great variety and complexity of phenomena in perceptual organization, it must be tested against various well-controlled experiments. The phenomenal world of perceptual organization is the starting point for the construction of this hypothesis, and it is also the world to which this hypothesis must return for verification of its psychological reality.

In this section, we will focus on a few representative experiments that support the topological hypothesis, starting with the visual sensitivity to distinction made in topology.

Visual sensitivity to distinctions made in topology. If topological invariants play a fundamental role in perceptual organization, such as in figure–ground discrimination, we could predict some experimental results that are not necessarily consistent with our everyday perceptual experiences, but that are consistent with topology. One of the basic experiments revealing the counterintuitive influence of topological properties on early visual processing involves the stimuli shown in Figure 1(a) (Chen, 1982). It turned out that the disk-and-annulus pair is more discriminable in a near-threshold "same–

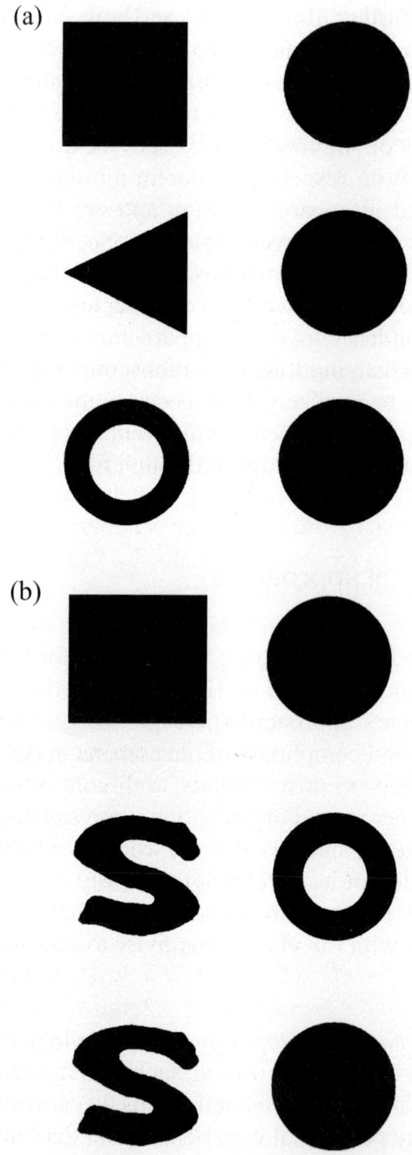

	% correct response	Area difference (mm^2)
(a)	43.5	220
	38.5	292
	64.5	254
(b)	35.6	310
	59.0	0
	41.1	314

Figure 1. **(a)** The three stimulus displays used to test visual sensitivity to distinction made in topology (adapted from Chen, 1982, Fig. 1); **(b)** each stimulus display was further controlled for luminous flux difference, spatial frequency components, perimeter length, and other featural factors (from Chen, 1990, Fig. 2).

different" task than the disk-and-square pair and the disk-and-triangle pair. Although an intuitive notion of shape similarity might lead one to expect the opposite, topology provides an explanation of the data: the disk and annulus differ topologically, in that the annulus contains a hole whereas the disk does not. Although phenomenally they look quite different in shape, the solid figures in the other two pairs are all topologically equivalent to each other, since any one of them can be modified to match any other by performing smooth deformation. On the other hand, smooth deformations cannot create or destroy holes, so the annulus and the disk are not topologically equivalent.

The topological account of this experiment was tested by further controlled experiments (Chen, 1990), in response to scepticism about the human ability to perceive topological properties. Counter explanations in favour of early feature analysis argued that the results were due to differences not in topological properties but in featural properties, such as luminous flux (Rubin & Kanwisher, 1985). As shown in Figure 1(b), stimuli, for example, an S-like figure and an annulus, which controlled for luminous flux, spatial frequency components, perimeter length, and other featural factors, were still more discriminable than other pairs of figures that are topologically equivalent, such as an S-like figure and a disk. It is interesting to note that, although "it has long been known that primate visual system has a primitive capacity—one that survives even bilateral removal of visual cortex—to detect differences in luminous flux" (Klüver, 1941), these experimental results, which ruled out the alternative explanation based on luminous flux, suggest that topological factors may play an even more primitive role in the discriminability of form than luminous flux does.

Topological invariants and correspondence tokens in apparent motion. As discussed previously, the analysis of the phenomenon of shape-changing transformations observed in apparent motion led us to consider topological invariants as candidates for the correspondence tokens in apparent motion (Chen, 1985). Two stimulus displays are successively presented: The first containing a single figure in the centre, and the second containing two figures located on either side of, and at the same distance from, the centre. In each presentation, subjects were required to choose one of two motion directions in a forced-choice procedure. These stimuli, shown in Figure 2, were designed to represent topological differences, such as one hole vs. no hole (stimuli a, b, c, d, and g), two holes vs. one hole (stimulus e), the inside/outside relationship (stimulus f), and connectivity (stimulus b). Various non-topological factors, such as luminous flux, spatial frequency components, terminators, were also controlled for. Subjects consistently reported a strong preference for motion from a central figure to a figure with the same topological invariants. These results shed new light on some long-standing debates about apparent motion in particular, and perceptual organization in general. For example, it is now clear that the question of whether motion perception precedes form perception or

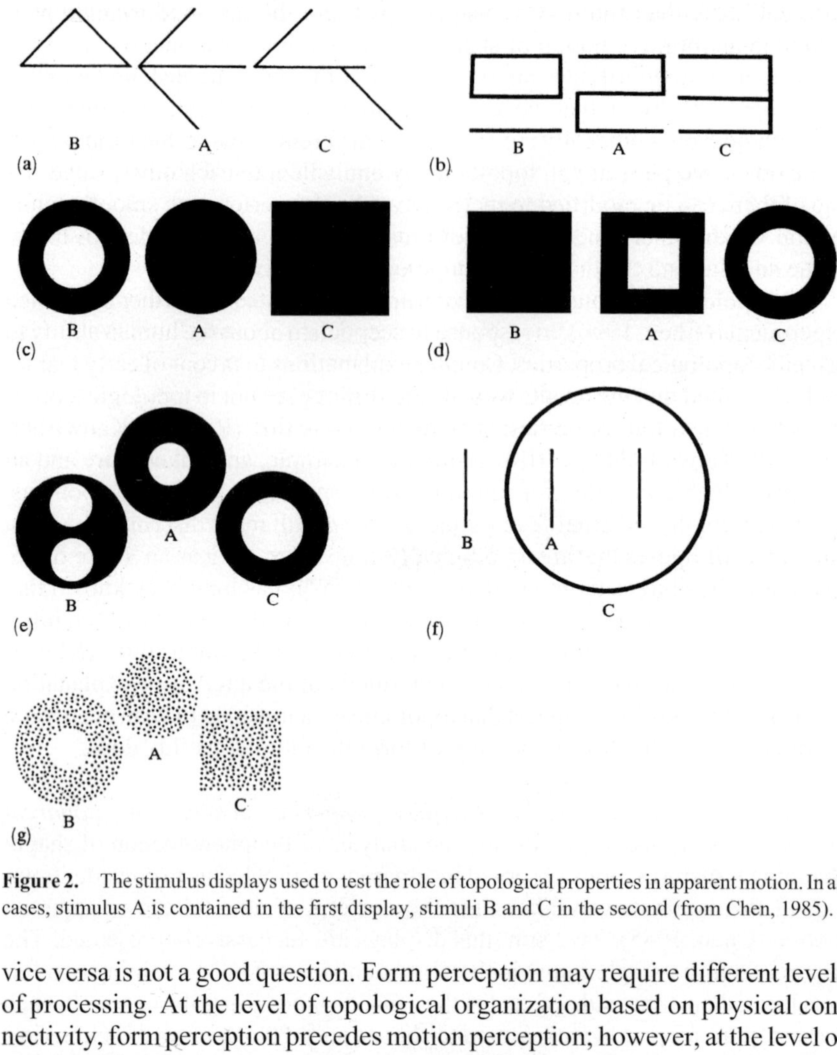

Figure 2. The stimulus displays used to test the role of topological properties in apparent motion. In all cases, stimulus A is contained in the first display, stimuli B and C in the second (from Chen, 1985).

vice versa is not a good question. Form perception may require different levels of processing. At the level of topological organization based on physical connectivity, form perception precedes motion perception; however, at the level of more detailed featural properties, say the differences between a solid square and triangle, motion perception may precede form perception, as is commonly observed in other studies. So, we cannot bluntly claim that "the correspondence tokens are not structured forms" (Ullman, 1979, p. 27) in apparent motion. Ullman's theory is noted for the proposal of rigidity constraint, which, as Marr pointed out, "enables us to solve the structure-from-motion problem unambiguously". But at the same time its limitation also comes from the rigidity assumption. As Marr also noted, a new theory may be needed when the observed object is not only moving but also changing. Nevertheless, Marr did not give any hint at what kind of a new theory it could be. The topological approach provides a new analysis of object identity over shape-changing motion perception.

Topological illusory conjunction. The hypothesis of early topological perception was also tested by employing the phenomenon of illusory conjunctions. In a series of experiments, which used the paradigm originally designed by Treisman (1986a) and controlled for various feature errors, we consistently observed the illusory conjunction of holes, illustrated in Figure 3 (Chen & Zhou, 1997). Subjects in our experiments perceived illusory hollow figures in which the conjoined holes underwent shape-changing transformations. This indicates that the holes were perceived as abstract topological entities available at an early stage. A major difficulty in supporting the early topological perception is that it is difficult to design stimuli that represent only topological distinctions without introducing differences in non-topological variables. Even

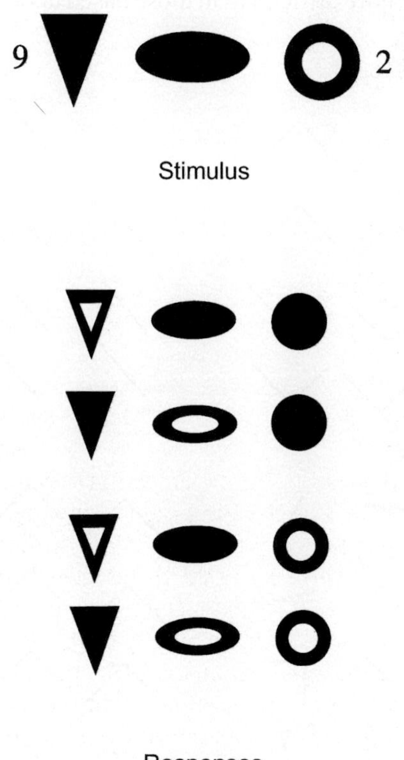

Figure 3. An example of stimulus displays used in the experiments of illusory conjunctions of holes and examples of reports counted as illusory conjunctions of holes. The subjects' primary task was to report correctly the two digits, and, as a secondary task, to report the shapes (from Chen & Zhou, 1997).

though various factors (e.g., luminous flux, spatial frequency components, and perimeter length) may be controlled under various conditions, in a single experiment there always seems to be room for an argument against the topological hypothesis in terms of confounding by non-topological features. This kind of confound seemed unavoidable before discovery of the illusory conjunction of holes. The key is that the holes in illusory conjunctions differ from those in the original stimuli, for example in shape, and they do not depend on detailed geometric properties or physical properties. It is therefore quite difficult to explain these results in terms of confounds based upon non-topological features.

The relation between topological perception and perception of other geometric properties: Relative salience of different geometric invariants in configural superiority effects. Pomerantz, Sager, and Stoever (1977) reported configural superiority effects: Discriminations based upon line orientation alone are often more difficult than those based upon certain line arrange-

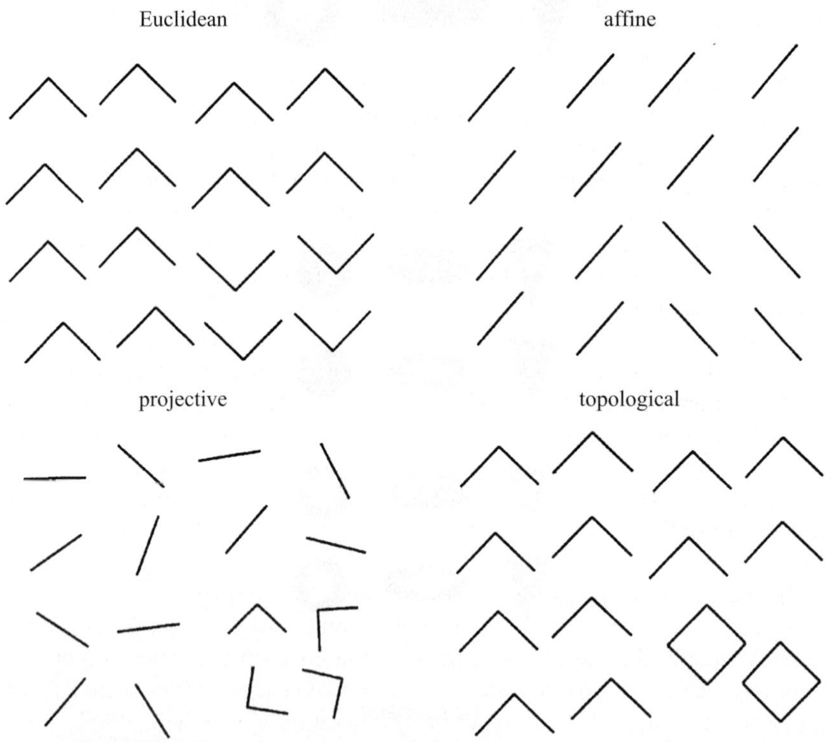

Figure 4. Some example stimulus patterns used in studying the relative salience of different geometric properties (from Todd, Chen, & Norman, 1998).

ments or configurations, as illustrated in Figure 4. This finding of configural superiority effects evidently provided a challenge to early feature analysis, in which sloped line segments were commonly considered the primitive units. However, it is interesting to note that although this challenge looks simple and direct, no convincing answer to it has been provided to date except the following topological account.

Applying the similar paradigm, Chen (1983, 1986) studied the relation between topological perception and perception of other geometric properties, and reported that the relative perceptual salience of different geometric properties is remarkably consistent with the hierarchy of geometries in the Klein Erlangen program (for an introduction to Erlangen program, see Aleksandrov, Kolyogorov, & Lavrent'ev, 1963). Some representative stimulus patterns from his study are shown in Figure 4. When the elements in the segregated region were topologically distinct from those in the remaining portions of the pattern, observers could identify the disparate quadrant with a mean reaction time of only 801 ms. When the disparate quadrant was defined by a projective property (collinearity) the reaction time increased to 968 ms. Furthermore, when the disparate quadrant was defined by an affine property (parallelism), the reaction time increased further to 1465 ms. Finally, when the disparate region could only be distinguished by the Euclidean property (orientation) of relative orientation, the reaction times increased still further to1941 ms. These data indicated that a similar type of stratification to the hierarchy of geometries defined by Klein's Erlangen program may occur in human form perception.

Inspired by the results obtained with 2-D forms, this hierarchy was successfully extended to 3-D forms (Todd et al., 1998). In this study, a match-to-sample task was performed, in which subjects compared configurations of line segments presented stereoscopically in different three-dimensional orientations. Several different structural properties of these configurations were manipulated, including the relative orientations of line segments (a Euclidean invariant), their coplanarity (an affine invariant), and their pattern of co-intersection (a topological invariant). Although the differences in these properties to be detected were all metrically equivalent, they varied dramatically in reaction times and error rates, which demonstrated again the same perceptual relative salience of Euclidean, affine, and topological structure for 3-D form as for 2-D form.

The theory of *early* topological perception has demonstrated its applicability to a wide spectrum of phenomena in perceptual organization. In addition to the ones already discussed, these phenomena concern the object superiority effect (e.g., Chen, 1986), texture discrimination (Chen, 1989), visual search (e.g., Zhou & Chen, 1996), competing organization (e.g., Chen, 1986), global precedence (e.g., Han, Humphreys, & Chen, 1999a), the relation between different organizational factors (e.g., Han, Humphreys, & Chen, 1999b), hemispheric asymmetry (e.g., Lan & Chen, 1996), and others.

As everything is difficult at its very beginning, this topological approach may be merely a first step in the long march to understanding vision, but importantly, we believe, a step in the correct direction.

REFERENCES

Aleksandrov, A.D., Kolmogorov, A.N., & Lavrent'ev, M.A. (Eds.) (1963). *Mathematics: Its contents, methods, and meaning* (K. Hirsch, Trans.). Cambridge, MA: MIT Press.

Chen, L. (1982). Topological structure in visual perception. *Science, 218,* 699–700.

Chen, L. (1983). *What are the units of figure perceptual representation?* (Studies in Cognitive Science No. 22). Irvine, CA: University of California, Irvine, School of Social Sciences.

Chen, L. (1985). Topological structure in the perception of apparent motion. *Perception, 14,* 197–208.

Chen, L. (1986). Topological perception: A possible dark cloud over computational approaches to vision [in Chinese]. In X.S. Qian (Ed.). *On cognitive sciences* (pp. 250–301). Shanghai, China: People's Press.

Chen, L. (1989). Topological perception: A challenge to computational approaches to vision. In R. Pfeifer et al. (Eds.), *Connectionism in perspective* (pp. 317–329). Amsterdam: Elsevier.

Chen, L. (1990). Holes and wholes: A reply to Rubin and Kanwisher. *Perception and Psychophysics, 47,* 47–53.

Chen, L. (1999). The theory of topological structure and functional hierarchy and its relations to foundations of cognitive science: A plenary talk. In *Proceedings of the Second International Conference on Cognitive Science* (pp. 16–22). Tokyo: Japanese Cognitive Science Society.

Chen, L., & Zhou, W. (1997). Holes in illusory conjunctions. *Psychonomic Bulletin and Review, 4,* 507–511.

Duncan, J. (1989). Parallel processing: Giving up without fight. *Behavioral and Brain Sciences, 12,* 402–403.

Han, S., Humphreys, G.W., & Chen, L. (1999a). Parallel and competitive processes in hierarchical analysis: Perceptual grouping and encoding of closure. *Journal of Experimental Psychology: Human Perception and Performance, 25,* 1411–1432.

Han, S., Humphreys, G.W., & Chen, L. (1999b). Uniform connectedness and classical Gestalt principles of perceptual grouping. *Perception and Psychophysics, 61,* 661–674.

Hurlbert, A., & Poggio, T. (1985). *Spotlight on attention.* Cambridge, MA: MIT Press.

Klüver, H. (1941). Visual function after removal of the occipital lobes. *Journal of Psychology, 11,* 23–45.

Kubovy, M., & Pomerantz, J. (1981). *Perceptual organization* (pp. 141–179). Hillsdale, NJ: Lawrence Erlbaum Associates Inc.

Lan, Z., & Chen, L. (1996). Left-hemisphere advantage for topological discrimination. *Investigative Ophthalmology and Visual Science, 37*(3 Suppl.), s365.

Marr, D. (1982). *Vision* (pp. 203–205). San Francisco: Freeman.

Pomerantz, J.R. (1981). Perceptual organization in information processing. In M. Kubovy & J. Pomerantz (Eds.), *Perceptual organization.* Hillsdale, NJ: Lawrence Erlbaum Associates Inc.

Pomerantz, J.R., Sager, L.C., & Stoever, R.J. (1977). Perception of wholes and of their component parts: Some configural superiority effects. *Journal of Experimental Psychology: Human Perception and Performance, 3,* 422–435.

Rubin, J., & Kanwisher, N. (1985). Topological perception: Holes in an experiment. *Perception and Psychophysics, 37,* 179–180.

Todd, J., Chen, L., & Norman, F. (1998). On the relative salience of Euclidean, affine, and topological structure for 3-D form discrimination. *Perception, 27,* 273–282.

Treisman, A. (1986a). Features and objects in visual processing. *Scientific American, 255*(5), 114B–125.

Treisman, A. (1986b). Properties, parts, and objects. In K. Boff, L. Kaufman, & J. Thomas (Eds.), *Handbook of perception and human performance* (Vol. 2, pp. 1–70). New York: Wiley.

Ullman, S. (1979). *The interpretation of visual motion*. Cambridge, MA: MIT Press.

Zhou, T.G., & Chen, L. (1996). Hierarchy of perceptual primitives: Evidence from search rates. *Investigative Ophthalmology and Visual Science, 37*(3 suppl.), s1361.

VISUAL COGNITION, 2001, *8* (3/4/5), 305–327

Symmetry, complexity and perceptual economy: Effects of minimum and maximum simplicity conditions

Slobodan Marković and Vasilije Gvozdenović
Laboratory of Experimental Psychology, University of Belgrade, Yugoslavia

According to Gestalt theory, the perceptual system works on economic principles and tends to reach the *maximum* efficiency (i.e., increase of quality, goodness, and accuracy) with *minimum* invested energy (i.e., reduction of processing load). In this study the effects of two concurrent stimulus constraints, symmetry and simplicity, were investigated with the following variables related to perceptual economy: Goodness judgement (Experiment 1), completion of semi-structured patterns (Experiment 2), duration of search for target patterns (Experiment 3), and the duration and accuracy of pattern detection (Experiment 4). The results suggest that the dominance of symmetry or simplicity depends upon the difficulty of the experimental task. Symmetry prevailed in less restrictive, more interesting, and easier perceptual tasks, such as goodness judgement and pattern completion (Experiments 1, 2, and, partly, Experiment 3), whereas simplicity prevailed in difficult and restricted conditions, such as the detection of briefly exposed stimuli (50 ms; Experiment 4). The results are discussed in the context of Koffka's concept of minimum and maximum simplicity. When the perceptual system has a small energy disposal, or when external conditions are difficult and restricted (minimum simplicity conditions), simplicity in stimulus pattern organization will be preferred. When the perceptual system has a large amount of energy, or when external situations are unrestricted and interesting (maximum simplicity conditions), fine and regular articulations of stimulus patterns will be preferred. Our study confirmed the prediction implied by the concept of minimum and maximum simplicity.

In his famous *Law of Prägnanz* Wertheimer stated that the phenomenal organization of a percept will be as "good" or *Prägnant* as the prevailing conditions allow (Koffka, 1935). Some authors identify the Law of Prägnanz with a, so called, Minimum principle, while "goodness" or *Prägnanz* quality is identified

Please address all correspondence to S. Marković, Faculty of Philosophy, Laboratory of Experimental Psychology, Čika Ljubina 18–20, 11000 Belgrade, Yugoslavia.
Email: smarkovi@f.bg.ac.yu

http://www.tandf.co.uk/journals/pp/13506285.html DOI:10.1080/13506280143000025

with the *simplicity* of perceptual organization (Attneave, 1982; Hatfield & Epstein, 1985; Hochberg & McAlister, 1953; Köhler, 1927, 1971; Leeuwenberg, 1971; Restle, 1982; van Leeuwen, 1990). According to this principle, the perceptual system tends to reduce its engagement to a minimum and thus to describe external world in the simplest possible way (for review see Hatfield & Epstein, 1985).

However, the perceptual system is not an isolated and closed system with an aim to establish equilibrium at the minimum state of energy. As Köhler has emphasized, it is a dynamic, open, and sophisticated natural system, which tends to reach the greatest possible *efficiency* of operation (Köhler, 1927, 1971). In this sense it is necessary to introduce a Maximum principle, which expresses a tendency toward increasing the quality of processing outcomes: That is the regularity, stability, and good articulation of the percept.

These hypothetical tendencies toward maximum representation with minimum energy refer to the two complementary aspects of energy distribution within the perceptual system, *entropy* and *dynamics*. The minimum tendency refers to the entropy domain, that is the total amount of available energy to be minimized (saved), whereas the maximum tendency refers to a domain of dynamics, or the amount of energy needed to process, and which has to be maximized (used).

STIMULUS CONSTRAINTS OF PERCEPTUAL ECONOMY

Perceptual economy is always relative to the given stimulus conditions: some stimulus patterns are processed more effectively and with smaller investments than others (see Figure 1). Existing models suggest that the various stimulus

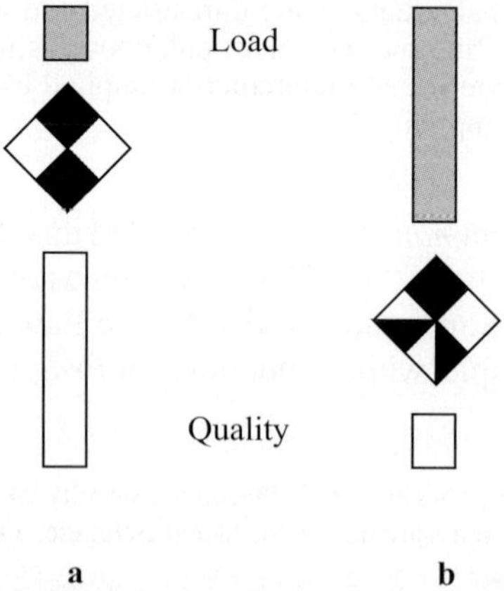

Figure 1. The pattern on the left (a) is processed more economically than the pattern on the right (b).

constraints of perceptual economy can be reduced into two basic categories, *regularity* and *complexity* (Boselie, 1988; Chipman, 1977; Leeuwenberg, 1971; Marković, 1995; Sekuler, 1994; van Leeuwen & van den Hof, 1991), whereas many other classifications of structural features of visual Gestalt are very similar to complexity-regularity model (e.g., Berlyne, 1974; Birkhoff, 1932; Eysenck, 1941, 1968).

Regularity includes symmetry and other forms of pattern invariance subject to given transformations (e.g., Garner, 1962; Gibson, 1979; Koffka, 1935; Shaw, McIntyre, & Mace, 1974; Shaw & Turvey, 1981). A number of studies have shown that symmetry is significantly correlated with perceptual economy. It is positively correlated with the quality of the percept, that is with subjective measures of figural "goodness" (Bear, 1973; Bell & Handle, 1976; Clement 1964; Garner & Clement, 1963; Hamada & Ishihara, 1988; Palmer, 1991; Szilagyi & Baird, 1977; Yodogawa, 1982), and negatively correlated with processing load variables, such as reaction-time (RT) measures (Attneave, 1955; Bell & Handle, 1976; Checkosky & Whitlock, 1973; Corballis & Roldan, 1974; Garner & Sutliff, 1974; Palmer & Hemenway, 1978; Royer, 1981; Wagemans, van Gool, & d'Ydewalle, 1991). Thus, all these studies suggest that more symmetric patterns are judged as perceptually better and processed faster than asymmetric ones (for review, see Wagemans, 1995).

The number of different elements within the pattern defines its simplicity-complexity: The greater the number of elements, turns, and other sorts of changes within the stimulus pattern, the greater the complexity. It can thus be identified with dimensions such as uniformity, homogeneity, continuity, and the like (Koffka, 1935). Some studies suggest that complexity is inversely related to perceptual economy: Simpler patterns are processed more effectively and easily than complex ones (Alexander & Carey, 1968; Attneave, 1955; Chipman, 1977; Frith, 1978; Hochberg & McAlister, 1953; Palmer, 1977; Royer & Weitzel, 1977).

In some theoretical approaches such as Garner's informational model (Garner, 1962) and Leeuwenberg's structural-information theory (Leeuwenberg, 1971, 1982) symmetry and the complexity are put into a common conceptual and metric framework. In Garner's model regularity is identified with so-called external redundancy/uncertainty (e.g., the invariance of a pattern under rotation and reflection), whereas internal redundancy/uncertainty refers to the internal complexity of pattern (e.g., the number of details).

Leeuwenberg's structural information theory is a model for quantifying pattern complexity in terms of the, so-called, coding system (Leeuwenberg, 1971, 1982). In this theory, the greater the number of different elements and rules, the greater the structural informational load; regularity (minimum number of rules) and simplicity (minimum number of elements) are aspects of the same coding system.

Thus, perceptual economy is considered to be high when stimulus patterns are *regular* and *simple* and reduced when the perceptual system is faced with *irregular* and *complex* patterns (see Figure 1). However, note that in Figure 1 regularity and simplicity coincide with each other (symmetric simple vs. asymmetric complex pattern). The question is what would happen if these two dimensions do not coincide, that is if symmetric complex are contrasted with asymmetric simple patterns. Which dimension would then be a better predictor of perceptual economy? One of the main purposes of this paper is to try to solve this dilemma by contrasting the effects of symmetry and complexity on perceptual economy. Contradictory predictions of symmetry and simplicity models are shown in Figure 2.

Previous studies do not offer a clear answer to the question: i.e., which dimension, symmetry or simplicity, dominantly determine a perceptual economy. This is because the aims of these studies were mainly oriented towards investigation of particular effects of either variable symmetry with constant complexity (Attneave, 1955; Bear, 1973; Bell & Handle, 1976; Checkosky & Whitlock, 1973; Clement, 1964; Corballis & Roldan, 1974; Garner & Clement 1963; Garner & Sutliff, 1974; Hamada & Ishihara, 1988; Palmer & Hemenway, 1978; Royer, 1981; Szilagyi & Baird, 1977; Wagemans et al., 1991), or variable complexity with constant symmetry (Alexander & Carey, 1968; Attneave, 1955; Chipman, 1977; Frith, 1978; Hochberg & McAlister, 1953; Palmer, 1977; Royer & Weitzel, 1977). These studies were not motivated to contrast the strength of symmetry and simplicity, directly, by simultaneous variation of both dimensions. One notable exception is the contrasting of *global* and *local* models of visual occlusion phenomena. However, these data do not indicate a clear advantage of either global (symmetry) or local (contour simplicity, good continuation) models (cf. Boselie, 1988, 1994; Boselie & Leeuwenberg, 1986; Boselie & Wouterlood, 1989; Sekuler, 1994).

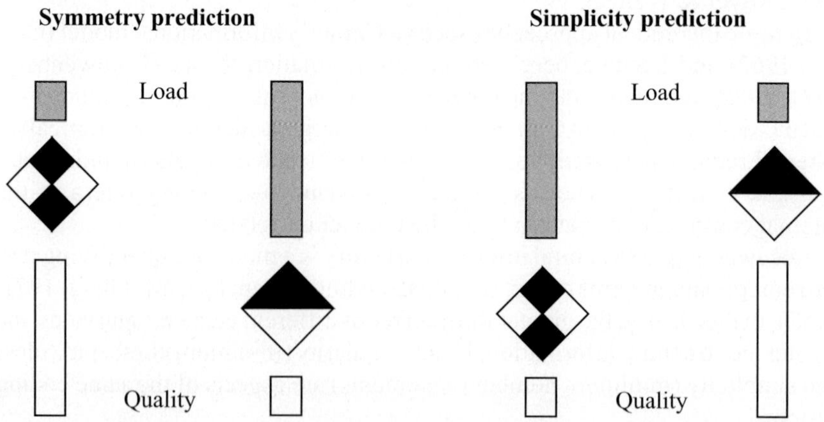

Figure 2. Contradictory predictions of perceptual economy by symmetry and simplicity models.

MINIMUM AND MAXIMUM SIMPLICITY

Koffka's concept of Minimum and Maximum simplicity can help us understand some possible reasons why there are no clear answer to the question which dimension, symmetry or simplicity, dominantly determines a perceptual economy (Koffka, 1935). According to this concept, the dominance of simplicity or symmetry depends on the energy state of the perceptual system. In so-called minimum simplicity conditions, that is, in situations when energy states are lower (e.g., low vigilance conditions) the perceptual system tends to save available energy, and, consequently, it "prefers" the *simplicity* of stimulus organization. The greater the simplicity of stimulus input, the smaller the processing load. However, in maximum simplicity conditions, the perceptual system has a greater energy disposal, which enables the articulation of rich and sophisticated perceptual Gestalten. In these conditions, minimizing energy usage is not as important as maximizing the quality of the percept, which is the reason why the perceptual system "prefers" the *regularity* over the simplicity of stimulus organization. In other words, both symmetry and simplicity are equally dominant constraints of perceptual economy: Symmetry prevails in greater energy state, whereas simplicity prevails in lower energy state.

PURPOSE OF THE STUDY

We argue that minimum and maximum simplicity conditions can be controlled through the manipulation of either perceptual task *demands*, or inner perceptual *motivation*. So, the higher energy state in maximum simplicity condition would be maintained in *easier* perceptual tasks (easy task low energy usage → high energy state), and in *interesting* tasks (high motivation → opening of additional energy resource → high energy state). On the other hand, the lower energy state in minimum simplicity condition would be established in more *demanding* tasks (difficult task → greater processing load → low energy state), and in *uninteresting* perceptual tasks (exhausting and uninteresting tasks → low perceptual arousal → low energy state).

The aim of this study was to evaluate the idea that minimum–maximum simplicity, that is to say, demands and interest of the perceptual task determine the dominance of given stimulus constraint (simplicity or symmetry). For this purpose, the following four perceptual tasks were defined. The first two tasks, *goodness judgement* (Experiment 1), and *pattern completion* (Experiment 2), were less demanding and more interesting, whereas the other two tasks, *perceptual search* (Experiment 3) and *pattern discrimination* (Experiment 4), were more difficult and uninteresting. According to the minimum–maximum simplicity hypothesis, we expected that symmetry would represent a dominant constraint for goodness judgement and completion, whereas simplicity would prevail in more demanding tasks such as search and discrimination.

STIMULI

The stimuli were generated in the following way. The symmetry axes divided the square into eight, equal triangular parts (see Figure 3). With four parts coloured black and four parts white, 13 basic patterns were generated. Similar method of stimulus generation was already employed by other authors (Prokhovnik, 1959; Royer, 1977; Royer & Weitzel, 1977). For the purpose of Experiments 1, 2, and 3 the shape of the referent square matrix was varied (patterns A, B, C, and D in Figure 4). Patterns A, B, C, and D were selected from the wider set of patterns used in a previous study of form cohesiveness perception (Marković, 1996): Patterns A and B have more cohesive (leaf-like) shapes, while patterns C and D have more disperse (star-like) shapes.

The 13 basic patterns can be distributed in two independent dimensions, symmetry and complexity. Symmetry and simplicity–complexity ranks for all stimulus patterns were specified (see Figure 3), giving three symmetry and four complexity ranks. The highest symmetry rank, S = 1, has patterns with two-fold mirror symmetry (i.e., dihedral symmetry group of order 2, or D_2) and a "swastika-like" pattern (i.e., cyclic group of order 4, or C_4). Rank S = 2 has patterns with single mirror symmetry (D_1), and the lowest rank, S = 3, has asymmetric patterns (i.e., invariant only after full circle rotation, C_1). The symmetry ranks

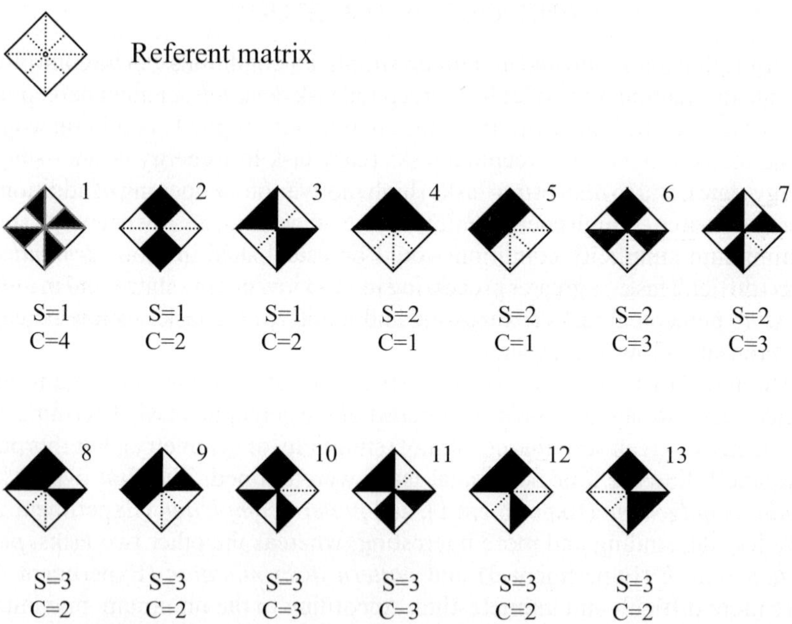

Figure 3. The referent square matrix and the 13 black–white patterns used as the stimuli. All patterns have their nominal numbers (1–13). Symmetry ranks (S) and simplicity–complexity ranks (C) are specified for each stimulus pattern.

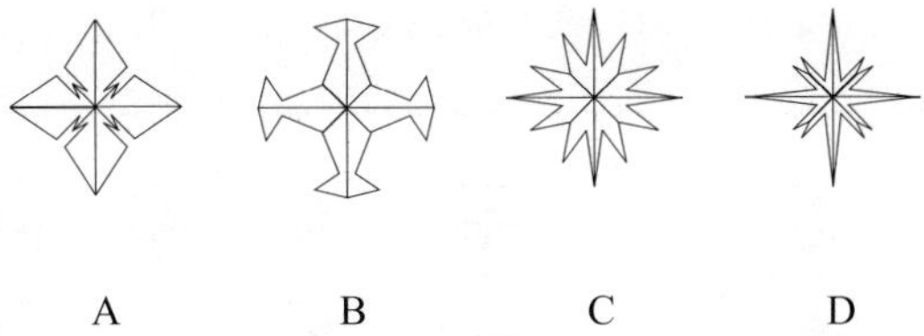

Figure 4. The shapes of referent matrices A, B, C, and D used for stimuli generation in Experiments 1, 2, and 3. See the text for details.

were derived from the subgroup–group relation. In our case the referent group was a "square symmetry", or dihedral group D_4. This group generates the subgroups D_2 and C_4 (rank S = 1). D_1 is subgroup of D_2 and it has lower order of symmetry (S = 2), and finally, C_1 has the lowest order of symmetry (S = 3). The four simplicity–complexity ranks (C) were derived from the number of black (or white) areas within the pattern: The smaller the number of areas, the higher the rank of simplicity–complexity: C = 1 (one area), C = 2 (two areas), C = 3 (three areas), and C = 4 (four areas).

On this basis, the systematic combination of four black and four white elements generated a closed and definite population of patterns. The patterns can be included in two independent (uncorrelated) distributions, one of the symmetry–asymmetry and another of the simplicity–complexity dimension. Regression analysis shows that two series of measures for 13 basic patterns symmetry (S) and simplicity–complexity (C) are not significantly correlated, $r^2 = .012$, $F(1, 11) = .13$, $p > .05$.

EXPERIMENT 1

In this experiment the figural goodness judgements of four sets of stimuli was investigated. The main purpose of this experiment was to evaluate which constraint, symmetry or simplicity–complexity, is the best predictor of goodness judgements.

Method

Subjects. Fifty-eight undergraduate students of the Department of Psychology, University of Belgrade (27 females and 31 males; mean age 20 years) participated in the experiment. All subjects had normal or corrected-to-normal vision.

Stimuli and design. Four sets (A, B, C, and D) each consisting of 13 black–white patterns. The stimuli were generated by the principle given in Figure 3. The shape of referent square patterns (A, B, C, and D; see Figure 4) defines each

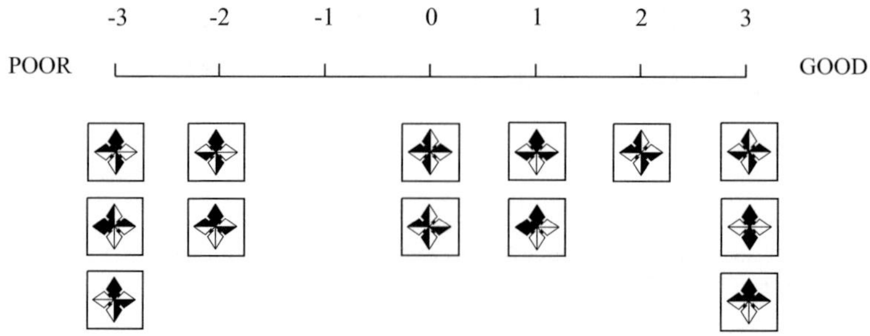

Figure 5. One of the possible arrangements of the cards below the scale.

set. A within-subjects design was used, with the factors set (4 levels) and pattern (13 levels).

Procedure. Four sets of stimulus cards (5 × 5 cm) were given to the subjects consecutively, one after another. The order of sets A, B, C, and D were counterbalanced among subjects using a Latin square method. The patterns within the set were shuffled (i.e., pseudorandomly) ordered. Subjects worked individually. They were asked to judge the goodness of each pattern within the given set using the seven-point bipolar scale, poor–good. Goodness was defined as "a visually well-arranged group of element" and as "a well-organized whole". The scale was put on the table in front of the subject, and he or she arranged the cards below the appropriate values (see Figure 5) while an experimenter recorded the judgements. The sessions (i.e., the judgements of all four sets) lasted about 10 minutes.

Results and discussion

The judgements were transformed from bipolar (–3 to 3) in unipolar form (1–7) form. The distributions of means and standard deviations for all four sets were are given in Figure 6.

Analysis of variance fails to show significant main effect of set, $F(3, 57) = .59$. However, the factor pattern was significant, $F(12, 57) = 268.25, p < .01$, as was the interaction of this factor with set $F(3, 12) = 3.18, p < .01$. This interaction is not unexpected because of great number of pattern levels.

Regression analysis indicated that symmetry rank is the most significant predictor of mean-goodness judgements for all four sets: The higher the symmetry, the greater the goodness (see Table 1).

The simplicity–complexity rank did not show good prediction of mean goodness judgements and was surprisingly poor with the determination coefficients being between $r^2 = .01$ and $r^2 = .05$.

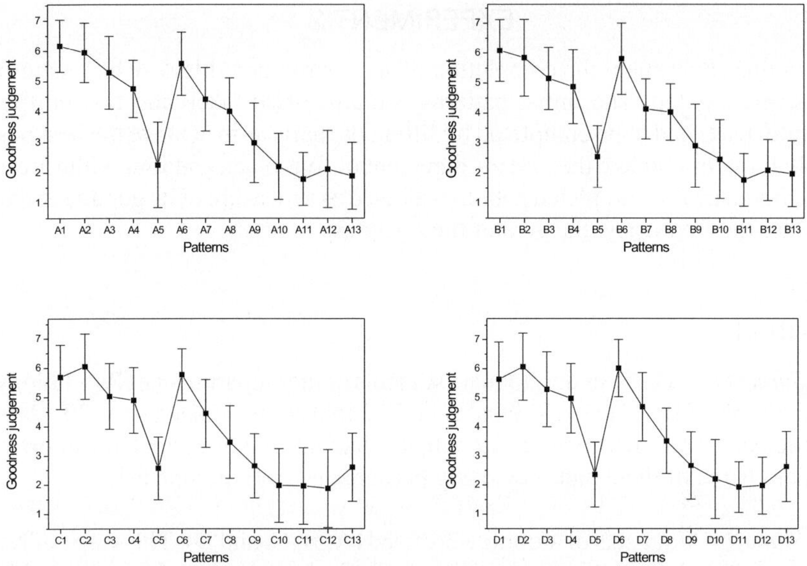

Figure 6. Results of Experiment 1: Distributions of means and standard deviations of goodness judgements for the sets A, B, C, and D.

Indicating that symmetry is the dominant stimulus constraint of goodness judgements, the results of the present experiment confirmed our expectation that symmetry would be the prevailing constraint under maximum simplicity conditions (less demanding tasks), such as goodness judgement. In Experiment 2 we used the pattern completion task in order to obtain further evidence about validity of this hypothesis and subjects were asked to complete semi-structured patterns into the best possible Gestalten. Similar to goodness judgement, the completion task reflected the maximum simplicity condition as well, because it was both easy and interesting and stimulus presentation was not restricted.

TABLE 1
Results of regression analyses for sets A, B, C, and D. Symmetry rank is a predictor, and goodness judgement is a dependent variable

Set	r^2	F*(1, 11)*	p
A	0.92	119.74	0.001
B	0.92	133.74	0.001
C	0.91	118.68	0.001
D	0.90	101.77	0.001

EXPERIMENT 2

In this experiment the completion of semi-structured black–white patterns was investigated. The initial patterns contained two black and two unfilled (white) parts had to be completed by filling the parts as to achieve the best possible form, or to make the best arrangement of four black and four white areas. The frequency of completed pattern was used as a measure of its goodness: The greater the frequency, the greater the goodness.

Method

Subjects. Thirty undergraduate students of the Department of Psychology, University of Belgrade (18 females and 12 males; mean age about 20 years) participated in Experiment 2. All subjects had normal or corrected-to-normal vision. None of them had previously participated in Experiment 1.

Stimuli. Four sets of stimuli were used (A, B, C, and D). The shape of referent pattern defines the sets (see Figure 4). Each set consisted of seven initial semi-structured patterns (two black and six white areas). Figure 7 shows the distribution of black areas within all seven initial patterns and some possible ways of their completion.

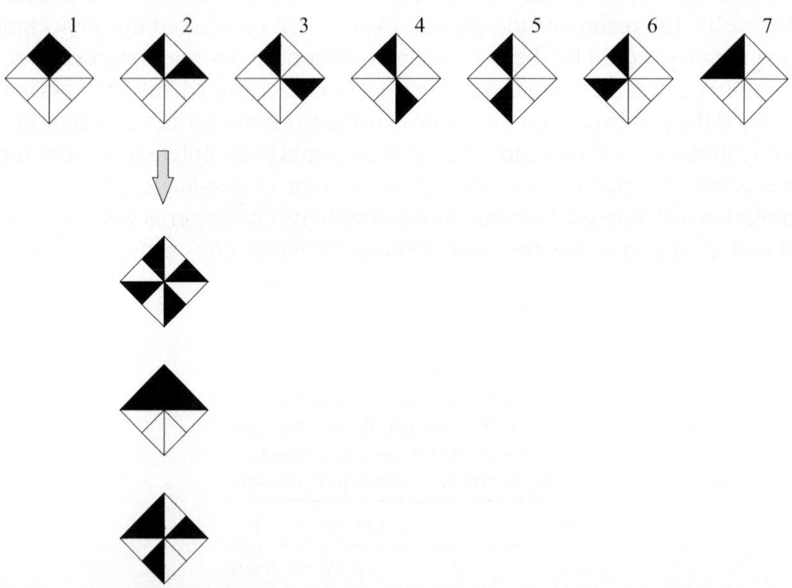

Figure 7. The distribution of black areas within all seven initial patterns. This principle was used for the generation of A, B, C, and D sets of initial patterns. Three out of fifteen possible completions of pattern 2 are shown.

Procedure. The four sets of stimulus cards (10 x 10 cm) were given to the subjects consecutively, one after another. The order of sets A, B, C, and D were counterbalanced between subjects using a Latin square method and the seven patterns within the set were pseudorandomly ordered. Subjects worked individually and were asked to fill the two parts in each pattern as to achieve the visually best possible configuration: That is to make the best arrangement of four black and four white areas. Subjects filled in the patterns with black marker pencils. The sessions (completion of all four sets) lasted about 15 minutes.

Results

The frequency distributions of 13 basic pattern completions for all four sets are shown in Figure 8. Regression analysis indicated that symmetry rank was a significantly good predictor of frequency of completion: The higher the symmetry, the greater the frequency (see Table 2).

Simplicity-complexity rank was not a significant predictor of frequencies. The coefficients of determination were between $r^2 = .00$ and $r^2 = .01$!

Similar to Experiment 1, results of the present experiment confirmed our hypothesis, suggesting that symmetry is the prevailing stimulus constraint in the maximum simplicity condition, that is to say in less demanding and more interesting tasks.

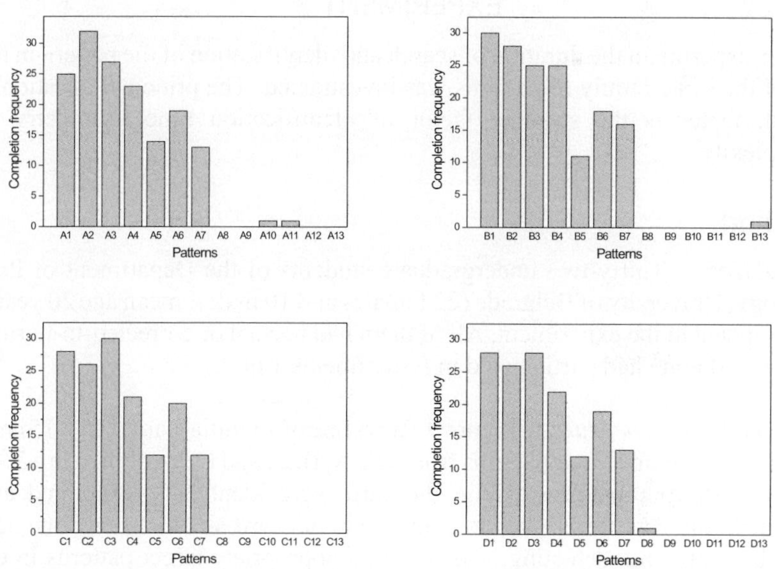

Figure 8. Results of Experiment 2: Frequency distributions of 13 basic pattern completions for sets A, B, C, and D.

TABLE 2
Results of regression analyses for sets A, B, C, and D. Symmetry rank is a predictor, and completion frequency is a dependent variable

Set	r^2	$F_{(1, 11)}$	*p*
A	0.88	82.62	0.001
B	0.85	62.15	0.001
C	0.89	98.00	0.001
D	0.87	83.75	0.001

The next two experiments focused on the minimum simplicity conditions: Specifically, demanding, exhausting, and uninteresting perceptual tasks. In these conditions we expected that the simplicity–complexity of stimulus patterns would play more important role than regularity (symmetry). In Experiment 3, subjects were asked to find the target pattern in a large pile of scattered patterns. The task required massive spatial search, but it was not temporally restricted. In Experiment 4 subjects were faced with a relatively simple same–different task, but the presentation times of stimuli were very short (50 ms). In other words, Experiments 3 and 4 represented two sorts of demands, detection of stimuli in spatially and temporally restricted conditions.

EXPERIMENT 3

In this experiment the duration of search and identification of the pattern in the set of the same family of patterns was investigated. The principal question is which factor is the stronger factor of identification time, symmetry or complexity.

Method

Subjects. Thirty-two undergraduate students of the Department of Psychology, University of Belgrade (22 females and 10 males; mean age 20 years) participated in the experiment. All of them had normal or corrected-to-normal vision and none had participated in Experiments 1 or 2.

Stimuli and procedure. Figure 9 shows one of 13 initial cards (15 × 15 cm). Each card contained four patterns from sets A, B, C, and D distributed in a 2 × 2 matrix. All four patterns within the card were identically structured and oriented. Subjects were asked to copy the initial card and to arrange the new card by searching, detecting, and selecting appropriate target patterns in the pile of little cards (5 × 5 cm). The pile was made by the random scattering of 104 patterns (four sets, A, B, C, and D, of 13 small cards times two; see Figure 10).

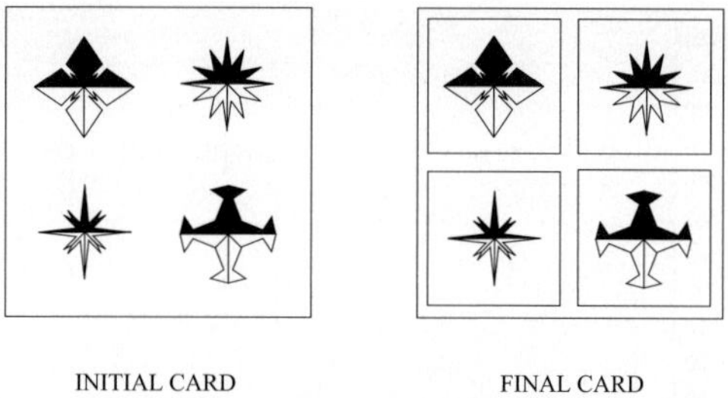

Figure 9. Initial card that contains four identically structured and oriented patterns from sets A, B, C, and D is on the left. The final card as the result of the copying of initial card is on the right.

The duration of the initial card copying was recorded and the copying time was measured in seconds, with an electronic clock, from when the initial card was put in front of the subject, and ending when copying was completed. The presentation order of 13 initial cards was randomized.

Design. A within-subjects design was used with the factor pattern structure (13 pattern structures).

Results

The distribution of copying-time means and standard deviations is shown in Figure 11. A one-way analysis of variance revealed a significant effect of pattern structure on copying time, $F(12, 31) = 37.34, p < .01$.

The linear regression indicated that symmetry rank was a good predictor of the mean copying time, $r^2 = .70$, $F(1, 11) = 25.98$, $p < .01$: The higher the

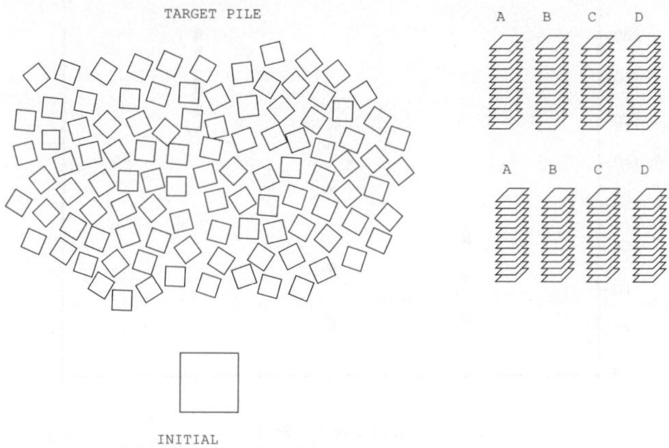

Figure 10. The experimental situation in Experiment 3 included the pile of 104 scattered cards and the initial card, which had to be copied by searching for the target card in the pile.

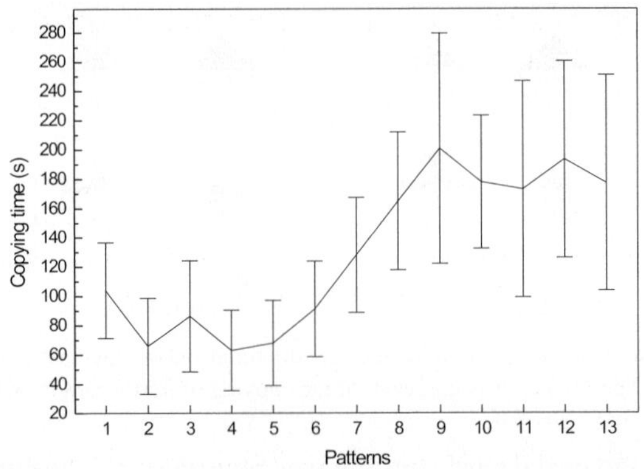

Figure 11. Results of Experiment 3: Distribution of copying-time means and standard deviations for 13 initial patterns.

symmetry rank, the faster the copying of initial card. However, a quadratic regression revealed a better prediction of symmetry rank, $r^2 = .87$, $F(1, 10) = 33.68$, $p < .01$ (see Figure 12). The simplicity–complexity rank did not reach significance, $r^2 = .05$, $F(1, 11) = .68$.

The results of the present experiment failed to confirm our expectation that simplicity–complexity is dominant constraint of copying time. However, more detailed inspection of Figure 12 suggests that the symmetry rank is significant predictor mainly due to the difference between asymmetric (S = 3) and symmetric (S = 1 and S = 2) patterns. When asymmetric patterns are excluded from regression analysis, then symmetry rank becomes a non-significant predictor,

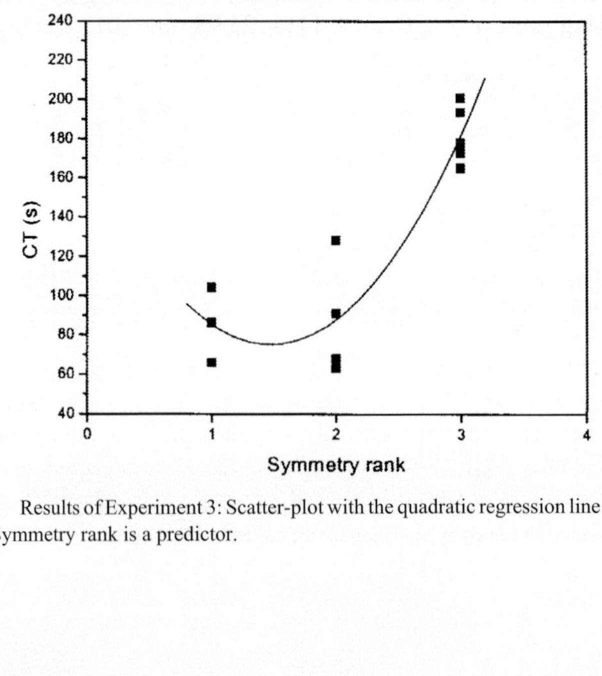

Figure 12. Results of Experiment 3: Scatter-plot with the quadratic regression line for the mean copying time. Symmetry rank is a predictor.

$r^2 = .00$, $F(1, 5) = .01$, but simplicity–complexity achieves significance, $r^2 = .60$, $F(1, 5) = 7.62$, $p < .05$.

Hence in the searching task, subjects were globally sensitive to the difference between asymmetric and symmetric patterns: Asymmetric patterns were more difficult to find in the pile than symmetric ones. However, they are not sensitive to the finer difference between less and more symmetric patterns. In this case, simplicity–complexity becomes the more important constraint: The greater the complexity, the more difficult it is to find the pattern. So, our hypothesis about the dominance of simplicity in searching tasks was partially confirmed because only the relative impact of simplicity–complexity on copying time has been revealed.

In this experiment, the task was demanding and exhausting but it was not temporally restricted. In Experiment 4, the duration of stimulus presentation was extremely restricted: Subjects had to compare two very briefly exposed patterns. According to Koffka's original formulation of minimum and maximum simplicity conditions, the reduction of exposure time is one of the most effective ways to induce minimum simplicity, in other words a low energy state (Koffka, 1935).

EXPERIMENT 4

This experiment was designed to evaluate the concept of minimum and maximum simplicity in more restrictive tasks, such as pattern discrimination (same–different task) in reduced temporal conditions. The hypothesis is that the detection and discrimination of extremely shortly exposed stimuli (50 ms) is a considerably more difficult and stressful task than goodness judgement and completion. The same–different paradigm was used to investigate the effect of pattern configuration (i.e., symmetry and complexity) on duration and correctness of stimulus detection.

Method

Subjects. Sixteen undergraduate students of the Department of Psychology, University of Belgrade (10 females and 6 males; mean age 20 years) participated in the experiment. All of them had normal or corrected-to-normal vision and none of them had participated in Experiments 1, 2, or 3.

Stimuli. Eleven, basic, black–white patterns were used for stimulus generation (see Figure 13). For each pattern a *same* and *different* pair was created. The same pair consisted of two identically oriented patterns (see Figure 14a), whereas the different pair included the basic pattern and its equivalent obtained by 90° clockwise rotation (Figure 14b), or the mirror version for the "swastika-like" pattern (C_4). The position of patterns within the *different* pair was bal-

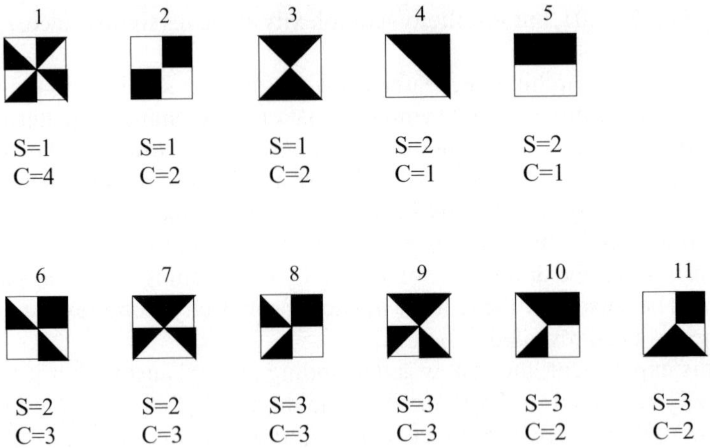

Figure 13. The 11 basic patterns used for the generating of stimuli in Experiment 4. The symmetry ranks (S) and the simplicity–complexity ranks (C) of patterns are shown.

anced left–right (Figure 14b,d). To establish the equal number of same and different pairs, the same pairs were made of equivalents of 11 basic patterns as well (Figure 14c), such that the 22 same and the 22 different pairs were created (44 in total). Stimuli were presented on the screen of IBM-compatible Pentium 2 personal computer. In order to avoid after-image effect a textural mask was used after stimulus presentation.

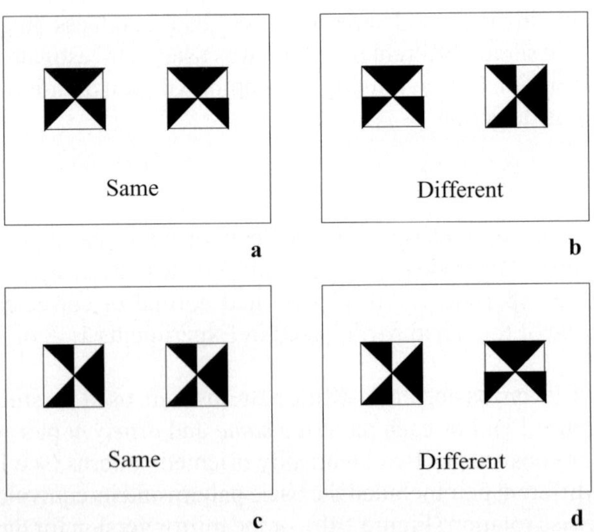

Figure 14. The same and different combinations. See text for details.

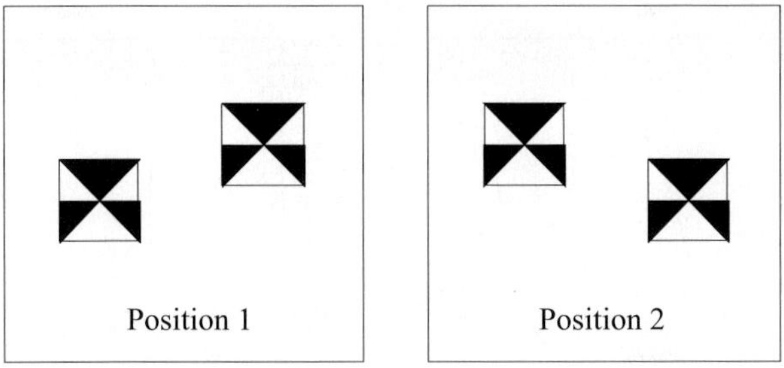

Figure 15. The spatial position of patterns within the stimulus pair.

To avoid the possibility of global symmetry of the *same* pairs, patterns were diagonally positioned (Figure 15). Then the number of stimuli was doubled (44 × 2 = 88), because each pattern could be in both positions, upper and lower (see Figure 15). Finally, each pair was presented twice, so the total number of stimuli increased to 176.

Procedure. Each trial comprised the following displays: Fixation point (500 ms), stimulus exposition (50 ms; about 10 × 10 cm) and textural mask (1000 ms; 10 × 10 cm). Fixation point, stimuli, and mask were centred on the computer screen. The distance between the screen and the observer's eyes was set at 50 cm. Subjects responded during mask presentation. The order of stimuli presentation was counterbalanced.

Subjects were asked to indicate whether the patterns within the exposed pair were completely the same (identically oriented) or different (differently oriented) by pressing one of two keys marked as same or different. The instructions stressed both speed and accuracy. The session began with a practice trial, which included the presentation of 20 stimuli. The RT (in ms) and the number of correct responses were recorded. The 88 RTs for the same responses were collapsed into 11 RTs by averaging the following situations: 2 presentations (first and second), 2 positions (upper, lower), and 2 equivalents (basic, rotated). So the RTs for all 11 patterns were obtained. The RTs for different responses were collapsed by averaging 2 presentations (first and second) × 4 positions (upper, lower, left, right). A similar principle was used for correct responses.

Design. A within-subjects design was used, with the factors same–different and pattern (11 patterns).

Results

The mean RTs and the mean proportions of correct responses for the same and different situations are shown in Figure 16. A two-way analysis of variance yielded no main effect of the factor same–different on RT, $F(1, 15) = .33$, a

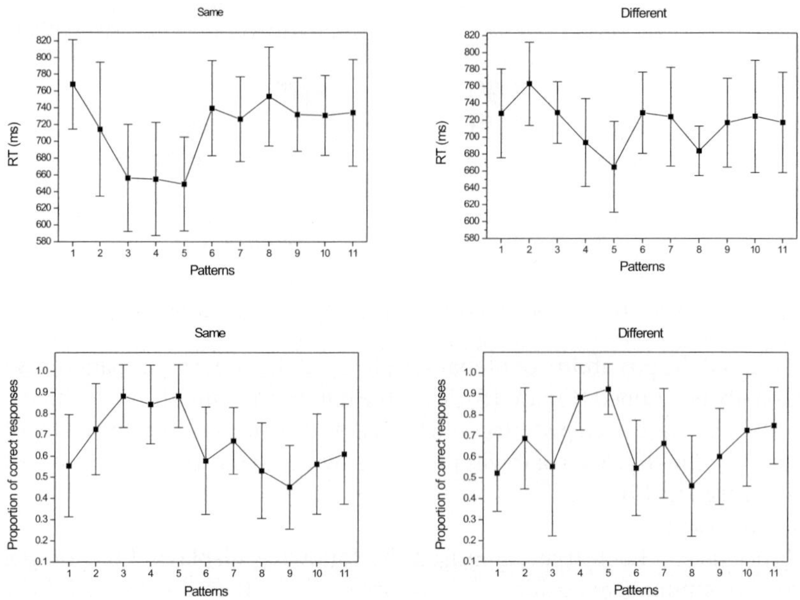

Figure 16. Results of Experiment 4: Mean RT and mean proportions of correct responses for the "same" and "different" situations.

main effect of factor pattern, $F(10, 150) = 18.59, p < .01$, and a significant interaction between these two factors, $F(10, 150) = 11.21, p < .01$. A two-way analysis of variance yielded no main effect of the factor same–different on proportion of correct responses, $F(1, 15) = .00$, a main effect of factor pattern, $F(10, 150) = 19.13, p < .01$, and a significant interaction between these two factors, $F(10, 150) = 3.67, p < .01$.

Only the same responses will be under the scope of our interest because they indicate the duration of figure detection. The different responses refer to the specific discrimination processes (e.g., comparisons 0° vs. 90° rotated figure, sharp vs. blurred texture, original vs. distorted image, etc.). A regression analysis has shown that the simplicity–complexity rank is a significantly good predictor of RT, $r^2 = .715$, $F(1, 9) = 22.60, p < .01$. The greater the simplicity, the faster the detection. Symmetry rank was not significant ($r^2 = .080$).

The simplicity–complexity rank showed good prediction of mean proportion of correct responses as well, $r^2 = .554$, $F(1, 9) = 11.19, p < .01$. The greater the simplicity, the more accurate the detection. The symmetry rank failed to achieve a significance, $r^2 = .288$, $F(1, 9) = 3.63, p > .05$.

The results of this experiment confirmed our expectation that simplicity–complexity is the prevailing constraint in the minimum simplicity condition, that is in demanding and exhausting perceptual tasks. These results also suggest that the role of simplicity is greater in temporally restricted conditions, than in demanding tasks that are not temporally restricted.

GENERAL DISCUSSION

The results of the present study generally support Koffka's idea that in so-called minimum simplicity conditions (i.e., in demanding, exhausting, and uninteresting tasks) the regularity prevails, whereas in maximum simplicity condition (i.e., in easy and interesting tasks) the simplicity is more important constraint (Koffka, 1935). Although this conception requires more extensive evaluation, some possible theoretical implications of minimum–maximum simplicity concept can be considered.

Minimum–maximum simplicity and perceptual organization

According to Koffka (1935), in minimum simplicity conditions (small energy disposal) the perceptual system tends to describe external stimulation in the simplest possible way, producing percepts that are uniform, homogenized, and reduced in details. However, in maximum simplicity conditions (greater energy disposal), the stimulus becomes articulated into sophisticated, regular, and meaningful Gestalten. Moreover, the additional energy resource can sometimes help the perceptual system to transform meaningless and chaotic stimulus patterns into the meaningful and well-structured percepts (e.g., perception of Rorschach figures).

This conception has great importance for understanding constraints of perceptual organization, because it suggests that there is no fixed hierarchy of organizational principles: The same stimulus elements can be bound together in different perceptual wholes, depending on inner perceptual states. So, in minimum simplicity conditions, the elements will be bound into the *simplest* possible structure, whereas in maximum simplicity conditions they will be bound into the *most regular* Gestalt.

The results of a previous study of visual occlusion support this idea (Marković, 1998). These results indicate that amodal completion of partly occluded figures in more complex stimulus conditions is driven by good continuation (minimum change of contour direction). In simpler stimulus conditions, the same stimulus patterns are completed by the symmetry principle: Interrupted contours of occluded figures are connected so that the greatest possible symmetry of completed figures was reached. Luccio's demonstrations yield the similar conclusions: In suboptimal observation (e.g., filling in the blind spot) the local simplicity prevails, destroying the regularity of whole configuration (Luccio, 1998).

Minimum–maximum simplicity and processing theories

Representation theories of perception fail to explain the variability of perceptuo-organizational principles. This failure is not the consequence of the "fact" that these theories do not take into account the domain of perceptual processes. On the contrary, they explicitly include the idea that the form of representation depends on processing constraints. For instance, Leeuwenberg's structural-information theory (Leeuwenberg, 1971, 1982; van der Helm & Leeuwenberg, 1996) predicts that the simplest description of a stimulus pattern will be preferred by the perceptual system, assuming that the simplest representation is the one that is the most economically processed. Leeuwenberg's model implies the same results of stimulus pattern encoding regardless of the variability of task demands, inner motivation, or presentation restrictions. It seems that the main problem with representational theories is not the dilemma between representation and process, but rather the question whether the processing is unique (i.e., single) or complex (i.e., composed of two or more stages).

The variability of organizational principles could be more successfully explained by theories that start from the two-stage model of perceptual process (Bruce & Morgan, 1975; Freyd & Tversky, 1984; Julesz, 1971; Locher & Nodine, 1987; Palmer & Hemenway, 1978; Sekuler & Palmer, 1992; see also Wagemans, 1995). The first stage is defined as a fast, preattentive process, which yields a rough representation of stimulus, whereas the second stage comprises a slower cognitively controlled attentive process, which leads towards a fine, scrutinized, and meaningful perceptual description. A similar distinction can be found in Kanisza's notion of primary and secondary processes (Kanizsa, 1979; Kanizsa & Gerbino, 1982; see also Luccio, 1998).

The predictions of a two-stage model referring to the dominance of organizational principles (simplicity vs. symmetry) are similar to the predictions of the minimum–maximum simplicity model. In temporally restricted conditions, a perceptual process will result in simple, rough representation, but if the perceptual system is given more time for processing, the rough representation will be refined into a well-articulated percept. The results of Experiment 4 confirmed one part of this prediction: For detection of briefly presented patterns (50 ms) how many elements the pattern consisted of was more important than how regular these elements were structured. However, the two-stage theories do not take into account the role of variability of inner energy resources in temporally unrestricted conditions (e.g., change of vigilance, arousal, visibility, spatial complexity of stimulus display, and the like). The results of Experiment 3 (searching task) suggest that an increase of task complexity can have a similar effect to temporal restriction (i.e., the impact of pattern simplicity), but this has to be more precisely evaluated in further studies.

In conclusion, our study suggests that there is no fixed hierarchy of organizational principles in perception, but that the dominance of principles (e.g., simplicity or regularity) depends on energy states within the perceptual system.

REFERENCES

Alexander, C., & Carey, S. (1968). Subsymmetries. *Perception and Psychophysics, 4*(2), 73–77.

Attneave, F. (1955). Symmetry, information, and memory for patterns. *American Journal of Psychology, 68*, 209–222.

Attneave, F. (1982). Prägnanz and soap bubble system: A theoretical exploration. In J. Beck (Ed.), *Organization and representation in perception* (pp. 11–29). Hillsdale, NJ: Lawrence Erlbaum Associates Inc.

Bear, G. (1973). Figural goodness and predictability of figural elements. *Perception and Psychophysics, 13,* 32–40.

Bell, H.H., & Handle, S. (1976). The role of pattern goodness in the reproduction of backward masked patterns. *Journal of Experimental Psychology: Human Perception and Performance, 2*(1), 139–150.

Berlyne, D.E. (1974). Novelty, complexity, and interestingness. In D.E. Berlyne (Ed.), *Studies in the new experimental aesthetics* (pp. 175–180). Washington, DC: Hemisphere Publishing Corporation.

Birkhoff, G.D. (1932). *Aesthetic measure.* Cambridge, MA: Harvard University Press.

Boselie, F. (1988). Local versus global minima in visual pattern completion. *Perception and Psychophysics, 43*(5), 431–445.

Boselie, F. (1994). Local and global factors in visual occlusion. *Perception, 23,* 517–528.

Boselie, F., & Leeuwenberg, E. (1986). A test of the minimum principle requires a perceptual coding system. *Perception, 15,* 331–354.

Boselie, F., & Wouterlood, D. (1989). The minimum principle and visual pattern completion. *Psychological Research, 51,* 93–101.

Bruce, V.G., & Morgan, M.J. (1975). Violations of symmetry and repetition in visual patterns. *Perception, 4,* 239–249.

Checkosky, S.F., & Whitlock, D. (1973). Effect of pattern goodness on recognition time in a memory research task. *Journal of Experimental Psychology, 100*(2), 341–348.

Chipman, S.F. (1977). Complexity and structure of visual pattern. *Journal of Experimental Psychology: General, 106*(3), 269–301.

Clement, D.E. (1964). Uncertainty and latency of verbal naming response as correlates of pattern goodness. *Journal of Verbal Learning and Behavior, 3,* 150–157.

Corballis, M.C., & Roldan, C.E. (1974). On the perception of symmetrical and repeated patterns. *Perception and Psychophysics, 16*(1), 136–142.

Eysenck, H.J. (1941). The empirical determination of an aesthetic formula. *Psychological Review, 48,* 83–92.

Eysenck, H.J. (1968). An experimental study of aesthetic preference for polygonal figures. *Journal of General Psychology, 79,* 3–17.

Freyd, J., & Tversky, B. (1984). Force of symmetry in form perception. *American Journal of Psychology, 97*(1), 109–126.

Frith, C.D. (1978). The subjective properties of complex visual patterns. In E.L.J. Leeuwenberg & H.F. Buffart (Eds.), *Formal theories of visual perception* (pp. 231–246). Chichester, UK: John Wiley & Sons.

Garner, W.R. (1962). *Uncertainty and structure as psychological concepts.* New York: John Wiley.

Garner, W.R., & Clement, D.E. (1963). Goodness of pattern and pattern uncertainty. *Journal of Verbal Learning and Verbal Behavior, 2,* 446–430.

Garner, W.R., & Sutliff, D. (1974). The effect of goodness on encoding time in visual pattern perception. *Perception and Psychophysics, 16*(3), 426–430.

Gibson, J.J. (1979). *The ecological approach to visual perception.* Boston: Houghton Mifflin.

Hamada, J., & Ishihara, T. (1988). Complexity and goodness of dot patterns varying in symmetry. *Psychological Research, 50,* 155–161.

Hatfield, G., & Epstein, W. (1985). The status of minimum principle in the theoretical analysis of visual perception. *Psychological Bulletin, 97*(20), 155–186.

Hochberg, J.E., & McAlister, E. (1953). A quantitative approach to figural "goodness". *Journal of Experimental Psychology, 46,* 361–364.

Julesz, B. (1971). *Foundations of cyclopean perception.* Chicago: University of Chicago Press.

Kanizsa, G. (1979). *Organization of vision.* New York: Praeger

Kanizsa, G., & Gerbino, W. (1982). Amodal completion: Seeing or thinking? In J. Beck (Ed.), *Organization and representation in perception* (pp. 167–190). Hillsdale, NJ: Lawrence Erlbaum Associates Inc.

Köhler, W. (1971). Zum Problem der Regulation [On the problem of regulation]. In M. Henle (Ed.), *The selected papers of Wolfgang Köhler* (pp. 305–326). New York: Liveright. (Original work published 1927).

Koffka, K. (1935). *Principles of Gestalt psychology.* London: Kegan, Paul, Trench & Trubner.

Leeuwenberg, E. (1971). A perceptual coding language for visual and auditory patterns. *American Journal of Psychology, 84*, 307–349.

Leeuwenberg, E. (1982). Metrical aspects of patterns and structural information theory. In J. Beck (Ed.), *Organization and representation in perception* (pp. 57–71). Hillsdale, NJ: Lawrence Erlbaum Associates Inc.

Locher, P.J., & Nodine, C.F. (1987). Symmetry catches the eye. In J.K. O'Regan & A. Levy–Schoen (Eds.), *Eye movements: From physiology to cognition* (pp. 353–361). Amsterdam: Elsevier.

Luccio, R. (1998). On Prägnanz. In L. Albertazzi (Ed.), *Shapes of form: From gestalt psychology and phenomenology to ontology and mathematics* (pp. 123–148). Dordrecht, The Netherlands: Kluwer.

Marković, S. (1995). Objective features of figural goodness: uniformity, compactness or symmetry? *Laboratorija za Eksperimentalnu Psihologiju* (LEP). Rep. 21. Serbia, Yugoslavia: Faculty of Philosophy, University of Belgrade.

Marković, S. (1996). *Figural cohesiveness and Prägnanz quality.* Unpublished manuscript.

Marković, S. (1999). Local and global factors in the occlusion phenomena: The effect on context complexity. *Perception* (suppl.), *28*, 117.

Palmer, H. (1977). Hierarchical structure in perceptual representation. *Cognitive Psychology, 9*(4), 441–474.

Palmer, S.E. (1991). Goodness, Gestalt, groups, and Garner: Local symmetry subgroups as a theory of figural goodness. In G.R. Lockhead & J.R. Pomerantz (Eds.), *The perception of structure* (pp. 23–39). Washington, DC: American Psychological Association.

Palmer, S.E., & Hemenway, K. (1978). Orientation and symmetry: Effects of multiple, rotational and near symmetries. *Journal of Experimental Psychology: Human Perception and Performance, 4*(4), 691–702.

Prokhovnik, S.J. (1959). Pattern variants on a square field. *Psychometrika, 24*(4), 329–341.

Restle, F. (1982). Coding theory as an integration of gestalt psychology and information processing theory. In J. Beck (Ed.), *Organization and representation in perception* (pp. 31–56). Hillsdale, NJ: Lawrence Erlbaum Associates Inc.

Royer, F.L. (1977). Information processing in the block design task. *Intelligence, 1,* 32–50.

Royer, F.L. (1981). Detection of symmetry. *Journal of Experimental Psychology: Human Perception and Performance, 7*(6), 1186–1210.
Royer, F.L., & Weitzel, K.E. (1977). Effects of perceptual cohesiveness on pattern recoding in the block design task. *Perception and Psychophysics, 21*(1), 39–49.
Sekuler, B.A. (1994). Local and global minima in visual completion: Effects of symmetry and orientation. *Perception, 23,* 529–545.
Sekuler, B.A., & Palmer, S.E. (1992). Perception of partly occluded objects: A microgenetic analysis. *Journal of Experimental Psychology: General, 121,* 95–111.
Shaw, R.E., McIntyre, M., & Mace, W. (1974). The role of symmetry in event perception. In R.B. McLeod & H.L. Pick Jr. (Eds.), *Essays in honor of James J. Gibson* (pp. 276–310). Ithaca, NY: Cornell University Press.
Shaw, R.E., & Turvey, M.T. (1981). Coalitions as models for ecosystems: A realist perspective on perceptual organization. In M. Kubovy & J.R. Pomerantz (Eds.), *Perceptual organization* (pp. 343–415). Hillsdale, NJ: Lawrence Erlbaum Associates Inc.
Szilagyi, P.G., & Baird, J.C. (1977). A quantitative approach to the study of visual symmetry. *Perception and Psychophysics, 22*(3), 287–292.
van der Helm, P.A., & Leeuwenberg, E.L.J. (1996). Goodness of visual regularities: A nontransformational approach. *Psychological Review, 103*(3), 429–456.
van Leeuwen, C. (1990). Perceptual-learning systems as conservative structures: Is economy an attractor? *Psychological Research, 52,* 145–152.
van Leeuwen, C., & van den Hof, M. (1991). What has happened to Prägnanz? Coding, stability or resonance. *Perception and Psychophysics, 50*(5), 435–448.
Wagemans, J. (1995). Detection of visual symmetries. *Spatial Vision, 9*(1), 9–32.
Wagemans, J., van Gool, L., & d'Ydewalle, G. (1991). Detection of symmetry in tachistoscopically presented dot patterns: Effects of multiple axes and skewing. *Perception and Psychophysics, 50*(5), 413–427.
Yodogawa, E. (1982). Symmentropy, an entropy-like measure of visual symmetry. *Perception and Psychophysics, 32*(3), 230–240.

VISUAL COGNITION, 2001, *8* (3/4/5), 329–348

On what is bound in figures and grounds

Mary A. Peterson and Jee Hyun Kim
University of Arizona, Tucson, USA

All else being equal, regions providing a quick, good match to object memories are likely to be seen as shaped figures rather than as shapeless grounds. Good matches to object memories occur only if the parts are properly bound spatially. If object memories are accessed in the course of perceptual organization even for regions ultimately seen as shapeless grounds, then binding of parts cannot require attention to figures. Novel silhouette primes were shown immediately before real or novel line drawings. The silhouette contours of half of the primes preceding real line drawings sketched a known shape on the outside, which nevertheless appeared to be a shapeless ground. At short prime-line drawing SOAs, observers took longer to categorize real line drawings following these experimental primes than control primes, suggesting that parts are properly bound spatially for regions perceived to be shapeless grounds, and further that object memories matching grounds are inhibited.

Early in the course of perceptual processing, certain regions in the visual field are assigned figural status and others are assigned ground status (see Figure 1). Figures and grounds have different properties. Figures have a definite shape that, if familiar, can be recognized; they appear to be things or objects. Grounds are not shaped by any contours they share with figures; they appear to simply continue behind the figures near those contours. Kahneman and Treisman (1984) proposed that when an object is first sensed (presumably after figure assignment), an "object file" is opened as a precursor to a perceived object. Information about object features (e.g., motion, brightness, colour, size) and object identity is entered into the object file as it becomes available. Object files segregate information belonging to different objects (Kahneman & Treisman, 1984); attention then binds together various features of objects (such as colour and form) (Treisman & Gelade, 1980).

Please address all correspondence to Dr. M.A. Peterson, Department of Psychology, University of Arizona, Tucson, AZ 85721, USA. Email: mapeters@u.arizona.edu

This research was supported by a National Science Foundation grant (BCS 9906063) to the first author. We thank Melissa Lin, Logan Trujillo, and especially Daniel Lampignano for their help with these experiments. Tia Kalla did an excellent job drawing the real line drawings we used to supplement the Snodgrass and Vanderwart set.

http://www.tandf.co.uk/journals/pp/13506285.html DOI:10.1080/13506280143000034

Figure 1. A. The Rubin vase–faces display illustrates the coupling between figural status and conscious recognition. As one steadily observes this display, figural status is alternately assigned to the black and white regions. The face profiles can be seen and recognized as such only when the black regions appear to be figure. When the white region appears to be the figure, the black region appears shapeless near the contours it shares with the black region. Similarly, the vase (goblet) can be seen/recognized only when the white region appears to be the figure; it cannot be seen/recognized when the black regions appear to be figures at the borders they share with the white region.

Wolfe and Bennett (1997) interpreted their visual search results as evidence that the parts within an object file remain spatially unordered unless attention is allocated to the location of the object file. Hence, an object in an unattended object file would be indistinguishable from a scrambled version of the same object. On this account, attention serves to "bind" the parts of the figure in the object file into their proper spatial relationships (Wolfe & Bennett, 1997). It is well known that good access to object memories requires the parts of the object to be arranged properly in space: Scrambled versions of objects, in which the parts have been spatially rearranged, cannot be correctly identified (Biederman, 1987; Cave & Kosslyn, 1993; Hummel & Biederman, 1992; Peterson, Harvey, & Weidenbacher, 1991). Thus, on Wolfe and Bennett's account, once attention binds together the parts of a figure within an object file, the conditions have been established for successful access to object memories.

Implicit in the reasoning about object files are the assumptions that object files (1) are established for figures but not for grounds, and (2) are precursors for access to object memories. From this line of reasoning, the assumption that object memories are accessed for figures and not for grounds follows. This assumption is common among perception researchers; it arises in part from the fact that grounds *appear* shapeless near the contours they share with figures (see also Peterson, 1999). However, the fact that grounds appear shapeless does not answer to the question of whether or not grounds were matched to object memories in the course of perceptual organization. Grounds might appear shapeless because of inhibitory connections between processes operating on opposite sides of a contour (Peterson, de Gelder, Rapcsak, Gerhardstein, &

Bachoud-Lévi, 2000). In the two experiments presented here, we investigated whether or not object memories are accessed in the course of perceptual organization for regions ultimately perceived to be shapeless grounds. Evidence indicating that access to object memories has occurred will be taken to imply that the parts of grounds are bound together properly prior to the assignment of figure and ground status.

In the present experiments, figure–ground displays were presented as primes for line drawing targets. The figure–ground primes were small, symmetric, enclosed, black silhouettes shown centred on a much larger white screen. (Samples are shown in Figure 2.) Participants were asked to just look at the primes; they made no response to them. Their task was to quickly judge whether a line drawing shown immediately after the prime portrayed a real or a novel object. (Sample line drawings are shown in Figure 3.) The critical trials were those involving line drawings of real objects. Half of the line drawings of real objects were preceded by control primes and half were preceded by experimental primes.

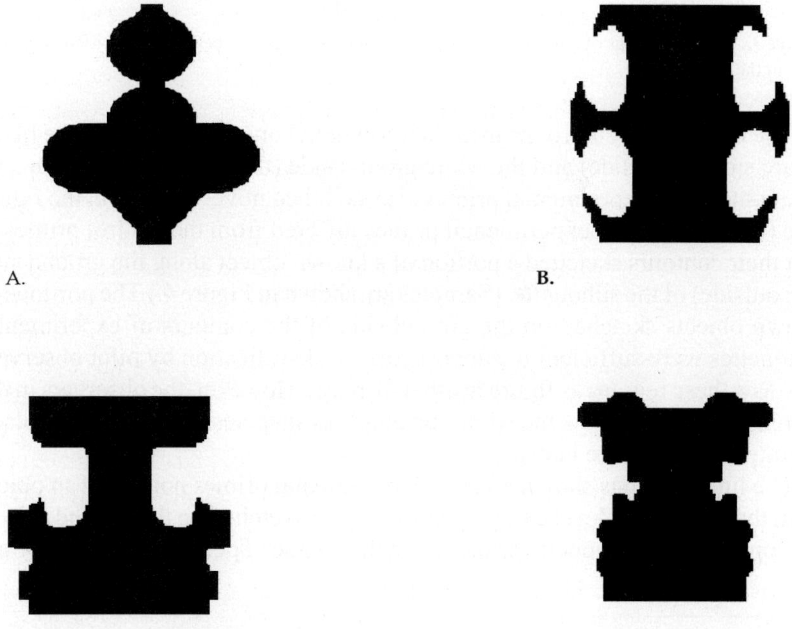

Figure 2. Samples of the silhouettes shown before the line drawings. These "control" silhouettes are low in denotivity along both side of their contours in that neither side of the contour provides a good match to an object memory.

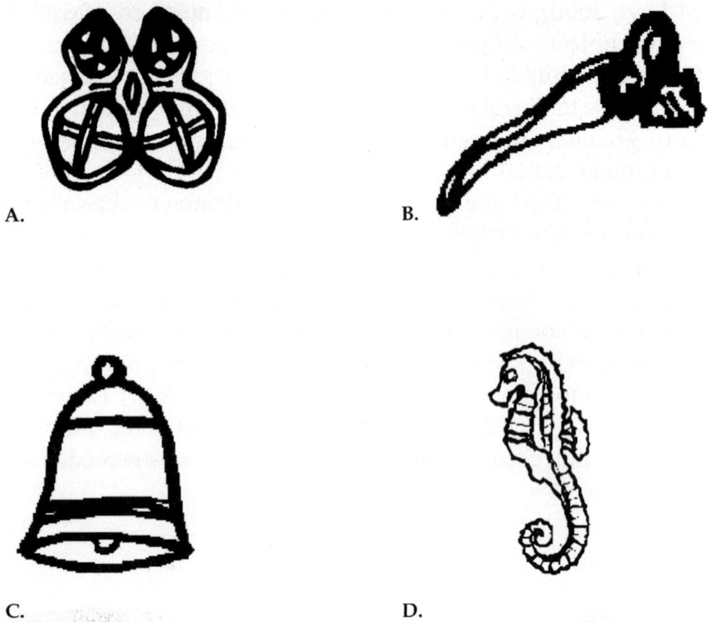

Figure 3. Line drawings of novel objects (A and B) and real objects (a bell in C and a sea horse in D) used in the experiment.

The contours of control primes sketched novel objects along both the black figure side (the inside) and the white ground side (the outside) (see Figure 3). The contours of experimental primes also sketched novel objects on the figure side (the inside). The experimental primes differed from the control primes in that their contours sketched a portion of a known object along the ground side (the outside) of the silhouette. (Samples are shown in Figure 4.) The portions of known objects sketched on the ground side of the contours of experimental silhouettes were sufficient to support correct identification by pilot observers who saw these regions as figure in other displays. However, the observers in the current experiments saw the white surrounds as shapeless grounds to the black silhouette figures (see later).

The line drawings shown after the experimental primes portrayed an object from the same basic level category as the object sketched on the ground side of the contour of the silhouette prime.[1] If, in the course of perceptual organization,

---

[1]The contours of the experimental silhouettes were not used to generate the line drawings. This is because we were interested in assessing whether or not pre-existing object memories were accessed during figure assignment. We were not interested in testing the different question of whether or not memories are established for novel ground regions (see Treisman & DeSchepper, 1996, and General Discussion, later).

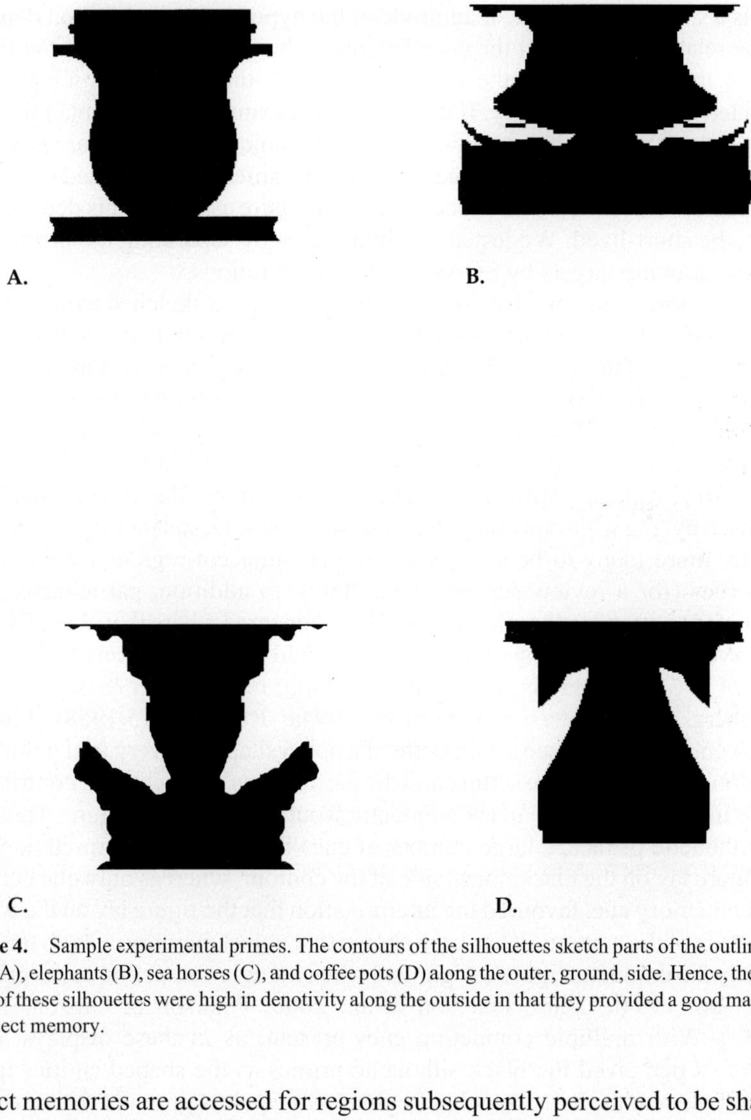

Figure 4. Sample experimental primes. The contours of the silhouettes sketch parts of the outlines of bells (A), elephants (B), sea horses (C), and coffee pots (D) along the outer, ground, side. Hence, the contours of these silhouettes were high in denotivity along the outside in that they provided a good match to an object memory.

object memories are accessed for regions subsequently perceived to be shapeless grounds, then reaction times to correctly classify the line drawings as real objects should differ depending upon whether they appear after an experimental or a control prime. A specific prediction about the direction of the difference arises from a model proposed by Peterson et al. (2000), which is one of a class of models predicting cross-contour inhibition in figure assignment (see also Sejnowski & Hinton, 1987; Vecera & O'Reilly, 1998). The Peterson et al. model predicts that object memories accessed for one side of a contour will be inhibited when more or stronger cues favour the interpretation that the other side is a shaped figure. The magnitude of the hypothesized inhibition depends on the relative strength of the cues favouring the interpretation that the figure lies on the other side of the contour. The hypothesized inhibition may be reflected in response latency. If it is, then participants will take longer to accurately report that line drawings portray familiar objects when they are preceded by experimental primes rather than by control primes. The proposed inhibition is expected to occur early in processing when figure assignment is determined, and to be short-lived. We tested this hypothesis by separating the primes and the line drawing targets by SOAs of different durations.

It is important to note that, although the real objects sketched along the outside of the vertical contours of the experimental primes may be clearly visible to the readers of this paper, they were not visible to the observers in the experiment.[2] A relatively large number of cues favoured the interpretation that the black silhouette, rather than the surrounding white region, was the shaped entity in the visual field (i.e., the figure). Silhouettes were always reflectionally symmetric around a vertical axis, and were much smaller in area than, and enclosed by, the white surround. Regions with these Gestalt configural properties are more likely to be seen as figure than adjacent regions lacking these properties (for a review see Peterson, 2000). In addition, participants were instructed to attend to the silhouettes, which appeared where they were fixating their eyes at the beginning of a trial. Fixated and attended regions are likely to be seen as figures (Baylis, Tipper, & Houghton, 1997; Driver & Baylis, 1998; Hochberg, 1971; Peterson & Gibson, 1994a; Rubin, 1915/1958). Finally, observers expected to see a silhouette of a novel shape on every trial before the line drawings. Hence, the setting and the participants' expectations contributed to the likelihood that the black silhouette would be seen as a figure. Thus, for the silhouette primes, a large number of cues favoured the interpretation that the figure lay on the black, inner side of the contour, whereas only one cue, the object memory cue, favoured the interpretation that the figure lay on the white, outer side of the contour. It has been shown that object memory cues do not necessarily the dominate figure assignment when a single competing cue is present (Peterson, 1994b, 2000; Peterson et al., 2000; Peterson & Gibson, 1993, 1994b). With multiple competing cues present, as in these displays, most observers perceived the black silhouette primes as the shaped entities in the visual field and the adjacent white regions as shapeless grounds. These conditions allowed us to test whether or not object memories are accessed for regions ultimately perceived to be shapeless grounds.

---

[2]Some observers did see the shapes in the ground. The data obtained from those participants were excluded before they were analysed. (See Methods section for details.)

EXPERIMENT 1

Method

Participants. Participants were 34 undergraduate students who enrolled in the experiment to partially fulfill a requirement for their introductory psychology class. Before the data were analysed, twelve participants were excluded: One because a system error occurred during the experiment, one because he was uncooperative, and nine because they reported becoming aware of the shapes in the grounds of the priming stimuli, typically after participating in more than two blocks of trials.[3] Data acquired from one other participant were excluded because he failed to make a response to 33% of the novel stimuli in one block of trials.

Stimuli and apparatus. The line drawings ($N = 84$) depicted 42 real and 42 novel objects. Novel objects were drawn from Kroll and Potter (1984). Many of the line drawings of real objects were taken from the Snodgrass and Vanderwart (1989) set; others were created for this experiment. Line drawings varied in height from 1.2° to 4.5°, and in width from 1.0° to 7.8°. Line drawings of real objects were divided into two sets (A and B). (See the Appendix for a listing of the objects in sets A and B.) For half of the participants, A was the primed set and B was the control set (i.e., A line drawings were preceded by experimental silhouettes and B line drawings were preceded by control silhouettes). For the other half of the subjects, this assignment was reversed. Across sets A and B, line drawings were matched for area, axis of elongation, word frequency of the object's name, number of symmetric versus asymmetric drawings, and number of living versus non-living objects. An additional 11 line drawings were used on practice trials.

The silhouettes were as described earlier; 42 were experimental silhouettes. These experimental silhouettes portrayed a portion of one of the known objects in either set A or set B along their outside edge. The experimental silhouettes were divided into two sets, A and B, matching the line drawing sets A and B. A given participant saw only 21 of the experimental silhouettes (either set A or set B silhouettes). The remaining 63 silhouettes shown on experimental trials ($N = 84$) were control silhouettes. Of these, 20 were inverted versions of other control stimuli in the set. Each silhouette subtended a visual angle of 3.4° in height; they ranged in width from 1.0° to 4.1°. Silhouettes were shown centred on a white screen, 23.3° wide by 16.4° high.

---

[3]Because a within-subjects design was used in this experiment, observers saw the stimuli repeatedly across different conditions. Observers who saw the shapes in the white surround region of the primes typically did so after being exposed to the stimuli numerous times. It is likely that, for these observers, the factors of attention and expectancy ceased to operate in favour of seeing the black silhouette as figures as the experiment progressed.

Stimuli were viewed from a distance of approximately 98 cm on an Optiquest monitor (Model V773). The experiment was run on an ACT personal computer equipped with a 166 MHz processor. Responses were made on a custom response box. The presentation software was the DMDX software developed by Jonathan C. Forster at the University of Arizona.

Procedure. During the experiment, a chin rest was used to keep participants' heads at a constant distance from the screen. Participants were told that their task was to distinguish between line drawings of real and novel objects as quickly and as accurately as possible. (Examples of each were shown.) They were told that a black silhouette would precede each line drawing and they would see many different black silhouettes, all of which would be novel and symmetrical around a vertical axis. Participants were asked to look at the silhouette, but to make no response to it. Each trial began with the presentation of a small fixation cross in the centre of the screen, on which participants were asked to fixate. When they were fixating properly, and were ready for the trial to begin, participants pressed a foot pedal. A black silhouette then appeared centred at fixation for 50 ms, and was followed by a blank white screen that varied in duration for each of five blocked SOA conditions (SOAs = 83, 200, 350, 500, and 650 ms). Next, a line drawing appeared (also centred at fixation) and remained on the screen until a response was made (or until 1.5 s had elapsed). Participants indicated whether the line drawing portrayed a real or novel object by pressing one of two keys. Pressing a key with the dominant hand indicated a real object; pressing a key with the non-dominant hand indicated a novel object. Reaction times (RTs) were measured for correct responses from the onset of the line drawing target. Following the participant's response, regardless of accuracy, the fixation cross for the next trial appeared.[4] No feedback was given.

We used a 50 ms exposure duration for the prime because pilot testing indicated that duration was sufficient for observers to obtain a clear percept of the black silhouette as figure. A 33 ms blank screen was inserted following the prime display in the shortest SOA condition so that all conditions included a blank between the prime and the target displays. This resulted in a smaller difference between the first two SOA conditions (117 ms) than between the other SOA conditions (150 ms). The 83 ms condition allows us to probe for evidence of access to object memories close to when the figure assignment was made for the prime displays. The longer SOA conditions allowed us to explore the time course of any priming we obtained.

All participants were exposed to all five SOA conditions. The order of SOA conditions was counterbalanced across subjects via a Latin square. Each SOA condition was comprised of two blocks, a priming block followed by an

---

[4]If no response was made within 1.5 s, the line drawing was removed and replaced by the fixation cross for the next trial.

uncoupling block. Within each block there were 11 practice trials followed by 84 experimental trials (comprised of 42 real and 42 novel line drawings). Neither silhouette nor line drawing stimuli used on practice trials, were included in the experimental trials, with the exception of two silhouettes that were shown in an inverted orientation on experimental trials. In the experimental block, an experimental prime silhouette preceded 21 of the real line drawings; a control silhouette preceded the other 21. Control silhouettes preceded all 42 novel line drawings. Trial types were randomly presented. No silhouettes or line drawings were repeated in the priming block. All silhouettes and line drawings were seen a second time in the uncoupling block.[5] During the uncoupling blocks, experimental primes preceded novel line drawings and control primes preceded all real object line drawings. (All silhouettes and line drawings were re-paired for the uncoupling block to prevent observers from learning paired associations between silhouettes and line drawings over the course of the experiment.) The results obtained on these uncoupling blocks will not be reported because the use of randomly presented trials prevented us from controlling the duration between the presentation of a silhouette prime and its paired line drawing during the uncoupling block. Observers were given a short break between the experimental and uncoupling blocks for a given SOA condition and a 5-min break between SOA blocks. Participation in this experiment took approximately 1.5 hours.

After they had participated in all five pairs of priming and uncoupling blocks, participants were asked whether they had seen any known objects in the white surrounds. As they were questioned, participants were shown pictures of three silhouettes and, for each, the object portrayed along the outer contour in the white surround was pointed out to them. (One of these silhouettes was designed especially for the debriefing so that the known object portrayed in the surround could be seen easily.) During these post-experiment questions, many observers formed the impression that they were supposed to see the objects portrayed on the outside of the silhouettes, and were embarrassed to admit they had not seen them. We certainly did not intend that observers see the white regions as shaped during the experiment. However, the fact that many participants felt they should have seen the shapes in the white surrounds when we questioned them gave us some confidence that those who said they had not seen shapes in the white regions were reporting honestly. At this stage, nine of the observers reported that they did see the shape portrayed by the white region adjacent to the black silhouette; they typically reported seeing shapes in the white regions after participating in more than two SOA conditions (hence, after seeing the silhouettes four times). The data from these participants were not analysed since we are interested in investigating whether or not priming can be obtained from

[5]One subject was not run in the 500 ms condition of the uncoupling block due to experimenter error.

regions perceived to be shapeless grounds, and these observers had potentially seen the white regions as shaped figures.[6]

Results

Mean RTs were calculated for each participant in each condition (primed and unprimed real objects, and novel objects). RTs that were more than two standard deviations from the individual's condition mean were excluded. This process was repeated until no outliers remained. Mean RTs obtained for both primed (P) and unprimed (UP) real object responses are shown in Table 1. A repeated measures analysis of variance (ANOVA) on these means showed a main effect of condition, $F(2, 21) = 35.09$, $p < .001$, indicating that RTs were longer for accurate novel responses (584 ms) than for accurate real responses (515 ms).

For each participant, the index of priming was the difference between the mean reaction time recorded on Unprimed and Primed trials (UP–P). These difference scores were entered into a one-way ANOVA with 5 SOA levels. A main effect of SOA was obtained, $F(4, 21) = 2.474$, $p = .051$. We conducted planned *t*-tests to investigate whether or not significant priming was obtained in each of the SOA conditions. As expected, observers' latency to respond to primed line drawings was longer than their latency to respond to unprimed line drawings in the shortest (83 ms) SOA condition, UP – P = –18.74 ms, $t(21) = -1.90$, $p < .05$, one tailed. This finding indicates that object memories matching the white grounds were accessed in the course of perceptual organization. Furthermore, the fact that the difference score is negative indicates that object memories matching regions seen as shapeless grounds are inhibited, as predicted by Peterson et al. (2000). No differences between the latency to respond to primed versus unprimed line drawings was observed for the 200, 350, or 650 ms SOA, all *ps* > .20. Post hoc tests indicated that the (UP – P) differences obtained in the 83 ms condition and the 350 ms condition were significantly different, $p < .03$, suggesting that no measurable inhibition remained in the 350 ms condition. Thus, the inhibition appears to be short-lived, as predicted by Peterson et al. (2000).

Unexpectedly, in the 500 ms SOA condition, observers' latency to respond to primed line drawings was again longer than their latency to respond to

[6]Because of the obvious demand character of the post-experiment questions, it is not clear that all of these observers really saw the shape sketched in the white surrounds. They often reported seeing shapes that were not sketched in the surrounds of the experimental silhouettes (i.e., shapes in the control set). Nevertheless, we did not inspect the data from any of the observers who reported seeing shapes in the white surround.

TABLE 1
Mean reaction times and (UP–P) differences obtained in the Priming Block of Experiment 1 as a function of stimulus onset asynchrony (SOA)

SOA														
83 ms			*200 ms*			*350 ms*			*500 ms*			*650 ms*		
UP	*P*	*Diff*	*UP*	*P*	*Diff*	*UP*	*P*	*Diff*	*UP*	*P*	*Diff*	*UP*	*P*	*Diff*
497.7	515.9	–18.2	503.4	505.2	–1.8	523.8	516.4	7.4	502.7	520.8	–18.0	506.7	501.5	5.2
(15.8)	(21.0)	(9.6)	(17.0)	(16.4)	(5.2)	(17.3)	(18.2)	(6.5)	(17.2)	(17.1)	(6.8)	(20.7)	(21.0)	(8.2)

Standard errors shown in parentheses. UP = unprimed; P = primed; Diff = UP–P.

unprimed line drawings, UP – P = –18.0, $t(20)$[7] = 2.67, $p < .02$, two tailed. The reappearance of inhibition in the 500 ms condition is surprising. We note that inhibition in the 500 ms condition was most evident among observers who saw the 500 ms condition either third or fourth in the sequence of conditions, and, hence, may be due to the repetition of the stimuli across three or four blocks rather than to the SOA itself. Unfortunately, the number of participants who received each order was too small to permit a sensitive test of this hypothesis. However, in Experiment 2, we used a between-subjects design in order to eliminate order effects, which may have contaminated the data obtained in other SOA conditions as well.

EXPERIMENT 2

Method

Participants. Participants were 132 undergraduate students who enrolled in the experiment to partially fulfill a requirement for their introductory psychology class. Before the data were analysed, 19 participants were excluded: One because of a shoulder injury that might have interfered with her ability to respond, one because he had been told about the experimental design before arriving at the laboratory, and 17 because they reported becoming aware of the shapes in the grounds of the priming stimuli. The percentage of students dropped for the last reason was half as large in Experiment 2 (13%) as in Experiment 1 (26%), probably because of the use of a between-subjects design in Experiment 2. Fifteen of the participants who saw the shapes in the surround were exposed to the primes for 350 ms or more, ample time to make an eye movement, and, hence, to change the balance of cues favouring the black and white regions as figures. (The other two subjects were in the 200 ms condition.)

Stimuli and apparatus. The stimuli and apparatus used in Experiment 2 were much the same as those used in Experiment 1, although new control silhouettes were added so that the experimental primes were not repeated in the uncoupling block, and none of the silhouettes was used in both an upright and an inverted orientation in the priming block. There were 84 control silhouettes, and 42 experimental silhouettes. As in Experiment 1, a given subject saw only 21 of the experimental silhouettes. Of the 84 control silhouettes, 63 were shown in both the priming block and the uncoupling block (they were paired with different line drawings in the uncoupling block); 21 were shown in the uncoupling block only as replacements for the 21 experimental silhouettes. In Experiment

[7] One subject was dropped from the analysis of the 500 ms condition of the priming block because of a high error rate. For the ANOVA, the condition mean was entered into the cell so there would be no missing data.

2, each silhouette was matched as closely as possible to the corresponding line drawing in curvature and size, while preserving the resolution and aspect ratio. The silhouettes subtended 2.1°–5.4° in height and 1.6°–5.6° in width. The line drawings subtended 2.1°–3.1° in height and 0.8°–4.3° in width. Across priming sets A and B, line drawings were matched for curvature (which had not been done in Experiment 1). Thus, the sets used in Experiment 2 were somewhat different from those used in Experiment 1 (leaf and pine tree were switched into set A and lamp and palm tree were switched into Set B). In the course of matching the two sets for curvature, they became slightly unmatched in the number of living things.

Procedure. When participants entered the laboratory they were assigned to one of the SOA conditions using a pseudo-random procedure that balanced experimenter and time of day across SOA conditions. In this experiment, the primes were exposed for the full duration of the SOA. Under these conditions, the shortest SOA used was 50 ms, and all adjacent SOA conditions differed by 150 ms. There were 23 participants in each of the 50 ms, 350 ms, and the 650 ms conditions and 21 participants in each of the 200 ms and 500 ms conditions.

Each observer participated in two blocks of trials, a priming block followed by an uncoupling block. Within each block, trials were presented in a random order. The instructions for this experiment were presented on the computer screen. Participants were able to ask the experimenter questions regarding the experiment at any time while reading the instructions or while participating in the practice trials. They were then left alone to perform the experimental trials. Participation in this experiment took approximately 20 min.

Results

Mean RTs were calculated for each participant in each condition (primed and unprimed real objects, and novel objects). RTs more than two standard deviations from the individual's condition mean were excluded. This process was repeated until no outliers remained. Mean RTs obtained for both primed and unprimed real object responses are shown in Table 2. For each participant, the difference was taken between the mean RT recorded on primed and unprimed trials.

It was obvious upon inspection of the overall means and standard errors that there were no differences between primed (P) and unprimed (UP) RTs in any of the SOA conditions. We noted, however, that much longer RTs were obtained in Experiment 2 than in Experiment 1. Consider the 83 ms SOA condition where inhibition was observed in Experiment 1. The mean UP RT was 516 ms, whereas the mean UP RT in the comparable short SOA condition of Experiment 2 (i.e., the 50 ms condition) was 573 ms, a difference of almost 60 ms. Inhibition applied to object memories accessed for regions determined to be

TABLE 2
Mean reaction times and (UP – P) differences obtained in Experiment 2 as a function of stimulus onset asynchrony (SOA)

SOA														
50ms			*200 ms*			*350ms*			*500ms*			*650ms*		
UP	*P*	*Diff*	*UP*	*P*	*Diff*	*UP*	*P*	*Diff*	*UP*	*P*	*Diff*	*UP*	*P*	*Diff*
Priming block, all subjects														
	(*N* = 23)			(*N* = 21)			(*N* = 23)			(N = 21)			(*N* = 23)	
573.3	573.8	–0.5	555.9	546.3	9.6	549.4	545.9	3.5	567.4	554.5	2.9	554.6	553.0	1.6
(17.6)	(14.5)	(9.5)	(18.3)	(15.9)	(8.8)	(18.6)	(17.1)	(7.0)	(18.9)	(20.8)	(8.2)	(16.4)	(15.6)	(6.2)
Priming block, subjects with $\overline{X}_{up} < 580$ ms														
	(*N* = 11)			(*N* = 13)			(*N* = 14)			(N = 11)			(*N* = 14)	
506.7	530.6	–24.0	505.5	507.5	-1.2	490.8	495.3	-4.6	498.6	490.9	7.8	505.9	505.1	–0.3
(15.6)	(18.5)	(6.7)	(14.4)	(16.7)	(9.3)	(13.9)	(16.3)	(9.8)	(13.6)	(17.0)	(12.4)	(13.2)	(10.7)	(7.6)
Uncoupling block, subjects with $\overline{X}_{up} < 580$ ms														
521.5	517.1	4.4	478.9	486.3	-7.4	476.0	474.2	1.8	479.0	480.0	–1.0	493.6	485.2	8.3
(22.1)	(26.5)	(15.8)	(10.7)	(13.0)	(8.4)	(10.5)	(11.4)	(7.5)	(12.7)	(12.5)	(9.3)	(17.6)	(16.6)	(12.0)

Standard errors shown in parentheses. UP = unprimed; P = primed; Diff = UP–P.

grounds is expected to be short-lived. Therefore, it would be difficult to observe inhibition if RTs are too long. Indeed, in both the 50 ms and 200 ms conditions of Experiment 2, the magnitude of the difference score (UP – P) was correlated with the mean RT on UP trials, $rs = 0.57$ and 0. 50 in the 50 ms and the 200 ms conditions, respectively, $ps < .02$. In other words, the longer the observers took to respond to the line drawings shown on unprimed trials, the more positive the (UP – P) difference score was (i.e., the less negative it was).

In Experiment 1, 77% of the observers had mean UP RTs that were less than 630 ms from the onset of the silhouette, whereas only 48% of the observers in Experiment 2 had mean UP RTs below that limit. Accordingly, we separately examined the difference scores of those observers in Experiment 2 whose UP RTs were less than 630 ms from the onset of the silhouette (i.e., observers with UP RT means less than or equal to 580 ms in the 50 ms condition). The mean RTs for this subset of participants is shown in the middle panel of Table 2. Planned comparisons showed that in the 50 ms condition, the subset of observers with mean UP RTs < 580 ms took significantly longer to respond to line drawings on primed trials than on unprimed trials, $t(10) = -3.567$, $p < .01$, two tailed. Thus, Experiment 2 replicates Experiment 1 when responses within the same RT range are examined.[8] Like Experiment 1, Experiment 2 indicates that object memories matching regions ultimately perceived to be shapeless grounds are inhibited.

Planned comparisons were conducted on the subset of observers whose mean UP RTs were ≤580 ms in the other SOA conditions as well. No significant (UP – P) difference scores were obtained in any other SOA condition, all $ts < 1.0$. Thus, inhibition does not seem to be sufficiently long-lived to be observed using this paradigm when the silhouettes are exposed for 200 ms or longer.

Performance on the uncoupling block provides a different, within-subjects measure of the longevity of priming.[9] Suppose residual priming lasts the approximately 2–3 min between the presentation of a primed line drawing in the priming block and the presentation of the same line drawing in an unprimed condition in the uncoupling block. Then, RTs for the previously primed line drawings should be longer than the previously unprimed line drawings. No such difference was found in the 50 ms condition, where significant inhibition

[8]The results of Experiment 1 are stronger when the data from the 77% of participants who responded within 630 ms of the onset of the prime are examined alone. Because of the 33 ms interstimulus interval between the offset of the silhouette primes and the onset of the line drawings in Experiment 1, the comparable subset of participants had UP RTs < 550 ms. The UP–P differences obtained in this subset of observers in the 83 ms SOA condition (–12.56) and the 500 ms SOA condition (–19.84) remained significantly greater than zero, $t(14) = 3.25$, $p < .01$, two tailed, and $t(12) = 2.98$, $p < .02$, two tailed.

[9]Uncoupling trials in Experiment 2 afford this analysis because experimental primes were not used in the uncoupling blocks of Experiment 2.

was observed in the priming block, or in any other condition, as can be seen in the bottom panel of Table 2, all *ps* > .05.

DISCUSSION

In the 83 ms and the 500 ms SOA conditions of Experiment 1, and the 50 ms condition of Experiment 2, observers required more time to accurately classify real line drawings that were preceded by experimental silhouettes than line drawings preceded by control silhouettes. The contours of experimental silhouettes sketched a basic level object along their outer (ground) side that was the same as that portrayed by the line drawing. The increased latency may reflect inhibition of object memories matched in the course of perceptual organization by regions determined to be grounds (see Peterson et al., 2000). Hence, these results are consistent with the proposal that in the course of figure assignment, object memories are accessed for both sides of contours, including the side of the contour later assigned ground status. Given that a good fit to an object memory is possible only when the spatial relationships between the parts has been properly specified, these effects indicate that parts are bound together before ground status is determined. Thus, it is not true that attention to figures is necessary to bind the parts together.

Experiments are currently underway to test whether attention to the spatial location of the prime is necessary to obtain effects such as those presented here. If it is, that would be consistent with recent research showing that attention is required for many perceptual phenomena (e.g., Mack & Rock, 1998; Nakayama & Joseph, 1998). Given that the present results reveal aspects of perceptual organization that do not result in conscious awareness, however, they may be observed even when attention is allocated elsewhere (see Moore & Egeth, 1997). Even if attention to the spatial location of the prime is shown to be necessary for these effects, the present results indicate that neither object files created for figures (but not for grounds) nor attention to those object files is necessary for access to object memories.

The inhibition obtained in the present experiments might be considered similar to negative priming (for review see Neill, Valdes, & Terry, 1995). Indeed, Treisman and DeSchepper (1996) reported that observers required to match a comparison shape to one of two novel figures on a probe trial were slower when the comparison shape was putatively seen as a ground on a prime trial than when it was a new novel figure. On the basis of these results, Treisman and DeSchepper (1996) proposed that memories for the shapes of grounds are stored even though they are novel, and have not been seen consciously. The question of whether or not object memories are established for novel shapes of grounds is an important one that requires further investigation (e.g., see Lampignano & Peterson, 2001; Luola, Kourtzi, & Shiffrar, 2000). However, we were addressing a different question in the present paper. We were concerned here with the question of whether or not memories of known objects are accessed in the course of figure assignment. Accordingly, in order not to confuse the two issues, we constructed the experimental primes so that the shape sketched on the high denotative side of their contours (i.e., the outside or the ground side) was not identical to the shape of the subsequently viewed line drawing. Instead, the high denotative side of the silhouette portrayed a different object with the same name as the object portrayed by the line drawing. Any effect of the prime on the line drawing target then must be mediated by a pre-existing object memory that can be accessed by different exemplars of the same object (e.g., two different sea horses, or two different owls). Consequently, the latency to respond to the line drawings used in the present experiments can be used to assess whether or not pre-existing object memories have been accessed for ground regions in the course of figure assignment.

Peterson et al. (2000) proposed that, when the cues strongly favour the assignment of figural status on one side of a contour and not the opposite side, processes assessing configural cues and accessing object memories on that opposite side would be inhibited. In the present experiments, this predicted inhibition was observed in the shortest SOA conditions. On the assumption that figure–ground assignment occurs early in the course of perceptual processing, an assumption supported by recent neurophysiological evidence (e.g., Zipser, Lamme, & Schiller, 1996), it is under such short SOA conditions that inhibition linked to figure and ground determination would be expected. The inhibition we observed was short lived; suggesting it is not the same as negative priming (see Neill et al., 1995). The inhibition observed in the present experiments is attributed to the fact that a region matching the object memory accessed by a line drawing was assigned ground status rather than figure status in experimental primes. In contrast, in negative priming experiments, the ignored elements (to which negative priming accrued) were always presented as figures rather than grounds. We expect that different inhibitory mechanisms account for these two types of effects.

The results of the present experiment are relevant to an alternative interpretation that has been offered for our previous experiments investigating object memory effects on figure assignment. In our previous research, participants made direct reports indicating which of two adjacent regions appeared to be the figure. One of the regions (the high denotative region) portrayed a known mono-oriented object. Participants were more likely to report seeing high denotative regions as figures when the stimuli were presented in an upright orientation rather than an inverted orientation. (In the upright orientation the objects portrayed by high denotative regions were shown in their canonical orientation.) We took these previous results as evidence that object memories can be accessed early in the course of perceptual organization (i.e., while Gestalt configural cues and depth cues are being assessed) and can affect which of two adjacent regions is assigned figural status. We reasoned that effects of object memories were not observed for inverted stimuli because object memories are accessed too late in time by inverted stimuli to affect an early perceptual outcome like figure assignment. (See Peterson, 1994a, for a summary.) Driver and Baylis (1995) offered an alternative interpretation of those results resting upon the fact that observers typically recognized the known objects portrayed by the high denotative regions when they see those regions as figures (although recognition need not accompany figural status; see Peterson et al., 2000). Driver and Baylis argued that, once observers recognized some familiar objects in the stimuli, they changed their task to one of searching for known objects rather than reporting the first figure assignment they perceived. In that case, observers' responses might not reflect object memory effects on initial figure assignment. The experiments that are reported in this paper contained no incentives to look for known shapes in the grounds of the prime silhouettes. Hence, they do not lend themselves to the alternative interpretation offered by Driver and Baylis (1995). Instead, these results show that in the course of figure assignment, object memories are accessed (and inhibited) for high denotative regions that are ultimately perceived to be shapeless grounds.

In conclusion, the results of the present experiments, combined with our previous results, show that the parts lying on both sides of contours are bound together sufficiently well to enable access to object memories early in the course of perceptual organization. This binding of parts and their spatial relationships clearly does not depend upon attention to figures and/or to object files created for figures but not for grounds. It remains possible that another form of binding may be needed for conscious perception of definite shape and conscious object recognition, both of which occur for figures but not for grounds (e.g., see Crick & Koch, 1990). One reason the results obtained in the present experiment support different conclusions than the results of visual search experiments (e.g., Wolfe & Bennett, 1997) is that the present experiment assesses aspects of perceptual organization that occur outside of conscious awareness, whereas visual search experiments assess conscious perception.

REFERENCES

Baylis, G.C., Tipper, S.P., & Houghton, G. (1997). Externally cued and internally generated selection: Differences in distractor analysis and inhibition. *Journal of Experimental Psychology: Human Perception and Performance, 23,* 1617–1630.

Biederman, I. (1987). Recognition by components: A theory of human image understanding. *Psychological Review, 94,* 115–147.

Cave, C.B., & Kosslyn, S.M. (1993). The role of parts and spatial relations in object identification. *Perception, 22,* 229–248.

Crick, F., & Koch, C. (1990). Towards a neurobiological theory of consciousness. *Seminars in Neuroscience, 2,* 263–275.

Driver, J., & Baylis, G.C. (1995). One-sided edge assignment in vision: 2. Part decomposition, shape description, and attention to objects. *Current Directions in Psychological Science, 4,* 201–206.

Driver, J., & Baylis, G.C. (1998). Attention and visual object segmentation. In R. Parasuraman (Ed.), *The attentive brain* (pp. 299–325). Cambridge, MA: The MIT Press.

Hochberg, J. (1971). Perception I: Color and shape. In J.W. Kling & L.A. Riggs (Eds.), *Woodworth and Schlossberg's experimental psychology* (3rd ed., pp. 395–474). New York: Hold, Rinehart, & Winston.

Hummel, J., & Biederman, I. (1992). Dynamic binding in a neural network for shape recognition. *Psychological Review, 99,* 480–517.

Kahneman, D., & Treisman, A. (1984). Changing views of attention and automaticity. In R Parasuraman (Ed.), *Varieties of attention* (pp. 29–61). New York: Academic Press.

Kroll, J.F., & Potter, M.C. (1984). Recognizing words, pictures, and concepts: A comparison of lexical, object, and reality decisions. *Journal of Verbal Learning and Verbal Behavior, 23,* 39–66.

Lampignano, D.W., & Peterson, M.A. (2001, March). *Memories for novel shapes seen as grounds?* Poster presented at the meeting of the Cognitive Neuroscience Society, New York, USA.

Luola, F., Kourtzi, Z., & Shiffrar, M. (2000). Surface segmentation cues influence negative priming for novel and familiar shapes. *Journal of Experimental Psychology: Learning, Memory, and Cognition, 26,* 929–944.

Mack, A., & Rock, I. (1998). *Inattentional blindness*. Cambridge, MA: The MIT Press.

Moore, C.M., & Egeth, H. (1997). Perception without attention: Evidence grouping under conditions of inattention. *Journal of Experimental Psychology: Human Perception and Performance, 23,* 339–352.

Nakayama, K., & Joseph, J.S. (1998). Attention, pattern recognition, and pop-out visual search. In R. Parasuraman (Ed.), *The attentive brain* (pp. 279–298). Cambridge, MA: The MIT Press.

Neill, W.T., Valdes, L.A., & Terry, K.M. (1995). Selective attention and the inhibitory control of cognition. In F.N. Dempster & C.J. Brainerd (Eds.), *Interference and inhibition in cognition.* San Diego: Academic Press.

Peterson, M.A. (1994a). Shape recognition can and does occur before figure–ground organization. *Current Directions in Psychological Science, 3,* 105–111.

Peterson, M.A. (1994b). The proper placement of uniform connectedness. *Psychonomic Bulletin and Review, 1,* 509–514.

Peterson, M.A. (1999). On the role of meaning in organization. *Intellectica, 28,* 37–51.

Peterson, M.A. (2000). Object perception. In E.B. Goldstein (Ed.), *Blackwell handbook of perception*. Oxford, UK: Blackwell.

Peterson, M.A., de Gelder, B., Rapcsak, S.Z., Gerhardstein, P.C., & Bachoud-Lévi, A.-C. (2000). Object memory effects on figure assignment: Conscious object recognition is not necessary or sufficient. *Vision Research, 40,* 1549–1567.

Peterson, M.A., & Gibson, B.S. (1993). Shape recognition contributions to figure–ground organization in three-dimensional display. *Cognitive Psychology, 25,* 383–429.

Peterson, M.A., & Gibson, B.S. (1994a). Object recognition contributions to figure-ground organization: Operations on outlines and subjectives contours. *Perception & Psychophysics, 56,* 551–564.

Peterson, M.A., & Gibson, B.S. (1994b). Must shape recognition follow figure–ground organization? An assumption in peril. *Psychological Science, 5,* 253–259.

Peterson, M.A., Harvey, E.H., & Weidenbacher, H.L. (1991). Shape recognition inputs to figure–ground organization: Which route counts? *Journal of Experimental Psychology: Human Perception and Performance, 17,* 1075–1089.

Rubin, E. (1958). Figure and ground. In D. Beardslee (Ed.), *Readings in perception* (M. Wertheimer, Trans.; pp. 35–101). Princeton, NJ: Van Nostrand. (Original work published 1915.)

Sejnowski, T.J., & Hinton, G.E. (1987). Separating figure from ground with a Boltzmann machine. In M. Arbib & A. Hanson (Eds.), *Vision, brain, and cooperative computation*. Cambridge, MA: MIT Press.

Snodgrass, J.G., & Vanderwart, M. (1980). A standardized set of 260 pictures: Norms for name agreement, image agreement, familiarity, and visual complexity. *Journal of Experimental Psychology: Human Learning and Memory, 2,* 174–215.

Treisman, A., & DeSchepper, B. (1996). Object tokens, attention, and visual memory. In T. Inui & J.L. McClelland (Eds.), *Attention and performance XVI: Information integration in perception and communication* (pp. 15–46). Cambridge, MA: MIT Press.

Treisman, A., & Gelade, G. (1980). A feature-integration theory of attention. *Cognitive Psychology, 12,* 97–136.

Vecera, S.P., & O'Reilly, R.C. (1998). Figure–ground organization and object recognition processes: An interactive account. *Journal of Experimental Psychology: Human Perception and Performance, 24,* 441–462.

Wolfe, J.M., & Bennett, S.C. (1997). Preattentive object files: Shapeless bundles of basic features. *Vision Research, 37,* 25–43.

Zipser, K., Lamme, V.A., & Schiller, P.H. (1996). Contextual modulation in primary visual cortex. *The Journal of Neuroscience, 16,* 7376–7389.

APPENDIX

Set A	**Set B**
axe	anchor
bell	duck
bone	elephant
boot	faucet
butterfly	flower
coffee pot	foot
dog	guitar
eagle	house
face	hydrant
grapes	jet plane
hand	leaf
lamp	Mickey Mouse
light bulb	owl
locomotive	pine tree
palm tree	pineapple
pig	rabbit
rhinoceros	sea horse
spray bottle	snow man
umbrella	teddy bear
woman	trumpet
wrench	watering can

VISUAL COGNITION, 2001, *8* (3/4/5), 349–358

Dynamics of perceptual grouping: Similarities in the organization of visual and auditory groups

Aleksandar Aksentijević
School of Psychology, Birkbeck College, University of London, UK
Mark A. Elliott
Institut für Allgemeine Psychologie, Universität Leipzig, Leipzig, Germany
Paul J. Barber
School of Psychology, Birkbeck College, University of London, UK

In vision, the Gestalt principles of perceptual organization are generally well understood and remain a subject of detailed analysis. However, the possibility for a unified theory of grouping across visual and auditory modalities remains largely unexplored. Here we present examples of auditory and visual Gestalt grouping, which share important organizational properties. In particular, similarities are revealed between grouping processes in apparent motion, auditory streaming, and static 2-D displays. Given the substantial difference in the context, within which the phenomena in question occur (auditory vs. visual, static vs. dynamic), these similarities suggest that the dynamics of perceptual organization could be associated with a common (possibly central) mechanism. If the relevance of supramodal invariants of grouping is granted, the question arises as to whether they can be studied empirically. We propose that a "force-field" theory, based on a differential-geometric interpretation of perceptual space, could provide a suitable starting point for a systematic exploration of the subjective properties of certain classes of auditory and visual grouping phenomena.

In this paper, we aim to show that the basis for multi-modal principles of perceptual organization may be evident from similarities between the Gestalt organization of visual and auditory stimuli. Although striking similarities have often been noted between certain classes of auditory and visual grouping

Please address all correspondence to A. Aksentijević, School of Psychology, Birkbeck College, University of London, Malet Street, London, WC1E 7HX, UK.
Email: a.aksentijevic@psyc.bbk.ac.uk

Mark A. Elliott is supported by Deutsche Forschungsgemeinschaft project grant SCHR 375/8-1. The authors are grateful to Greg Davis for his helpful comments on an earlier draft of the paper.

http://www.tandf.co.uk/journals/pp/13506285.html DOI:10.1080/13506280143000043

contexts (Bregman, 1990, pp. 173–181; Koffka, 1935), the possibility that these similarities represent general, modality-independent invariants of perceptual organization is still an open issue. Further, the notion that perceptual organization may be based on modality-independent principles remains for the most part unexplored. Rather than speculate on the neural correlates of these principles, we examine some of the evidence in support of a common framework for the systematic study of visual and auditory Gestalt phenomena. For this purpose, the paper is divided into three sections. In the first section, a simple grouping situation is described and discussed with reference to both auditory and visual contexts. The second section briefly addresses the similarities between three well-known instances of perceptual grouping: Namely, the auditory streaming effect, static visual displays (Bregman, 1990, p. 173), and apparent motion (Wertheimer, 1912). Finally, in the third section, these similarities are briefly discussed with a view to introducing a common framework for the study of auditory and visual Gestalt phenomena.

INSTANCES OF GROUPING IN VISION AND AUDITION

Consider the display in Figure 1a. The line segments are mutually equidistant along the abscissa and tend to be perceived as forming a single zigzag line. With the increase in the vertical separation between the alternating segments, the percept changes into two horizontal collinear groups (Figure 1b). Shifting the upper group horizontally relative to the lower one so that they completely coincide results in a sequence of line-segment pairs (Figure 1c). In addition, there is the intermediate case where the relationship between the vertical and horizontal distance produces a multistable percept. One such "unstable" solution is represented in Figure 1d. The display can be interpreted as a single zigzag line, two horizontal lines, or even as a sequence of slanted segment pairs.

In all four instances, the perceptual outcome is mediated by the horizontal/vertical relationships. Changing the horizontal distance between the segments will, depending on the other conditions, either increase or decrease the grouping stability of the percept. Thus, other things being equal (e.g., the contrast between the lines and the ground and the length of the segments), organization of the elements in this example is governed by two factors—the vertical separation and the horizontal separation of the segments.

The previous example serves a dual purpose. First, it demonstrates that the interaction of the two factors generally produces several stable grouping solutions, in this case a single zigzag group (Figure 1a), two horizontally collinear groups (Figure 1b), or a sequence of line-segment pairs (Figure 1c). In addition, under appropriate conditions, the display can produce a number of unstable or ambiguous perceptual solutions (Figure 1d).

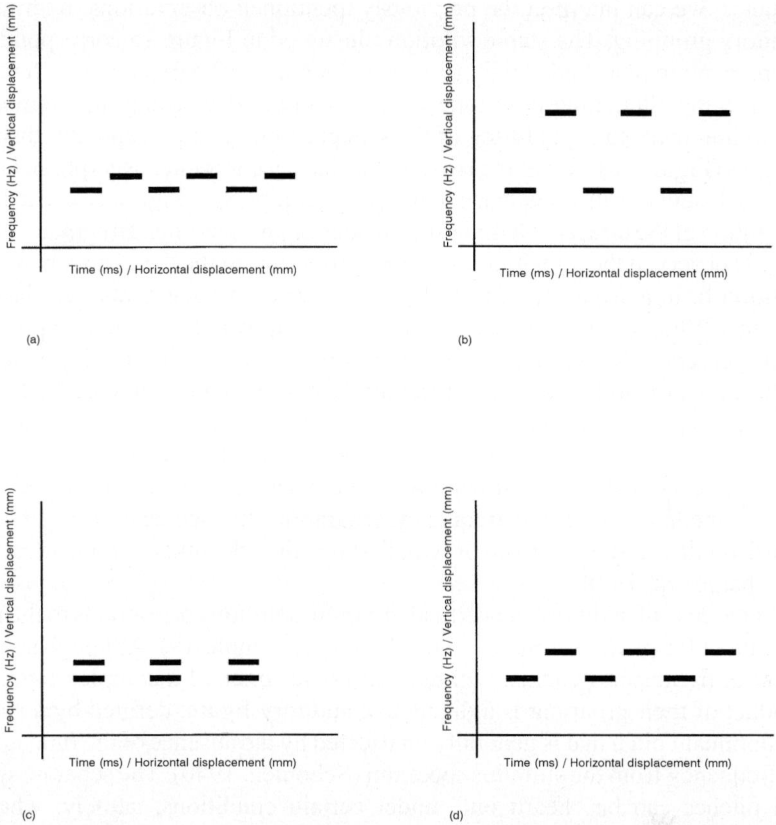

Figure 1. **(a)** A stable (auditory and visual) grouping solution. The sequence is perceived as a zigzag line or a single auditory stream. In the former case, the abscissa represents horizontal, and the ordinate, vertical displacement (in mm). In the auditory context, the abscissa represents time (in ms), and the ordinate represents frequency (in Hz). **(b)** The second stable solution. The sequence has split into two horizontal collinear groups (or auditory streams). **(c)** The third stable solution. In the visual context, the display is interpreted as a sequence of line-segment pairs. In the auditory grouping context, the figure corresponds to a sequence of harmonic complex tones. **(d)** An unstable solution. The sequence is perceived either as a zigzag line, or two horizontal (or three slanted) groups. In the auditory context, the figure corresponds to the situation where single- and multi-stream solutions are equally probable.

Second, the example represents a visual illustration of a well-known auditory phenomenon—the streaming effect. When a sequence of alternating high and low tones is played at an appropriate speed, the listener perceives two separate streams (high and low). According to Bregman (1990, p. 47), the effect illustrates the general principle of auditory stream segregation. How does the streaming effect relate to the earlier visual example? To all intents and purposes, the streaming effect and its visual analog are governed by identical dynamics. Substituting frequency for the vertical, and time for the horizontal distance, we can interpret the previously mentioned observations in terms of auditory grouping. The stable solution illustrated in Figure 1a corresponds to the perception of a single auditory stream. Increasing the frequency difference between the alternating pure-tone segments and/or decreasing their temporal separation leads to the splitting of the sequence into two perceptually distinct streams (Figure 1b). When the two streams have a common onset (phase angle 0°), the listener hears a sequence of harmonic complexes (Figure 1c). In a demonstration of the effects of temporal coincidence on streaming, Bregman (1990, p. 213) observed the transition from the "harmonic" to the "one-stream" stable solution from a sequence of two alternating pure-tone segments each lasting 250 ms. When the inter-stream temporal overlap was 50%, the components were perceptually assigned to different streams. Once the overlap reached 88%, the segments belonging to different streams were fused into unified "vertical" percepts, which sounded like complex tones. Finally, under the right circumstances, both stable solutions would become equally available (Figure 1d). As Bregman noted: "In the streaming effect, when the sequence is played with an intermediate speed and frequency separation, the sequence can often be heard as either a single stream or two, first one then the other organization taking charge" (p. 199).

In the case of audition, the vertical grouping solution corresponds to the perception of the pitch of complex tones (harmonic complexes). Although several spectral frequencies coexist within a harmonic series of a complex tone, the product of their grouping is a distinctive auditory figure, defined by a single predominant pitch that is generally unaffected by the absence of the fundamental frequency from the stimulus spectrum (Schouten, 1940). The separate spectral pitches can be "heard out" under certain conditions, namely, when a conscious effort is made to analyse the complex percept (see von Helmholtz, 1863/1954).[1]

This suggests that the spectral components of complex tones represent the fundamental descriptors, or building blocks of music and speech. According to some investigators (e.g., Terhardt, 1986) harmonics may operate in a way that is remarkably similar to the function of edges and contours in early visual feature analysis. Although such an analogy appears plausible, a dose of caution is called for. In the absence of an appropriate empirical framework, the analogy between visual contours and harmonics cannot be carried too far. Although the previous illustration points to a similarity between the auditory and visual contexts, the correspondence is not perfect. To illustrate, harmonics do not "circumscribe" a complex tone in the sense in which contours delineate a visual object. This is because sound possesses only one dimension analogous to spatial extension—that of pitch (see Kubovy, 1981, for a detailed discussion on the

[1] Audibility of individual harmonics also depends on factors such as timbre and the amount of musical training.

criteria for translation of visual into auditory form). At the same time, the similarity between the dynamics of visual and auditory grouping does not end at the level of pure tones. At the next level, complex (musical) tones themselves group according to the Gestalt principles (see Bregman, 1990, pp. 461–471, for experimental evidence on melodic grouping). Similarly, in vision, the principles discussed in the context of simple line segments guide the organization of two-dimensional objects.

The phenomenon of auditory stream segregation represents an important manifestation of the organizing potential of the auditory system. In agreement with the earlier visual examples, the simple grouping context provides a limited number of stable grouping solutions. Further, these grouping outcomes are a function of the interaction between stimulus frequency and temporal factors—stimulus duration and the interstimulus interval (ISI). In other words, the closer together the tones are in terms of frequency or time, the more easily they will be assigned to a single stream. Further, stream formation is facilitated by continuous/smooth transition. Tones of different frequency connected (fully or partially) by a frequency glide tend to be grouped into single streams (Bregman & Dannenbring, 1973).

Another factor, which facilitates auditory grouping, is spectral similarity. Harmonically related tones with a common onset also tend to form a coherent percept. In order for the partials (pure-tone components of harmonic complex tones) to fuse into a single percept, the harmonic ratio has to be maintained within relatively narrow margins. Simultaneously stretching (or compressing) the frequency separations between the harmonics by 7% (on a log scale; approximate harmonic-ratio margin: 1.86 to 2.14) destroys the sensation of harmonic pitch (Cohen, 1980; Slaymaker, 1970). The lower partials are then usually heard as individual tones, while the higher ones are perceived as an undifferentiated tonal buzz. Similarly, mistuning a low harmonic by between 3% and 6% will cause the shifted harmonic to be perceived as separate from the (weakened) harmonic complex (Moore, Glasberg, & Peters, 1985).

COMMON FACTORS INFLUENCING GROUPING IN VISION AND AUDITION

Although the parallel between the static visual displays in Figure 1 and auditory streaming is intuitively appealing, it might invite premature speculation. Even though the dependence of the streaming effect on the changes in the pitch/time relationship has been established, there seems to be no direct evidence that the static displays presented here behave in the same manner. Indirect evidence, though, is provided by the phenomenon of apparent motion (Wertheimer, 1912). As a visual, yet dynamic, phenomenon, apparent motion could provide the necessary link between the previously described visual and auditory grouping examples. Briefly, the perception of two (or more) successive light flashes changes as a function of the distance between the flashes, the size of the ISI, and the intensity of the flashes. (Here it should be noted that the effect could be generalized to more complex stimulus configurations.) As the ISI is increased, the perception changes from simultaneity (less than 30 ms) and partial movement (30–60 ms), to optimum (about 60 ms) and phi movement (60–200 ms). Finally, at ISIs of above 200–400 ms, no movement is perceived (Graham, 1965). According to Körte's (1915) third law as the speed of presentation increases, distance between flashes must be reduced in order for the impression of smooth motion to be preserved. This clear interdependence of spatial and temporal factors characterizes not only apparent motion, but as already mentioned, the auditory streaming effect. Specifically, for a given pure-tone segment duration, the speed of presentation must be reduced as the frequency difference between the segments increases, if the alternating tones are to be perceived as a single stream. Bregman (1990, p. 462) generalized this observation to music, referring to melodic motion that is preserved through a trade-off between frequency separation and speed.

More intriguing is the apparent parallel between Körte's third law and the interactions associated with the static visual displays described earlier. Let us look again at Figure 1a. If we gradually increase the vertical distance between the segments, the figure will eventually cease to be perceived as a single zigzag line. In fact, the pattern will have fragmented into a set of weakly grouped segments, and then into two horizontal collinear groups (Figure 1b). The figure is perceived as a single group as long as the ratio between the vertical and horizontal distance is maintained within a certain range. Similarly, the continuous "motion" between flashes can be observed only within a certain range of values of the distance/time ratio ($V = s/t$), as observed by Körte. This simple demonstration suggests that the same dynamics govern grouping in three different contexts: Apparent motion, auditory stream segregation, and its visual analog (although the list could be longer). Discrete auditory and visual stimuli are *connected* in some way and the patterns of connection are a function of the spatial or spatio-temporal relationships obtaining between the stimuli. The question then arises as to the apparent correspondence between the "horizontal" spatial dimension in the visual streaming example, and the temporal dimension of the apparent motion and auditory streaming effects.

A POSSIBLE FRAMEWORK FOR THE STUDY OF PERCEPTUAL ORGANIZATION

The comparison between the static and moving visual and auditory contexts reveals numerous commonalities, which are, at least in principle, open to empirical investigation. First, the perceptual impact of a particular arrangement of stimuli (salience of individual stimuli and their grouping) depends on the totality of spatial and spatio-temporal relationships obtaining between them—illusory contours cease to be contours if a single element of the figure is displaced. A harmonic complex is weakened if a harmonic is mistuned, and an auditory stream is broken if one of the segments exceeds a certain frequency margin. This dependence of the perceptual effect on the entirety of spatial and temporal relationships obtaining between objects and events (context) evokes the classical Gestalt proposition that the percept represents more than the sum of its parts. Second, spatial or spatio-temporal proximity in vision is in a sense equivalent to proximity in audition, defined in terms of time and pitch (Kubovy, 1981). Further, proximity and similarity are related in both modalities, despite the fact that the embedding dimensions are different. This statement requires elaboration. It is well known from Gestalt demonstrations that other things being equal, the more mutually similar the two objects, the more easily they will group. Similarly, the larger the difference between the objects, the closer together they have to be in order to be grouped. From this, an analogy can be drawn with audition where factors such as timbre (Bregman, 1990, p. 19) and localization (e.g., Cherry, 1953; Kubovy & Howard, 1976) interact with pitch/time proximity to assist organization.

The analogy between auditory and visual grouping contexts described in this paper rests on several assumptions, the most important of which is that the observed similarities are real, relevant, and open to experimental investigation. At the same time, they must not blind one to the important anatomical, functional, and ecological differences between the two modalities (see, e.g., Julesz & Hirsh, 1972). As is evident from the case of harmonic/vertical grouping (Figure 1c), even for simple grouping situations, the analogy can be maintained only to a limited (albeit considerable) extent. Yet, in the light of numerous important differences, one could argue that the systematic study of supramodal invariants of organization might provide important clues about the function of the neural correlates of perception in general.

These considerations prompt the question as to what kind of formal model could embrace the supramodal grouping invariants described here. Mainstream psychology never accepted the original attempt by Köhler (1920/1929) to incorporate the Minimum Principle into perception, partly because of the unsustainable psychophysical parallelism of the "physical Gestalten" model. According to the Minimum Principle (also known as the law of *Prägnanz*), the mind organizes the world in a way that minimizes expenditure of energy. In perception, the principle manifests itself as the general tendency towards simplicity (regularity, symmetry, and fewer independent units). Despite its intuitive appeal and some empirical support, the Minimum Principle still inhabits the domain of speculation.

Without venturing into a detailed exposition, we propose that a reformulation of the Minimum Principle within the framework of surface topology/analytical geometry might provide a link between the primitive relational properties of auditory and visual grouping phenomena, and experimental psychology.

What would be the starting assumptions for such a model? First, the organizing potential of the perceptual system could be represented by a perceptual "space", into which objects and events are embedded. Second, objects and events can be conceptualized as force fields, which affect the geometry of perceptual space.[2] Third, these force fields and their interactions can be represented as patterns of distortion on a surface of finite (and in the first instance, uniform) elasticity. The "elasticity" of perceptual space reflects the limited processing potential of the perceptual system(s) and is assumed to be obtainable from appropriate psychophysical measurements. According to this view, the salience of an object or event (its psychophysical profile) is reflected in the strength of its force field, and thus in the extent of deformation it imposes on perceptual space. It follows that the introduction of a new object would result in (1) the reduced salience of the first object, and (2) a change in the pattern of distortion. If two objects (or events) are sufficiently close to one another, they will create a common distorted region (basin). Depending on the spatial or spatio-temporal relationships between the objects, different patterns of distortion will be obtained.

The other important point concerns the relationship between perceptual space and the perceptual system. The Minimum Principle can be formalized as the sensitivity of the perceptual system to the minimal paths or *geodesics* in perceptual space. To illustrate, the length of a geodesic joining identical collinear objects (e.g., collinear line segments or pure tones of identical pitch) is determined by the distance between them. With a change in the spatial or spatio-temporal relationship, the curvature of the common region changes, altering the metric of perceptual space. Thus, although the physical distance between the objects might remain the same, the overall amount of distortion would increase, and with it the length of the geodesic joining the two objects. Conversely, the less distorted the common region, the more easily the objects will be grouped. The same would be true in the situation where a pair of identical objects is juxtaposed with a pair of different objects. Other things being equal, the former will create a more symmetrical (less distorted) basin, and thus be more easily grouped.

Analysis of the general geometrical properties of the patterns of distortion could provide a means for relating the perceptually transparent dynamics of grouping to psychophysical measurement, and, eventually, neurophysiological data.

---

[2] The notion of a two-dimensional visual "space", whose geometry is affected by force interactions between simple visual stimuli, can be found in Watson (1978).

CONCLUSIONS

Understanding the principles of perceptual organization remains a major task for psychological science. Three examples (two visual and one auditory) described here demonstrate that at least some of these principles operate across sensory modalities. Further, the apparent similarity between static and moving visual and auditory contexts suggests a form of spatio-temporal equivalence that needs to be addressed by any general model of perceptual grouping. Although systematic investigation of grouping-related neural dynamics holds considerable promise, the current state of knowledge leaves room for complementary approaches. A theory of grouping based on a "force field" interpretation of the Minimum Principle might represent such an approach.

REFERENCES

Bregman, A.S. (1990). *Auditory scene analysis*. Cambridge, MA: MIT Press.

Bregman, A.S., & Dannenbring, G.L. (1973). The effect of continuity on auditory stream segregation. *Perception and Psychophysics, 13*(2), 308–312.

Cherry, E.C. (1953). Some experiments on the recognition of speech with one and with two ears. *Journal of the Acoustical Society of America, 25,* 975–979.

Cohen, E.A. (1980). Pitch processing of non-harmonic tones: A search for an auditory mechanism that recognizes spectral patterns. *Journal of the Acoustical Society of America, 68* (Suppl. 1), S110.

Graham, C.H. (1965). Perception of movement. In C. Graham (Ed.), *Vision and visual perception* (pp. 575–588). New York: Wiley.

Julesz, B., & Hirsh, I.J. (1972). Visual and auditory perception—an essay of comparison. In E.E. David Jr. & P.B. Denes (Eds.), *Human communication: A unified view* (pp. 283–340). New York: McGraw-Hill.

Köhler, W. (1929). Physical Gestalten. In W.D. Ellis (Ed.), *A source book of Gestalt psychology*. New York: Humanities Press. (Original work published 1920.)

Körte, A. (1915). Kinomatoscopische Untersuchungen. *Zeitschrift für Psychologie der Sinnesorgane, 72,* 193–296.

Koffka, K. (1935). *Principles of Gestalt psychology*. New York: Harcourt, Brace & World.

Kubovy, M. (1981). Pitch segregation and indispensable attributes. In M. Kubovy & J. Pomerantz (Eds.), *Perceptual organization* (pp. 55–98). Hillsdale, NJ: Lawrence Erlbaum Associates Inc.

Kubovy, M., & Howard, F.P. (1976). Persistence of a pitch-segregating echoic memory. *Journal of Experimental Psychology: Human Perception and Performance, 2,* 531–537.

Moore, B.C., Glasberg, B.R., & Peters, R.W. (1985). Relative dominance of individual partials in determining the pitch of complex tones. *Journal of the Acoustical Society of America, 77,* 1853–1860.

Schouten, J.F. (1940). The residue and the mechanism of hearing. *Proceedings of the Koninklijke Nederlandsche Akademie von Wetenschappen, 43*, 991–999.

Slaymaker, F.H. (1970). Chords from tones having stretched partials. *Journal of the Acoustical Society of America, 47,* 1569–1571.

Terhardt, E. (1986). Gestalt principles and music perception. In W.A. Yost & C.A. Watson (Eds.), *Auditory processing of complex sounds* (pp. 157–166). Hillsdale, NJ: Lawrence Erlbaum Associates Inc.

von Helmholtz, H.L.F. (1954). *On the sensations of tone as a physiological basis for the theory of music*. (A.J. Ellis, Trans. Original work published 1863). New York: Dover.

Watson, A. (1978). A Riemann geometric explanation of the visual illusions and figural after-effects. In E.L.J. Leeuwenburg & H.F.J.M. Buffart (Eds.), *Formal theories of visual perception* (pp. 140–169). New York: Wiley.

Wertheimer, M. (1912). Experimentelle Studien über das Sehen von Bewegung. *Zeitschrift für Psychologie, 61,* 161–265.

VISUAL COGNITION, 2001, *8* (3/4/5), 359–379

Visual extinction and awareness: The importance of binding dorsal and ventral pathways

Gordon C. Baylis, Christopher L. Gore, and P. Dennis Rodriguez
University of South Carolina, USA
Rebecca J. Shisler
University of Georgia, USA

Patients with visual extinction were tested on three tasks involving stimulus identification and localization. In the first experiment, in which patients were to identify and localize stimuli, they demonstrated high levels of contralesional omissions. This primarily occurred under conditions of double simultaneous stimulation (DSS), consistent with the character of extinction. In contrast, when patients had to simply localize or count stimuli in Experiment 2, their contralesional omissions were very low. Similarly, when patients were to identify stimuli without localizing them (Experiment 3) they again showed very low contralesional error rates. These results support the view (Baylis, Driver, & Rafal, 1993) that visual extinction may be greatest when information about location cannot be bound to information about identity.

Our visual experience has the compelling quality of being unitary in nature. That is, we are aware of a single, unified visual world in which we act. Although this unitary nature is of obvious value, even a necessity given the singular nature of the world we live in, it is unclear how our brains ensure that it is achieved. Very early on, the visual input is directed to a large number of visual areas that are specialized for the processing of different visual features such as colour and motion. For example, for an observer to be aware of a red ball in a particular location they must be simultaneously aware of the shape, the colour, and the location.

Please address all correspondence to G.C. Baylis, Attention and Perception Laboratory, Department of Psychology, University of South Carolina, Columbia, SC 29208, USA. Email: gordon@sc.edu

This work was supported by a grant from the National Science Foundation (SBR 96-16555) and by generous intramural funding from the University of South Carolina. We thank all the patients who generously volunteered their time in this study.

http://www.tandf.co.uk/journals/pp/13506285.html DOI:10.1080/13506280143000052

The problem of how multiple, separately processed, sensory attributes are brought together has been termed the "binding problem". In the real world the binding problem for the example of a red ball may be much more complex due to the presence of another object in the field of view. In fact, there are typically many more objects in the field of view. For instance, we may be required to bind "square" with "green" and a different location to be aware of both a red ball as well as a green box. Although all the features must reach awareness together, they must be combined correctly. Otherwise the observer may become aware of a green ball, or a red box—objects that have no basis in reality.

The importance of correctly binding together features into object percepts is underscored by the work of Treisman and others (e.g., Treisman & Gelade, 1980; Treisman & Kanwisher, 1998). Under appropriate conditions, typically outside of focused attention, observers may report miscombined features—so called illusory conjunctions. However, further work (e.g., Baylis, Driver, & McLeod, 1992; Prinzmetal, Presti, & Posner, 1986) has suggested that preattentive visual parsing constrains illusory conjunctions such that features are rarely miscombined outside of the same perceptual group. However, the claim that illusory conjunctions are confined to a given perceptual group remains controversial (see Treisman, 1998).

The present study is based on the possibility of a binding problem that may lead to a much more severe deficit of visual perception. The particular source of a binding problem that we are concerned with here is the division of the visual system into a dorsal and a ventral stream. For some time it has been suggested that the multiple visual areas of the brain can be conceptualized as being divided in this way (Ungerleider & Mishkin, 1982). The dorsal stream, running from the dorsal occipital lobe into the parietal lobe, is concerned with scene-based properties such as location and motion (see, e.g., Andersen, 1999). The ventral stream, running from ventral occipital areas into the lower part of the temporal lobe, analyses object-based properties such as shape and colour (see, e.g., Baylis, Rolls, & Leonard, 1985, 1987; Lueschow, Miller, & Desimone, 1994). The correct binding of the dorsal "where" system to information in the ventral "what" system would seem essential for unified awareness of objects within a visual scene. Baylis, Driver, and Rafal (1993) suggested that a failure to bind information from the two visual streams together may underlie the neuropsychological deficit of visual extinction. The purpose of the present study is to test this proposal.

Extinction is a relatively common neurological sign following unilateral brain damage. First described by Oppenheim (1885), extinction is typically assessed by the process termed "clinical confrontation". The clinician presents a stimulus, typically a moving finger, in the patient's field of view contralateral to the lesion (contralesional), on the same side (ipsilesional), or both. A patient with extinction will correctly detect a single contralesional stimulus, but when presented with stimuli in both fields may report only the ipsilesional stimulus.

The classical account, and hence the name, is that the presence of an ipsilesional stimulus "extinguishes" the contralesional percept.

The fact that single contralesional stimuli are detected suggests that visual extinction cannot represent a failure of sensory input to the brain. However, sensory accounts of extinction (e.g., Bender, 1952) can account for the double simultaneous stimulation (DSS) effect in a straightforward manner. With single contralesional stimulation, the weakened stimulus might still be registered, but when in competition with a strong stimulation in the ipsilesional field such a weakened contralesional stimulus might not get detected. Indeed, in many cases (see Berti et al., 1992) a mild deficit in detecting single contralesional stimuli may exist, but may be obscured by a ceiling effect of performance in this condition.

An alternative characterization of extinction is as an attentional deficit, similar to neglect (Bisiach & Vallar, 1988; di Pellegrino & De Renzi, 1995; Weinstein, 1994). The proposition that extinction is a deficit of attention, rather than a sensory deficit, means that extinguished stimuli are processed to some extent, although not to the level of awareness. Volpe, LeDoux, and Gazzaniga (1979) studied four patients with lesions to the parietal cortex leading to extinction. These patients were presented with one or two objects in a tachistoscope, and had to determine if the two objects were the same or different. Although they were able to make this comparison correctly, when asked to identify the objects, patients were only able to name the ipsilesional object and not the object on the contralesional side. These results suggest that the contralesional objects were partially analysed—sufficiently to allow a determination if it was different to the ipsilesional object, but not enough to allow conscious perception.

Volpe et al. (1979) took their results to support the notion that extinction is an attentional deficit, because contralesional information is processed to some extent. Conversely Farah, Monheit, and Wallace (1991; cf. Berti et al., 1992) showed that the pattern of deficits observed could be explained equally well in terms of sensory degradation. They produced the same pattern of data in normal subjects simply by degrading sensory stimuli on one side of a display. These subjects were unable to identify the degraded stimuli, but were accurate in judging whether the stimuli in the two hemifields matched. Furthermore, the difference between intact matching and deficient identification disappeared when both tasks were run as a forced choice task, with equal difficulty. Thus, the results of Volpe et al. could equally be taken to support a sensory view of extinction in which the contralesional stimulus was merely "highly degraded", such that conscious identification could not occur, but a simple comparison with the ipsilesional stimulus was still possible.

However, Posner, Walker, Friedrich, and Rafal (1984) provided indirect evidence that extinction is a deficit in attention. A visual target stimulus was presented with a priming cue on either the same side (a valid cue) or the opposite side (an invalid cue) of a target (Posner, 1980). Patients with lesions to the parietal lobe were found to perform poorly on detecting contralesional stimuli on "invalid" trials (Posner et al., 1984). That is, when attention was directed to the ipsilesional side by a cue, and a target appeared on the contralesional side, patients were very slow to detect those targets. In contrast, the performance of these patients was relatively normal for contralesional targets on valid trials. That is, if patients' attention was directed first to the contralesional side, detection of a target on that side was relatively normal. Based on this pattern of results, Posner et al. suggested that parietal lesions may produce a deficit in the inability to *disengage* attention from ipsilesional events to shift toward contralesional events.

The patients studied by Posner et al. (1984) were selected by lesion, rather than having the symptom of extinction, but in all cases the lesion sites are very similar to those typically associated with extinction and neglect, and some of the patients showed extinction at the time of testing. A disengagement deficit could explain the extinction of contralesional stimuli. With only a single contralesional stimulus, the only "cue" to direct attention to that side, would be the contralesional stimulus. In contrast, in DSS trials attention may be directed first to the stimulus in the unimpaired ipsilesional field. Patients may fail to report the contralesional stimulus because they cannot disengage from the ipsilesional side (see also Milner, 1997).

The view that extinction represents a failure of ipsilesional disengagement entails that patients first direct their attention to the ipsilesional side. This is likely, given that the ipsilesional stimulus is typically judged as appearing subjectively earlier than the contralesional stimulus (Rorden et al., 1997). A test of this view came from Karnath (1988) who asked patients to report contralesional events prior to ipsilesional events or did not require them to report ipsilesional events at all. By removing the need to disengage attention from ipsilesional objects, he found that patients could then respond to the contralesional stimuli (Karnath, 1988).

A study by Baylis et al. (1993) provides strong support for the notion that visual extinction represents a failure in awareness of stimuli that are none the less processed by the visual system. In this study, patients were presented with coloured letter stimuli in the two hemifields. They were asked to identify the letter in each field, or name the colour of the stimuli. Extinction was greatest when the stimuli in the two fields were the same on the task relevant dimension. Therefore, if a patient was presented with an "E" in both fields in the letter naming task, they were more likely to miss the contralesional stimulus than when they were presented with an "O" in one field and an "E" in the other. These results demonstrate that the extinguished items must be processed by the visual system, otherwise the modulation of extinction by item repetition could not have occurred. These results provide, therefore, evidence against simple sensory accounts for extinction (cf. Rafal & Robertson, 1995). Using an entirely different paradigm, Marzi et al. (1996) showed that extinguished items are, none the less, processed. In this study patients had to detect the presence of items in a display regardless of their location. The reaction time to detect items when one was present in both fields was lower than when a single ipsilesional item was present. This target redundancy effect occurred even on trials on which the patient was unaware of the contralesional item. Thus these extinguished contralesional items still produced a target redundancy effect, and must have been processed.

None the less, the results of Baylis et al. (1993) may appear counter to intuition. After all one might predict that the presence of information in the ipsilesional field might be expected to prime the detection of the same or similar information in the contralesional field. In fact, Karnath (1988) did show such a facilitation in the case that stimuli in the two fields were *similar*. Furthermore, Ward, Goodrich, and Driver (1994) showed that grouping between visual stimuli based on Gestalt principles such as similarity may reduce visual extinction. Baylis et al. (1993) explained this apparent contradiction in terms of the distinction between types and tokens (Kanwisher, 1987). It was suggested that unilateral brain lesions may lead to a reduced capacity to generate tokens in the contralesional hemifield. As a result, tokens can be generated if they are unique (i.e., either with single contralesional stimulus, or with different—or even similar—stimuli in the two hemifields). By contrast, when the same token has to be generated in the contralesional hemifield after one just produced in the ipsilesional field (in the case of same stimuli), this is difficult, similar to the case of repetition blindness (Kanwisher, 1987, 1991). This view explains the facilitation seen by Karnath in terms of priming of the types, without an effect on the production of tokens. At the core of this explanation is the fact that interventions at many different levels of processing may affect the probability that a patient becomes aware of a given contralesional stimulus. Sensory priming or low-level grouping (Ward et al., 1994) may predominate and tend to increase the probability of awareness of a contralesional item. Alternatively, higher level attentional competition for token formation may predominate, reducing the probability that a contralesional stimulus is noticed. (An essentially similar explanation was proposed by Ward et al., 1994.)

Our present view of these data represents a related but distinct theory, coming from the viewpoint that perception represents the generation of percepts to "explain" the sensory data presented to the perceptual system. Thus when a subject becomes aware of the percept of "an E on the right", this can be seen as a perceptual "explanation" of the sensory stimulation processed by the brain—in this case the representation of location (the right field location) and featural information (the "E quality"). The production of this percept clearly requires integration of visual information from the dorsal and ventral pathways (see Ungerleider & Haxby, 1994; Ungerleider & Mishkin, 1982). If the ability to integrate this information is reduced on one side of space due to a lesion, we can now explain the effect of sameness in reducing the probability that a contralesional stimulus will be perceived. In the case of an "O" on the left in addition to the "E" on the right, after the perception of an "E" on the right, both "O quality" and "left stimulation" remain to be "explained" by perception, and so the percept of an "O" on the left may be forced. On the other hand, when the contralesional stimulus has the same featural information (here by being an "E"), then there is less necessity to have a percept of an "E" on the left. This is because the presence of "E quality" may be more or less explained by the "E" on the ipsilesional side. Therefore, the weak signal of left stimulation is, by itself, less likely to force a percept when accompanied by unexplained featural information.

The current proposal goes beyond the notion that perception involves binding of dorsal and ventral information. Indeed we suggest that to be aware of a percept it must have information from dorsal and ventral pathways bound together. We propose that when information cannot be bound together in this way, the observer may not be aware of visual information that is none the less processed by their brain. We propose that visual extinction may represent, at least in part, such a failure of binding, probably as a result of an anatomical interruption of the connections between the dorsal and ventral pathways.

In the present study, we investigate visual extinction beginning with the task used by Baylis et al. (1993). We then tested patients with two additional tasks designed to test the proposal that extinction is due to a failure to produce "tokens" by the binding of information from dorsal and ventral sensory streams. In these tasks, it was not necessary to bind information between the two streams, and therefore it might be predicted that extinction would be reduced or absent.

EXPERIMENT 1

Participants were presented with visual stimuli that consisted of letters displayed in either red or green in the left or right hemifield, or both (i.e., DSS). They were required to name either the colour of the letter presented and its location (colour task), or the letter presented and it location (shape task). There were three main hypotheses for this experiment. The first was that there would be a greater proportion of errors for DSS trials than for single stimulus trials. The second hypothesis was that, on these DSS trials there would be more errors when the two stimuli were the same. The final hypothesis was that this effect of sameness should only apply on the task-relevant dimension.

Methods

Participants. Six participants from HealthSouth Rehabilitation Hospital were recruited for inclusion on one or all of these three experiments. The lesion localization, sex, and age and brief clinical details are given next, with reconstructions according to the method of Rorden and Brett (in press).

AS was 53 year-old right handed Caucasian female with 12 years of education. She was admitted following a large cerebrovascular accident (CVA) to the right hemisphere. She showed marked left-sided weakness, especially of the lower body. She demonstrated evidence of complete sensory loss on the left lower body, and of tactile extinction in the upper body. She demonstrated a marked right gaze preference, but no visual field defects. On clinical confrontation she showed left-sided visual extinction that was severe and consistent. She was alert and well oriented, with no deficits of memory. An MRI demonstrated a large infarct involving both the basal ganglia and lower layers of frontal cortex. Damage included the caudate and putamen, centrum semiovale, and the outer part of the corona radiation.

CS was a 42-year-old right-handed Caucasian female with a baccalaureate education. She had presented with an aneurysm at the bifurcation of the middle cerebral artery (MCA). At surgery, the inferior division of the MCA was entirely clipped, with no distal flow, resulting in an infarct in the right parieto temporal region. Following surgery she was well oriented with intact memory and speech. She demonstrated left-sided weakness, slight left-sided facial droop, and slight right deviation of gaze. She displayed no visual field defects, and inconsistent visual extinction by clinical confrontation.

NS was an 81-year-old, right-handed Caucasian female with 10 years of education. She had an embolic lesion to the right parietal and occipital lobe. She was well oriented with some left lower-body weakness. Although she initially showed severe visual neglect, at the time of testing she showed no neglect, but displayed extinction to clinical confrontation. She had normal acuity with small peripheral field defects on the left hemifield. All testing was carried out outside of these areas. In addition to visual extinction, she showed severe tactile extinction, but no auditory perceptual deficits.

SJ was a 53-year-old right-handed Caucasian male with 12 years of education. He had a small ischemic lesion to the right parietal lobe. He was well oriented, and had some left-sided weakness, especially to his upper body and face. He showed some visual neglect and severe visual extinction to clinical confrontation, although visual acuity was normal. He also showed severe tactile extinction in his left upper body, along with slight tactile sensory loss on his left side.

TH was a 67-year-old, right-handed Caucasian male with 12 years of education. He had an embolic lesion to the right parietal lobe that had occurred 3 years prior to testing. He was well oriented, and showed very slight tactile extinction on his left hemibody (as far as could be tested, given that he had undergone two above-the-knee amputations), and visual extinction on clinical confrontation.

WY was a 68-year-old, right-handed Caucasian man with 10 years of education. He had a large embolic lesion to the right parietal lobe, extending into the

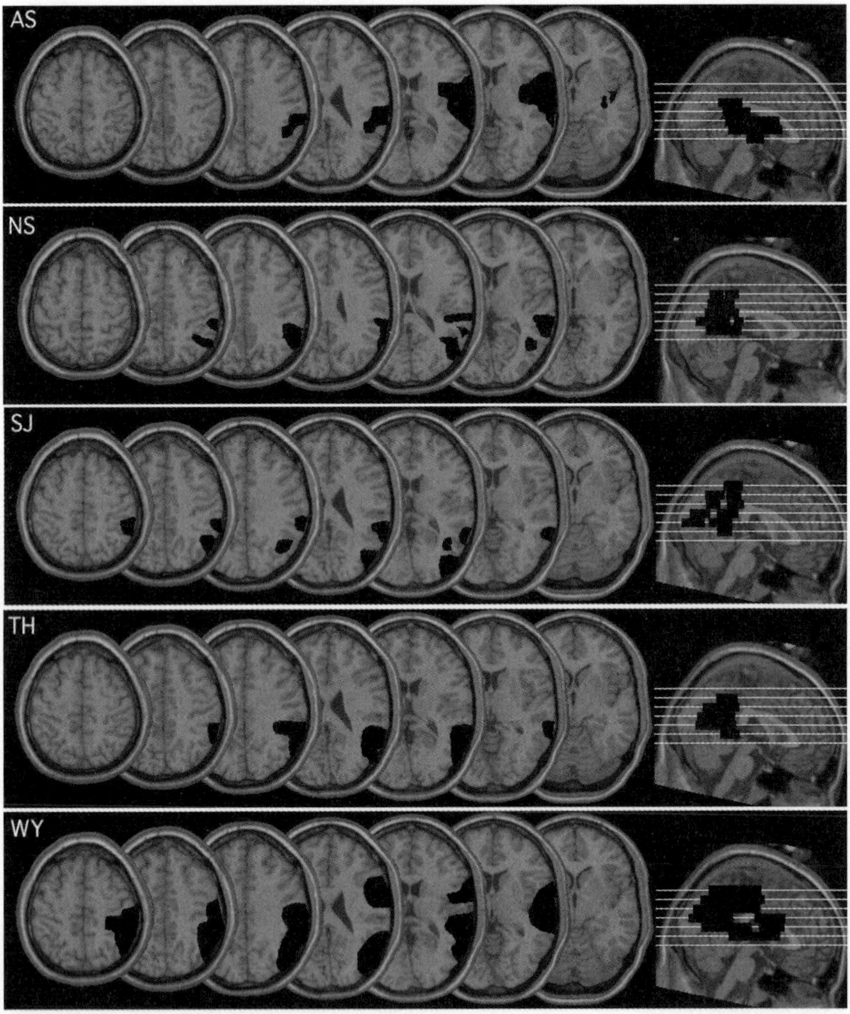

Figure 1. Reconstruction of the lesions, based on CT and MRI scans. No scan was available for CS.

frontal lobe. He presented with left-sided weakness, especially of the lower hemibody, some tactile sensory loss, and neglect and extinction to clinical confrontation. He was well-oriented, and initially he had right deviation of gaze, although this had resolved at the time of testing. He showed normal visual acuity (when corrected by his existing spectacles), and no visual field defects.

Apparatus. Tasks were run on a Dell Pentium computer with a 20-inch monitor. Participants were seated approximately 1 m from the monitor.

Stimuli. The stimuli consisted of the letters "E" and "O" presented in either red or green at approximately 15° to the left or right of a fixation point that was present at all times. The stimuli were adjusted in size until a patient was able to read them with ease, and the total stimulus duration was titrated so that patients made no more than 25% errors of omission in single contralesional trials.

Design. There were two variants of the task: A colour task and a shape task. In the colour task, patients were asked to verbally report the colour at each location; while for the shape task they had to report the letter at each location. In each case patients were asked to make a forced choice between the two alternatives and "nothing" while pointing to each side. There were 42 trials with seven types of display, each presented six times in a pseudorandom order. The seven types of display are as follows:

Catch trials: No stimulus was presented.
Single left target: A single red or green letter was presented on the left only.
Single right target: A single red or green letter was presented on the right.

For DSS conditions, two stimuli were presented, with conditions as follows, described initially for the colour task (letter task in parentheses):

DSS same relevant, same irrelevant: The same letter was presented simultaneously on the left and right, in the same colour.
DSS same relevant, different irrelevant: The same coloured letter was presented on both sides, although the letters were different. (For the letter task the same letter was presented to the left and right, but in different colours.)
DSS different relevant, same irrelevant: The same letter was presented in different colours to both sides. (For the letter task different letters were presented to the left and right in the same colours.)
DSS different: Different letters in different colours were presented in the left and right fields.

Procedure. The task was explained to the patient by the experimenter, and it was emphasized that only the task-relevant dimension of the stimuli should be considered and reported. The patient was instructed to point to each side in turn and report the stimulus, or lack of a stimulus on that side. If a patient failed to mention one side they were asked about it, and reminded of their instructions. Each trial began with the experimenter asking if the patient was ready, then pressing the <SPACE BAR> on the key board to begin each trial. The patient reported the stimuli either as they were present or immediately afterwards.

Stimuli were initially presented for 400 ms, but this was adjusted up (if patients made more than 15% errors on single stimulus trials) or down (if they made no errors on DSS trials). This automated algorithm determined an appropriate stimulus duration from the possible values of 33, 50, 100, 150, 250, 400, 600, 1000, or 2000 ms. Having established stimulus parameters for a particular patient, these were all kept exactly the same for that patient in Experiments 1, 2, and 3. In carrying out this adjustment we ensured that there was moderate extinction, but not frank neglect for contralesional stimuli. This enabled us to demonstrate a reduction in extinction when binding of identity and location was not required (in Experiments 2 and 3). At different parameters of stimulus size, eccentricity, and duration, extinction might be apparent in Experiments 2 and 3. Although the initial stimulus duration adjustment was carried out on the task used in Experiment 1, subsequent testing of the patients was carried out on all five tasks in semi-random order in each case over a period of 2 weeks or less. In Table 1, the total number of experimental blocks performed by each patient in each experiment are shown.

Results

Extinction on DSS. We found that the number of errors of omission in reporting contralesional stimuli increased dramatically under conditions of DSS. The mean error proportions under single and DSS presentations collapsed across the two tasks are shown in Figure 2. A paired samples *t*-test comparing the proportion of errors in reporting the contralesional stimulus in the

TABLE 1
The total number of blocks of experimental trials carried out on each patient

	Patient					
Task	*AS*	*CS*	*NS*	*SJ*	*TH*	*WY*
Exp 1 colour	2	4	2	2	2	2
Exp 1 letter	2	3	2	2	1	2
Exp 2	2	4	4	2	2	1
Exp 3 colour		3	2	3		2
Exp 3 letter		2	2	2		2

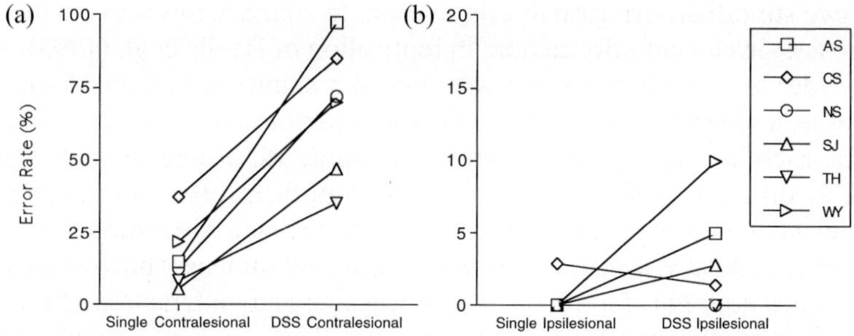

Figure 2. The effects of DSS on contralesional (a) and ipsilesional (b) error rates. For each patient the number of errors (in the vast majority of cases errors of omission) under single and DSS conditions are plotted. Each curve represents data for a single patient.

single contralesional to the number of these errors in the DSS condition showed that DSS trials were missed significantly more often than single left trials, $t(5) = 6.7, p < .001$. This difference on performance for single left and DSS trials shows that there is clear extinction, rather than neglect, seen on this task.

Effect of stimulus sameness. Baylis et al. (1993) showed that in visual extinction, an increase in the number of extinguished trials was seen when the stimuli in the two fields were the same with respect to the quality that patients had to report. By contrast, whether or not the stimuli were the same on the quality that patients did *not* report appeared to have no effect on the amount of visual extinction. The error data are sorted according to sameness on the relevant dimension in Figure 3a, and sorted according to sameness on the irrelevant dimension in Figure 3b. The data shown in these graphs suggests that sameness on the task-relevant dimension modulate visual extinction. That is, when the two fields contained stimuli that were the same on the task-relevant dimension, the item on the contralesional side was more likely to be missed than when there

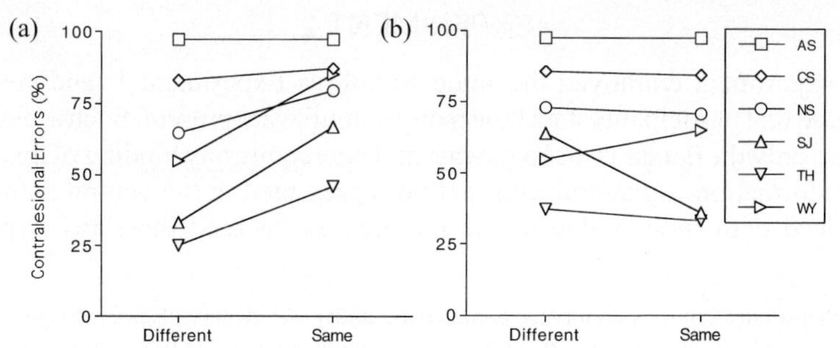

Figure 3. The effect of sameness on (a) the task–relevant and (b) task-irrelevant stimulus dimension on the level of extinction under DSS. Each point represents data collapsed across two conditions of DSS, with each curve representing a single patient.

were two stimuli differing on this dimension. In contrast, this was not the case for the task-irrelevant information, in replication of Baylis et al. (1993).

In order to test whether there was indeed a significant effect of stimulus sameness, a repeated measures ANOVA was performed on the data with two factors, each having two levels: irrelevant (same vs. different), and relevant (same vs. different). This analysis revealed a significant effect for sameness on the relevant dimension such that more errors were made when stimuli were the same, $F(1, 5) = 12.9, p < .02$. There was no effect of sameness on the task-irrelevant dimension, $F(1, 5) = 0.7$, n.s., nor was there any interaction of relevant and irrelevant dimensions, $F(1, 5) = 0.6$, n.s. That is, there was no greater extinction when the two stimuli were the same on the task-irrelevant dimension. Therefore, this experiment provides a clear replication of the results found by Baylis et al. (1993).

Sameness of stimuli leading to an increase in visual extinction is consistent with the view that extinction results from a failure to generate "tokens" in the contralesional field (see Baylis et al., 1993; Rafal & Robertson, 1995). If this is so, then token production first requires that the observer binds together stimulus features (such as shape and colour) within the ventral visual pathway and then binds them to a particular spatial location, as coded by the dorsal visual pathway. This may explain why interruption of the pathway linking the parietal lobe with the temporal lobe is commonly seen in patients with visual extinction. Our view explains extinction as a failure to bind featural (ventral) and location (dorsal) information together, and predicts that without such a requirement for binding, extinction may not occur. This view entails that extinction is at least in part dependent on the task requiring information from dorsal and ventral streams are bound together. Therefore, it would be expected that even if the same stimuli were used, extinction would not be seen if the patients were asked to respond to the stimuli in a way that does not require binding of features and location.

EXPERIMENT 2

This experiment employed the same stimuli as Experiment 1, and yet only required that participants state how many stimuli were present. Such a task may require only the dorsal visual pathway, and not require any binding of this location information to featural information represented in the ventral pathway.[1] If indeed extinction is due to the requirement to bind these two types of

[1]Other studies in our laboratory have studied the ability of patients with extinction to count up to eight stimuli. In these studies, the error rates, although appreciable (see Dehaene & Cohen, 1994; Humphreys, 1998), are lower than those on tasks like Experiment 1. However, it is clear that this experiment may only require patients to subitize the 0, 1, or 2 stimuli, a task that may not take place entirely within the dorsal pathway (see Sathian et al., 1999).

information, then it would be predicted that very few contralesional stimuli would be missed for DSS trials.

Method

All aspects of the method were the same as in Experiment 1 except as noted.

Design. A single task was used with seven types of stimuli that were the same as those used in Experiment 1.

Procedure. Stimuli were presented in the same manner, and for the same durations for each participant as was used in experiment 1. Patients were asked to ignore what colour or shape the letters were, but merely to count whether 0, 1, or 2 were present in the display. The experimenter entered these responses into the computer for subsequent analysis.

Results

The error rates in the four different DSS conditions were not different in any patient, and so all DSS data was collapsed together. There were no catch trials in which a patient erroneously stated that there was a nonzero number of letters present, and only two trials in which a patient missed a single ipsilesional stimulus, and said there were zero letters in the display. Thus the only critical data are the mean numbers of missed stimuli in the single contralesional and the pooled DSS conditions. The mean proportion of errors of omission in single and DSS trials are given in Figure 4. A planned comparison revealed that there was no difference between error rates for single left stimulus trials, and single right stimulus trials ($p > .20$). Similarly, there was no increase in errors of omission for left stimuli in DSS versus single left stimulus trials ($p > .10$). These comparisons suggest that no extinction will be seen when participants are simply required to enumerate stimuli.

In order to determine whether these results are different from those seen in Experiment 1, we carried out a paired samples t-test between the contralesional error rate for DSS trials in Experiment 1 versus Experiment 2. Note that the stimuli in these two conditions were the same; what differed in these two experiments was whether the participants had to identify and localize stimuli, or simply enumerate them. This analysis showed that subjects made significantly more errors in Experiment 1 than in Experiment 2, $t(5) = 4.15, p < .01$.

These results support the notion that extinction is observed only in tasks where the participant has to bind featural and location information. However, it is possible that the reason Experiment 2 failed to produce any extinction is due to the fact that there is no requirement to identify stimuli. Clearly identification is required in Experiment 1 where a large amount of visual extinction is seen,

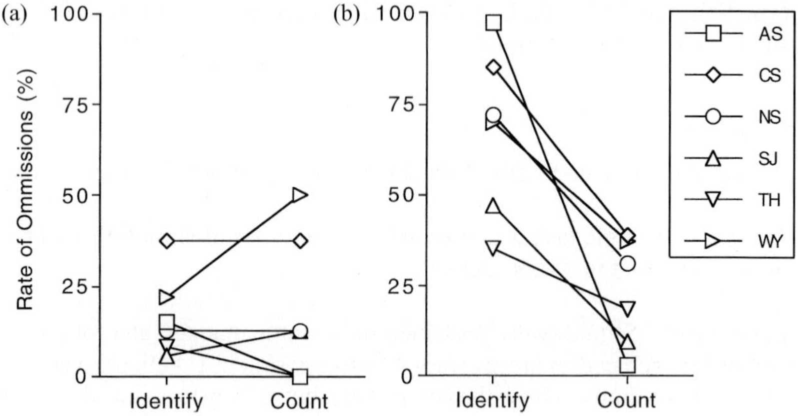

Figure 4. The difference between the contralesional error rates in Experiment 1 and Experiment 2. **(a)** For each patient the error rate for single contralesional stimuli in Experiment 1 is compared to the rate of omissions in this condition in Experiment 2. **(b)** The mean contralesional error rate across the four different conditions of DSS in Experiment 1 is compared to the rate of omissions (presumably contralesional) in Experiment 2.

and thus could be the sole underlying cause of the extinction. This led to the design of Experiment 3 in which the *only* requirement is to identify stimuli.

EXPERIMENT 3

This experiment was to examine whether patients with extinction would be able to identify items in the contralesional field if they were not required to bind them to a particular location. This is to test the notion that contralesional errors of omission were much less in Experiment 2 due to the lack of a requirement to bind information from the dorsal and ventral visual pathways.

Method

All aspects of the method followed Experiment 1 except as noted.

Participants. Four patients with extinction took part in this experiment: CS, NS, SJ, and WY. Clinical details were given previously.

Design. There were two tasks, analogous to those in Experiment 1, in which the patient was asked about the letters, or the colours of the stimuli. Each followed the same design with the only difference the nature of the forced-choice question that was asked after the display. Both tasks were carried out with exactly the same stimulus and timing parameters as those used for Experiment 1. There were 13 conditions, based on the 7 in Experiment 1:

- *Catch trials*: No stimulus was presented.
- *Single contralesional* and *single ipsilesional*: Each of these was further subdivided into trials when the patient was asked about the stimulus that was present or catch trials asking about the stimulus that was not in the display. So, in the letter task, following an "E" in the contralesional field, participants could either be asked about an "E" or an "O".
- DSS trials with *same relevant, different irrelevant*, and *same relevant, same irrelevant* were similarly subdivided into trials where the patient was asked about the present or absent stimuli.
- DSS trials with *different relevant* stimuli (i.e., *different relevant, different irrelevant* and *different relevant, same irrelevant*) were divided according to whether patients were tested about the stimulus in the ipsilesional or contralesional field. These last trials are clearly the crucial trials in our analysis.

Procedure. The thirteen conditions were presented with equal probability each three times in pseudorandom order in each block of 39 trials. Patients were instructed to pay attention just to the letters or just to the colours, and it was emphasized that they did not have to remember where the stimuli were. The tasks of letter identification and colour identification were blocked. Displays were presented at the same duration as Experiment 1 and 300 ms after the display a question appeared on the screen. In the letter task the question was of the form "Was there an 'E' present?", or "Was there a green letter?" in the colour task. The experimenter read this question out loud. The patient then answered "yes" or "no". In a minority of trials the patient said that they did not know. In these cases the experimenter insisted: "If you are not sure you must guess", until the patient made a yes or no response. As soon as the patient responded the experimenter entered the response into the computer for automated scoring. The forced-choice procedure was adopted because an earlier attempt to ask patients to report the letters without their location failed—patients always said "an E, *on the right*", etc. Thus in order to ensure that patients were not (against instructions) carrying out a location and identity task, we used the present procedure. This does, of course, raise the possibility that the forced-choice task having two alternatives was slightly easier that the identity task, where at each location three possibilities (e.g., E, O, or nothing) existed. This slight change in task should be accounted for in our harsh guessing-correction procedure.

Treatment of data. Since it is possible that patients were adopting a guessing strategy on this task, we have employed the most conservative guessing correction to all the misses in this task. For every time that a patient said that a stimulus was not present, we might propose that an equal number of times the patient simply guessed that the stimulus was present, and would have been correct. To account for this, we have therefore doubled the error rates for Experiment 2 in every case in the following analyses and figures.

Results

The error rates for each of the patients for each of the 13 conditions are shown in Figure 5, along with their corresponding error rates for the 7 conditions of Experiment 1. The first point to be noted is the absence of false alarms—that is trials when a patient said that a stimulus was present when in fact it was not. This shows that the correct identifications were not simply due to a bias to say "yes", and that our estimated (i.e., doubled) error rates represent an overestimate of the underlying failure to detect. Note that the only two conditions where we can be sure we are testing the identification of items on the left are the single left stimulus trials, and the DSS trials with different stimuli in the two fields. A correct response on DSS same stimuli trials may be due to correctly identifying the left stimulus, or more likely as a result of identifying the stimulus on the right.

For each patient, the total number of errors on single stimulus trials was no different than the numbers of errors present in Experiment 1. This was confirmed by a paired samples *t*-test, $t(3) = 0.02$, n.s.. The large difference between this experiment and experiment 1 was in terms of the error rates in the DSS conditions. The crucial comparison is between error rates for the DSS different trials, comparing errors when the left stimulus was tested here to the contralesional error rate in Experiment 1. As confirmed by a *t*-test there were fewer errors in this experiment than Experiment 1, $t(3) = 3.25$, $p < .05$. Thus removing the need to localize stimuli led to a major reduction in the extinction effect seen with DSS. Even though extinction (as evidenced by the difference between error rates on single contralesional and DSS trials) had been greatly reduced, there was still a small numeric trend for the error rates on DSS trials to be higher than those on single contralesional trials. A paired *t*-test showed this trend to be non-significant, $t(3) = 0.94$, $p = .4$. Nonetheless we cannot be sure that requiring only identification removes extinction completely.

GENERAL DISCUSSION

In three experiments we provide evidence that visual extinction may, at least in part, represent a failure to bind together information from the dorsal and ventral visual pathways. In the first experiment, all patients demonstrated a large number of contralesional omissions under conditions of DSS. In these tasks, patients had to report the identity or the colour of a letter presented in each visual hemifield. Since this required the patients to be aware of particular stimuli at particular locations, it may be expected to require the observer to bind together the location information from the parietal lobe, with colour or shape

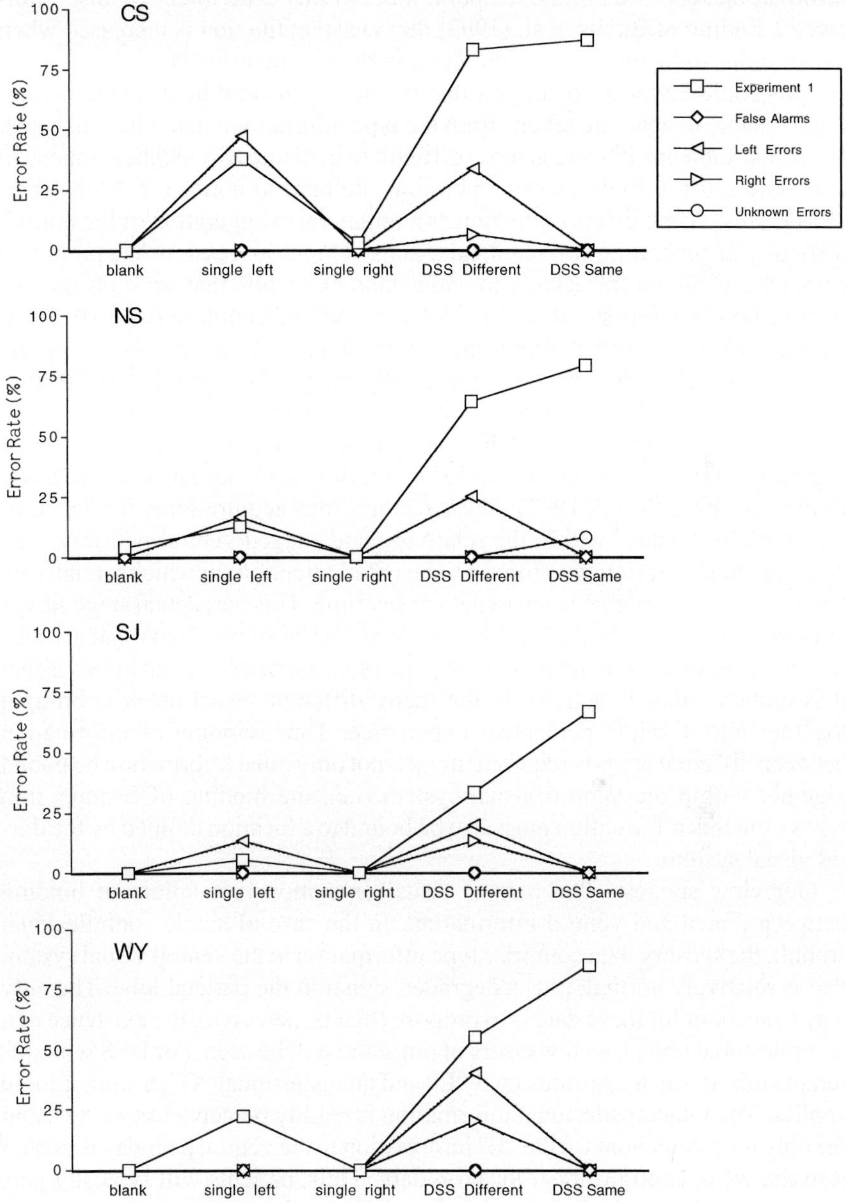

Figure 5. For the four patients who took part in Experiment 3, the pattern of data in Experiments 1 and 3 are compared. Note that the error rates plotted here for Experiment 3 are twice the observed error rates, to account for successful guesses in the most conservative manner possible. Note also that many types of errors are not possible in all stimulus conditions in Experiment 3.

information processed in the temporal lobe. In this experiment we also replicated a finding of Baylis et al. (1993) that visual extinction is increased when the stimulus to be identified is the same in the two hemifields.

This could be taken to suggest that the damaged right hemisphere is relatively unable to generate tokens from the type information that it has analysed. In normal subjects, it is much more difficult to generate two identical tokens in succession; for example, word repetitions are hard to notice (cf. Kanwisher, 1987). This characterizes extinction as a unilateral exaggeration of the normal difficulty in generating two identical tokens in rapid succession. We propose a somewhat different framework to understand extinction that parallels the difference between types and tokens. A large body of literature (e.g., Baylis & Driver, 1995; Treisman & Kanwisher, 1998; Wolfe & Bennett, 1997) supports the view that the entire visual field is rapidly analysed to some level of feature analysis without the need for attention or awareness. We suggest that such a featural analysis occurs in the contralesional field in patients with extinction or neglect (cf. Baylis & Baylis, in press; Driver, Baylis, Goodrich, & Rafal, 1994; Driver, Baylis, & Rafal, 1992). These features may acquire some further combination into "types" within the relatively undamaged ventral pathway. The next step in perception we propose to be entail attention, in which a relatively few objects are available to awareness at any time. This perceptual stage serves to construct a model of the world to account for the sensory data that are currently processed. A crucial part of the perceptual experience of an object is that it is unitary—that is activity in the many different visual areas is brought together into a single perceptual experience. Thus, binding of information between different areas is required. In fact, not only must information be bound together within the ventral visual system (i.e., the binding of features into types), but this information must also be bound to a location defined by the dorsal visual system.

Our view suggests that part of visual extinction is a failure of binding between dorsal and ventral information. In the case of single contralesional stimuli, the sensory data comprise type information in the ventral visual system that is relatively normal, plus a degraded signal in the parietal lobe. The only way to account for these data is to propose (that is, perceive), the existence of a contralesional object, so few errors of omission will be seen. For DSS with different stimuli, say a contralesional "E" and an ipsilesional "O", a similar logic applies. The intact ipsilesional information is readily perceived as an "O", and the only way to account for the "E" information in the ventral pathway is to bind it to the weak contralesional location data. Thus, patients will typically perceive a contralesional stimulus when it is different from the ipsilesional stimulus. A different situation arises when stimuli are the same, for example an "E" on both sides. Here, the only type information is "E", and the dorsal areas provide a strong ipsilesional location signal and a weak contralesional signal. The "E" type information can be accounted for simply in terms of the ipsilesional item. Here, it is not necessary to posit (i.e., perceive) a contralesional stimulus to account for this.

This account suggests that extinction will result from a combination of two effects in the brain—a weakening of the dorsal location signal, and a weakening of the ability to bind dorsal and ventral information. In the case of one of the more common lesions to cause extinction—parietal damage—it is straightforward to see how the lesion can lead to such a compromise. First these lesions will damage the parietal lobe itself, but also typically interrupt the connection of the parietal lobe to the temporal lobe.

Our account explains the pattern of data in an extinction task and also makes the prediction that tasks that do not require binding of dorsal and ventral information will lead to far fewer contralesional omission errors. This was tested in the present study by experiments in which purely dorsal (Experiment 2), or purely ventral (Experiment 3) information could be used to solve the task. In these tasks, contralesional error rates were drastically reduced in the DSS conditions to a level that was no higher than error rates observed with a single contralesional stimulus. Note that the stimulus parameters used were chosen such that performance in Experiment 1 was at neither a floor nor a ceiling. With other stimulus parameters, it is possible, indeed likely that extinction will be seen in experiments such as Experiments 2 and 3 (see also Ward et al., 1994). Furthermore, we suggest that our view can account for the findings of Vuilleumier and Rafal (1999). In this study, contralesional extinction was less when patients were simply asked to enumerate the number of different shapes (analogous to our Experiment 3). This task, which we would argue does not require binding between temporal and parietal information, was contrasted to a task in which patients had to localize the shapes in which error rates were much higher. This localization task of Vuilleumier and Rafal would require parietal information, perhaps bound to information from the temporal lobe.

Our results support the notion that an important component of visual extinction is a deficient ability to bind information in the dorsal and ventral visual pathways. In tasks that do not require this binding, visual extinction tends to be less than in tasks that require such binding. Such a relation may suggest that a crucial component of awareness of visual stimuli is the ability to bind together information around them.

REFERENCES

Andersen, R.A. (1999). Multimodal integration for the representation of space in the posterior parietal cortex. *Philosophical Transactions of the Royal Society, B352,* 1421–1428.

Baylis, G.C., & Baylis, L.L. (in press). Effects of brain damage on selective reaching. In S. Jackson (Ed.), *Selection and action*. London: University College London Press.

Baylis, G.C., & Driver, J. (1995). One-sided edge-assignment in vision: 1. Figure–ground segmentation and attention to objects. *Current Directions in Psychological Science, 4,* 201–206.

Baylis, G.C., Driver, J., & McLeod, P. (1992). Movement and proximity constrain miscombinations of colour and form. *Perception, 21,* 201–218.

Baylis, G., Driver, J., & Rafal, R. (1993). Visual extinction and stimulus repetition. *Journal of Cognitive Neuroscience, 5*(4), 453–466.

Baylis, G.C., Rolls, E.T., & Leonard, C.M. (1985). Selectivity between faces in the responses of a population of neurons in the cortex in the superior temporal sulcus of the monkey. *Brain Research, 342,* 91–102.

Baylis, G.C., Rolls, E.T., & Leonard, C.M. (1987). Functional subdivisions of the temporal lobe neocortex. *Journal of Neuroscience, 7,* 330–342.

Bender, M.B. (1952). *Disorders in perception.* Springfield, IL: Thomas.

Berti, A., Allport, A., Driver, J., Dienes, Z., Oxbury, J., & Oxbury, S. (1992). Levels of processing for stimuli in an "extinguished" visual field. *Neuropsychologia, 30,* 403–415.

Bisiach, E., & Vallar, G. (1988). Hemineglect in humans. In F. Boller & J. Grafman (Eds.), *Handbook of neuropsychology* (Vol. 1, pp. 195–222). Amsterdam: Elsevier.

Dehaene, S., & Cohen, L. (1994). Dissociable mechanisms of subitizing and counting: Neuropsychological evidence from simultanagnosic patients. *Journal of Experimental Psychology: Human Perception and Performance, 20,* 958–975.

di Pellegrino, G., & De Renzi, E. (1995). An experimental investigation on the nature of extinction. *Neuropsychologia, 33*(2), 153–170.

Driver, J., Baylis, G.C., Goodrich, S., & Rafal, R. (1994). Axis-based neglect of visual shapes. *Neuropsychologia, 32,* 1353–1365.

Driver, J., Baylis, G.C., & Rafal, R. (1992). Preserved figure–ground segregation and symmetry perception in visual neglect. *Nature, 360,* 73–75.

Farah, M.J., Monheit, M.A., & Wallace, M.A. (1991). Unconscious perception of "extinguished" visual stimuli: reassessing the evidence. *Neuropsychologia, 29,* 949–958.

Humphreys, G.W. (1998). Neural representations of objects in space: A dual coding account. *Philosophical Transactions of the Royal Society, B353,* 1341–1351.

Kanwisher, N. (1987). Repetition blindness: Type recognition without token individuation. *Cognition, 27,* 117–143.

Kanwisher, N. (1991). Repetition blindness and illusory conjunctions: Errors in binding visual types with tokens. *Journal of Experimental Psychology: Human Perception and Performance, 17,* 404–421.

Karnath, H.O. (1988). Deficits of attention in acute and recovered visual hemineglect. *Neuropsychologia, 26,* 27–43.

Lueschow, A., Miller, E.K., & Desimone, R. (1994). Inferior temporal mechanisms for invariant object recognition. *Cerebral Cortex, 5,* 523–531.

Marzi, C.A., Smania, N., Martini, M.C., Gambina, G., Tomelleri, G., Palmara, A., Allesandrini, F., & Prior, M. (1996) Implicit redundant-targets effect in visual extinction. *Neuropsychologia, 34,* 9–22.

Milner, A.D. (1997). Neglect, extinction, and the cortical streams of visual processing. In P. Thier & H.-O. Karnath (Eds.), *Parietal lobe contributions to orientation in 3D space* (Experimental Brain Research series, No. 25, pp. 3–22). Heidelberg, Germany: Springer.

Oppenheim, H. (1885). *Neurologisches Zentralblatt, 4,* 529.

Posner, M.I. (1980). Orienting of attention. *Quarterly Journal of Experimental Psychology, 32*(1), 3–25.

Posner, M.I., Walker, J.A., Friedrich, F.J., & Rafal, R.D. (1984). Effects of parietal injury on covert orienting of visual attention. *Journal of Neuroscience, 4,* 1863–1874.

Prinzmetal, W., Presti, D.E., & Posner, M.I. (1986). Does attention affect visual feature integration? *Journal of Experimental Psychology: Human Perception and Performance, 12,* 361–369.

Rafal, R., & Robertson, L. (1995). The neurology of visual attention. In M.S. Gazzaniga (Ed.), *The cognitive neurosciences*. Cambridge, MA: MIT Press.
Rorden, C., & Brett, M. (in press). Stereotaxic display of brain lesions. *Behavioural Neurology*.
Rorden, C., Mattingley, J.B., Karnath, H.-O., & Driver, J. (1997). Visual extinction and prior entry: Impaired perception of a temporal order with intact motion perception after unilateral pariental damage. *Neuropsychologia, 35,* 421–433.
Sathian, K., Simon, T.J., Peterson, S., Patel, G.A., Hoffman, J.M., & Grafton, S.T. (1999). Neural evidence linking visual object enumeration and attention. *Journal of Cognitive Neuroscience, 11,* 36–51.
Treisman, A. (1998). Feature binding, attention and object perception. *Philosophical Transactions of the Royal Society, B353,* 1295–1306.
Treisman, A., & Gelade, G. (1980). A feature-integration theory of attention. *Cognitive Psychology, 12,* 97–136.
Treisman, A.M., & Kanwisher, N.G. (1998). Perceiving visually presented objects: Recognition, awareness and modularity. *Current Opinion in Neurobiology, 8,* 18–26.
Ungerleider, L.G., & Haxby, J.V. (1994). "What" and "where" in the human brain. *Current Opinions in Neurobiology, 4*(2), 157–165.
Ungerleider, L.G., & Mishkin, M. (1982). Two cortical visual systems. In D.J. Ingle, M.A. Goodale, & R.J.W. Mansfield (Eds.), *Analysis of visual behavior* (pp. 549–586). Cambridge, MA: MIT Press.
Vuilleumier, P., & Rafal, R.D. (1999). "Both" means more than "two": Localizing and counting in patients with visuospatial neglect. *Nature Neuroscience, 2,* 783–784.
Volpe, B.T., LeDoux, J.E., & Gazzaniga, M.S. (1979). Information processing of stimuli in an "extinguished" visual field. *Nature (London), 282,* 722–724.
Ward, R., Goodrich. S., & Driver, J. (1994). Grouping reduces visual extinction: Neuropsychological evidence for weight-linkage in visual selection. *Visual Cognition, 1,* 101–129.
Weinstein, E.A. (1994). Hemineglect and extinction. *Neuropsychological Rehabilitation, 4*(2), 221–224.
Wolfe, J.M., & Bennett, S.C. (1997). Preattentive object files: Shapeless bundles of basic features. *Vision Research, 37,* 25–43.

VISUAL COGNITION, 2001, *8* (3/4/5), 381–410

A multi-stage account of binding in vision: Neuropsychological evidence

Glyn W. Humphreys

Behavioural Brain Sciences Centre, University of Birmingham, UK

I review neuropsychological evidence on the problems patients can have in binding together the attributes of visual stimuli, following brain damage. The evidence indicates that there can be several kinds of binding deficit in patients. Damage to early visual processing within the ventral visual stream can disrupt the binding of contours into shapes, though the binding of form elements into contours can still operate. This suggests that the process of binding elements into contour is distinct from the process of binding contours into shapes. The latter form of binding seems to operate within the ventral visual system. In addition, damage to the parietal lobe can disrupt the binding of shape to surface information about objects, even when the binding of elements into contours, and contours into shapes, seems to be preserved. These findings are consistent with a multi-stage account of binding in vision, which distinguishes between the processes involved in binding shape information (in the ventral visual stream) and the processes involved in binding shape and surface detail (involving interactions between the ventral and dorsal streams). In addition, I present evidence indicating that a further, transient form of binding can take place, based on stimuli having common visual onsets. I discuss the relations between these different forms of binding.

Please address all correspondence to Glyn W. Humphreys, Behavioural Brain Sciences Centre, School of Psychology, University of Birmingham, Birmingham, B15 2TT, UK. Email: g.w.humphreys@bham.ac.uk

This work was supported by grants from the European Union and from the Medical Research Council, UK. I am extremely grateful to HJA and GK for all their time and for their ability to make research fun as well as interesting. My thanks go also to all of my colleagues who contributed to the different parts of the work reported here: Muriel Boucart, Caterina Cinel, Anne Giersch, Dietmar Heinke, Nikki Klempen, Illona Kovacs, Gudrun Nys, Andrew Olson, Jane Riddoch, and Jeremy Wolfe. Many thanks also to Gordon Baylis for his insightful comments on an earlier draft of this paper.

http://www.tandf.co.uk/journals/pp/13506285.html DOI:10.1080/13506280143000061

THE BINDING PROBLEM IN VISION

There is considerable evidence, from neurophysiology, neuropsychology, and studies of functional brain imaging, that visual processing involves decomposition of the signal into separable dimensions, with these dimensions being processed to some degree in different neural areas (e.g., see Desimone & Ungerleider, 1989; Humphreys, 1999; Tootell et al., 1995; Ungerleider & Haxby, 1994; Watson et al., 1993; Zeki, 1993). Given this functional decomposition in image processing, it is clearly important to understand both how different visual dimensions are inter-related (e.g., colour and shape), and how elements within a dimension are integrated when they belong to a common object (e.g., so there is grouping of local parts into a more global shape). The question of how information is integrated between and within visual dimensions, is typically labelled as "the binding problem".

Historically, two major solutions have been offered to explain the binding problem. One is that binding is solved by "going serial"—attending to the location of each object in the field in a serial fashion. Cells at higher levels of the visual system tend to have relatively large receptive fields (e.g., see Gross, Rocha-Miranda, & Bender, 1972). This is useful for achieving viewpoint invariance for recognition, but carries the risk of incorrect feature binding, since cells may be activated by features belonging to different objects that happen to fall within the same receptive field. This problem can be overcome by selective attention. Attention to a location increases the activation of features that fall there, so that these features are activated over and above others present in the visual field at that time (see Brefczynski & de Yoe, 1999; Hillyard, Vogel, & Luck, 1998). As a consequence features at an attended location will activate high-level cells involved in pattern recognition more than features at unattended locations, enabling the attended features to be bound by the high-level cells. This notion of binding being modulated by attention to location is perhaps articulated most clearly in Feature Integration Theory (Treisman, 1998; Treisman & Gelade, 1980). Physiological evidence consistent with this account has been reported by Moran and Desimone (1985), who showed that selective attention to the location of a stimulus can dynamically shift the receptive field properties of cells in area V4 of the monkey. Their evidence suggested that cells behaved as if their receptive fields were tuned to the locations of attended stimuli.

However, attention to location is not the only way that a competitive advantage could be given to visual features, so that only these features can be bound at higher levels of processing. Chelazzi, Miller, Duncan, and Desimone (1993), for instance, demonstrated a form of selective processing by feature priming. They showed that cells may be primed by prior expectation, with features consistent with the expectation being activated more rapidly than those inconsistent with the expectation (see also Motter, 1994). Again the net result should be that only the primed features should be available for binding. Unlike the spatial attention account, when there is top-down priming, the features selected do not need to cover contiguous spatial locations. For example, the whole of an animal could be selected by pre-activating cells for an expected colour, even if parts of the object are occluded by other objects.

The second major account of binding proposes that features are linked by temporal properties of neural processing, perhaps the best-known account being that binding is based on temporal synchrony in the firing of cell (e.g., see Eckhorn, 1999; Singer & Gray, 1995). If cells responsive to the features of a single object fire at the same time, then the brain has a temporal code to enable these features to be bound together and to prevent binding between the features of different objects. This account is supported primarily by physiological evidence showing time-locked firing of cells when stimulus elements group (see Singer & Gray, 1995, for a review), though there is also some behavioural evidence for temporal synchronization in the input being important for feature binding in humans (e.g., Elliott & Müller, 1998; Fahle, 1993).

The previous approaches are not mutually inconsistent, and it may be that one way that attention conveys a competitive advantage on processing is by improving the synchrony of firing for attended elements. Nevertheless both the FIT and temporal synchrony accounts tend to emphasize a single solution to the binding problem. In this paper I will review neuropsychological evidence on binding in vision, and, on the basis of this evidence, I argue that several binding processes operate in vision. Furthermore, these contrasting binding processes are associated with different neural sites. I discuss the evidence in relation to theories that make a formal distinction between the binding of form information and the binding of form and surface detail (e.g., Grossberg & Mingolla, 1985; Grossberg & Pessoa, 1998), and in relation to the major accounts of visual binding already discussed.

EFFECTS OF PARIETAL DAMAGE ON VISUAL BINDING: IMPAIRMENTS AND PRESERVATIONS

Damage to the parietal lobes has long been known to produce a variety of spatial disorders, including poor localization of visual stimuli (e.g., Stark, Coslett, & Saffran, 1996; see also DeRenzi, 1982; Ungerleider & Mishkin, 1982, for early reviews). For example, patients may point inaccurately to a visual location, though their pointing under proprioceptive guidance may be relatively intact (e.g., Balint, 1909; Holmes, 1918). Similarly, when copying stimuli, patients with unilateral parietal damage can mislocalize parts of objects, and reproduce stimuli from the contralesional side of space on the ipsilesional side (Bisiach, Capitani, Luzzatti, & Perani, 1981). And, given a task such as reading aloud the letters within a letter string, patients with parietal damage can make numerous mislocalization errors, reporting the letters correctly but in the wrong spatial order (e.g., Baylis, Driver, Baylis, & Rafal, 1994; Hall, Humphreys, & Cooper, 2001; Shallice & Warrington, 1977). There appears to be an impaired binding of visual form to space, perhaps due to damage to the space that visual form is bound to.[1]

Parietal damage is also associated with impaired binding between shape and surface properties of objects. Friedman-Hill, Robertson, and Treisman (1995) reported that a patient (RM) with Balint's syndrome,[2] following bilateral parietal damage, made large numbers of "illusory conjunction" (IC) errors when asked to identify multiple coloured letters, even under prolonged viewing conditions. For example, given the presence of a red B and a blue C in the field, RM might report that there was a red C and a blue B. IC errors can be induced in normal observers when stimuli are presented relatively briefly and are not fully attended (e.g., Treisman & Schmidt, 1982; though see Donk, 1999). However, when stimuli are given long exposures, and attention fully allocated, such errors are normally (and fortunately!) rare. The ICs found with RM even under these conditions demonstrate an impairment in binding. There may be poor localization of stimuli along each dimension, preventing accurate integration of shape and colour, or there may be a detriment in attending to the location of each stimulus in turn, in order to bind each shape with its colour (cf. Treisman, 1998). Deficits in binding shape and colour attributes have also been documented in the contralesional field of patients with unilateral parietal damage (e.g., Cohen & Rafal, 1991).

These results suggest that the parietal lobe plays an important role in visual binding. In particular, the parietal lobe seems important for linking visual stimuli to some stable representation of space, and also for allocating attention to the locations of stimuli. Following parietal damage there is poor visual localization of shapes, and poor integration of shape and surface detail (at least when there are multiple, competing, shapes and surfaces present). The association between poor visual localization and impaired integration of shape and surface detail is consistent with the proposal of FIT, that attention to location is necessary to ensure appropriate feature binding in multi-element displays (see Treisman, 1998). It may also be, though, that poor spatial representation disrupts integration across stimulus dimensions directly, without attentional modulation. We elaborate this proposal further in the General Discussion.

However, even though parietal damage can disrupt some types of visual binding, other types of binding seem to be relatively intact. For instance, the mislocalization errors apparent in letter reading tasks seem to involve the

---

[1]Our thanks to Gordon Baylis for this last suggestion.

[2]The term Balint's syndrome is applied to patients showing two primary behavioural symptoms: Poor identification of multiple visual stimuli ("simultanagnosia"), and poor visual localization, following the first description of such a case by Balint (1909).

migration of whole forms (letters), consistent with the letter features themselves being bound before mislocalization occurs (Baylis et al., 1994; Hall et al., 2001). Also even in patients with bilateral parietal damage, who have profound problems in spatial localization and in integrating the form and colour of multiple objects, there can be relatively intact recognition of single objects (Robertson, Treisman, Friedman-Hill, & Grabowecky, 1997). The relative preservation of object recognition suggests that the ability to bind the parts within objects can be largely preserved in such cases.

Perhaps the most dramatic example of some form of binding continuing to operate despite parietal damage comes from studies of visual extinction. Visual extinction occurs when patients are able to report the presence of single stimuli presented in either their contralesional or their ipsilesional field; however, when contra- and ipsilesional stimuli are presented simultaneously, the contralesional stimulus cannot be reported (or sometimes even detected) (e.g., Karnath, 1988). Extinction is consistent with parietal damage leading to a spatial bias in attention, which is allocated to the ipsilesional stimulus in preference to the contralesional one. Interestingly, several studies have now shown that extinction can be modulated by grouping relations between the contra- and ipsilesional stimuli. In particular, extinction is reduced when the stimuli group relative to when they do not group. In some instances, this recovery from extinction is contingent on local relations between collinear edges (Gilchrist, Humphreys, & Riddoch, 1996), but effects due to common brightness, connectedness and surroundedness can also be found (see Humphreys, 1998). Effects can also be altered according to whether two elements fall in appropriate occlusion relations behind objects (Mattingly, Davis, & Driver, 1997), and they can be demonstrated with widely separated elements provided that the elements conform to a familiar shape (e.g., a — and > making up a →; see Ward, Goodrich, & Driver, 1994). Effects of grouping on extinction can even occur based on the activation of stored representations alone, when there are no Gestalt relations between elements that would lead to their grouping in a bottom-up fashion. Kumada and Humphreys (2001) tested extinction in two-letter words (be, go) relative to two-letter nonwords (bo, ge, created by exchanging the letters across the words). They found that there was better detection of two letters that formed words than two letters that formed nonwords, even though there are no bottom-up cues that favour the grouping of letters in words compared with nonwords. These data suggest that the letters were bound by activating a common stored representation, that exists for a word but not for a nonword. In all of these examples, the fact that recovery from extinction occurs indicates that stimuli in the contralesional field must be processed to at least a level at which they can enter into grouping relationships with ipsilesional items. The grouping effects also take place despite the presence of parietal damage. It appears that some forms of binding of elements into groups can be effected in neural areas unaffected by the parietal damage.

There is also evidence for extinction being determined by the "goodness" of objects, rather than by their spatial locations, in patients with bilateral parietal damage. For example, in a study with one of the two patients featured in the present paper, GK, Humphreys, Romani, Olson, Riddoch, and Duncan (1994) compared the selection of stimuli that differed in how well their parts grouped into a shape. Though single stimuli could be detected, there was impaired detection of the less good stimulus when both were presented simultaneously. This occurred even though GK was severely impaired at localizing the stimuli that were selected relative to a fixed reference point (a fixation cross). Here it appears that there can be binding of elements into a more global shape despite there being both parietal damage and poor spatial localization. Explicit localization is not a prerequisite for the binding of form elements.

EFFECTS OF OCCIPITO-TEMPORAL DAMAGE ON VISUAL BINDING

A somewhat different pattern of visual disturbances can be found in patients who have sustained damage to their ventral visual system, typically involving pathways between the occipital and temporal cortices. Damage to the ventral visual system is classically associated with disorders of object recognition (visual agnosia), although aspects of spatial perception can be largely intact (see chapters in Humphreys, 1999). Thus, patients may be impaired at making simple perceptual judgements about objects but may nevertheless be able to reach and grasp the same object appropriately (e.g., Milner & Goodale, 1995). The copying of such patients does not lead to gross mislocalization of object parts (from one side of space to another), and, when asked to identify letters in strings, patients with left ventral damage do not show mislocalization errors (though they do have abnormally prolonged identification times; see Behrmann, Plaut, & Nelson, 1998; Humphreys, 1998). Hence the ability to integrate visual stimuli into a stable spatial representation can be preserved.

On the other hand, the recognition of single objects, words and faces can be severely disrupted by damage to the ventral visual system (though there may be some hemispheric specialization for the processing of words and faces; see Farah, 1990). In many instances, the recognition disorder seems to be perceptual in nature, and to involve poor grouping of local elements into perceptual wholes. For example, patients may have poor discrimination of Gestalt grouping relations based on proximity and similarity (e.g., Milner et al., 1991). Patients may also tend to use local detail within objects to segment the stimulus into parts that are then used in isolation for recognition. In one example, the agnosic patient HJA, whom we discuss in more detail later, was given a black and white photograph of a paintbrush. He stated that "it appears to be two things close together; a longish wooden stick and a shorter, darker object, though this can't be right or you would have told me" (that there were two objects rather than one present) (see Humphreys & Riddoch, 1987). The patient reported by Butter and Trobe (1994) similarly thought that there were several objects present when he was given line drawings to identify. Furthermore, unlike normal subjects, agnosic patients can find it relatively more difficult to identify line drawings than silhouettes of the same stimuli (Butter & Trobe, 1994; Lawson & Humphreys, 1999; Riddoch & Humphreys, 1987). This is consistent with the internal details in line drawings being unhelpful for recognition in such patients, even though normally we may be facilitated by using the internal details to compute the part structure of objects. There seems to be an impairment in the inter-play between grouping and segmentation, that leads to a mis-parsing of perceptual wholes. This mis-parsing can come about because grouping of parts to wholes is relatively weak when compared with segmentation operations between parts.

Consistent with there being impaired grouping of parts to wholes in some agnosic patients, performance is further impaired when fragmented forms are presented (Boucart & Humphreys, 1992) and when overlapping forms are given (Butter & Trobe, 1994; DeRenzi & Lucchelli, 1993; Riddoch & Humphreys, 1987). These conditions stress the processes involved in grouping and organizing the spatial relations between edge contours, and in segmenting them from background forms in an appropriate manner, relative to when single objects are presented with full contours.

These deficits in agnosic patients suggest that object recognition depends on processes that bind edge contours into their correct spatial relations, and that support appropriate segmentation between "figural" elements and elements occupying the perceptual "ground". Grouping and segmentation processes are impaired by damage to the ventral visual system, even though stimuli can be localized. In addition, to the best of our knowledge, there have been no reports of agnosic patients showing abnormal increases in IC reports of shape and surface detail, when required to identify multiple items in the field. There are suggestions here that the processes that bind contours into more wholistic shapes (the processes that are impaired in some agnosics), are not dependent on explicit localization (and note the pattern of intact recognition poor localization in Balint's syndrome, discussed earlier), and binding of parts to wholes may also be separable from the processes that bind shape and surface detail. Given the lesions that lead to agnosia, the process of binding contours into shape also appears to be localized within the ventral visual system.

FRACTIONATING THE BINDING PROCESS IN AGNOSIA

Recently, in collaboration with Anne Giersch, Muriel Boucart, and Illona Kovacs, I have been able to examine the impairments in binding shape information in the agnosic patient HJA (Giersch, Humphreys, Boucart, & Kovacs,

2000). A first study evaluated HJA's ability to group local forms elements into contours, based on the presence of oriented, collinear edge fragments. HJA was given stimuli such as those shown in Figure 1, composed of multiple Gabor patches. In one part of each image, the Gabor patches were collinear with one another and, if grouped, formed a circular shape. Distractor patches, at random orientations, were also presented and they could fall at random locations within the image. When the spacing between the target contours is kept constant, the ease of detecting the target decreases as more distractor elements are present. Thus, a threshold for detecting the target shape can be computed as a function of the number of distractors in the image (see Kovacs, 2000). Earlier studies had demonstrated that HJA had clear impairments in object identification that seemed to be related to processes of grouping contours into shapes (e.g., effects of overlapping shapes, of line drawings vs. silhouettes, and poor identification of fragmented forms, etc.; see Boucart & Humphreys, 1992; Riddoch &

Figure 1. Display of Gabor patches with some local elements aligned to form a shape from grouping by collinearity.

Humphreys, 1987). However, much to our surprise, HJA turned out to have a normal threshold for detecting the shape made up from the collinear edge fragments. The process of binding local edge fragments into a contour seemed to be intact.

Nevertheless, HJA remained impaired on other tasks in which contours had to be integrated into shapes. One example is presented in Figure 2. HJA was given the stimulus configuration shown at the top of each shape triplet (presented here within a single box) followed by the two other stimuli presented underneath, which were exposed on the screen below where the original shape triplet had appeared. The task was to detect as quickly as possible which of the two following shape configurations was the same as the one he had just seen. The configurations were exposed as overlapping line drawings (SUP), occluded shapes (OCC), silhouettes (SIL), and spatially separated shapes (SEP). The data for HJA, elderly controls, and young controls are given in Figure 3. HJA was slower than all of the control subjects, but this is not particularly surprising and could be a general effect of his brain lesion. More interesting is that HJA manifested a selective deficit with occluded figures, which were even worse than overlapping figures here (condition SUP). This indicates that HJA had particular difficulty in dealing with occlusion, a condition in which edge elements may be computed behind objects and in which the depth relations between the shapes

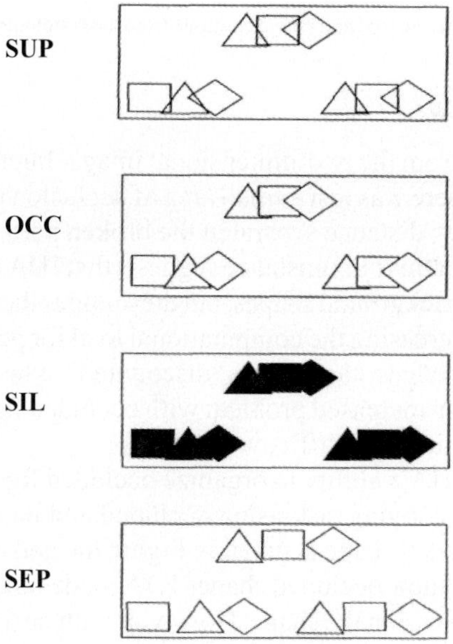

Figure 2. Example displays of the type used by Giersch et al. (2000). On each trial the top shapes in each box were presented first, followed by the lower shapes on the left and right of the screen. The task was to choose which of the bottom shapes matched the top one.

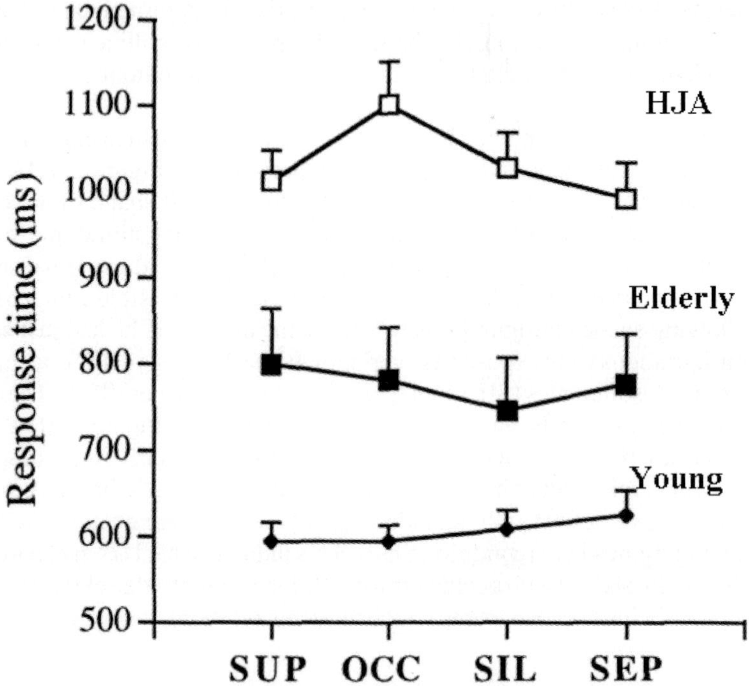

Figure 3. The data from HJA, elderly, and young controls, from the matching task using displays such as those shown in Figure 2.

have to be articulated from the two-dimensional image. Interestingly, HJA was most impaired when there was just a small area of occlusion for the background shapes, so that a narrow distance separated the broken parts of their edge contours. A difficulty under this circumstance suggests that HJA was computing the occluded edges of the background shapes, but these edges then disrupted performance—perhaps by increasing the computational load for perceptual organization, especially when edges have to be "discounted" when they are formed behind an occluder. The increased problem with occluded figures suggests that this last process is particularly difficult for HJA.

In a further test of HJA's ability to organize occluded figures appropriately, we gave him a simple copying task using occluded and non-occluded shapes. An example non-occluded shape is given in Figure 4a, and occluded shapes in Figure 4b and 4c. With non-occluded shapes HJA made no errors and he never drew a connecting line within the shape. However, with occluded shapes he did sometimes mistakenly draw in the occluded line as if it were present in the front shape; see Figure 4b(i) and 4c(ii). This again suggests that HJA did compute the occluded edge from the visible collinear edges in the background shape, but

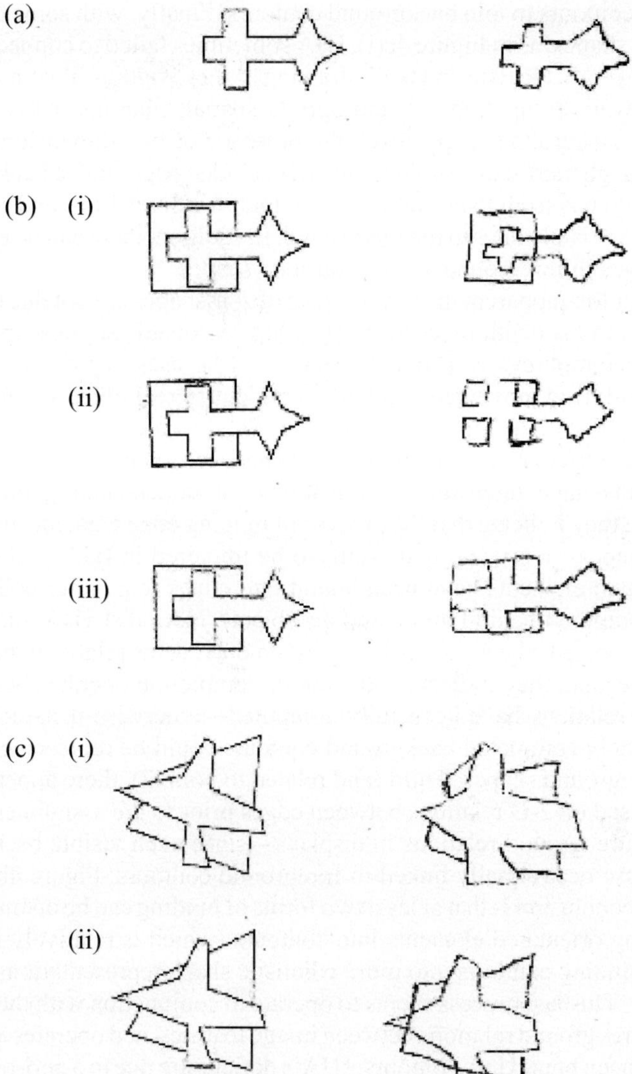

Figure 4. Examples of the stimuli given to HJA for copying (on the left) along with some example copies (on the right).

this "virtual" line was then used as if it were really present. He also made other errors with occluded shapes. Errors such as those shown in Figure 4b(ii) seemed to reflect segmentation of the background shape based on the T junctions formed between the foreground and background shapes, and errors such as those illustrated by Figure 4b(iii) seemed to reflect continuation of the foreground contours to join background contours. Finally, with some complex background shapes, as in Figure 4c(i), HJA sometimes failed to connect collinear edges. Overall, the data on HJA's drawing of these figures illustrate that he has difficulty in computing the appropriate spatial relations between foreground and background shapes from the presence of two-dimensional (2-D) edges. Although there can be completion of occluded edges in the background, these edges do not seem to be "labelled" for their depth relations and so can be represented as visible lines in the foreground. In addition, there can be grouping between edges in foreground and background shapes.

The difficulties apparent in HJA's copies of 2-D shapes are not due to a general problem in his depth perception. HJA has reasonable stereoscopic depth perception (Humphreys & Riddoch, 1987) and he uses depth cues such as stereopsis and head movements to help him identify real objects (Chainay & Humphreys, 2001). The difficulties shown in Figure 4 are particular to the use of 2-D shape cues to resolve depth relations between shapes.

The results have interesting implications for understanding binding in vision. First, they indicate that the process of binding edge elements into more wholistic shapes—a process that seems to be impaired in HJA—takes place after orientated elements have been bound into edges (e.g., after collinearity has been computed behind an occluding object). Note that HJA's ability to compute connected edges from collinear fragments seems relatively intact (cf. Figure 1). Second, they indicate that contour completion operates before figure–ground relations have been fully computed—otherwise it is difficult to understand how completed background contours could be represented incorrectly in foreground shapes. Third (and related to point 2), there appears to be grouping based on 2-D relations between edges prior to the assignment of the edges to figure–ground relations in displays—since even visible background elements were occasionally linked to foreground contours, Figure 4b(ii) and 4b(iii). Our conclusion is that at least two forms of binding can be distinguished here: Binding orientated elements into contours (which is relatively intact in HJA), and binding contours into more wholistic shape representations (which is impaired). This last process seems to operate in conjunction with the assignment of figure–ground relations between image features, and operates after elements have been bound into contours. HJA's deficits are due to a peri-operative stroke that led to bilateral lesions affecting the lingual, fusiform, and posterior, inferior temporal gyri (see Riddoch, Humphreys, Gannon, Blott, & Jones, 1999, for an MRI scan). From his deficits we may propose that the process of binding contours into more wholistic shapes takes place in these posterior, inferior regions of the ventral visual stream. His ability to group orientated elements into contours, though, may be based on interactions within earlier visual areas (even V1) spared by the lesions. There is indeed recent evidence for grouping by collinearity within such early cortical regions (e.g., Gilbert, Ito, Kapadia, & Westheimer, 2000).

FRACTIONATING THE BINDING PROCESS IN BALINT'S SYNDROME (SIMULTANAGNOSIA)

We have discussed the problems associated with visual binding in patients with bilateral lesions of parietal cortex, who presented with Balint's syndrome. These patients may be able to report the attributes of single stimuli quite well, but are impaired when presented with multiple items (see Friedman-Hill et al., 1995). In particular, such patients may make abnormally high numbers of IC responses when multiple stimuli are exposed, under conditions where normal subjects make few such errors. Yet, patients with parietal lesions can also be sensitive to grouping relations in images, as demonstrated by the effects of grouping on recovery from extinction. What are the relations between these two apparently contrasting results?

Caterina Cinel, Jeremy Wolfe, Nikki Klempen, Andrew Olson, and I examined this issue in a patient with Balint's syndrome, GK (Humphreys, Cinel, Wolfe, Olson, & Klempen, 2000). GK suffered bilateral parietal lesions from two consecutive strokes in 1986. Following this he has a number of neuropsychological problems including simultanagnosia (see Cooper & Humphreys, 2000), attentional dyslexia (Hall et al., 2001), and a mild problem in word finding. He also shows visual extinction. With stimuli presented above and below fixation, extinction is non-spatial and influenced by the perceptual "goodness" of the stimuli—"good" stimuli tend to be reported and "poor" stimuli are extinguished (Humphreys et al., 1994). With stimuli presented horizontally there is spatial extinction, with right-side items tending to be reported and left-side items extinguished. This spatial extinction effect is modulated by grouping between the left- and right-side stimuli; there is less extinction when stimuli group relative to when they do not group (see Boutsen & Humphreys, 2000; Gilchrist et al., 1996; Humphreys, 1998). The effects of grouping on both spatial and non-spatial extinction indicate that some forms of binding continue to operate, despite GK's parietal lesions and neuropsychological deficits.

In contrast to the binding processes apparent in studies of extinction, GK showed poor binding when asked to report the surface and shape properties from multiple items in the field. For example, given three coloured letters and asked to report the colour and identity of just the central letter at fixation, about 32% of the responses appeared to be ICs, miscombining either the shape or colour of the central letter with one of the other letters present. With single stimuli, few errors were made (see also Friedman-Hill et al., 1995). We assessed the relations between binding effects on extinction and ICs in full report tasks by presenting GK with shapes such as those presented in Figure 5. Shapes fell either to the left or right of fixation, and when two shapes were present they could group in a variety of ways. Both could be squares (same shape and aligned collinear edges), or both circles (same shape only); the shapes could have the same or opposite contrast polarities (both white, both black, or one

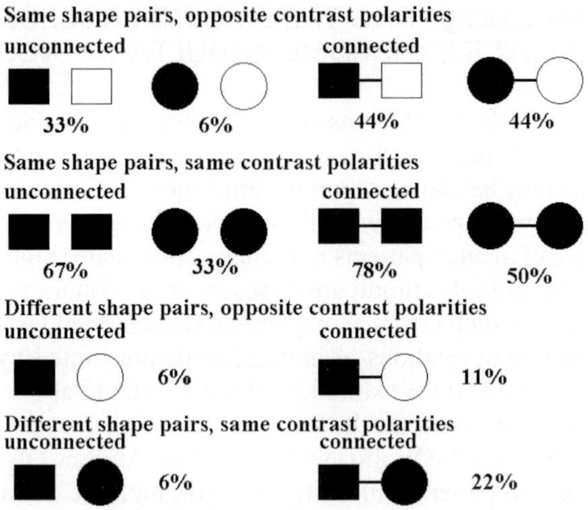

Figure 5. The shapes given to GK in a study comparing the effects of grouping on extinction and illusory conjunctions. On each trial, only one pair of shapes was presented, against the background of a complete grey screen. One shape fell to the left and one to the right of fixation.

white and one black, against a grey background); the shapes could be connected or unconnected. All combinations of shapes appeared, in the different shape and contrast polarity conditions (i.e., each shape appeared equally to the left or right of fixation, as did each contrast polarity). The stimuli were presented at the centre of a computer monitor for 1 s, and GK was asked to report the shapes and letters present. The percentage of correct reports is shown in Figure 5. The results were quite clear. There was better report of shapes when they grouped than when they did not group. For example, when the two shapes were the same, performance improved relative to when they differed; performance also improved when the shapes had the same rather than opposite contrast polarities and when they were connected relative to when they were unconnected. When only one shape was present, report was generally good (87% correct for single shapes in the left field and 90% correct for single letters in the right field). In the two shape conditions, many of the errors made by GK appeared to be "visual extinctions", in that he would report the presence of only one shape. The rate of extinction errors was affected by grouping. When the stimuli had different shapes and contrast polarities, extinction responses were made on 67% of the trials when the items were unconnected (on all of these trials, GK reported the shape and colour of the stimulus in his right field). However, when the same stimuli were connected, extinction errors occurred on just 33% of trials. When the stimuli were connected, there was less extinction for the item in the left field. These data confirm previous findings on the effects of grouping on extinction (Boutsen & Humphreys, 2000; Gilchrist et al., 1996; Humphreys, 1998).

In addition to making extinction errors, GK also made errors by misreporting the attributes of the items. For instance, when the stimuli had different shapes and contrast polarities, he sometimes made errors by pairing the shape in the right field with the colour in the left, and vice versa (e.g., black square, white circle → white square, black circle). We termed these "feature exchange" errors. These errors may reflect incorrect bindings of shape and surface details, or they may simply be misidentifications of the attributes present. To discriminate these possibilities, we assessed the number of feature misidentifications made in other conditions where "feature exchange" errors could not occur because the two stimuli shared one of the critical attribute (e.g., when the stimuli had the same colour or when they had the same shape). On these trials, GK could make an unambiguous feature misidentification error by reporting an attribute not present in the display (e.g., white square, black square → white square, black circle; here the response "circle" can be classed as a feature misidentification, since this shape was not present). Feature exchange errors could stem from two feature misidentifications being made concurrently to the two shapes present on a trial. The likelihood of feature exchange errors occurring by chance, then, can be estimated from the probability that two feature misidentification errors would occur on the same trial (taking the data from the unambiguous feature misidentification trials). The rates of observed feature exchanges, relative to those expected by chance combinations of feature misidentifications, are given in Figure 6. Feature exchange errors occurred at a rate substantially higher than that expected by chance co-occurrences of feature misidentifications. We conclude that feature exchanges reflected incorrect bindings of shape and surface properties. The data presented in Figure 6 also illustrate that feature exchange errors tended to occur with more frequency

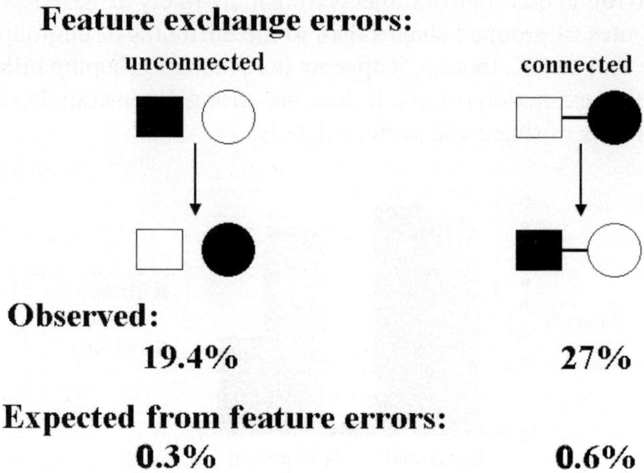

Figure 6. Example of illusory conjunction and feature error responses that could be made to displays where the shapes differed and had opposite contrast polarities.

when the shapes were connected than when they were unconnected. Remember, however, that more extinction responses occurred on trials with unconnected shapes than on trials with connected shapes; this means that the opportunity for feature exchange errors was reduced when the shapes were unconnected. When the probabilities for chance combinations of feature misidentifications are adjusted for extinction trials, we find that, by chance, we would expect more feature exchanges with connected than with unconnected shapes (on 0.6 as opposed to 0.3% of the trials when stimuli had both different shapes and contrast polarities). Relative to these estimated chance levels, the rates of feature exchange errors did not differ for connected and unconnected shapes.

The data shown in Figures 5 and 6 come from a study that measured full report of the stimuli. However, this same pattern was replicated in other experiments in which detection of a shape–colour pairing was assessed using two-alternative forced-choice techniques (Humphreys et al., 2000, Exp. 6). Such techniques reduce the likelihood that IC errors are caused by GK forgetting the pairings of shape and surface detail during report.

Our finding, that ICs of shape and surface detail were not clearly affected by a grouping factor, such as connectedness, contrasts with data from control subjects. For example, when displays of coloured letters are used, illusory reports of letter colour combinations are more likely when the different coloured letters occur within a syllable boundary relative to when they occur across syllable boundaries (Prinzmetal, Treiman, & Rho, 1986). Migrations of colour appear to be more frequent between letters that form a syllabic group. Similarly, ICs of colour and form are affected by common movement of the items (Baylis, Driver, & McLeod, 1992). Using the same displays as those employed with GK, we also found that control subjects were more likely to make ICs responses to the attributes of grouped shapes than to the attributes of ungrouped shapes (see Figure 7). For GK, though, it appears that, though grouping influences the likelihood that extinction occurs, it does not strongly constrain his perception of combinations of shape and surface details.

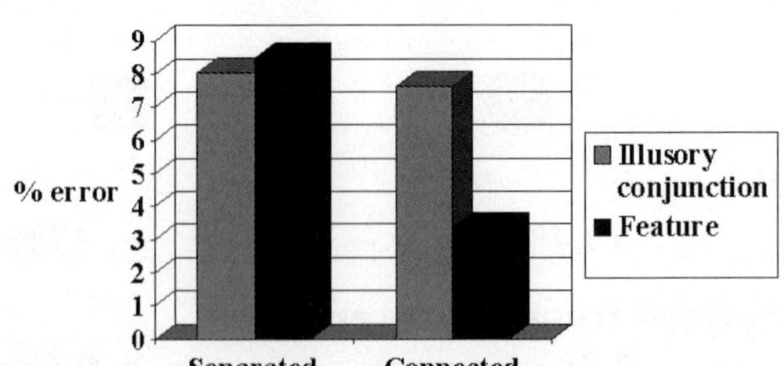

Figure 7. Data from control subjects examining the effects of grouping on illusory conjunctions of form and surface detail (see Humphreys et al., 2000).

We conclude that the lesions to GK's parietal lobes do result in a deficit in binding shape and surface details of objects together, but that this problem occurs after shapes have been bound into perceptual groups. As a consequence of grouping having already taken place, surface properties tend to migrate between whole shapes. The problems might occur because GK has difficulty in bringing visual attention to bear on the common location occupied by shape and surface information, enabling shapes and surface details from different objects to compete. As we have noted, normal subjects do show effects of grouping on ICs of shape and surface detail (e.g., Baylis et al., 1992; Prinzmetal et al., 1986). This might be because activation within the form system influences the allocation of attention to the area occupied by a dominant group (see Humphreys & Riddoch, 1993; Vecera & Farah, 1994), so limiting the likelihood of illusory conjunctions involving properties of stimuli outside that group. For GK, the damage to his parietal system impairs such interactions, allowing properties of multiple, grouped stimuli still to be miscombined. A fuller framework for these results is presented in the General Discussion.

GROUPING OVER TIME AS WELL AS SPACE

So far, we have focused on how binding operates between visual elements across space. However, we have also recently found neuropsychological evidence for forms of binding based on the common temporal onset of visual stimuli. This binding seems to be relatively transient, and it is not maintained when stimuli are presented for longer durations. Transient binding by common onset may provide one way in which visual information is provisionally organized, until more sustained binding processes generate stable perceptual representations.

Our evidence for binding by common onset comes again from single case work conducted with patient GK. In the studies reported previously, GK manifested clear visual extinction when stimuli were presented for durations of around 1 s. Interestingly, a different pattern of performance is found when shorter stimulus durations are used. Gudrun Nys, Jane Riddoch, Dietmar Heinke, and I had GK identify letters that were presented either in isolation to his left or right visual field or simultaneously to both fields. The stimuli were unmasked but presented for different durations across blocks of trials. The results are given in Figure 8. On two-letter trials, all of GK's errors involved him reporting the letter in the right but not the left visual field. Figure 8 shows three things: (1) GK's report of a single letter in his right field was superior to that of a single left-field letter, and there was a small improvement in report over time; (2) GK's ability to report a left-field letter improved over time; (3) GK's ability to report two letters was initially *better* than his ability to report a single letter on the left, but, if anything, two-letter reports decreased as the stimulus exposure increased. At the longer stimulus durations (above 450 ms),

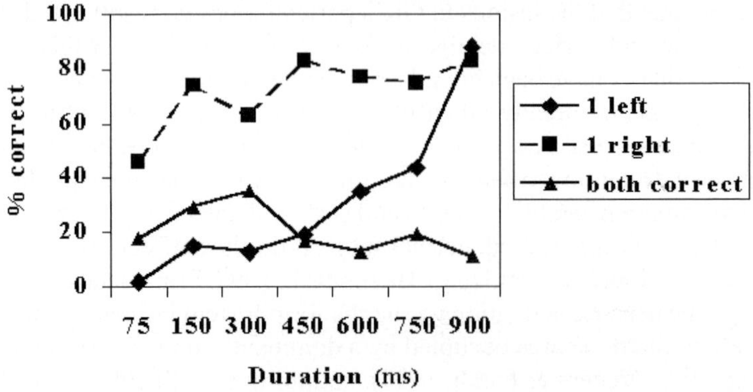

Figure 8. The percentage correct letter reports made by GK as a function of the stimulus exposure duration.

there was an extinction effect: The report of a single left letter was better than the report of the left letter on two-letter trials. However, the opposite result occurred at the briefer durations (300 ms or below). Then there was better report of the left letter in a two-letter pair than a single letter on the left.

To our knowledge, this last pattern of performance, with the report of two items being better than the report of a single item in an impaired field, has been reported once previously in a patient with parietal damage, by Goodrich and Ward (1997), who coined the term "anti-extinction" to describe it. Goodrich and Ward suggested that anti-extinction was produced by a form of response-based grouping, when the same task was applied to bilaterally presented stimuli. In our case, though, this account is insufficient since the same task was always applied but we found that performance changed from a pattern of anti-extinction to one of extinction as a function of the stimulus duration. In addition, in other experiments we have found that the anti-extinction effect with GK is as large when different tasks are performed on the two stimuli as when the same task is performed. An alternative account is that anti-extinction reflects a form of temporary binding between the bilateral stimuli. On this account, the item in the left field is bound to the item in the right field for a short time following the common onset of the stimuli, and this enables it to be recovered for report along with the right field stimulus. However, this form of binding effect is transient. When stimuli are presented for longer durations, more sustained processes of binding come into play, in which case there is recovery from extinction based on grouping by properties of shape and surface detail (see Figure 5), rather than by common onset. Consistent with the view that common onsets are necessary for the effect, we failed to find evidence for anti-extinction in studies that had the stimuli defined by offsets of contours from pre-masks.

One further proposal is that the anti-extinction effect is not due to binding but to the common onsets cueing attention to an area of field containing both left and right field items. Due to this, both items can be recovered by attention on some trials. However, when the stimuli remain for longer durations another form of attentional bias may influence performance—for instance, GK may make an eye movement to the right-most letter, and this disrupts report of the left-side item. We have assessed this last proposal in two ways. First, we measured GK's eye movements when he performed the letter report tasks. We found that eye movements had little impact on the anti-extinction effect: The effect occurred on trials where GK made no eye movement when the stimuli were present and on trials where he made an eye movement to the right-most letter. For example, Figure 9 presents data summed across two stimulus durations (320 and 480 ms), illustrating the percentage correct letter reports in single left and two-letter trials as a function of whether he made an eye movement whilst the display was on the screen. It is clear that an anti-extinction effect arose in both instances.

Second, we had GK carry out an identification task with three letters. Two letters were created by new onsets and fell in the left and right visual fields (as before). The third letter was created by the offsetting of contours from a central pre-mask, that fell at fixation. The presentations making up a typical trial are illustrated in Figure 10. Our idea here was as follows. Let us suppose that the onsets from the left and right flanking stimuli cue GK's attention to that area of field. It should follow that, when he attends to that area, he should also attend to the location of the letter at fixation, even though that was created by an offset rather than an onset. Accordingly, on trials where GK reports the left letter (signifying attention has been drawn to that location), he should also be likely to report the central letter (especially as he has a bias to report the right-most of two letters). On the other hand, if the two onset letters are temporarily bound into a group by their common onset, and the central letter is not, then the flanker letters may be reported when the central letter is not. We presented a pre-mask

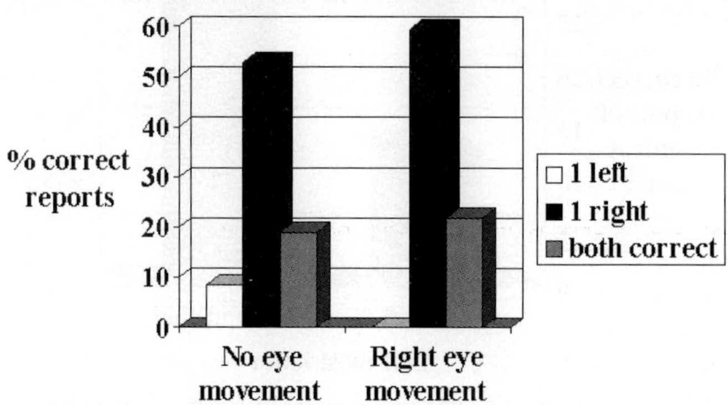

Figure 9. Percentage correct identification responses made by GK on single left, single right, and two-letter trials, as a function of whether no eye movement or a rightwards eye movement was made during stimulus presentation (data are summed across two stimulus durations, 320 and 480 ms).

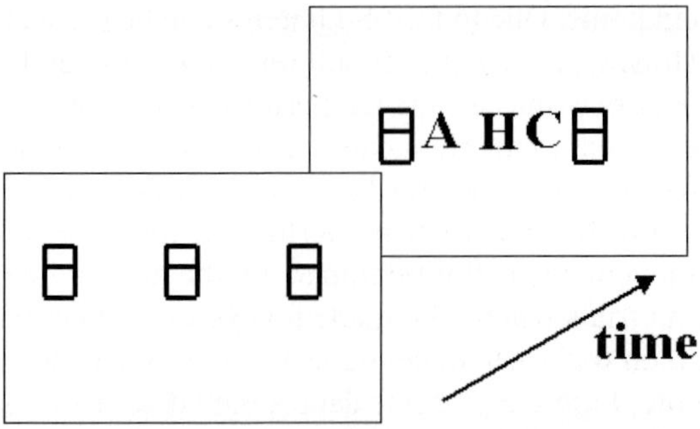

Figure 10. The three-letter displays used in the study of temporal grouping and anti-extinction. The two flanker letters were created by luminance onsets (black on a white screen). The central letter was created by offsetting contours from a pre-mask presented at fixation.

for 500 ms, followed by the letter display for 300 ms (to generate an anti-extinction effect). We found that, contrary to an attentional account, GK was not good at identifying the central letter on trials where he reported the left letter correctly—on these trials he identified less than 25% of the central letters. In fact, GK's report of the central letter was better when the left letter was not reported than when it was (see Figure 11), even though his attention is more likely to be more shifted to the right when the left letter was not reported.

The data from this last study comparing onsets and offset stimuli suggest that common onsets do not produce anti-extinction by cueing attention to a wider area of field, which is then selected. The data are however consistent with a binding account which holds that stimuli grouped by common onset are briefly linked and made available for report together. Stimuli not defined in the

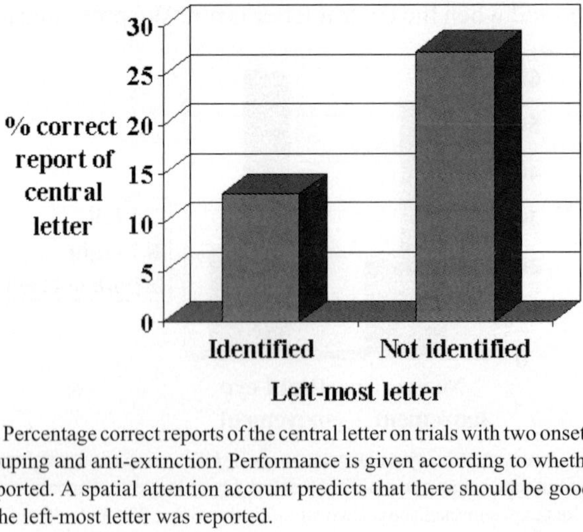

Figure 11. Percentage correct reports of the central letter on trials with two onset letters, in the study of temporal grouping and anti-extinction. Performance is given according to whether the left-most onset letter was reported. A spatial attention account predicts that there should be good report of the central letter when the left-most letter was reported.

same way (e.g., those defined by an offset rather than an onset) do not form part of the same group, and are not made available for report along with the onset letters.

One other interesting point to note here is that binding by time seems to operate unconsciously. GK, like other patients with neglect, shows an effect of "prior entry" (see Rorden, Mattingley, Karnath, & Driver, 1997). When bilateral stimuli are presented simultaneously he overwhelmingly reports that the right stimulus precedes the left (on over 90% of trials), and even with left-side stimuli presented for 450 ms before right-side stimuli he still reported that the right stimulus appeared first on 75% of trials (see Figure 12). This is consistent with a bias in spatial selection. However, with brief stimulus presentations, report of bilateral stimuli was improved when they appeared simultaneously relative to when the left stimulus has its onset 450 ms earlier then the right one.

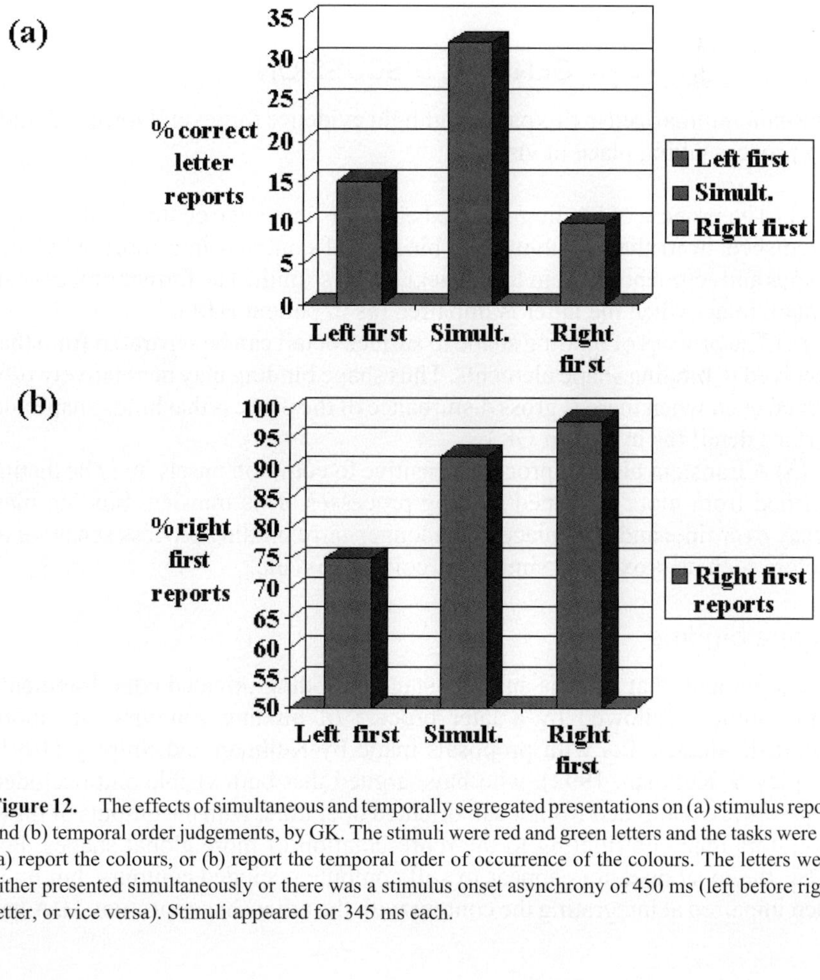

Figure 12. The effects of simultaneous and temporally segregated presentations on (a) stimulus report and (b) temporal order judgements, by GK. The stimuli were red and green letters and the tasks were to (a) report the colours, or (b) report the temporal order of occurrence of the colours. The letters were either presented simultaneously or there was a stimulus onset asynchrony of 450 ms (left before right letter, or vice versa). Stimuli appeared for 345 ms each.

The contrast between temporal order judgements and item report is shown in Figure 12. Simultaneous onset improves report of left-side stimuli, but GK perceives the right stimulus as appearing earlier than the left one. I conclude that binding by temporal onset is dissociated from conscious perception. Conscious perception, reflected in temporal order judgements, seems to reflect GK's biased selection, which favours stimuli on the right.

Temporary binding, by common onset, may provide one way to generate a rapid representation of the world, even though this representation will likely be noisy since it may be insensitive to factors such as the similarity or even proximity of stimuli. Consequently, a more sustained representation may be developed later in time, which is sensitive to grouping relations between image features. I suggest that selection of both representations by GK is biased to the right, with the strength of binding determining how well the left stimulus is reported along with the right one.

GENERAL DISCUSSION

The data summarized in this paper highlight evidence for several forms of binding process taking place in vision.

(1) The process of binding oriented elements into edge contours can be distinguished from that involving the binding of contours into more wholistic shapes and segmenting them from background stimuli. The former process can remain intact when the latter is impaired (as in patient HJA).

(2) The process of binding shape to surface detail can be separated from that involved in binding shape elements. Thus shape binding may be relatively preserved even when there is gross disturbance of the process that binds shape and surface detail (as in patient GK).

(3) A transient binding process, sensitive to common onsets, may be distinguished from more sustained binding processes. This transient binding may decay over time and be replaced by a longer-term binding process sensitive to factors such as proximity, similarity, collinearity, etc.

Shape binding

The argument, that there is an early stage of coding oriented edge fragments into contours followed by a later process of binding contours into more wholistic shapes, fits with proposals made by Kellman and Shipley (1991; Shipley & Kellman, 1992), who have argued that both visible and occluded contours are computed from local, oriented operators, with the outputs of these operators then contributing to the representation of more global shapes. For HJA, the local operators appear to still compute occluded contours, but he is then impaired at integrating the contour with the other shapes present. HJA has bilateral damage affecting the lingual and fusiform gyri and the inferior posterior temporal gyrus. His deficits in integrating contours into shapes suggest that this binding process normally operates in these now-damaged visual areas of cortex. In contrast, the ability to link oriented fragments into edges may depend on the preserved regions of early visual cortex (V1/V2). There is evidence for these latter visual areas being activated by illusory contours (Grosof, Shapley, & Hawken, 1993; Redies, Crook, & Creutzfelt, 1986; Sheth, Sharma, Rao, & Sur, 1996; von der Heydt & Peterhans, 1989; see also Mendola, Dale Fischl, Liu, & Tootell, 1999, for evidence from fMRI), and more global perceptual structures may emerge from long-range interactions between the neurons in these regions (Gilbert et al., 2000; Gilbert & Wiesel, 1989). However, we suggest that the computation of more complex spatial relations, to enable multiple edges to be integrated into wholistic shapes, requires the involvement of later visual areas, that may competitively weight one emerging perceptual group against others. These later, integrative processes are impaired in HJA (see also Riddoch & Humphreys, 1987).

The evidence from GK converges with the argument that the binding of edges into shapes operates within the ventral visual system, since, like other patients with parietal damage, GK shows relatively intact binding of shapes even though he is grossly impaired at selecting multiple shapes and at localizing stimuli, once selected (see Humphreys et al., 1994, for evidence on localization). This is consistent with the intact binding operating in the ventral visual system. The fact that grouping between elements reduces extinction in such patients further indicates that grouping can operate prior to attention being brought to bear on the shapes present. This runs contrary to an attentional account of binding, which stresses that binding is dependent on attention being applied to a spatial region, to favour those features over others in the field (cf. Treisman, 1998). However, it should be noted that the effects of binding on extinction have typically been shown using relatively simple visual displays where, when the elements group, only a single object is present. It may be that attention is useful, if not also necessary, when multiple shapes are present, when there is increased competition for selection of the features between the different objects.

A stronger argument, that attention is not necessary for form binding even when multiple stimuli are present, comes from studies of visual search in normal human observers. Here there are data indicating that search for targets defined by a conjunction of form elements can be efficient and apparently spatially parallel under some circumstances. For example, search is efficient when the distractor items are homogeneous, and so form a separate group from the conjunction target (Duncan & Humphreys, 1989; Humphreys, Quinlan, & Riddoch, 1989). Search is also efficient if all the features in the display group into a single two- or three-dimensional object (Donnelly, Humphreys, & Riddoch, 1991; Humphreys & Donnelly, 2000), or if, once grouped, the target then has a unique three-dimensional orientation relative to the homogeneous distractors (Enns & Rensink, 1991). Highly efficient search does not seem dependent on the serial application of visual attention. Now one possibility suggested by these data is that the ventral visual system operates to group features together to form object descriptions at different levels—including that of the whole display, if the multiple items form a coherent group (Duncan & Humphreys, 1989). If the display-level description is sufficient to support the discrimination between the target and the distractors, then search is highly efficient. If the description is not sufficient in this way (e.g., if grouping links the target to distractor elements; see Rensink & Enns, 1995), then attention is required to help segment the display, by activating features within some regions of the display over others (e.g., to enable selective grouping to take place over parts of the display). On this view, pre-attentive binding within the ventral visual system must normally be allied with attentional segmentation, to enable individual objects to be segmented and identified in complex (multi-object) scenes.

Binding shape and surface detail

Although there is evidence for the binding of shape features in patients with parietal damage, the same patients can also be shown to be impaired at integrating shape and surface properties of objects, when multiple objects are present (e.g., GK here, see also Cohen & Rafal, 1991; Friedman-Hill et al., 1995). The findings with patient GK further indicate that binding within the shape domain has relatively little effect on ICs of shape and surface detail (Humphreys et al., 2000). From this it can be inferred that the process of binding contours into shapes, and the process of assigning surface detail to those shapes, can be functionally separated. Such a distinction is suggested by recent computational approaches to vision, such as the FAÇADE model of Grossberg and colleagues (e.g., Grossberg & Mingolla, 1985; Grossberg & Pessoa, 1998). These authors propose the perception of surface properties of objects depends on two operations. First, a process of boundary formation, performed by a "Boundary contour system" (BCS), that uses grouping processes such as collinearity and good continuation to form bounded contours of shapes. Second, a process of "filling in", within the bounded regions, performed by a "feature contour system" (FCS). Activation within the FCS generates the surface properties of objects. For patients such as GK, we may propose that processing within the BCS is relatively intact, but that there is a deficit within the FCS.

What is the nature of the deficit in binding form and surface detail? According to an attentional account, GK's impairment may arise because of damage to his visual attentional system, which prevents selective activation of the common location shared by the colour and form of an object. Because of poor attention, colours from multiple items in the field are available to be combined with a given shape, so that illusory conjunctions arise. Alternatively, there may be poor co-registration of colour and shape within a master map of locations within the parietal lobe, enabling colours from one object to be mis-attributed to another. On this last view, an accurate co-registration process would normally make it possible for colour and shape to be combined even without attention to their common location. For patients such as GK, though, the process is disrupted by lesions to the master location map. We note that there is evidence from search in normal subjects for super-additivity when multiple form–colour conjunctions are present (Linnell & Humphreys, in press; Mordkoff, Yantis, & Egeth, 1990), and also in segmentation tasks when form and colour boundaries coincide (Kubovy, Cohen, & Hollier, 1999). These last results suggest that bindings of colour and form do not always depend on selective attention, though the parietal role may still play an important mediating role for co-registration.

In normal observers there is evidence that illusory conjunctions are sensitive to grouping between stimuli: ICs occur more frequently between the attributes belonging to one perceptual group than between attributes belonging to separate perceptual groups (Baylis et al., 1992; Prinzmetal et al., 1986; see also Figure 7 here). This was not the case for GK, though there were clear effects of grouping on extinction. The data from normal subjects may be explained in terms of there being interactions between form grouping in the ventral visual system, and activation within the parietal lobe. Strong grouping for elements in one location may lead to greater associated activation for neurons representing the same location within the parietal lobe, and this may reduce the chance of co-registration with surface information from other locations. GK's parietal damage may limit these interactions. As a consequence, surface details from multiple objects may compete to be registered with shape information, even when the objects do not group. Due to this, IC errors may occur even between separate objects.

Transient and sustained binding

In addition to the evidence on form binding and on the integration of form and surface detail, we have also reported evidence that there can be temporary binding of stimuli based on their common onset. Indeed, with brief presentations, it is possible to witness "anti-extinction" in which there can be recovery of a contralesional stimulus when its onset coincides with the onset of an ipsilesion item, even when the contralesional stimulus cannot be reported in isolation. Our evidence on the triple-letter identification task (Figure 10) further suggests that this anti-extinction effects did not come about by the onsets cueing attention to a shared area of field. Rather the anti-extinction effect we have reported seems due to the onset stimuli being bound together, so that they can be reported even when a central offset letter is not.

We only found an anti-extinction effect with short stimulus presentations (Figure 8). With longer exposures, there was improved report of single contralesional items whilst, if anything, report of the contralesional stimulus decreased on two-item trials. This transition, from anti-extinction to extinction, was not caused by rightwards eye movements at longer stimulus exposures; anti-extinction occurred both when no eye movements occurred during a display and when a rightwards eye movement was initiated. The transition can be accounted for if the binding by common onset is transient, and so becomes ineffective over time. This transient form of binding is replaced over time by more sustained binding, sensitive to form and surface-based grouping relations between items in the field. Thus, extinction, at long durations, is affected by grouping. In a patient such as GK, these two forms of binding operate against a bias in stimulus selection, favouring stimuli in the right over those in the left visual field. Sustained binding may enable observers to generate a veridical representation of the world, with elements organized by similarity of shape and suurface detail. Transient binding, in contrast, may yield a "quick and dirty" representation, insensitive to higher-order grouping factors but sensitive to the presence of a potential perceptual group. These two forms of binding may also be generated by different neural processes, with oscillatory firing patterns of neurons being important for sustained but not transient binding (cf. Singer & Gray, 1995). Resolution of these issues clearly requires further research.

REFERENCES

Balint, R. (1909). Seelenahmung des "Schauens": Optische ataxie, raumliche Storung der Aufmerkamsamkeit. *Manatschrift fur Psychiatrie und Neurologie, 25*, 51–81.

Baylis, G.C., Driver, J., Baylis, L.L., & Rafal, R.D. (1994). Reading of letters and words in a patient with Balint's syndrome. *Neuropsychologia, 32*, 1273–1286.

Baylis, G.C., Driver, J., & McLeod, P. (1992). Movement and proximity constrain miscombinations of colour and form. *Perception, 21*, 201–218.

Behrmann, M., Plaut, D., & Nelson, J. (1998). A literature review and new data supporting an interactive account of letter-by-letter reading. *Cognitive Neuropsychology, 15*, 7–52.

Bisiach, E., Capitani, E., Luzzatti, C., & Perani, D. (1981). Brain and conscious representation of outside reality. *Neuropsychologia, 24*, 739–767.

Boucart, M., & Humphreys, G.W. (1992). The computation of perceptual structure from collinearity and closure: Normality and pathology. *Neuropsychologia, 30*, 527–546.

Boutsen, L., & Humphreys, G.W. (2000). Axis-based grouping reduces visual extinction. *Neuropsychologia, 38*, 896–905.

Brefczynski, J.A., & de Yoe, E.A. (1999). A physiological correlate of the "spotlight" of visual attention. *Nature Neuroscience, 2*, 370–374.

Butter, C.M., & Trobe, J.D. (1994). Integrative agnosia following progressive multifocal leukoencephalopathy. *Cortex, 30*, 145–158.

Chainay, H., & Humphreys, G.W. (2001). The real-object advantage in agnosia: Evidence of a role for shading and depth in object recognition. *Cognitive Neuropsychology, 18*, 175–191.

Chelazzi, L., Miller, E.K., Duncan, J., & Desimone, R. (1993). A neural basis for visual search in inferior temporal cortex. *Nature, 363*, 345–347.

Cohen, A., & Rafal, R.D. (1991). Attention and feature integration: Illusory conjunctions in a patient with a parietal lobe lesion. *Psychological Science, 2*, 106–110.

Cooper, A.C.G., & Humphreys, G.W. (2000). Coding space within but not between objects: Evidence from Balint's syndrome. *Neuropsychologia, 38,* 723–733.

DeRenzi, E. (1982). *Disorders of space exploration and cognition.* New York: John Wiley.

DeRenzi, E., & Lucchelli, F. (1993). The fuzzy boundaries of apperceptive agnosia. *Cortex, 29*, 187–215.

Desimone, R., & Ungerleider, L.G. (1989). Neural mechanisms of visual processing in monkeys. In E. Boller & J. Grafman (Eds.), *Handbook of neuropsychology, Vol. II.* Amsterdam: Elsevier Science.

Donk, M. (1999). Illusory conjunctions are an illusion: The effects of target–nontarget similarity on conjunction and feature errors. *Journal of Experimental Psychology: Human Perception and Performance, 25*, 1207–1233.

Donnelly, N., Humphreys, G.W., & Riddoch, M.J. (1991). Parallel computation of primitive shape descriptions. *Journal of Experimental Psychology: Human Perception and Performance, 17*, 561–570.

Duncan, J., & Humphreys, G.W. (1989). Visual search and stimulus similarity. *Psychological Review, 96*, 433–458.

Eckhorn, R. (1999). Neural mechanisms of visual feature binding investigated with microelectrodes and models. *Visual Cognition, 6*, 231–266.

Elliott, M.A., & Müller, H.M. (1998). Synchronous information presented in 40Hz flicker enhances visual feature binding. *Psychological Science, 9*, 277–283.

Fahle, M. (1993). Figure–ground discrimination from temporal information. *Proceedings of the Royal Society, B254*, 199–203.

Farah, M.J. (1990). *Visual agnosia: Disorders of object recognition and what they tell us about normal vision.* Cambridge, MA: MIT Press.

Friedman-Hill, S., Robertson, L.C., & Treisman, A. (1995). Parietal contributions to visual feature binding: Evidence from a patient with bilateral lesions. *Science, 269*, 853-855.

Giersch, A., Humphreys, G.W., Boucart, M., & Kovacs, I. (2000). The computation of occluded contours in visual agnosia: Evidence for early computation prior to shape binding and figure-ground coding. *Cognitive Neuropsychology, 17,* 731–759.

Gilbert, C., Ito, M., Kapadia, M., & Westheimer, G. (2000). Interactions between attention, context and learning in primary visual cortex. *Vision Research, 40*, 1217–1226.

Gilbert, C., & Wiesel, T.N. (1989). Columnar specificity of intronsic horizontal and corticocortical connections in cat visual cortex. *Journal of Neuroscience, 9*, 2432–2442.

Gilchrist, I., Humphreys, G.W., & Riddoch, M.J. (1996). Grouping and extinction: Evidence for low-level modulation of selection. *Cognitive Neuropsychology, 13*, 1223–1256.

Goodrich, S.J., & Ward, R. (1997). Anti-extinction following unilateral parietal damage. *Cognitive Neuropsychology, 14*, 595–612.

Grosof, D.H., Shapley, R.M., & Hawken, M.J. (1993). Macaque V1 neurons can signal "illusory" contours. *Nature, 257*, 219–220.

Gross, C.G., Rocha-Miranda, C.E., & Bender, D.B. (1972). Visual properties of neurons in inferotemporal cortex. *Journal of Neurophysiology, 35*, 96–111.

Grossberg, S., & Mingolla, E. (1985). Neural dynamics of form perception: Boundary completion, illusory figures, and neon color spreading. *Psychological Review, 92*, 173–211.

Grossberg, S., & Pessoa, L. (1998). Texture segregation, surface representation and figure–ground separation. *Vision Research, 38*, 2657–2684.

Hall, D.A., Humphreys, G.W., & Cooper, A.C.G. (2001). Neuropsychological evidence for case-specific reading: Multi-letter units in visual word recognition. *Quarterly Journal of Experimental Psychology, 54A,* 439–467.

Hillyard, S.A., Vogel, E.K., & Luck, S.J. (1998). Sensory gain control (amplification) as a mechanism of selective attention: Electrophysiological and neuroimaging evidence. *Philosophical Transactions of the Royal Society, B353*, 1257–1270.

Holmes, G. (1918). Disturbances of spatial orientation and visual attention. *British Journal of Ophthalmology, 2*, 449–516.

Humphreys, G.W. (1998). Neural representation of objects in space: A dual coding account. *Philosophical Transactions of the Royal Society, B353*, 1341–1352.

Humphreys, G.W. (1999). Integrative agnosia. In G.W. Humphreys (Ed.), *Case studies in the neuropsychology of vision* (pp. 41–58). Hove, UK: Psychology Press.

Humphreys, G.W., Cinel, C., Wolfe, J., Olson, A., & Klempen, N. (2000). Fractionating the binding process: Neuropsychological evidence distinguishing binding of form from binding of surface features. *Vision Research, 40*, 1569–1596.

Humphreys, G.W., & Donnelly, N. (2000). 3D constraints on spatially parallel shape processing. *Perception and Psychophysics, 62,* 1060–1085.

Humphreys, G.W., Quinlan, P.T., & Riddoch, M.J. (1989). Grouping processes in visual search: Effects with single- and combined-feature targets. *Journal of Experimental Psychology: General, 118*, 258–279.

Humphreys, G.W., & Riddoch, M.J. (1987). *To see or not to see: A case study of visual agnosia.* Hove, UK: Lawrence Erlbaum Associates Ltd.

Humphreys, G.W., & Riddoch, M.J. (1993). Interactions between object and space vision revealed through neuropsychology. In D.E. Meyer & S. Kornblum (Eds.), *Attention and performance XIV: Synergies in experimental psychology, artificial intelligence, and cognitive neuroscience* (pp. 143–162). Cambridge, MA: MIT Press.

Humphreys, G.W., Romani, C., Olson, A., Riddoch, M.J., & Duncan, J. (1994). Non-spatial extinction following lesions of the parietal lobe in humans. *Nature, 372*, 357–359.

Karnath, H.-O. (1988). Deficits of attention in acute and recovered visual hemi-neglect. *Neuropsychologia, 26*, 27–43.

Kellman, P.J., & Shipley, T.F. (1991). A theory of visual interpolation in object perception. *Cognitive Psychology, 23*, 141–221.

Kovacs, I. (2000). Human development of perceptual organization. *Vision Research, 40*, 1301–1310.

Kubovy, M., Cohen, D.J., & Hollier, J. (1999). Featured integration that routinely occurs without focal attention. *Psychonomic Bulletin and Review, 6*, 183–203.

Kumada, T., & Humphreys, G.W. (2001). Lexical recovery from extinction: Interactions between visual form and stored knowledge modulate visual selection. *Cognitive Neuropsychology, 18,* 465–478.

Lawson, R., & Humphreys, G.W. (1999). The effects of view in depth on the identification of line drawings and silhouettes of familiar objects. *Visual Cognition, 6*, 165–196.

Linnell, K.J., & Humphreys, G.W. (in press). Visual search within versus across dimensions: A case for within-dimension grouping. *British Journal of Psychology.*

Mattingly, J.B., Davis, G., & Driver, J. (1997). Pre-attentive filling in of visual surfaces in parietal extinction. *Science, 275*, 671–674.

Mendola, J.D., Dale, A.M., Fischl, B., Liu, A.K., & Tootell, R.B.H. (1999). The representation of illusory and real contours in human cortical vissual areas revealed by funcitonal magnetic resonance imaging. *Journal of Neuroscience, 19*, 8560–8572.

Milner, A.D., & Goodale, M.A. (1995). *The visual brain in action.* Oxford, UK: Oxford University Press.

Milner, A.D., Perrett, D.I., Johnston, R.S., Benson, P.J., Jordan, T.R., Heeley, D.W., Bettucci, D., Mortara, F., Mutani, R., Terazzi, E., & Davidson, D.L.W. (1991). Perception and action in "visual form agnosia". *Brain, 114*, 405–428.

Moran, J., & Desimone, R. (1985). Selective attention gates visual processing in the extra-striate cortex. *Science, 229*, 782–784.

Mordkoff, J.T., Yantis, S., & Egeth, H.E. (1990). Detecting conjuncitons of color and form in parallel. *Perception and Psychophysics, 48*, 157–168.

Motter, B.C. (1994). Neural correlates of selective attention for color or luminance in extrastriate area V4. *Journal of Neuroscience, 14,* 2178–2189.

Prinzmetal, W., Treiman, R., & Rho, S.H. (1986). How to see a reading unit. *Journal of Memory and Language, 25*, 461–475.

Redies, C., Crook, J.M., & Creutzfelt, O.D. (1986). Neural response to borders with and without luminance gradients in cat visual cortex and dorsal lateral geniculate nucleus. *Experimental Brain Research, 61*, 49–81.

Rensink, R.A., & Enns, J. (1995). Pre-emption effects in visual search: Evidence for low-level grouping. *Psychological Review, 102*, 101–130.

Riddoch, M.J., & Humphreys, G.W. (1987). A case of integrative visual agnosia. *Brain, 110*, 1431–1462.

Riddoch, M.J., Humphreys, G.W., Gannon, T., Blott, W., & Jones, V. (1999). Memories are made of this: The effects of time on stored knowledge in a case of visual agnosia. *Brain, 122*, 537–559.

Robertson, L.C., Treisman, A., Friedman-Hill, S., & Grabowecky, M. (1997). A possible connection between spatial deficits and feature binding in a patient with parietal damage. *Journal of Cognitive Neuroscience, 9*, 295–317.

Rorden, C., Mattingley, J.B., Karnath, H.O., & Driver, J. (1997). Visual extinction and prior entry: Impaired perception of temporal order with intact motion perception after parietal injury. *Neuropsychologia, 35*, 421–433.

Shallice, T., & Warrington, E.K. (1977). The possible role of selective attention in acquired dyslexia. *Neuropsychologia, 15*, 31–41.

Sheth, B.R., Sharma, J., Rao, S.C., & Sur, M. (1996). Orientation maps of subjective contours in visual cortex. *Science, 274*, 2110–2115.

Shipley, T.F., & Kellman, P.J. (1992). Perception of partly occluded objects and illusory figures: Evidence for an identity hypothesis. *Journal of Experimental Psychology: Human Perception and Performance, 18*, 106–120.

Singer, W., & Gray, C.M. (1995). Visual feature integration and the temporal correlation hypothesis. *Annual Review of Neuroscience, 18*, 555–586.

Stark, M., Coslett, H.B., & Saffran, E. (1996). Impairment of an egocentric map of locations: Implications for perception and action. *Cognitive Neuropsychology, 13*, 481-524.

Tootell, R.B.H., Reppas, J.B., Kwong, K., Malach, R., Born, R.T., Brady, T.J., Rosen, B.R., & Belliveau, J.W. (1995). Functional analysis of human MT and related visual cortical areas using magnetic resonance imaging. *Journal of Neuroscience, 15*, 3215–3230.

Treisman, A. (1998). Feature binding, attention and object perception. *Philosophical Transactions of the Royal Society, B353*, 1295–1306.

Treisman, A., & Gelade, G. (1980). A feature-integration theory of attention. *Cognitive Psychology, 12*, 97–136.

Treisman, A., & Schmidt, H. (1982). Illusory conjunctions in the perception of objects. *Cognitive Psychology, 14*, 107–141.

Ungerleider, L.G., & Haxby, J.V. (1994). "What" and "where" in the human brain. *Current Opinions in Neurobiology, 4*, 157–165.

Ungerleider, L.G., & Mishkin, M. (1982). Two cortical visual systems. In D.I. Ingle, M.A. Goodale, & R.J.W. Manfield (Eds.), *Analysis of visual behavior.* Cambridge, MA: MIT Press.
Vecera, S.P., & Farah, M.J. (1994). Does visual attention select objects or locations? *Journal of Experimental Psychology: General, 123*, 146–160.
von der Heydt, R., & Peterhans, E. (1989). Mechanisms of contour perception in monkey visual cortex: I. Lines of pattern discontinuity. *Journal of Neuroscience, 9*, 1731–1748.
Ward, R., Goodrich, S., & Driver, J. (1994). Grouping reduces visual extinction: Neuropsychological evidence for weight-linkage in visual selection. *Visual Cognition, 1*, 101–130.
Watson, J.D.D., Myers, G.R., Frackowiak, R.S.J., Hajnal, V.J., Woods, R.P., Mazziota, J.C., Ship, S., & Zeki, S. (1993). Area V5 of the human brain: Evidence from a combined study using positron emission tomography and magnetic resonance imaging. *Cerebral Cortex, 3*, 79–84.
Zeki, S. (1993). *A vision of the brain.* Oxford, UK: Blackwell.

VISUAL COGNITION, 2001, *8* (3/4/5), 411–430

Between-object binding and visual attention

Greg Davis
Centre for Brain and Cognitive Development, Department of Psychology, Birkbeck College, University of London, UK

Many previous studies have found that we can attend pairs of visual features (e.g., colour, orientation) more efficiently when they belong to the same "object" compared to when they belong to separate, neighbouring objects (e.g., Behrmann, Zemel, & Mozer, 1998; Egly, Rafal, & Driver, 1994). This advantage for attending features from the same object may reflect stronger binding between these features than arises for pairs of features belonging to separate objects. However, recent findings described by Davis, Welch, Holmes, and Shepherd (in press) suggest that under specific conditions this same-object advantage can be reversed, such that attention now spreads more readily between features belonging to separate neighbouring objects than between features of the same object. In such cases it would appear that features belonging to separate visual objects are more strongly bound than features of the same object. Here I review these findings and present the results of a new study. Together these data suggest that magnocellular processes in the human visual system bind together features from separate objects, whereas parvocellular processes bind together features from the same object.

INTRODUCTION

In contrast to the relatively simple stimuli employed in the laboratory, natural scenes typically comprise bewildering arrays of colours, textures, and shapes. To guide behaviour effectively in such complex environments, our visual systems must be able to determine, and to designate, which colour, shape, and texture "features" in a given scene belong to which objects. That is, as other papers in this special issue address, from the many separately coded features yielded by early stages of visual processing, vision must form unitary representations that can be recognized and acted upon (see, e.g., Elliott & Müller, 1998; Usher & Donnelly, 1998). This "binding" together of individual features into unitary representations may serve numerous functions in vision, and the

---

Please address all correspondence to G. Davis, Centre for Brain and Cognitive Development, Department of Psychology, Birkbeck College, Malet Street, London WC1E 7HX, UK. Email: g.davis@psyc.bbk.ac.uk

http://www.tandf.co.uk/journals/pp/13506285.html DOI:10.1080/13506280143000205

representations created to serve, for example, object recognition may be different from those created for other purposes, such as grasping an object (e.g., Milner & Goodale, 1995). With this in mind, I shall therefore restrict my discussion here to the types of binding involved in solving a second major problem when processing natural scenes: The selection of relevant information.

Much of the information in complex natural scenes may often be irrelevant to us. In order to optimize processing of relevant information in such scenes, our visual systems incorporate a variety of mechanisms referred to under the umbrella term "selective attention" (e.g., Duncan, 1984; Lavie & Driver, 1996). These mechanisms of attention were envisaged, in several early studies, to behave as a "spotlight" or "zoom lens", enhancing processing within an approximately circular region of the visual field independently of the shapes of objects situated there (e.g., Eriksen & Eriksen, 1974). However, a substantial body of subsequent evidence has challenged this view, suggesting that many aspects of attention are "object-based" (Duncan, 1984; Egly, Rafal, & Driver, 1994; Watson & Kramer, 1999). That is, rather than simply selecting a circular region of the visual field, our attention may select whole object-like units formed by the binding-together of multiple individual stimulus features. On such a view, when we attend to one feature in a scene (e.g., an edge or patch of colour), our attention also tends to select all the other features belonging to the same "object" as that feature, due to their being bound together. The units selected by attention are conventionally described as "objects" (see, e.g., Duncan, 1984), and for economy I shall adopt this terminology here. However, this does not imply that the representations governing our attention in this way need be the same as those that support our recognition, or those that we intuitively regard, as objects. Further, even the nature of the "objects" selected by attention may in principle change according to the particular task and stimuli employed.

The two-target paradigm

Some of the most compelling evidence that our attention selects whole "objects", rather than circular regions of space, derives from "two-target" studies where observers are asked to make speeded judgements regarding pairs of target features (shape, colour, or texture elements) located at different parts of the visual field. For example, in the case of Figure 1A, observers might be asked to compare two squashed-ring elements, one at the top left of the display and one at the bottom left. A crucial manipulation in these experiments concerns whether the two target features pertain to a single object (e.g., the left object in Figure 1A) or alternatively to two different objects (as in Figure 1B). Note that the two pairs of target features are otherwise identical and are equidistant from each other in the two displays. Thus, if attention were to behave like a spotlight, it could equally well encompass the pair of target features in Figure 1A as those

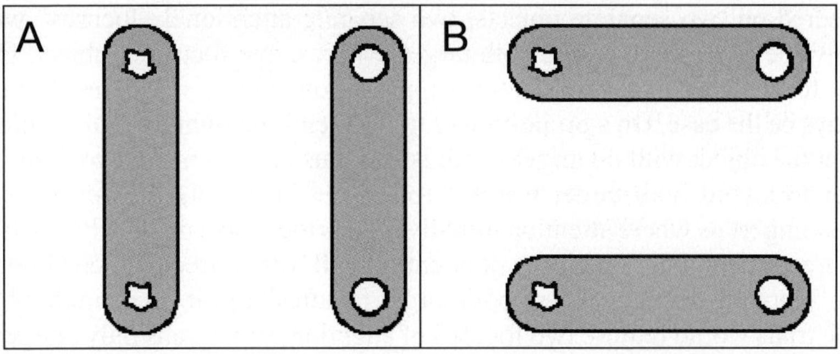

Figure 1. Typical "two-target" displays. **A:** Both target features (squashed-ring elements) appear on single object, in this case the left object. **B:** One target feature appears on each of the objects. Note that the target features (squashed-ring elements) are identical and equidistant from each other in the two displays.

in Figure 1B. In such a case we should expect the target features to be equally rapidly compared in the two displays. However, if, as object-based accounts suggest, attention selects whole object representations, then a different pattern might be expected. When attention selects one target feature (one squashed-ring element), attention should also encompass all the other features belonging to that object. Accordingly, when both target features belong to the same object as in Figure 1A, attention would therefore encompass both target features, allowing them to be compared easily. However, this tendency to select whole objects would not ease comparison of the two target features when both features appeared on separate objects as in Figure 1B. In such a case, when attention selects one target feature in Figure 1B, encompassing the whole of the object to which that feature belongs, it would not necessarily encompass the other target feature in the display, possibly slowing comparison of the two target features.

Since the 1980s many studies have employed this basic design (Behrmann, Zemel, & Mozer, 1998; Duncan, 1984; Lavie & Driver, 1996). These have typically found that in displays comprising pairs of objects, such as those in Figure 1, target features are compared (or otherwise judged) more rapidly and accurately when they seem to belong to the same object than when they appear to belong to different objects (see Lavie & Driver, 1996, for a review). Such findings provide strong support for the view that our attention selects whole objects rather than circular regions of space, though a precise explanation for how such patterns of performance arise remains a matter of controversy. One popular model ascribes advantages for within-object feature comparisons (i.e., where both target features belong to the same object) over between-object comparisons (i.e., where the features belong to different objects) to a difficulty in attending to more than one object at a time (Duncan, 1984; Duncan, Humphreys, & Ward, 1997). On such an account, when two target features appeared on two separate objects, two separate attentional "focuses" would *always* be required to attend both target features, one focus per object. However, for trials where the two features appeared on a single object this would not always be the case. On a proportion of trials attention might by chance initially select the object with no target features and thus have to make two focuses in order to attend both target features (one to each object). However, on the remaining trials where attention initially selects the object on which both target features appear, only one focus of attention will be required to attend both targets. Thus for displays where both target features appear on a single object, some trials would require two focuses of attention, some trials only one, yielding a performance benefit over trials where the target features appear on different objects, and where two focuses of attention are always required.

This conventional "one-object" account has recently been challenged by Davis, Driver, Pavani, and Shepherd (2000) who suggested that although attention may indeed select whole objects, performance benefits and costs seen in previous studies may not reflect a fixed inability to attend more than one "object" at a time. As was the case in many previous studies where the displays comprised two objects of equal size and complexity, two objects between them constitute twice the overall amount of perceptual information as a single object. Thus, when features appear on the same object (as in Figure 1A) and attention can be restricted to just one of the objects in some trials, attention would have to select only half the perceptual information in the display. In contrast, when target features each appear on different objects and attention must always select both objects in a display (either one at a time or both at once), all the information in the display must be attended, twice as much information as when only one object is attended. Davis and colleagues therefore suggested that the amount of attended information, rather than the number of attended objects, is crucial in determining performance.

In order to test their new account, Davis et al. (2000) compared performance in displays comprising two small objects versus one large object (see, e.g., Figure 2A). The two types of display were designed to comprise roughly the same amount of perceptual information overall (compare Figure 2A with Figure 2B), and to differ only in the number of "objects" they comprised. If attention can select only one object at a time as suggested by conventional accounts, then the displays comprising one large object should be more efficiently attended than the two object displays, where in many cases two attention "focuses" would be required, one to each object. On the other hand, if the amount of information that must be attended, rather than the number of objects *per se*, is crucial in governing performance, the two display types should be equally well attended as they comprise approximately the same amount of information overall. On trials requiring a "same" response, the target features in each display were two notches that could both be triangular (e.g., Figures 2A and 2B), or both rectangular. On trials requiring a "different" response, one notch of each type would

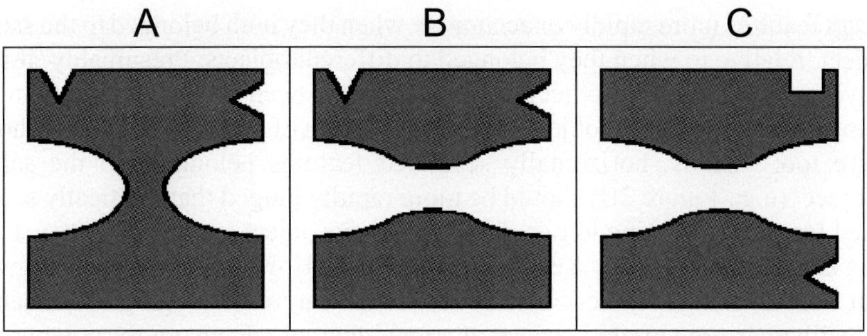

Figure 2. Typical displays employed by Davis et al. (2000). **A:** Display comprising one large object. **B:** Display comprising two small objects, which is similar in appearance to A and comprises a similar amount of perceptual information overall. In this case, the two target features (two triangular "notches" cut from the upper object) are described as "horizontally separated", both appearing on the same object. **C:** A second two-small-object display, similar to B except that now the two target features are "vertically separated", one feature belonging to each separate object. Note that whereas in B both features were triangular notches, now one feature is a square notch (upper object) and one a triangular notch (lower object).

be presented (one triangular, one rectangular; e.g., Figure 2C). Observers had to determine as quickly as possible whether the two notches were of the same or different types, and press one of two buttons on a computer keyboard to indicate their response. Within the two-object displays, these features could be horizontally separated, appearing on a single object (as in Figure 2B), or vertically separated, appearing on two separate objects (as in Figure 2C). Similar horizontally and vertically separated features were also presented in the one-object displays, although these always pertained to the single (large) object (e.g., horizontally separated features in Figure 2A). Davis and colleagues found equivalent performance overall for the two display types, suggesting that, when other factors are equated, two objects can be as easily attended as one.

This equal performance for one versus two object displays raises an immediate question: How can we be sure that observers' attention in the Davis et al. (2000) study had really treated the two-small-object displays to comprise two objects, and the one-large-object displays only one object? If, for example, their attention had somehow treated the two-object displays as comprising a single "object" rather than two objects as Davis et al. intended, this might account for the equality of performance in the two cases. Alternatively, if the one-large-object displays had been treated as comprising two separate "objects" by attention, this too would render the findings uninformative as attention would be selecting two objects in both one- and two-object displays. In order to test these possibilities, Davis et al. individually analysed horizontally and vertically separated features in the one- and two-object displays.

Let us first consider the two-object displays. In many previous studies, when presented with a display comprising two objects, observers compared pairs of target features more rapidly or accurately when they both belonged to the same object, relative to when they belonged to different objects. Presumably, if the Davis et al. (2000) two-object displays had also been treated by attention as comprising two separate objects, this same pattern of performance should hold there too. That is, horizontally separated features belonging to the same "object" (e.g., Figure 2B) should be more rapidly judged than vertically separated features belonging to two different objects object (e.g., Figure 2C). This was indeed the case (Davis et al., 2000, Exp. 2). However, it might be argued that this advantage for horizontally separated features belonging to the same object had arisen simply because of some inherent advantage for comparing horizontally separated features over vertically separated features, independently of whether or not the features belonged to the same object. To preclude this latter possibility, Davis et al. compared the patterns of results in their two-small-object displays to similar conditions in their one-large-object displays. If the advantage for horizontally separated features (belonging to the same object in the two-object displays) over vertically separated features (on different objects) had arisen simply because of inherent advantages in comparing horizontal features, then this pattern of results should also hold in the very similar one-large-object displays. Conversely, if the advantage for horizontally separated features in the two-object displays had arisen because they belonged to the same object whereas vertically separated features belonged to different objects, this pattern should not be evident in the one-large-object displays, where vertically and horizontally separated features belonged to the same object.

Davis et al. (2000) found that for the one-large-object displays, vertically and horizontally separated features were compared equally rapidly and accurately, indicating that no inherent advantage for horizontally separated features held, once both horizontally and vertically separated features belonged to the same object. Rather, the more rapid detection of horizontally than vertically separated features in the two-object displays appeared to have arisen due to horizontally separated features there belonging to the same "object", with vertically separated features belonging to separate objects. The two-object displays had thus given rise to patterns in performance expected for pairs of separate objects: A performance advantage for features belonging to the same object. However, the minor differences between the one and two object displays of Davis et al. had caused the one-large-object displays to control attention and performance as would be expected for a single large object.

Davis et al. (2000) concluded that a display comprising two objects can be attended as efficiently as a display comprising only one object, provided that the two displays constitute the same amount of perceptual information overall. Such a finding seems to contradict the view that attention can select only one object at a time, as that would predict substantial performance advantages overall for displays comprising only one object. Instead, Davis et al. suggested that it was the amount of perceptual information overall constituted by the attended objects, not the number of attended objects *per se* that was crucial in limiting attention and performance.

Davis, Welch, Holmes, and Shepherd (in press) have since extended the analysis of Davis et al. (2000) to six- versus three-object displays, where three objects comprise approximately the same amount of information as six objects. These new displays comprised three small versions of the one- and two-object displays used by Davis et al. (2000) to yield three and six objects respectively (Figures 3A and 3B). Again the task was to make same/different judgements concerning pairs of notches on the objects. In a given display, the notches could either both be rectangular (e.g., Figure 3A), both be diagonal (e.g., Figure 3C), or one of each type of notch (Figure 3B). The notches could appear on any object in the display, with the position of one target notch holding no predictive value with regard to the position of the other. That is, one notch might fall on one "pair" of neighbouring objects in a six-object display and the other notch could either appear within that same pair of objects (1/3 of six-object trials; Figures 3B and 3C) or on another pair of objects (2/3 of six-object trials; e.g., Figure 3D). Identical variations in target positions arose in the three-large-object displays. This new study found equivalent performance for the six-small-object and three-large-object displays, again suggesting that the number of objects in a display did not affect how efficiently that display was attended.

The new study also analysed individual conditions within the six-small-object and three-large-object displays in order to check that the six-object displays had been perceived to comprise three pairs of separate objects (i.e., six objects), and the three-object displays three large objects. Whenever the two target notches fell within a single pair of small objects in the six-object displays, horizontally separated features (on the same object) were more rapidly compared than vertically separated features belonging to two separate objects. Note that this is the same pattern as seen in the original Davis et al. (2000) study for pairs of objects in their two-object displays. Moreover, for similar conditions in the three-large-object displays where both features appeared on a single large object, vertically separated features and horizontally separated features were compared equally rapidly, as Davis et al. (2000) had found in their one-large-object displays. Thus, each pair of objects in the six-object displays (Figure 3B) had yielded patterns expected for a pair of two, separate "objects", whereas each large-object in the three-object displays (Figure 3A) gave rise to patterns expected for a single large object.

These new results suggest that six-object displays can be attended as efficiently as three-object displays provided the amount of information is equated in the two cases. Such a conclusion seems to provide strong support for the Davis et al. (2000) proposal that the amount of information attended, rather the number of objects *per se*, is crucial in governing our attention and performance. However, one obvious weakness in their account was that it lacked an index of "amount of information". In response to this absence, Davis et al. (in press)

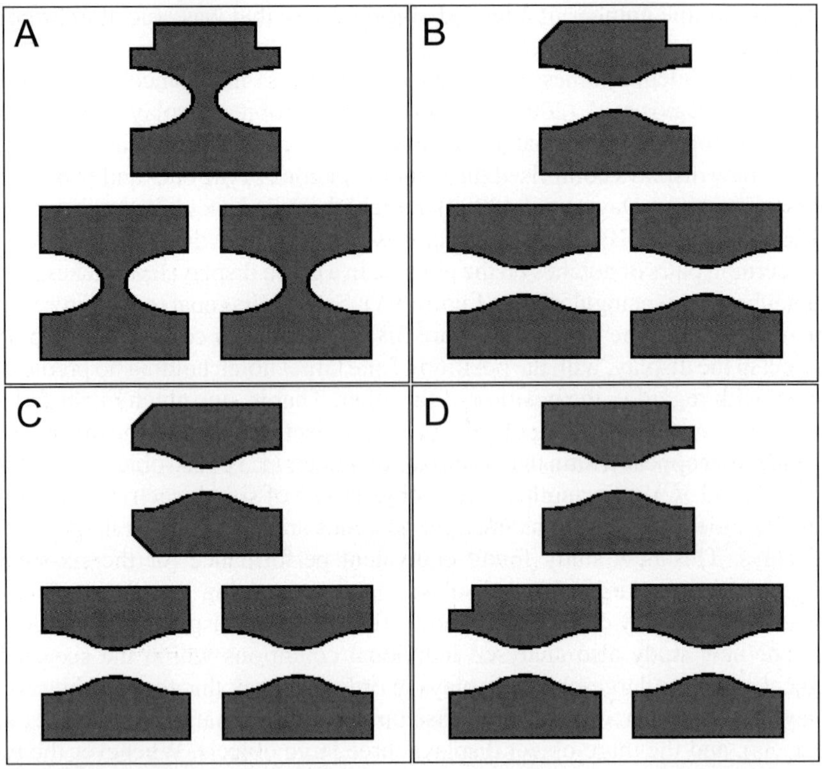

Figure 3. Typical displays employed by Davis et al. (in press) when comparing attention to six versus three objects. **A:** Three-large-object display in which both target features (two square notches cut from the top-left and top-right corners of the top-most object) appear on the same object and are horizontally separated. **B:** Six-small-object display comprising three "pairs" of small objects. Note that this display is very similar to the three-object displays. In this case, the two target features features (one square notch, one diagonal) are horizontally separated and appear on a single small object (the uppermost object). **C:** Another six-small-object display in which the two target features (two diagonal notches) both appear within a single "pair" of small neighbouring objects, but, in contrast to A and B, the features are now vertically separated, each belonging to a different object within that pair of objects. **D:** Six-object-display in which the two target notches do not appear in the same "pair" of objects: Now one feature appears on the top-most pair of objects, the other on the bottom-left pair of objects.

have proposed a model of object-based attention involving two types of binding in human vision, which forms the basis of the current study. In addition to binding together of features that belong to the same "object", this new account also assumes that some binding arises between features from separate objects.

A new model of visual attention limitations

As I discussed earlier, many previous studies have found that in displays comprising two small objects, pairs of features belonging to a single object are more rapidly compared than features belonging to separate objects: a "same-object advantage". Davis et al. (2000) similarly found a robust same-object advantage in their two-object displays, but the minor physical difference between those displays and their one-large-object displays (a small connecting region in the centre of the display) had given rise to a different pattern of performance in the two display types. These results seem to confirm that the two-object displays were attended as containing two separate objects, whereas the one-large-object displays were attended as a single object.

In one of their studies, Davis et al. (in press) used exactly the same stimuli and procedure as the Davis et al. (2000) study, but with one crucial modification. In their original experiment, Davis et al. (2000) had presented the object(s) in a display for a substantial period of time (1.6 s) before the target features were presented. The new study, in contrast, presented the objects and target features simultaneously. This modification had a profound influence upon the patterns of performance seen in the two-object versus one-object displays. Now, Davis and colleagues (in press) found no evidence of a same-object advantage. Rather, a robust "different-object advantage" was now yielded whereby, compared with similar conditions in the one-large-object displays, features belonging to separate objects in the two-object displays were *more* rapidly compared than features belong to the same object.

An immediate objection to such a finding might be that both the one-object and two-object displays were now attended as though they comprised only a single object, or alternatively that both the two-object and one-object displays had been attended as though they comprised two separate objects. However, both of these explanations would predict the same patterns of results in the one- and two-object displays, whereas Davis et al. (in press) found different patterns. When the features and objects were presented simultaneously, binding between target features was *stronger* when they belonged to separate visual objects in the two-object displays than when they belonged to the same object. Davis et al. (in press) next attempted to replicate this new "different-object advantage" in displays comprising three versus six objects (Figures 3A and 3B). In their first study, Davis et al. (in press) had found robust same-object advantages within pairs of small objects in their six object displays that did not arise within single large objects within their three object displays (Figures 3A and 3B). As for the Davis et al. (2000) comparison of one- versus two-object displays, that study had presented the objects in each display for a substantial period of time in each trial before the target features were presented. In their final experiment, Davis et al. (in press) now replicated their comparison of six- versus three-object displays but presented the two target features simultaneously with the objects rather than after a substantial delay. This manipulation of the delay between presentation of objects and presentation of target features again had a profound effect upon the patterns of performance when both target features fell on a single pair of objects in the six-object displays. Now, with other possible factors partialled out (e.g., inherent advantages for horizontally or vertically separated features), robust different-object advantages were found: Features belonging to separate objects were more rapidly compared than features belonging to the same object.

In order to explain these effects of the delay between object presentation and feature presentation (the "object-feature delay"), Davis et al. (in press) proposed a new account, which will be tested here in a further study. This new model is essentially a modified version of a model proposed by Humphreys (1998), with which it is compared and contrasted in the Discussion section of this paper. The Davis et al. account can be summarized as two proposals:

(1) That individual pairs of features belonging to the same object are bound together by within-object "links", driven primarily by parvocellular processes, whereas pairs of features belonging to different nearby objects are bound by similar between-object "links", driven by magnocellular processes.

(2) That the overall number and strength of these links, and not the number of attended objects *per se*, forms the primary limitation on our visual attention.

The former of these two proposals can readily account for the effects of object-feature delays in the Davis et al. (in press) studies. The parvocellular pathway in vision continues to code stimuli for a prolonged period after their onset, whereas, in contrast, the magnocellular pathway has a relatively transient (short-lived) response to the onset of stimuli (e.g., Livingstone & Hubel, 1988). Thus, when the objects in the Davis et al. displays were presented for a substantial period of time before onset of features, the parvocellular system should still be responding strongly to the objects by the time the features were presented, predicting strong binding of features from the same object. In contrast, by that time, much of the transient magnocellular coding of the objects should have waned, and binding of features from separate objects should thus be relatively weak. This predicted greater strength of binding for features from the same object should then predict superior performance for features belonging to the same object: A "same-object advantage", as Davis and colleagues found.

When instead, objects and features are presented simultaneously, transient responses within the magnocellular pathway should still be responding robustly to the onset of the objects while the features are being coded, such that binding of features from separate objects should be strong. Under these alternative conditions, parvocellular coding of the objects and hence binding of features from the same object may be relatively weak compared to the substantial response of magnocellular mechanisms. In such a case, this new model would predict strong binding of features from different objects compared to the binding between features from the same object, correctly predicting a "different-object advantage" as Davis et al. (in press) found.

The second proposal of Davis et al. (in press) was primarily intended to account for the equal *overall* performance that they found for six-small-object versus three-large-object displays. As the two display types (being very similar in size and appearance) comprised approximately the same number of features, they would on the Davis et al. model also have formed the same number of links overall, since each pair of features is bound either by a within- or between-object link. Therefore if the *number* of links alone limited our attention, the two display-types should be attended equally well. This was the case with the Davis et al. (in press) first study where the objects were presented for a substantial period of time before the target features were presented. However, when instead, the objects and features were presented simultaneously, the six-object displays employed by Davis et al. were attended slightly *more* efficiently than the three-object displays, even though the number of links required to bind features in the two displays was presumably still the same.

To account for this latter finding, Davis and colleagues (in press) suggested that the average *strength* of the links coding a display, as well as their number, affects how efficiently the display is attended. On such an assumption, when features and objects were presented simultaneously (strengthening between-object links relative to within-object links), this would be expected to have differential effects on performance in six-object versus three-object displays. A display comprising six small objects would on the Davis et al. model comprise more between-object links and fewer within-object links overall than a comparable display comprising three large objects. Thus, any strengthening of between-object links should strengthen more of the links in the six-object display than in the three-object display, and this would be expected to benefit performance on six-object relative to three-object displays.

However, although this new model can provide an explanation for the Davis et al. (in press) findings, much more evidence will be required before the account as a whole can be widely accepted. Although the delay between presentation of features and the presentation of objects does seem to affect the strength of within- and between-object binding, it is far from certain whether this effect is due to the relative activation of magnocellular versus parvocellular pathways. Here, therefore, I describe a new study, based on one of the studies described in Davis et al. (in press), which is intended to provide a further test of magnocellular coding for between-object "links". Whereas parvocellular pathways tend to be responsive to a broader range of spatial frequencies, magnocellular pathways appear to be primarily sensitive only to low-spatial frequencies (see, e.g., Livingstone & Hubel, 1988). If this is indeed the case, and if between-object links are primarily driven by magnocellular processes, then by selectively removing low-spatial frequency aspects of an attended stimulus it should be possible to selectively weaken between-object links while leaving within-object links relatively unaffected. In order to test these assumptions, I therefore replicated, in all but one aspect, one of the studies described by

Davis et al., in which six-object displays were compared to three-object displays, with the target features and objects being presented simultaneously. These conditions had previously given rise to robust different-object advantages within pairs of objects in the six object displays, compared to other similar conditions within single large objects of the three-object displays. However, I now manipulated distribution of spatial frequencies within the stimuli and I expected that this would significantly alter the pattern of results yielded.

METHOD

Observers

Seven observers from the Department Subject Panel were recruited. Four were female, three male, their ages ranging from 18 to 29 years, with a mean of 22. Each was paid £5.00.

Displays

The stimuli were presented on a Sony 17" screen with a Power Macintosh G3 computer running "Vscope" experiment-generator software (Enns & Rensink, 1992). Figure 4A illustrates a typical display in the three-large-object condition, whereas Figure 4B illustrates a typical six-small-object display. These figures are drawn to scale: From top to bottom the objects the actually measured 24 cm vertically, subtending approximately 26° of visual angle at the viewing distance of 50 cm. From this dimension, all other stimulus dimensions can be calculated given the scaled figure. A feedback symbol (+ or –) immediately followed each response, appearing centrally and subtending 0.5° of visual angle.

In the case of six-object trials, displays were either presented with two pairs of objects in the upper half of the screen, one pair below, or vice versa (as illustrated in, e.g., Figure 4B), and identical variations held for the three-object displays. Note that as for the Davis et al. (2000, in press) studies, each pair of objects or single large object was presented only in the illustrated orientations (see Figures 2 and 3). This was because pilot observations indicated that when pairs of objects in the six-object displays were constructed with one object on the left and one on the right, the gap between those objects was seen as symmetrical around its major axis, the vertical axis. This symmetry caused the white gap to be seen as a vase-like single figure, and the dark objects to become ground, which was undesirable given the importance of controlling the number of figural objects seen.

The stimuli were produced by passing each pair of small objects in the six-object displays and each single large object in the three-object displays of Davis et al. (in press) through a high-pass Gaussian filter in Adobe Photoshop with the cut-off radius set to 2 pixels. Each stimulus filtered measured 212 × 212 pixels. This process selectively removed low spatial frequency energy from the

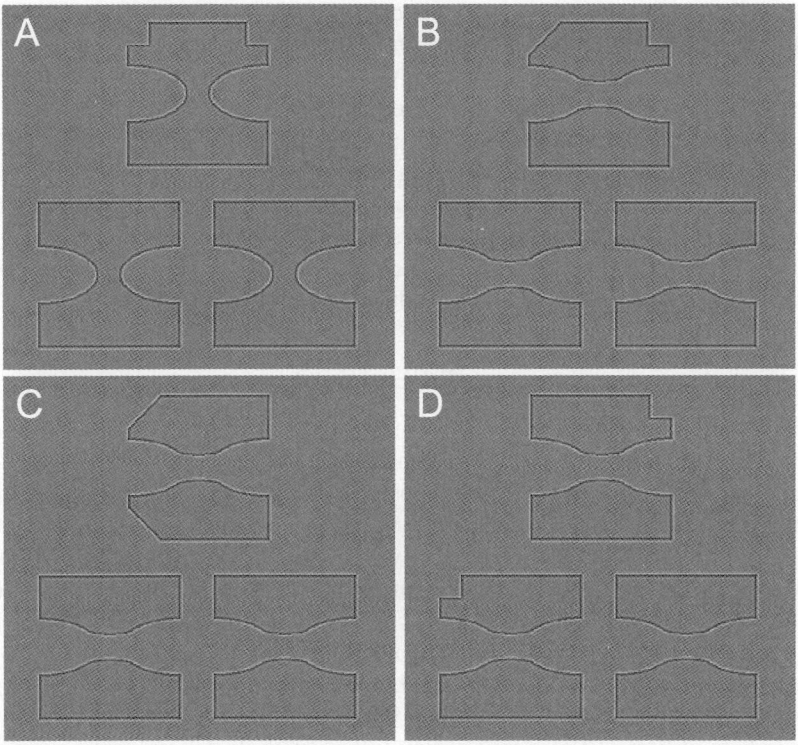

Figure 4. Typical displays employed in the current study, which are the same as those illustrated in Figure 3, except that low-spatial frequency elements have now been removed from each pattern.

stimulus, a manipulation that should decrease activation of the magnocellular pathway (Livingstone & Hubel, 1988).

Procedure

Target features could be square or diagonal notches and were equally likely to appear at any of the four possible "corner" locations of any of the objects in a given display. Three-large-object displays comprised half the trials, and six-small-object displays the other half. The notches could appear on any object in the display, with the position of one target notch holding no predictive value with regard to the position of the other. That is, one notch might fall on one pair of objects in a six-object display and the other notch could either appear within that same pair of objects (as in Figures 4B and 4C) or on any of the other objects in the display (Figure 4D). Identical variations arose in the three-large-object displays.

The order in which different trial-types were presented was randomized. Each observer viewed 10 blocks of 60 trials, the first 4 of which were excluded as practice as for all studies in Davis et al. (2000, in press). Observers were instructed to focus their gaze at the centre of the screen, and to try to attend all of the objects in a display simultaneously. When the target features were presented, observers had to press the correct button as quickly and accurately as possible, to indicate whether the two notches were the same or different in shape. Observers pressed one key on a computer keyboard when the two notches had the same shape (i.e., both square, or both diagonal: e.g., Figures 4A and 4C) and another key when the notches had different shapes (i.e., one diagonal, one square: e.g., Figure 4B), which was equally likely. Following each response, the screen cleared and a feedback symbol was presented

RESULTS

Trials where the features were the same (both square notches or both diagonal notches) or different (one diagonal, one square) were pooled so as to yield a minimum of 30 trials per cell for all possible comparisons. For six-object displays, performance was compared for trials where the two target features appeared on a single small object (i.e., were horizontally separated as in Figure 4B) versus on two separate neighbouring objects (i.e., vertically separated within a single "pair" of objects as in Figure 4C). An identical comparison of horizontally versus vertically separated features was also conducted for trials within the three-object displays where both features appeared on a single large object. Means of median RTs for these four conditions are graphed in Figure 5 (error bars indicate ±1 standard error). Filled symbols denote data points for three-object conditions, whereas open symbols denote data points for six-object conditions. The left pair of data points indicates horizontally separated targets, and the right pair vertcally separated ones. Inspection of Figure 5 suggests that different patterns arose within pairs of small objects in the six-object displays versus for single large objects in the three-object displays. Horizontally separated features (same object) appear to have been detected faster than vertically separated features (different object) for the six-small-objects displays, although this pattern does not hold to nearly the same extent for the three-large-objects displays.

These RT data were analysed using a two-way within-subjects ANOVA, display-type (features on a single large object in the three-object displays versus within a "pair" of neighbouring objects in the six-object displays) × horizontal/vertical target displacement, that yielded a main effect of display-type, $F(1, 6) = 22.29, p < .01$, and a main effect of horizontally versus vertically-separated targets, $F(1, 6) = 11.54, p < .02$. Crucially, moreover, these two factors interacted significantly, $F(1, 6) = 13.69, p < .02$, indicating that the six-object-displays had yielded significantly different patterns of performance for vertically versus horizontally separated features from the three-object displays. Planned comparisons revealed the source of this interaction. For features

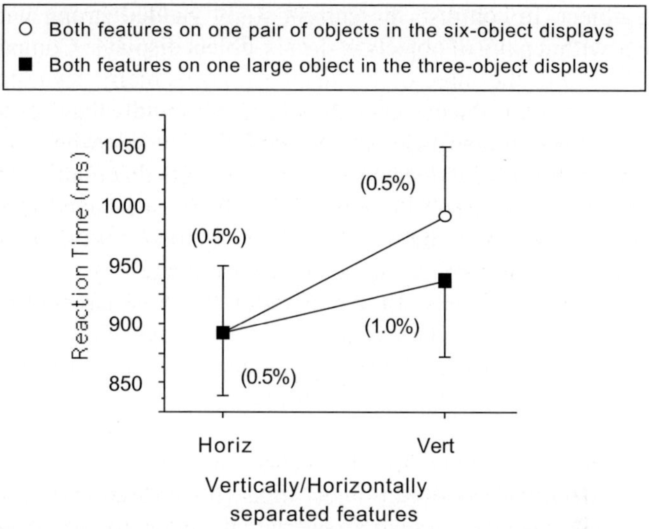

Figure 5. Graph of intersubject means of median RTs for trials where both target features were presented on a single large object in the three-large-object displays (filled symbols) versus on a single pair of small objects in the six-small-object displays (open symbols). The left pair of data points graphs horizontally separated features, the right pair vertically separated features. In the six-object displays, horizontally separated features belonged to the same small object (see Figure 4B), whereas vertically separated features belonged to two different small objects (see Figure 4C). In the three-large-object displays, both horizontally and vertically separated features belonged to the same object (e.g., see Figure 4A). Percentage error rates for each condition are in parentheses.

appearing within a single pair of objects in the six-small-object displays, vertically separated targets (which pertained to two different small objects) were detected more slowly than horizontally separated targets (both of which pertained to the same small object: $t(6) = 5.2, p < .02$. This effect is typical for pairs of objects (see my description of Davis et al., 2000, in the Introduction). However, this advantage for horizontally over vertically separated features did not arise to nearly the same degree in the three-object displays, $t(6) = 1.79$, n.s. Similar analyses of error-rates, which were less than 1% in all conditions, also found no significant main effects or interactions that could threaten my interpretation of the RT data (all Fs < 1).

In all but one aspect, the current study was identical to a previous one described in Davis et al. (in press), but patterns of performance in the two studies were very different. In the six-object displays employed by the Davis et al. study, when both target features appeared on a single "pair" of objects (i.e., two neighbouring objects as in Figures 4B and 4C), a substantial different-object advantage was found. That is, compared to parallel conditions in the three-object displays, vertically separated features belonging to *separate* objects were compared more rapidly than horizontally separated features belonging to the *same* object. In contrast, the current study yielded strong within-object advantages within pairs of objects in the six-object displays: Compared to parallel conditions in the three-object displays, horizontally separated features belonging to the *same* object were compared more rapidly than vertically separated features belonging to different objects. This reversal in the patterns of performance in the six-object displays strongly suggests that relative to the Davis et al. study, between-object links were selectively weakened in the current experiment such that now between-object comparisons were *less* rapid than within-object comparisons: A "same object advantage".

Overall performance was also compared in the three-large-object displays (901 ms, 1% errors) versus the six-small-object displays (932 ms, 1% errors), in a one-way within-subjects ANOVA. This analysis found a near-significant effect of six-object versus three-object displays, $F(1,6)=4.71, p=.07$, suggesting a tendency for three-object displays to be attended more efficiently than six-object displays. Recall that in the Davis et al. (in press) studies, conditions that particularly *strengthen* between-object links (features and objects presented simultaneously) also gave rise to an overall advantage for six-object displays over three-object displays. This advantage was attributed to the greater proportion of between-object links coding six-object displays than three-object displays. On this same logic, conditions that greatly *weaken* between-object links should instead benefit three-object displays over six-object displays, as coding three-object displays would required fewer (weak) between-object links than coding six-object displays. The current study provides evidence in support of this proposal: Evidence for substantial weakening of between-object links is associated with an overall tendency for three-object displays to be more efficiently attended than six-object displays.

DISCUSSION

The stimuli employed in the current study, produced by removal of low spatial frequencies from the Davis et al. (in press) stimuli, seem to have given rise to a selective weakening of between-object binding. This manipulation of spatial frequency distributions within each display would also be expected to weaken the response of magnocellular pathways to the stimuli. The current findings therefore seem to provide a further link between magnocellular processing and between-object binding, providing support for the model of Davis et al. (in press) that proposes between-object binding to be driven by the magnocellular pathway.

As I discussed earlier, models of attention that assume we can attend only to one or four objects at a time, do not seem able to explain several of the findings described in Davis et al. (in press). Rather, only the Davis et al. model seems able to account for both the current data, their own findings, and for several other robust findings in the literature. Additionally their approach can provide an explanation for some intriguing new data presented by Humphreys in the current issue, relating to a recently discovered phenomenon known as "anti-extinction" (Goodwich & Ward, 1997). "Extinction" refers to a failure of some neurological patients with right hemisphere damage to report the presence of objects presented to their left when a second object is presented simultaneously to their right, even though in the absence of other objects they can accurately report left-side objects (see, e.g., Mattingley, Davis, & Driver, 1997). However, "anti-extinction" refers to the converse case, where some patients exhibit *better* coding of the object to their left in the presence of an object to their right, than when the object is presented alone (Goodwich & Ward, 1997). Humphreys demonstrates in his current study both extinction *and* anti-extinction within the same patient. Specifically, when stimuli were presented only briefly to the patient, anti-extinction was found in that the left object was more likely to be noticed when a right-hand object was also presented than when the left stimulus was presented alone. However, when the stimuli were instead presented for longer intervals, the patients ceased to show anti-extinction and began to show extinction; noticing the object to their left *less* often when presented with a right-hand stimulus than when the left stimulus was presented alone.

Humphreys' findings (this issue) seem to indicate that when two objects are presented briefly, it is relatively easy for the patient to attend to and therefore to notice both right- and left-hand objects when they are presented briefly. However, when the objects are presented for longer periods of time, it becomes harder (relative to the baseline of a single object presented on the left) for the patient to attend and thus notice both objects. These effects of duration upon the patient's ability to attend two objects resemble findings described by Davis et al. (in press) for normal observers. In the Davis et al. studies, when the objects were present only briefly before observers' attention could locate and compare target features, Davis and colleagues found that two features from separate objects could be attended and thus compared very rapidly (relative to features from the same object). However, when the objects were presented for a substantial period of time before the features could be attended, observers found it much harder to attend features from two separate objects (relative to features from the same object). Davis et al. concluded that the effects of duration in their task arose due to the binding of features from separate objects ("between-object links") being driven by transient processes in the magnocellular stream of human vision. Such processes would respond most vigorously to briefly presented stimuli (both to their onset and offset) allowing the features of separate objects too be bound together and attended, but would be far less responsive overall to stimuli presented for a prolonged period of time.

A similar explanation could account for Humphreys' new findings (this issue). In each trial where two objects were presented, the patient's attention might be expected to select the right-hand object (due to a rightward spatial bias in their attention). When the stimuli were presented briefly, emphasizing magnocellular responses in guiding attention, such that between-object binding should be strong, the patient's attention should also select the left-hand object due to its features being strongly bound to those of the right-hand object. Such a tendency would predict a relatively good performance in detecting the presence of the left-hand object, as Humphreys found. Conversely, when instead the two objects were presented for a longer period of time, this between-object binding should become weaker as the magnocellular response subsides shortly after the stimuli have been presented. In such a case, due to the weak binding between the features of the right and left objects, the patient's attention should not be expected to spread to the features of the left-hand object, predicting (as Humphreys found) that the patient should tend not to notice the left hand stimulus.

The Davis et al. (in press) account therefore seems to provide a powerful tool for explaining patterns of performance in previous object-based attention studies. As mentioned earlier, this account is very similar to that of Humphreys (1998), which proposed that within-object links in the ventral stream of the visual system (which is primarily driven by the parvocellular pathway) bind together pairs of features belonging to the same object. This part of his account is identical in the Davis et al. proposals. In contrast, Humphreys suggested that their was *no* direct binding between features of the same object, though up to four whole "objects" could be maintained in attention via other binding mechanisms in the dorsal stream (which is driven by the magnocellular pathway). Each one of this latter type of link was proposed to bind together two whole object representations.

The Humphreys (1998) account does not seem well suited to explaining two aspects of the Davis et al. (in press) data. First, when features and objects were presented simultaneously in their tasks, a "different-object advantage" was found. That is, features from different objects were more rapidly compared (presumably due to being more strongly bound together) than were features from the same object. On Humphreys' model, features from the same object are not directly bound together. Rather, in order to compare two features from the same object, these features must first be bound into two separate objects by within-object links, and these "objects" must then be bound to each other by processes in the dorsal stream. That is, a pair of features from two separate objects would have to bound together via two sets of within-object links (one within each object) and via a link between the two objects. On the other hand, features from the same object are bound *directly* together. It is therefore difficult to see how the Humphreys account can ever predict stronger binding of features from separate objects, than from the same object, as Davis et al. (in press) found.

Next, in common with several other authors (e.g., Pylyshyn, 1989), Humphreys (1998) proposed that our attention is limited to four objects at a time. However, as I discussed earlier, such a conclusion is not consistent with the Davis et al. (in press) finding that their six-small-object displays can be attended as efficiently as their three-large-object displays. In contrast, the Davis et al. model proposes that attention is limited by the number and strength of within-object and between-object links formed when attending a stimulus. Such a proposal *is* able to explain the equivalent performance in the six- and three-object displays, due to their comprising a similar number of features overall and thus presumably a similar number of links.

SUMMARY

To conclude, the Davis et al. (in press) proposals seem able to explain several recent findings that are not readily accounted for by previous models of attention, particularly those models that assume we can attend only a fixed number of objects at once (e.g., Duncan et al., 1997; Pylyshyn, 1989). In common with other approaches to understanding the role of feature-binding in guiding visual attention (e.g., Duncan, 1984; Humphreys, 1998), Davis et al. suggested that features from the same "object" are directly bound together in the ventral stream, and that this processing is primarily driven by sustained processes in the parvocellular pathway. However, in contrast to previous studies of visual attention, Davis et al. also concluded that features from nearby/neighbouring objects are also *directly* bound together and that this binding can be stronger than that between features of the same object. They suggested that this latter type of binding may be driven by the magnocellular system, and the current findings provide further evidence for this view.

Here, I employed precisely the same procedure as that used by Davis et al. (in press), but selectively removed low-spatial frequency elements from their stimuli. This manipulation was intended to minimize activation of magnocellular processes, which on the Davis et al. account should also minimize the strength of binding between features from different objects. This manipulation appears to have affected performance in precisely the manner predicted by the Davis et al. model. Whereas under virtually the same conditions, Davis et al. had found evidence for stronger binding of features from different objects than from the same object, my new study now found evidence of very weak binding between features from different objects.

Although the Davis et al. (2000, in press) studies were intended primarily to reveal mechanisms of visual attention, they have also been informative as to the types of binding process that arise in vision. An implicit assumption of many previous studies has been that binding will tend to be stronger within a particular "object" (however this is defined) than between two objects. However, in conjunction with the results reported here, the Davis et al. findings suggested that under some circumstances this is not the case, particularly when magnocellular mechanisms are activated. In future studies I hope to provide further tests of the Davis et al. (in press) model, and to examine how early stages of visual processing can determine which types of binding will be treated as within-object links, and which as between-object links.

REFERENCES

Behrmann M., Zemel, R.S., & Mozer, M.C. (1998). Object-based attention and occlusion: Evidence from normal participants and a computational model. *Journal of Experimental Psychology: Human Perception and Performance, 24*(4), 1–27.

Davis, G., Driver, J., Pavani, F., & Shepherd, A. (2000). Reappraising the apparent costs of attending to two separate visual objects, *Vision Research, 40*(10), 1323–1332.

Davis, G., Welch, V.L., Holmes, A., & Shepherd, A. (in press). Is attention limited to a fixed number of objects?

Duncan, J. (1984). Selective attention and the organisation of visual information. *Journal of Experimental Psychology: General, 113,* 501–517.

Duncan, J., Humphreys, G., & Ward, R. (1997). Competitive brain activity in visual attention. *Current Opinion in Neurobiology, 7*(2), 255–261.

Egly, R., Rafal, R.D., & Driver, J. (1994). Shifting visual attention between objects and locations: Evidence from normal and parietal lesion subjects. *Journal of Experimental Psychology: General, 123,* 161–177.

Elliott, M.A., & Müller, H.J. (1998). Synchronous information presented in 40-Hz flicker enhances visual feature binding. *Psychological Science, 9,* 277–283.

Enns, J.T., & Rensink, R.A. (1992). *Vscope software and manual: Vision testing software for the Macintosh.* Vancouver, Canada: Micropsych Software.

Eriksen, B.A., & Eriksen, C.W. (1974). Effects of noise letters on identification in a nonsearch task. *Perception and Psychophysics, 16,* 143–149.

Goodrich, S.J., & Ward, R. (1997). Anti-extinction following unilateral parietal damage. *Cognitive Neuropsychology, 14*(4), 595–612.

Humphreys, G.W. (1998). Neural representation of objects in space: A dual coding account. *Philosophical Transactions of the Royal Society, Series B—Biological Sciences, 353*(1373), 1341–1351.

Humphreys, G.W. (this issue). A multi-stage account of binding in vision: Neuropsychological evidence. *Visual Cognition, 8*(3/4/5), 381–410.

Lavie, N., & Driver, J. (1996). On the spatial extent of attention in object-based visual selection. *Perception and Psychophysics, 58*(8), 1238–1251.

Livingstone, M.S., & Hubel, D.H. (1988). Segregation of colour, form and depth—anatomy, physiology and perception. *Science, 240*(4853), 740–749.

Mattingley, J.B., Davis, G., & Driver, J. (1997). Preattentive filling-in of visual surfaces in parietal extinction. *Science, 275*(5300), 671–674.

Milner, D.A., & Goodale, M.A. (1995). *The visual brain in action.* Oxford, UK: Oxford University Press.

Pylyshyn, Z. (1989). The role of location indices in spatial perception: A sketch of the FINST spatial-index model. *Cognition, 32,* 65–97.

Usher, M., & Donnelly, N. (1998). Visual synchrony affects binding and segmentation in perception. *Nature, 394,* 179–182.

Watson, S.E., & Kramer, A.F. (1999). Object-based visual selective attention and perceptual organization. *Perception and Psychophysics, 61*(1), 31–49.

VISUAL COGNITION, 2001, *8* (3/4/5), 431–466

Context-sensitive binding by the laminar circuits of V1 and V2: A unified model of perceptual grouping, attention, and orientation contrast*

Rajeev D.S. Raizada and Stephen Grossberg

Department of Cognitive and Neural Systems, Boston University, USA

A detailed neural model is presented of how the laminar circuits of visual cortical areas V1 and V2 implement context-sensitive binding processes such as perceptual grouping and attention. The model proposes how specific laminar circuits allow the responses of visual cortical neurons to be determined not only by the stimuli within their classical receptive fields, but also to be strongly influenced by stimuli in the extra-classical surround. This context-sensitive visual processing can greatly enhance the analysis of visual scenes, especially those containing targets that are low contrast, partially occluded, or crowded by distractors. We show how interactions of feedforward, feedback, and horizontal circuitry can implement several types of contextual processing simultaneously, using shared laminar circuits. In particular, we present computer simulations that suggest how top-down attention and preattentive perceptual grouping, two processes that are fundamental for visual binding, can interact, with attentional enhancement selectively propagating along groupings of both real and illusory contours, thereby showing how attention can selectively enhance object representations. These simulations also illustrate how attention may have a stronger facilitatory effect on low contrast than on high contrast stimuli, and how pop-out from orientation contrast may occur. The specific functional roles which the model proposes for the cortical layers allow several testable neurophysiological predictions to be made. The results presented here simulate only the boundary grouping system of adult cortical architecture. However, we also discuss how this model contributes to a larger neural theory of vision that suggests how intracortical and intercortical feedback help to stabilize development and learning within these cortical

Please address all correspondence to S. Grossberg, 677 Beacon Street, Boston, MA 02215, USA. Email: steve@cns.bu.edu

R.D.S.R. supported in part by the Defense Advanced Research Projects Agency and the Office of Naval Research (ONR N00014-95-1-0409), the National Science Foundation (NSF IRI 97-20333), and the Office of Naval Research (ONR N00014-95-1-0657); S.G. supported in part by the Defense Advanced Research Projects Agency and the Office of Naval Research (ONR N00014-95-1-0409), the National Science Foundation (NSF IRI 94-01659), and the Office of Naval Research (ONR N00014-92-J-1309 and ONR N00014-95-1-0657).

*Technical Report CAS/CNS TR-2000-008.

http://www.tandf.co.uk/journals/pp/13506285.html DOI:10.1080/13506280143000070

circuits. Although feedback plays a key role, fast feedforward processing is possible in response to unambiguous information. Model circuits are capable of synchronizing quickly, but context-sensitive persistence of previous events can influence how synchrony develops. Although these results focus on how the interblob cortical processing stream controls boundary grouping and attention, related modelling of the blob cortical processing stream suggests how visible surfaces are formed, and modelling of the motion stream suggests how transient responses to scenic changes can control long-range apparent motion and also attract spatial attention.

INTRODUCTION: CONTEXTUAL EFFECTS AND BINDING IN VISUAL CORTEX

This paper continues the development of a neural model aimed at providing a unified explanation of how the laminar circuits of visual cortical areas V1 and V2 interact with the LGN to control cortical development, learning, perceptual grouping, and attention (Grossberg, 1999a; Grossberg, Mingolla, & Ross, 1997; Grossberg & Raizada, 2000; Grossberg & Williamson, 2001; Ross, Mingolla, & Grossberg, 2000). In particular, the model has begun to clarify how preattentive and attentive perceptual mechanisms are intimately linked within the laminar circuits of visual cortex, notably how bottom-up, top-down, and horizontal cortical connections interact within the cortical layers. To this end, we quantitatively simulate a number of phenomena about visual contextual processing, contrast-sensitive grouping, and attention to illustrate the model's predictive power. In this regard, it has long been known that a neuron's response to stimuli inside its classical receptive field (CRF) can be strongly influenced by stimuli outside in the surround (e.g., Blakemore & Tobin, 1972; Maffei & Fiorentini, 1976; Nelson & Frost, 1978). Only more recently, however, has the functional importance of these contextual effects for real-world visual processing been widely appreciated (e.g., Allman, Miezin, & McGuinness, 1985; Gilbert & Wiesel, 1990; Grossberg, 1994; Grossberg & Mingolla, 1985; Kapadia, Ito, Gilbert, & Westheimer, 1995; Knierim & Van Essen, 1992; Lamme, 1998; Polat, Mizobe, Pettet, Kasamatsu, & Norcia, 1998; Sillito, Grieve, Jones, Cudeiro, & Davis, 1995; Sugita, 1999; von der Heydt, Peterhans, & Baumgartner, 1984).

A particularly vivid example of a contextual effect is the collinear grouping of oriented stimuli, which enhances the detection of grouped targets (Kapadia et al., 1995; Polat & Sagi, 1993) and of smooth contours (Field, Hayes, & Hess, 1993; Kovacs & Julesz, 1993), and which also gives rise to the percept of illusory contours (Kanizsa, 1979) when the inducing stimuli also cause a brightness difference across the two sides of the collinear group (Grossberg, 1994; Grossberg & Mingolla, 1985). Psychophysical evidence suggests that grouping occurs without the need for top-down attention (Moore & Egeth, 1997). Perceptual grouping mechanisms are particularly needed for detecting targets that are surrounded by distractors or that are of low contrast. The relevance of contrast for such grouping is further illustrated by recent neurophysiological studies of cortical area V1, which have shown that the contextual effects are contrast-dependent, with low-contrast targets being facilitated by collinear flankers, but high-contrast targets being depressed, as shown in Figure 1 (Kapadia, Westheimer, & Gilbert, 1998; Polat et al., 1998).

Top-down attention can also be viewed as a form of contextual processing, in that it plays an important role when a target is surrounded by distractors, but may have much less effect when a target is presented on its own (De Weerd, Peralta, Desimone, & Ungerleider, 1999; Motter, 1993). Attentional effects have been observed throughout visual cortex, including many recent studies of attention in V1 (e.g., Brefczynski & DeYoe, 1999; Ito & Gilbert, 1999; Roelfsema, Lamme, & Spekreijse, 1998; Somers, Dale, Seiffert, & Tootell, 1999; Watanabe, Sasaki, Nielsen, Takino, & Migakawa, 1998). Like collinear grouping, attention also has its greatest facilitatory effect when the target is low contrast, as illustrated in the study by De Weerd et al. (1999; data shown in Figure 2c). Moreover, attention interacts in important ways with other

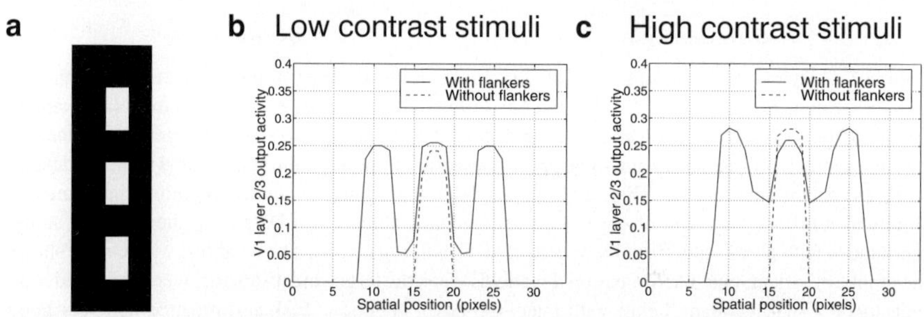

Figure 1. Contrast-dependent perceptual grouping in primary visual cortex, showing how collinear flankers have a net facilitatory effect at low stimulus contrasts, but then "cross over" into being net inhibitory at high contrasts. **(a)** Example stimuli of the sort used by Kapadia et al. (1998), consisting of three bars of equal contrast: a central target bar, and two collinear flankers. The image shown here is an actual stimulus that was presented to the model network. **(b)** Cross-section of V1 layer 2/3 neural activity in the model, in response to low contrast bar stimuli. The solid line shows activity when the target and flankers are presented together, with the responses to each of the bar corresponding to a "hump" of activity in the cross-section. Above-threshold layer 2/3 groupings form between the collinear bars, as shown by the regions of non-zero activity filling the inter-bar spaces. The dotted line shows the neural response to the central target bar alone, presented without any flankers. It can be seen that the target bar elicits more activity when the flankers are present, showing that the grouping has a net facilitatory effect at this low stimulus contrast. **(c)** Same set of V1 layer 2/3 cross-sections as in (b), but now with all three bars presented at high contrast. Strong above-threshold collinear groupings form between the bars, but the net effect of the flankers on the target is nonetheless inhibitory. By "net inhibitory", we mean that the central stimulus elicits a weaker response when the flankers are present than when they are absent, with "net facilitatory" meaning the reverse. Thus, the net facilitatory effect of the flankers in panel (b) can be seen by the fact that the solid with-flankers activity trace is above the dotted without-flankers line. In (c), the relative positions of these two lines have switched, indicating that the flankers have now "crossed over" into being net inhibitory.

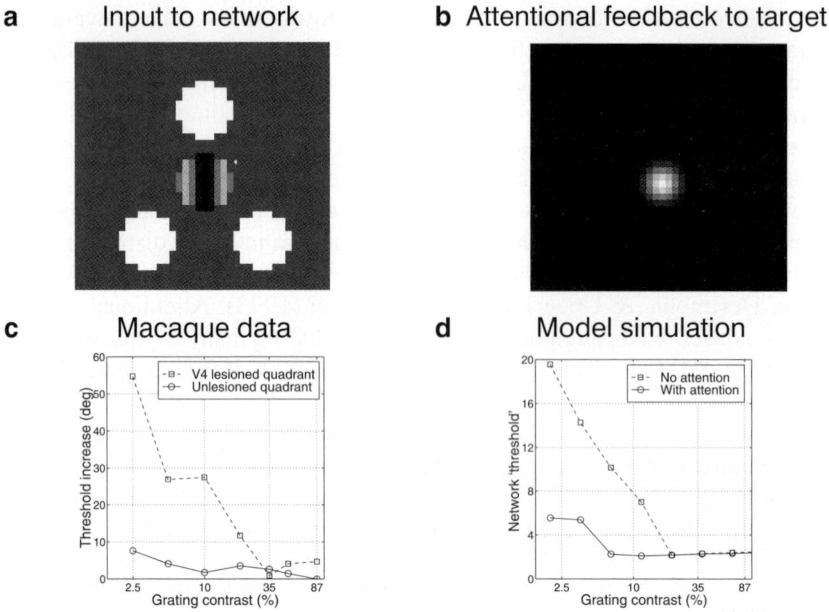

Figure 2. Attention has a stronger facilitatory effect on low contrast stimuli than it does at high contrasts, as shown in the study by De Weerd et al. (1999) and the model's simulation of it. **(a)** Example stimuli of the sort used by De Weerd et al., consisting of a variable-contrast oriented grating surrounded by three distractor discs. The image shown here is an actual stimulus that was presented to the model network. **(b)** Attentional feedback directed in the model to the location of the target grating, implemented simply as a diffuse Gaussian of corticocortical feedback activity. **(c)** Data from the macaque study, reproduced with permission from De Weerd et al. (1999, Figure 3b). The solid line with circles shows the monkeys' orientation discrimination thresholds when the target and distractors were presented in an unlesioned visual quadrant, hence with intact top-down attention. Task performance was very good across all conditions, even when the target grating was very low contrast. The dashed line with squares shows that when the stimuli were presented in a visual quadrant from which V4 had been lesioned, hence impairing top-down attention, task performance was still good at high grating contrasts, but degraded significantly as the contrast reduced. Hence, top-down attention has more of an effect on low contrast stimuli. **(d)** Model simulation of the De Weerd et al. data. In the model, attention can simply be turned on and off, rather than by having to lesion any higher-level cortical areas. Indeed, these higher task-encoding areas, presumably in prefrontal and inferotemporal cortex, are not simulated in the present model, which considers only V1 and V2. Thus, the Gaussian of attention is positioned over the target grating by specifying its coordinates in the simulation computer program, rather than by being steered by a simulated higher cortical area. The network's "behavioural threshold" is simply operationalized as the reciprocal of V1 layer 2/3 oriented activity, since these are the cells that pass information about the grating's orientation forward to higher areas.

contextual effects, in particular with grouping: Attention can spread itself along visual groupings (Davis & Driver, 1997; He & Nakayama, 1995), and can propagate along both real and illusory contours (Moore, Yantis, & Vaughan, 1998; Roelfsema & Spekreijse, 1999), as illustrated later in Figures 4 and 5. We have elsewhere argued that top-down attention and related feedback pathways are mechanisms whereby the cortex can stabilize its initial development and subsequent learning (Grossberg, 1980, 1999a, b; Grossberg & Williamson, 2001).

Another important contextual effect is orientation contrast, in which an element whose orientation differs from that of its neighbours "pops out" from the background. Such effects have been observed psychophysically, and also neurophysiologically in V1 (Knierim & Van Essen, 1992; Nothdurft, 1991; Nothdurft, Gallant, & Van Essen, 1999; Sillito et al., 1995). Like grouping, this mechanism is particularly useful for picking out targets which are surrounded by distractors, as shown for example in Figure 3.

The process of visual binding is very closely related to these contextual processes; it too is needed most when the visual scene is cluttered with distractors.

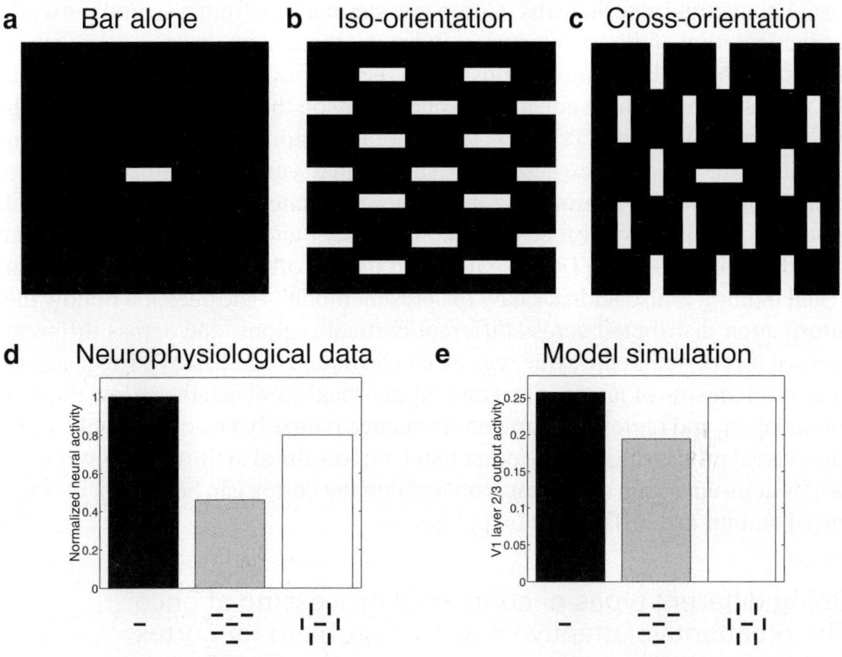

Figure 3. Orientation contrast in V1 and in the neural model. **(a–c)** Stimuli of the sort used by Knierim and Van Essen (1992). The neural responses elicited by an isolated bar are recorded, then compared with responses when the same bar is embedded either in an iso-orientation or cross-orientation texture surround. The images shown here are the actual stimuli that were presented to the model network. **(d)** Neurophysiological data from macaque V1, adapted with permission from Knierim and Van Essen (1992, Figure 10). The icons along the *x*-axis indicate that the stimuli presented were of the sorts shown in (a), (b), and (c) respectively. It can be seen that both sorts of texture surrounds have a suppressive effect on neural activity, compared to when the bar is presented on its own, but that the orthogonal surround produces less suppression. This is consistent with the perceptual effect that the bar seems to "pop-out" from the orthogonal background but not from the iso-orientation surround. **(e)** Model simulation of the orientation contrast effect. It can be seen here too that both kinds of surround have a net inhibitory effect, with the cross-orientation surround being less suppressive.

Indeed, when there is just a single visual element in a display the binding problem cannot arise. It is therefore unsurprising that many experimental studies of binding have concentrated on the effects discussed previously, in particular grouping and attention (for recent reviews, see Gray, 1999, on the relations between binding and Gestalt grouping, and Reynolds & Desimone, 1999, and Treisman, 1999, on binding and attention).

Discussions of the neural processes underlying binding are often somewhat vague. In this paper, we will attempt to address this problem by proposing specific and testable neurophysiological substrates for two visual processes that are fundamental for binding, namely attention and grouping. In particular, we suggest detailed laminar circuits in V1 and V2 for implementing these processes, and propose ways in which they can interact with each and with other visual contextual mechanisms. Computer simulations from a neural network implementation of this architecture will be presented, demonstrating the viability of the proposed scheme and illustrating the details of its operation. Although the model proposed here concentrates primarily on the spatial aspects of binding, rather than possible relations to temporal phenomena such as neural synchronization, it has elsewhere been shown that variants of this model are capable of rapidly synchronizing their emergent states during both perceptual grouping and attentional focusing; see Grossberg and Grunewald (1997) and Grossberg and Somers (1991). An important but often overlooked aspect of visual binding is also addressed by the present model—the question of how the information distributed across different cortical regions, and across different cortical layers within the same region, can be bound together. We suggest specific mechanisms of intercortical and intracortical feedback that allow the different layers and regions of cortex to influence mutually and even synchronize their visual processing. On the other hand, our results also illustrate how a very fast bottom-up sweep of information through the cortex can be sufficient if the visual stimuli are sufficiently unambiguous.

Doing different types of contextual processing at once: The preattentive/attentive interface problem for cortex and for cortical models

The neurophysiological studies mentioned earlier provide compelling evidence that the processes of preattentive perceptual grouping and top-down visual attention coexist within the same cortical areas, namely V1 and V2.

We wish to argue that the ability of the cerebral cortex to implement these different contextual processes all at once, within the same brain areas, is a more non-trivial functional feat than is widely appreciated. In particular, although the individual tasks of implementing attention and perceptual groupings such as illusory contour grouping may, considered separately, be relatively tractable, the task of performing both processes at once within the same cortical circuit raises the difficult problem of distinguishing the preattentive from the attentive, the external from the internal: The cortex must be able to tell the difference between activity that conveys information about objects in the environment as opposed to activity that has arisen purely as a result of top-down cortical processing.

For attention, this problem is as follows: Top-down attention can enhance the firing of cells that are already active, but if it were to produce above-threshold activity in the absence of any bottom-up retinal input, then the brain would be in danger of hallucinating—activity in V1 and V2 gets passed up to higher areas regardless of how it was caused, and these higher areas would have no means of telling the internally and externally created signals apart. It has, in fact, been elsewhere suggested how a breakdown in this process *can* lead to hallucinations, such as during the positive symptoms of schizophrenia (Grossberg, 2000).

Four possible mechanisms would each seem to provide plausible solutions to this problem. However, we will argue that they all fail, and that a more subtle solution utilizing the laminar architecture of cortex must be used instead.

First, it seems that cortex could ensure that top-down attention on its own never produces above-threshold activity simply by keeping attentional feedback very weak. However, numerous physiological studies show that attention can exert extremely powerful effects in visual cortex, for example modulating the activity of MST cells by 113% (Treue & Maunsell, 1996). As well as being strongly facilitatory, attention can also be strongly suppressive, causing neurons to respond weakly even when their receptive fields contain stimuli that would otherwise elicit optimal responses (Reynolds, Chelazzi, & Desimone, 1999).

A second possibility, often adopted by other computational models, would be to make top-down feedback have a purely multiplicative effect on cortical firing (e.g., Neumann & Sepp, 1999), for instance by having feedback act exclusively on NMDA channels, which open only when the post-synaptic cell is active (e.g., Lumer, Edelman, & Tononi, 1997). This would ensure that only already existing activity could be enhanced. However, this possibility fails to account for the fact mentioned earlier that attention can be inhibitory, as well as facilitatory. In particular, there is psychophysical and neurophysiological evidence that attention has a facilitatory on-centre and suppressive off-surround form (Caputo & Guerra, 1998; Downing, 1998; Mounts, 2000; Smith, Singh, & Greenlee, 2000; Vanduffell, Tootell, & Organ, 2000). Moreover, there is evidence that corticocortical feedback axons act on both non-NMDA and NMDA channels (Cauller & Connors, 1994).

The third possible way of solving the preattentive/attentive interface problem would be if the cortex were to enforce the simple rule that only those cells whose CRFs contain visual stimuli should be allowed to be active. However, here the functional difficulties of simultaneously implementing multiple types of contextual processing start to become apparent. This would-be rule is disobeyed by neurons that respond to Kanizsa-type illusory contours. Such neurons give above-threshold responses without having *any* visual stimuli within their CRFs, and are known to exist in V2 (Peterhans & von der Heydt, 1989; von der Heydt et al., 1984) and possibly also in V1 (Nguyen & Lee, 1999). Responses to illusory contours induced by offset gratings have also been found in V1 (Grosof, Shapley, & Hawken 1993; Redies, Crook, & Creutzfeldt, 1986; Sheth, Sharma, Rao, & Sur, 1996). Although the receptive fields of neurons responding to such stimuli are not completely empty, since they contain line endings, they do not contain any stimuli that have the same orientation as the illusory contour itself.

Thus, cortex is faced with the problem of ensuring that top-down attention can have only a modulatory effect on bottom-up stimuli, even though groupings like an illusory contour can generate suprathreshold responses at positions that do not receive bottom-up inputs. A fourth possible solution, then, might be simply to ensure that attentional and perceptual grouping are kept firmly separated in cortical processing. However, as mentioned previously and illustrated in Figures 4 and 5, there exists neurophysiological and psychophysical evidence that attention actually propagates along both real and illusory contour groupings (He & Nakayama, 1995; Moore et al., 1998; Roelfsema et al., 1998; Roelfsema & Spekreijse, 1999). Thus attention and grouping are intimately linked within the same neural circuitry. That is why we refer to this as an *interface* problem. How, then, are their different, even apparently contradictory, properties generated at an appropriately designed cortical interface?

The experiment by Moore et al. (1998) provided a particularly elegant demonstration that attention can flow along illusory contours. They presented subjects with two "pacmen" stimuli which together induced an illusory Kanizsa rectangle. That is, the two pacmen were separated by retinally unstimulated space, but were perceived as jointly forming a single object in virtue of the illusory contours that connected them. Moore et al. then cued attention to one end of the illusory bar by briefly flashing one of the pacmen, and found that the reaction time to a probe stimulus presented at the other end of the bar was improved, showing that the speed-enhancing effect of attention had spread from one side of the illusory contour to the other. In a control condition when the illusory contours were blocked, but all other aspects of the stimuli left the same, the reaction time advantage was now restricted only to the cued pacman inducer. Thus, attention was able to spread across the retinally unstimulated space separating the pacmen if, and only if, they were already joined by a preattentively formed illusory contour grouping. Because attention did not create any new groupings, but merely enhanced ones the inducers had already formed, its preattentive/attentive interface constraint remained unviolated.

Given, then, that the candidate solutions considered above to the preattentive/attentive interface problem all fail, how does the cortex succeed? The

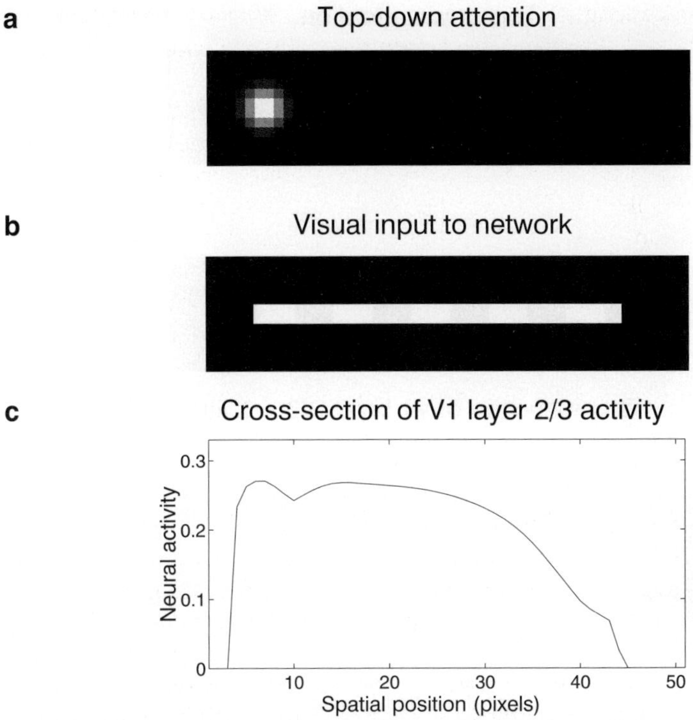

Figure 4. Demonstration of attention flowing along the neural representation of a visual boundary in V1 of the neural model. A similar result was found neurophysiologically by Roelfsema et al. (1998) and Roelfsema and Spekreijse (1999). **(a)** A diffuse Gaussian of top-down attention directed to the end of a line, **(b)**, which was presented as visual input to the model network. **(c)** Cross-section of V1 layer 2/3 activity elicited by the line visual stimulus with the attention directed to the left-most end. Attention can enter layer 2/3 via two routes, both of which render the attentional enhancement subthreshold via a balance of excitation and inhibition. In one route, attentional feedback passes into layer 6, is folded back up into the modulatory on-centre off-surround layer 6 → 4 path, and then passes up into layer 2/3. In the second route, attentional feeds back into in V1 layer 1, where it is collected by the apical dendrites of layer 2/3 pyramidal cells and also by the dendrites of inhibitory interneurons with their soma and axons in layer 2/3 but dendrites in layer 1 (Lund & Wu, 1997). It can be seen that attention enhances the end to which it is directed, but that this enhancement flows along the length of the line beyond the range of the attentional Gaussian itself, gradually decaying over distance. This lateral flow is carried by long-range horizontal axons from pyramidals in layer 2/3. The slight dip in neural activity next to the maximally boosted region at the left-most end is due to the off-surround layer 6 → 4 inhibition which attention also induces.

fact that cortex does indeed succeed in solving the problem is evidenced by the co-existence and mutual interaction within V1 and V2 of the two crucial contextual effects of top-down attention and preattentive perceptual grouping. We suggest that the question of how cortex integrates these diverse and seemingly conflicting tasks is one that must be addressed by any descriptively adequate computational model of contextual processing.

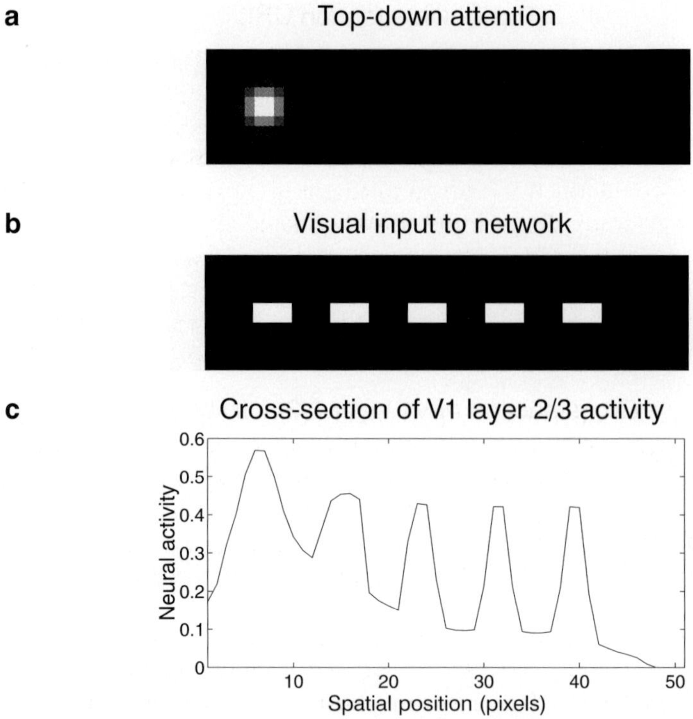

Figure 5. Demonstration of attention flowing along the neural representation of an illusory contour in V1 of the neural model. A similar result was demonstrated psychophysically by Moore et al. (1998). **(a)** A diffuse Gaussian of top-down attention directed to the end of a dotted line, **(b)**, which was presented as visual input to the model network. **(c)** Cross-section of V1 layer 2/3 activity elicited by the dotted line visual stimulus and the attention directed to the left-most end. Note that regions of above-threshold layer 2/3 activity form between the segments of the dotted line, preattentively completing the neural representation of the boundary contour. As in Figure 4, attention flows along the neural representation of the contour, carried by the long-range layer 2/3 horizontal axons linking pyramidal cells, which are firing above-threshold. Note that without the preattentive completion of the layer 2/3 boundary representation, attention on its own would have been able only to provide a subthreshold prime to the neurons whose classical receptive fields fall on the gaps in the dotted line. The attentional enhancement extends well beyond the range of the top-down feedback Gaussian itself.

We now present a neural model of V1 and V2, which proposes a specific solution to this problem using known properties of cortical laminar design, and which shows in computer simulations how the contextual effects of attention, perceptual grouping, and orientation contrast can all be simultaneously implemented. The model builds on and extends previous work presented in Grossberg (1999a), Grossberg et al. (1997), and Grossberg and Raizada (2000).

MODEL NEURAL NETWORK

The laminar architecture of the present model is constructed out of two fundamental building blocks: an on-centre off-surround circuit running from layer 6 to layer 4, and intrinsic horizontal connections in layer 2/3 which perform collinear integration and perceptual grouping. Each of these two subcircuits has assigned to it a well-defined functional role, and is constructed from model neurons with empirically determined connectivity and physiological properties, as summarized in Table 1. When these building blocks are connected together according to the known anatomy of V1 and V2, as shown in Figure 6, a cortical network is formed whose properties can be understood from the interactions of the functional subcircuits, but whose behaviour is much richer than that of any subcircuit taken individually.

Attention in the model is mediated by a new mechanism that we call *folded feedback* (Grossberg, 1999a), whereby signals from higher cortical areas, and also the V1 supragranular layers, pass down into V1 layer 6 and are then "folded" back up into the feedforward stream by passing through the layer 6 → 4 on-centre off-surround path (Figure 6b), thus giving attention an on-centre off-surround form, enhancing attended stimuli and suppressing those that are ignored.

A key prediction of the model is that the on-centre of the 6 → 4 path is modulatory (or priming, or subthreshold), consistent with the finding that layer 4 EPSPs elicited by layer 6 stimulation are much weaker than those caused by stimulation of LGN axons or of neighbouring layer 4 sites (Stratford, Tarczy-Hornoch, Martin, Bannister, & Jack, 1996), and also with the fact that binocular layer 6 neurons synapse onto monocular layer 4 cells of both eye types without reducing these cells' monocularity (Callaway, 1998, p. 56). We suggest that the on-centre excitation is inhibited down into being modulatory by the overlapping and broader off-surround. Thus, although the centre excitation is weak, the suppressive effect of the off-surround inhibition can be strong. Because attentional excitation passes through the 6 → 4 path, it inherits this path's properties: The attentional on-centre is modulatory, able to enhance existing activity but only slightly to elevate neurons' baseline firing rates in the absence of visual input (Luck, Chelazzi, Hillyard, & Desimone, 1997), but the off-surround can select strongly against unattended stimuli. The model would still be supported if weak suprathreshold excitatory responses in layer 4 could be created by layer 6 stimulation, as long as these responses meet the crucial condition that they be too weak to cause suprathreshold groupings to occur within the horizontal connections of layer 2/3.

Several routes exist through which feedback from higher cortex can reach V1 layer 6, as shown in Table 1. Figure 6b illustrates the route whereby feedback signals pass into layer 1, where the majority of V2 feedback axons terminate (Rockland & Virga, 1989), and then stimulate the apical dendrites of layer

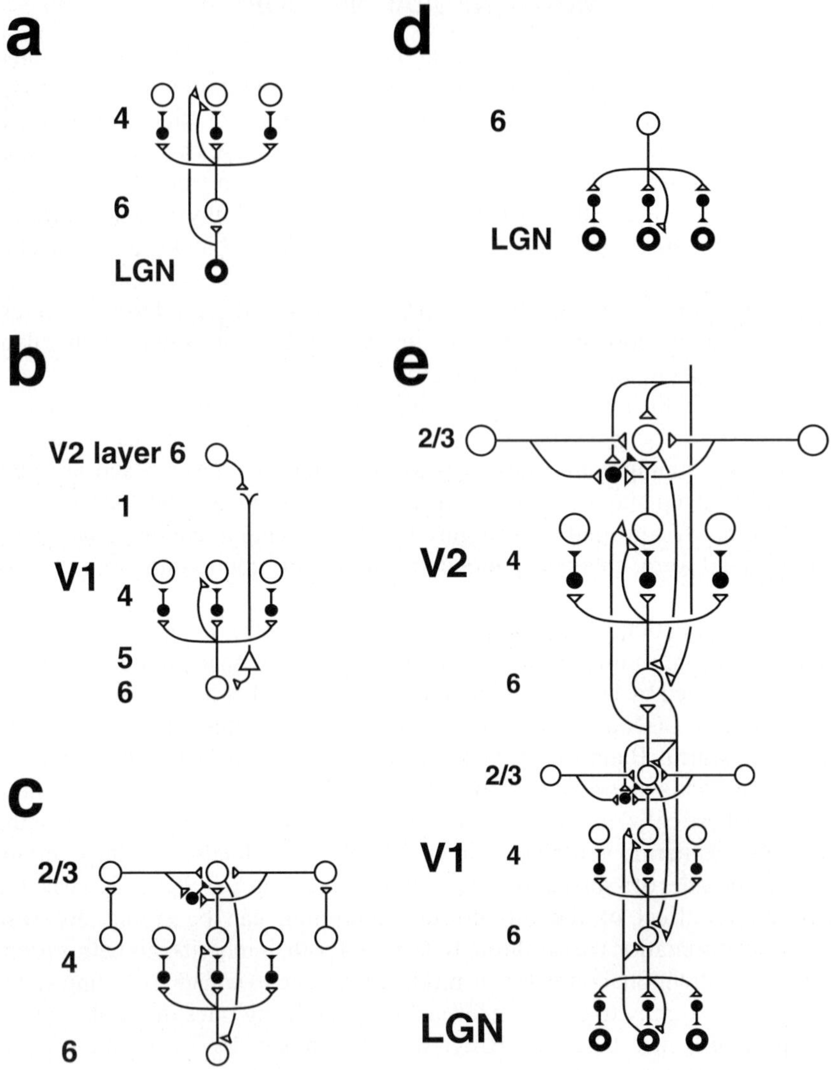

Figure 6. How known cortical connections join the layer 6 → 4 and layer 2/3 building blocks to form the entire V1/V2 laminar model. Inhibitory interneurons are shown filled in. **(a)** The LGN provides bottom-up activation to layer 4 via two routes. First, it makes a strong connection directly into layer 4. Second, LGN axons send collaterals into layer 6, and thereby also activate layer 4 via the 6 → 4 on-centre off-surround path. Thus, the combined effect of the bottom-up LGN pathways is to stimulate layer 4 via an on-centre off-surround, which provides divisive contrast normalization (Grossberg, 1973, 1980; Heeger, 1992) of layer 4 cell responses (see Appendix). **(b)** Folded feedback carries attentional signals from higher cortex into layer 4 of V1, via the modulatory 6 → 4 path. Corticocortical feedback axons tend preferentially to originate in layer 6 of the higher area and to terminate in the lower cortex's layer 1 (Salin & Bullier, 1995, p. 110), where they can excite the apical dendrites of layer 5 pyramidal cells

(continued opposite)

5 pyramidal cells whose axons send collaterals into layer 6 (Gilbert & Wiesel, 1979; Lund & Boothe, 1975), where the attentional signals are "folded" back up into the 6 → 4 on-centre off-surround. Reversible deactivation studies of monkey V2 have shown that feedback from V2 to V1 does indeed have an on-centre off-surround form (Bullier et al., 1996), and moreover that the V1 layer whose activation is most reduced by cutting off V2 feedback is layer 6 (Sandell & Schiller, 1982).

We suggest that the mechanism of folded feedback is also used to help select the final layer 2/3 grouping. If the visual information coming into the brain is unambiguous, then the correct groupings could, in principle, form due to the first incoming wave of activation across layer 2/3 horizontal connections. However, in response to scenes or images with multiple grouping possibilities, the initial groupings that are formed in layer 2/3 may need to be pruned to select those that are correct. Like attentional signals from higher cortex, the groupings that start to form in layer 2/3 also feed back into the 6 → 4 path (Figure 6c), to enhance their own positions in layer 4 via the 6 → 4 on-centre, and to suppress input to other groupings via the 6 → 4 off-surround. There exist direct layer 2/3 → 6 connections in macaque V1, as well as indirect routes via layer 5 (Table 1). This competition between layer 2/3 groupings, via layer 2/3 → 6 → 4 → 2/3 feedback, causes the strongest groupings to be selected, while it suppresses weaker groupings, ungrouped distractors, and noise. The interlaminar feedback also binds the cortical layers together into functional columns.

---

whose axons send collaterals into layer 6 (the triangle in the figure represents such a layer 5 pyramidal cell). Several other routes through which feedback can pass into V1 layer 6 exist (see Table 1 for references). Having arrived in layer 6, the feedback is then "folded" back up into the feedforward stream by passing through the 6 → 4 on-centre off-surround path (Bullier, Hupé, James, & Girard, 1996). **(c)** Connecting the 6 → 4 on-centre off-surround to the layer 2/3 grouping circuit: like-oriented layer 4 simple cells with opposite contrast polarities compete (not shown) before generating half-wave rectified outputs that converge onto layer 2/3 complex cells in the column above them. Like attentional signals from higher cortex, groupings that form within layer 2/3 also send activation into the folded feedback path, to enhance their own positions in layer 4 beneath them via the 6 → 4 on-centre, and to suppress input to other groupings via the 6 → 4 off-surround. There exist direct layer 2/3 → 6 connections in macaque V1, as well as indirect routes via layer 5 (Table 1). **(d)** Top-down corticogeniculate feedback from V1 layer 6 to LGN also has an on-centre off-surround anatomy, similar to the 6 → 4 path. The on-centre feedback selectively enhances LGN cells that are consistent with the activation that they cause (Sillito, Jones, Gerstein, & West, 1994), and the off-surround contributes to length-sensitive (endstopped) responses that facilitate grouping perpendicular to line ends. **(e)** The entire V1/V2 circuit: V2 repeats the laminar pattern of V1 circuitry, but at a larger spatial scale. In particular, the horizontal layer 2/3 connections have a longer range in V2, allowing above-threshold perceptual groupings between more widely spaced inducing stimuli to form (Amir, Harel, & Malach, 1993). V1 layer 2/3 projects up to V2 layers 6 and 4, just as LGN projects to layers 6 an 4 of V1. Higher cortical areas send feedback into V2 which ultimately reaches layer 6, just as V2 feedback acts on layer 6 of V1 (Sandell & Schiller, 1982). Feedback paths from higher cortical areas straight into V1 (not shown) can complement and enhance feedback from V2 into V1.

TABLE 1

Connection in model	*Functional interpretation*	*Selected references*
LGN → 4	Strong oriented LGN input	Blasdel and Lund (1983), Ferster et al. (1996, cat)
LGN → 6	LGN input sharpened by 6 → 4 on centre off-surround	Blasdel and Lund (1983)
6 → 4 spiny stellates	Modulatory on-centre of the 6 → 4 on-centre off-surround	Stratford et al. (1996, cat), Callaway (1998, p. 56)
6 → 4 inhibitory interneurons	Off-surround of the 6 → 4 on-centre off-surround	McGuire et al. (1984, cat), Ahmed et al. (1997, cat)
4 inhib.int → 4 inhib.int.	Context-dependent normalization of off-surround inhibition	Ahmed et al. (1997, cat), Tamas et al. (1998, cat)
4 → 2/3 pyramidals	Feedforward of stimuli with bottom-up support	Fitzpatrick et al. (1985), Callaway and Wiser (1996)
2/3 pyr. → 2/3 pyr	Long-range collinear integration along RF axes	Bosking et al. (1997, shrew), Schmidt et al. (1997, cat)
2/3 pyr. → 2/3 inhib.int.	Keep outward grouping subthreshold (Bipole property)	McGuire et al. (1991), Hirsch and Gilbert (1991, cat)
2/3 inhib.int → 2/3 inhib.int.	Normalize 2/3 inhibition (2-against-1 part of bipole property)	Tamas et al. (1998, cat)
V1 2/3 pyr. → V2 layer 4	Feedforward of V1 boundary groupings into V2	Van Essen et al. (1986), Rockland and Virga (1990)
V1 2/3 pyr. → V2 layer 6	Feedforward V1 groupings into V2 6 → 4 on centre off-surround	Van Essen et al. (1986, p. 470)
V1 layer 6 → LGN	Modulatory on-centre off-surround feedforward	Sillito et al. (1994, cat), Montero (1991, cat)
Feedback routes into V1 layer 6		
V2 layer 6 → V1 layer 1	Standard intercortical laminar feedback (Salin & Bullier, 1995, p. 110)	Rockland and Virga (1989)
1 → 6 (within a layer 5 pyr.)	Corticocortical fdbk into 6: Lay 5 pyr., apic.dend. in 1, axon in 6.	Lund and Boothe (1975, Fig. 7), Gilbert and Wiesel (1979, cat)
V2 (unknown layer) → V1 layer 6	Direct corticocortical feedback into V1 layer 6	Gattass et al. (1997, Fig. 4)
2/3 → 6	Boundary grouping feedback into 6 → 4 on-centre off-surround	Blasdel et al. (1985, Fig. 13), Kisvarday et al. (1989, Fig. 7)
1→ 5	Corticocortical fdbk into 5: Lay 5 pyr. with apic.dend. in 1	Valverde (1985, Fig. 24o), Peters and Sethares (1991, p. 7)
2/3 → 5	Part of indirect 2/3 → 6	Lund and Boothe (1975, Fig. 8), Callaway and Wiser (1996)
5 → 6	Continuation of indirect routes into 6, via 5	Blasdel et al. (1985, Fig. 17), Kisvarday et al. (1989, Fig. 7)

All references are to macaque monkeys unless otherwise noted.

The fact that both attention and perceptual grouping share the properties of enhancing weak stimuli, and of suppressing signals from nearby rival inputs, can thus be parsimoniously explained by the hypothesis that both processes share the $6 \rightarrow 4$ folded feedback path. This laminar architecture also resolves the preattentive-attentive interface problem described previously, since despite their shared properties and coexistence side by side within V1 and V2, attention and grouping behave quite differently in parts of visual space where there is no bottom-up visual stimulus. Above-threshold boundary groupings *can* form over regions with no bottom-up support, e.g., illusory contours. These groupings form in layer 2/3. However, the only way top-down attentional signals can enter layer 2/3 is by first passing through a pathway in which a balance of overlapping excitation and inhibition damps down the attentional feedback into being subthreshold, or priming. Thus, attention can only modulate layer 2/3, but cannot on its own cause above-threshold activation, and its internal/external problem is thereby resolved.

In the earlier version of this model presented in Grossberg and Raizada (2000), the only pathway via which attention could enter layer 2/3 was the folded-feedback layer $6 \rightarrow 4 \rightarrow 2/3$ circuit described earlier. Since the majority of feedback axons from higher cortical areas terminate in V1 layer 1 (Rockland & Virga, 1989), we also discussed the possibility that attentional signals may modulate layer 2/3 more directly by stimulating the layer 1 apical dendrites of layer 2/3 pyramidals. Lund and Wu (1997) have shown that there exist inhibitory interneurons in layer 2/3 macaque V1 that also have dendrites in layer 1. Hence, we suggested that there may also exist a balance of excitation and inhibition keeping this direct attentional path into layer 2/3 modulatory, or subthreshold, just as the layer $6 \rightarrow 4$ off-surround overlaps with and balances $6 \rightarrow 4$ the on-centre. Going beyond this earlier paper, we have now implemented these connections in the present simulations (see equations 20 and 21 in the Appendix). As will be discussed later, the extended model incorporating these anatomical connections is still able to keep top-down feedback's facilitatory effect within layer 2/3 purely modulatory.

The notion of activity being subthreshold, or modulatory, is given a simple instantiation in the model's equations: Layer 2/3 activity below a fixed value, Γ, produces no output from the cells in that layer. When the input activity starts to exceed Γ, the output starts to climb from zero at the same rate, as described in equation 13 (see Appendix). In both V1 and V2, Γ was fixed at 0.2 for all the simulations performed. Because this layer 2/3 signal function is continuous, and gives the output the same gain as the input, the behaviour of the network changes continuously and predictably if Γ is changed: Smaller values would tend to allow stronger layer 2/3 bipole groupings to form, for example allowing V1 groupings to bridge over slightly larger visual gaps than otherwise. Larger values would tend slightly to weaken the groupings, and to mean that larger top-down attention signals would be required to influence the groupings that do form.

We also extend the network dynamics of the model presented in Grossberg and Raizada (2000) in another respect. In that study, we showed how the model could simulate the finding by Polat et al. (1998) that neurons in cat V1 responding to a low-contrast target Gabor stimulus are net facilitated by the presence of collinear flanking Gabor patches, but when the target is high-contrast, the effect of the flankers "crosses over" into being net inhibitory. The simulation in the Grossberg and Raizada (2000) paper showed that a long-range range V2 grouping between the flanking elements fed back a subthreshold prime to the V1 location of the central target Gabor, facilitating it by raising it above threshold at low-contrasts. However, shunting $6 \rightarrow 4$ inhibition from the flankers also had a divisive effect on neural responses to the target, lowering their gain and causing the net effect of the flankers to be suppressive at high-target contrasts. Thus, this simulation showed how contrast-dependent perceptual grouping can emerge as a result of network behaviour, without needing to take into account possible differential effects of contrast on individual excitatory and inhibitory neurons.

Substantial neurophysiological evidence exists, however, showing that at high stimulus contrasts, inhibition starts to predominate over excitation as a combined result of several diverse factors: Inhibitory interneurons have higher gains than excitatory pyramidal cells at high contrast (McCormick, Connors, Lighthall, & Prince, 1985), inhibitory synapses depress less than excitatory synapses (Varela, Song, Turrigiano, & Nelson, 1999), with synapses from inhibitory interneurons onto pyramidals in fact actively facilitating (Markram, Wang, & Tsodyks, 1998; Reyes et al., 1998; Thomson, 1997). This complex mixture of pre- and post-synaptic factors cannot be completely captured without greatly complicating the existing model; we approximate the total net effect on inhibition by passing the population inhibitory activity through a sigmoidal signal function, as shown in equations 16 and 17 (see Appendix). This signal function starts off at low values, and then rapidly increases as higher contrast stimuli cause greater levels of inhibitory activation. Since the network pyramidals gradually saturate at increasing contrasts, the net effect is for inhibition to start to predominate (cf. Grossberg, 1970; Grossberg & Kelly, 1999; Somers et al., 1998; Stemmler, Usher, & Niebur, 1995). By extending the previous model in this way, the model can capture an even wider range of contrast-sensitive grouping effects. An example is the simulation of recent data from Kapadia et al. (1998) presented in Figure 1.

RESULTS

The model presented here captures several aspects of visual contextual processing. The following simulations and explanations illustrate how the laminar architecture of cortex brings about this behaviour.

Attention has a greater effect on low-contrast stimuli

As was remarked in the introduction, top-down attention is needed most when a visual target is of low salience due to being surrounded by distractors, or being of low contrast. It would therefore be functionally advantageous for attention to provide a strong boost to low contrast targets, but to have a relatively weaker effect at high contrasts. This is exactly what was observed in the recent behavioural study of macaque monkeys by De Weerd et al. (1999). The monkeys' task was to discriminate the orientation of a variable-contrast grating patch that was surrounded by distractors. Stimuli of this sort were presented to the model network, as shown in Figure 2a. De Weerd et al. placed the stimuli in either an unlesioned visual quadrant, or ones in which lesions had been made to cortical areas V4 or TEO, both of which are known to play important roles in visual attention. Their finding, illustrated in Figure 2c, was that the absence of these attentional regions severely impaired the monkeys' performance when the target grating was low contrast, but had relatively little effect when the target was high contrast. As can be seen from Figure 2d, the model simulation produces very similar behaviour. Here, the "behavioural threshold" of the network is simply operationalized as the reciprocal of the activity of the V1 layer 2/3 cells that respond to vertical orientations. Because the model only simulates V1 and V2, rather than higher areas such as prefrontal cortex, which presumably control the behavioural responses made by the macaque, the network does not literally have a "behavioural threshold". However, the layer 2/3 neurons that respond to vertical orientations are the cells that would pass forward information about the grating's orientation to higher areas. The greater the activity of these cells, the stronger and hence the more discriminable is the information passed forward. Since high discriminability would result in a low behavioural threshold, and vice versa, the simplest way of embodying this process in an equation is to take the reciprocal. Instead of having to lesion higher cortical areas, we are able simply to turn attention on and off in the model; attention is implemented as a diffuse Gaussian of unoriented cortical feedback directed to the target's location.

In the model, attention aids discrimination by boosting the neural representation of the target through the layer $6 \rightarrow 4$ on-centre, and also via the direct attentional projection into layer 2/3. It also suppresses the distractors, which fall into attention's layer $6 \rightarrow 4$ off-surround. However, these facts alone are not enough to explain why attention facilitates the lower contrast targets more than the high contrast ones. This behaviour follows from two closely related network phenomena: shunting inhibition and neural saturation. High-contrast stimuli induce strong $6 \rightarrow 4$ on-centre excitation at their own locations, but also bring with them divisive shunting inhibition from the overlapping $6 \rightarrow 4$ off-surround, thereby reducing their own contrast gain. Hence, lower contrast stimuli have higher gain and can therefore be boosted more by attention. Similarly, the simple fact of neural saturation means that cells which are firing far below their maximal rate can be significantly boosted by attention, but cells that are pushed close to saturation by high contrast stimuli cannot.

Orientation contrast

Another important contextual effect exhibited by the model network is orientation contrast, in which stimuli that are embedded in orthogonally oriented texture surrounds are seen to "pop-out", whereas stimuli in iso-orientation surrounds do not (Knierim & Van Essen, 1992; Nothdurft, 1991; Northdurft et al., 1999; Sillito et al., 1995). This perceptual effect is reflected in the activity of V1 neurons: Although both iso- and cross-orientation surrounds have a net suppressive effect on the neural response to an isolated bar, the cross-orientation surround is significantly less suppressive (Knierim & Van Essen, 1992; data shown in Figure 3d). Examples of the types of stimuli used by Knierim & Van Essen are shown in Figure 3a–c. These images were in fact presented as stimuli to the model network. As shown in Figure 3e, model V1 neurons exhibit the same qualitative pattern of behaviour. The explanation for this is simply that in the model, layer $6 \rightarrow 4$ iso-orientation off-surround inhibition is stronger than the cross-orientation inhibition. The key question is: How did the inhibition come to be that way? The relative strengths of the iso- and cross-orientation inhibitory projective fields were not specified by hand, but instead were self-organized in the developmental laminar model of Grossberg and Williamson (2001), which used the same laminar architecture as the present model, but without the corticocortical attentional connections. In the course of that model's self-organizing development, the synapses tracked the statistics of visual inputs that were presented to the network. These inputs contained visual structure, in particular straight edges, which caused iso-orientation correlations between neurons positioned along the length of the edge. The inhibitory synapses tracked these iso-orientation correlations, with the result that the iso-orientation inhibition grew stronger than that for cross-orientations.

Attention flows along real and illusory contours

As remarked in the Introduction, the ability of attention to flow along real and illusory contours places important constraints on visual cortical processing. Attention must be able to flow along contour groupings that are already preattentively active, but cannot cause above-threshold activity on its own. The fact that attention does indeed flow along groupings is no mere epiphenomenon, but is the key mechanism uniting spatial and object-based attention in early visual cortex. In particular, attention can thereby selectively enhance an entire object by propagating along its boundaries.

Grossberg and Raizada (2000) simulated the study by Roelfsema et al. (1998), including the delayed time-course of attentional enhancement, caused by the time needed for attention to propagate along the representation of the curve. Here we show in more detail the spatial spread of attention along a real or illusory curve, illustrated in Figures 4 and 5. In both cases, a Gaussian of diffuse attentional feedback directed to one end of a line stimulus causes excitation that does not just boost the directly attended location, but also spreads along some of the length of the line, even when the line is physically discontinuous but perceived as forming a collinear grouping (see Figure 5).

This lateral spread of attentional excitation is carried by the long-range horizontal connections in layer 2/3 of V1 and V2. As described earlier in this section, later, there exist two routes by which attention can get into layer 2/3. The main route is that attention passes into layer 6, is then folded back up into the layer 6 → 4 on-centre off-surround path, where the balance between the on-centre excitation and the overlapping off-surround inhibition ensures that the attentional enhancement that can then feed on into layer 2/3 is purely subthreshold. The second route is the direct attentional connection into layer 2/3, illustrated in Figure 6e and described in equations 20 and 21 (see Appendix). The model layer 2/3 contains inhibitory interneurons as well as excitatory pyramidal cells, in order to control the formation of groupings through layer 2/3 horizontal connections, and the attentional feedback synapses onto both of them, again providing a balance of suppressive and facilitatory forces, which ensures that attentional enhancement remains subthreshold. Although this subthreshold signal would on its own be unable fully to activate layer 2/3, it can none the less boost preattentively formed collinear groupings that form along the line stimuli, and, in the case of the dotted line, bridge over the gaps of retinally unstimulated space. Note that in both cases, the attentional enhancement gradually declines with distance from the attention focus, due to decay of neural activity. The rate of fall-off with distance is smaller in V2 than in V1, due to the longer-range layer 2/3 horizontal connections found in the higher area (Amir et al., 1993).

Contrast-sensitive grouping and inhibition

Contextual effects can be either facilitatory or inhibitory, depending on stimulus contrast. In particular, the effect of collinear flankers on a target can "crossover" from being net excitatory at low contrasts to being net suppressive at high-contrasts, either when the central target alone varies in contrast (Polat et al., 1998), or when the target and flankers all vary in contrast together. As discussed earlier in this section, several pre- and post-synaptic factors may contribute to the predominance of inhibition over excitation at higher stimulus contrasts, although network-level effects alone can be sufficient to account for the Polat et al. (1998) data, as shown in our previous paper (Grossberg & Raizada, 2000).

Figure 1 shows a crossover effect using three bars of equal contrast, as demonstrated experimentally by Kapadia et al. (1998). The flanking bars exert both excitatory and inhibitory effects on the central target. At low contrasts, the layer $6 \rightarrow 4$ inhibitory sigmoidal signal function still takes low values, and inhibition is weaker than the collinear layer 2/3 excitation, giving a net facilitatory effect (Figure 1b). At higher stimulus contrasts, the total amount of inhibition starts to fall into the rapidly growing section of the sigmoidal inhibitory signal function, allowing inhibition from the flankers to overwhelm the excitation that they also supply, making their net effect suppressive (Figure 1c).

DISCUSSION

The neural model presented here shows how visual cortex can implement several types of contextual processing at once, and also allow them to interact. In doing so, it builds upon and extends the simulations presented in Grossberg et al. (1997), Grossberg and Raizada (2000), and Grossberg and Williamson (2001). Moreover, the model proposes specific functional roles for known laminar circuits to carry out the contextual processing, and suggests how attention and perceptual grouping can interact within this laminar circuitry to solve the preattentive/attentive interface problem.

As far as we are aware, no other existing model meets the challenge of this problem by attempting to emulate cortex's ability to perform attention and perceptual grouping simultaneously. Whereas the functional importance of top-down attention is clear, the formation of illusory contours may at first sight appear to be an almost epiphenomenal consequence of the seemingly more fundamental process of collinear facilitation. However, illusory contours can perform a crucial task that mere facilitation cannot: They can actively close incomplete boundaries, a process that requires that cells with unstimulated CRFs can nonetheless become active. This boundary closure can guide surface reconstruction, complete boundaries over visual gaps caused by the blind-spot and retinal veins, and also provide enhanced information for the recognition of partially occluded objects (Grossberg, 1994). Several other models of collinear grouping in V1 produce facilitation but not illusory contours, and hence are unable to capture this important aspect of cortical processing (Li, 1998; Sommers et al., 1998; Stemmler et al., 1995; Yen & Finkel, 1998). Those models that do implement illusory contours either leave out any consideration top-down cortical feedback (Heitger, von der Heydt, Peterhans, Rosenthaler, & Kubler, 1998; Williams & Jacobs, 1997), fail to capture the on-centre off-surround form of attention by treating top-down feedback as having a purely excitatory multiplicative effect (Neumann & Sepp, 1999), or treat "re-entrant" feedback signals from higher areas "as if they were signals from real contours in the periphery entering via 4Cα" (Finkel & Edelman, 1989, p. 3197), thereby creating the risk of perceptual hallucinations. Conversely, many models of top-down feedback in visual processing do not implement perceptual grouping (e.g., Harth, Unnikrishnan, & Pandya, 1987; Mumford, 1992; Olshausen, Anderson, & Van Essen, 1993; Rao & Ballard, 1999; Tsotsos et al., 1995; Ullman, 1995; Usher & Niebur, 1996) therefore leaving untouched what we suggest are crucial design constraints that shape the functional laminar architecture of cortex.

In our previous paper (Grossberg & Raizada, 2000), we presented simulations of the earlier version of this model, which differed from the present one only in lacking the direct attentional connections into layer 2/3, and the layer 6 → 4 inhibitory signal function. Three types of behaviour were simulated in the earlier paper: attention protecting a target from the suppressive effect of flankers (Reynolds et al., 1999), the time-course of attention flow along a curve (Roelfsema et al., 1998), and contrast-sensitive perceptual grouping of Gabor patches (Polat et al., 1998). As can be seen from the simulations presented in the current paper, these properties still hold in the extended version of the model, although here they are applied to different, but related, sets of stimuli. Thus, the new extensions to the model maintain and extend its previous qualitative patterns of behaviour, although the exact quantitative behaviour is not identical, due to the addition of the new circuitry.

These modelling results also bear upon other issues concerning cortical coding. For example, in response to unambiguous visual information, a boundary grouping can start to form very rapidly in response to a feedforward sweep of signal from layer 4 to layer 2/3. Thus the existence of cortical feedback does not preclude fast cortical processing (Thorpe, Fize, & Marlot, 1996). Intracortical feedback is predicted to become increasingly important when multiple groupings of the image or scene are possible. Even here, the model's selection of a final grouping can often converge within one or at most a few feedback cycles between layers 4 → 2/3 → 6 → 4. Intercortical feedback may be needed when attention must select some cue combinations over others, based on higher-order constraints. The model shows how very high-order constraints can, in principle, modulate even low-order feature detectors by propagating across multiple cortical regions via their layers 6, without ever fully activating their groupings in layer 2/3. An open experimental question concerns whether and how such a propagating priming effect is attenuated as a function of the number of cortical regions that are traversed. It has also been simulated how these grouping and attentional circuits may rapidly synchronize, even generating fast synchronizing oscillations under some conditions (Grossberg & Grunewald, 1997; Grossberg & Somers, 1991).

All of these statements require qualification, however. For example, the context-dependent persistence of previously grouped images may interfere with the synchrony of subsequent groupings, as illustrated by the model of

Francis, Grossberg, and Mingolla (1994). Also, the fact that attention-induced increases in firing rate can propagate along perceptual groupings (see Figures 4 and 5), thereby selectively enhancing object representations, shows that synchronous activation of an object by attention is not necessary in all cases (Roelfsema et al., 1998). Finally, one needs to emphasize that all the explanations and simulations presented previously, and those in earlier papers about this evolving cortical model, concern only processing of visual boundaries within the interblob stream of visual cortex, as opposed to the processing of surface brightness and colour within the blob stream. Boundary groupings within the interblob stream are predicted, in the absence of surface featural information, to be invisible, or amodal. Hence, all of the results in this series of papers strictly concern only the salience of boundary groupings, not the perception of the surfaces that these boundaries enclose. Visibility is predicted to be a property of surface representations within the blob stream, with these surfaces arising due to the filling-in of brightness and colour within closed boundary groupings formed in the interblob stream (Grossberg, 1994). Whereas contour salience and visibility often covary, this is not always the case: For example, Glass patterns (Glass, 1969) contain highly salient concentric contour groupings, but do not induce any brightness differences that would cause bright Ehrenstein-like circular surfaces to be visible. Another limitation of the present model is that it does not describe how transient responses to changing or moving stimuli can rapidly attract visual attention. One major pathway for this mechanism is likely to be the "where" dorsal cortical stream. Recent models of motion processing clarify the key role of these transient responses (Baloch, Grossberg, Mingolla, & Nogueira, 1999; Chey, Grossberg, & Mingolla, 1997, 1998), and also how they can attract visual attention (Grossberg, 1998).

Several studies providing important data on grouping and also attention in V1 have recently been carried out by Charles Gilbert and colleagues. In particular, Kapadia et al. (1998) used oriented line stimuli of the sort shown in Figure 1a to investigate the spatial arrangement of contextual facilitation and inhibition induced by flanking lines which were of the same orientation as the target. They found that the flankers were facilitatory when they were placed to be approximately collinear with the target line, but were inhibitory when they were located to its sides. In the present model, stimuli induce a pool of layer 6 $\rightarrow$ 4 off-surround inhibition around them which extends in all directions, as shown in Figure 7, and also induce a more strongly anisotropic region of layer 2/3 facilitation, oriented primarily collinearly with the stimulus itself (Figure 8). These regions of facilitation and inhibition spatially overlap. However, the collinear excitation at the ends of an oriented line can be strong enough to overwhelm the inhibition that is also generated there, giving a net facilitatory effect, especially at low stimulus contrasts. Thus, we suggest that the existence of a net excitatory effect at locations collinear with a line ending does not imply that the inhibitory off-surround is restricted to being present only by the line's sides. In

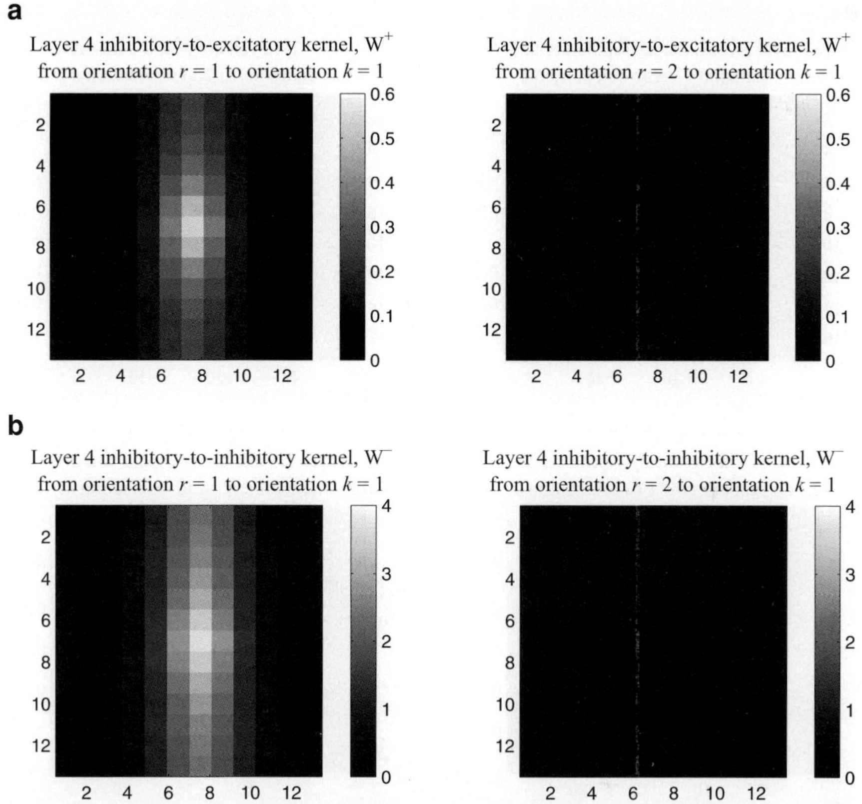

Figure 7. **(a)** The inhibitory-to-excitatory off-surround kernels in layer 4, W^+. Only the kernels operating on vertically oriented cells are shown, since those operating on horizontally oriented cells are the same, but rotated by 90°. **(b)** The inhibitory-to-inhibitory off-surround kernels in layer 4, W^-. Again, only the vertical kernels are shown.

fact, the existence of off-surround inhibition at a line ending can be very useful functionally, for example in generating end-cuts (Grossberg & Mingolla, 1985).

Ito and Gilbert (1999) examined the interaction of top-down attention and collinear facilitation in V1 of macaque monkeys that were performing a brightness comparison task. Although this study is pioneering in investigating the interaction of these visual processes, we have not simulated their neural data here since their results were not consistent across the two monkeys from which recordings were made. In one monkey, focal attention directed to a target line was found to increase the facilitatory effect upon that line of a collinear flanker. In the other monkey, the opposite effect was found. Several factors might contribute to this discrepancy. As remarked by Ito and Gilbert themselves, the monkeys had undergone different amounts of training. Another possibility is

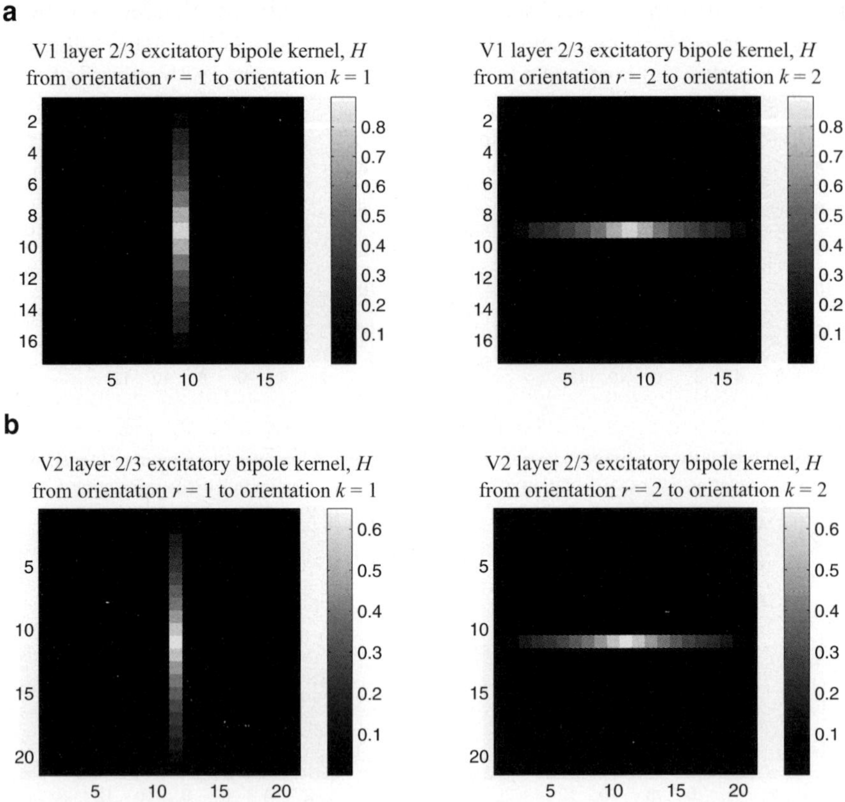

Figure 8. **(a)** The bipole-grouping kernels in V1 layer 2/3, H. Since bipole facilitation is collinear, the cross-orientation bipole kernels have approximately zero strength. They are not shown. **(b)** The bipole-grouping kernels in V2 layer 2/3, H^{V2}. Note that they are longer-range than the corresponding V1 kernels.

that the requirements of the behavioural task were not well-suited for probing the most commonly needed functions of attention and grouping: As we argued in the Introduction, these processes are needed most when a visual target is weak or low-contrast, and hence hard to detect. In such circumstances, one would expect both processes, and their interaction, to be facilitatory. However, in the Ito and Gilbert study, the target was bright and easily detectable, and the task was to discriminate its brightness as accurately as possible. Thus, a simple net facilitation of neural activity could actually hinder the monkey's brightness judgement. This conflict between the specific task demands and the most common ecological uses of attention and grouping may partially account for the differences between the monkeys. In the present model, a possible mechanism that might underlie such a difference would be the width of the attentional focus directed at the target line. If the focus is narrow, it will enhance the target, but attention's off-surround will actively suppress the collinear flanker, and attention will tend to reduce the flanker's facilitatory effect. If the focus is slightly wider, the attentional on-centre will fall on both target and flanker, and the facilitatory effect of the collinear grouping will be enhanced.

Because the present model assigns specific functional roles to many aspects of cortical laminar circuitry, many testable predictions can be derived from it. Several such predictions are presented in the conclusion of Grossberg and Raizada (2000). The simulations presented here extend and broaden the scope of the model, and also generate new predictions over and above those already presented. Perhaps the most directly testable of these concern the spread of attention along illusory as well as real contour groupings (see Figures 4 and 5). We suggest that there should exist measurable neurophysiological correlates of such flow, in particular in layer 2/3 of V2 and possibly also of V1. This could be tested by replicating the Roelfsema et al. (1998) study, but having the monkeys trace curves made of dashed instead of solid lines. V2 neurons lying along the empty parts of the dashed lines should fire as a result of collinear grouping (von der Heydt et al., 1984), and we predict that attention to the traced curve should be able to enhance such firing, just as in the case where the complete contour is physically present. It also follows from the model that attentional enhancement should be more pronounced for low contrast stimuli (see the simulation of the De Weerd et al., 1999, data in Figure 2). Thus, using low contrast dashed lines should make it easier to observe the predicted attentional effect.

REFERENCES

Ahmed, B., Anderson, J.C., Martin, K.A.C., & Nelson, J.C. (1997). Map of the synapses onto layer 4 basket cells of the primary visual cortex of the cat. *Journal of Comparative Neurology, 380,* 230–242.

Allman, J., Miezin, F., & McGuinness, E. (1985). Stimulus specific responses from beyond the classical receptive field: Neurophysiological mechanisms for local–global comparisons in visual neurons. *Annual Review of Neuroscience, 8,* 407–430.

Alonso, J.M., & Martinez, L.M. (1998). Functional connectivity between simple cells and complex cells in cat striate cortex. *Nature Neuroscience, 1*(5), 395–403.

Amir, Y., Harel, M., & Malach, R. (1993). Cortical hierarchy reflected in the organization of intrinsic connections in macaque monkey visual cortex. *Journal of Comparative Neurology, 334,* 19–46.

Baloch, A.A., Grossberg, S., Mingolla, E., & Nogueira, C.A.M. (1999). Neural model of first-order and second-order motion perception and magnocellular dynamics. *Journal of the Optical Society of America, A16,* 953–978.

Blakemore, C., & Tobin, E.A. (1972). Lateral inhibition between orientation detectors in the cat's visual cortex. *Experimental Brain Research, 15,* 439–440.

Blasdel, G.G., & Lund, J.S. (1983). Termination of afferent axons in macaque striate cortex. *Journal of Neuroscience, 3*(7), 1389–1413.

Blasdel, G.G., Lund, J.S., & Fitzpatrick, D. (1985). Intrinsic connections of macaque striate cortex: Axonal projections of cells outside lamina 4C. *Journal of Neuroscience, 5*(12), 3350–3369.

Bosking, W., Zhang, Y., Schofield, B., & Fitzpatrick, D. (1997). Orientation selectivity and the arrangement of horizontal connections in tree shrew striate cortex. *Journal of Neuroscience, 17*(6), 2112–2127.

Brefczynski, J.A., & DeYoe, E.A. (1999). A physiological correlate of the "spotlight" of visual attention. *Nature Neuroscience, 2,* 370–374.

Bullier, J., Hupé, J.M., James, A., & Girard, P. (1996). Functional interactions between areas V1 and V2 in the monkey. *Journal of Physiology (Paris), 90*(3–4), 217–220.

Callaway, E.M. (1998). Local circuits in primary visual cortex of the macaque monkey. *Annual Review of Neuroscience, 21,* 47–74.

Callaway, E.M., & Wiser, A.K. (1996). Contributions of individual layer 2–5 spiny neurons to local circuits in macaque primary visual cortex. *Visual Neuroscience, 13,* 907–922.

Caputo, G., & Guerra, S. (1998). Attentional selection by distractor suppression. *Vision Research, 38*(5), 669–689.

Cauller, L.J., & Connors, B.W. (1994). Synaptic physiology of horizontal afferents to layer I in slices of rat SI neocortex. *Journal of Neuroscience, 14*(2), 751–762.

Chey, J., Grossberg, S., & Mingolla, E. (1997). Neural dynamics of motion grouping: From aperture ambiguity to object speed and direction. *Journal of the Optical Society of America, A14,* 2570–2594.

Chey, J., Grossberg, S., & Mingolla, E. (1998). Neural dynamics of motion processing and speed discrimination. *Vision Research, 38,* 2769–2786.

Davis, G., & Driver, J. (1997). Spreading of visual attention to modally versus modally completed regions. *Psychological Science, 8,* 275–281.

De Weerd, P., Peralta, M.R., Desimone, R., & Ungerleider, L.G. (1999). Loss of attentional stimulus selection after extrastriate cortical lesions in macaques. *Nature Neuroscience, 2,* 753–758.

Downing, C.J. (1988). Expectancy and visual-spatial attention: Effects on perceptual quality. *Journal of Experimental Psychology: Human Perception and Performance, 14*(2), 188–202.

Ferster, D., Chung, S., & Wheat, H. (1996). Orientation selectivity of thalamic input to simple cells of cat visual cortex. *Nature, 380,* 249–252.

Field, D.J., Hayes, A., & Hess, R.F. (1993). Contour integration by the human visual system: Evidence for a local "association field". *Vision Research, 33,* 173–193.

Finkel, L.H., & Edelman, G.M. (1989). Integration of distributed cortical systems by reentry: A computer simulation of interactive functionally segregated visual areas. *Journal of Neuroscience, 9,* 3188–3208.

Fitzpatrick, D., Lund, J.S., & Blasdel, G.G. (1985). Intrinsic connections of macaque striate cortex: Afferent and efferent connections of lamina 4C. *Journal of Neuroscience, 5*(12), 3329–3349.

Francis, G., Grossberg, S., & Mingolla, E. (1994). Cortical dynamics of feature binding and reset: Control of visual persistence. *Vision Research, 34,* 1089–1104.

Gattass, R., Sousa, A., Mishkin, M., & Ungerleider, L. (1997). Cortical projections of area V2 in the macaque. *Cerebral Cortex, 7*(2), 110–129.

Gilbert, C.D., & Wiesel, T.N. (1979). Morphology and intracortical projections of functionally characterised neurones in the cat visual cortex. *Nature, 280,* 120–125.

Gilbert, C.D., & Wiesel, T.N. (1990). The influence of contextual stimuli on the orientation selectivity of cells in primary visual cortex of the cat. *Vision Research, 30,* 1689–1701.

Glass, L. (1969). Moire effect from random dots. *Nature, 223,* 578–580.

Gove, A., Grossberg, S., & Mingolla, E. (1995). Brightness perception, illusory contours, and corticogeniculate feedback. *Visual Neuroscience, 12*(6), 1027–1052.

Gray, C.M. (1999). The temporal correlation hypothesis of visual feature integration: Still alive and well. *Neuron, 24,* 31–47.

Grosof, D.H., Shapley, R.M., & Hawken, M.J. (1993). Macaque V1 neurons can signal "illusory" contours. *Nature, 365,* 550–552.

Grossberg, S. (1970). Neural pattern discrimination. *Journal of Theoretical Biology, 27*(2), 291–337.
Grossberg, S. (1973). Contour enhancement, short term memory, and constancies in reverberating neural networks. *Studies in Applied Mathematics, 52,* 217–257. Reprinted in S. Grossberg (1982), *Studies of mind and brain.* Dordrecht, The Netherlands: D. Reidel Publishing Company.
Grossberg, S. (1980). How does a brain build a cognitive code? *Psychological Review, 87,* 1–51.
Grossberg, S. (1994). 3-D vision and figure–ground separation by visual cortex. *Perception and Psychophysics, 55*(1), 48–120.
Grossberg, S. (1998). How is a moving target continuously tracked behind occluding cover? In T. Watanabe (Ed.), *High-level motion processing: Computational: neurobiological, and psychophysical perspectives* (pp. 1–30). Cambridge, MA: MIT Press.
Grossberg, S. (1999a). How does the cerebral cortex work? Learning, attention, and grouping by the laminar circuits of visual cortex. *Spatial Vision, 12,* 163–187.
Grossberg, S. (1999b). The link between brain learning, attention, and consciousness. *Consciousness and Cognition, 8,* 1–44.
Grossberg, S. (2000). How hallucinations may arise from brain mechanisms of learning, attention, and volition. *Journal of the International Neuropsychological Society, 5,* 583–592.
Grossberg, S., & Grunewald, A. (1997). Cortical synchronization and perceptual framing. *Journal of Cognitive Neuroscience, 9*(1), 117–132.
Grossberg, S., & Kelly, F. (1999). Neural dynamics of binocular brightness perception. *Vision Research, 39,* 3796–3816.
Grossberg, S., & Mingolla, E. (1985). Neural dynamics of form perception: Boundary completion, illusory figures, and neon colour spreading. *Psychological Review, 92*(2), 173–211.
Grossberg, S., Mingolla, E., & Ross, W.D. (1997). Visual brain and visual perception: How does the cortex do perceptual grouping. *Trends in Neurosciences, 20*(3), 106–111.
Grossberg, S., & Raizada, R.D.S. (2000). Contrast-sensitive perceptual grouping and object-based attention in the laminar circuits of primary visual cortex. *Vision Research, 40,* 1413–1432.
Grossberg, S., & Somers, D. (1991). Synchronized oscillations during cooperative feature linking in a cortical model of visual perception. *Neural Networks, 4*(4), 453–466.
Grossberg, S., & Williamson, J.R. (2001). A neural model of how visual cortex develops a laminar architecture capable of adult perceptual grouping. *Cerebral Cortex, 11,* 37–58.
Harth, E., Unnikrishnan, K.P., & Pandya, A.S. (1987). The inversion of sensory processing by feedback pathways: A model of visual cognitive functions. *Science, 237,* 184–187.
He, Z.J., & Nakayama, K. (1995). Visual attention to surface in three-dimensional space. *Proceedings of the National Academy of Sciences, USA, 21,* 11155–11159.
Heeger, D.J. (1992). Normalization of cell responses in cat striate cortex. *Visual Neuroscience, 9*(2), 181–197.
Heitger, F., von der Heydt, R., Peterhans, E., Rosenthaler, L., & Kubler, O. (1998). Simulation of neural contour mechanisms: Representing anomalous contours. *Image and Vision Computing, 16,* 407–421.
Hirsch, J.A., Alonso, J.M., Reid, R.C., & Martinez, L.M. (1998). Synaptic integration in striate cortical simple cells. *Journal of Neuroscience, 18*(22), 9517–9528.
Hirsch, J.A., & Gilberg, C.D. (1991). Synpatic physiology of horizontal connections in the cat's visual cortex. *Journal of Neuroscience, 11*(6), 1800–1809.
Ito, M., & Gilbert, C.D. (1999). Attention modulates contextual influences in the primary visual cortex of alert monkeys. *Neuron, 22,* 593–604.
Kanisza, G. (1979). *Organization in vision: Essays on Gestalt perception.* New York: Praeger.
Kapadia, M.K., Ito, M., Gilberg, C.D., & Westheimer, G. (1995). Improvements in visual sensitivity by changes in local context: Parallel studies in human observers and in V1 of alert monkeys. *Neuron, 15,* 843–856.

Kapadia, M.K., Westheimer, G., & Gilbert, C.D. (1998). Spatial distribution and dynamics of contextual interactions in cortical area V1. (From *Society for Neuroscience Abstracts*, Abstract No. 789.6.)

Kisvarday, Z.F., Cowey, A., Smith, A.D., & Somogyi, P. (1989). Interlaminar and lateral excitatory amino acid connections in the striate cortex of monkey. *Journal of Neuroscience, 9*(2), 667–682.

Knierim, J.J., & Van Essen, D.C. (1992). Neuronal responses to static texture patterns in area V1 of the alert macaque monkey. *Journal of Neurophysiology, 67,* 961–980.

Kovacs, I., & Julesz, B. (1993). A closed curve is much more than an incomplete one: Effect of closure in figure–ground segmentation. *Proceedings of the National Academy of Sciences, USA, 90*(16), 7495–7497.

Lamme, V.A.F. (1998). The neurophysiology of figure–ground segregation in primary visual cortex. *Journal of Neuroscience, 15,* 1605–1615.

Li, Z. (1998). A neural model of contour integration in the primary visual cortex. *Neural Computation, 10,* 903–940.

Luck, S.J., Chelazzi, L., Hillyard, S.A., & Desimone, R. (1997). Neural mechanisms of spatial selective attention in areas V1, V2, and V4 of macaque visual cortex. *Journal of Neurophysiology, 77,* 24–42.

Lumer, E.D., Edelman, G.M., & Tononi, G. (1997). Neural dynamics in a model of the thalamocortical system. I. Layers, loops and the emergence of the fast synchronous rhythms. *Cerebral Cortex, 7,* 207–227.

Lund, J.S., & Boothe, R.G. (1975). Interlaminar connections and pyramidal neuron organisation in the visual cortex, area 17, of the macaque monkey. *Journal of Comparative Neurology, 159,* 305–334.

Lund, J.S., & Wu, C.Q. (1997). Local circuit neurons of macaque monkey striate cortex: IV. Neurons of laminae 1–3A. *Journal of Comparative Neurology, 384,* 109–126.

Maffei, L., & Fiorentini, A. (1976). The unresponsive regions of visual cortical receptive fields. *Vision Research, 16,* 1131–1139.

Markram, H., Wang, Y., & Tsodyks, M. (1998). Differential signalling via the same axon of neocortical pyramidal neurons. *Proceedings of the National Academy of Sciences, USA, 95,* 5323–5328.

McCormick, D.A., Connors, B.W., Lighthall, J.W., & Prince, D.A. (1985). Comparative electrophysiology of pyramidal and sparsely spiny stellate neurons of the neocortex. *Journal of Neurophysiology, 54,* 782–806.

McGuire, B.A., Gilbert, C.D., Rivlin, P.K., & Wiesel, T.N. (1991). Targets of horizontal connections in macaque primary visual cortex. *Journal of Comparative Neurology, 305*(3), 370–392.

McGuire, B.A., Hornung, J.P., Gilbert, C.D., & Wiesel, T.N. (1984). Patterns of synaptic input to layer 4 of cat striate cortex. *Journal of Neuroscience, 4*(12), 3021–3033.

Montero, V.M. (1991). A quantitative study of synaptic contacts on interneurons and relay cells of the cat lateral geniculate nucleus. *Experimental Brain Research, 86,* 257–270.

Moore, C.M., & Egeth, H. (1997). Perception without attention: Evidence of grouping under conditions of inattention. *Journal of Experimental Psychology: Human Perception and Performance, 23*(2), 339–352.

Moore, C.M., Yantis, S., & Vaughan, B. (1998). Object-based visual selection: Evidence from perceptual completion. *Psychological Science, 9,* 104–110.

Motter, B.C. (1993). Focal attention produces spatially selective processing in visual cortical areas V1, V2 and V4 in the presence of competing stimuli. *Journal of Neurophysiology, 70,* 909–919.

Mounts, J.R.W. (2000). Evidence for suppressive mechanisms in attentional selection: Feature singletons produce inhibitory surrounds. *Perception and Psychophysics, 62,* 969–983.

Mumford, D. (1992). On the computational architecture of the neocortex. II. The role of corticocortical loops. *Biological Cybernetics, 66,* 241–251.

Nelson, J.I., & Frost, B.J. (1978). Orientation-selective inhibition from beyond the classic visual receptive field. *Brain Research, 139,* 359–365.

Neumann, H., & Sepp, W. (1999). Recurrent V1–V2 interaction in early visual boundary processing. *Biological Cybernetics, 81,* 425–444.

Nguyen, M., & Lee, T.S. (1999). Spatiotemporal dynamics of subjective contour formation in primate V1 and V2. (From *Society for Neuroscience Abstracts,* Abstract No. 7.3.)

Nothdurft, H.C. (1991). Texture segmentation and pop-out from orientation contrast. *Vision Research, 31,* 1073–1078.

Nothdurft, H.C., Gallant, J.L., & Van Essen, D.C. (1999). Response modulation by texture surround in primate area V1: Correlates of "popout" under anaesthesia. *Vision Neuroscience, 16,* 15–34.

Olshausen, B.A., Anderson, C.H., & Van Essen, D.C. (1993). A neurobiological model of visual attention and invariant pattern recognition based on dynamics routing of information. *Journal of Neuroscience, 13,* 4700–4719.

Peterhans, E., & von der Heydt, R. (1989). Mechanisms of contour perception in monkey visual cortex. II. Contours bridging gaps. *Journal of Neuroscience, 9,* 1749–1763.

Peters, A.G., & Sethares, C. (1991). Organization of pyramidal neurons in area 17 of monkey visual cortex. *Journal of Comparative Neurology, 306,* 1–23.

Polat, U., Mizobe, K., Pettet, M.W., Kasamatsu, T., & Norcia, A.M. (1998). Collinear stimuli regulate visual responses depending on cell's contrast threshold. *Nature, 391,* 580–584.

Polat, U., & Sagi, D. (1993). Lateral interactions between spatial channels: Suppression and facilitation revealed by lateral masking experiments. *Vision Research, 33,* 993–999.

Przybyszewski, A.W., Foote, W., & Pollen, D.A. (1998). Contrast gain control of the LGN neurons by V1. *Visual Neuroscience, 17,* 485–494.

Rao, R.P.N., & Ballard, D.H. (1999). Predictive coding in the visual cortex: A functional interpretation of some extra-classical receptive field effects. *Nature Neuroscience, 2,* 79–87.

Redies, C., Crook, J.M., & Creutzfeldt, O.D. (1986). Neuronal responses to borders with and without luminance gradients in cat visual cortex and dorsal lateral geniculate nucleus. *Experimental Brain Research, 61,* 469–481.

Reid, R.C., & Alonso, J.M. (1995). Specificity of monosynaptic connections from thalamus to visual cortex. *Nature, 378,* 281–284.

Reyes, A., Lujan, R., Rozov, A., Burnashev, N., Somogyi, P., & Sakmann, B. (1998). Target-cell-specific facilitation and depression in neocortical circuits. *Nature Neuroscience, 1,* 279–285.

Reynolds, J., Chelazzi, L., & Desimone, R. (1999). Competitive mechanisms subserve attention in macaque areas V2 and V4. *Journal of Neuroscience, 19,* 1736–1753.

Reynolds, J.H., & Desimone, R. (1999). The role of neural mechanisms of attention in solving the binding problem. *Neuron, 24,* 19–29.

Rockland, K.S. (1994). The organization of feedback connections from area V2 (18) to V1 (17). In A. Peters & K.S. Rockland (Eds.), *Cerebral cortex* (Vol. 10, pp. 261–299). New York: Plenum Press.

Rockland, K.S., & Virga, A. (1989). Terminal arbors of individual "feedback" axons projecting from area V2 to V1 in the macaque monkey: A study using immunohistochemistry of anterogradely transported phaseolus vulgaris-leucoagglutinin. *Journal of Comparative Neurology, 285*(1), 54–72.

Rockland, K.S., & Virga, A. (1990). Organization of individual cortical axons projecting from area V1 (area 17) to V2 (area 18) in the macaque monkey. *Visual Neuroscience, 4*(1), 11–28.

Roelfsema, P.R., Lamme, V.A.F., & Spekreijse, H. (1998). Object-based attention in the primary visual cortex of the macaque monkey. *Nature, 395,* 376–381.

Roelfsema, P.R., & Spekreijse, H. (1999). Correlates of a gradual spread of attention over a traced curve in macaque area V1. (From *Society for Neuroscience Abstract,* Abstract No. 7.2.)

Ross, W.D., Mingolla, E., & Grossberg, S. (2000). Visual cortical mechanisms of perceptual grouping: Interacting layers, networks, columns, and maps. *Neural Networks, 13,* 571–588.

Salin, P., & Bullier, J. (1995). Corticocortical connections in the visual system: Structure and function. *Physiological Reviews, 75*(1), 107–154.

Sandell, J.H., & Schiller, P.H. (1982). Effect of cooling area 18 on striate cortex cells in the squirrel monkey. *Journal of Neurophysiology, 48*(1), 38–48.

Schiller, P.H. (1992). The ON and OFF channels of the visual system. *Trends in Neurosciences, 15*(3), 86–92.

Schmidt, K.E., Goebel, R., Löwel, S., & Singer, W. (1997). The perceptual grouping criterion of colinearity is reflected by anisotropies of connections in the primary visual cortex. *European Journal of Neuroscience, 9,* 1083–1089.

Sheth, B.R., Sharma, J., Rao, S.C., & Sur, M. (1996). Orientation maps of subjective contours in visual cortex. *Science, 274,* 2110–2115.

Sillito, A.M., Grieve, K.L., Jones, H.E., Cudeiro, J., & Davis, J. (1995). Visual cortical mechanisms detecting focal orientation discontinuities. *Nature, 378,* 492–496.

Sillito, A.M., Jones, H.E., Gerstein, G.L., & West, D.C. (1994). Feature-linked synchronization of thalamic relay cell firing induced by feedback from the visual cortex. *Nature, 369,* 479–482.

Smith, A.T., Singh, K.D., & Greenlee, M.W. (2000). Attentional suppression of activity in the human visual cortex, *Neuroreport, 11,* 271–277.

Somers, D.C., Dale, A.M., Seiffert, A.E., & Tootell, R.B. (1999). Functional MRI reveals spatially specific attentional modulation in human primary visual cortex. *Proceedings of the National Academy of Sciences, USA, 96,* 1663–1668.

Somers, D.C., Todorov, E.V., Siapas, A.G., Toth, L.J., Kim, D., & Sur, M. (1998). A local circuit approach to understanding integration of long-range inputs in primary visual cortex. *Cerebral Cortex, 8,* 204–217.

Stemmler, M., Usher, M., & Niebur, E. (1995). Lateral interactions in primary visual cortex: A model bridging physiology and psychophysics. *Science, 269,* 1877–1880.

Stratford, K.J., Tarczy-Hornoch, K., Martin, K.A.C., Bannister, N.J., & Jack, J.J.B. (1996). Excitatory synaptic inputs to spiny stellate cells in cat visual cortex. *Nature, 382,* 258–261.

Sugita, Y. (1999). Grouping of image fragments in primary visual cortex. *Nature, 401,* 269–272.

Tamas, G., Somogyi, P., & Buhl, E.H. (1998). Differentially interconnected networks of GABAergic interneurons in the visual cortex of the cat. *Journal of Neuroscience, 18*(11), 4255–4270.

Thomson, A.M. (1997). Activity-dependent properties of synaptic transmission at two classes of connections made by rat neocortical pyramidal axons in vitro. *Journal of Physiology, 502,* 131–147.

Thorpe, S., Fize, D., & Marlot, C. (1996). Speed of processing in the human visual system. *Nature, 381,* 520–522.

Treismann, A. (1999). Solutions to the binding problem: Progress through controversy and convergence. *Neuron, 24,* 105–110.

Treue, S., & Maunsell, J.H.R. (1996). Attentional modulation of visual motion processing in cortical areas MT and MST. *Nature, 382,* 539–541.

Tsotsos, J., Culhane, S., Wai, W., Lai, Y., Davis, N., & Nuflo, F. (1995). Modeling visual attention via selective tuning. *Artificial Intelligence, 78,* 507–547.

Ullman, S. (1995). Sequence seeking and counter streams: A computational model for bidirectional information flow in the visual cortex. *Cerebral Cortex, 5,* 1–11.

Usher, M., & Neibur, E. (1996). Modeling the temporal dynamics of its neurons in visual search: A mechanism for top-down selective attention. *Journal of Cognitive Neuroscience, 8,* 311–327.

Valverde, F. (1985). The organizing principles of the primary visual cortex in the monkey. In A Peters & E.G. Jones (Eds.), *Cerebral cortex* (Vol. 3, pp. 205–257). New York: Plenum.

Vanduffel, W., Tootell, R.B., & Orban, G.A. (2000). Attention-dependent suppression of metabolic activity in the early stages of the macaque visual system. *Cerebral Cortex, 10,* 109–126.

Van Essen, D.C., Newsome, W.T., Maunsell, J.H., & Bixby, J.L. (1986). The projections from striate cortex (V1) to areas V2 and V3 in the macaque monkey: Asymmetries, areal boundaries, and patchy connections. *Journal of Comparative Neurology, 244*(4), 451–480.
Varela, J.A., Song, S., Turrigiano, G.G., & Nelson, S.B. (1999). Differential depression at excitatory and inhibitory synapses in visual cortex. *Journal of Neuroscience, 19,* 4293–4304.
von der Heydt, R., Peterhans, E., & Baumgartner, G. (1984). Illusory contours and cortical neuron responses. *Science, 224,* 1260–1262.
Watanabe, T., Sasaki, Y., Nielsen, M., Takino, R., & Miyakawa, S. (1998). Attention-regulated activity in human primary visual cortex. *Journal of Neurophysiology, 79,* 2218–2221.
Williams, L.R., & Jacobs, D.W. (1997). Stochastic completion fields: A neural model of illusory contour shape and salience. *Neural Computation, 9,* 837–858.
Wiser, A.K., & Callaway, E.M. (1997). Ocular dominance columns and local projections of layer 6 pyramidal neurons in macaque primary visual cortex. *Visual Neuroscience, 14,* 241–251.
Yen, S.C., & Finkel, L.H. (1998). Extraction of perceptually salient contours by striate cortical networks. *Vision Research, 38*(5), 719–741.

APPENDIX: MODEL EQUATIONS

Retina

The model retina has at each position (i, j) both an ON-cell, u^+_{ij}, whose receptive field has the form of a narrow on-centre and a Gaussian off-surround, and an OFF-cell, u^-_{ij}, with a narrow off-centre and a Gaussian on-surround (Schiller, 1992). As is observed *in vivo*, these ON and OFF cells feed forward into ON and OFF channels of the LGN, and enable the network to respond both to light increments and to light decrements. The retinal cell activities caused by constant visual inputs I have the equilibrium values:

$$u^+_{ij} = I_{ij} - \sum_{pq} G_{pq}(i, j, \sigma_1) I_{pq}, \tag{1}$$

and

$$u^-_{ij} = -I_{ij} + \sum_{pq} G_{pq}(i, j, \sigma_1) I_{pq}, \tag{2}$$

where $G_{pq}(i, j, \sigma)$ is a two-dimensional Gaussian kernel, given by:

$$G_{pq}(i, j, \sigma) = \frac{1}{2\pi\sigma^2} \exp\left(-\frac{1}{2\sigma^2}((p-1)^2 + (q-i)^2) \right). \tag{3}$$

The Gaussian width parameter was set to: $\sigma_1 = 1$.

Lateral geniculate nucleus

The ON and OFF cells of the LGN, v^+_{ij} and v^-_{ij}, are excited by the half-wave rectified ON and OFF cells of the retina, respectively. These retinal inputs are also multiplicatively gain-controlled by on-centre off-surround feedback from V1 layer 6 (Gove, Grossberg, & Mingolla, 1995; Przybyszewski, Foote, & Pollen, 1998; Sillito et al., 1994). Layer 6 cells, x_{ijk}, at position (i, j) and of all orientations, k, send on-centre excitation, A_{ij}, to LGN neurons at the same position, and send a two-dimensional Gaussian spread of off-surround inhibition, B_{ij}, to LGN neurons at the same and nearby positions, as shown in Figure 6d:

$$\frac{1}{\delta_v}\frac{d}{dt} v^+_{ij} = -v^+_{ij} + (1 - v^+_{ij})[u^+_{ij}]^+(1 + A_{ij}) - (1 + v^+_{ij})B_{ij}, \tag{4}$$

and

$$\frac{1}{\delta_v}\frac{d}{dt}v_{ij}^{-} = -v_{ij}^{-} + (1 - v_{ij}^{-})[u_{ij}^{-}]^{+}(1 + A_{ij}) - (1 + v_{ij}^{-})B_{ij}. \tag{5}$$

In equations 4 and 5, the layer 6 on-centre off-surround feedback terms, A_{ij} and B_{ij}, are given by:

$$A_{ij} = C_1 \sum_k x_{ijk}, \tag{6}$$

and

$$B_{ij} = C_2 \sum_{pqk} G_{pq}(i, j, \sigma_1) x_{ijk}, \tag{7}$$

where the off-surround Gaussian, $G_{pq}(i, j, \sigma_1)$ is defined by equation (4), and the notation $[u_{ij}^{+}]^{+}$ signifies half-wave rectification, $[u_{ij}^{+}]^{+} = \max(u_{ij}^{+}, 0)$. The parameters for the LGN were: $\delta_v = 1.25$, $C_1 = 1.5$, $C_2 = 0.075$.

LGN inputs to cortical simple cells

At each position, (i, j), and for each orientation, k, the model has a even-symmetric simple cell with two parallel elongated parts: an ON subregion, R_{ijk}, which receives excitation from LGN ON cells beneath it and is inhibited by LGN OFF cells at the same position; and an OFF subregion, L_{ijk}, which has the converse relation to the LGN channels (Hirsch, Alonso, Reid, & Martinez, 1998; Reid & Alonso, 1995). This physiology is embodied in the equation for the ON subregion by subtracting the half-wave rectified LGN OFF channel, $[v_{pq}^{-}]^{+}$, from the rectified ON channel, $[v_{pq}^{+}]^{+}$, and convolving the result with the positive lobe of a Difference-of-Offset-Gaussians (DOOG) kernel, $[D_{pqij}^{(k)}]^{+}$, which has the simple cell subfield's characteristic oriented elongated shape. The OFF subregion, L_{ijk}, is similarly constructed:

$$R_{ijk} = \sum_{pq}([v_{pq}^{+}]^{+} - [v_{pq}^{-}]^{+})[D_{pqij}^{(k)}]^{+}, \tag{8}$$

and

$$L_{ijk} = \sum_{pq}([v_{pq}^{-}]^{+} - [v_{pq}^{+}]^{+})[-D_{pqij}^{(k)}]^{+}, \tag{9}$$

where the oriented DOOG filter $D_{pqij}^{(k)}$ is given by:

$$D_{pqij}^{(k)} = G_{pq}(i - \delta\cos\theta, j - \delta\sin\theta, \sigma_2) - G_{pq}(i + \delta\cos\theta, j + \delta\sin\theta, \sigma_2), \tag{10}$$

with $\delta = \sigma_2/2$ and $\theta = \pi(\kappa - 1)/K$, where k ranges from 1 to $2K$, K being the total number of orientations. For simplicity, the number of orientations was set to $K = 2$ (vertical and horizontal) in the present simulations. The width parameter for the DOOG filter was $\sigma^2 = 0.5$.

At an oriented contrast edge, a suitably oriented simple cell of the correct polarity will have its ON subfield stimulated by a luminance increment and its OFF subfield stimulated by an equal but opposite decrement. The optimal nature of this stimulus is embodied in the following equation, in which simple cell activity is the rectified sum of the activities of each subfield, minus their difference:

$$S_{ijk} = \gamma[R_{ijk} + L_{ijk} - |R_{ijk} - L_{ijk}|]^{+}. \tag{11}$$

Recent physiological studies have confirmed that layer 4 simple cells that are sensitive to opposite contrast polarities pool their outputs at layer 2/3 complex cells (Alonso & Martinez, 1998). In order to make the simulations manageable, cells in layers 6 and 4 were implemented with their simple cell inputs already pooled, thus halving the number of cells. Since the present model is not used to simulate any polarity-specific interactions in these layers, this simplification leaves the output unaffected. Thus, the polarity-pooled input from LGN to cortical layers 6 and 4 was calculated as the term C_{ijk}, which pools over opposite-polarity simple cells:

$$C_{ijk} = S_{ijk} + S_{ij(k+K)}, \tag{12}$$

where k ranges from 1 to K. The parameter for the simple cell responses, was set to $\gamma = 10$.

Layer 6 cells

V1 layer 6 cells, x_{ijk}, receive input from the LGN (Blasdel & Lund, 1983), which, as described previously, is represented by the contrast-polarity pooled oriented input, C_{ijk}. They also receive two types of folded-feedback excitation. The first type is intracortical feedback from above-threshold pyramidal cells in V1 layer 2/3, z_{ijk}, as shown in Figure 6c (Blasdel, Lund, & Fitzpatrick, 1985; Kisvarday, Cowey, Smith, & Somogyi, 1989). These are passed through a thresholding signal function, F, given by:

$$F(z_{ijk}, \Gamma) = \max(z_{ijk} - \Gamma, 0), \tag{13}$$

where Γ is the threshold value. The second type of folded feedback is intercortical attentional feedback from V2, x_{ijk}^{V2} (Sandell & Schiller, 1982), originating in V2 layer 6 (Rockland & Virga, 1989), as shown in Figure 6b. The feedback axons from V2 terminate predominantly in V1 layer 1 (Rockland, 1994). There exist several routes through which these layer 1 signals can pass down into layer 6, notably via the layer 1 apical dendritic tufts of layer 5 pyramidals with axon collaterals in layer 6 (Gilbert & Wiesel, 1979; Lund & Boothe, 1975; see also Table 1). These paths are not explicitly implemented in the present model.

In attentional simulations, an additional term, *att*, is added to the excitatory channel, implementing a two-dimensional Gaussian spread of attentional signals, centred on the attended location and exciting all orientations equally. This attentional term is applied both to V1 and to V2. In the non-attentional simulations, $att = 0$. Thus:

$$\frac{1}{\delta_C}\frac{d}{dt}x_{ijk} = -x_{ijk} + (1 - x_{ijk})\left(\alpha C_{ijk} + \phi F(z_{ijk}, \Gamma) + V_{21}x_{ijk}^{V2} + att\right). \tag{14}$$

This equation was solved at equilibrium, giving:

$$x_{ijk} = \frac{\alpha C_{ijk} + \phi F(z_{ijk}, \Gamma) + V_{21}x_{ijk}^{V2} + att}{1 + \alpha C_{ijk} + \phi F(z_{ijk}, \Gamma) + V_{21}x_{ijk}^{V2} + att}. \tag{15}$$

The equations for layer 6 of V2 are identical to those just given for V1, with the exception that the V2 $\rightarrow$ V1 feedback term, $V_{21}x_{ijk}^{V2}$, is now absent. Parameters for the terms in the layer 6 equation were: $\delta_C = 0.25, \alpha = 0.5, \phi = 2.0, \Gamma = 0.2, V_{21} = 1$.

Layer 4 activity

Model spiny stellate cells in layer 4, y_{ijk}, as well as receiving the contrast-polarity pooled oriented input, C_{ijk}, described previously, also receive on-centre off-surround input from layer 6, as shown in Figure 6a. The on-centre consists of excitatory connections from layer 6, x_{ijk}, to layer 4 spiny stellates at the same position and of the same orientation (Stratford et al., 1996; Wiser & Callaway,

1997). The off-surround input is caused by medium-range projections from layer 6 onto layer 4 inhibitory interneurons (Ahmed, Anderson, Martin, & Nelson, 1997; McGuire, Hornung, Gilbert, & Wiesel, 1984). The spatial distribution and strength of these connections are determined by a two-dimensional kernel, W^{+}_{pqrijk}, which is in the present model a linearly scaled version of a self-organized 6 → 4 inhibitory kernel grown in the developmental study by Grossberg and Williamson (2001) using the same network architecture, but without the corticocortical feedback connections. The spatial distribution of this kernel, which is approximately Gaussian, is shown in Figure 7a. Therefore, the distribution of the off-surround inhibition in the present model is not hand-crafted by an algebraic equation, but is instead the product of a self-organized equilibrium reached by the same network architecture in response to naturally structured visual inputs.

As remarked in the Results section, the version of the model presented here extends that of Grossberg and Raizada (2000) by considering the complex mixture of pre- and post-synaptic factors which collectively contribute to the tendency for the total amount of inhibition to predominate over excitation at high stimulus contrasts. We approximate the total net effect of these factors by passing the population inhibitory activity through a sigmoidal signal function, f, defined as follows:

$$f(x) = \mu \frac{x^n}{\nu^n + x^n}. \tag{16}$$

This function is a sigmoid, ranging in output value from zero to μ, attaining half its maximum value at $x = \nu$, and with the steepness of the sigmoid controlled by the exponent n. In the present simulations, the following parameter values were used: $\mu = 2, \nu = 1.1, n = 6$.
Thus, the equation for layer 4 spiny stellates is:

$$\frac{1}{\delta_C}\frac{d}{dt} y_{ijk} = -y_{ijk} + (1 - y_{ijk})\left(C_{ijk} + \eta^{+} x_{ijk}\right) - (y_{ijk} + 1) f\left(\sum_{pqr} W^{+}_{pqrijk} m_{pqr}\right). \tag{17}$$

This was solved at equilibrium, giving:

$$y_{ijk} = \frac{C_{ijk} + \eta^{+} x_{ijk} - f\left(\sum_{pqr} W^{+}_{pqrijk} m_{pqr}\right)}{1 + C_{ijk} + \eta^{+} x_{ijk} + f\left(\sum_{pqr} W^{+}_{pqrijk} m_{pqr}\right)}. \tag{18}$$

Layer 4 inhibitory interneurons, m_{ijk}, also receive on-centre off-surround input, the on-centre again coming from layer 6 cells with the same position and orientation, x_{ijk}, and the off-surround inhibition coming via the spatial kernels, W^{-}, of the other inhibitory interneurons in layer 4 (Ahmed et al., 1997). These inhibitory-to-inhibitory synapses help to normalize the total amount of inhibition present at a given position in layer 4. Thus:

$$\frac{1}{\delta_m}\frac{d}{dt} m_{ijk} = -m_{ijk} + \eta^{-} x_{ijk} - m_{ijk} f\left(\sum_{pqr} W^{+}_{pqrijk} m_{pqr}\right). \tag{19}$$

As with the inhibitory-to-excitatory kernels, W^{+}, the inhibitory-to-inhibitory kernels, W^{-}, are also linearly scaled versions of the kernels which were self-organized in the model of Grossberg and Williamson (2001). They have a very similar spatial structure to the W^{+} kernels, but are a little stronger, as shown in Figure 7b. Parameters for layer 4 were: $\delta_m = 0.01875$, $\eta^{+} = 2.1$, $\eta^{-} = 1.5$.

Layer 2/3

The pyramidal cells in layer 2/3, z_{ijk}, receive excitatory input from layer 4 cells, y_{ijk}, at the same position and orientation (Callaway & Wiser, 1996), and also long-range bipole excitation from the thresholded outputs of other layer 2/3 pyramidals with collinear, coaxial receptive fields, $F(z_{ijk})$ (Bosking, Zhang, Schofield, & Fitzpatrick, 1997; Schmidt, Goebel, Löwel, & Singer, 1997). Inhibitory interneurons in layer 2/3, s_{ijk}, also synapse onto these pyramidals, as shown in Figure 6c. As with the inhibitory kernels in layer 4, W^+ and W^-, the layer 2/3 cells synapse onto each other through linearly scaled versions of the self-organized kernels grown in the model of Grossberg and Williamson (2001). The excitatory-to-excitatory, long-range bipole kernels, H, are shown in Figure 8. As well the long-range excitation, layer 2/3 pyramidals also receive short-range inhibition from inhibitory interneurons at the same position and of the same orientation, s_{ijk} (McGuire, Gilbert, Rivlin, & Wiesel, 1991). This inhibition operates through a self-organized short-range kernel, T^+.

As remarked in the Results section, the present model extends that presented in Grossberg and Raizada (2000) by considering the possibility that attentional feedback might enter layer 2/3 directly, as well as via the indirect layer 6 $\rightarrow$ 4 folded feedback path. In the direct path, feedback signals in layer 1 are collected by the apical dendrites of layer 2/3 pyramidals, and also by the dendrites of layer 2/3 inhibitory interneurons with dendrites in layer (Lund & Wu, 1997). Thus, attention is carried directly into layer 2/3 by both excitatory and inhibitory neurons, creating a balance of excitation and inhibition which keeps the net effect of attention subthreshold, or modulatory. The coefficients that determine the relative inputs of attention into the layer 2/3 excitatory and inhibitory cells are denoted by a^{23}_{excit} and a^{23}_{inhib}, respectively.

Thus, the full equation for layer 2/3 pyramidals is as follows:

$$\frac{1}{\delta_z}\frac{d}{dt}z_{ijk} = -z_{ijk} + (1 - z_{ijk})\left(\lambda[y_{ijk}]^+ + \sum_{pqr} H_{pqrijk} F(z_{pqr},\Gamma) + a^{23}_{excit}att\right) - (z_{ijk} + \psi)\sum_r T^+_{rk} s_{ijr}. \quad (20)$$

The layer 2/3 inhibitory interneurons, s_{ijk}, receive excitation from layer 2/3 pyramidals, through the kernels H, and are inhibited by other layer 2/3 interneurons at the same position but of all orientations, via the self-organized short-range kernel, T^- (Tamas, Somogyi, & Buhl, 1998). Like the layer 2/3 pyramidals, they also receive direct attentional input, when attention is present:

$$\frac{1}{\delta_s}\frac{d}{dt}s_{ijk} = -s_{ijk} + \sum_{pqr} H_{pqrijk} F(z_{pqr},\Gamma) + a^{23}_{inhib}att - s_{ijk} T^-_{rk} s_{ijr}. \quad (21)$$

Parameters for layer 2/3 were: $\delta_z = 0.0125, \delta_s = 2.5, \lambda = 1.5, \psi = 0.5, a^{23}_{excit} = 3, a^{23}_{inhib} = 0.5$.

Feedforward projections from V1 to V2

The thresholded output of V1 layer 2/3 projects forward to layers 6 and 4 of V2, x^{V2}_{ijk} and y^{V2}_{ijk} respectively, following the same pattern as the LGN forward projections to layers 6 and 4 of V1, as shown in Figure 6e. Hence:

$$\frac{1}{\delta_C}\frac{d}{dt}x^{V2}_{ijk} = -x^{V2}_{ijk} + (1 - x^{V2}_{ijk})\left(V^6_{12}F(z_{ijk},\Gamma) + \phi F(z^{V2}_{ijk},\Gamma) + att\right). \quad (22)$$

and

$$\frac{1}{\delta_C}\frac{d}{dt}y^{V2}_{ijk} = -y^{V2}_{ijk} + (1 - y^{V2}_{ijk})\left(V^4_{12}F(z_{ijk},\Gamma) + \eta^+ x^{V2}_{ijk}\right) - (y^{V2}_{ijk} + 1)f\left(\sum_{pqr} W^+_{pqrijk} m^{V2}_{pqr}\right). \quad (23)$$

All other equations and parameters for V2 are exactly the same as for the corresponding layers of V1, except that the length of the V2 bipole kernel, H^{V2}, is greater than that of V1, reflecting the fact that intrinsic horizontal connections have a longer range in V2 than in V1 (Amir et al., 1993), and also that illusory contours can form between more widely spaced inducers in V2 than in V1 (Sheth et al., 1996). The V2 bipole kernels are shown in Figure 8b. Parameters for the forward projection from V1 to V2 were: $V_{12}^{6} = 1, V_{12}^{4} = 5$.

Network inputs for the simulations

The simulations presented in this paper all used the same set of network parameters. The strengths of the raw inputs and, where applicable, the attentional Gaussians, were as follows: crossover simulation (Figure 1): low contrast raw input strength, I = 0.1, high contrast raw input strength, I = 0.6; De Weerd et al. (1999) simulation (Figure 2): distractor contrast = 20%, peak value of attentional Gaussian = 0.05; Knierim and Van Essen (1992) simulation (Figure 3): raw input strength, I = 0.2; simulation of attention flow along a real contour (Figure 4): raw input strength, I = 0.08, peak value of attentional Gaussian = 0.02; simulation of attention flow along an illusory contour (Figure 5): raw input strength, I = 0.3, peak value of attentional Gaussian = 0.02. All of the attentional simulations used an attentional Gaussian with a standard deviation of 1.5.

Self-organized kernels

The kernels, which were self-organized in the study by Grossberg and Williamson (2001), are represented here graphically (Figures 7 and 8), except for the single-pixel layer 2/3 inhibitory kernels, T^{+} and T^{-}, which had the following self-organized equilibrium values. $T_{11}^{+} = 0.9032$; $T_{21}^{+} = 0.1384$, $T_{12}^{+} = 0.1282$, $T_{22}^{+} = 0.8443$. $T_{11}^{-} = 0.2719$, $T_{21}^{-} = 0.0428$, $T_{12}^{-} = 0.0388$, $T_{22}^{-} = 0.2506$. T^{+} in V2 was 0.625 times the value of T^{+} in V1.

VISUAL COGNITION, 2001, *8* (3/4/5), 467–487

Selection can be performed effectively without temporal binding, but could be even more effective with it

Kyle R. Cave

Department of Psychology, University of Southampton, UK

Experiments using spatial cues and spatial probes provide strong evidence for an attention mechanism that chooses a location and selects all information at that location. This selection process can work very quickly; so quickly that selection probably begins before segmentation and grouping. It can be implemented in a neural network simply and efficiently without temporal binding. In conjunction with this spatial attention, however, temporal binding can potentially enhance visual selection in complex scenes. First, it would allow a target object to be selected without also selecting a superimposed distractor. Second, it could maintain representations of objects after attention has moved to another object. Third, it could allow multiple parts of an object or scene to be selected, segmented, and analysed simultaneously. Thus, temporal synchrony should be more likely to appear during tasks with overlapping targets and distractors, and tasks that require that multiple objects or multipart objects be analysed and remembered simultaneously.

A single visual object can be expected to trigger activity in many different neurons distributed across separate cortical areas. Evidence comes both from computational demonstrations of the advantages of distributed representations (McClelland & Rumelhart, 1986; Rumelhart & McClelland, 1986) and physiological demonstrations of separate visual areas in cortex (Felleman & Van Essen, 1991). How can all the activity from a single object be linked together? At least three different solutions have been proposed. First, the many neurons firing in response to one object could all be connected to a single high-level neuron that represents the entire combination (binding by conjunction units). Second, attentional mechanisms can select a subset of the visual input and filter

---

Please address all correspondence to K.R. Cave, Department of Psychology, University of Southampton, Southampton SO17 1BJ, UK. Email: kc@coglit.soton.ac.uk

Thanks to Nick Donnelly, Giovanni Galfano, John Hummel, Werner X. Schneider, and Shui-I Shih for very helpful comments.

---

http://www.tandf.co.uk/journals/pp/13506285.html DOI:10.1080/13506280143000089

out the rest, so that only information about a single object is represented in higher-level cortical structures (attentional binding). Third, all of the neurons responding to a single object could fire in synchrony (temporal binding). Ideally, only one of these mechanisms would be used, and the task of explaining binding would be fairly straightforward. However, the available evidence suggests otherwise. There is strong and consistent physiological evidence that the first two binding mechanisms play important roles in vision, and there is good reason to believe that the third mechanism is important in human vision as well.

BINDING BY CONJUNCTION UNITS

Physiological studies of visual neurons show a hierarchy of complexity in their response properties, starting at the retina and passing through the LGN and V1 and on to the ventral pathway structures in the inferior temporal lobe (Felleman & Van Essen, 1991). Neurons in the lower stages of this hierarchy have small receptive fields and respond to simple visual properties such as colour, orientation, and motion. The information about a single object is split across different neurons, but they will all be close together, allowing the features of the object to be loosely "bundled" (Wolfe & Cave, 1999). Neurons at the upper stages have large receptive fields, and some respond to complex, multipart stimuli such as faces and hands. This hierarchy is apparently able to produce single neurons that respond to the combinations of features and properties belonging to a single object, or to the combination of components that make up a complex object. Ghose and Maunsell (1999) argue that there are so many neurons in cortex that each object that is learned can be represented by its own neuron or set of neurons. However, the conjunction units that have been measured so far generally seem to be devoted mainly to stimuli, such as faces and hands, that are the most significant and most familiar for the animals being tested, suggesting that some other method must be used with less familiar objects.

A conjunction unit by itself is a very limited representation, because it cannot adequately represent both the conjunction and the identity of the individual components (Fodor & Pylyshyn, 1988; Hummel & Biederman, 1992). Furthermore, the necessary connections for the conjunctive representations that Ghose and Maunsell propose presumably cannot be formed instantly. Binding by conjunction units might work in an environment in which all of the object representations can be prewired or learned over a long training period, but it does not explain our extreme flexibility in learning new complex objects quickly and easily. Attentional binding and temporal synchrony are more dynamic, and explain how short-term object representations can be formed quickly and with limited exposure to the object.

ATTENTIONAL BINDING

One advantage of a system in which each combination of features is represented by its own neuron is that it can represent many different objects simultaneously. If conjunction units are not available for every object present, then it becomes difficult to represent each object in a way that maintains information about which features belong to which object and avoids illusory conjunctions (Prinzmetal, 1981; Treisman & Schmidt, 1982). One way to prevent confusion in combining features is to limit the number of objects represented in the system at any one time. There is now abundant evidence for a visual attention mechanism that limits visual processing by enhancing information from some locations and inhibiting information from others. (For reviews, see Cave & Bichot, 1999, and van der Heijden, 1993.) Described here are some experiments from our laboratory that illustrate the spatial nature of this selection process and demonstrate some of its other important aspects as well.

Feature-driven location selection

Kim and Cave (1995) measured the degree to which target and distractor locations were selected or inhibited during conjunction search. On 25% of the trials, the search stimulus was followed by a spatial probe (a small black dot) at one of the locations that had just been occupied by one of the elements in the search array (see Figure 1). Response times to this probe reflected the degree to which each location was selected during the search. As expected, the location with the target object (a red square) received the most attention, but responses were also fairly fast at locations with distractors that shared the target colour (red circles) or the target shape (green squares), indicating that these locations also received a certain amount of attention. The slowest probe responses were for those locations that had a distractor with neither of the relevant target features (green circles).

Note that location is irrelevant in this search task. Yet it is the *location* of the target that is selected, because the spatial probe also enjoys the benefits of attention when it appears at the target's location. In a task that requires selection of a target with a particular colour and shape, the target is selected by first determining the location with those properties, and then selecting that location. This indirect type of selection has been described as "feature-driven location selection" (Shih & Sperling, 1996).

Kim and Cave (1995) also combined the spatial probe task with a feature search, in which the target was a red circle among red squares. Probes at the target location produced faster responses than those at distractor locations, even though some probes appeared only 30 ms after the target. The exact timing of attentional effects is difficult to determine from behavioural experiments such as these, because we do not know at which processing stage the effects occur or at what time the different stages occur. Nonetheless, the feature search

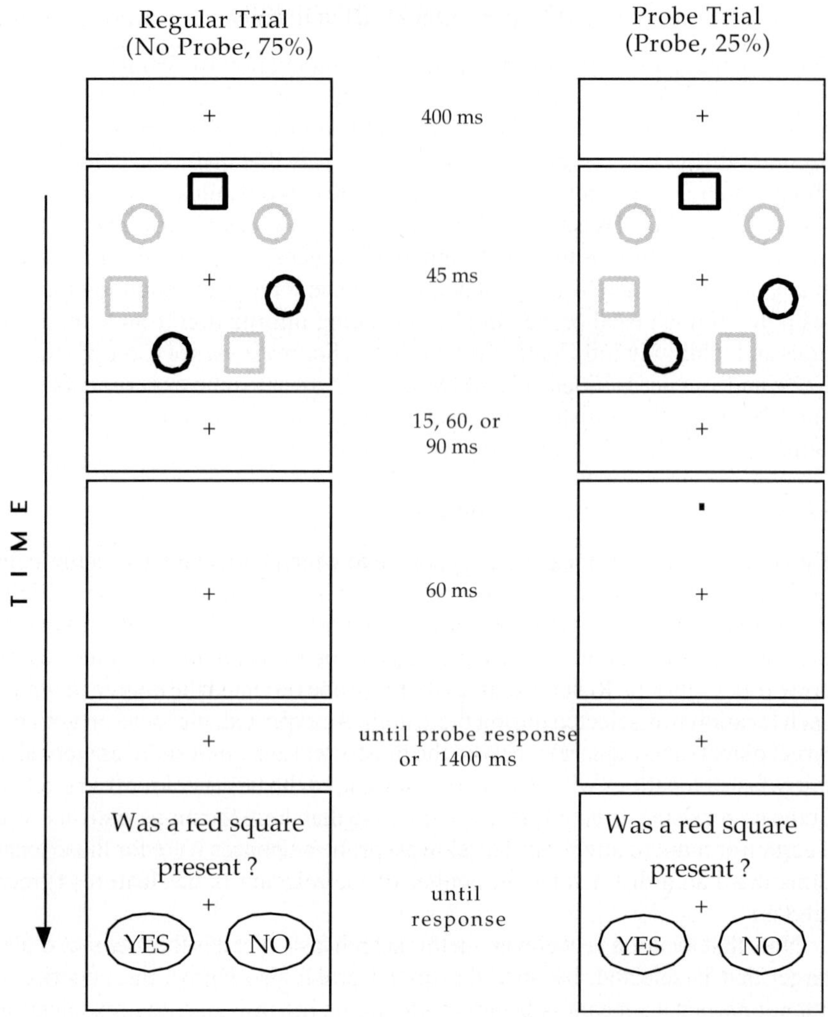

Figure 1. The sequence of displays for the regular and probe trials in Kim and Cave (1995). Red shapes are shown here in black, and green shapes are shown here in grey. Participants responded as quickly as possible when they detected a probe dot.

experiment suggests that a location can be selected very quickly after a stimulus appears.

Cave and Zimmerman (1997) demonstrated feature-driven location selection in a very different search task, in which participants searched for one specified letter in an array of letters. As before, response times were faster to spatial probes at the target letter location than at distractor letter locations, suggesting that the location with the shape features belonging to the target letter was selected, allowing that letter to be processed more fully and confirmed as the target. Responses to probes at distractor locations near the target were slower than those for locations far from the target. This pattern indicates that nearby distractors interfere more with target identification, and underscores the importance of location in selection. (See Bahcall & Kowler, 1999; Caputo & Guerra, 1998; and Mounts, 2000a, b, for additional demonstrations of this flanking inhibition.)

Spatial attention is often compared to a spotlight that facilitates processing of the target location (Posner, Snyder, & Davidson, 1980), but this flanking inhibition would only appear with attention that inhibits distractor locations. Additional evidence for selection by distractor inhibition comes from search experiments by Cepeda, Cave, Bichot, and Kim (1998). They probed target locations, distractor locations, and blank locations between the search array elements. Probe responses were slow for distractor locations, but fast at target and blank locations, indicating that inhibition was focused specifically on distractor locations.

Modeling spatial selection without synchrony

We have designed a model to demonstrate how a relatively simple set of neural networks can produce the feature-driven location selection found in these experiments, as well as other attentional phenomena from experiments using spatial cueing, visual search, and distractor interference (Cave, 1999; Cave, Kim, Bichot, & Sobel, 2001). This model (like many other network models, including Koch & Ullman, 1985; Olshausen, Anderson, & Van Essen, 1993; Tsotsos et al., 1995; Wolfe & Gancarz, 1996) starts with the assumption that visual processing occurs within a hierarchy of spatial maps. Information starts at the lowest level of the hierarchy and travels up to the top, with some information about location being lost at each step (see Figure 2). The maps at the lowest level of the hierarchy consist of neural units that respond to one particular feature value (a colour or orientation) within a small receptive field. Each unit in the next level up has a larger receptive field, because it receives input from a small region of the maps at the lowest level. The third level units have even larger receptive fields, receiving their inputs from a region of the second-level maps, and so on up to the top of the hierarchy. At the top level, there are just a few units, each representing a particular colour or orientation anywhere in the visual field.

This hierarchical architecture corresponds to that found in physiological studies of the ventral pathway (Ungerleider & Haxby, 1994; Ungerleider & Mishkin, 1982). It creates a problem when multiple objects are present simultaneously in the visual field: At the bottom level, information from each object will be represented separately from the others at its own location. However, as information travels up the hierarchy, information from the different objects

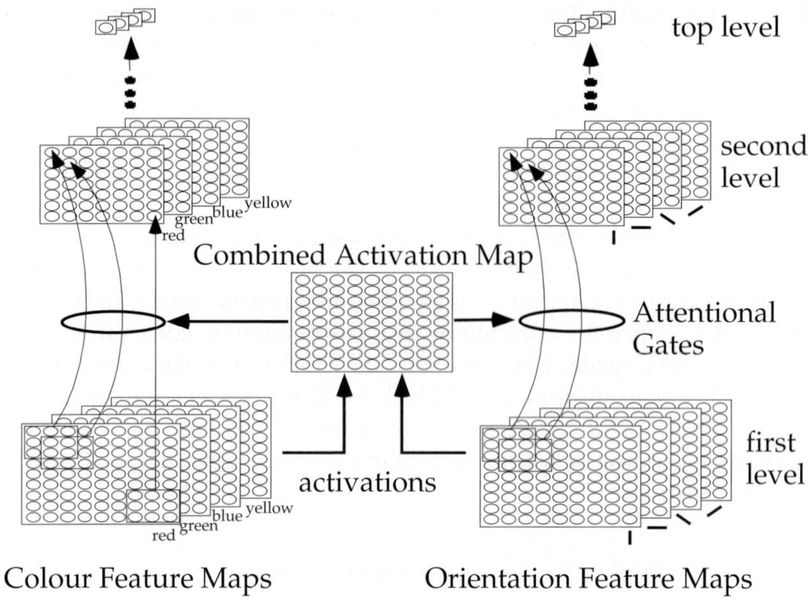

Figure 2. The main structures of the FeatureGate model. Two types of feature maps are shown, representing colour and orientation. At the top of each hierarchy are units responding to a specific colour or orientation anywhere within the visual field. The flow of feature information upward through each hierarchy is controlled by attentional gates.

converges, making it impossible to determine which colours and orientations belong together (see Schneider, 1995). Thus, identifying each object is complicated by the interference from other objects.

The attentional mechanism of the model is designed to prevent this interference. It works by inhibiting information from some locations so that information from one location can be represented at the top level free of interference. Each connection from one location on one level to the level above is controlled by an attentional gate that limits the amount of activation traveling up the connection. The degree to which each gate is open is determined by the features present at that location. It will be open more if its location contains a unique feature that does not appear at nearby locations, and it will be open more if its location contains a feature known to belong to the target. Because of this feature-driven gating mechanism, the model is named FeatureGate.

FeatureGate does not always select a target on the first pass. If it selects a distractor, it inhibits the selected location and allows a new location to be represented at the top level. This process can be repeated to produce a serial scan of locations. The search times produced by FeatureGate correspond to those produced by human subjects engaged in feature and conjunction search (Treisman & Gelade, 1980; Wolfe, Cave, & Franzel, 1989), and in feature searches with a singleton distractor (Theeuwes, 1994). When FeatureGate receives a location cue, it can produce an attentional gradient like those found by Downing and Pinker (1985) and LaBerge and Brown (1989). Its individual elements show activation patterns similar to those recorded by Luck, Chelazzi, Hillyard, and Desimone (1997) and by Moran and Desimone (1985). (More details are included in Cave et al., 2001.)

FeatureGate can account for many of the phenomena demonstrated in visual attention experiments. It works with very simple networks that have mainly short local connections, allowing it to explain how attentional effects such as those in Kim and Cave's (1995) feature search can arise so quickly. Furthermore, unlike a similar model proposed by Crick and Koch (1990a, b), it does not rely on temporal synchrony to tag selected locations. FeatureGate demonstrates that much of what a visual attention mechanism must do can be accomplished straightforwardly by neurons sensitive only to firing rate, and not to precise timing patterns or temporal synchrony.

Selecting objects from two locations simultaneously

FeatureGate illustrates the central principle of attentional binding, that ambiguity about which features belong together can be eliminated by limiting processing to one location at a time. The idea that attention is limited to a single location has generally been accepted after Posner et al. (1980) found that they could only produce attentional facilitation at two cued locations simultaneously if they were next to one another. More recent experiments, however, show that under some conditions two locations can be selected simultaneously (Bichot, Cave, & Pashler, 1999; Castiello & Umiltà,1992; Kramer & Hahn, 1995). At first it seems that selecting two locations should be difficult or impossible in a system relying on attentional binding, but a closer look at Bichot et al.'s task reveals that these results are consistent with attentional binding. Their stimulus consisted of a circular array of circles and squares. Two shapes were red, and the rest were green. The participants pressed one button if the two red objects were the same shape and another if they were not. Once the two locations with red have been selected, participants do not need to bind shape and location; they can perform the task without knowing which shape belongs at which location. Within a hierarchy such as FeatureGate, if the two red locations are both selected, their features will be represented simultaneously at the top. If both the curvature of a circle and the straight edges and angles of a square are active together, the "different" response is appropriate. If only one type of shape feature is active, the "same" response should be produced. This strategy of judging same or different based on a combination of the features from two objects should also be possible in Kramer and Hahn's experiment, although it will be more error-prone because the feature differences among their five-letter stimuli would be harder to discriminate than the differences between Bichot et al.'s circles and squares. Thus, simultaneous selection of the two locations is possible if interference between the two target shapes is not a problem.

Grouping

Unlike some models (Grossberg, Mingolla, & Ross, 1994; Müller, Humphreys, & Donnelly, 1994), FeatureGate can inhibit distractors and select targets without first organising display elements into groups. None the less, grouping clearly plays an important role in visual perception, and any explanation of binding must explain not only how features are bound together into objects, but how objects are bound together into groups. One example of the effects of grouping comes from Harms and Bundesen (1983), who asked participants to report a target letter in the centre of the display while ignoring two distractors to the left and right of the target. The target could appear in one of two colours, and one of the two distractors was the same colour as the target. The distractor that shared the target's colour interfered more with target identification than the other.

Harms and Bundesen's experiment shows that a distractor sharing a target's colour is to some extent grouped with the target and selected along with it (see also Driver & Baylis, 1989, and Baylis & Driver, 1992). Their results do not, however, indicate whether this selection is mediated by location. Kim and Cave (2001) combined Harms and Bundesen's task with a spatial probe task to show that the location with the distractor sharing the target colour receives more attention (or less inhibition) than the location with the other distractor. They concluded that each trial began with the selection of the centre location, which was known to contain the target, but that the selected area then expanded to include the colour group containing the target. Another experiment by Kim and Cave (1999) demonstrated that grouping also affected the allocation of attention to different locations in a conjunction search task. In that experiment, the location with a distractor element that shared a feature (colour or shape) with the search target received more attention if it was part of a group that included the target and other distractors sharing the same feature with the target.

This group selection can be implemented with a simple addition to FeatureGate. There are two ways in which top-down information can be introduced to FeatureGate to guide selection. When a target location is known in advance, the units controlling the attentional gates for those locations can be activated directly. When nonspatial features of the target, such as colour or orientation, are known in advance, the target feature units representing these features can be activated. These units trigger a top-down mechanism that activates each location that has a specified feature. In Kim and Cave's (2001) task, a trial begins with activation applied directly to the units that control the attentional gates for the centre location that contains the target. With that location selected, the features there, including the target colour, are represented at the top of the hierarchy (see Figure 3). The new addition to FeatureGate is a set of connections from these units at the top of the hierarchy to the target feature units. This activation to the target feature units causes locations with the target colour to be selected and locations with the other colour to be inhibited (see Figure 4). Thus, the target-colour distractor will to some extent be selected along with the target, and its shape features will also be somewhat activated at the top level, where they can interfere with target identification, as found by Harms and Bundesen (more details are included in Cave et al., 2001).

These new connections between the top level and the target feature units create a feedback loop that allows the selected area to change and develop depending on the stimulus. Once one part of an object is selected, this feedback will cause the rest of the object to be selected if it has the same colour, texture, or other features as the originally selected part. This mechanism will also allow attention to move with a moving object (Kahneman, Treisman, & Gibbs, 1992).

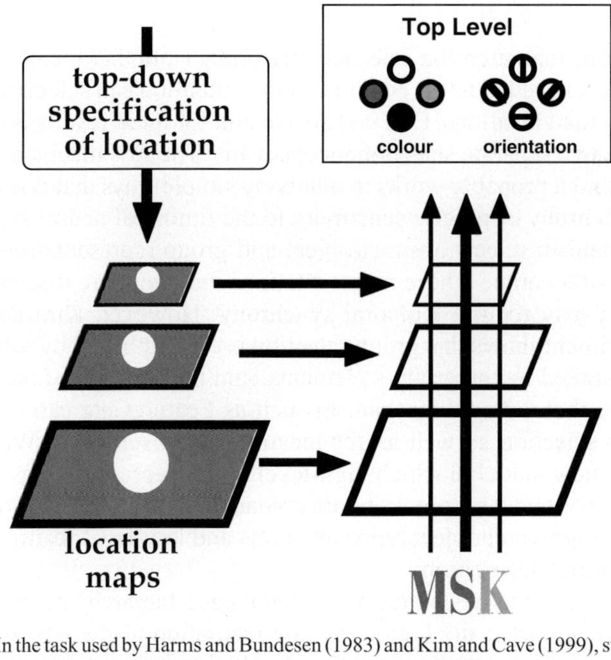

Figure 3. In the task used by Harms and Bundesen (1983) and Kim and Cave (1999), subjects attend to the middle letter while ignoring the distractors on either side. The target location is activated in the combined activation maps, so that its colour and other features are most strongly active at the top level.

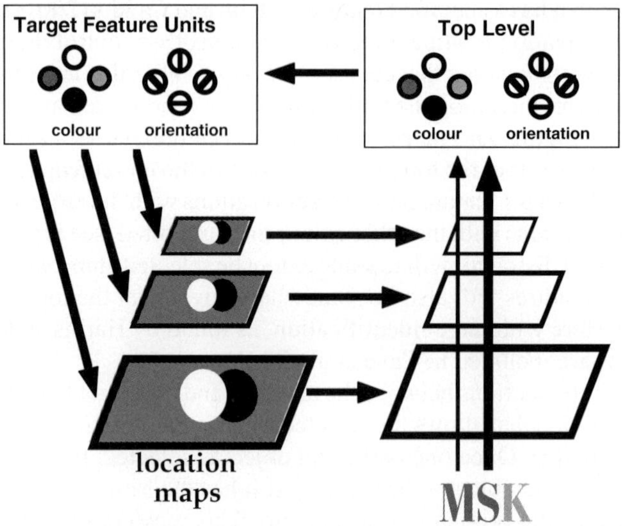

Figure 4. The target's features represented at the top level are fed back into the target feature units. As a result, the top-down mechanism inhibits the distractor location with the nontarget colour more than the distractor location with the target colour.

Selecting objects rather than locations

Demonstrations that attention selects entire groups and that it can move with moving objects have led to the conclusion that attention can select objects and groups rather than locations. One way to account for these results is to assume that there are two separate selection mechanisms. The first mechanism selects by location, and it probably works in relatively simple ways that do not require temporal synchrony or precise sensitivity to the timing of neural signals. The second mechanism selects abstract object and group representations that are independent of location. These representations may be more distributed, and this selection may require temporal synchrony. However, Kim and Cave's (2001) experiment shows that group selection is accomplished by selecting the locations occupied by the group's elements, and the addition of the feedback loop suggests that a single mechanism such as FeatureGate can account for object-based selection as well as for location-based selection. We are now developing a new model in which high-level object representations can guide selection of locations. This object-based guidance of location selection forms a link between high-level object representations and low-level features without relying on temporal synchrony.

The new model is like FeatureGate in that it has a hierarchy of spatial maps, from high-resolution at the bottom to low-resolution at the top. In the new model, however, the properties driving individual units become more complex at higher levels of the hierarchy. Orientations and line terminators are represented by individual units in the bottom layer, combinations of these features are represented at the intermediate levels, and complete letters are represented at the top level (see the left side of Figure 5). This hierarchy is able to recognize a letter based on its simple features.

The new model is able to search for a specified target letter, and to select locations with features belonging to that letter. This object-driven search is accomplished through a top-down selection mechanism that is location-based, but directed by the high-level representation of the target letter (see the right side of Figure 5). Because selection still relies on the gating of each location as

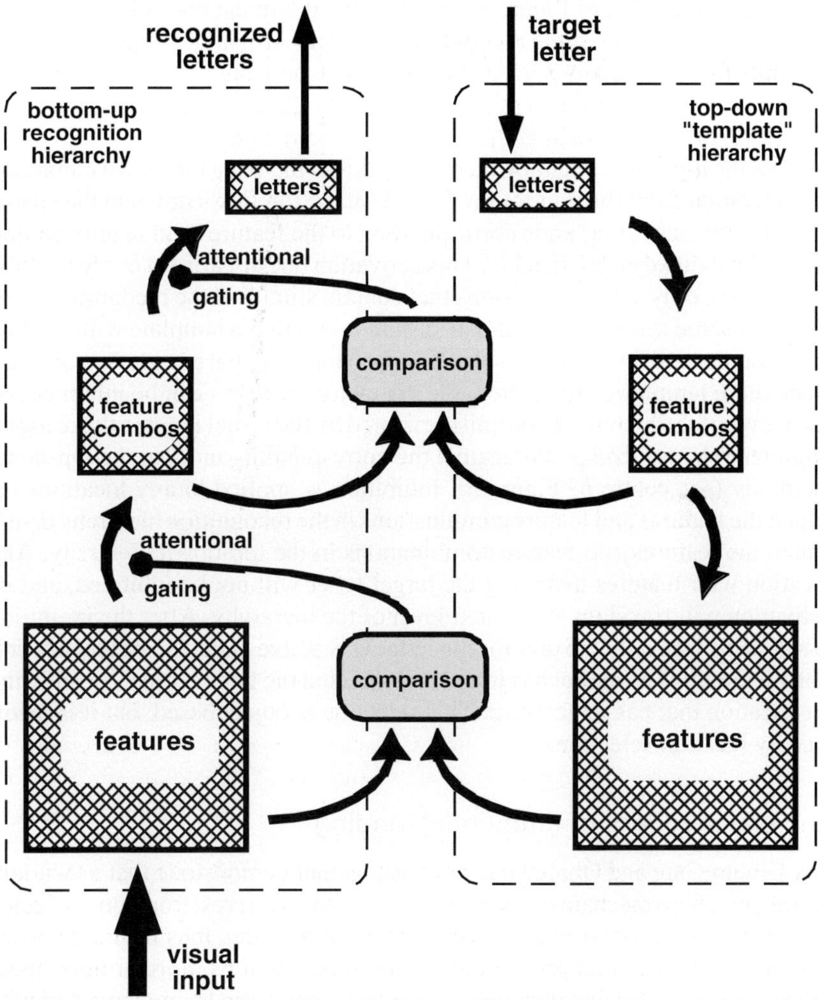

Figure 5. The main structures of the ObjectGate model.

in FeatureGate, but is ultimately controlled by a location-independent object representation, the model is called "ObjectGate" (Shi & Cave 1998, 2001).

The top-down selection mechanism takes the form of a hierarchy that mirrors that of the recognition hierarchy, but it is driven from the top down rather than from the bottom up. First one of the units at the top level is activated, representing the letter that is to be the target of a visual search. Then a search stimulus array is introduced to the bottom of the recognition hierarchy. Assume that the target letter, activated at the top of the top-down hierarchy, is U, and that the input at the bottom of the recognition hierarchy contains features making up three letters: U, N, and P. As activation travels up to the top of the recognition hierarchy (on the left of Figure 5), free of any attentional control, the units for U, N, and P at the top of the recognition hierarchy will all be highly activated, but units for other letters such as O will also be activated by combinations of features from U, N, and P. The model produces illusory conjunctions without attention, just as Treisman and Schmidt (1982) predict.

Now the top-down attention mechanism kicks in. In the top-down hierarchy, the activation from the unit for the letter U at the top flows down to the spatial maps below, activating units corresponding to the features and feature combinations that make up the letter U. This activation doesn't arise at every location in the maps; only at those locations that contain stimuli in the recognition hierarchy. In some sense, the top-down system is creating a template with the features appropriate for the target letter U at each location that has a letter stimulus. Once these templates are created, the distractor locations can be inhibited. At each level of the hierarchy, the units activated by the visual input in the recognition hierarchy are compared against the corresponding units in the top-down hierarchy (see centre of Figure 5). Inhibition is applied to any locations for which the features and feature combinations in the recognition hierarchy do not match the features and feature combinations in the top-down hierarchy. Any location with features matching the target letter will not be inhibited, and its activation will travel up to the next level of the hierarchy. After the inhibition has done its job, only the unit for the letter U is active at the top of the recognition hierarchy. The model has found and selected the target object by selecting the location that has its features. This selection is object based, but it is mediated by location selection.

The effectiveness of attentional binding

The FeatureGate and ObjectGate models together demonstrate that a location-based selection mechanism can allow only the features from one selected object to pass on to the final stages of visual processing, thus insuring correct binding of features and preventing illusory conjunctions. Furthermore, these models demonstrate that these selection mechanisms can be implemented with simple neural networks. The speed with which attentional effects arise in Kim and Cave's feature search suggest that spatial selection is implemented with mechanisms such as those in FeatureGate, in which most of the work is done by local networks, each involving a small number of units. The speed of attention also suggests that selection can begin before segmentation is completed (contrary to assumptions by Gray, 1999). Furthermore, the speed suggests that selection does not need to wait for the formation of patterns of temporal synchrony (although see von der Malsburg's, 1999, arguments that some types of synchrony can arise quickly). In sum, much of the data from experiments that have been conducted up to now on visual attention and binding can be accounted for by straightforward location selection that does not rely on neural synchrony or precise timing of neural signals.

TEMPORAL BINDING

One goal in building FeatureGate and ObjectGate is to take location selection as far as possible in accounting for demonstrated attentional effects. These mechanisms are robust and simple, and require little coordination across regions and little precision in timing. It seems likely that the visual system follows the same strategy, employing location selection and attentional binding whenever possible because of their reliability. In fact, a visual system with location selection as its only binding mechanism would be reasonably powerful and flexible.

However, the human visual system is regularly called upon to perform tasks much more challenging than those in most current attention experiments. We are able to detect subtle differences in complex configurations of objects and object parts, even when the objects are partially superimposed. The flexibility required goes beyond what can be achieved with location-based selection systems such as FeatureGate and ObjectGate. In the following subsections three problems are described that human visual systems handle quite well, but that pose serious challenges for any location-based selection mechanism operating by itself. Temporal synchrony, like attention binding, provides a mechanism to select target information apart from distractor information, but unlike attentional binding, it does not require selection of a location. There is nothing inherent in any of these visual processing problems that makes temporal synchrony the only possible solution, but if temporal synchrony could be used to link information represented across different neurons, these problems would be much easier to solve.

Selection of a target object with a distractor superimposed

Usually different objects occupy different locations, making location selection an effective way to select objects. However, in some circumstances multiple objects are superimposed so that to some extent they occupy the same locations, making it difficult to select one object's location without selecting the other. None the less, we are able to attend to one object or scene while to some extent ignoring a superimposed distractor object or scene. Neisser and Becklen (1974) showed participants a movie made by superimposing two scenes. In one, a group of people were bouncing a ball back and forth among them, while in the other, two pairs of hands were visible, engaged in a sort of game. Participants were instructed to attend to one scene or the other, and their memory performance after viewing the video indicated that they were generally successful in focusing their attention. Another set of experiments using much simpler stimuli (a rectangle and a line superimposed) showed that there are costs involved in shifting attention from one object to another (Duncan, 1984). To some extent, the separation of overlapping stimuli seems to be aided by perceiving them at different depths, but there are still some difficult questions left unanswered. How are superimposed objects at different depths represented neurally? Furthermore, in stimuli such as Duncan's or Neisser and Becklin's in which there are no cues from stereopsis or other depth cues, before the two stimuli can be assigned to two different depths, there must be some way to link together all the components of one overlapping stimulus so that they can be selected and separated apart from the other. What sort of mechanism is required?

The first thing to note about these tasks is that a location selection mechanism is not as helpless in these circumstances as some have assumed. The amount of overlapping contour between target and distractor is small. When guided by the feedback in ObjectGate, a location selection mechanism with enough precision could select most of the target contours without selecting much of the distractor contours. In fact, Cave and Kosslyn (1989) found evidence that in a task similar to Duncan's, a visual image-like template was used to select the target without selecting the superimposed distractor. Thus with only attentional binding, at least some visual processing should be possible even with overlapping objects.

Nevertheless, visual processing would be much easier in these circumstances if binding were possible independently of location, and neural synchrony provides one alternative. One suggestive piece of evidence comes from a binocular rivalry study by Fries, Roelfsema, Engel, König, and Singer (1997). Rivalry is, of course, an extreme case of superimposed stimuli, and the neural recordings in this study showed a higher level of neural synchrony when rivalrous stimuli were presented to the two eyes. Perhaps synchrony is necessary under rivalry to keep the features of one stimulus separate from the features of the superimposed distractor.

Maintaining episodic representations of objects after spatial attention moves to a new object

The main disadvantage of attentional binding is that it allows for the binding of only one object at a time. This limitation is consistent with claims that difficult attentional tasks such as conjunction search require serial scanning from one object to the next (Treisman & Gelade, 1980). However, our visuo-spatial memories are clearly capable of maintaining representations of multiple objects simultaneously. Much current research in active vision is devoted to minimizing the role of visual memory, but we undeniably have a well-developed ability to remember multiple visual objects. If you first survey a new room, noting all the pieces of furniture, and then close your eyes, you are able to navigate around the room fairly well. You will have to feel your way around because the location of each object is not represented precisely, but you are certainly able to maintain multiple objects and their approximate locations in memory simultaneously.

Kahneman and Treisman (1984) proposed that once an object is selected, all of its features are bound together and stored in an "object file", where they are maintained after attention shifts to another object. These object files have to be flexible enough to represent feature combinations that have never been seen before, so it seems unlikely that they could be implemented with only conjunction units. As noted by Hummel and Biederman (1992) and by Luck and Vogel (1998), however, neural synchrony provides a flexible mechanism by which multiple object files could be maintained simultaneously. Luck and Vogel also show that short-term memory capacity for visual objects is a bit less than four objects, which is perhaps what would be expected if these object representations are maintained by synchrony within separate neural groups, each firing independently of the other.

Representing multipart objects and complex configurations

The third problem is related to the second in that it requires the maintenance of information about multiple entities simultaneously. While the second involved the maintenance of memories after visual processing was completed, the third involves the maintenance of multiple components in the course of visual processing. Many complex objects consist of multiple parts, and many complex scenes consist of multiple objects. As Rensink (2000) suggests, it may be possible to extract some information about the setting of a scene (the "gist") using statistics of low-level structures, without binding features together. Most complex visual discriminations, however, will require some type of binding. Some of these objects and scenes can be analysed fully by serially attending to one component after another, identifying each by itself, and gradually building a representation of the entire configuration in memory. Others, however, may not be identifiable without considering all the components together. For these stimuli, the entire object or scene must be selected, but the features belonging to each component must also be bound together and kept separate from the rest. If conjunction units are not available to represent these configurations, then some sort of dynamic binding is necessary.

Hummel and Biederman (1992; see also Hummel, this issue; Hummel & Stankiewicz, 1996, 1998) argue strongly for the need to represent this type of complex structure in human vision. They introduce models that decompose an object into individual parts, and then use neural synchrony to represent each part separately from the others. The units representing each part fire rapidly in succession, so that over time their activations together trigger a representation of the entire object. Thus representations of the object, its parts, and some of the spatial relationships between the parts are all active simultaneously.

The same problem arises in identifying complex scenes, although it is not addressed directly by these models. Figure 6, which comes from Biederman (1981), shows an example. This scene is instantly recognizable as an office, even though the components making up the scene are not recognizable as office furniture, but are simple blocks and cylinders. The colours, textures, and other local cues that could be quickly extracted and used to find the gist are not there. Furthermore, each object, when selected and examined in isolation, is not very informative. Recognition of these scenes depends on the many different spatial

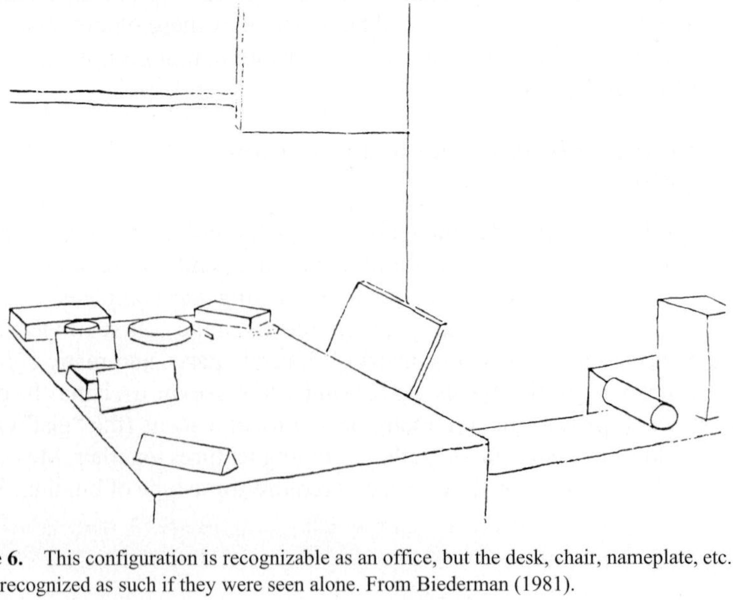

Figure 6. This configuration is recognizable as an office, but the desk, chair, nameplate, etc. would not be recognized as such if they were seen alone. From Biederman (1981).

relationships among the different components, and it probably requires that many different feature bindings be maintained simultaneously. Neural synchrony provides one method of doing this. The matrix of dots used by Parton, Donnelly, and Usher (this issue) is another example. In order for it to be perceived as a set of rows or columns, the entire stimulus must be represented while each row or column is also represented as a separate unit.

It should be noted that although the models by Hummel and colleagues are capable of representing configurations of object parts, they are still limited (like most object recognition models) in that they can only receive input from one object at a time. For these models to work, there must be some selection mechanism that prevents information about distractor objects from interfering. Hummel and Stankiewicz (1998) do explore how attention can contribute to their model's performance, but their attention mechanism only determines whether the parts of an object fire in synchrony or out of synchrony; it does not filter out distractor objects. In theory, this selection could also be done via temporal synchrony. Although Hummel has not incorporated this into his models, this type of synchrony-based target selection was suggested by Crick and Koch (1990a, b). However, it might be more efficient and straightforward to have a location selection mechanism to regulate the input to the object recognition model without relying on synchrony. In other words, complex object recognition might best be accomplished by a combination of location selection (to select the target object and inhibit distractor objects) and temporal synchrony (to represent each component of the target object separately).

WHERE TO LOOK FOR TEMPORAL BINDING

In physiological studies over the past decade, neural synchrony has been difficult to pin down. It appears in some circumstances and not in others, suggesting that if it is used in binding, it is not the only available mechanism. The findings reviewed here show why temporal binding might not always be used. A wide variety of different experiments suggest the presence of an attention mechanism that selects locations quickly and efficiently. Models such as FeatureGate and ObjectGate demonstrate that this location selection can be implemented with simple excitation and/or inhibition of locations. These models can execute the selection and binding necessary in many visual attention tasks without relying on temporal binding. Given the simplicity of these mechanisms and the fact that they can be implemented mainly with short-range connections, these mechanisms should be fast and reliable, and thus there is good reason for the visual system to employ location selection and attentional binding whenever possible.

However, there are limits to what can be accomplished with attentional binding, and visual processing of complex objects and scenes apparently goes beyond those limits. Some other method of binding is probably required with overlapping targets and distractors, and with tasks that require the maintenance of information about a number of objects or that require the identification of complex configurations or multipart objects. There is no guarantee that neural synchrony is employed in these tasks, but it is a promising candidate.

If neural synchrony can be used in binding, it is probably not used in every situation, and there may be many visual tasks that can be performed either with it or without it. This optional nature of temporal binding would explain why it has been difficult to characterize when it will appear and when it will not in physiological studies. If the conclusions described here are correct, then experimentalists trying to measure neural synchrony should focus on those tasks that are difficult or impossible to accomplish with location selection, because these are the tasks in which temporal synchrony is most likely to be employed.

REFERENCES

Bahcall, D., & Kowler, E. (1999). Attentional interference at small spatial separations. *Visual Research, 39,* 71–86.

Baylis, G.C., & Driver, J. (1992). Visual parsing and response competition: The effect of grouping factors. *Perception and Psychophysics, 51,* 145–162.

Bichot, N.P., Cave, K.R., & Pashler, H. (1999). Visual selection mediated by location: Feature-based selection of noncontiguous locations. *Perception and Psychophysics, 61,* 403–423.

Biederman, I. (1981). On the semantics of a glance at a scene. In M. Kubovy & J.R. Pomerantz (Eds.), *Perceptual organization* (pp. 213–253). Hillsdale, NJ: Lawrence Erlbaum Associates Inc.

Caputo, G., & Guerra, S. (1998). Attentional selection by distractor suppression. *Vision Research, 38,* 669–689.

Castiello, U., & Umiltà, C. (1992). Splitting focal attention. *Journal of Experimental Psychology: Human Perception and Performance, 18,* 837–848.

Cave, K.R. (1999). The FeatureGate model of visual selection. *Psychological Research, 62,* 182–194.

Cave, K.R., & Bichot, N.P. (1999). Visuo-spatial attention: Beyond a spotlight model. *Psychonomic Bulletin and Review, 6,* 204–223.

Cave, K.R., Kim, M.-S., Bichot, N.P., & Sobel, K.V. (2001). *Visual selection within a hierarchical network: The FeatureGate model.* Manuscript in preparation.

Cave, K.R., & Kosslyn, S.M. (1989). Varieties of size-specific visual selection. *Journal of Experimental Psychology: General, 118,* 148–164.

Cave, K.R., & Zimmerman, J.M. (1997). Flexibility in spatial attention before and after practice. *Psychological Science, 8,* 399–403.

Cepeda, N.J., Cave, K.R., Bichot, N.P., & Kim, M.-S. (1998). Spatial selection via feature-driven inhibition of distractor locations. *Perception and Psychophysics, 60,* 727–746.

Crick, F., & Koch, C. (1990a). Some reflections on visual awareness. In *Symposia on Quantitative Biology, Vol. 55.* Plainview, NY: Cold Spring Harbor Press.

Crick, F., & Koch, C. (1990b). Towards a neurobiological theory of consciousness. *Seminars in the Neurosciences, 2,* 263–275.

Downing, C.J., & Pinker, S. (1985). The spatial structure of visual attention. In M.I. Posner & O.S.M. Marin (Eds.), *Attention and performance XI: Mechanisms of attention.* Hillsdale, NJ: Lawrence Erlbaum Associates Inc.

Driver, J., & Baylis, G.C. (1989). Movement and visual attention: The spotlight metaphor breaks down. *Journal of Experimental Psychology: Human Perception and Performance, 15,* 448–456.

Duncan, J. (1984). Selective attention and the organization of visual information. *Journal of Experimental Psychology: General, 113,* 501–517.

Felleman, D.J., & Van Essen, D.C. (1991). Distributed hierarchical processing in the primate cerebral cortex. *Cerebral Cortex, 1,* 1–47.

Fodor, J.A., & Pylyshyn, Z.W. (1988). Connectionism and cognitive architecture: A critical analysis. *Cognition, 28,* 3–71.

Fries, P., Roelfsema, P.R., Engel, A.K., König, P., & Singer, W. (1997). Synchronization of oscillatory responses in visual cortex correlates with perception of interocular rivalry. *Proceedings of the National Academy of Sciences USA, 94,* 12699–12704.

Ghose, G.M., & Maunsell, J. (1999). Specialized representations in visual cortex: A role for binding? *Neuron, 24,* 79–85.

Gray, C.M. (1999). The temporal correlation hypothesis of visual feature integration: Still alive and well. *Neuron, 24,* 31–47.

Grossberg, S., Mingolla, E., & Ross, W.D. (1994). A neural theory of attentive visual search: Interaction of boundary, surface, spatial, and object representations. *Psychological Review, 101,* 470–489.

Harms, L., & Bundesen, C. (1983). Color segregation and selective attention in a nonsearch task. *Perception and Psychophysics, 33,* 11–19.

Hummel, J.E. (this issue). Complementary solutions to the binding problem in vision: Implications for shape perception and object recognition. *Visual Cognition, 8*(3/4/5), 489–517.

Hummel, J.E., & Biederman, I. (1992). Dynamic binding in a neural network for shape recognition. *Psychological Review, 99,* 480–517.

Hummel, J.E., & Stankiewicz, B.J. (1996). An architecture for rapid, hierarchical structural description. In T. Inui & J.L. McClelland (Eds.), *Attention and performance XVI: Information integration in perception and communication* (pp. 93–121). Cambridge, MA: MIT Press.

Hummel, J.E., & Stankiewicz, B.J. (1998). Two roles for attention in shape perception: A structural description model of visual scrutiny. *Visual Cognition, 5,* 49–79.

Kahneman, D., & Treisman, A. (1984). Changing views of attention and automaticity. In R. Parasuraman & D.R. Davies (Eds.), *Varieties of attention*. San Diego, CA: Academic Press.

Kahneman, D., Treisman, A., & Gibbs, B.J. (1992). The reviewing of object files: Object-specific integration of information. *Cognitive Psychology, 24,* 175–219.

Kim, M.-S., & Cave, K.R. (1995). Spatial attention in visual search for features and feature conjunctions. *Psychological Science, 6,* 376–380.

Kim, M.S., & Cave, K.R. (1999). Grouping effects on spatial attention in visual search. *Journal of General Psychology, 126*, 326–352.

Kim, M.S., & Cave, K.R. (2001). Perceptual grouping via spatial selection in a focused-attention task. *Vision Research, 41,* 611–624.

Koch, C., & Ullman, S. (1985). Shifts in selective visual attention: Towards the underlying neural circuitry. *Human Neurobiology, 4,* 219–227.

Kramer, A.F., & Hahn, S. (1995). Splitting the beam: Distribution of attention over noncontiguous regions of the visual field. *Psychological Science, 6,* 381–386.

LaBerge, D., & Brown, V. (1989). Theory of attentional operations in shape identification. *Psychological Review, 96*, 101–124.

Luck, S.J., Chelazzi, L., Hillyard, S.A., & Desimone, R. (1997). Neural mechanisms of spatial selective attention in areas V1, V2, and V4 of macaque visual cortex. *Journal of Neurophysiology, 77,* 24–42.

Luck, S.J., & Vogel, E.K. (1998). Response from Luck and Vogel. *Trends in Cognitive Sciences, 2,* 78–80.

McClelland, J.L., & Rumelhart, D.E. (1986). *Parallel distributed processing: Vol. 2: Psychological and biological models*. Cambridge, MA: MIT Press.

Moran, J., & Desimone, R. (1985). Selective attention gates visual processing in the extrastriate cortex. *Science, 229,* 782–784.

Mounts, J.R.W. (2000a). Attentional capture by abrupt onsets and feature singletons produces inhibitory surrounds. *Perception and Psychophysics, 62,* 1485–1493.

Mounts, J.R.W. (2000b). Evidence for suppressive mechanisms in attentional selection: Feature singletons produce inhibitory surrounds. *Perception and Psychophysics, 62,* 969–983.

Müller, H.J., Humphreys, G.W., & Donnelly, N. (1994). SEarch via Recursive Rejection (SERR): Visual search for single and dual form-conjunction targets. *Journal of Experimental Psychology: Human Perception and Performance, 20,* 235–258.

Neisser, U., & Becklen, R. (1974). Selective looking: Attending to visually specified events. *Cognitive Psychology, 7,* 480–494.

Olshausen, B.A., Anderson, C.H., & Van Essen, D.C. (1993). A neurobiological model of visual attention and invariant pattern recognition based on dynamic routing of information. *Journal of Neuroscience, 13,* 4700–4719.

Parton, A., Donnelly, N., & Usher, M. (this issue). The effects of temporal synchrony on the perceived organization of elements in spatially symmetric and asymmetric grids. *Visual Cognition, 8*(3/4/5), 637–654.

Posner, M.I., Snyder, C.R.R., & Davidson, B.J. (1980). Attention and the detection of signals. *Journal of Experimental Psychology: General, 109,* 160–174.

Prinzmetal, W. (1981). Principles of feature integration in visual perception. *Perception and Psychophysics, 4,* 330–340.

Rensink, R.A. (2000). Seeing, sensing, and scrutinizing. *Vision Research, 40,* 1469–1487.

Rumelhart, D.E., & McClelland, J.L. (1986). *Parallel distributed processing: Vol. 1: Foundations.* Cambridge, MA: MIT Press.

Schneider, W.X. (1995). VAM: A neuro-cognitive model for visual attention control of segmentation, object recognition, and space-based motor action. *Visual Cognition, 2,* 331–375.

Shi, W., & Cave, K.R. (1998, November). *How to select both objects and locations.* Paper presented at the Psychonomic Society annual meeting, Dallas, TX, USA.

Shi, W., & Cave, K.R. (2001). Object recognition and spatial selection. *Manuscript in preparation.*

Shih, S.-I., & Sperling, G. (1996). Is there feature-based attentional selection in visual search? *Journal of Experimental Psychology: Human Perception and Performance, 22,* 758–779.

Theeuwes, J., (1994). Endogenous and exogenous control of visual selection. *Perception, 23,* 429–440.

Treisman, A.M., & Gelade, G. (1980). A feature integration theory of attention. *Cognitive Psychology, 12,* 97–136.

Treisman, A.M., & Schmidt, H. (1982). Illusory conjunctions in the perception of objects. *Cognitive Psychology, 14,* 107–141.

Tsotsos, J., Culhane, S.M., Wai, W., Lai, Y., Davis, N., & Nuflo, F. (1995). Modeling visual attention via selective tuning. *Artificial Intelligence, 78,* 507–545.

Ungerleider, L.G., & Haxby, J.V. (1994). "What" and "where" in the human brain. *Current Opinion in Neurobiology, 4,* 157–165.

Ungerleider, L.G., & Mishkin, M. (1982). Two cortical visual systems. In D.J. Ingle, M.A. Goodale, & R.J.W. Mansfield (Eds.), *Analysis of visual behavior* (pp. 549–586). Cambridge, MA: MIT Press.

van der Heijden, A.H.C. (1993). The role of position in object selection in vision. *Psychological Research, 56,* 44–58.

von der Malsburg, C. (1999). The what and why of binding: The modeler's perspective. *Neuron, 24,* 95–104.

Wolfe, J.M., & Cave, K.R. (1999). The psychophysical evidence for a binding problem in human vision. *Neuron, 24,* 11–17.

Wolfe J.M., Cave K.R., & Franzel S.L., (1989). Guided Search: An alternative to the feature integration model for visual search. *Journal of Experimental Psychology: Human Perception and Performance, 15,* 419–433.

Wolfe, J.M., & Gancarz, G. (1996). Guided Search 3.0: A model of visual search catches up with Jay Enoch 40 years later. In V. Lakshminarayanan (Ed.), *Basic and clinical applications of vision science* (pp. 189–192). Dordrecht, The Netherlands: Kluwer Academic.

VISUAL COGNITION, 2001, *8* (3/4/5), 489–517

Complementary solutions to the binding problem in vision: Implications for shape perception and object recognition

John E. Hummel

Department of Psychology, University of California, Los Angeles, USA

Behavioural, neural, and computational considerations suggest that the visual system may use (at least) two approaches to binding an object's features and/or parts into a coherent representation of shape: Dynamically bound (e.g., by synchrony of firing) representations of part attributes and spatial relations form a structural description of an object's shape, while units representing shape attributes at specific locations (i.e., a static binding of attributes to locations) form an analogue (image-like) representation of that shape. I will present a computational model of object recognition based on this proposal and empirical tests of the model. The model accounts for a large body of findings in human object recognition, and makes several novel and counter intuitive predictions. In brief, it predicts that visual priming for attended objects will be invariant with translation, scale, and left–right reflection, whereas priming for unattended objects will be invariant with translation and scale, but sensitive to left–right reflection. Five experiments demonstrated the predicted relationships between visual attention and patterns of visual priming as a function of variations in viewpoint. The implications of these findings for theories of visual binding and shape perception will be discussed.

HUMAN OBJECT RECOGNITION

The most important property of the human capacity for object recognition is our ability to recognize objects despite variations in the image presented to the retina. This ability takes two forms. The most commonly studied is recognition despite variations in viewpoint. We can recognize objects in a wide variety of views even though different views can present radically different images to the

Please address all correspondence to J.E. Hummel, Department of Psychology, University of California, 405 Hilgard Ave., Los Angeles, CA 90095-1563, USA.
Email: jhummel@lifesci.ucla.edu

This research was supported by NSF Grant 9709023 and by grants from the UCLA Academic Senate.

http://www.tandf.co.uk/journals/pp/13506285.html DOI:10.1080/13506280143000214

retina. This capacity is particularly challenging to understand because human object recognition is robust to some but not all variations in viewpoint. Recognition is invariant with the location of the image on the retina, left–right (mirror) reflection (Biederman & Cooper, 1991a), scale (Biederman & Cooper, 1992), and, to a lesser degree, rotation in depth (see Lawson, 1999, for a thorough review). However, it is sensitive to rotation in the picture plane (as when an object is upside-down; Jolicoeur, 1985, 1990; Lawson, 1999; Tarr & Pinker, 1989, 1990). The second form of object constancy is our ability to generalize recognition over variations in object shape. This capacity has at least two familiar and important manifestations. First, we are good at recognizing objects as members of a class, such as "chair" or "car", rather than just as specific instances, such as "my office chair" or "Toyota Camry". And second, we easily recognize novel members of known object classes: The first time we see a Dodge Viper, it is easy to recognize it as a car, even if we have never before seen a car with exactly that shape.

Together, these properties are challenging to explain because they defy explanation in terms of simple geometric laws. A system based strictly on the laws of projective geometry—e.g., that used those laws to match the information in an object's two-dimensional (2-D) image to a 3-D model the object's shape (e.g., Lower, 1987; Ullman, 1989, 1996)—would be equally able to accommodate all variations in viewpoint (which the human is not) but would not tolerate variations in an object's shape (which the human does).

These and other properties of human object recognition have led some researchers to postulate that we recognize objects on the basis of *structural descriptions* specifying an object's parts (or features) in terms of their spatial relations to one another (Biederman, 1987; Clowes, 1967; Marr & Nishihara, 1978; Palmer, 1977; Sutherland, 1968; Winston, 1975). The most explicit such theory to date is Biederman's (1987) *recognition by components* and its variants (Bergevin & Levine, 1993; Dickinson, Pentland, & Rosenfeld, 1992; Hummel & Biederman, 1992; Hummel & Stankiewicz, 1996a, 1998). According to this theory, objects are recognized as collections of simple volumes (*geons*; Biederman, 1987) in particular categorical relations. For example, a coffee mug would be represented as a curved cylinder (the handle) side-attached to a straight vertical cylinder (the body). The relations are critical: If the curved cylinder were attached to the top of the straight cylinder, then the object would be a bucket rather than a mug. This type of representation provides a natural account of many properties of human object recognition. Note that it will not change if the mug is translated across the visual field, moved closer to or farther from the viewer, or left–right (mirror) reflected. But rotating the mug 90° about the line of sight (so that the body is horizontal and the handle is on top) will change the description. Like human object recognition, this description is sensitive to rotations about the line of sight, but insensitive to translation, scale, left–right reflection, and some rotations in depth. It is also insensitive to things such as the exact length of the handle or the exact width of the body, making it a suitable basis for recognizing many different mugs as members of the same general class (Biederman, 1987; Hummel & Stankiewicz, 1998).

Consistent with this proposal, there is evidence that the visual system explicitly represents an object's parts (Biederman, 1987; Biederman & Cooper, 1991b; Tversky & Hemenway, 1984) in terms of their spatial relations (Hummel & Stankiewicz, 1996b; Palmer, 1978; Saiki & Hummel, 1996, 1998a, b), and that these representations are used in the service of object recognition (Biederman & Cooper, 1991b; Hummel & Stankiewicz, 1996b; Saiki & Hummel, 1996, 1998b). If these properties were all that were true of human object recognition, then we could conclude that recognition is based on generating and matching structural descriptions, as postulated by Clowes (1967) and Sutherland (1968), and later by Palmer (1977), Marr (1982; Marr & Nishihara, 1978), and Biederman (1987). However, several additional findings indicate that structural descriptions cannot provide a complete account of our ability to visually recognize objects. To understand why, it is necessary to consider the computational problem of generating and representing explicit structural descriptions.

Consider generating the description *curved cylinder side-attached to straight cylinder* from the image of a coffee mug (Hummel & Biederman, 1992). First, it is necessary to segment the object's local features (e.g., contours and vertices) into parts-based groups so that the features of one part do not interfere with the interpretation of the other. Likewise, any higher-level interpretations of the parts' attributes (e.g., the shapes of their cross sections and axes, their aspect ratio, etc.) must also be bound into sets. Next, the representation of *curved cylinder* must be bound to the agent role of *side-attached*, and *straight cylinder* to the patient role. An important problem for structural description concerns the nature of these bindings. Bindings can be either *dynamic* or *static*. A dynamic binding is one in which a single representational unit can be used in many different combinations. For example, one unit (or collection of units) might represent cylinders and another might represent the side-attached relation; a cylinder side-attached to another part would be represented by explicitly tagging these units as bound together (e.g., by synchrony of firing; Gray & Singer, 1989; Hummel & Biederman, 1992; von der Malsburg, 1981/1994). Because tags are assigned to units dynamically, the same units can enter into different conjunctions at different times. A static binding is one in which a separate unit is pre-dedicated for each conjunction. For example, one unit might respond to cylinders side-attached to other parts, another might respond to cylinders above other parts, and so forth. Structural description requires dynamic binding (Hummel & Biederman, 1992). The number of units required to pre-code all possible part–relation conjunctions would be prohibitive (growing exponentially with the number of relations).

More importantly, static binding sacrifices the independence of the bound attributes: The fact that a cylinder side-attached to something is more similar to a cylinder above something than to a slab above something is completely lost in a representation where each part–relation binding is coded by a separate unit. This loss of similarity structure is a fundamental property of static binding that cannot be overcome even with sophisticated static codes, such as Smolensky's (1990) tensor products (Holyoak & Hummel, 2000; Hummel & Biederman, 1992). Dynamic binding is thus a necessary prerequisite to structural description.

The problem is that dynamic binding imposes a bottleneck on processing: It is necessarily time consuming and capacity limited, and there is substantial evidence that it requires visual attention (Hummel & Stankiewicz, 1996a; Luck & Beach, 1998; Luck & Vogel, 1997). The limitations of dynamic binding are problematic for structural description theories of object recognition. Structural description cannot be faster or more automatic than dynamic binding, but object recognition apparently is. Face recognition in the macaque is accomplished to a high degree of certainty based on the *first* set of spikes to reach inferotemporal cortex (at least for overlearned stimuli; Oram & Perrett, 1992). Clearly, the macaque visual system recognizes faces without waiting around for several sets of desynchronized spikes. People also recognize objects very rapidly. Intraub (1981) showed that people can recognize common objects presented at the rate of 10 per second (see also Potter, 1976). These findings suggest that object recognition is much too fast to depend on dynamic binding for structural description. Similarly, although dynamic binding—and therefore structural description—requires visual attention, object recognition apparently does not, as shown by findings of both negative priming (e.g., Tipper, 1985; Treisman & DeSchepper, 1996) and positive priming (Stankiewicz, Hummel, & Cooper, 1998) for ignored objects.

COMPLEMENTARY SOLUTIONS TO THE BINDING PROBLEM

Both the strengths of the structural description account of shape perception (its ability to account for the flexibility of human object recognition, as well as the role explicit parts and relations in shape perception) and its weaknesses (its inability to account for the speed and automaticity of object recognition) stem from its ability to represent parts independently of their relations, and the resulting need for a dynamic solution to the binding problem. The question is how the visual system profits from the strengths of this approach without suffering its limitations.

Hummel and Stankiewicz (1996a) hypothesized that the visual system solves this problem by adopting a hybrid solution to the binding problem. Their model, *JIM.2* (so named because it is the successor to Hummel & Biederman's,

1992, *JIM* model), uses dynamic binding to generate structural descriptions of object shape when an object is attended, and uses static binding to maintain the separation of an object's parts when an object is ignored (or when dynamic binding otherwise fails). The basic idea starts with the observation that static binding—in which separate units responding to separate conjunctions of properties—is not capacity limited in the way that dynamic binding is. The theory predicts that when the visual system succeeds in segmenting an object into its parts, shape perception will have the characteristics of a structural description: Recognition will be largely invariant with variations in viewpoint, and part attributes will be represented independently of one another, and of the parts' interrelations. When the visual system fails to segment an image into its parts (e.g., due to inattention or insufficient processing time), shape perception will have the characteristics of the statically bound representation: It will be more sensitive to variations in viewpoint, and part attributes will not be represented independently of their spatial relations.

This paper presents the most recent version of this theory—a model I shall refer to as *JIM.3*, as it is the successor of *JIM.2*—and reviews several experiments that have been conducted to test its predictions (Stankiewicz & Hummel, 2000; Stankiewicz et al., 1998). In addition to accounting for a wide variety of findings in human shape perception and object recognition, *JIM.2* and *JIM.3* predict a number of counterintuitive relationships between visual attention and patterns of visual priming. As elaborated later, attended images should prime themselves, scaled and translated versions of themselves, and left–right reflections of themselves; by contrast, ignored images should prime themselves, scaled and translated versions of themselves, but not left–right reflections of themselves. Five experiments tested these (and other) predictions of the model, and all the predictions were supported by the empirical results.

THE MODEL

Space limitations preclude describing the model in detail, so I will describe it only in broad strokes, and note important departures from the *JIM.2* model of Hummel and Stankiewicz (1996a). The model is an eight-layer artificial neural network that takes a representation of the contours in an object's image as input, and activates a representation of the object's identity as output (Figure 1). Units in the first three layers represent local image features, including contours (layer 1), vertices and axes of symmetry (layer 2), and the shape properties of surfaces (e.g., layer 3). The explicit coding of object surfaces represents a significant departure from the models of Hummel and Biederman (1992) and Hummel and Stankiewicz (1996a). Each surface is represented in terms of five categorical properties of its shape: whether it is *elliptical* (i.e., is bounded by a single contour without sharp discontinuities) vs. *non-elliptical*

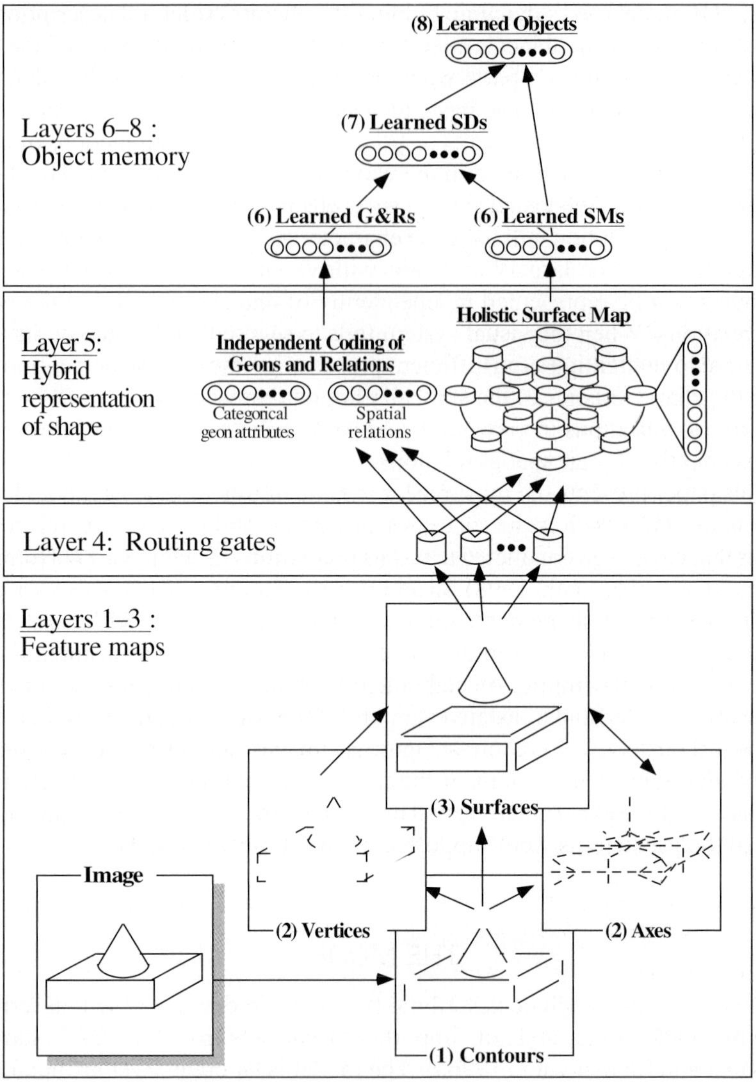

Figure 1. Illustration of *JIM.3*'s overall architecture. Units in layer 1 represent the contours in an object's image. Units in layer 2 represent vertices where contours coterminate and axes of symmetry between contours belonging to the same surface. Units in layer 3 represent the shape properties of object surfaces. Units in layer 4 gate the output of layer 3 to the independent geon shape units and the surface map in layer 5. Although the layer 4 gating units are depicted as a simple one-dimensional array in the figure, in the model they are distributed spatially over the visual field, like the local feature units in layers 1–3. Layer 5 is divided into two components: The independent units represent the shape attributes of an object's geons, and the units in the surface map represent shape attributes of surfaces at each of 17 location in a circular reference frame. Units in layers 6–8 encode patterns of activation in layer 5 (i.e., structural descriptions of objects) into long-term memory for recognition. See text for details.

(i.e., bounded by multiple contours that meet at vertices); the degree to which its axes of symmetry are *parallel*, *expanding* (i.e., wider at one end than the other), *concave* (i.e., wider at both ends than in the middle), or *convex* (i.e., wider in the middle than at either end); whether its major axis is *curved* or *straight*; whether it is *truncated* (meaning that some of its axes of symmetry terminate in the midsegments of its bounding contour or contours), or *pointed* (meaning that all its axes terminate at vertices where its contours meet); and whether it is *planar* (i.e., exists in a single 2-D plane in 3-D space) or *non-planar* (i.e., is curved in 3-D space). These properties are inferred from the properties of the vertices and axes of symmetry within a surface, and are used in subsequent layers of the model to infer the shape attributes of the geons to which the surfaces belong.

The local features coded in the model's first three layers group themselves into sets corresponding to geons by synchrony of firing: Lateral excitatory and inhibitory interactions cause the units in layers 1–3 to fire in synchrony when they represent features of the same geon, and out of synchrony when they belong to separate geons (Hummel & Biederman, 1992; Hummel & Stankiewicz, 1996a). The units in layer 3 activate units in layer 5 that represent an object's geons in terms of their shape attributes (e.g., whether a geon has a straight cross section or a curved cross section, whether its sides are parallel or non-parallel, etc.) and the configuration of their surfaces; interactions among the units in layer 5 compute the spatial relations among geons (e.g., whether a given geon is above or below another, larger than or smaller than another, etc.). Units in layer 6 learn to respond to specific patterns of activation in layer 5 (i.e., specific geons in specific relations), and units in layers 7 and 8 learn to respond to combinations of these patterns (i.e., collections of geons in particular relations). Together, the units in layers 6–8 constitute the model's long-term memory for known objects.

The synchrony relations established in layers 1–3 are preserved in layers 4–6, where they serve to bind together the various attributes of a geon's shape, and to bind geons to their spatial relations. However, the lateral interactions that establish synchrony and asynchrony take time, so initially (i.e., in the first several iterations [tens of ms] after an image is presented) all the features in an image will tend to fire at once, whether they belong to the same geon or not. The inhibitory interactions that cause the features of separate geons to fire out of synchrony with one another also require visual attention, so if an object is never attended, its features will never group themselves into parts-based sets (Hummel & Stankiewicz, 1996a, 1998). The model's fourth layer is a collection of inhibitory gates that project the instantaneous outputs of layer 3 (surface properties) to layer 5 (geons and relations) (Hummel & Stankiewicz, 1996a). The interactions between layers 3, 4, and 5 allow the model to capitalize on the dynamic binding of features into parts-based sets when synchrony can be established, and prevent catastrophic failure when it cannot.

Layer 5: The representation of object shape

Layer 5 is divided into two components: A collection of units that represent geon shape attributes independently of one another and of the geons' interrelations (the left-hand side of layer 5 in Figure 1), and a holistic *surface map*, which represents the shape attributes of an object's surfaces (the same shape attributes coded in layer 3) separately at each of several locations in a circular reference frame (right-hand side of layer 5 in Figure 1).[1] The independent shape units represent the shape of a geon in terms of five categorical attributes (cf. Biederman, 1987): whether its cross-section is *straight* (like that of a brick) or *curved* (like that of a cylinder); whether its major axis is *straight* or *curved*; whether its sides are *parallel* (like those of a brick), *expanding* (like a cone or wedge), *convex* (like a football) or *concave* (narrower in the middle than at the ends); and whether the geon is *pointed* (like a cone) or *truncated* (like a cylinder or truncated cone). These attribute units are capable of distinguishing 31 different kinds of geons.[2] For example, a brick has a straight cross-section, a straight major axis, parallel sides, and is truncated; a curved cone has a round cross-section, a curved major axis, expanding sides, and is pointed. Additional units code whether a geon's aspect ratio is *flat* (like a disk), *intermediate* (like a cube), or *elongated* (like a pipe). Other units code the spatial relations between geons (specifically, whether a given geon is *above*, *below*, *beside*, *larger-than*, and/or *smaller-than* other geons in an object).

These units represent geons attributes and relations independently in the sense that a unit that responds to a given property will respond to that property in the same way regardless of the geon's other properties. That is, separate units

---

[1]In *JIM.2*, the units in the holistic map represent, not surface properties, but geon attributes (the same attributes represented on the independent units). The shift to surface properties in the current version of the model is more a matter of convenience (i.e., simply copy surface features rather than having to use them to compute geon properties) than a strong theoretical claim. I am not theoretically committed to any particular vocabulary of features in the surface map; there is simply no empirical or theoretical basis for choosing a specific vocabulary at this time. The only strong theoretical claims about the surface map are that it is (a) holistic, (b) invariant with translation and scale, and (c) able to be activated automatically (i.e., without attention or other provisions for dynamic binding).

[2]This is a substantial improvement over the eight different kinds of geons the Hummel and Biederman (1992) and Hummel and Stankiewicz (1996a) models are capable of distinguishing. The previous models are incapable of distinguishing pointed geons from truncated geons, and are incapable of distinguishing different kinds of non-parallelism in a geon's sides. The difference between the current model and the previous models stems from the fact that the current model uses the vertices and axes in an object's image to infer the properties of the object's surfaces, and uses the surface properties to infer the properties of the geons. That is, the mapping from vertices and axes to geon properties is a two-stage mapping in the current model. By contrast, the previous models infer geon properties directly from vertex and axis properties (i.e., a one-stage mapping). It is tempting to speculate that geon properties are not linearly separable in the space of vertex and axis properties, and therefore cannot be unambiguously computed in a one-stage mapping.

are responsible for representing separate attributes and relations. This independence has two important consequences. First, it makes the representation completely invariant with translation, scale, and left–right reflection (the relations *left-of* and *right-of* are both coded simply as *beside*; Hummel & Biederman, 1992), and relatively insensitive to rotation in depth; it also permits the model to respond to the shapes of an object's parts independently of their relations and vice versa. The second consequence of the independence is that it makes the representation heavily dependent on synchrony of firing to bind geon attributes and relations into geon-based sets. For example, if the local features of the cone in Figure 1 fire in synchrony with one another and out of synchrony with the local features of the brick, then the properties of the cone will fire out of synchrony with the properties of the brick; together, resulting activation vectors will unambiguously specify that a cone is on top of a larger brick. However, if the local features of the cone happen to fire in synchrony with those of the brick, then the properties of the two geons will be superimposed on the independent units. The resulting pattern of activation cannot distinguish a cone and a brick from a cylinder and a wedge, or even from a single geon with a combination of cone and brick properties. That is, when dynamic binding fails, the representation formed on the independent units of layer 5 is effectively useless (cf. Hummel & Biederman, 1992; Hummel & Stankiewicz, 1996a).

The holistic surface map is much less sensitive to such binding errors than are the independent geon attribute and relation units. This component of layer 5 is a collection of units that represent the shape attributes of an object's surfaces at each of 17 locations in a circular reference frame (see the right-hand side of layer 5 in Figure 1). The map is holistic in the sense that each unit codes a static binding of one property to one location in the map (cf. Hummel, 2000; Hummel & Stankiewicz, 1996b). The units in layer 4 gate the instantaneous outputs of layer 3 (surface shape properties) to the independent units of layer 5 and to specific locations in the map: Surface properties are projected to the map in a way that preserves their topological relations (i.e., surfaces in adjacent locations in layer 3 project to adjacent locations in the surface map; see Hummel & Stankiewicz, 1996a, for details).[3] As a result, the units in the surface

[3]Units in layer 4 have circular receptive fields in layer 1. Different units have receptive fields of different sizes and locations, so that, collectively, they cover the entire visual field. Layer 4 units gate the connections between layer 3 units (surface features) and units in layer 5 (both the independent units on the left-hand side [layer 5i], and the units in the holistic surface map on the right-hand side [layer 5s]). A layer 4 gating unit, *i*, will become active at time *t* if all the layer 1 contour units with non-zero outputs at time *t* are: (1) contained entirely with its receptive field (i.e., if the gating unit can "see" all the contour units that are currently generating outputs), and (2) are not contained entirely within the receptive field of any other unit, *j*, whose receptive field is contained wholly within *i*'s receptive field. When *i* becomes active, it enables the connections of layer 3 surface units to send their outputs to: (1) the independent units in layer 5, and (2) those units in the surface map whose locations *relative to the surface map* are the same as the features' locations

(Continued overleaf)

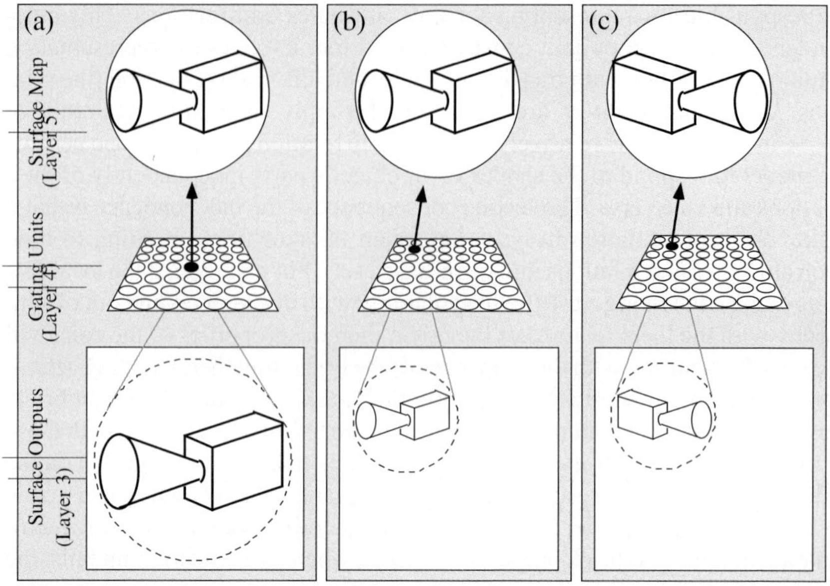

Figure 2. Illustration of the mapping of layer 3 (surface feature unit) outputs to the surface map of layer 5 via the gating units of layer 4. Adjacent surfaces in layer 3 project to adjacent locations in the map in a way that discards their absolute locations and sizes in the image. (a) and (b) illustrate that the same image in different locations and sizes in layer 3 produce exactly the same representation on the surface map. The image in (c) is a left–right reflection of the image in (b), so the representation of (c) is a left–right reflection of the representation of (b) on the surface map.

map maintain the separation of geon attributes even when multiple geons fire at the same time. (Different geons, occupying different locations in the image, will project to different locations in the map.) Although the mapping from layer 3 to the surface map preserves the topological relations of the surfaces, it discards their absolute locations and sizes in the image. Thus, the representation formed on the surface map is sensitive to rotation (both in depth and in the picture plane) and left–right reflection (compare Figures 2b and 2c), but it is invariant with translation and scale (compare Figures 2a and 2b).

(Footnote 3–continued)
relative to i's receptive field. For example, surface features in the upper left of *i*'s receptive field will project their outputs to the upper-left of the surface map (i.e., the corresponding layer 3-to-layer 5 connections will be enabled); features in the centre of the receptive field will project their outputs to the centre of the surface map, etc. These gating operations, which can all be performed in a strictly feed-forward fashion, cause the representation generated on the surface map to be invariant with translation and scale. That is, due to the operation of the layer 4 gating units, a given shape will have the same representation in the surface map regardless of its size or location in the image. See Hummel and Stankiewicz (1996a) for details.

The independent units and the surface map work together to permit the model to generate structural descriptions of object shape when dynamic binding succeeds, and to permit recognition of objects in familiar views even when dynamic binding fails. When an object image is first presented for recognition, all the local features in the image (contours, vertices, axes, and surfaces) will tend to fire at once, whether they belong to the same geon or not. In layer 5, the resulting pattern of activation on the independent units blends all properties of all the geons in the image, but the pattern on the surface map keeps the geons spatially separate (see Figure 3a). Although the blended representation on the independent units is useless for specifying the object's identity, the holistic representation on the surface map can specify the object's identity, provided the object is depicted in a familiar view. The initial (globally synchronized) burst of activation in layers 1–3 also serves as the units' first opportunity to exchange excitatory and (when the stimulus is attended) inhibitory signals. The excitatory signals encourage features belonging to the same geon to continue to fire in synchrony with one another, and the inhibitory signals encourage the features of separate geons to fire out of synchrony with one another (see Hummel & Stankiewicz, 1996a, 1998), so as processing proceeds, the object's geons

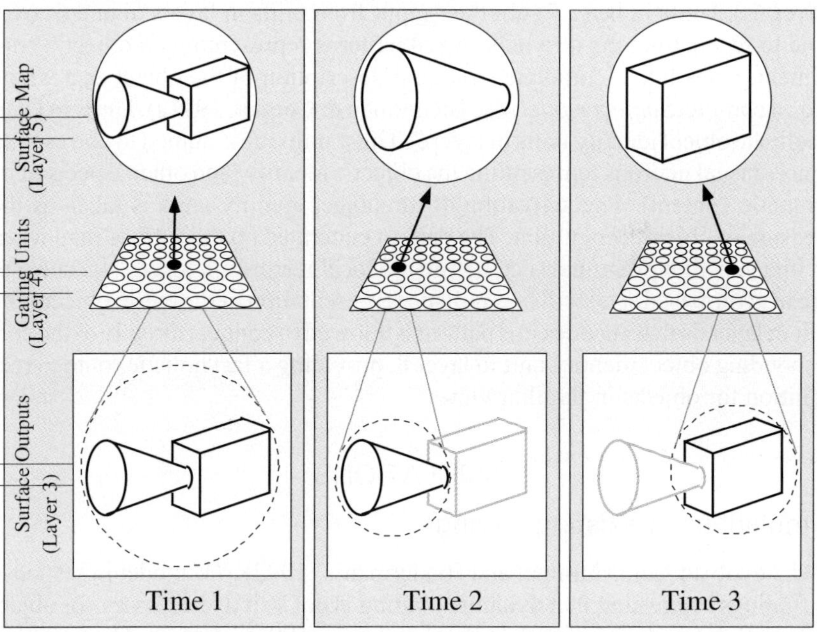

Figure 3. Illustration of the representation formed on the surface map as a function of the synchrony relations among the features of an object's geons. When all the features of an object fire at once (time 1), the separation of the object's surfaces is preserved in their separate locations in the surface map. After the objects' geons have desynchronized their outputs (times 2 and 3), individual geons are projected to the surface map one at a time.

come to fire out of synchrony with one another. In layer 5, the resulting series of patterns of activation constitute a structural description specifying the object's geons in terms of their shape attributes, spatial relations, and the topological relations of their constituent surfaces. This structural description can specify the object's identity even if it is depicted in a novel view, and even if the object is a novel member of a known object category (i.e., even if its shape differs somewhat from the shape of familiar members of the category).

Layers 6–8: Encoding shapes into long-term memory

The patterns of activation generated in layer 5 are encoded into the model's long-term memory by a simple kind of unsupervised Hebbian learning (see Hummel & Saiki, 1993). Patterns of activation generated on the independent units are learned by individual units in layer 6 (one unit per pattern; layer 6i in Figure 1), as are patterns of activation generated on the surface map (layer 6s in Figure 1). That is, each unit in layer 6 learns to respond to the shape attributes of one geon (or collection of geons) and its relations to other geons in the object (layer 6i), or to the arrangement of surfaces in a geon (or collection of geons) (layer 6s). Units in layer 7 sum their input from units in layers 6i and 6s over time to reconstruct the desynchronized patterns representing an object's constituent geons into a complete structural description of the object as a whole (i.e., a complete *object model*; see Biederman & Cooper, 1991a). Units in layer 7 activate object identity units in layer 8. These units are assumed to correspond to non-visual neurons representing the object's identity (and other aspects of its semantic content). The activation of the object identity units is taken as the measure of object recognition. The pattern generated on the surface map when an image is first presented (i.e., before the local features in layers 1–3 come to fire in geon-based sets) will be a holistic representation of the entire object. The unit in layer 6s that encodes this pattern is allowed to connect directly to the corresponding object identity unit in layer 8, providing a fast holistic route to recognition for objects in familiar views.

SIMULATIONS

Simulations of existing findings

JIM.3 evolved from Hummel and Biederman's (1992) *JIM* model in response to findings suggesting that dynamic binding is not strictly necessary for object recognition (as did Hummel & Stankiewicz's, 1996a, *JIM.2*). The resulting model is substantially more complicated than *JIM*. It is therefore important to show that it can still account for the findings against which *JIM* was tested—namely, the effects of various transformations in viewpoint on recognition performance. To this end, the model was trained on one view of each of 20 simple

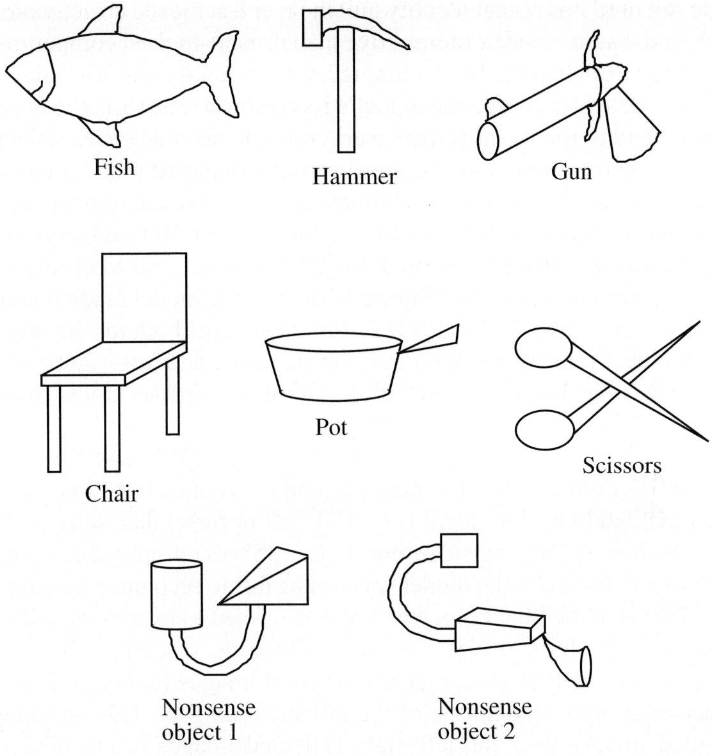

Figure 4. Eight of the twenty object images on which *JIM.3* was trained.

objects,[4] and tested for its ability to recognize those objects in new (untrained) views. A subset of the images on which *JIM.3* was trained is depicted in Figure 4. The objects were designed to be structurally complex: Most have several parts, many (such as the fish) contain ambiguous segmentation cues, and most are left–right asymmetrical. The model was trained by presenting each view once, and allowing the units in layers 6–8 to encode its representation on layer 5 (i.e., the object's structural description) into long-term memory (see Hummel & Stankiewicz, 1996a). It was then tested for its ability to recognize the images on which it was trained, translated versions of those images (i.e., with the same image translated to a new location in the visual field), scaled versions of the images, left–right reflections of the images, and images rotated 45°, 90°, 135°, and 180° in the picture plane. In all the simulations described here, I allowed the

[4]All objects had at least two parts (most had three or more). They comprised: a car, a cat, a chair, a fish, a revolver, a hammer, a house, the cone-on-a-brick object in Figure 1, a telephone, a cooking pot, a sailboat, a pair of scissors, a pair of eyeglasses, a teacup, a teapot, a sliding board, and four nonsense objects.

model to run until one object identity unit in layer 8 achieved an activation of at least 0.5, and was at least 0.2 more active than its next-highest competitor (activations range from 0 to 1). The "winning" object identity unit was taken as the model's response. I recorded the model's recognition time (RT: the number of iterations it had to run to satisfy these criteria) and accuracy (i.e., whether the winning unit corresponded to the object actually depicted in the image).

Figure 5 shows the model's performance on the trained, translated, scaled and reflected images (the RTs shown are means over 10 runs), and Figure 6 shows its performance on the rotated images (mean RT and error rate over 10 runs). Errors are not reported in Figure 5 because the model made no errors in these simulations. Like *JIM* and *JIM.2*, *JIM.3* accounts both for the invariance of human object recognition with translation, scale, and left–right reflection, and for the detrimental effects (on both response time and accuracy) of rotation in the picture plane. Importantly, it also accounts for the "cusp" in the rotation function at 180°: *JIM.3*, like people (see Jolicoeur, 1985) and like *JIM* (see Hummel & Biederman, 1992), is faster and more accurate to recognize images that are completely upside-down (i.e., 180° off upright) than images that are slightly less than perfectly upside-down (e.g., 135° off upright; see Figure 6).

As shown in Figure 5, the model was just as fast to recognize translated and scaled versions of the images on which it was trained as to recognize the original images themselves. It was somewhat slower to recognize the left–right reflected images than to recognize the original images (although it was perfectly accurate in its recognition of the reflected images). This advantage for the original images over the left–right reflected images in the model's RT

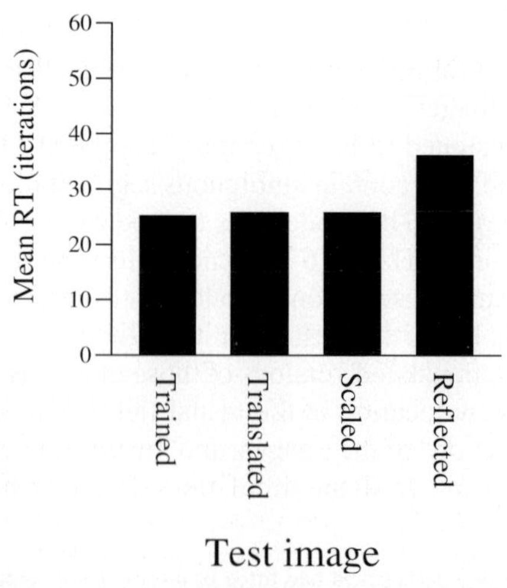

Figure 5. *JIM.3*'s recognition performance (recognition time, RT) with the images on which it was trained, and translated, scaled, and left–right reflected versions of those images. RTs reflect means over 10 runs of all 20 objects.

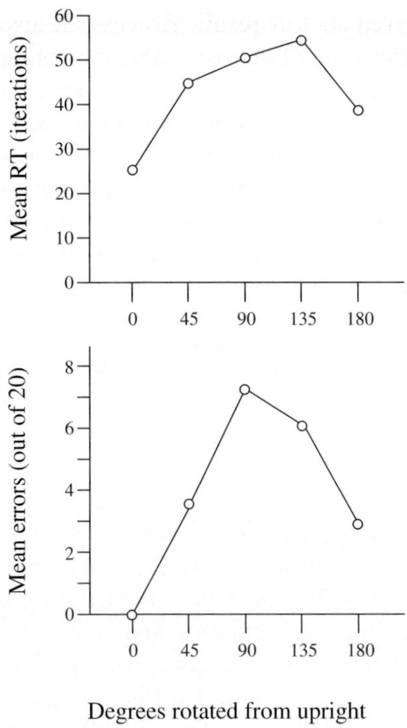

Figure 6. *JIM.3*'s recognition performance (RT and errors) with the images on which it was trained (0°), and 45°, 90°, 135°, and 180° rotated versions of those images. Rotations were in the picture plane.

performance reflects the operation of the holistic surface map: The stored holistic object representation (in the direct connection from layer 6s to layer 8) allows the model to recognize an object in a familiar view based solely on the first pattern of activation generated on the surface map. Because the surface map is invariant with translation and scale, this makes recognition of translated and scaled images just as fast as recognition of familiar images. However, the surface map is not invariant with left–right reflection, so recognition of reflected images requires the model to decompose the image into parts and generate a structural description. The resulting structural description is invariant with left–right reflection, but the process of generating it takes time. Hence, recognition of left–right reflected images is slower than recognition of the original images. At first sight, this result seems to be inconsistent with the fact that Biederman and Cooper (1991a) showed that visual priming is completely invariant with left–right reflection (in the sense that images visually primed their left–right reflections just as much as they primed themselves). However, Biederman and Cooper measured visual priming over long prime-probe delays (on the order of minutes), and they did not report subject's response times recognizing familiar objects in unfamiliar left–right orientations. As discussed in detail shortly, *JIM.3* predicts this result. However it also predicts that short-term priming (i.e., on the order of seconds rather than minutes) will be sensitive to left–right reflection, and that it will take slightly longer to recognize familiar objects in unusual left–right orientations (although accuracy should be high). The former prediction (about short-term priming) turns out to be correct, as discussed shortly (Stankiewicz et al., 1998); to the best of my knowledge, the latter prediction remains untested (although there are well-known effects of non-canonical viewpoints on the time required for recognition; see Lawson, 1999).

Novel predictions

The fundamental theoretical tenet underlying *JIM.3* (and *JIM.2*) is that the visual system uses two solutions to the binding problem for the representation of object shape, and that these solutions have complementary properties: Dynamic binding is "expensive", requiring both visual attention and time to establish, but results in structural descriptions that specify object properties independently, and is therefore highly flexible (e.g., among other things, it is robust to variations in viewpoint and the metric properties of an object's shape); by contrast, static binding is "inexpensive", requiring neither attention nor time to establish, but results in a representation that lacks the flexibility of a structural description. This tenet leads to the general prediction that the visual representation of an attended image should differ *qualitatively* from the visual representation of an unattended image. One specific manifestation of this general prediction is that attended images should visually prime both themselves and their left–right reflections (by virtue of the structural description generated on the independent units), whereas ignored images should prime themselves (by virtue of the holistic surface map), but not their left–right reflections.[5]

To illustrate the implications of this relationship between attention and priming, I tested the model for its ability to recognize the trained images after either the objects' independent representations had been primed (layer 6i), or their holistic representations had been primed (layer 6s), or both had been primed. (The simulation results in Figure 5 serve as a baseline condition, in

[5] One very important (and very hard) problem the model does not solve is the figure–ground segmentation problem. Like the vast majority of all computational models of object recognition, *JIM.3* can "view" only one object at a time. We assume that when an object is ignored, its features occasionally fire, but when they do, they all fire in synchrony with one another (i.e., all ignored objects are forced to share a single "time slice" in the oscillatory firing; see Hummel & Stankiewicz, 1998). This account predicts that the relationship between attention and patterns of priming should vary as a function of how many ignored objects there are in the visual field: The more ignored objects, the smaller the probability that any given one of them will have the opportunity to fire by itself within any fixed amount of time. In addition, with multiple ignored objects, there may be the opportunity for binding errors, even in the surface map, if two or more objects happen to fire at the same time. We have yet to investigate these possibilities empirically.

which neither representation had been primed.) I primed these representations by turning up the gain (i.e., the growth rate in the activation function) on the units in layer 6i and/or 6s (respectively), which allows them to become active faster in response to input from layer 5.[6] The assumptions underlying this manipulation are the following: (1) If an image is attended, then the representation of that image on both the independent units and the surface map will become active and therefore be primed; hence, to simulate priming for attended images, I primed both layer 6i and layer 6s. (2) If an image is ignored, then its (holistic) representation in the surface map will become active, but no useful representation will be activated on the independent units; to simulate priming for ignored images, I therefore primed layer 6s, but not layer 6i. (3) Priming for the surface map is less enduring than priming for the independent units. (This latter was less an a priori assumption than a hypothesis suggested by the Stankiewicz et al. 1998, data summarized later. However, by assuming it, the model provides a straightforward account of a subtle and counterintuitive aspect of those data.) To simulate the effects of long-term priming of attended images, I primed layer 6i but not layer 6s. I then tested the model with the trained images and recorded its RT with each. I operationalized priming as the difference between the mean RT (over objects and runs) in the unprimed condition (Figure 5) minus the mean RT in each primed condition (layer 6i only, layer 6s only, or both 6i and 6s).

Figure 7 shows the simulation results (i.e., magnitude of priming in iterations) in the three priming conditions (both layer 6i and 6s primed, only 6i primed, and only 6s primed). Based on the characteristics of the independent and holistic representations in layer 5, it is possible to turn these simulation results into specific behavioural predictions about the relationship between visual attention and priming for various kinds of object images. First consider the model's predictions regarding short-term priming—i.e., when the probe trial (i.e., the second presentation of an image) follows immediately after the prime trial (Figures 8 and 9). Recall that the independent representation, but not the holistic representation, is (1) invariant with left–right reflection but (2) requires visual attention. Therefore, attended images should visually prime both themselves and their left–right reflections, whereas ignored images should prime themselves but not their left–right reflections. There are four components to this prediction (see Figure 8). (1) A person who attends to an image on one trial (the prime), and then immediately sees the very same image on the next (probe) trial should profit from priming in both the independent representation (because the image was attended) and the holistic representation

[6]It is arguably more realistic to assume the priming resides, not in the units, but in the mapping between representations (i.e., in the connections between units; see Cooper, Biederman, & Hummel, 1992). However, for the purposes of the current simulations, the two produce equivalent results.

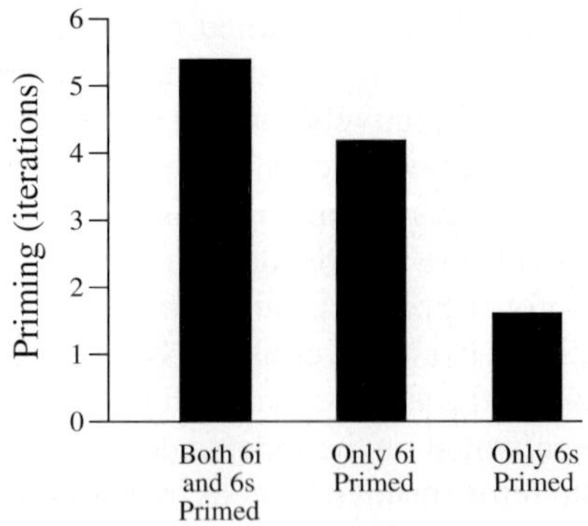

Figure 7. *JIM.3*'s recognition performance in the priming conditions expressed as magnitude of priming: RT on unprimed simulation runs (Figure 5) minus RT on primed simulation runs (both 6i and 6s primed, only 6i primed or only 6s primed).

(because the prime and probe images were identical, and the prime-probe delay was short); that is, the magnitude of priming in this case should be equivalent to the magnitude of priming in the *both 6i and 6s* condition (Figure 8, attended/identical). (2) A person who attends to an image on the prime trial and then immediately sees its left–right reflection on the probe trial should profit from priming in the independent representation (because the image was attended, and the independent representation is invariant with left–right reflection), but should not profit from priming in the holistic representation (because the holistic representation is sensitive to left–right reflection); the magnitude of priming in this case should be equivalent to the magnitude of priming in the *6i only*

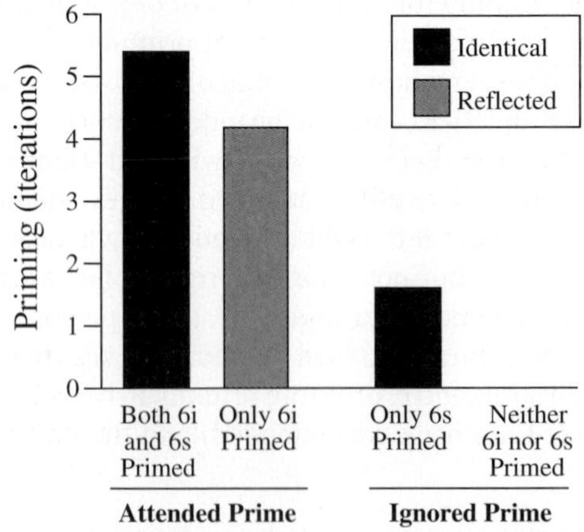

Figure 8. *JIM.3*'s predictions regarding the relationship between attention (i.e., whether the prime image is attended or ignored) and visual priming for identical images and left–right reflections. See text for details.

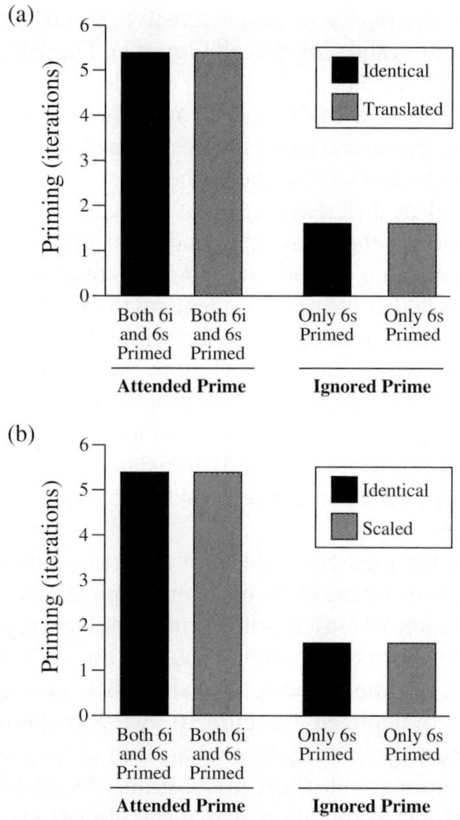

Figure 9. *JIM.3*'s predictions regarding the relationship between attention (i.e., whether the prime image is attended or ignored) and visual priming for identical images (a and b), translated images (a), and scaled images (b). See text for details.

condition (Figure 8, attended/reflected). (3) A person who ignores an image on the prime trial and then immediately sees the same image on the probe trial should not profit from priming in the independent representation (because the image was not attended), but should profit from priming in the holistic representation (because the prime and probe images were identical, and the prime-probe delay was short); that is, the magnitude of priming in this case should be equivalent to the magnitude of priming in the *6s only* condition (Figure 8, ignored/identical). (4) Finally, a person who ignores an image on the prime trial and then immediately sees its left–right reflection on the probe trial should profit neither from priming in the independent representation (because the image was not attended), nor from priming in the holistic representation (because the probe image was the left–right reflection of the prime); that is, there should be no priming at all (Figure 8, ignored/reflected).

Although the holistic representation is sensitive to left–right reflection, it is invariant with translation and scale (recall Figure 3). The pattern of visual priming effects should therefore be substantially simpler if the left–right reflected probe images are replaced with probes that are either translated relative to the prime (i.e., so that the prime and probe images are presented in different parts of the visual field) or scaled relative to the prime (i.e., so that the prime and probe images are presented in different sizes). In this case, the only variable that should matter is whether the prime is attended or ignored: Attended images should profit from priming in both the independent and holistic representations, regardless of whether the probe is identical to the prime (Figure 9a and b, attended/identical), translated relative to the prime (Figure 9a, attended/translated), or scaled relative to the prime (Figure 9b, attended/scaled); ignored images should profit from priming in the holistic representation but not the independent representation, regardless of whether the probe is identical to the prime (Figure 9a and b, ignored/identical), translated relative to the prime (Figure 9a, ignored/translated) or scaled relative to the prime (Figure 9b, ignored/scaled).

Finally, consider the predicted effects of attention and viewpoint for long prime-probe delays (i.e., on the order of several minutes, as in the experiments of Biederman & Cooper, 1991a). If priming in the holistic representation (layer 6s) is short lived (i.e., persists for seconds but not minutes; Stankiewicz et al., 1998), then with long prime-probe delays, all holistic priming will disappear, resulting in the pattern depicted in Figure 10. A few properties of this pattern are notable. First, the magnitude of priming in all conditions is lower than in the corresponding conditions with short prime-probe delays (the one exception being the ignored/reflected condition, which was already at zero even for short prime-probe delays). Second, priming in all the ignored conditions goes to

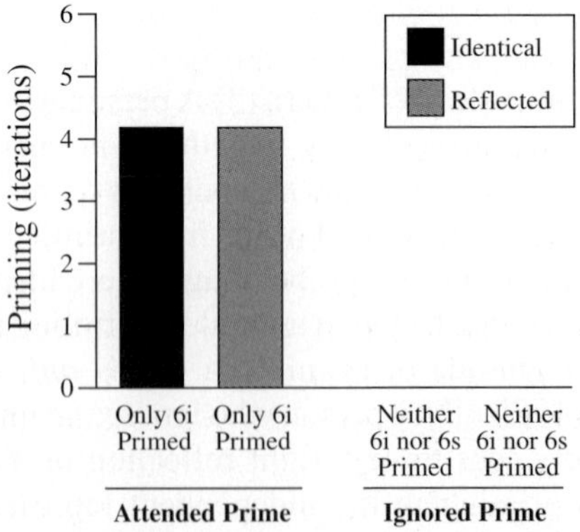

Figure 10. *JIM.3*'s predictions regarding the relationship between attention (i.e., whether the prime image is attended or ignored) and visual priming for identical images and left–right reflections over long prime-probe delays. See text for details.

zero. And third, priming in the attended/reflected condition is equivalent to priming in the attended/identical condition: That is, over long prime-probe delays, priming is completely invariant with left–right reflection, as reported by Biederman and Cooper (1991a). The predicted advantage for attended/identical images over attended/reflected images in the short prime-probe delay simulations is due to the holistic (layer 6s) priming in the identical condition. With long prime-probe delays, this advantage is predicted to disappear, with the result that images prime their left–right reflections just as much as they prime themselves.

TESTS OF THE MODEL'S PREDICTIONS

Brian Stankiewicz and his colleagues (Stankiewicz & Hummel, 2001; Stankiewicz et al., 1998; see also Stankiewicz, 1997) ran five experiments to test these predictions. In the basic paradigm with short prime-probe delays, trials were grouped into prime/probe pairs. Each prime trial began with a fixation cue (a cross in the centre of the screen), followed by an empty box either left or right of fixation. The box was followed by two line drawings of objects: One appeared inside the box, and the other outside the box (on the other side of fixation). The subject's task was to name the object that appeared inside the box, ignoring the other object. The precue box served both as an endogenous attentional cue (subjects knew to attend to the image in the box) and as an exogenous attentional cue (its abrupt onset automatically attracts attention). The images remained on the computer screen for 165 ms, and were then masked. The entire prime trial (from precue to mask) lasted only 195 ms, which is too brief to permit a saccade to the attended image. After a 2 s pause, the prime trial was followed by the corresponding probe trial, which presented a fixation cue in the centre of the screen, followed by a single line drawing either in the centre of the screen (Stankiewicz et al.; Stankiewicz & Hummel, Exp. 2), or in a new location off fixation (i.e., a location occupied by neither the attended nor the ignored image during the prime trial; Stankiewicz & Hummel, Exp. 1). The subject's task was to name the object depicted in the line drawing. In addition to the paired trials producing short prime-probe delays, one experiment (Stankiewicz et al., Exp. 3) investigated the effects of priming for attended and ignored images over delays lasting several minutes (as in Biederman & Cooper, 1991a). In this experiment, any prime object that was not probed on the trial immediately following the prime was probed in a separate block of trials at the very end of the experiment: If the probe trial presented the ignored object from the immediately preceding prime trial, then the (un-probed) attended object was presented in the probe block at the end of the experiment; and if the probe trial presented the attended image from the immediately preceding prime trial, then the (un-probed) ignored object was presented at the end of the experiment. This long-delay probe condition permitted Stankiewicz et al. to compare the effects of attention (and viewpoint) on short-delay priming (i.e., delays lasting a few seconds) to their effects on long-delay priming (i.e., delays lasting several minutes).

In all these experiments, the critical manipulation was the relationship between the probe image and the images presented on the corresponding prime trial (see Table 1). The probe either depicted the object that was attended on the prime trial (the *attended* condition), the object that was ignored on the prime trial (the *ignored* condition), or an object the subject had not previously seen in the experiment (the unprimed *baseline* condition). In the attended and ignored conditions, the probe image could either be: (1) identical to the corresponding prime image (the *identical* condition; Stankiewicz et al., 1998; Stankiewicz & Hummel, 2001), (2) a left–right reflection of the prime image (the *reflected* condition; Stankiewicz et al.), (3) identical to the prime image except for its location in the visual field (the *translated* condition; Stankiewicz & Hummel, Exp. 1), (4) identical to the prime except for its size (the *scaled* condition; Stankiewicz & Hummel, Exp. 1), or (5) an image of a different object with the same basic-level name as the object depicted in the prime trial (the *different exemplar* control condition; Stankiewicz et al., Exp. 2). For example, if the prime presented an image of a jumbo jet (basic level name "airplane"), the probe image in the different exemplar condition would depict a small private

TABLE 1
Summary of conditions in the Stankiewicz et al. (1998) and Stankiewicz and Hummel (2001) experiments

Prime-probe relationship	*Attention condition*: *Attended*	*Attention condition*: *Ignored*	*Unprimed baseline*
Identical	SHC: 1,2,3 SH: 1,2 LD	SHC: 1,2,3 SH: 1,2 LD	
Left–right reflected	SHC: 1,2,3 LD	SHC: 1,2,3 LD	
Translated	SH: 1	SH: 1	SHC: 1,2,3 SH: 1,2 LD
Scaled	SH: 2	SH: 2	
Different exemplar	SHC: 2	SHC: 2	

Table entries indicate which conditions appeared in which experiments. Letters refer to papers: "SHC" denotes Stankiewicz et al. (1998) and "SH" denotes Stankiewicz and Hummel (2001). Numbers refer to experiments in corresponding experiments (Experiments 1, 2, and 3 in SHC, and Experiments 1 and 2 in SH). "LD" indicates that the corresponding condition was run in both the *long prime-probe delay* and *short prime-probe delay* conditions (Stankiewicz et al., 1998, Exp. 3); all conditions not so marked were run in the *short prime-probe delay* condition only.

plane such as a Cessna (basic level name "airplane"). The different exemplar control condition serves as a basis for estimating what fraction of any observed priming is specifically visual (i.e., reflects priming in visual representations), as opposed to non-visual (e.g., priming for an object's name or concept; see Biederman & Cooper, 1991a, b, 1992). I will not discuss this condition further except to note that the majority of the priming observed in the experiments summarized here is specifically visual, and that none of the effects summarized here are attributable to the non-visual components of the priming (see Stankiewicz et al. for details). In all five of the experiments, priming was operationalized as the time it took subjects to name an object in the unprimed baseline condition minus the time it took them to name the objects in the corresponding primed condition.

The results of all five experiments are strikingly consistent with the behavioural predictions of the model. Consider first the role of attention in short-delay priming for images and their left–right reflections (Figure 11). As predicted (Figure 8), attended images primed both themselves and their left–right reflections, whereas ignored imaged primed themselves, but not their left–right reflections. Also as predicted, the advantage for identical images over their left–right reflections in the attended condition was the same as the advantage for identical images over their left–right reflections in the ignored condition (about 50 ms. in both cases). That is, the effects of attention (attended vs. ignored) and view (identical vs. reflected) were strictly additive. Next consider the predicted role of attention in priming for translated and scaled images, and recall that the model predicts that, although ignored images should not prime their left–right reflections, priming for ignored images should none the less be invariant with translation and scale (Figure 9). Consistent with this prediction, ignored images primed translated versions of themselves just as much as they primed themselves (Figure 12a), and primed scaled versions of themselves just as much as they primed themselves (Figure 12b). Also as predicted, although short-delay priming did not vary as a function of translation or scaling for either the attended or ignored images, priming for attended images was generally

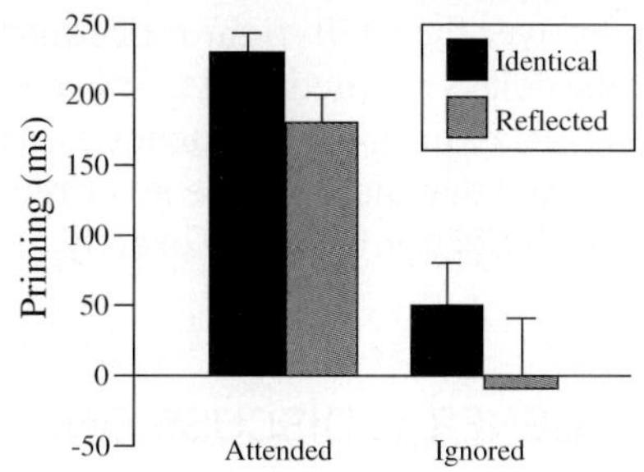

Figure 11. Patterns of visual priming for attended and ignored identical and reflected images (data from Stankiewicz et al., 1998, Exp. 1). See text for details.

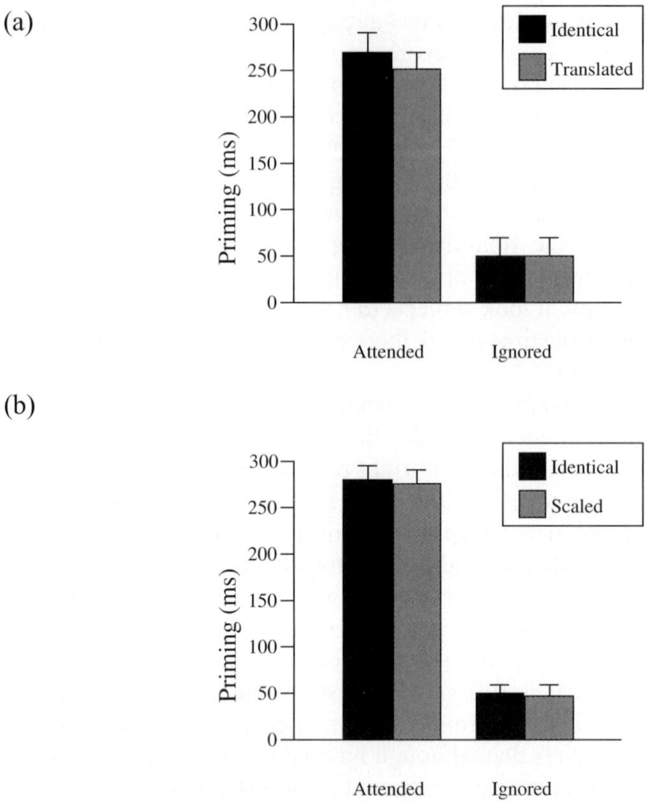

Figure 12. Patterns of visual priming for attended and ignored identical (a and b), translated (a), and scaled (b) images. The data in (a) are from Stankiewicz and Hummel (2001, Exp. 1); those in (b) are from Stankiewicz and Hummel (2001, Exp. 2). See text for details.

much larger than priming for ignored images. Finally, consider the effects of attention and view (identical vs. reflected) over long prime-probe delays (Figure 13). In contrast to short prime-probe delays, which show a priming advantage for identical images over their left–right reflections (as predicted by the model), long prime-probe delays are predicted to show no such advantage: The model predicts that long-delay priming for attended images will be invariant with left–right reflection, and that there will be no priming for ignored images (Figure 10). This pattern of effects is borne out exactly in the experimental data (Figure 13).

GENERAL DISCUSSION

Many aspects of the human capacity for shape perception and object recognition indicate that we represent an object's shape in terms its parts and their

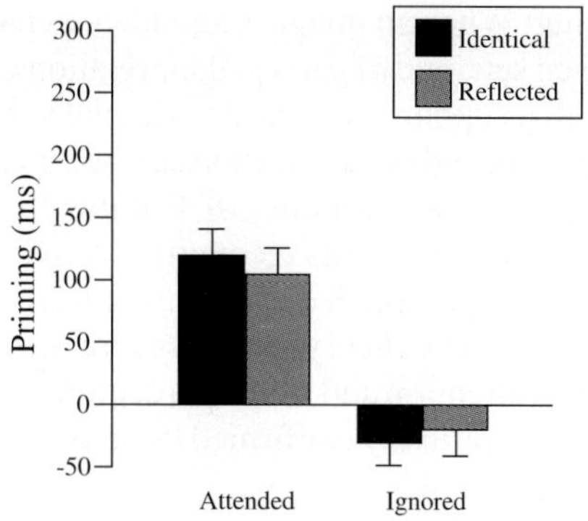

Figure 13. Patterns of visual priming for attended and ignored identical and reflected images over long prime-probe delays (data from Stankiewicz et al., 1998, Exp. 3). See text for details.

categorical spatial relations. The view-invariances and sensitivities characterizing human object recognition are captured precisely by the structural description model of Hummel and Biederman (1992; Hummel & Stankiewicz, 1996a). Structural descriptions also provide a natural account of both our ability to recognize objects as members of a general class (Biederman, 1987; Marr, 1982) and as specific instances (Hummel & Stankiewicz, 1998). More direct evidence for the role of structural descriptions in shape perception comes from studies showing that our visual systems explicitly represent objects in terms of their surfaces (Nakayama & He, 1995; Nakayama & Shimojo, 1992) and parts (Biederman, 1987; Biederman & Cooper, 1991b), and from studies showing that we represent the spatial relations among an object's parts both explicitly and independently of the parts they relate (Hummel & Stankiewicz, 1996a; Saiki & Hummel, 1996, 1998a, b; see also Palmer, 1978). The role of structural descriptions in shape perception is also supported by our ability to appreciate the relational similarity between shapes, independently of whether similar parts stand in corresponding relations (see Hummel, 2000, for a review). At the same time, however, the speed and automaticity of object recognition suggest that the visual system is not bound by the capacity limits imposed by this approach to representing object shape: Because of the computational demands of dynamic binding, generating a structural description from the information in an object's 2-D image is necessarily time consuming and attention demanding; by contrast, object recognition is both fast and automatic (see Hummel & Stankiewicz, 1996a, for a review).

JIM.3 is a computational instantiation of a theory of how the human visual system exploits the flexibility and expressive power of explicit structural descriptions when it attends to an object's image, without suffering catastrophic failures of recognition when it does not. According to this theory (and its predecessor, *JIM.2*; Hummel & Stankiewicz, 1996a), the visual system solves this problem by adopting two complementary approaches to the problem of visual feature binding: When an image is attended, dynamic binding of local features into parts-based sets, and of parts to their relations, results in an explicit structural description that supports recognition despite variations in the view in which an object is depicted, and even variations in the object's exact 3-D shape; when an image is ignored, static binding of features to locations in a semi-object-centred reference frame permits recognition provided the image depicts the object in a familiar view (although even in this case, recognition is invariant with translation and scale). The theory makes several novel predictions about the relationship between attention and shape perception, and all the predictions tested to date have been empirically confirmed (Stankiewicz & Hummel, 2001; Stankiewicz et al., 1998).

JIM.3 accounts for a very large number of findings in human shape perception and object recognition, and is entirely consistent with many others. Like its predecessors, *JIM* (Hummel & Biederman, 1992) and *JIM.2* (Hummel & Stankiewicz, 1996a), *JIM.3* provides a direct account of the major view-invariances and view-sensitivities characterizing human object recognition. It also provides an account of the role of categorical shape attributes in object recognition, and of the human capacity to recognize objects at multiple levels of abstraction (e.g., as "a car," or "a Honda Civic," or "my Honda Civic"; cf. Hummel & Stankiewicz, 1998). It is also consistent with our ability to represent an object's parts independently of one another, and of their spatial relations, and suggests a direct basis for appreciating the relational similarity of objects composed of different parts (see Hummel, 2000; Hummel & Holyoak, 1997). More generally, in its ability to account for the known properties of human shape perception, and to successfully predict previously unknown properties, the model illustrates how the strengths and limitations of dynamic binding map onto the strengths and limitations of human shape perception: Both are flexible, and permit the generation of sophisticated structured representations; and both are inherently capacity limited and therefore require finite working memory and attentional resources (cf. Hummel & Holyoak, 1997).

In recent years, models based on varieties of *view-matching*—in which objects are recognized by matching holistic representations of the precise locations of their 2-D features directly to memory (e.g., Edelman, 1998; Poggio & Edelman, 1990; Riesenhuber & Poggio, 1999; Tarr & Bülthoff, 1995)—have become the dominant account of human object recognition in the literature (for reviews, see Hummel, 2000; Lawson, 1999). According to these models, all of shape perception is based on representations akin to the holistic surface map of the current theory. Accordingly, they can only account for the properties of object recognition that stem directly from that kind of representation. Theories in this tradition account for only a fraction of the view-invariances of human object recognition, and are inconsistent with most other aspects of shape perception—most notably, all those phenomena that stem from our ability to represent features or parts independently of their configuration (i.e., virtually all the interesting properties of human shape perception; see Hummel, 2000). *JIM.3*, like *JIM.2*, acknowledges the important role of holistic representations in our ability to recognize objects without the aid of visual attention. But by integrating these holistic representations into explicit relational descriptions, the current theory also provides a natural account of all the phenomena that depend on our ability to represent an object's parts and relations independently. In turn, the model's capacity to do so depends entirely on its ability to solve the dynamic binding problem.

REFERENCES

Bergevin, R., & Levine, M. D. (1993). Generic object recognition: Building and matching course descriptions from line drawings. *IEEE Transactions on Pattern Analysis and Machine Intelligence, 15,* 19–36.

Biederman, I. (1987). Recognition-by-components: A theory of human image understanding. *Psychological Review, 94*(2), 115–147.

Biederman, I., & Cooper, E.E. (1991a). Evidence for complete translational and reflectional invariance in visual object priming. *Perception, 20,* 585–593.

Biederman, I., & Cooper, E.E. (1991b). Priming contour deleted images: Evidence for intermediate representations in visual object recognition. *Cognitive Psychology, 23,* 393–419.

Biederman, I., & Cooper, E.E. (1992). Size invariance in visual object priming. *Journal of Experimental Psychology: Human Perception and Performance, 18,* 121–133.

Clowes, M.B. (1967). Perception, picture processing and computers. In N.L. Collins & D. Michie (Eds.), *Machine intelligence* (Vol. 1, pp. 181–197). Edinburgh, UK: Oliver & Boyd.

Cooper, E.E., Biederman, I., & Hummel, J.E. (1992). Metric invariance in object recognition: A review and further evidence. *Canadian Journal of Psychology, 46,* 191–214.

Dickinson, S.J., Pentland, A.P., & Rosenfeld, A. (1992). 3-D shape recovery using distributed aspect matching. *IEEE Transactions on Pattern Analysis and Machine Intelligence, 14,* 174–198.

Edelman, S. (1998). Representation is representation of similarities. *Behavioural and Brain Sciences, 21,* 449–498.

Gray, C.M., & Singer, W. (1989). Stimulus specific neuronal oscillations in orientation columns of cat visual cortex. *Proceedings of the National academy of Sciences, USA, 86,* 1698–1702.

Holyoak, K.J., & Hummel, J.E. (2000). The proper treatment of symbols in a connectionist architecture. In E. Dietrich & A. Markman (Eds.), *Cognitive dynamics: Conceptual change in humans and machines* (pp. 229–264). Hillsdale, NJ: Lawrence Erlbaum Associates Inc.

Hummel, J.E. (2000). Where view-based theories break down: The role of structure in shape perception and object recognition. In E. Dietrich & A. Markman (Eds.), *Cognitive dynamics: Conceptual change in humans and machines* (pp. 157–185). Hillsdale, NJ: Lawrence Erlbaum Associates Inc.

Hummel, J.E., & Biederman, I. (1992). Dynamic binding in a neural network for shape recognition. *Psychological Review, 99,* 480–517.

Hummel, J.E., & Holyoak, K.J. (1997). Distributed representations of structure: A theory of analogical access and mapping. *Psychological Review, 104,* 427–466.

Hummel, J.E., & Saiki, J. (1993). Rapid unsupervised learning of object structural descriptions. In *Proceedings of the fifteenth annual conference of the Cognitive Science Society* (pp. 569–574). Hillsdale, NJ: Lawrence Erlbaum Associates Inc.

Hummel, J.E., & Stankiewicz, B.J. (1996a). An architecture for rapid, hierarchical structural description. In T. Inui & J. McClelland (Eds.), *Attention and performance XVI: Information integration in perception and communication* (pp. 93–121). Cambridge, MA: MIT Press.

Hummel, J.E., & Stankiewicz, B.J. (1996b). Categorical relations in shape perception. *Spatial Vision, 10,* 201–236.

Hummel, J.E., & Stankiewicz, B.J. (1998). Two roles for attention in shape perception: A structural description model of visual scrutiny. *Visual Cognition, 5,* 49–79.

Intraub, H. (1981). Identification and processing of briefly glimpsed visual scenes. In D. Fisher, R.A. Monty, & J.W. Sender (Eds.), *Eye movements: Cognition and visual perception* (pp. 181–190). Hillsdale, NJ: Lawrence Erlbaum Associates Inc.

Jolicoeur, P. (1985). The time to name disoriented natural objects. *Memory and Cognition, 13,* 289–303.

Jolicoeur, P. (1990). Identification of disoriented objects: A dual systems theory. *Mind and Language, 5,* 387–410.

Lawson, R. (1999). Achieving visual object constancy across plane rotation and depth rotation. *Acta Psychologica, 102,* 221–245.

Lower, D.G. (1987). The viewpoint consistency constraint. *International Journal of Computer Vision, 1,* 57–72.

Luck, S.J., & Beach, N.J. (1998). Visual attention and the binding problem: A neurophysiological perspective. In R.D. Wright (Ed.), *Visual attention* (pp. 455–478). New York: Oxford University Press.

Luck, S.J., & Vogel, E.K. (1997). The capacity of visual working memory for features and conjunctions. *Nature, 390,* 279–281.

Marr, D. (1982). *Vision*. San Francisco: W.H. Freeman.

Marr, D., & Nishihara, H.K. (1978). Representation and recognition of three dimensional shapes. *Proceedings of the Royal Society of London, Series B, 200,* 269–294.

Nakayama, K, & He, Z.J. (1995). Attention to surfaces: Beyond a Cartesian understanding of focal attention. In T.V. Papathomas, C. Chubb, A. Gorea, & E. Kowler (Eds.), *Early vision and beyond* (pp. 181–186). Cambridge, MA: MIT Press.

Nakayama, K., & Shimojo, S. (1992). Experiencing and perceiving visual surfaces. *Science, 257,* 1357–1363.

Oram, M.W., & Perrett, D.I. (1992). The time course of neural responses discriminating different views of the face and head. *Journal of Neurophysiology, 68,* 70–84.

Palmer, S.E. (1977). Hierarchical structure in perceptual representation. *Cognitive Psychology, 9,* 441–474.

Palmer, S.E. (1978). Structural aspects of similarity. *Memory and Cognition, 6,* 91–97.

Poggio, T., & Edelman, S. (1990). A neural network that learns to recognize three-dimensional objects. *Nature, 343,* 263–266.

Potter, M.C. (1976). Short-term conceptual memory for pictures. *Journal of Experimental Psychology: Human Learning and Memory, 2,* 509–522.

Riesenhuber, M., & Poggio, T. (1999). Hierarchical models of object recognition in cortex. *Nature Neuroscience, 11,* 1019–1025.

Saiki, J., & Hummel, J.E. (1996). Attribute conjunctions and the part configuration advantage in object category learning. *Journal of Experimental Psychology: Learning, Memory, and Cognition, 22,* 1002–1019.

Saiki, J., & Hummel, J.E. (1998a). Connectedness and part-relation integration in shape category learning. *Memory and Cognition,* 26, 1138–1156.

Saiki, J., & Hummel, J.E. (1998b). Connectedness and the integration of parts with relations in shape perception. *Journal of Experimental Psychology: Human Perception and Performance, 24,* 227–251.

Smolensky, P. (1990). Tensor product variable binding and the representation of symbolic structures in connectionist systems. *Artificial Intelligence, 46,* 159–216.
Stankiewicz, B.S. (1997). *The role of attention in viewpoint-invariant object recognition.* Unpublished doctoral dissertation, University of California, Los Angeles, USA.
Stankiewicz, B.S., & Hummel, J.E. (2001). Automatic priming for translation- and scale-invariant representations of object shape. *Manuscript submitted for publication.*
Stankiewicz, B.J., Hummel, J.E., & Cooper, E.E. (1998). The role of attention in priming for left–right reflections of object images: Evidence for a dual representation of object shape. *Journal of Experimental Psychology: Human Perception and Performance, 24,* 732–744.
Sutherland, N.S. (1968). Outlines of a theory of visual pattern recognition in animals and man. *Proceedings of the Royal Society of London, Series B, 171,* 95–103.
Tarr, M.J., & Bülthoff, H.H. (1995). Is human object recognition better described by geon structural descriptions or by multiple views? Comment on Biederman and Gerhardstein (1993). *Journal of Experimental Psychology: Human Perception and Performance, 21,* 1494–1505.
Tarr, M.J., & Pinker, S. (1989). Mental rotation and orientation dependence in shape recognition. *Cognitive Psychology, 21,* 233–283.
Tarr, M.J., & Pinker, S. (1990). When does human object recognition use a viewer-centered reference frame? *Psychological Science, 1*(4), 253–256.
Tipper, S.P. (1985). The negative priming effect: Inhibitory effects of ignored primes. *Quarterly Journal of Experimental Psychology, 37A,* 571–590.
Treisman, A., & DeSchepper, B. (1996). Object tokens, attention, and visual memory. In T. Inui & J.L. McClelland (Eds.), *Attention and performance XVI: Information integration in perception and communication* (pp. 15–46). Cambridge, MA: MIT Press.
Tversky, B., & Hemenway, K. (1984). Objects, parts, and categories. *Journal of Experimental Psychology: General, 113,* 169–193.
Ullman, S. (1989). Aligning pictoral descriptions: An approach to object recognition. *Cognition, 32,* 193–254.
Ullman, S. (1996). *High-level vision: Object recognition and visual cognition.* Cambridge, MA: MIT Press.
von der Malsburg, C. (1994). The correlation theory of brain function. In E. Domany, J.L. van Hemmen, & K. Schulten (Eds.), *Models of neural networks II* (pp. 95–119). Berlin: Springer. (Original work published 1981.)
Winston, P. (1975). Learning structural descriptions from examples. In P. Winston (Ed.), *The psychology of computer vision* (pp. 157–209). New York: McGraw-Hill.

VISUAL COGNITION, 2001, *8* (3/4/5), 519–530

Flexible cortical gamma-band correlations suggest neural principles of visual processing

Reinhard Eckhorn, Andreas Bruns, Mirko Saam, Alexander Gail, Andreas Gabriel, and Hans Joerg Brinksmeyer

Physics Department, Philipps-University Marburg, Germany

We summarize recent studies of our group from the primary visual cortex V1 of behaving monkeys referring to the hypothesis of spatial feature binding by γ-synchronization (30–90 Hz). In agreement with this hypothesis the data demonstrates decoupling of γ-activities among neural groups representing figure and ground. As γ-synchronization in V1 is restricted to cortical ranges of few millimeters, feature binding may equivalently be restricted in visual space. Closer inspection shows that the restriction in synchrony is due to far-reaching travelling γ-waves with changing phase coupling. Based on this observation we extend the initial binding-by-synchronization hypothesis and suggest object continuity to be coded by phase continuity. It is further argued that the spatial phase changes of the V1 γ-waves in general will also limit lateral phase coupling to higher levels of processing. Instead of phase-locked γ-coupling, corticocortical cooperation among γ-processes may be mediated by mutual amplitude modulations that are more reliable than phase synchrony over larger distances. The relevance of this concept of corticocortical binding is demonstrated with subdural recordings from human subjects performing cognitive tasks. The experimental results are discussed on the basis of network models with spiking neurons.

SYNCHRONIZATION AND CORTICAL COOPERATIVITY

The neural mechanisms of cortical cooperativity, including perceptual feature binding and interactions among different levels of visual processing, are still largely unknown. How are local features flexibly grouped into actually perceived objects and events, and how do their current representations interact

Please address all correspondence to R. Eckhorn, Philipps-University, Physics Department, Neurophysics Group, Renthof 7, D-35032 Marburg, Germany.
Email: reinhard.eckhorn@physik.uni-marburg.de

This research was supported by grants Ec 53/7-3 and Ro 529/12-1 from the DFG to R. Eckhorn. We thank U. Thomas, W. Gerber, A. Rentzos, and P. Muth for their excellent technical assistance and Professor R. Bauer for his help in recordings.

http://www.tandf.co.uk/journals/pp/13506285.html DOI:10.1080/13506280143000098

with visual memory and other higher-order processes? It has been proposed that binding of spatially distributed features and inter-areal cooperations are supported by fast synchronized rhythms in neurons processing a common task, for example the coding of a visual object (Reitboeck, 1983; Malsburg & Schneider, 1986). This hypothesis attracted attention when synchronized γ-oscillations (30–90 Hz) were found in the visual cortex of anaesthetized cats (Eckhorn et al., 1988; Gray, Koenig, Engel, & Singer, 1989) and awake monkeys (Frien, Eckhorn, Bauer, Woelbern, & Kehr, 1994; Kreiter & Singer, 1992). However, γ-synchronization is restricted in monkey V1 to a range of few millimeters, even if the cortical representation of a (homogeneous) stimulus is much larger (Frien & Eckhorn, 2000). Hence, the observed range of γ-synchronization probably provides an upper limit for dynamically emerging patches of γ-synchronization during visual processing. According to the synchronization hypothesis, this should result in restricted feature binding in visual space. Since we do not have perceptual evidence for such a restriction, we suggest γ-phase *continuity* (as opposed to synchrony) as a basis for a less restrictive type of lateral signal coupling, because such phase coupling has been found to cover larger cortical ranges (Eckhorn & Gabriel, 1999). Furthermore, if visual processing involves cooperativity among patches of γ-synchronization across different cortical areas, equivalent restrictions for phase coupling as within a single area may hold. In fact, although γ-synchronization has been found between neural groups with overlapping receptive fields in adjacent visual areas (cat area 17/18: Brosch & Eckhorn, 1992; Eckhorn et al., 1988; monkey V1/V2: Frien et al., 1994), evidence from subdural recordings in humans suggests that inter-areal interactions are generally not reflected by stable phase coupling in the γ-range (Bullock et al., 1995; Menon et al., 1996; Towle et al., 1998). Instead, they may be mediated by covarying *strengths*, i.e., covarying amplitudes, accessible by correlated amplitude envelope time courses.

Here, we present data from monkey and human cortical recordings showing the different types of γ-interactions (intra-areal phase coupling and phase continuity as well as long-range inter-areal amplitude coupling), and we extend the initial binding-by-synchronization hypothesis by including these types of γ-coupling. Subsequently, we present a related model in order to discuss potential neural network properties underlying the experimental results.

EXPERIMENTAL EVIDENCE

Flexible decoupling of γ-activity is capable of supporting figure–ground segregation

The binding-by-synchronization hypothesis suggests coupling of γ-activities representing the same object. Accordingly, neural groups representing different scene segments should decouple their γ-activities. This prediction has been tested with a static figure–ground stimulus and μ-electrode recordings of local field potentials (LFP) in V1 of awake monkeys, simultaneously from inside and outside the figure's representational area (Figure 1A; Gail, Brinksmeyer, & Eckhorn, 2000). Time-resolved analysis with respect to stimulus onset of spectral coherence revealed the following results: (1) There is substantial stimulus-specific coupling of γ-activity between groups of neurons representing the same scene segment (figure or ground). When the receptive fields of recording pairs lie both within the figure or both within the background, γ-coherence is stronger than in a prestimulus condition with a homogeneous grey screen. (2) Stimulus-specific late γ-coherence (about 100–250 ms post stimulus onset) is strongly reduced across the figure–ground contour (Figure 1B) compared to the situation with a continuous surface. (3) Coherence of the early, stimulus-locked broad-band responses is not significantly reduced across the contour. (4) Coherence of low-frequency components does not show a difference between the figure-to-ground versus the continuous condition.

These data particularly show that decoupling of late γ-activity at a contour representation in V1 is potentially responsible for figure–ground segregation (and not the low frequencies or early transient broad-band responses). In a previous study with quite a similar experimental arrangement, Lamme and Spekreijse (1998) had ruled out synchronization as an indicator of a dynamic feature-binding process in monkey V1. Differences to our results may be due to their use of multiple unit activity and cross-correlation as coupling measure, which showed also less reliable decoupling in our data than LFP γ-coherence.

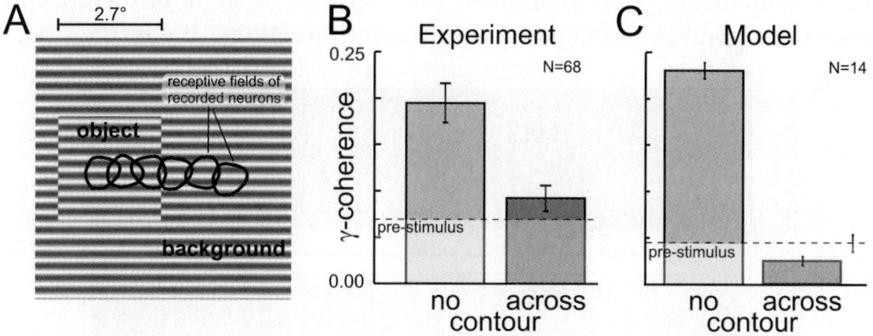

Figure 1. Coherence of γ-activity is reduced across the representation of an object's contour. **A:** Schema of visual grating stimulus and positions of receptive fields. **B:** A continuous grating induced a substantial increase in LFP γ-coherence (left bar, $N = 68$ recording pairs from two monkeys) compared to the prestimulus condition with a homogenous grey screen (dashed horizontal line). Introduction of the figure–ground contour by phase-shifting a part of the grating reduces LFP γ-coherence between inside and outside representations almost to the prestimulus level from about 100 ms poststimulus (right bar). (A and B modified from Gail, Brinksmeyer, & Eckhorn, 2000). **C:** Coherence in the model also shows strong reductions when a contour intersects the receptive fields of the recordings (for the model see Discussion; C modified from Saam, Gabriel, Al-Shaikhli, & Eckhorn, 2000). Coherence within each segment (object or background) remains high (data not shown).

In conclusion, these results from our group support the classical binding-by-synchronization hypothesis.

Phase continuity but not synchrony of γ-waves is present across large cortical distances

As the lateral synchronization range of stimulus-induced γ-activity in monkey V1 is limited to patches of about 5 mm diameter (measured by coherence; Frien & Eckhorn, 2000), visual objects with larger cortical representations cannot be coded by synchrony of a single patch. In order to understand the reasons for this limitation, former recordings were inspected in more detail, revealing spatio-temporal activity patterns, interpretable as long-ranging γ-waves. Across linearly arranged cortical recording positions relative phases at a given moment change continuously in space and vary randomly but smoothly in time from phase lead over synchronization to phase lag within periods of about 100 ms (Figure 2A). For detecting such continuous phase couplings a new method for single-trial responses has been developed (Eckhorn & Gabriel, 1999). It revealed that the relative phases among the recording positions are symmetrically distributed around zero delay and that their variance increases on average linearly with cortical distance (Figure 3). We want to note that averaging across the variable phases, which is inherent in the typical use of cross-correlation and coherence measures, leads to diminished or no coupling. Hence, the classical pairwise coupling measures do not capture the fact that there is still a non-trivial phase relationship between distant recording sites mediated by the phase continuity. In conclusion, γ-oscillations in striate cortex, as so far observed, can be interpreted as waves propagating in different directions, suggesting that the

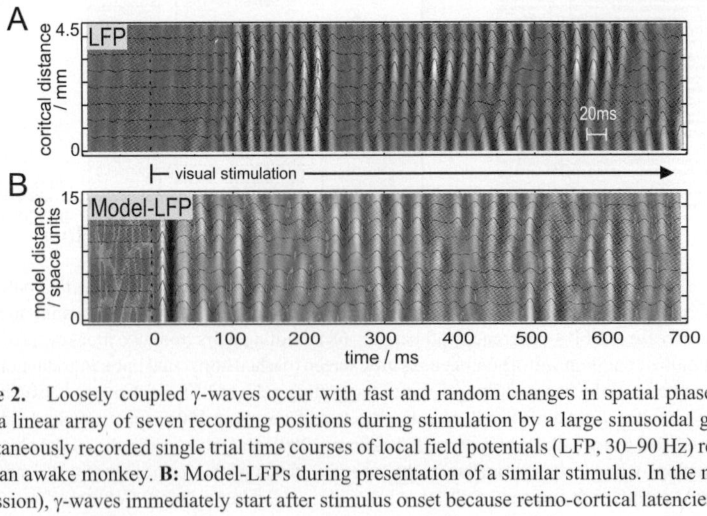

Figure 2. Loosely coupled γ-waves occur with fast and random changes in spatial phase relations along a linear array of seven recording positions during stimulation by a large sinusoidal grating. **A:** Simultaneously recorded single trial time courses of local field potentials (LFP, 30–90 Hz) recorded in V1 of an awake monkey. **B:** Model-LFPs during presentation of a similar stimulus. In the model (see Discussion), γ-waves immediately start after stimulus onset because retino-cortical latencies were not included. (Modified from Saam, Gabriel, Al-Shaikhli, & Eckhorn, 2000.)

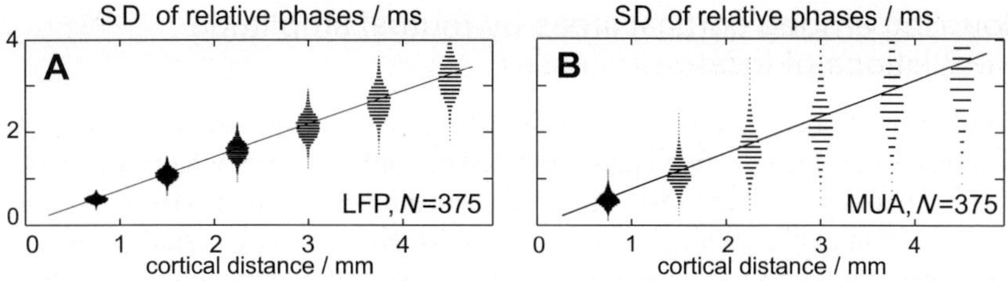

Figure 3. Random phase-jitter increases with cortical distance (measured as standard deviation of relative phases). **A:** Local field potentials, LFP. **B:** Multiple unit activity (MUA), simultaneously recorded by the same μ-electrodes in V1 of awake monkeys. (Modified from Saam et al., 2000.)

zero-delay correlation previously reported by several groups including ours (reviews in Eckhorn, 1999; Gray, 1999) shows not a steady state but only the average of the randomly changing phase delays.

If continuity of γ-waves (with variable phase relations) potentially supports the coding of object continuity, their extent over object representations in V1 and the related visual fields should be much larger than that covered by a patch of synchronized γ-components (as measured by γ-coherence). This is indeed the case in monkey V1 as Figure 4 (A and B) shows. The effective ranges of synchronization are three to four times smaller than those of the continuous waves (estimated from the half-height decline in Figure 4 (A and B).

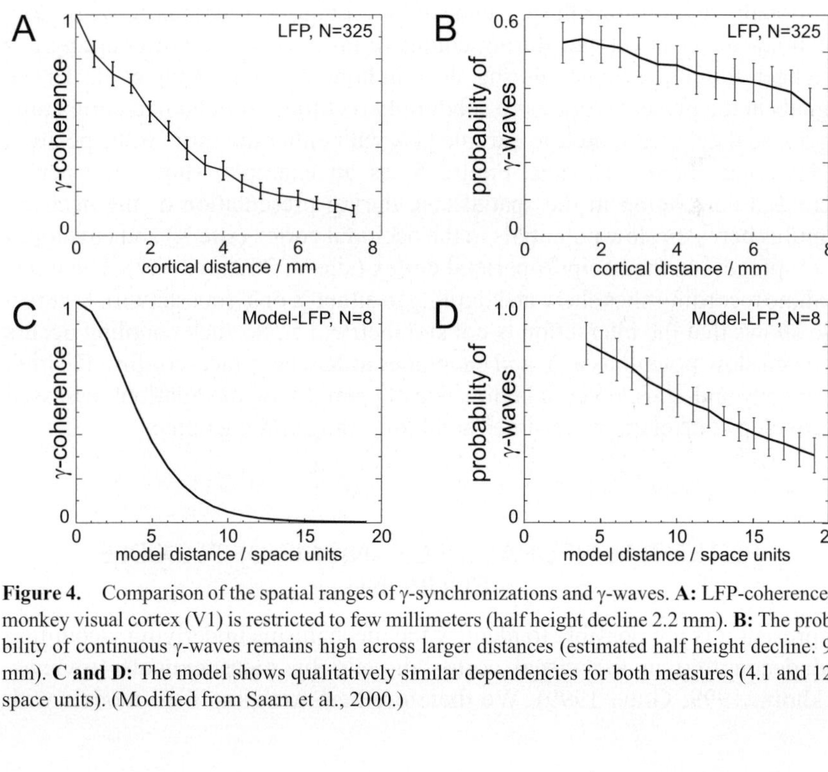

Figure 4. Comparison of the spatial ranges of γ-synchronizations and γ-waves. **A:** LFP-coherence in monkey visual cortex (V1) is restricted to few millimeters (half height decline 2.2 mm). **B:** The probability of continuous γ-waves remains high across larger distances (estimated half height decline: 9.5 mm). **C and D:** The model shows qualitatively similar dependencies for both measures (4.1 and 12.8 space units). (Modified from Saam et al., 2000.)

Coupling among cortical areas by mutual amplitude modulations of local γ-processes

A rather limited cortical range of classical γ-coherence or correlation (i.e., stable phase coupling) has been demonstrated not only for microelectrode recordings in monkeys, but also for subdural recordings in humans (Bullock et al., 1995; Menon et al., 1996; Towle et al., 1998). Nonetheless, visual processing across several levels requires some form of cooperation between different cortical areas. A local patch of γ-synchronization at one site may modulate the mean amplitude of another patch at a remote site, leading to coordinated amplitude time courses of the otherwise independent processes in the γ-range, whose phases and even frequencies need not be related at all. Therefore we tested the possibility that local γ-activities may interact via their amplitude envelopes, which are largely independent of small differences in activation delays of parallel projections. Given that the γ-envelope signals are transmitted and can be recorded extracellularly as slow potentials, correlations between pairs of envelopes, between slow potentials and envelopes, or both should be observable.

It has recently been shown in subdural recordings from human subjects that task-specific correlations between γ-envelopes do in fact occur independently of stable phase coupling (Bruns, Eckhorn, Jokeit, & Ebner, 2000). Here we additionally demonstrate the presence of long-range correlations between slow potentials and γ-envelopes during cognitive tasks. This type of coupling has also been found previously during sleep in human EEGs (Witte et al., 1997). Signals in the present work were subdurally recorded from human cortex during a visual delayed-match-to-sample task with either the form or the position of an object being relevant. Figure 5, as an example, shows transiently increased correlation in the spatial task during presentation of the decision stimulus between slow potentials in the occipital cortex (site X) and envelopes of a γ-process in the occipito-parietal cortex (site Y, 30 mm away). The intermediate recording sites show no coupling to either X or Y (not shown). Figure 5 also shows that the interaction is not symmetric, i.e., no such coupling occurs between slow potentials at Y and envelopes at X. These facts confirm the high specificity and, thus, potential relevance of γ-amplitude modulations, assessed as envelope correlations, for inter-areal long-range interactions.

POTENTIAL NEURAL MECHANISMS OF FLEXIBLE γ-COUPLING

At present it is not possible to identify the mechanisms underlying γ-coupling and decoupling in the visual cortex directly by measurements (reviews: Eckhorn, 1999; Gray, 1999). We therefore here use simplified models with

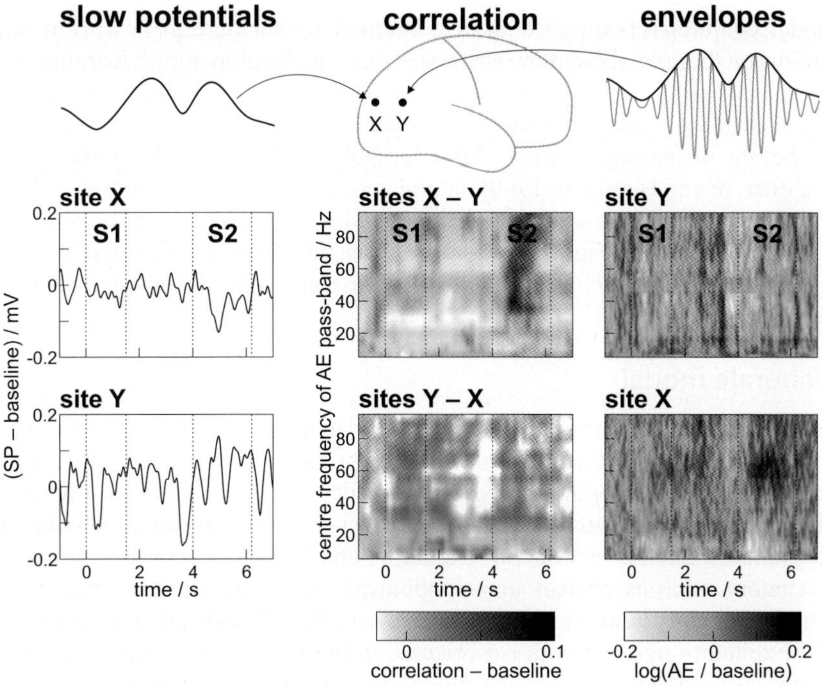

Figure 5. Event-related changes of correlation between slow potentials (SP, 0.02–5 Hz) and amplitude envelopes (AE) at two cortical sites (X and Y) during the spatial task. Stimulation periods are marked by dashed lines (S1 and S2: presentation of first and second stimulus; last line: mean response time). Envelopes of bandpass signals (bandwidth ±5 Hz) were calculated for centre frequencies between 5 Hz and 95 Hz. Time-resolved correlation was determined for each AE frequency band and trial (correlation length 640 ms). Correlations were then averaged across trials ($N = 57$), and baseline correlation was subtracted (middle column). For comparison, the left and right columns show event-related changes of average slow potentials and envelopes, which were actually not used for the correlation analysis.

spiking neurons to discuss potential mechanisms (Saam & Eckhorn, 2000; Saam et al., 2000).

Intra-areal limitation of γ–synchronization

In the primary visual cortex there are dense horizontal connections, which provide a possible neural substrate for mediating synchronization. However, lateral spike velocities in the visual cortex are slow (e.g., Bringuier, Chavane, Glaeser, & Fregnac, 1999), which suggests strong influences on synchronization behaviour (Ritz, Gerstner, Fuentes, & van Hemmen, 1994; Traub, Whittington, & Jefferys, 1997) and synaptic learning (Markram & Tsodyks, 1996). In order to test how lateral transmission delays may limit the size of synchronization patches, finite spike velocities are used for the lateral connections in a *simple one-layer model* (Saam & Eckhorn, 2000). In the initial phase of this model, coupling is homogeneous in its strength, so that there are no a priori constraints on the spatial coupling structures that can develop during learning. For the same reason, the inputs to the model are slightly synchronized stochastic signals without gradients in spatial correlations (mimicking spontaneous activity before visual experience). After temporal Hebbian learning (Kempter, Gerstner, & van Hemmen, 1999), lateral connection strength and thereby synchronization becomes spatially restricted, which corresponds to the observations in monkey V1 (Figures 3 and 4A). Thus, the spatial restriction of cortical γ-synchronization patches may, among other reasons, be due to lateral activation delays.

Elaborate model

For the next steps of argumentation a more elaborate model is used (being still compatible with the previous results; again, the lateral connections have axonal delays increasing proportionally with distance; Saam et al., 2000). Spiking neurons are arranged in four retinotopic layers of different preferred stimulus orientations. Each layer contains excitatory and inhibitory neurons (ratio 4:1). Excitatory neurons project to neighbouring inhibitory neurons. The latter inhibit excitatory neurons within the same neighbourhood in all orientation layers. Excitatory neurons with iso-orientation preference and coaxially aligned receptive fields are coupled via modulatory synapses (Eckhorn, Reitboeck, Arndt, & Dicke, 1990). To account for stochastic inputs from brain regions excluded from the model, all neurons receive mutually uncorrelated broadband noise.

Gamma decoupling across figure-ground contour

In the figure–ground experiment the respective representations in monkey V1 are decoupled in their γ-activities. On the other hand, the same neural groups show substantial γ-coupling when they represent a single scene segment. We interpret the observed γ-decoupling as a blockade of lateral coupling at the position of the contour representation within V1 (Gail et al., 2000). The *elaborate model* supports this notion. When we extract model-LFPs, using relative positions and integration ranges comparable to the experimental arrangement and determine coherence values across the contour representation, they are reduced to the baseline level (Figure 1C). Taking into account the structure of the model, this behaviour can be explained by the following effects. First, neurons responding preferentially to the surface texture stimulus are only weakly activated at the contour (which has a different orientation in the present example). Second, their activity is even more reduced due to the orientation-independent inhibition induced by the strongly activated neurons at the contour. Third, neurons representing the surface (texture) in the vicinity of the contour therefore do not receive modulatory input from these inhibited neurons at the contour representation. This considerably reduces coupling among neurons representing the surface near both sides of the contour. The special implementation of the model, using orientation selective layers, has been chosen for the sake of comparability with the experimental data. It does not mean a confinement of general validity, since any object border constitutes a discontinuity in at least one visual feature dimension, and therefore an analogous argumentation always holds, based on the low activity of neurons with feature selectivity different from that of the contour. Alternatively, decoupling may be mediated by neurons activated by a contour and acting via pre-synaptic inhibition at those synapses that support lateral phase coupling in situations without contours. Future experimental and model work has to be done in order to prove the existence of these or other mechanisms.

Object continuity may be coded by phase continuity of γ-waves

The propagating γ-waves mentioned in the Experimental Evidence section are generated across wide cortical extents when large stimuli drive neighbouring neural groups in a sustained way. Their local generation is particularly supported by neighbouring neural groups of similar feature preference during simultaneous activation (e.g., Frien & Eckhorn, 2000). Experimental data showed that local phase coupling includes also neural groups that are only weakly driven by a stimulus (Frien & Eckhorn, 2000; Koenig, Engel, & Singer, 1995). It suggests that local phase coupling can emerge among neurons coding different feature values, and thus bind them across object surfaces. However, global intra-areal phase continuity among patches of coherent γ-activities deserves additional explanations that are also derived from the *elaborate model*.

Generation of travelling γ-waves with varying phase shifts

Local groups of excitatory neurons in the visual cortex share inhibitory feedback neurons (Braitenberg & Schuez, 1991). When a corresponding model network is activated by "visual" stimulation, simultaneous rhythmic chopping in the γ-range turns up in the local group (Figure 2B), mediated by fast local feedback inhibition. More extended γ-waves are explained in the *elaborate model* by the weak lateral coupling and the activation delays, consistent with the experimental data. Quantitative analyses of relative phase relations in the γ-waves show a similar increase in variance with distance as in the cortical recordings (not shown). In addition, distance dependence of γ-coherence and γ-wave probability is compared in Figure 4. From these plots the cortical extents of γ-synchronization and γ-waves can be estimated as the half-height decline. Patches of γ-coherence are three to four times smaller than those of the γ-waves.

In conclusion, as phase coupling of γ-waves is randomly but smoothly varying in space and time, phase continuity may be a potential code for defining object continuity in visual cortex (Eckhorn & Gabriel, 1999).

Coupling among different cortical areas

A restricted range of γ-synchronization is likely to be characteristic not only of lateral interactions within the same cortical area, but also of inter-areal coupling (as also pointed out in the Experimental Evidence section). This is supported by an extension of the previously mentioned one-level model to a two-level model representing two cortical areas (e.g., V1 and V2). Hebbian learning in this model of forward inter-areal connections reveals that level 2 receptive fields tend to cover just the range of γ-synchronization fields at level 1 (Saam & Eckhorn, 2000). (This, by the way, gives one possible explanation why the sizes of receptive fields in mammalian visual systems increase from lower to higher cortical areas.) The convergence from a patch of synchronized level 1 neurons to a single level 2 neuron will generally cause level 2 neurons with non-overlapping receptive fields to receive incoherent inputs, and thus display incoherent γ-activities. Phase coupling at this level may nevertheless arise, involving the emergence of an additional separate coupling dynamics that may be independent of level 1 activity (possibly characterized by different frequencies). In such a scenario, phase coupling between different cortical areas in the γ-range would generally not occur (at least among retinotopically non-corresponding patches).

However, long-range inter-areal cooperation is a basic postulate in present concepts of brain function. We assume that a substantial part of this cooperation may be mediated by interdependent amplitude modulations among distant γ-processes via bundles of parallel axonal connections. Given a patch of γ-activity whose amplitude is temporally modulated (e.g., by a sensory stimulus), the amplitude envelope signal could, at a distant projection target, be extracted by synaptic summation with time constants matching the temporal characteristics of the envelope. Such longer time constants are not needed in cases where differences in axonal delays lead to a broad temporal dispersion between spikes reaching the target cells. Finally, the extracted envelope component of a distant γ-process may interact with local γ-processes, modulating their amplitudes. Hence, basic neural properties are sufficient to explain how remote patches of γ-activities, although being subject to different local dynamics, could become correlated in their amplitudes and thus be coordinated or "bound" on a larger spatial scale.

Conclusion

We have presented three possible coupling mechanisms among γ-processes that can well co-exist in the cortex and can serve different purposes in binding and association. Two of them add an extension to the original binding-by-synchronization hypothesis.

REFERENCES

Braitenberg, V., & Schuez, A. (1991). *Anatomy of the cortex.* Berlin: Springer.

Bringuier, V., Chavane, F., Glaeser, L., & Fregnac, Y. (1999). Horizontal propagation of visual activity in the synaptic integration field of area 17 neurons. *Science, 283*, 695–699.

Brosch, M., & Eckhorn, R. (1992). Synchronization rules of stimulus-induced oscillations between areas 17 and 18. *European Journal of Neuroscience, 5*(Suppl.), 1079.

Bruns, A., Eckhorn, R., Jokeit, H., & Ebner, A. (2000). Amplitude envelope correlation detects coupling among incoherent brain signals. *NeuroReport, 11*, 1509–1514.

Bullock, T.H., McClune, M.C., Achimowicz, J.Z., Iragui-Madoz, V.J., Duckrow R.B., & Spencer, S.S. (1995). EEG coherence has structure in the millimeter domain: Subdural and hippocampal recordings from epileptic patients. *Electroencephalography and Clinical Neurophysiology, 95*, 161–177.

Eckhorn, R. (1999). Neural mechanisms of visual feature binding investigated with microelectrodes and models. *Visual Cognition, 6*, 231–265.

Eckhorn, R., Bauer, R., Jordan, W., Brosch, M., Kruse, W., Munk, M., & Reitboeck, H.J. (1988). Coherent oscillations: A mechanism of feature linking in the visual cortex? Multiple electrode and correlation analyses in the cat. *Biological Cybernetics, 60*, 121–130.

Eckhorn, R., & Gabriel, A. (1999). Phase continuity of fast oscillations may support the representation of object continuity in striate cortex of awake monkey. *Society for Neuroscience Abstracts, 25*, 677.

Eckhorn, R., Reitboeck, H.J., Arndt, M., & Dicke, P. (1990). Feature linking via synchronization among distributed assemblies: Simulations of results from cat visual cortex. *Neural Computation, 2*, 293–307.

Frien, A., & Eckhorn, R. (2000). Functional coupling shows stronger stimulus dependency for fast oscillations than for low-frequency components in striate cortex of awake monkey. *European Journal of Neuroscience, 12*, 1466–1478.

Frien, A., Eckhorn, R., Bauer, R., Woelbern, T., & Kehr, H. (1994). Stimulus-specific fast oscillations at zero phase between visual areas V1 and V2 of awake monkey. *NeuroReport, 5*, 2273–2277.

Gail, A., Brinksmeyer, H.J., & Eckhorn, R. (2000). Contour decouples gamma activity across texture representation in monkey striate cortex. *Cerebral Cortex, 10*, 840–850.

Gray, C.M. (1999). The temporal correlation hypothesis of visual feature integration: Still alive and well. *Neuron, 24*, 31–47.

Gray, C.M., Koenig, P., Engel, A.K., & Singer, W. (1989). Oscillatory responses in cat visual cortex exhibit inter-columnar synchronization which reflects global stimulus properties. *Nature, 338*, 334–337.

Kempter, R., Gerstner, W., & van Hemmen, J.L. (1999). Hebbian learning and spiking neurons. *Physical Review, E59*, 4498–4514.

Koenig, P., Engel, A.K., & Singer, W. (1995). Relation between oscillatory activity and long-range synchronization in cat visual cortex. *Proceedings of the National Academy of Sciences of the USA, 92*, 290–294.

Kreiter, A., & Singer, W. (1992). Oscillatory neuronal responses in the visual cortex of the awake macaque monkey. *European Journal of Neuroscience, 4*, 369–375.

Lamme, V.A.F., & Spekreijse, H. (1998). Neuronal synchrony does not represent texture segregation. *Nature, 396*, 362–366.

Malsburg, C. von der, & Schneider, W. (1986). A neural cocktail-party processor. *Biological Cybernetics*, *54*, 29–40.

Markram, H., & Tsodyks, M. (1996). Redistribution of synaptic efficacy between neocortical pyramidal neurons. *Nature*, *382*, 807–810.

Menon, V., Freeman, W.J., Cutillo, B.A., Desmond, J.E., Ward, M.F., Bressler, S.L., Laxer, K.D., Barbaro, N., & Gevins, A.S. (1996). Spatio-temporal correlations in human gamma band electrocorticograms. *Electroencephalography and Clinical Neurophysiology*, *98*, 89–102.

Reitboeck, H.J. (1983). A multi-electrode matrix for studies of temporal signal correlations within neural assemblies. In H. Haken, E. Basur, H. Flohr, & A.J. Mandell (Ed.), *Synergetics of the brain* (pp. 174–182). Berlin: Springer.

Ritz, R., Gerstner, W., Fuentes, U., & van Hemmen, J.L. (1994). A biologically motivated and analytically soluble model of collective oscillations in the cortex: II. Application to binding and pattern segmentation. *Biological Cybernetics*, *71*, 349–358.

Saam, M., & Eckhorn, R. (2000). Lateral spike conduction velocity in visual cortex affects spatial range of synchronization and receptive field size without visual experience: A learning model with spiking neurons. *Biological Cybernetics*, *83*, L1–L9.

Saam, M., Gabriel, A., Al-Shaikhli, B., & Eckhorn, R. (2000). Neural mechanisms of figure–ground segregation: Recordings from awake monkey and a model with spiking neurons. In C. Freska, G. Baratoff, & H. Neumann (Eds.), *Dynamische Perzeption*, volume 9 of *Proceedings in Artificial Intelligence* (pp. 27–32). Berlin: infix.

Towle, V.L., Syed, I., Berger, C., Grzesczcuk, R., Milton, J., Erickson, R.K., Cogen, P., Berkson, E., & Spire, J.P. (1998). Identification of the sensory/motor area and pathologic regions using ECoG coherence. *Electroencephalography and Clinical Neurophysiology*, *106*, 30–39.

Traub, R.D., Whittington, M.A., & Jefferys, J.G.R. (1997). Gamma oscillation model predicts intensity coding by phase rather than frequency. *Neural Computation*, *9*, 1251–1264.

Witte, H., Putsche, P., Eiselt, M., Hoffmann, K., Schack, B., Arnold, M., & Jaeger, H. (1997). Analysis of the interrelations between a low-frequency and a high-frequency signal component in human neonatal EEG during quiet sleep. *Neuroscience Letters*, *236*, 175–179.

VISUAL COGNITION, 2001, *8* (3/4/5), 531–547

Objective assessment of the functional role of spike train correlations using information measures

Stefano Panzeri and Huw D.R. Golledge

Neural Systems Group, Department of Psychology, University of Newcastle, UK

Fashan Zheng

Department of Experimental Psychology, University of Oxford, UK

Martin J. Tovée and Malcolm P. Young

Neural Systems Group, Department of Psychology, University of Newcastle, UK

The functional role of correlations between neuronal spike trains remains strongly debated. This debate partly stems from the lack of a standardized analysis technique capable of accurately quantifying the role of correlations in stimulus encoding. We believe that information theoretic measures may represent an objective method for analysing the functional role of neuronal correlations. Here we show that information analysis of pairs of spike trains allows the information content present in the firing rate to be disambiguated from any extra information that may be present in the temporal relationships of the two spike trains. We validate and illustrate the method by applying it to simulated data with variable degrees of known synchrony, and by applying it to recordings from pairs of sites in the primary visual cortex of anaesthetized cats. We discuss the importance of information theoretic analysis in elucidating the neuronal mechanisms underlying object identification.

INTRODUCTION

It is suggested that the responses of neurons are bound together by temporal correlations between their spike trains when they respond to the same object or feature (von der Malsburg, 1981). Such correlations could help solve the so-called binding problem by tagging the responses of neurons responding to an

Please address all correspondence to F. Zheng, Department of Experimental Psychology, University of Oxford, South Parks Road, Oxford OX1 3UD, UK.
Email: fashan.zheng@psy.ox.ac.uk

Supported by a Wellcome Trust project grant to M.P. Young and M.J. Tovée. We are grateful to S. Schultz and A. Treves for many useful discussions on information theory and for their contributions to previous collaborations.

http://www.tandf.co.uk/journals/pp/13506285.html DOI:10.1080/13506280143000106

object and disambiguating those responses from responses to other objects. Thus, neurons could synchronize when co-stimulated by a single object and desynchronize when stimulated by separate objects, synchronization between neuronal populations then being used to implement associations between elementary visual features coded by units in the visual cortex. This hypothesis has been the subject of extensive neurophysiological investigations over recent years. Although several groups have reported experimental evidence from the visual system in support of this theory (for a review see Singer, 1999), the role played by synchronous firing in visual feature binding remains controversial (see, e.g., Shadlen & Movshon, 1999), and far from being understood. Part of the controversy originates from the fact that some studies have found no evidence for a role of correlations in feature binding (de Oliveira, Thiele, & Hoffman, 1997; Golledge et al., 1999; Lamme & Spekreijse, 1998; Zheng et al., 1999). It is possible that one or more methodological factors contribute to the continuing uncertainty about this issue. Almost all the reported neurophysiological evidence in favour or against the temporal binding hypothesis relies upon the assessment of the significance of peaks in cross-correlograms (CCGs; Perkel, Gerstein, & Moore, 1967), and of their modulation with respect to stimulus configuration. Although investigating stimulus modulation of peaks (or of other features) of CCGs can clearly bear on the role of synchrony in binding, it does not address the critical issue of *how much* synchrony tells the brain about the configuration of objects in the visual field. This question is particularly important as it is well known that firing rates of individual cells are often strongly related to features of the sensory world (Adrian, 1926) and even to perceptual judgements (see, e.g., Britten, Shadlen, Newsome, & Movsho, 1992). Firing rate modulations can potentially contribute to the association of features in a variety of ways (Shadlen & Movshon, 1999). Therefore, the specific contribution of synchrony (or in general of correlations between the firing of cells) as a mechanism for binding should be assessed against the contribution of independent firing rate modulation to the encoding of objects in the visual field.

To address these issues, an analysis of the characteristics of CCGs is insufficient. We show here that information theory can instead be used to address the specific contribution of synchronized or correlated firing to visual feature binding, and to compare the contribution of synchrony against that of firing rates. Information theory allows one to take the point of view of an observer trying to reconstruct the stimulus configuration based solely on the observation of the activity of the neuronal population, and to determine to what degree the presence of correlated firing helps in identifying the stimulus. We now review some of the problems related to traditional CCG analysis, and we discuss how information theory could overcome these limitations. We first validate the method using simulated data, and then we present information theoretic analyses of neurophysiological experiments that we performed to test the binding by synchrony hypothesis. We show that information theory can lead to a much less equivocal understanding of the role of correlated firing in encoding visual information. We then discuss the implication of the proposed approach for more general understanding of the role of correlated firing in brain function.

Ambiguities in conventional cross-correlation analysis

The CCG represents a histogram of the probability of a spike from one neuron or multiunit activity (MUA) at a given time relative to a reference spike of a second neuron or MUA. Although cross-correlation is clearly capable of identifying synchrony between neurons, a number of factors limit the usefulness of the technique.

Several aspects of the analysis of CCGs present problems or are incomplete. First, CCG analysis itself does not provide a criterion to choose which periods of a response epoch should be analysed. Since, in most cases, moving stimuli are employed, the response varies with time and it may be that correlations are present or are stimulus modulated for only a short period in the response (Gray, Engel, Konig, & Singer, 1992). This short period is not necessarily related simply to the response peak, although some studies have analysed only the period in which the peak of the response is made to a moving stimulus (Engel, Konig, & Singer et al., 1991; Kreiter & Singer, 1996). Second, the width of the time window over which correlations should be assessed is arbitrary. Using long windows (e.g., much larger than the width of CCG peaks) may "wash out" transient correlations. Narrow windows centred upon the PSTH peak may ignore the part of the responses that contains most of the information about the stimuli (e.g., in firing rate modulations). Third, if the window length used to assess correlations is varied between stimulus conditions (e.g., Kreiter & Singer, 1996) then an undesirable extra source of variation is introduced when the stimulus conditions are compared. Information theory can mitigate some of these problems by providing a criterion for the selection of time windows, by identifying the windows in which most information is actually transmitted.

Many previous studies also differ in the methods used to quantify the temporal structure in CCGs. Some studies rely on the fitting of a damped sine wave to the CCG (Konig, 1994), a method that requires further arbitrary criteria for accepting a fit as significant (Young, Tanaka, & Yamane, 1992). Other methods quantify solely the likelihood that any peak in the CCG did not arise by chance (de Oliveira et al., 1997; Golledge et al., 1999). Analysis of the significance of a peak or of structure in the CCG must be made in relation to the flanks of the CCG. What length of flank is chosen will affect the significance of peaks. However, downstream neurons are unlikely to be able to compare the likelihoods of spikes occurring at lags of tens of milliseconds against the likelihood of simultaneous spikes. Also, the parameters of a CCG do not themselves quantify the informational contribution of synchronous firing.

Conventional CCG analysis techniques attempt to assess correlation in a manner independent of the firing rate in order to disambiguate synchronous modulations from firing rate variations. It is unlikely, though, that any downstream detector of the synchronous discharge of neurons would be capable of assessing the significance of correlation independent of the firing rate. It is more likely that it would make use of the actual number of coincident spikes available in its integration time window. Therefore cross-correlation peaks and firing rate modulation are likely to be closely linked in transmitting information to downstream neurons, and an analysis of the functional role of synchrony should be able to take this into account.

Most studies that appear to show stimulus-dependent synchrony have employed relatively strongly stimulated cells. An important prediction of the temporal correlation hypothesis is that synchrony should encompass the responses of sub-optimally stimulated neurons (Konig, Engel, Roelfsema, & Singer, 1995). A thorough test of this hypothesis requires the study of cells that fire very few spikes. The number of spikes included in the calculation of a CCG of course affects the precision with which correlations can be detected. Variations in the number of evoked spikes, rather than a true change in correlation between the neurons, could thus affect comparisons between optimal and sub-optimal stimuli. To avoid such problems some studies impose stringent limits on the number of spikes contributing to a CCG (e.g., Hata, Tsumoto, Sato, & Tamura, 1991) which effectively preclude the analysis of low firing rate responses. While analysing cells firing at low rates may be a challenge for CCG analysis, it is tractable for analyses developed from information theory (Panzeri, Schultz, Treves, & Rolls, 1999).

We believe that the continuing methodological ambiguities that attend studies of spike train correlations can be greatly reduced by employing methods based upon information theory (Shannon, 1948), as detailed next.

Information theory and neuronal responses

Information theory (Shannon, 1948) measures the statistical significance of how neuronal responses co-vary with the different stimuli presented at the sensory periphery. In other words, it determines how much information neuronal responses carry about the particular set of stimuli presented during an experiment. Unlike other simpler measures, like those of signal detection theory, which take into account only the mean response and its standard deviation, information theory allows one to consider the role of the entire probability distributions. A measure of information thus requires sampling experimentally the probabilities of neuronal responses. This is done by choosing a certain stimulus set when designing the experiment; by presenting each stimulus *s* several times, with a probability of presentation $P(s)$ set by the experimenter; and by constructing from the repeated presentations an empirical probability histogram $P(r|s)$ of a neuronal response *r* to all stimuli *s* in the set. The information measure is performed by computing the distance between the conditional response probabilities $P(r|s)$ and the unconditional response probability $P(r) = \Sigma s\, P(r|s)P(s))$, as follows (Cover & Thomas, 1991; Shannon, 1948):

$$I(S;R) = \sum_{s} P(s) \sum_{r} P(r|s) \log_2 \frac{P(r|s)}{P(r)}. \tag{1}$$

If the conditional response probabilities $P(r|s)$ differ among stimuli, our knowledge about what stimulus was presented increases after the observation of one neuronal spike train. Equation (1) quantifies this fact. The further apart from each other are the stimulus–conditional response probabilities, the higher is the information value. Equation (1) thus quantifies how well an observer could discriminate between different stimulus conditions, based on a single response trial.

There are several advantages in using information theory to quantify how reliably the activity of a set of neurons encodes the events in the sensory periphery (Borst & Theunissen, 1999; Rieke, Warland, deRuyter van Steveninck, & Bialek, 1996). First, information theory puts the performance of neuronal responses on a scale defined at the ratio level of measurement. For example, an increase of 30% of the peak height of a cross-correlogram does not tell us how this relates to synchrony-based stimulus discrimination, but values of information carried by synchronous firing have a precise meaning. Information theory measures the reduction of uncertainty about the stimulus following the observation of a neuronal response on a logarithmic scale. One bit of information corresponds to a reduction by a factor of two in the stimulus uncertainty. A second advantage of information theory in this context is that it does not require any specific assumption about the distance between responses or the stationarity of the processes, and it can therefore lead to objective assessments of some of the hypotheses.

It is worth noticing that information values are always relative to the stimulus set used, and that testing a neuron with different stimuli may lead to rather different information values. The intrinsic dependency of mutual information values on the nature of stimulus set allows us to test whether different encoding strategies are used by visual cortical neurons when dealing with external correlates of a different nature. This is of interest because one of the predictions of the binding-by-synchrony hypothesis is that synchrony is particularly important when stimulus configurations requiring some kind of associations are included, and less important in other situations. Information theory thus provides a natural framework to test this theory.

METHODS

The example data presented here come from a study performed to re-examine the findings of Gray, Konig, Engel, and Singer (1989). Some of the data has been presented previously (Golledge et al., 1999). Briefly, data were recorded from paired sites in area 17 of adult cats, which were anaesthetized with 0.5–1.1% halothane and paralysed with gallamine triethiodide. Multi-unit signals were recorded with tungsten in glass microelectrodes, amplified (× 10,000 gain), bandpass filtered (500–10,000 Hz) and digitized at 25 KHz. Multiunit recordings were considered instead of single units because they have been widely employed in previous studies of neuronal synchrony (Brosch, Bauer, & Eckhorn, 1997; Engel et al., 1991; Gray et al., 1989; Kreiter & Singer, 1996; Lamme & Spekreijse, 1998). Receptive fields (RFs) were non-overlapping in most cases, whilst in some cases there was partial overlap between the two RFs. Stimuli were based upon those employed by Gray et al. (1989), and they are plotted in Figure1. RFs were mapped by characterizing qualitatively, by means of presentations of bars and grating stimuli in different parts of the visual field, the bounding edges that surrounded the RF. For each cell the orientation-tuning curve was defined using bar stimuli in 10° orientation steps. The spatial frequency of each site was also qualitatively characterized. Once two RFs were mapped and the orientation tuning defined, bar stimuli were swept across the RFs such that they always crossed the centre of the mapped receptive fields simultaneously. Bar stimuli had a width based upon an intermediate value between the spatial frequency preferences of the two sites. Stimuli were presented as white bars against a black background, Michelson contrast = 0.93.

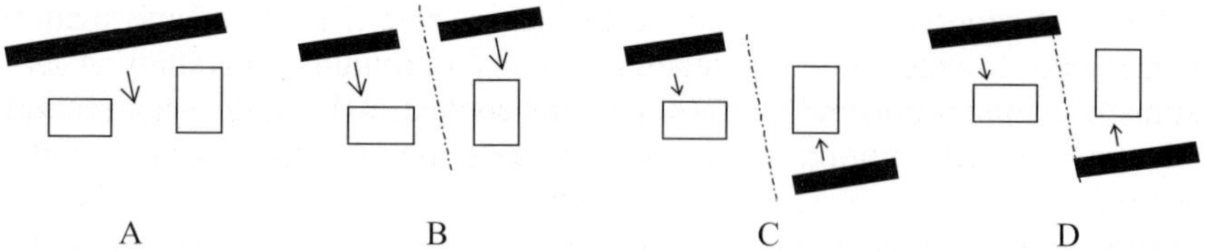

Figure 1. Stimulus set. Dashed line represents the midline between the two RFs. These schematic RFs and stimuli are used throughout to denote stimulus configurations in graphical representations of the data. Only one direction of sweep is shown; in all cases the stimuli were swept across the RF in the opposite direction as well. **A:** Whole bar—an unequivocally single object that co-stimulates both RFs. Theory and some previous results predict strong synchrony in this case. **B:** Split bar—a pair of bars, which co-stimulates the RF but retains the cue of "common motion", synchrony may be enhanced (Gray et al., 1989) but less than for the whole bar condition. **C:** Split opposing bars—bars moving in opposing directions but that cross the RF centres simultaneously, there was a gap between the two bars equivalent to the gap in stimulus B. In this case synchrony is predicted by the temporal correlation hypothesis to be minimal. **D:** Opposing bars—this stimulus differs from stimulus C only in the absence of a gap between the two bars moving in opposing directions. Synchrony is likely to be reduced, the meeting of the bars could conceivably enhance synchrony over the split opposing bar condition.

Each stimulus sweep lasted for 2–4 s and began and ended at least 1° outside the RFs.

We compared the results for four stimulus conditions that differed in their Gestalt properties (Rock & Palmer, 1990) such that they would be expected to cause differing amounts of synchrony between the paired sites if temporal correlation plays a role in feature binding (Figure 1). Stimuli were presented 30 or 40 times in a random sequence. Conventional cross-correlograms (Perkel et al., 1967) were calculated with a bin size of 1 ms over the entire response epoch using a sliding correlation window of 300 ms. The statistical significance of peaks in the CCGs was quantified using the Z-score of the maximal bin within the central 10 bins of the CCG (zero lag ± 5 ms).

Assessing the role of correlated firing in transmitting information

We recorded from two sites, and for each stimulus presentation we quantified r_1, r_2, the response of sites 1 and 2 respectively. We usually quantified the response as the number of spikes recorded from each site in windows of 100 ms (although other window lengths were considered; see the Results section).

From the repeated presentations of the stimuli we constructed the probability $P(r_1, r_2|s)$ of occurrence of a joint and simultaneous responses r_1, r_2 of a pair of recording sites. We then used the probabilities $P(r_1,r_2|s)$ to compute, through equation (1), the information extracted from the joint and simultaneous knowledge of responses r_1, r_2 of a pair of recording sites. Expressed in terms of $P(r_1,r_2|s)$, Equation (1) takes the following form:

$$I_2 = \sum_s P(s) \sum_r P(r_1, r_2 | s) \log_2 \frac{P(r_1, r_2 | s)}{P(r_1, r_2)}. \quad (2)$$

Of course, the information obtained from the joint observation of spike counts reflects the contribution of independent firing rate modulations to different stimuli of both sites, and also the information that may be gained (or lost) because the cells tend to fire together more than expected by chance. We wanted to separate out the specific impact of correlated firing on information transmission. For this purpose, we also computed a joint response probability by first randomly shuffling the order of trials for each stimulus. Shuffling the trial order destroys all the within-trial temporal correlations between the two spike trains. The shuffled joint probability distribution $P_{sh}(r_1,r_2|s)$ obtained in this way reflects only independent rate modulations, and it is the response probability that one would get in absence of any correlation between the two recording sites. We then calculated the information obtained from the shuffled probability distribution,

$$I_{2sh} = \sum_s P(s) \sum_r P_{sh}(r_1, r_2 | s) \log_2 \frac{P_{sh}(r_1, r_2 | s)}{P_{sh}(r_1, r_2)}. \quad (3)$$

We called it the "shuffled population information". It reflects, by construction, only the information in the rates. The subtraction of the shuffled population information (equation 3) from the simultaneous population information (equation 2) is thus a suitable quantification of the contribution of the statistical correlation between the cells to stimulus grouping.

Since the neuronal response probabilities were estimated empirically from repeated presentations of the same stimulus, neurophysiological information measures are plagued by a systematic error (or bias). An analytical procedure has been developed, that allows the computation of the systematic error, and its subtraction from the raw information values, in order to get unbiased and reliable information estimates (Panzeri & Treves, 1996). The bias term is a relatively simple function of response probabilities:

$$BIAS = \frac{1}{2NS \ln 2}\left[\sum_{s}(R_s - 1) - R + 1)\right], \tag{4}$$

where N is the number of trials per stimulus, S is the total number of stimulus conditions, and R is the number of relevant response classes across all stimuli (i.e., the number of different responses with non-zero probability of being observed). R_s is the number of relevant response classes to stimulus s (Panzeri & Treves, 1996). The bias correction procedure works well if there are at least as many trials per stimulus N as response classes R (Panzeri & Treves, 1996). In our case, if the number of response R was around 15–16 we could obtain unbiased estimates, given the 30–40 trials per stimulus available. Since we computed the information in the joint spike times and in relatively short windows, this condition was usually satisfied. If for example the maximum number of spikes per time window per cell was 3, there were up to 16 possible joint responses. When the firing rates were higher than that, we compressed the number of possible responses as follows. When computing the response probabilities $P(r_1,r_2|s)$, we have grouped the response firing rates into four classes per each neuron. The classes were equidistant between the minimum and maximum response observed per cell. In this way, there were in total 16 response classes for the joint probability and information calculations. Binning the responses into sub-classes of course decreases the information. However, it is preferable to obtain an information value that is approximated because of binning than to get an estimate that is out of statistical control because of undersampling and biases. Hence, the information estimations were unbiased and as accurate as possible given the amount of data.

RESULTS

We first assessed the efficacy of the information analysis of correlated firing by applying it to simulated spike trains containing variable amounts of synchrony.

Correlated spike trains were simulated using a method employed by Shadlen and Newsome (1998). In brief, there were two cells, each receiving 300 excitatory and 300 inhibitory inputs, each modelled as a Poisson process. Spikes were generated through a simple integrate-and-fire mechanism; the decay constant of the cell membrane was set to 20 ms, and the threshold for firing was set so that the output firing rate of the neuron was as close as possible to the mean rate of its inputs over the firing rate range used here (Shadlen & Newsome, 1998). Responses to two stimuli were simulated. The degree of synchrony between the neurons was varied by varying the fraction of common inputs to the two cells, either in a stimulus-independent or in a stimulus-dependent way. We simulated 50 trials per each stimulus presentation, and we computed the information in the simultaneous and the shuffled observation as described in methods section. For response quantification, the simulated spikes were counted in a window 50 ms long.

We report the results of the simulations in Figure 2. In the first example there was no temporal correlation between the activity of the two simulated neurons (Figure 2A), because there were no inputs shared by the two neurons. However, the mean firing rates were different to different stimuli, and so there was some information in the firing rates. The application of the information method gives the right result: There is information in the firing rates (as determined by the shuffled information), and no extra information in the correlated firing (Figure 2B). In the second example, the two neurons had the same firing rates as before, but there was some degree of synchrony because 10% of the inputs were shared (Figure 2C). The resulting correlation should be very weakly stimulus modulated, and in this case the information in the correlated firing is expected to be small but non-zero. Figure 2D shows that in this case the information analysis showed that the majority of information is carried by the independent rate modulations, and that there is a very small increase of information if the correlation between neurons is also taken into account. Since this correlation is very small and very weakly stimulus-modulated, the small increase of information is due to the fact that the correlation between the mean responses of the neurons is negative, and the trial-by-trial correlation between the variability of the neuronal responses is positive (Oram, Foldiak, Perret, & Sengpiel, 1998; Panzeri et al., 1999). We last considered the case when there was very little information in the rates, because each neuron presented approximately the same output rate to all the stimuli. However, in the first stimulus condition there was very high synchrony (90% of shared inputs; Figure 2E), and in the second stimulus condition there was no synchrony (0% of common inputs; Figure 2F). Applying the information theoretic analysis to this case (Figure 2G), we found that all the information was conveyed by correlated firing. Negligible information was present in the rates. Hence, the information theoretic analysis could effectively assess the stimulus coding mechanisms of the simulated neurons. Thus, the shuffled value reflects the amount of information carried by the firing

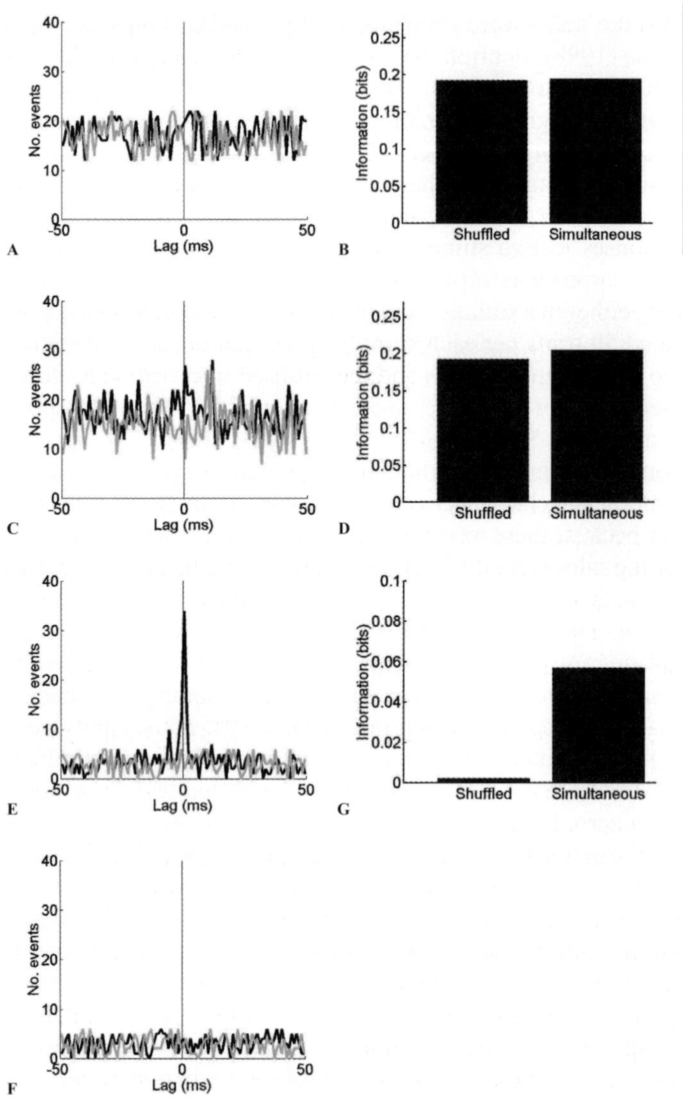

Figure 2. Testing the method with integrate-and-fire simulations. **Panels A and B:** The method is tested on pairs of simulated neurons with no shared connections. Firing rate of neuron 1 is 10 Hz to stimulus 1, and 20 Hz to stimulus 2. Firing rate of neuron 2 is 20 Hz to stimulus 1, and 10 Hz to stimulus 1. Panel A reports the CCG. Throughout the figure, dark lines show the raw CCG, light grey lines represent the shift-predictor. Panel B reports the information values. **Panels C and D:** Simulation of another neuronal pair with firing rates as in the top row, but this time with 10% of shared connections. Panel C shows the CCG, and panel B reports the information values. **Panels E, F, and G:** Simulation of a pair of neurons with constant firing rate across stimuli, but with different degrees of synchronization across the two stimuli (see text). Panels E and F report the CCG in the first and second stimulus condition respectively. Panel G shows the results of information analysis.

rate, whereas the difference of the simultaneous and shuffled information value reflects the amount of information carried by the correlations between the spikes of the two cells.

We next applied the information and CCG techniques to the neurophysiological recordings, and we endeavour to assess the specific contribution of synchrony between pairs of recording sites in associating visual features into objects, and to compare this to the contribution from firing rates. We present three examples of information analysis of correlated pairs of recording sites in the primary visual cortex of anaesthetized cats. For the information computation, the stimulus set used was composed of the four visual stimuli reported in Figure 1, and of the "no stimulus" conditions. Responses to the no-stimulus condition were obtained from the inter-trial recordings, taking care to eliminate the first 100 ms after the end of the previous stimulation, in order to avoid possible transient "off" responses. In this way, the stimulus set includes configurations involving the presence of zero, one and two objects.

In Figure 3 we examined a pair of sites whose receptive fields were non-overlapping and separated by 3°. Throughout, we refer to the separation of the receptive fields in terms of degrees of visual angle between the edges of the RFs. Both sites were orientation selective. The difference between tuning curve peak orientations was 70°. The stimulus orientation and speed was moderately sub-optimal for the first RF, and optimal for the second RF. The CCG (computed over the whole stimulus presentation epoch) showed significant modulations of the peak with stimulus configuration. There was a much higher level of synchrony for the continuous bar stimulus than for other discontinuous stimuli as previous studies have found (Brosch et al., 1997; Gray et al., 1989). The sites' firing rates were significantly modulated, as shown by the PSTHs. For example, site 2 showed a significant increase in firing rate when one of the two stimuli involving opposing bars were presented. To assess and compare the contribution of firing rates and of synchrony to the discrimination between stimulus configurations, we computed the information carried by the response pairs about the stimuli, and we compared the information carried by simultaneous responses to that carried by the shuffled responses. The latter quantifies how much the stimuli can be discriminated on the base of the firing rates only. We used sliding windows of width ranging from 25 to 200 ms for evaluating information. Here and in the following examples we present only the results for the 100 ms sliding windows, as the information in the correlations was maximal in this case. For some of the response windows, the information carried in the unshuffled condition is higher than the information in the shuffled condition. However, for other windows, shuffling the data actually increased the information (this is because the stimulus independent part of the CCG actually tends to decrease the information in this case). When considering the window in which maximal information was passed, the increase of information conveyed by modulations of synchronous firing was approximately 10% of the information

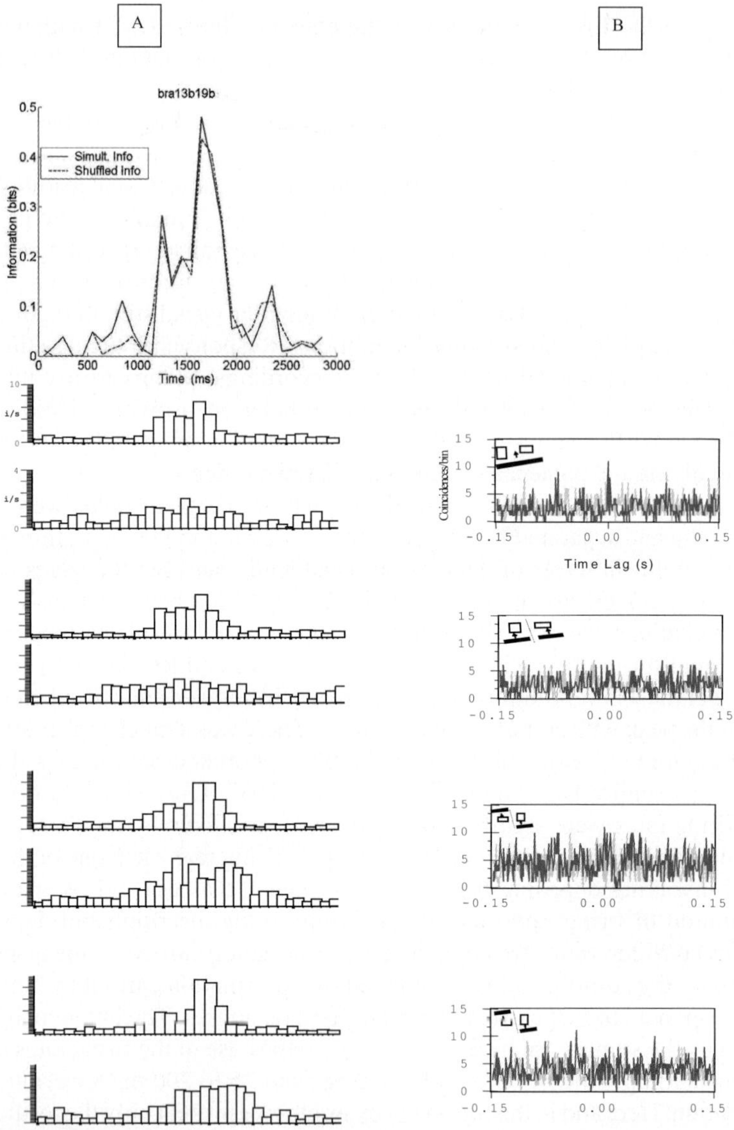

Figure 3. Example data from a non-overlapping receptive field pair. **Column A, upper graph:** Information present in the responses of the two RFs shown over the entire length of the stimulus sweep (3 s); solid line represents the information present in both the firing rate and correlations, dashed line represents information present in the firing rate alone after the temporal structure is lost by shuffling of the responses. **Lower graphs** represent the PSTHs for the two RFs for each stimulus condition. Y-axis represents spike rate in impulses per second, x-axis is time on the same scale as the information figure. **Column B** shows CCGs for each stimulus condition, the condition is shown as an icon in the upper left corner of the figure; dark lines show the raw CCG, light grey lines represent the shift-predictor, numbers in the upper right corner represent the Z-score for the statistical significance of the CCG peak.

that is conveyed just by independent rate modulations. Across all the windows analysed, the specific contribution of synchrony to information transmission (i.e., the difference between shuffled and unshuffled information) was at most 0.08 bits. This amount is appreciable but rather small relative to the peak information conveyed by the rates only, which is approximately 0.45 bits. This suggests that, where there is a tendency to fire in temporal coincidence in a stimulus dependent way, the information transmitted by synchrony may nonetheless be a secondary coding mechanism.

In Figure 4 we show a second pair of cells, whose cross-correlograms showed low frequency (~20 Hz) oscillations across all conditions. The RFs were partially overlapping (by 1.3°), and both sites were orientation selective, the distance between the tuning peaks was 40°. Again, however, all the information conveyed by the pair of sites can be attributed to rate modulations, and the specific contribution of synchrony is negligible for every time window considered. In Figure 5 we show another example of correlated pairs, in which there was strong correlation across all stimulus conditions, with similar peaks and Z scores. The RFs were separated by 5.9°. This pair of cells conveys most information by the firing rates. When considering the window of maximal information transmission, the contribution of synchrony *decreases* the total information conveyed by rates only. Thus, in this case correlations are not useful for stimulus encoding.

We plotted above the information results for sliding windows of 100 ms. However, we also carried out the same analysis using also windows of 50 and 200 ms length. The results were very similar to that presented for the 100 ms window. On average across the small population considered, the shuffled information and the simultaneous information peaked at 100 ms. However, the deviations from the values obtained with the shorter or longer window were small (within 5%) and not statistically significant. A systematic analysis of the information properties across time of a larger neuronal population will be reported elsewhere (in preparation).

DISCUSSION

In this paper we have discussed some problems related to CCG assessment of the role of temporal correlations between action potentials emitted by different neurons, and shown that using information theory can alleviate some problems of a pure CCG analysis. We have developed and presented an information theoretic formalism specifically devoted to assessing the role of synchrony in information encoding, and to comparing the role of synchrony to that of firing rate modulations. An application of this information theoretic formalism to neurophysiological recordings illustrated that information theory is extremely effective at clarifying the different encoding mechanisms used by neuronal populations for representing particular sets of stimuli. We have also shown that

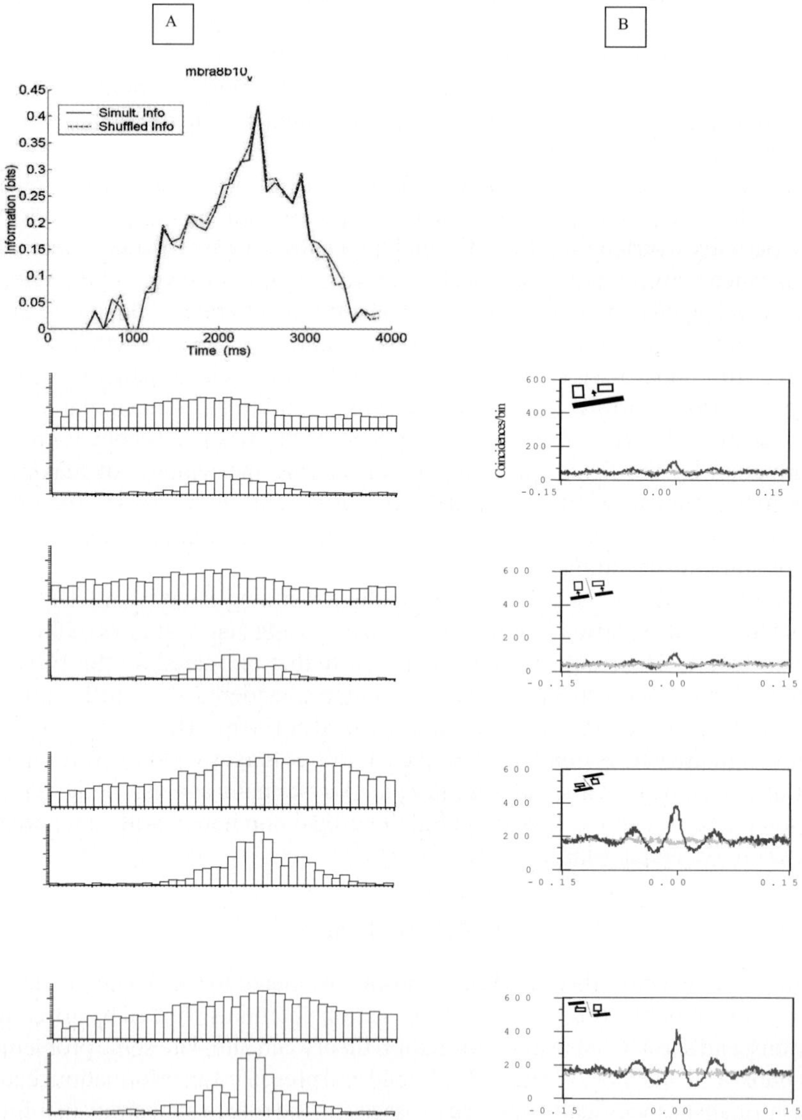

Figure 4. Information content, PSTHs, and CCGs for an overlapping RF pair that displayed pronounced oscillatory activity. Conventions as in Figure 3.

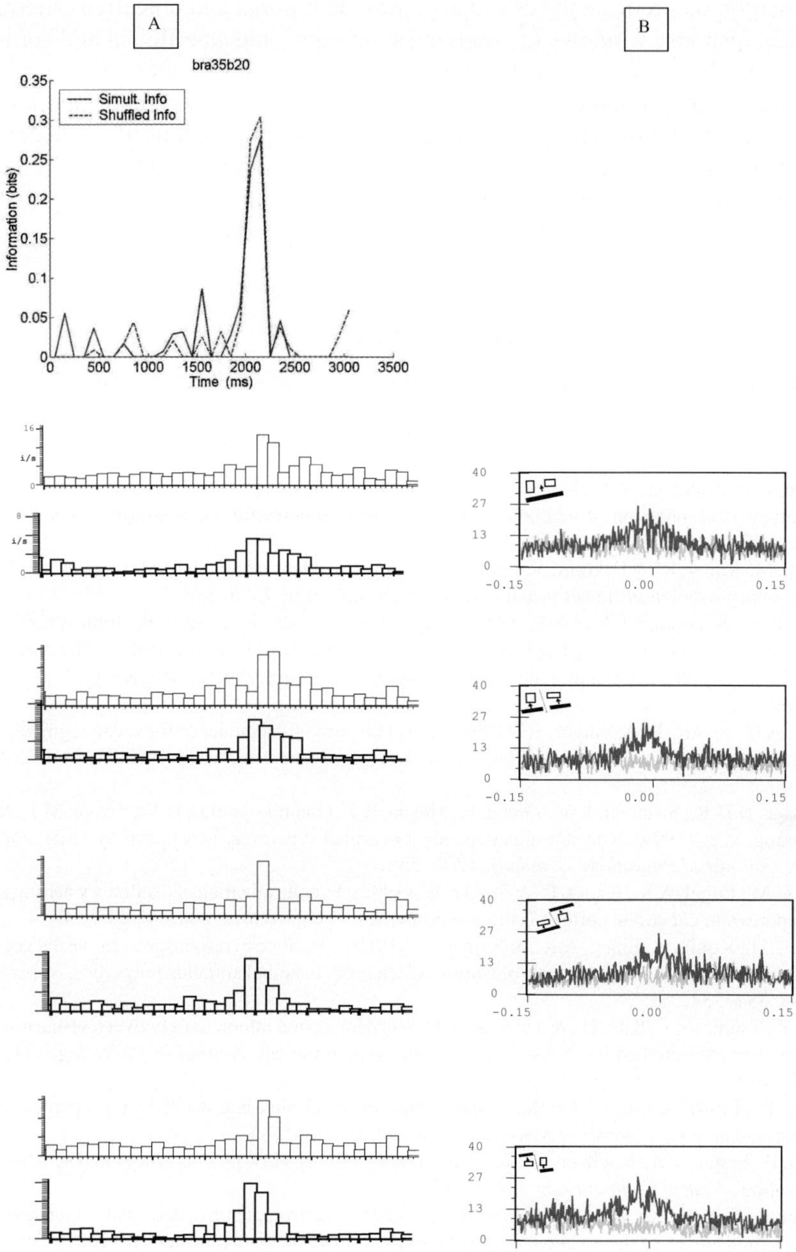

Figure 5. Information content, PSTHs, and CCGs for a non-overlapping RF pair that showed synchrony in all stimulus conditions. Conventions as in Figure 3.

information theoretic analyses can also provide rational and objective criteria to select response windows for studying synchrony, and an efficient and compact means by which to visualize the behaviour and significance of neuronal responses as a function of time. We are confident that the systematic application of these techniques to spike trains recorded from populations of visual cortical neurons will clarify some of the open and controversial questions on the neuronal mechanisms underlying object recognition and feature binding.

REFERENCES

Adrian, E.D. (1926). The impulses produced by sensory nerve endings: Part 1. *Journal of Physiology (London), 61,* 49–62.

Borst, A., & Theunissen, F.E. (1999). Information theory and neural coding. *Nature Neuroscience, 2,* 947–957.

Britten, K.H., Shadlen, M.N., Newsome, W.T., & Movshon, J.A. (1992). The analysis of visual motion: A comparison of neuronal and psychophysical performance. *Journal of Neuroscience, 12,* 4745–4765.

Brosch, M., Bauer, R., & Eckhorn, R. (1997). Stimulus dependent modulations of correlated high-frequency oscillations in cat visual cortex. *Cerebral Cortex, 7,* 70–76.

Cover T.M., & Thomas J.A. (1991). *Elements of information theory.* New York: John Wiley.

de Oliveira, S.C., Thiele, A., & Hoffman, A. (1997). Synchronization of neuronal activity during stimulus expectation in a direction discrimination task. *Journal of Neuroscience, 17,* 9248–9260.

Engel, A.K., Konig, P., & Singer, W. (1991). Direct physiological evidence for scene segmentation by temporal coding. *Proceedings of the National Academy of Sciences, USA, 88,* 9136–9140.

Golledge, H.D.R., Scannell, J.W., Zheng, F., Mason, R.J., Giannikopoulos, D.V., Tovée, M.J., & Young, M.P. (1999). Non stimulus-dependent neuronal synchrony in cat primary visual cortex. *Journal of Physiology (London), 520P,* 53P.

Gray, C.M., Engel, A.K., Konig, P., & Singer, W. (1992). Synchronization of oscillatory neuronal responses in cat striate cortex: Temporal properties. *Visual Neuroscience, 8,* 337–347.

Gray, C.M., Konig, P., Engel, A.K., & Singer, W. (1989). Oscillatory responses in cat visual cortex exhibit inter-columnar synchronization which reflects global stimulus properties. *Nature, 338,* 334–337.

Hata, Y., Tsumoto, T., Sato, H., & Tamura, H. (1991). Horizontal interactions between visual cortical neurones studied by cross-correlation analysis in the cat. *Journal of Physiology, 441,* 593–614.

Konig, P. (1994). A method for the quantification of synchrony and oscillatory properties of neuronal activity. *Journal of Neuroscience Methods, 54,* 31–37.

Konig, P., Engel, A.K., Roelfsema, P.R., & Singer, W. (1995). How precise is neuronal synchronization? *Neural Computation, 7,* 469–485.

Kreiter, A.K., & Singer, W. (1996). Stimulus-dependent synchronization of neuronal responses in the visual cortex of the awake macaque monkey. *Journal of Neuroscience, 16,* 2381–2396.

Lamme, V.A.F., & Spekreijse, H. (1998). Neuronal synchrony does not represent texture segmentation. *Nature, 396,* 362–366.

Oram, M.W., Foldiak, P., Perrett, D.I., & Sengpiel, F. (1998). The "Ideal Homunculus": decoding neural population signals. *Trends in Neurosciences, 21,* 259–265.

Panzeri, S., Schultz, S.R., Treves, A., & Rolls, E.T. (1999). Correlations and the encoding of information in the nervous system. *Proceedings of the Royal Society of London Series B-Biological Sciences, 266,* 1001–1012.
Panzeri, S., & Treves, A. (1996). Analytical estimates of limited sampling biases in different information measures. *Network, 7,* 87–107.
Perkel, D.H., Gerstein, G.L., & Moore, G.P. (1967). Neuronal spike trains and stochastic point processes: II. Simultaneous spike trains. *Biophysical Journal, 7,* 419–440.
Rieke, F., Warland, D., deRuyter van Steveninck, R., & Bialek, W. (1996). *Spikes: Exploring the neural node.* Cambridge, MA: MIT Press.
Rock, I., & Palmer, S. (1990). The legacy of Gestalt psychology. *Scientific American, 263,* 84–90.
Shadlen, M.N., & Movshon, J.A. (1999). Synchrony unbound: A critical evaluation of the temporal binding hypothesis. *Neuron, 24,* 67–77.
Shadlen, M.N., & Newsome, W.T. (1998). The variable discharge of cortical neurons: Implications for connectivity, computation and coding. *Journal of Neuroscience, 18,* 3870–3896.
Shannon, C.E. (1948). A mathematical theory of communication. *ATandT Bell Labs. Technical Journal, 18,* 3870–3896.
Singer, W. (1999). Neuronal synchrony: A versatile code for the definition of relations? *Neuron, 24,* 49–65.
von der Malsburg, C. (1981). The correlation theory of brain function. In E. Domany, J.L. van Hemmen, & K. Schulten, (Eds.), *Models of neural networks. Vol. I.* Berlin: Springer.
Young, M.P., Tanaka, K., & Yamane, S. (1992). On oscillating neuronal responses in the visual cortex of the monkey. *Journal of Neurophysiology, 67,* 1464–1474.
Zheng, F., Golledge, H.D.R., Scannell, J.W., Giannikopoulos, D.V., Mason, R.J., Tovée, M.J., & Young, M.P. (1999). Comparison of synchrony and firing rate in striate cortical neurons of anaesthetized cat. *Journal of Physiology (London), 520P, 47P.*

VISUAL COGNITION, 2001, *8* (3/4/5), 549–563

The effects of lorazepam on visual integration processes: How useful for neuroscientists?

Anne Giersch

Unité INSERM 405, Département de Psychiatrie, Hôpitaux Universitaires de Strasbourg, 1 place de l'hôpital, 67091 Strasbourg Cedex, France

The effects of psychotropic drugs can be seen as a reversible lesion of the central nervous system. We studied the effect of lorazepam, a benzodiazepine facilitating the fixation of GABA on the $GABA_A$ receptor. Evidence will be reviewed that lorazepam affects integration processes, using static fragmented pictures or compound stimuli. It will be shown how these effects can be dissociated from other peripheral or central effects of the drug. As a whole, the results suggest that lorazepam improves the detection of discontinuities between collinear elements, but impairs the detection of discontinuities between two parallel line-ends. Recent results will be presented that support the hypothesis that lorazepam does not affect integration processes themselves but modulates the mechanisms involved in the processing of discontinuities, i.e., the processing of line-ends and/or the production of virtual lines orthogonal to the line-ends. An understanding of the effects of the drug might give insights into the way these signals are used and modulated by the visual system.

Recent studies suggested that lorazepam, a benzodiazepine, affects not only several aspects of memory but also the processing of visual information, especially integration and segmentation processes. The hypothesis was raised that lorazepam may modulate the processing of discontinuities. The objective of the present paper is to clarify this hypothesis, and discuss to what extent it might be useful for neuroscientists.

At first sight, the difficulties raised by the use of drugs might discourage any attempt to use them as a tool to study the normal functioning of the brain. Indeed, the action of psychoactive drugs is diffuse; they may have effects at different levels of processing, and these different effects may interact. In particular, benzodiazepines have sedative effects affecting performance in all tasks.

Please address all correspondence to A. Giersch, Hôpitaux Universitaires de Strasbourg, INSERM U405, Département de Psychiatrie I, 1, pl de l'Hôpital, 67091 Strasbourg Cedex, France. Email: giersch@alsace.u-strasbg.fr

http://www.tandf.co.uk/journals/pp/13506285.html DOI:10.1080/13506280143000115

However, drug studies offer some very specific advantages, in particular those based on the use of benzodiazepines. First, it should be emphasized that a single intake of benzodiazepine is totally innocuous. This is especially the case in studies exploring the cognitive effects of the drug, as the dose used in those studies is much lower than an anaesthetic dose. The only contra-indications of the drug are respiratory insufficiency and known allergy, and all the effects on the central nervous system are reversible. At low doses, the pharmacological effect of benzodiazepines is relatively specific. Benzodiazepines fixate on a benzodiazepine receptor, and this fixation facilitates in turn the fixation of GABA on the $GABA_A$ receptor. The fixation of GABA on the $GABA_A$ receptor finally results in chlorine entering the cell and the cell being hyperpolarized. Benzodiazepines modulate the effect of the neurotransmitter but have no direct effect on the GABA receptor, and no direct effect on the polarity of the cell (at least at the dose used). In particular, they have no effect if GABA is not present. Hence, the effects observed are not the result of some alien effect of the drug, but are likely to occur in non-treated volunteers, when GABA is released in the synaptic gap. Another advantage is that a single intake of the drug affects cognitive functions for 2 to 3 hours only: There is no time for complex and long-term compensatory mechanisms to take place. Healthy volunteers can be taken as their own controls and experiments can be reproduced as many times as needed. This means that knowledge concerning the effects of the drug can be accumulated with time. Under these conditions, the various effects of the drug can become a subject of interest rather than a drawback.

Besides its classical therapeutic effects (hypnotic, anxiolytic, myorelaxant, and antiepileptic), lorazepam has also amnestic properties, which have been extensively studied (Brown, Brown, & Bowes, 1989; Curran, 1991; Vidailhet et al., 1994). Visuo-perceptual effects of lorazepam have been studied more recently, after the fortuitous observation that lorazepam impaired the identification of fragmented pictures (Legrand et al., 1995; Vidailhet et al., 1994).

Ophthalmological effects of lorazepam have been checked. Lorazepam impairs the oculomotor balance, but leaves visual acuity and accommodation unimpaired (Giersch, Boucart, Speeg-Schatz, Muller-Kauffmann, & Danion, 1996). All following experiments were conducted in monocular vision, to avoid any interference of the oculomotor effects of the drug on performance.

Lorazepam impairs contrast sensitivity. Treated subjects need a higher contrast than placebo treated subjects to detect the presence of a stimulus. The results reported in the literature concerning a specific effect on low or high spatial frequency are more controversial (Blin, Mestre, Paut, Vercher, & Audebert, 1993; Harris & Phillipson, 1995; Maddock, Casson, Lott, Carter, & Johnson, 1993). We manipulated the size of the stimuli in several experiments to check for this variable. The effects we describe in the following could not be explained in terms of a specific effect on low or high spatial frequencies (Giersch, 1999; Giersch, Boucart, & Danion, 1997).

A series of experiments have shown that lorazepam affects integration and segmentation processes (Giersch, 1999; Gierson, Boucart, Danion, Vidailhet, & Legrand, 1995; Giersch et al., 1996, 1997; Giersch & Lorenceau, 1999), but probably not directly. As a rule, the effects of the drug on form perception appear to depend on the arrangement of line-ends (Giersch, 1999; Giersch et al., 1997). An effect of the arrangement of line-ends was first observed with compound letters (Giersch et al., 1997), and then confirmed with more simple stimuli. In one of these tasks, subjects had to take decisions concerning the presence or the absence of a discontinuity between two line-segments (Giersch, 1999). Stimuli were composed of collinear or parallel elements, with or without a discontinuity (Figure 1). Stimuli were presented on the screen one at a time for 150 ms each.

Placebo-treated subjects performed faster when a discontinuity was present than when it was absent, but there was no performance difference for stimuli composed of collinear or parallel elements. In lorazepam-treated subjects, however, the advantage for discontinuous stimuli as compared to continuous stimuli increased when line-segments were collinear but disappeared when line-segments were parallel. These opposite effects cannot be accounted for by a sedative effect, which should have resulted in similar effects in all conditions. Similar effects of the arrangement of the line-ends were observed in other tasks, with other stimuli, like fragmented squares, moving diamonds, or moving line-segments (Giersch, 1999; Giersch & Lorenceau, 1999). However, even when lorazepam impaired integration processes, that is when treated subjects were slowed down and made more errors, they were still able to do the task, showing that at least part of the integration processes are spared. The relative preservation of visual integration abilities, together with what is known about the pharmacological effects of benzodiazepines, suggested that lorazepam only modulated the processing of discontinuities. Enhancement of the responses to line-ends might account for facilitation of the detection of the discontinuity in

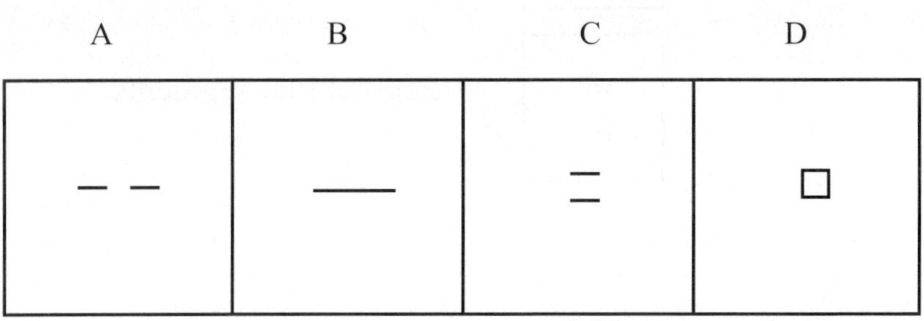

Figure 1. Examples of stimuli used in the gap detection task, composed of **(A)** collinear and discontinuous, **(B)** collinear and continuous, **(C)** parallel and discontinuous, or **(D)** parallel and continuous elements. The length of stimuli with collinear and continuous elements was 1° at a distance of 57 cm. The size of the gap between discontinuous elements was 0.28°.

the case of collinear elements. In the case of two parallel line segments, numerous studies have shown that the alignment of line-ends induces the perception of an orthogonal virtual line (Gove, Grossberg, & Mingolla, 1995; Lesher & Mingolla, 1993; von der Heydt & Peterhans, 1989; Westheimer & Li, 1996). In our task, enhanced responses to line-ends can induce the perception of a rectangle instead of two parallel lines. This might account for a difficulty in detecting the discontinuity between two parallel elements.

The hypothesis that lorazepam modulates the processing of discontinuities led to the following question concerning the normal functioning of visual perception in humans. We have already noticed that all effects observed in lorazepam-treated subjects are likely to occur in healthy volunteers. This means that if lorazepam indeed modulates the processing of discontinuities, such modulations should also occur in non-treated healthy volunteers. We tested this hypothesis with a modified priming paradigm (Giersch & Fahle, 2001), with sequences of two consecutive stimuli. The stimuli were composed of collinear or parallel line-segments (Figure 2).

Subjects had to decide for the first and second stimulus successively whether they included a discontinuity on the right or on the left side. Performance observed after the first stimuli did not differ across conditions. It varied, however, for the second stimulus. When the two consecutive stimuli were identical in terms of the arrangement of their line-segments, subjects were faster when the two gaps were on the same side than when they were on opposite sides. In constrast, when the two consecutive stimuli differed in terms of the arrangement of their line-segments (one stimulus composed of collinear elements and the other one of parallel elements), subjects were slower when the two

a

b

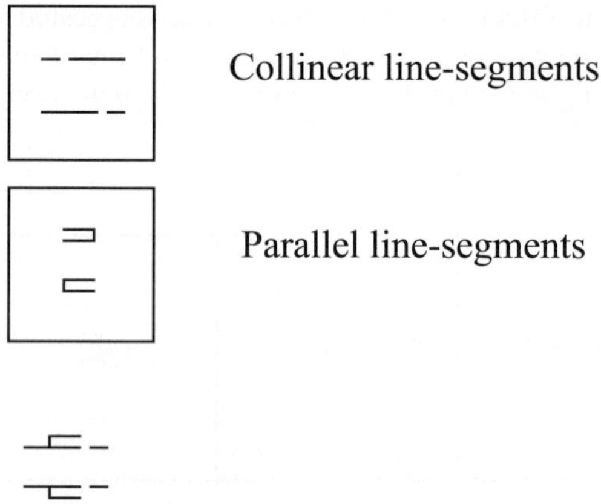

Figure 2. **(a)** Illustration of the stimuli used in Experiment 1, either collinear (upper panel) or parallel (lower panel). The stimuli were displayed one at a time. **(b)** The stimuli are drawn superimposed to illustrate the fact that the stimuli were displayed so that the discontinuities on one side were always in the same location on the screen.

consecutive gaps were on the same side than when they were on opposite sides. An illustration of this profile of results is illustrated later in Figure 4 (placebo-treated subjects). We were able to show that this effect is not simply due to a change in the global form between the two consecutive stimuli. It was still there if the two consecutive stimuli were very similar, and a change in the global form was not enough to induce this result (left-hand side of Figure 3). Neither was it due to an orthogonality between the two following gaps. The same results were observed even if the gaps were superimposed, and the orthogonality of the two gaps was not enough to induce the results (right-hand side of Figure 3). Moreover, RT variations are orientation and location dependent. They disappear if the two following stimuli are orthogonal and decrease if they are displaced one relative to another. These results show that different mechanisms underlie the detection of discontinuities between collinear and parallel elements and that these mechanisms are modulated very fast.

If lorazepam modulates the processing of discontinuities, as suggested by previous investigations, it may act by affecting the modulations normally observed in healthy volunteers. We tested this hypothesis by using the same modified priming paradigm just described. RT modulations were expected to

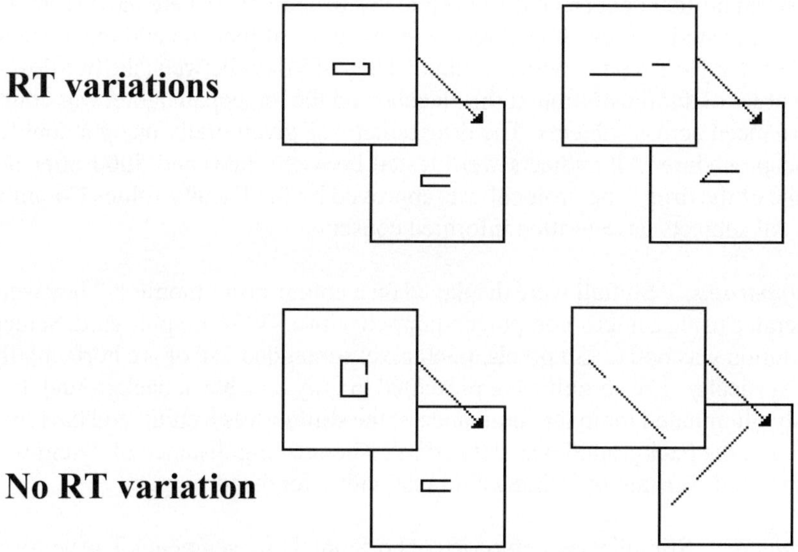

Figure 3. Illustration of the stimuli used to check the impact of the similarity of the global form of the stimuli (on the left) and of the orthogonality of the gaps (on the right) in the RT variations observed in the modified priming paradigm. Even when the two consecutive stimuli are very similar (top left), RT variations are still observed, and a difference in the global form of the stimuli is not enough to induce RT variations (bottom left). Similarly, variations of RTs are still observed when the two consecutive gaps are superimposed (top right), and an orthogonality of the two following gaps is not enough to induce RT variations (bottom right).

vary in amplitude after the intake of lorazepam so that gaps between collinear elements would be detected faster than gaps between parallel elements, reproducing this way the effect observed in preceding studies. This could be achieved by several means, especially (1) by increasing the disadvantage for stimuli composed of parallel elements when they are preceded by stimuli composed of collinear elements with a gap on the same side; otherwise, (2) by decreasing the disadvantage for stimuli composed of collinear elements when they are preceded by stimuli composed of parallel elements with a gap on the same side. Alternatively, the effects of lorazepam on visual perception could be unrelated to the modulations observed in healthy volunteers. In that case, the advantage for gaps between collinear elements over gaps between parallel elements should have the same amplitude when the gaps are part of the first or second stimulus in the priming sequence.

EXPERIMENT 1

Method

Subjects. Subjects were 12 paid students of the University of Strasbourg. They had normal or corrected-to-normal visual acuity and were naive as to the aim of the study. Each subject received one dose of placebo and one dose of 0.038 mg/kg lorazepam, with a minimal delay of 8 days between the two doses. The order of administration of the placebo and the lorazepam tablet was counterbalanced across subjects. The drug tablet was given orally using a double-blind procedure. All subjects were tested between 2h00 and 3h00 after the intake of the drug. The protocol was approved by the Faculty Ethics Committee. All subjects gave written informed consent.

Apparatus. Stimuli were displayed on a colour raster monitor. They were generated using a micro-computer equipped with a SVGA graphic card. Screen resolution was 640 × 480 pixels. Each pixel subtended 2.4' of arc horizontally and vertically. The stimuli were presented in gray on a black background. In a dimly illuminated room the luminance of the stimuli was 8 cd/m^2 and the luminance of the background was 0.04 cd/m^2. The viewing distance of 57 cm was maintained constant by using a chin rest with a forehead support.

Stimuli. Stimuli were composed of horizontal line-segments. The width of the lines was 1 pixel (2.4' of arc). Stimuli with a horizontal gap were composed of two collinear line-segments: a 7 pixel-long line-segment (16.8' of arc) and a 21 pixel-long line-segment (50.4' of arc), separated by a gap of 7 pixels (16.8' of arc). The gap was located either on the right or the left side. Stimuli with a vertical gap were composed of two 12 pixel-long parallel line-segments (28.8' of arc) separated by a gap of 7 pixels (16.8' of arc). A vertical line linked the ends of the two line-segments on one side, leaving a gap at the other end (Figure 2). The stimuli were arranged so that the gaps on one side were all at the same location on the screen, whatever the type of stimuli (Figure 2 below).

Procedure. A first stimulus was presented in the centre of the screen. The subjects were instructed to decide whether a gap was present on the right or on the left side. They pressed a right or left keyboard button according to the side of the gap. The stimulus stayed on the screen until the subjects gave their response, and then disappeared (the screen went black), followed by a second stimulus after a delay of 100 ms. Subjects were instructed to decide again on which side the gap was located, and the stimulus disappeared after they gave their response. After a delay of 100 ms during which a mask was displayed, and an additional delay of 1000 ms during which the screen remained black, the sequence started again. The gaps of the first and second stimulus in each sequence were either composed of collinear or parallel elements, resulting in four possible conditions: (1) Both the first and the second stimulus were composed of collinear line-segments; (2) the first stimulus was composed of collinear line-segments and the second one was composed of parallel line-segments; (3) both stimuli were composed of parallel line-segments; (4) the first stimulus was composed of parallel line-segments and the second one was composed of collinear line-segments. In each condition, the gap was either on the same side or on opposite sides in the two consecutive stimuli, defining a total of eight experimental conditions. The characteristics of the trials were randomly and equally represented: the side of the gap in the first and in the second stimulus, the position of the horizontal collinear elements (see Figure 2), and the eight experimental conditions. The onset of the stimulus activated the computer clock, which was stopped when the subject pressed a key. Errors were signalled by a 300 ms sound, initiated after the execution of the response. These trials were not replaced, and these RTs were not taken into account in the following analysis. When there was an error for the first stimulus of a sequence, RTs observed for the second stimulus were also excluded from the analysis.

Analogue self-ratings of sedation. All subjects used a set of visual scales to assess their subjective state 1h45 after the intake of the drug. Each scale consisted of a 100 mm ungraduated horizontal line, anchored by contrasting states of mind. Subjects were asked to regard each line as a continuum and to rate their feelings at the time by placing a vertical mark across each line. The scales were scored by measuring the length in mm from the positive end of each line to the subject's mark. Nine of these scales assessed complementary aspects of sedation (Bond & Lader, 1974). The mean score of these nine scales was calculated for each subject and was taken as a measure of sedation.

Results

Mean RTs were higher after the intake of lorazepam (528 ms) than after the intake of placebo (437 ms): $F(1, 11) = 67.8, p < .001$. The mean error rate was lower than 5% after the intake of placebo (2%) but also after the intake of lorazepam (4.5%). No significant main effects or interaction were observed in the analysis of errors. There was never more than one error difference between the two treatment groups, whatever the experimental condition. For this reason, the analyses on error rates are not detailed any further. Mean RTs are displayed in Figure 4.

RTs after the first stimuli were similar when stimuli were composed of collinear or parallel elements, after the intake of placebo (455 ms vs. 454 ms, $F < 1$)

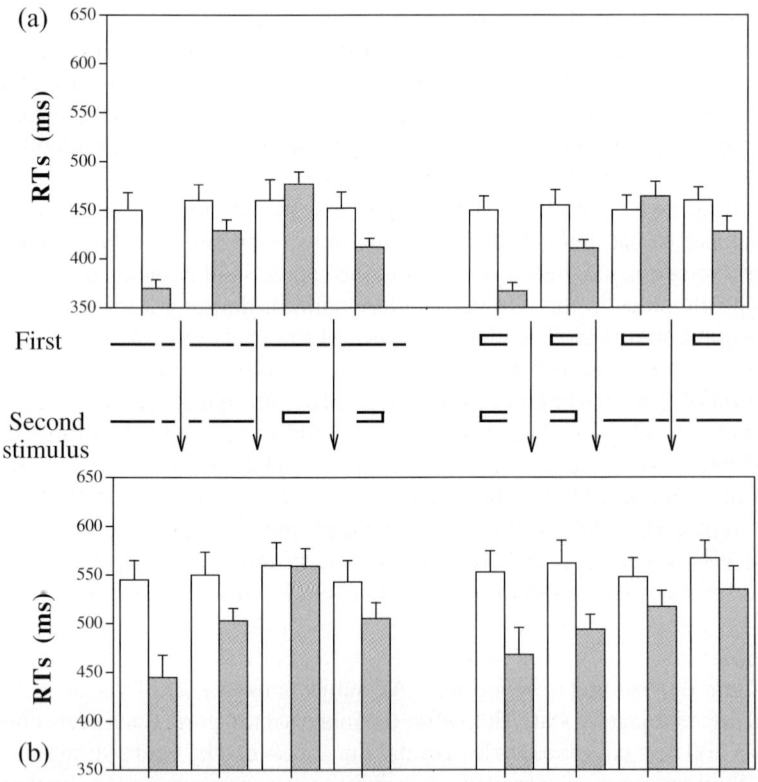

Figure 4. Mean RTs in Experiment 1 averaged across the 12 subjects (with standard errors) for the first stimulus (columns in white) and for the second stimulus (columns in black), as a function of the experimental condition and the treatment, (a) placebo or (b) lorazepam. The experimental conditions are defined by the collinear or parallel type of stimulus displayed at the first position, the type of stimulus displayed at the second position, and the relative side of the discontinuities (on the same side vs. on opposite sides). The proportions of right and left gaps were identical in all conditions.

as after the intake of lorazepam (549 ms when elements were collinear vs. 558 ms when elements were parallel, $F(1, 11) = 1.6$, n.s.). In contrast, RTs to the second stimulus varied as a function of the experimental conditions, and these variations differed after placebo and after lorazepam, as shown by a significant interaction between treatment, first stimulus type (composed of collinear or parallel elements), gap location (on the same or on opposite sides in the two consecutive stimuli) and the relative arrangement of the two stimuli (identical vs. different): $F(1, 11) = 6.8, p < .05$. We will describe the results observed after the intake of placebo and lorazepam.

Placebo. When the two consecutive stimuli were arranged in the same way, subjects were faster when the two gaps were on the same side than when they were on opposite sides. The magnitude of this effect was of 60 ms when both stimuli were composed of collinear elements, $F(1, 11) = 25.4$, $p < .001$, and 43 ms when both stimuli were composed of parallel elements, $F(1, 11) = 21.9, p < .001$. In contrast, when the first and second stimulus differed in terms of how their line-segments were arranged, RTs to the second stimulus were higher when the gap was on the same side in the two stimuli than when it was on opposite sides. The magnitude of this effect was of 35 ms when the first stimulus was composed of collinear elements and the second one was composed of parallel elements $F(1, 11) = 61, p < .005$. It was of 37 ms when the order of the sequence was reversed $F(1, 11) = 13.4, p < .005$.

Lorazepam. When the two consecutive stimuli were arranged in the same way (both composed of collinear elements or both composed of parallel elements), subjects were faster when the two gaps were on the same side than when they were on opposite sides. However, this effect was significant only for stimuli composed of collinear elements. In this condition, RTs were lower by 58 ms when gaps were on the same side than when they were on opposite sides: $F(1, 11) = 13.1, p < .005$. In contrast, when both stimuli were composed of parallel elements, RTs were only 26 ms lower when the two gaps were on the same side than when they were on opposite sides, $F(1, 11) = 1.2$, n.s. These effects resulted in a significant interaction between the stimulus type (composed of collinear or parallel elements) and the gap location (on the same or on opposite sides): $F(1, 11) = 5.2, p < .05$.

When the first and second stimulus differed regarding the arrangement of their line-segments, an effect of the gap side was observed again, but only when the first stimulus was composed of collinear elements, as suggested by a significant interaction between the first stimulus type (composed of collinear or parallel elements) and the gap location (on the same or on opposite sides): $F(1, 11) = 24.6, p < .001$. When the first stimulus was composed of collinear elements and the second one was composed of parallel elements, RTs were higher by 54 ms when the gap was on the same side in the two stimuli than when it was on opposite sides, $F(1, 11) = 30.1, p < 001$. In contrast, when the first stimulus was composed of parallel elements and the second one of collinear elements, RTs were lower by 18 ms when the gap was on the same side in the two stimuli than when it was on opposite sides, $F(1, 11) = 2$, n.s. These effects resulted in a 43 ms advantage for stimuli composed of collinear elements over stimuli composed of parallel elements, but only when the two consecutive stimuli differed in terms of the arrangement of their line-segments and had a gap on the same side (Figure 4): $F(1, 11) = 58.6, p < .001$.

Analogue self-ratings of sedation. Self–rated sedation increased significantly with the drug, $F(1, 11) = 23, p < .001$. After the intake of a placebo, the mean sedation score was lower (14) than after the intake of lorazepam (34.4).

Correlations. Pearson correlations with Bonferroni corrections were conducted for placebo- and lorazepam-treated subjects. There was no correlation between sedation scores and performance, as assessed under each experimental condition, or overall performance (RTs or errors averaged over all experimental conditions). There was only one significant correlation, when we calculated the RT and error differences across conditions. As already noted, when the two consecutive stimuli were composed of collinear elements, RTs were faster when the gaps were on the same side in both stimuli than when they were on the opposite side. The amplitude of this RT advantage increased with the sedation rating, but only when subjects were treated with lorazepam, as suggested by a positive correlation between these two variables: $r = 0.76$, $N = 12$, $p < .005$.

Discussion

Responses to the first stimulus are not different for stimuli composed of collinear or parallel elements. When a first stimulus composed of collinear elements is followed by a stimulus composed of parallel elements, lorazepam-treated subjects are slower in the same way as placebo-treated subjects, when the two consecutive gaps are on the same side than when they are on opposite sides. In the reverse order however (first stimulus composed of parallel elements), RT variations disappear in lorazepam-treated subjects, unlike placebo-treated subjects. These effects result in an advantage for gaps located between two collinear line-segments over gaps located between parallel elements. This advantage replicates the results observed in preceding experiments, but only in some very specific conditions, when the two consecutive stimuli differ in terms of the arrangement of their line-segments and have a gap on the same side.

The lack of lorazepam effect for the first stimulus may have been due to the spatial uncertainty of the gap location. We checked this hypothesis in a control experiment by exploring whether focalizing attention on the location of the discontinuity was enough to restore an advantage for stimuli composed of collinear elements in lorazepam-treated subjects.

EXPERIMENT 2

Method

We replicated Experiment 1 by replacing the first stimulus by a red dot appearing to the right or left of a fixation point. The red dot was in the same location as the gap in Experiment 1, and subjects were instructed to press on a right or left response button according to the location of the red dot. As in Experiment 1, their response was followed by a 100 ms delay and a stimulus composed of either collinear or parallel elements. To ensure that attention would be focused on the location of the red dot, the gap accompanying the following stimulus was on the same side as the dot in 75% of the trials (60 trials for each type of stimulus), and on the other side in 25% of the trials (20 trials for each type of stimulus).

Subjects were randomly assigned to one of two parallel groups of 10 subjects each: a placebo group and a lorazepam 0.038 mg/kg group. All subjects were investigated between 3h00 and 3h30 after the intake of the drug. Sedation was evaluated in the same way as in the preceding study, before and 2h30 after the intake of the drug.

Results

There was no effect of treatment except a general slowing down. RTs (in both groups) were faster by 33 ms when the gap and the dot were on the same side than when they were on opposite sides, $F(1, 9) = 18, p < .001$. Even when the gap was on the same side as the dot, there was no significant advantage for stimuli composed of collinear elements as compared to stimuli composed of parallel elements (2 ms in the placebo group, $F < 1$, and 11 ms in the lorazepam group, $F(1, 9) = 2.9$, n.s). As in Experiment 1, errors rates were low after the intake of placebo (2%), and also after the intake of lorazepam (4.7%). No significant main effects or interaction were observed in the analysis of errors. There was never more than one error difference between the two treatment groups, whatever the experimental condition.

Self-rated sedation was similar in both groups before the intake of the drug (21.4 and 21.6, $F < 1$). After the intake of the drug, it was significantly higher in the lorazepam group (43.2) than in the placebo group (22), $F(1, 18) = 8, p < .05$. No significant correlation was found between self-rated sedation and performance.

Discussion

The results of Experiment 2 show that focalizing attention on the location of the discontinuity is not enough to restore an advantage for stimuli composed of collinear elements in lorazepam-treated subjects. The lack of a performance difference between stimuli composed of collinear or parallel stimuli in the present experiments suggests that lorazepam does not act directly on the processes involved in the processing of discontinuities but rather affects the normal modulations of the processing of discontinuities, arising slowly as a consequence of the processing of a first gap.

An explanation in terms of a sedative effect is unlikely for three reasons. First, there was no correlation between self-rated sedation and the advantage for stimuli composed of collinear elements over those composed of parallel elements. Second, the only significative correlation was found between sedation and the RT advantage observed when two consecutive stimuli were composed of collinear elements with a gap on the same side rather than on opposite sides. This correlation shows that the amplitude of the RT effect increases with sedation induced by lorazepam. In contrast, the critical effect observed after the intake of lorazepam, that is the advantage for gaps between collinear elements over gaps between parallel elements, does not arise from the increase in the amplitude of an RT effect. In fact, there is a flattening of RT variations after the intake of lorazepam when a stimulus composed of parallel elements is followed by a stimulus composed of collinear elements. Third, the asymmetry of the results observed when the first stimulus is composed of collinear or parallel elements also supports the idea of some specific effect of lorazepam. Indeed, nonspecific effects of lorazepam on priming, motor responses or other processes underlying RT variations should have resulted in similar effects when the first stimulus was composed of collinear or parallel elements, especially as effects were similar after the intake of placebo.

The processing of the gap between two collinear line-segments probably involves the activation of the processing of line-ends. Enhanced responses to line-ends may facilitate the detection of a discontinuity between collinear elements. However, the simplicity of the task may allow a response before this activation is complete, explaining why performance is equivalent for first stimuli composed of collinear and parallel elements even after the intake of lorazepam. The fact that the present task is particularly easy is supported by the observations that error rates are very low and that RTs are faster than in preceding experiments (455 ms in placebo-treated subjects vs. 522 ms for analogue stimuli when the task involved a discrimination between continuous and discontinuous stimuli—Giersch, 1999). Moreover, a slow modulation of the processing of line-ends is supported by several studies. Bolz and Gilbert (1986) and Sillito (1992; Sillito, Grieve, Jones, Cudeiro, & Davis, 1995; Sillito, Jones, Gerstein, & West, 1994) have proposed that the processing of line-ends involves an inhibitory feedback on the cells coding the line-ends. This feedback may slowly enhance the contrast between continuous and discontinuous information. Yu and Levi (1999) have also proposed a slowly developing modulation of the response of cells coding line-ends. They measured the contrast threshold for the detection of a masked target. When the mask was long enough to encroach on end-zones, the masking effect decreased, revealing "psychophysical end-stopping". Yu and Levi showed that the reduction of the masking effect was observed only when the mask onset and the target onset were separated by a time interval of at least 70 ms, and developed fully for intervals of 150–200 ms. A slowly developing modulation of the processing of line-ends may explain the lack of effect of lorazepam for the first stimulus.

Yet, lorazepam did not affect the consequences of the processing of a gap between two collinear line-segments, at least at the time interval used in the present experiment. It selectively erased the RT variations observed after the display of a stimulus composed of parallel elements. When elements are parallel, enhancing the responses to aligned line-ends enhances the production of an amodal line orthogonal to the line-ends. In the case of our stimuli, this amodal line is produced exactly in the location of the discontinuity and may impair the detection of the discontinuity between parallel elements. Enhancing the detection of a discontinuity between two parallel elements may thus involve the inhibition of the production of the amodal orthogonal line or the inhibition of the responses to line-ends. As with stimuli composed of parallel elements, these modulations may be optimal only after the response of the subjects. Hence, the lack of RT variations observed in lorazepam-treated subjects when the first stimulus is composed of parallel elements suggests two possibilities. Lorazepam may impair (1) the inhibition of the production of an orthogonal amodal line, or (2) the inhibition of the processing of line-ends arising after the display of a first stimulus composed of parallel elements. As these effects are location-dependent and are at the root of the effects of the gap's side, an impairment of these effects explains the lack of RT variations for the second stimulus, especially when the second stimulus is composed of parallel elements. When the second stimulus is composed of collinear elements, a lack of inhibition of the processing of line-ends may also account for the lack of RT variations. Finally, a lack of inhibition of orthogonal amodal lines is also compatible with these results, given that orthogonal amodal lines may help to detect a gap between collinear elements, by helping to interpret the gap as resulting from an occlusion. However, further studies are needed to unravel the precise mechanisms underlying the modulations of the processing of discontinuities.

In this series of experiments, the contrast between stimuli composed of collinear and parallel elements has been a useful means of distinguishing between non-specific and specific effects of the drug. This conflict between the two types of stimuli may also reveal something significant concerning the normal functioning of the visual system, especially how it adapts to the processing of different types of discontinuities. Parallel investigations in non-treated healthy volunteers and lorazepam-treated subjects should help to gain a better understanding of the mechanisms of these modulations. As discontinuities play an important role in integration processes, these modulations should also affect the way visual information is linked together. However, a full and convincing understanding of the mechanisms underlying these modulations requires investigations in the electrophysiological field. It may be useful to study how lorazepam affects binding at an electrophysiological level, and how modulations of the integration processes are reflected for example in the coding of line-ends, or in the synchronization of oscillation phenomena, which may also play an important role in integration processes. The drug, acting at both behavioural and electrophysiological levels, may then help to draw the link between both levels. These possibilities make the drug particularly interesting for neuroscientists.

REFERENCES

Blin, O., Mestre, D., Paut, O., Vercher, J.L., & Audebert, C. (1993). GABA-ergic control of visual perception in healthy volunteers: Effects of midazolam, a benzodiazepine, on spatio-temporal contrast sensitivity. *British Journal of Clinical Pharmacology*, *36*, 117–124.

Bolz, J., & Gilbert, C.D. (1986). Generation of end-inhibition in the visual cortex via interlaminar connections. *Nature*, *320*, 362–365.

Bond, A., & Lader, M. (1974). The use of analogue scales in rating subjective feelings. *British Journal of Medical Psychology*, *47*, 211–218.

Brown, M.W., Brown, J., & Bowes, J.B. (1989). Absence of priming coupled with substantially preserved recognition in lorazepam-induced amnesia. *Quarterly Journal of Experimental Psychology*, *41A*, 599–617.

Curran, H.V. (1991). Benzodiazepines, memory and mood: A review. *Psychopharmacology*, *105*, 1–8.

Giersch, A. (1999). A new pharmacological tool to investigate integration processes. *Visual Cognition*, *6*, 267–297.

Giersch, A., Boucart, M., & Danion, J.-M. (1997). Lorazepam, a benzodiazepine, induces atypical distractor effects with compound letters: A role for line-ends in the processing of compound letters. *Visual Cognition*, *4*, 337–372.

Giersch, A., Boucart, M., Danion, J.-M., Vidailhet, P., & Legrand, F. (1995). Effects of lorazepam on perceptual integration of visual forms in healthy volunteers. *Psychopharmacology*, *119*, 102–114.

Giersch, A., Boucart, M., Speeg-Schatz, C., Muller-Kauffmann, F., & Danion, J.-M. (1996). Lorazepam impairs perceptual integration of visual forms: A central effect. *Psychopharmacology*, *126*, 260–270.

Giersch, A., & Fahle, M. (in press). Modulations of the processing of line discontinuities in selective attention conditions? *Perception & Psychophysics*.

Giersch, A., & Lorenceau, J. (1999). Effects of a benzodiazepine, lorazepam, on motion integration and segmentation: An effect on the processing of line-ends? *Vision Research*, *39*, 2017–2025.

Gove, A., Grossberg, S., & Mingolla, E. (1995). Brightness perception, illusory contours, and corticogeniculate feedback. *Visual Neuroscience*, *12*, 1027–1052.

Harris, J.P., & Phillipson, O.T. (1995). Effects of lorazepam on human contrast sensitivity. *Psychopharmacology*, *117*, 379–384.

Legrand, F., Vidailhet, P., Danion, J.-M., Grangé, D., Giersch, A., Van Der Linden, M., & Imbs, J.L. (1995). Time course of the effects of diazepam and lorazepam on perceptual priming and explicit memory. *Psychopharmacology*, *118*, 475–479.

Lesher, G.W., & Mingolla, E. (1993). The role of edges and line-ends in illusory contour formation. *Vision Research*, *33*, 2253–2270.

Maddock, R.J., Casson, E.J., Lott, L.A., Carter, C.S., & Johnson, C.A. (1993). Benzodiazepine effects on flicker sensitivity: Role of stimulus frequency and size. *Progress in Neuro-Psychopharmacology and Biological Psychiatry*, *17*, 955–970.

Sillito, A.M. (1992). GABA mediated inhibitory processes in the function of the geniculo-striate system. In R.R. Mize, R.E. Marc, & A.M. Sillito (Eds.), *Progress in brain research* (Vol. 90, 349–384). Amsterdam: Elsevier Science Publishers.

Sillito, A.M., Grieve, K.L., Jones, H.E., Cudeiro, J., & Davis, J. (1995). Visual cortical mechanisms detecting focal orientation discontinuities. *Nature*, *378*, 492–496.

Sillito, A.M., Jones, H.E., Gerstein, G.L., & West, D.C. (1994). Feature-linked synchronization of thalamic relay cell firing induced by feedback from the visual cortex. *Nature*, *369*, 479–482.

Vidailhet, P., Danion, J.-M., Kauffman-Muller, F., Grangé, D., Giersch, A., Van Der Linden, M., & Imbs, J.L. (1994). Lorazepam and diazepam effects on memory acquisition in priming tasks. *Psychopharmacology*, *115*, 397–406.

von der Heydt, R., & Peterhans, E (1989). Mechanisms of contour perception in monkey visual cortex: 1. Lines of pattern discontinuities. *Journal of Neuroscience*, *9*, 1731–1748.

Westheimer, G., & Li, W. (1996). Classifying illusory contours by means of orientation discrimination. *Journal of Neurophysiology*, *75*, 523–528.

Yu, C., & Levi, D.M. (1999). The time course of psychophysical end-stopping. *Vision Research*, *39*, 2063-2073.

VISUAL COGNITION, 2001, *8* (3/4/5), 565–578

Visual development in human infants: Binding features, surfaces, and objects

Scott P. Johnson

Department of Psychology, Cornell University, Ithaca, USA

The development of visual binding in humans has been investigated with psychophysical tasks assessing the extent to which young infants achieve perceptual completion of partly occluded objects. These experiments lead to two conclusions. First, neonates are capable of figure–ground segregation, but do not perceive the unity of a centre-occluded object; the ability to perceive object unity emerges over the first several postnatal months. Second, by 4 months, infants rely on a range of Gestalt visual information in perceiving unity, including common motion, alignment, and good form. This developmental pattern is thought to be built on the ability to detect, and then utilize, appropriate visual information in support of the binding of features into surfaces and objects. Evidence from changes in infant attention, computational modelling, and developmental neurophysiology is cited that is consistent with this view.

The visual environment is a complex arrangement of object surfaces that are only partly visible at any given point in space and time because of the ubiquity of occlusion: Surfaces near to the observer in the optic array often overlap those that are more distant. Despite this complexity, however, an observer with a mature visual system is able to perceive surfaces as belonging to coherent entities with distinct boundaries at various distances, and not as a collection of fragments that undergo continual changes in appearance. Moreover, we are able to join separate surfaces into unified percepts of objects that maintain distinct attributes and identities over spatiotemporal transformations. Only under limited circumstances, such as reported in challenging search experiments that may bear little resemblance to real-world perceptual tasks (e.g., Treisman &

Please address all correspondence to S.P. Johnson, Department of Psychology, Uris Hall, Cornell University, Ithaca, NY 14853, USA. Email: sj75@cornell.edu

Preparation of this article was supported by NSF Grant SBR-991079. I wish to thank my many colleagues for their invaluable contributions to this research, including, but not limited to Dick Aslin, Gavin Bremner, Kerri Johnson, Peter Jusczyk, Denis Mareschal, José Náñez, Alan Slater, Carter Smith, and Liz Spelke, and especially the infants and parents who participated in the studies.

---

http://www.tandf.co.uk/journals/pp/13506285.html DOI:10.1080/13506280143000124

Schmidt, 1982), or in observers with cortical damage (e.g., Goodale, Milner, Jakobson, & Carey, 1991), do veridical object percepts routinely fail to obtain in adults.

These remarkable achievements have often been described as the visual system's solution to the "binding problem" (Roskies, 1999). This term encompasses a variety of perceptual phenomena, including integration of intermodal stimuli, consolidation of visual information that is extended over space and time, conjoining such object features as colour and shape, and perception of the unity of partly occluded objects. In the present paper, I discuss insights that can be brought to bear on the binding problem from developmental studies using psychophysical methods with human infants between birth and 4 postnatal months of age. The experiments employ an "object unity" task, which incorporates two complementary processes: *unit formation*, or perception of the connectedness of edges across a spatial gap, and *surface segregation*, or detection of relative depth of two or more visible surfaces. I also discuss theoretical implications and speculation concerning the emergence of veridical object percepts across infancy. To anticipate, there is no current evidence in favour of the hypothesis that infants are born with mature object perception skills. However, such skills develop rapidly over the first few postnatal months. Mechanisms of the development of unit formation may include improvements in attentional skills and utilization of appropriate visual information, accompanied by cortical maturation.

INFANTS' PERCEPTION OF OBJECT UNITY

Figure 1A depicts a "rod-and-box" display consisting of a center-occluded object whose visible ends, protruding from behind a box, are aligned and undergo common lateral translation. Kellman and Spelke (1983) used this display, and others, to explore the conditions under which 4-month-olds would perceive the unity of the rod parts. They used a *habituation* paradigm in which an infant was first presented with the rod-and-box display until looking declined to a preset criterion. After reaching habituation, infants viewed two test displays, a complete rod (Figure 1B) and a "broken" rod (Figure 1C), which contained a gap in the space formerly occupied by the box. Each test display matched the visible portions of the rod surfaces in the habituation display, but the infants looked longer at the broken rod. Given that infants often look longer at a posthabituation display that is relatively novel, rather than at a relatively familiar display (Bornstein, 1985), these results imply that the infants perceived the unity of the rod parts in the habituation stimulus. Infants in a control condition viewed a rod-and-box display whose constituent parts were arranged so as to preclude unity percepts, and subsequently exhibited no consistent test display preference. This result mitigates against the likelihood of an inherent

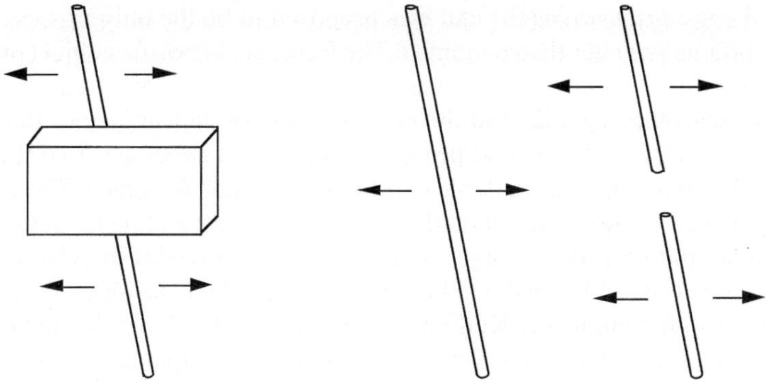

Figure 1. Displays employed in past research to investigate young infants' perception of partly occluded objects (adapted from Kellman & Spelke, 1983). **A:** A partly occluded rod moves relative to a stationary occluder. **B:** Complete rod. **C:** Broken rod. After habituation to A, infants often show a preference for C relative to B, indicating perception of the rod's unity in A.

preference for the broken rod that could account for the outcome of the unified-object condition.

Since the original studies, research on perception of object unity has taken two directions. The first is a series of explorations of the visual information used by infants to achieve unit formation in partly occluded object displays. The second consists of investigations of the origins of unit formation in infancy. Each is discussed in turn.

HOW DO INFANTS ACHIEVE UNIT FORMATION?

Kellman and Spelke (1983) reported robust unit formation when 4-month-olds viewed rod-and-box displays in which the rod parts underwent common motion relative to a stationary occluder. In contrast, however, 4-month-olds do not appear to perceive the unity of static partly occluded surfaces, nor surfaces that move along with the occluder. Kellman and Spelke posited that young infants are not able to take advantage of the full range of available visual cues when engaged in perceptual tasks, such as perception of object unity. Rather, infants were assumed to rely exclusively on the common motion of the rod parts, failing to use other cues such the rod parts' collinearity, the similarity of their surfaces, and so on. In Gestalt terms, then, young infants appear sensitive to common fate, but not good continuation, good form, or symmetry. In contrast, older infants and adults utilize these latter cues, as well as motion, to perceive unity (cf. Craton, 1996).

To account for these results, Kellman (1996) delineated a two-process account of development of perception of object unity. The first process was denoted *edge-insensitive* (EI) and was proposed to be the only process available to infants younger than 6 months. The EI process specifies object unity by relying on motion, but not other cues such as the orientation of edges as they intersect with the occluder and the configuration or appearance of the partly occluded surfaces. The second process was denoted *edge-sensitive* (ES) and was proposed to become available to infants older than 6 months. The ES process exploits a range of cues, including edge orientation and surface configuration. Under the ES process, object unity will be perceived if the visible edges are *relatable* (i.e., if they were to be extended behind the occluder, they would meet at an obtuse angle; see Kellman & Shipley, 1991). Given that the ES process is unavailable to young infants, they would not be capable of unity perception based on visual information other than motion.

A wealth of recent evidence is inconsistent with this view, and indicates that young infants utilize several Gestalt cues, in addition to common motion, in perceiving object unity. Johnson and Aslin (1996) began these more recent investigations by testing the Kellman (1996) prediction that 4-month-olds would perceive unity in any display in which two visible rod parts undergo common motion. We observed infants in four conditions, using computer-generated displays, as well as control conditions to rule out the likelihood of any inherent test display preference. (The control conditions consisted of displays in which rod surfaces did not move together behind the occluder.) The first group of infants viewed a rod-and-box display (Figure 2A) against a textured background (a grid of dots), and subsequently exhibited a consistent, statistically reliable posthabituation preference for the broken rod. This result replicates the original findings of Kellman and Spelke (1983) in its suggestion that the infants perceived the unity of the rod parts during habituation. The second group of infants viewed a rod-and-box display against a solid black background with no texture elements, and showed no reliable posthabituation preference. The next experiment used a *misaligned* rod display (against a textured background) in which the rod parts were not aligned, but were relatable, according to the Kellman and Shipley (1991) criteria for edge relatability (Figure 2B). These infants showed no test display preference. A fourth group of infants viewed a *nonaligned* rod display (against a textured background) in which the rod parts were neither aligned nor relatable (Figure 2C). These infants preferred the *complete* rod during test. In none of the four accompanying control conditions was there a consistent test display preference. On the logic that posthabituation looking times reflect novelty preferences, this pattern of results suggests that the infants in the first condition perceived the unity of the partly occluded rod. In contrast, percepts in the second and third conditions appear to have been indeterminate, and infants in the fourth condition seem to have perceived the rod parts as disjoint objects. Taken together, these findings indicate that unity perception does not appear to be driven exclusively by common motion, because common motion was available in all four displays. Rather,

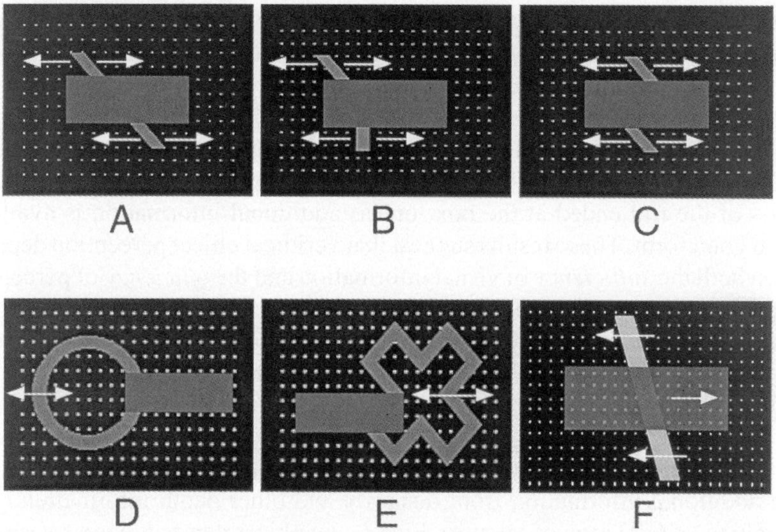

Figure 2. Displays employed to investigate the role of edge orientation, object form, and surface appearance in young infants' object perception. **A:** Rod parts are aligned across the occluder. **B:** Rod parts are not aligned, but are relatable (if extended, they would meet behind the occluder). **C:** Rod parts are neither aligned nor relatable. Four-month-old infants perceive unity only in A, underscoring the importance of edge alignment to unit formation. **D and E:** Edges at the rod/box intersections are not aligned, but good form supports perception of object unity. **F**: The box appears transparent under some conditions to 4-month-olds, suggesting that surface appearance aids in perceptual segregation. (A–C: adapted from Johnson & Aslin, 1996; D–E: adapted from Johnson, Bremner, Slater, & Mason, 2000. F: adapted from Johnson & Aslin, 2000.)

other cues, such as edge orientation and the presence of background texture, also support young infants' perception of object unity. Further experiments have revealed that good form supports unit formation (Figures 2D and 2E; Johnson et al., 2000), and that young infants perceive transparency in some displays, suggesting that the infants bound together surfaces with different reflectance characteristics in segregating the display into a translucent and an opaque layer (Figure 2F; Johnson & Aslin, 2000). (See also Craton, 1996; Johnson & Aslin, 1998; Jusczyk, Johnson, Spelke, & Kennedy, 1999; Needham, 1998.)

To account for these results, I have proposed a *threshold model* (Johnson 1997, 2000; Johnson & Aslin, 1996), positing that young infants' veridical surface segregation relies on several subprocesses, rather than a single cue (such as motion). If any of these subprocesses are disrupted, veridical object perception may be precluded. Nakayama and colleagues (Nakayama, He, & Shimojo, 1996; Nakayama & Shimojo, 1990; Nakayama, Shimojo, & Silverman, 1989) noted that in order to segregate surfaces in an occlusion display, the observer must determine in which depth plane each surface resides (a process called *depth placement*), and determine which contours in the scene belong with which objects (*contour ownership*). Depth placement relies on depth cues, and accretion and deletion of background texture, for example, aids perceptual segregation of the rod and box surfaces into their constituent depth planes. Contour ownership may rely on edge alignment, and when rod edges are nonaligned, infants appear to perceive them as belonging to separate objects, as if the contours of the rod ended at the box, unless additional information is available from good form. These results suggest that veridical object perception depends upon both the *sufficiency* of visual information and the *efficiency* of perceptual and/or cognitive skills, and that unit formation and surface segregation are multiply determined by independent sources of information. Unit formation and surface segregation, on this account, proceeds from an initial analysis of individual feature elements (cf. Marr, 1982): edge orientations, surface intersections (e.g., T-, L-, and X-junctions), and surface motions. From here, a viewer-centred description of relative distances of surfaces is constructed, incorporating additional information from disparity and other depth information (e.g., accretion and deletion of texture). Finally, an object-centred representation of the visual environment is realized, incorporating complete "object permanence" (Piaget, 1954). As described in the next section, the surface description does not appear to be available to human infants until several months after birth, and mature object-centred representations take longer still.

HOW DOES PERCEPTION OF OBJECT UNITY DEVELOP IN HUMAN INFANTS?

Kellman and Spelke (1983) interpreted 4-month-olds' success at object unity tasks as evidence for object perception skills that were functional at birth: "Humans may begin life with the notion that the environment is composed of things that are coherent, that move as units independently of each other, and that tend to persist, maintaining their coherence and boundaries as they move" (p. 521). When newborn infants were tested using similar procedures, however, these infants responded during test with the *opposite* looking time pattern than 4-month-olds: A significant preference for the complete rod (Slater et al., 1990). Concurrent experiments controlled for competing interpretations of the neonates' responses (e.g., familiarity rather than novelty preferences, an inability to detect each of the visible surfaces or segregate figure from ground, and so on), leading Slater et al. to conclude that these infants did not perceive object unity. Rather, neonates appeared to perceive disjoint rod surfaces in the rod-and-box display.

These two findings point to the time between birth and 4 months as the period during which veridical responses to object occlusion emerge. In an initial attempt to pin down more precisely the time course of development of unit formation, we found that 2-month-olds exhibited no preference for either a broken or complete rod test display after habituation to a rod-and-box display (Johnson & Náñez, 1995), suggesting that 2 months of age represents a time of transition from perception of disjoint objects in the display (the neonates' response) to unit formation (the 4-month-olds' response). Recall, however, the stipulations of the threshold model: It might have been that we supplied insufficient visual information to support unit formation in a population that might be expected to have relatively inefficient perceptual skills. This hypothesis was tested by presenting 2-month-old infants with rod-and-box displays in which more of the rod was visible as it moved back and forth, either by reducing box height, or by incorporating strategically placed gaps in the box (Johnson & Aslin, 1995). In each condition, the infants showed a consistent posthabituation preference for the broken rod relative to the complete rod, implying perception object unity during habituation. (Control groups did not exhibit this preference.) Thus perception of object unity may be a skill that, although fragile in its earliest form, is available to even very young infants if given adequate perceptual support (cf. Kawataba, Gyoba, Inoue, & Ohtsubo, 1999).

The Johnson and Aslin (1995) finding of perception of object unity in 2-month-olds raises an important question: Might neonates also perceive object unity, if given additional perceptual support? This possibility was investigated by Slater, Johnson, Brown, and Badenoch (1996), who presented neonates rod-and-box displays that were richer in visual information for surface segregation, relative to the display employed by Slater et al. (1990): Reduced occluder height, increased separation in depth between the rod and box, background texture (to increase the salience of the depth differences between surfaces), and so on. Even with this additional information, however, the neonates did not appear to respond to object unity: They showed a clear and reliable posthabituation preference for the complete rod, relative to the broken rod.

MECHANISMS OF DEVELOPMENT

To summarize the evidence to date on development of perception of object unity, neonates appear to perceive a partly occluded object as comprised of disjoint surfaces, implying that at birth, humans may experience what Piaget (1952, 1954) called a "sensory tableaux", or a mosaic of disconnected, fragmented shapes. The process of binding these fragments into coherent, segregated surfaces and objects develops rapidly such that incipient unit formation emerges by 2 months, and by 4 months, infants utilize a range of visual information in object perception tasks, including orientation, motion, shape, depth, texture, and colour (Johnson, 2000).

It is clear, then, that unit formation and surface segregation skills develop rapidly in the human infant with the onset of visual experience. At present there is no single developmental account that encompasses the entire range of evidence, but the threshold model holds promise in identifying important theoretical links to other approaches that might help explain the emergence of these skills. The heart of the model is the contention that improvements in information-processing proficiency underlie development of the ability to bind features into coherent surface and object percepts. This contention is supported by recent evidence from studies of infant eye movements, connectionist modelling, and developmental neurophysiology, presented in the next section.

Eye movements

It seems probable that at least part of the differences in performance on the object unity task across the first few months after birth is rooted in improvements in attentional skills: The more proficient infants become at information pickup, the more likely it is that they will be able to detect and utilize that information in perceptual tasks. Recording of eye movements can serve as an important tool to investigate this possibility. To date, however, there have been no reports in the literature of infants' scanning of moving objects, and few reports of longitudinal investigations of changes in individual infants' eye movement patterns (see Bronson, 1994, 1997). Johnson and Johnson (in press) recorded scanning patterns in thirteen 2- and 3.5-month-old infants engaged in free viewing of partly occluded rod displays. We predicted that 3.5-month-olds, relative to 2-month-olds, would scan more often in the rod's vicinity, more often on both visible rod parts, and less often in uninformative regions of the display. Several noteworthy findings emerged. First, as predicted, older infants produced a higher proportion of fixations per second than did younger infants. Second, older infants scanned more extensively (across the display), whereas younger infants scanned less often in the vicinity of the bottom rod part (see Figure 3). Younger infants' fixations in the bottom part of the display were more frequent, however, with longer display times. We did not obtain evidence concerning the infants' perception of object unity in this study, but these results

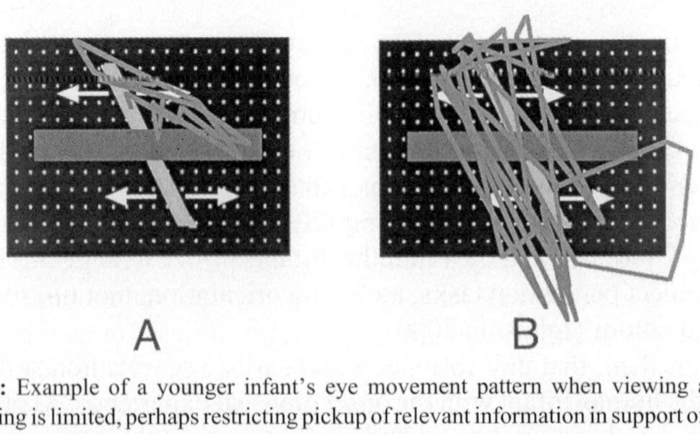

Figure 3. **A:** Example of a younger infant's eye movement pattern when viewing an occlusion display; scanning is limited, perhaps restricting pickup of relevant information in support of visual binding. **B:** Example of an older infant's scanning, which is more extensive, suggestive of superior information pickup.

indicate that the period in infancy during which unit formation undergoes rapid improvement is accompanied by important advances in scanning efficiency.

Connectionist modelling

Mareschal and Johnson (1999, in press) devised computational models of the development of perception of object unity. These models were programmed with standard connectionist architectures (i.e., input, hidden, and output layers) using backpropagation as a training algorithm, and endowed with sensitivity to visual information that has been found to influence infants' perception of object unity (object orientation, motion, and accretion and deletion of background texture). They were then presented with input that represented partly occluded object displays in which rod parts moved back and forth behind an occluder, and emerged from either side. That is, the rod was both fully and partly visible during each excursion across the display. The models were also equipped with a transient memory, such that after a rod became occluded, a trace of its now-hidden portion remained. After varying amounts of exposure to a subset of the possible occlusion events, the models were tested for perception of object unity while presented with events in which the rod parts did not emerge from behind the occluder. The results were positive: The models reliably perceived unity in most of the test events. The extent to which the models learned, and learning efficiency, were highly dependent on the training environment—which events were presented during training (i.e., which cues were made available), and how long training was allowed. Surface binding, then, arose from an initial perceptual sensitivity combined with transient memory and experience viewing objects that became occluded and again fully visible.

Developmental neurophysiology

Recent speculation concerning the visual system's ability to bind perceptual features has centred on the role of synchronized oscillatory firing patterns across neural assemblies (e.g., Singer, 1993, 1994; Singer & Gray, 1995). Binding is achieved when attention towards an object activates constellations of feature detectors throughout the visual system. Individual stimuli will tend to activate unique cell assemblies, with the global activity of assemblies' subcomponents functioning to bind together stimulus attributes. The "glue" that binds together unique object representations is the synchrony of neuronal discharges. In humans, this binding process appears largely nonfunctional at birth. A potential bottleneck in this process, therefore, might be rooted in limitations in synchronization of neural groupings. Notably, young infants' cortical discharges are characterized by a relatively high degree of neural "noise" or incoherence that impedes efficient neural transduction, and may restrict, for example, contrast sensitivity and other low-level visual functions (Skoczenski & Aslin, 1995; Skoczenski & Norcia, 1998). There is every reason to believe that more sophisticated perceptual functions, such as unit formation and surface segregation, are also compromised. Cell circuitries in infants analogous to those in adults, therefore, may be engaged to some extent by a particular display, yet the totality could be insufficient to activate appropriate responses to object properties. This suggestion is consistent with the tenets of the threshold model in stressing the necessity of sufficiency of visual information to achieve veridical percepts.

A second consideration is the likelihood that veridical object percepts are limited by deficiencies in horizontal and vertical connectivities within and between areas of the immature visual system. Burkhalter (1993; Burkhalter, Bernardo, & Charles, 1993), for example, reported that vertical connections within V1 and V2 begin to develop prenatally, perhaps supporting analysis of local features in visual scenes with the onset of visual experience. Horizontal connections within cortical layers, in contrast, show a much more protracted developmental trajectory, and were sparse even in a 4-month-old. Connections between areas V1 and V2 also mature during this period. Along with the construction of new circuitries arising from these connections is extensive pruning of existing synapses, a process that likewise requires months (or longer) to reach maturity (Huttenlocher & de Courten, 1987). This developmental sequence is consistent with the ontogeny of perception of object unity after birth that we have observed, which would seem to require integration of information across the visual field, and therefore coordination across local circuitries in visual cortex.

RELATIONS TO OTHER EXTANT EVIDENCE

Evidence on the development of visual binding sketched out in the previous sections dovetails well with other current evidence and accounts of feature binding and perceptual segregation. First, Sireteanu (2000) described a programmatic series of experiments exploring infants' segregation of stimuli from texture differences (e.g., variations in orientation or density of individual line segments). The earliest evidence for texture-based segregation in these experiments was 2 months, but improvements continued to be observed over the first several years in children tested for detection of texture differences in more complex patterns. Second, Kovács (2000) presented findings from experiments that investigated contour integration in stimuli consisting of Gabor elements that were oriented either randomly or along a path. Gabor elements are small patches of alternating black and white that are presented against a gray background. These elements match receptive field properties of orientation-selective simple cells in V1, and are thus well-suited to probing the interactions of low-level visual mechanisms (in the present case, to perceive a continuous path specified by the alignment of the elements). Kovács did not report evidence from infants, but observed marked improvement in performance in children from 5 to 14 years, suggesting that integration of information across the visual field is characterized by a protracted developmental profile. Both Sireteanu and Kovács discussed their findings in terms of maturation of long-range cortical interactions (e.g., horizontal connections in layers 2 and 3 of V1), an account consistent with the evidence on perception of object unity in infancy outlined previously.

Finally, Hummel and Biederman (1992) devised a connectionist model of object recognition that instantiated many of the principles outlined previously in the progression from figure–ground segregation to binding features into coherent object percepts. This model was equipped with banks of feature detectors composing the input layer, and subsequent layers that combined the resulting computations (such as local connectivities and discontinuities) into object parts (known as geons), and eventually matched the perceived collection of geons to a series of stored templates to arrive at an ultimate description of the object. The model used temporal synchrony as the binding mechanism: Individual cells, tuned to local line orientations, fired together to form "fast enabling links" capable of detecting longer contours. The goal of the model was to explore object recognition, rather than simply object perception, and therefore contained more sophisticated mechanisms (such as stored representations of geons and templates of complete objects) than required by an account of the development of visual binding. Nevertheless, this approach shares much in spirit with developmental considerations. Biederman (1996) has suggested that object recognition proceeds in children in analogous fashion to categorization and word learning: By the acquisition of a "vocabulary" of objects. The first entries into this vocabulary will be relatively simple, or "entry-level" objects (analogous to entry-level, or basic, categorization), followed by more complex objects. Notably, the Hummel and Biederman model of object recognition contains built-in representations of geons and objects. Future connectionist models of the development of object recognition must account for how these representations come to exist in the first place.

CONCLUSIONS

The evidence recounted in this paper supports a view of the development of visual binding that stresses the importance of both *experience-independent* and *experience-dependent* mechanisms. The experience-independent mechanisms are evinced by an assemblage of visual functions at birth, such as attention towards contour and motion (Slater, 1995), and figure–ground segregation (Slater et al., 1990). Experience-dependent developmental mechanisms involve processes such as changes in synaptic strengths and increased synchronization of the firing of neurons in various visual areas in response to environmental stimulation (Bailey & Kandel, 1995; Shatz, 1992). These two kinds of mechanism may combine in their contributions to the shaping of the visual system during infancy, because edges and motion provide critical information for surface segregation, and both kinds of cue are central to young infants' (and adults') unit formation.

REFERENCES

Bailey, C.H., & Kandel, E.R. (1995). Molecular and structural mechanisms underlying long-term memory. In M.S. Gazzaniga (Ed.), *The cognitive neurosciences* (pp. 19–36). Cambridge, MA: MIT Press.

Biederman, I. (1996). Visual object recognition. In S.M. Kosslyn & D. N. Osherson (Eds.), *Visual cognition: Vol. 2. An invitation to cognitive science* (2nd ed., pp. 121–165). Cambridge, MA: MIT Press.

Bornstein, M.H. (1985). Habituation of attention as a measure of visual information processing in human infants: Summary, systematization, and synthesis. In G. Gottlieb & N.A. Krasnegor (Eds.), *Measurement of audition and vision in the first year of postnatal life: A methodological overview* (pp. 253–300). Norwood, NJ: Ablex.

Bronson, G.W. (1994). Infants' transitions toward adult-like scanning. *Child Development*, *65*, 1243–1261.

Bronson, G.W. (1997). The growth of visual capacity: Evidence from infant scanning patterns. In C. Rovee-Collier & L.P. Lipsitt (Eds.), *Advances in infancy research* (Vol. 11, pp. 109–141). Norwood, NJ: Ablex.

Burkhalter, A. (1993). Development of forward and feedback connections between areas V1 and V2 of human visual cortex. *Cerebral Cortex*, *3*, 476–487.

Burkhalter, A., Bernardo, K.L., & Charles, V. (1993). Development of local circuits in human visual cortex. *Journal of Neuroscience*, *13*, 1916–1931.

Craton, L.G. (1996). The development of perceptual completion abilities: Infants' perception of stationary, partially occluded objects. *Child Development*, *67*, 890–904.

Goodale, M.A., Milner, A.D., Jakobson, L.S., & Carey, D.P. (1991). A neurological dissociation between perceiving objects and grasping them. *Nature*, *349*, 154–156.

Hummel, J.E., & Biederman, I. (1992). Dynamic binding in a neural network for shape recognition. *Psychological Review*, *99*, 480–517.

Huttenlocher, P.R., & de Courten, C.H. (1987). The development of synapses in striate cortex of man. *Human Neurobiology*, *6*, 1–9.

Johnson, S.P. (1997). Young infants' perception of object unity: Implications for development of attentional and cognitive skills. *Current Directions in Psychological Science*, *6*, 5–11.

Johnson, S.P. (2000). The development of visual surface perception: Insights into the ontogeny of knowledge. In C. Rovee-Collier, L. Lipsitt, & H. Hayne (Eds.), *Progress in infancy research* (Vol. 1, pp. 113–154). Mahwah, NJ: Lawrence Erlbaum Associates Inc.

Johnson, S.P., & Aslin, R.N. (1995). Perception of object unity in 2-month-old infants. *Developmental Psychology*, *31*, 739–745.

Johnson, S.P., & Aslin, R.N. (1996). Perception of object unity in young infants: The roles of motion, depth, and orientation. *Cognitive Development*, *11*, 161–180.

Johnson, S.P., & Aslin, R.N. (1998). Young infants' perception of illusory contours in dynamic displays. *Perception*, *27*, 341–353.

Johnson, S.P., & Aslin, R.N. (2000). Infants' perception of transparency. *Developmental Psychology, 36,* 808–816.

Johnson, S.P., Bremner, J.G., Slater, A., & Mason, U. (2000). The role of good form in young infants' perception of partly occluded objects. *Journal of Experimental Child Psychology*, *76*, 1–25.

Johnson, S.P., & Johnson, K.L. (in press). Young infants' perception of partly occluded objects: Evidence from scanning patterns. *Infant Behavior and Development.*

Johnson, S.P., & Náñez, J.E. (1995). Young infants' perception of object unity in two-dimensional displays. *Infant Behaviour and Development, 18*, 133–143.

Jusczyk, P.W., Johnson, S.P., Spelke, E.S., & Kennedy, L.J. (1999). Synchronous change and perception of object unity: Evidence from adults and infants. *Cognition, 71*, 257–288.

Kawataba, H., Gyoba, J., Inoue, H., & Ohtsubo, H. (1999). Visual completion of partly occluded grating in infants under 1 month of age. *Vision Research, 39*, 3586–3591.

Kellman, P.J. (1996). The origins of object perception. In R. Gelman & T. Au (Eds.), *Handbook of perception and cognition: Perceptual and cognitive development* (2nd ed., pp. 3–48). San Diego: Academic Press.

Kellman, P.J., & Shipley, T.F. (1991). A theory of visual interpolation in object perception. *Cognitive Psychology, 23*, 141–221.

Kellman, P.J., & Spelke, E.S. (1983). Perception of partly occluded objects in infancy. *Cognitive Psychology, 15*, 483–524.

Kovács, I. (2000). Human development of perceptual organization. *Vision Research, 40*, 1301–1310.

Mareschal, D., & Johnson, S.P. (1999). Developmental mechanisms in the development of object unity. In M. Hahn & S.C. Stoness (Eds.), *Proceedings of the twenty-first annual conference of the Cognitive Science Society* (pp. 343–348). Mahwah, NJ: Lawrence Erlbaum Associates Inc.

Mareschal, D., & Johnson, S.P. (in press). Learning to perceive object unity: A connectionist account. *Developmental Science.*

Marr, D. (1982). *Vision.* San Francisco: Freeman.

Nakayama, K., He, Z.J., & Shimojo, S. (1996). Visual surface representation: A critical link between lower-level and higher-level vision. In S.M. Kosslyn & D.N. Osherson (Eds.), *Visual cognition: Vol. 2. An invitation to cognitive science* (2nd ed., pp. 1–70). Cambridge, MA: MIT Press.

Nakayama, K., & Shimojo, S. (1990). Toward a neural understanding of visual surface representation. *Cold Spring Harbor Symposia on Quantitative Biology, 40*, 911–924.

Nakayama, K., Shimojo, S., & Silverman, G.H. (1989). Stereoscopic depth: Its relation to image segmentation, grouping, and the recognition of occluded objects. *Perception, 18*, 55–68.

Needham, A. (1998). Infants' use of featural information in the segregation of stationary objects. *Infant Behavior and Development, 21*, 47–76.

Piaget, J. (1952). *The origins of intelligence in children.* New York: International Universities Press.

Piaget, J. (1954). *The construction of reality in the child.* New York: Basic Books.

Roskies, A.K. (1999). The binding problem. *Neuron, 24*, 7–9.

Shatz, C.J. (1992). The developing brain. *Scientific American, 267*, 60–67.

Singer, W. (1993). Synchronization of cortical activity and its putative role in information processing and learning. *Annual Review of Physiology, 55*, 349–374.

Singer, W. (1994). Putative functions of temporal correlations in neocortical processing. In C. Koch & J.L. Davis (Eds.), *Large-scale neuronal theories of the brain* (pp. 201–237). Cambridge, MA: MIT Press.

Singer, W., & Gray, C.M. (1995). Visual feature integration and the temporal correlation hypothesis. *Annual Review of Neuroscience, 18*, 555–586.

Sireteanu, R. (2000). Texture segmentation, "pop-out," and feature binding in infants and children. In C. Rovee-Collier, L. Lipsitt, & H. Hayne (Eds.), *Progress in infancy research* (Vol. 1, pp. 183–249). Mahwah, NJ: Lawrence Erlbaum Associates Inc.

Skoczenski, A.M., & Aslin, R.N. (1995). Assessment of vernier acuity development using the "equivalent intrinsic blur" paradigm. *Vision Research, 35*, 1879–1887.

Skoczenski, A.M., & Norcia, A.M. (1998). Neural noise limitations on infant visual sensitivity. *Nature, 391*, 697–700.

Slater, A. (1995). Visual perception and memory at birth. In C. Rovee-Collier & L.P. Lipsitt (Eds.), *Advances in infancy research* (Vol. 9, pp. 107–162). Norwood, NJ: Ablex.
Slater, A., Johnson, S.P., Brown, E., & Badenoch, M. (1996). Newborn infants' perception of partly occluded objects. *Infant Behavior and Development*, *19*, 145–148.
Slater, A., Morison, V., Somers, M., Mattock, A., Brown, E., & Taylor, D. (1990). Newborn and older infants' perception of partly occluded objects. *Infant Behavior and Development*, *13*, 33–49.
Treisman, A., & Schmidt, H. (1982). Illusory conjunctions in the perception of objects. *Cognitive Psychology*, *14*, 107–141

VISUAL COGNITION, 2001, *8* (3/4/5), 579–592

Induced gamma-band responses in the human EEG are related to attentional information processing

Matthias M. Müller and Thomas Gruber
Cognitive Neuroscience, Department of Psychology, University of Liverpool, UK

Synchronized neural activity in the frequency range above 20 Hz, the gamma-band, has been proposed as a signature of temporal feature binding. Here we suggest that selective attention facilitates synchronization of neural activity. Selective attention can be guided by bottom-up, stimulus driven, or top-down task-driven processes. Both processes will cause that stimuli are processed preferentially. While bottom-up processes might facilitate synchronization of neurons due to the salience of the stimulus, top-down processes may bias information selection by facilitating synchronization of neurons coding a certain location in space and/or of neurons related to the processing of certain features. Animal as well as human EEG studies support the notion of a link between induced gamma-band responses and attentive, sensory stimulus processing.

INTRODUCTION

Information processing in the visual system requires the activity of many visual areas (Felleman & van Essen, 1991; Tootell, Dale, Sereno, & Malach, 1996; Ungerleider, 1995; Ungerleider & Haxby, 1994; Zeki, 1993). In addition, there is empirical evidence that distinct regions of information processing remain segregated through higher areas in the brain and can be divided into the ventral pathway, which is thought to be specialized for the analysis of object features (colour, shape, etc.—the "what" system) and the dorsal pathway specialized for the analysis of motion and the spatial relationships between objects (the "where" system) (Ungerleider, 1995; Ungerleider & Haxby, 1994). Given the anatomical organization of the visual cortex, which suggests a hierarchically organized information analysis (Felleman & van Essen, 1991) the question

Please address correspondence to M.M. Müller, Cognitive Neuroscience and Neuropsychology, Department of Psychology, University of Liverpool, Eleanor Rathbone Building, Liverpool L69 7ZA, UK. Email: m.mueller@liverpool.ac.uk

We would like to thank Mark Elliott for excellent editorial help. The reported work was supported by the Deutsche Forschunggemeinschaft and the Human Frontier Science Program.

http://www.tandf.co.uk/journals/pp/13506285.html DOI:10.1080/13506280143000133

emerges of how a particular visual object is represented in the brain? One possibility is that the object is coded by a Hebbian-like neuronal cell assembly distributed across the different functional visual areas by means of synchronized firing of cells in a frequency range above 20 Hz, i.e., in the gamma-band (Eckhorn, 1988; Gray & Singer, 1987; Malsburg & Schneider, 1986; Milner, 1974; Singer et al., 1997; Singer & Gray, 1995).

A number of animal studies have shown that synchronized neural activity in the visual cortex of anaesthetized cats and behaving monkeys is related to the grouping properties of features such as simple bar stimuli or gratings (for an overview, see Singer & Gray, 1995, and elsewhere in this issue). From these studies it is known that high-frequency neural responses are (1) neither time nor phase locked to the onset of a stimulus, thus being *induced* as opposed to *evoked*, (2) showed a variance in the frequency range from 30 to 80 Hz in cat visual cortex (Castelo-Branco, Neuenschwander, & Singer, 1998; Eckhorn et al., 1988; Engel, König, Gray, & Singer, 1990; Gray, Engel, König, & Singer, 1990; Singer & Gray, 1995) and up to 90 Hz in the awake behaving monkey (Eckhorn, Frien, Bauer, Woelbern, & Kehr, 1993), and (3) occurred in bursts, which last between 100 and about 300 ms (Eckhorn, Reitboeck, Arndt, & Dicke, 1990; Gray, Engel, König, & Singer, 1992). However, one limitation of most of the animal studies is their restriction to simple visual stimuli. Moving bar or grating stimuli require only low-level processing by individual neurons, which respond to simple features, such as orientation, to which they are tuned. Such an environment is not comparable to the rather complex visual scenes the brain is usually confronted with.

In the "real" world, the brain is confronted with an enormous amount of visual input at any given moment. By virtue of capacity limitations in information processing selective filtering of the perceptual input permits only a limited number of stimuli being processed at a given time (Neisser, 1967). Thus, selective attention is needed to focus the limited cognitive processing resources on a particular array of the available information while attenuating irrelevant signals (Hillyard, Mangun, Woldorff, & Luck, 1995; Posner, Snyder, & Davidson, 1980). What are the mechanisms that guide selective attention? In general, the distinction can be made between a bottom-up or stimulus-driven, and a top-down, task-driven processes (see Kastner & Ungerleider, 2000; Treisman, 1998). Bottom-up attentive processes are defined by the salience of a certain stimulus, defined by simple features such as orientation and colour, the dissimilarity between the stimulus and surrounding distractor stimuli and by Gestalt principles (Kastner & Ungerleider, 2000). In a search array, such stimuli pop-out automatically, e.g., a horizontal line among vertical lines (Treisman & Gelade, 1980; Treisman & Gormican, 1988). This situation becomes totally different when subjects are asked to search for a target defined by a "conjunction" of simple features such as an "O" among many "Qs", or to detect a certain target stimulus in a series of stimuli. Here, top-down processes are necessary to facilitate visual information processing of stimuli displayed at a certain (attended) location or of particular attributes (Desimone, 1998; Desimone & Duncan, 1995).

Recently, Kastner and Ungerleider (2000) published an excellent overview of their model of how top-down visual attention affects neural processing. They showed empirical evidence for the following mechanisms (p. 321):

- enhancement of neural responses to an attended stimulus
- filtering of unwanted information
- increase of baseline activity at the attended location in the absence of a visual stimulus
- increase of stimulus salience by enhancing the neuron's sensitivity.

In addition to the mechanisms reviewed by Kastner and Ungerleider, we will argue here that attention facilitates synchronization of neural activity as a further possible mechanism. Synchronization of action potentials can serve as a flexible and powerful mechanism to increase the signal compared to the background noise and thus allows for preferential processing. Synchronization could occur "automatically" and pre-attentively as in bottom-up stimulus-driven processing. This might result in the well-known pop-out of salient stimuli under some conditions. On the other hand, top-down task-driven attentive processing will bias visual information processing in favour of a target stimulus or a certain location. In this case, the "attentive brain" facilitates synchronization of neurons coding a certain location in space due to the retinotopic organization of visual cortex, and/or of neurons related to the processing of certain features.

A number of animal as well as human studies seem to support our notion that synchronization of high frequency oscillations are related to the attentive processing of a stimulus. In the 1970s, Rougeul-Buser and co-workers reported an attentional modulation of 40 Hz neural activity in parietal cortex and thalamus of the awake behaving cat (see Rougeul-Buser & Buser, 1994). When the animals watched a glass cage with a living mouse in it, they found a dramatic increase in 40 Hz activity as compared to an empty-cage condition. Similar increases in 40 Hz activity were observed during explorative behaviour of the cats. The authors interpreted their findings firstly as "intense wakefulness" but later as an indicator of focused attention. Murthy and colleagues (Murthy, Aoki, & Fetz, 1994; Murthy & Fetz, 1992) reported an increase of synchronized gamma-band responses (GBRs) in monkey sensorimotor cortex only when monkeys had to perform a sensorimotor integration task, which required animals' attention as compared to repetitive wrist movements. Steriade, Amzica, and Contreras (1996) reported increased synchronized GBRs as a function of cortical arousal and concluded that "the conventional notion of a totally desynchronized cortical activity upon arousal should be revised as fast rhythms are enhanced and synchronized within intracortical networks during brain activation" (p. 392). Supportive empirical evidence for this notion was presented by the work of Wolf Singer's group in Frankfurt. They showed a facilitation of cortical gamma-band synchronization in cat visual cortex upon activation of the mesencephalic reticular formation (Munk, Roelfsema, König, Engel, & Singer, 1996). In extension to that study, intracortical synchronization in the 20–65 Hz frequency range in areas 17 and 18 was reported to become more effective as a function of central activation (Herculano-Houzel, Munk, Neuenschwander, & Singer, 1999). Most interestingly, an increase of oscillatory modulation but a decrease in frequency with higher cortical activation was found. Furthermore, in a visuomotor integration task, zero time-lag synchronization was observed between cat parietal visual areas and motor cortex during attentive processing of visual stimuli, which required a motor response (Roelfsema, Engel, König, & Singer, 1997).

Early research in humans has also suggested a close relation between attention and high frequency responses in the human brain. Sem-Jacobsen, Petersen, Dodge, Lazarte, and Holman (1956) demonstrated by means of intracortical recordings that high frequency responses in occipital areas were only present when the patient was attentively looking to a complex cartoon in order to observe details. No such activity was present when the patient was confronted with a blank cardboard. On the basis of EEG recordings, Sheer (Sheer, 1970, 1989; Spydell & Sheer, 1982) hypothesized that 40 Hz EEG activity covariates with focused arousal, which in today terms can roughly be translated to selective attention. When subjects performed a problem solving task, 40 Hz EEG activity increased selectively over the hemisphere, which was related to the task as compared to a resting condition (Spydell & Sheer, 1982). In addition, muscle electromyographic (EMG) activity was analysed, since it is known that the EMG activity is in the gamma-band range (Cacioppo, Tassinary, & Fridlund, 1990). It was shown that the measured gamma-band response was not related to possible muscle artifacts. However, one of the problems of the previous designs, including the one of Rougeul-Buser et al., is their control against a relaxing condition. Recent research, reported later, has used designs, which assured that the general level of arousal between conditions is comparable, allowing to gather more conclusive data on the link between attentional processing and human EEG gamma-band responses. In the following we will show some empirical evidence that induced GBRs in the human EEG are linked to attentional processing of stimuli. Based upon the previously introduced distinction between stimulus-driven bottom-up and task-driven top-down attentional processing, in the first section we will describe studies, which used stimuli based on Gestalt principles. In the second section we will recapitulate studies showing the link between top-down attentional processing and GBRs.

BOTTOM-UP STIMULUS DRIVEN ATTENTIONAL PROCESSING

A series of studies have demonstrated that induced GBRs in the human EEG are related to the perception of a stimulus based on some of the major Gestalt principles, like common motion, colinearity, "gute Gestalt" (good figure), and, recently, common colour. Most of these studies have in common that the object automatically pops-out, and thus are a good example of bottom-up stimulus-driven attentive processes. Lutzenberger, Pulvermüller, Elbert, and Birbaumer (1995) found increased gamma-band power when lines in a visual quarter field moved coherently, giving the impression of a waterfall compared to a condition during which the lines were moving randomly. Related to that, in one series of experiments we (Müller et al., 1996) aimed at mimicking the work in animals as closely as possible. Based on the experiment by Gray, König, Engel, and Singer (1989) in which it was shown that V1 neurons with non-overlapping receptive fields synchronized their activity when stimulated with a long moving bar, and no such synchronization was optained when two small bars were moving in opposite direction, we presented our subjects a long, coherently moving bar and two small bars moving in opposite directions. We observed a significant increase of gamma-band power on posterior electrode sites with a latency of about 250–300 ms when subjects attended the long bar compared with the condition during which subjects attended to the two bars moving in opposite directions. This finding was replicated in a subsequent follow-up study (Müller, Elbert, & Rockstroh, 1997; Müller, Junghöfer, Elbert, & Rockstroh, 1997). In addition, we (Gruber, Keil, & Müller, 2000) showed that an increase in gamma-band power was also present when a figure was formed by the principles of common colour and motion operationalized by small squares.

Besides moving stimuli, other stimuli that induce bottom-up attentional processing were used as well in human EEG studies. Tallon-Baudry and co-workers (Tallon, Bertrand, Bouchet, & Pernier, 1995; Tallon-Baudry, Bertrand, Delpuech, & Pernier, 1996; Tallon-Baudry, Bertrand, Wienbruch, Ross, & Pantev, 1997) used illusionary Kaniza triangles (colinearity). When confronting their subjects with illusionary triangles and non-triangles ("Pac men" are rotated that they gave no illusion of a triangle), they found and replicated a significant increase in induced gamma power at occipital electrodes for the illusionary triangles with a latency of about 250–350 ms (Tallon et al., 1995; Tallon-Baudry, Bertrand, & Wienbruch, 1997). Recently, Herrmann, Mecklinger, and Pfeifer (1999), using illusionary triangles and squares, were not able to replicate the findings with respect to induced GBRs, but they also found an augmentation in evoked gamma-band responses. Interestingly, they found the biggest increase in early phase-locked gamma-band activity for illusionary squares, which were defined as targets. They also elicited the largest N100 and P300 in the evoked potential. In particular the increased N100, which is in about the same latency range as the evoked GBR, confirms the attentional modulation of automatic perceptual processes (LaBerge, 1995).

In a recent study, we (Keil, Müller, Ray, Elbert, & Gruber, 1999) presented our subjects a rotating bistable black and white face drawing, which—when standing vertically—was perceived as either a sad or happy face. No face perception was possible when the figure was oriented horizontally. Thus, the face popped-out automatically at a certain rotation angle. Results showed a significant increase in gamma power at occipital electrodes when subjects were able to perceive the face. Confirming our findings, Rodriguez et al. (1999) have shown an increase in gamma-band power with a latency of about 230 ms when subjects were confronted with so-called Mooney faces (black/white shapes of faces) as compared to when these figures were presented upside-down, prohibiting identification of the arrangement of features as a face. To summarize, there is some body of evidence that bottom-up stimulus-driven visual information processing is related to induced GBRs in the human brain. The topographical distribution of gamma-band power in these studies show a maximum at parieto-occipital electrode sites, which allows to speculate that neurons from visual cortices have contributed to that activity.

TOP-DOWN ATTENTIONAL PROCESSING

As of today, a series of human EEG studies are published, which can be summarized under the heading top-down attentional information processing. In one of our studies, we instructed our subjects in a block design to either attend to a long moving bar presented in one visual hemifield or to ignore it (Müller, 1998; Müller, Gruber, & Keil, 2000). Results showed an increase of more than 67% of spectral power in a distinct gamma frequency range at occipito-parietal electrodes when attention was focused on the moving bar as compared to when the moving bar was ignored. In addition to the power increase, we observed that the attention effect was prominent shortly after motion onset remaining prominent throughout the epoch while the bar was in motion and that spectral power peaked in the time window 256 512 ms after motion onset. These results are supported by a whole head MEG study, in which subjects were instructed to either attend to coherently moving bars or to a tone sequence (Sokolov et al.,1999). When subjects shifted their attention to the visual modality the authors reported of a significant increase of 40 Hz activity over occipital cortices.

Recently, we (Gruber, Müller, Keil, & Elbert, 1999) used a high density electrode montage to study the attentional modulation of induced GBRs. In addition, we investigated whether a shift in the topographical distribution of the GBR to the hemisphere contralateral to the to-be-attended side after the onset of an attention direction cue can be observed. We hypothesized that the attention direction cue should facilitate synchronization in the contralateral hemisphere for faster stimulus processing. This hypothesis was based on the anatomy of the visual system which projects visual input from the left visual field to the right hemisphere and vice versa. Results showed significantly higher gamma power on parieto-occipital electrode sites contralateral to the attended half-screen as compared to when the identical half of the screen was ignored. This shift of increased gamma power occurred after the cue, being supportive for our hypothesis. In general, the increase was more pronounced when the left visual hemifield was attended. Such a hemispheric asymmetry was frequently reported in spatial visual attention tasks using visual evoked potentials (Heilman, 1995; Palmer & Tzeng, 1990; Posner & Dehaene, 1994; Posner & Petersen, 1990) and PET (Corbetta, Miezin, Shulman, & Petersen, 1993; Corbetta, Shulman, Miezin, & Petersen, 1995). In their study, Corbetta and co-workers (1993) reported an asymmetrical activation of the parietal cortex when attending to the left or the right visual field. Attention to the left visual field was mostly controlled by one region in the right parietal cortex, whereas attention to the right field was controlled more bilaterally by a left parietal and a distinct right parietal region. Thus, our results fit with anatomical asymmetries related to visual spatial attention.

Two further studies must be mentioned in this section. In a visual search study, Tallon-Baudry and co-workers presented their subjects the famous Dalmatian dog picture or a similar picture in which no dog was present (Tallon-Baudry, Bertrand, Delpuech, & Pernier, 1997). While subjects were still "naive" with respect to the hidden Dalmatian, there was no difference in gamma-band power between the presentation of the dog and the no-dog picture. After the presence of the Dalmatian was indicated to the subjects, a marked increase in gamma power at occipital and right parietal electrodes with a latency of 280 ms was the consequence, which, however, was also present when subjects were shown the no-dog pictures. Similar to the visual search arrays as used, for example, by Treisman or Luck and co-workers (see Treisman, 1998, for an overview; Luck, Fan, & Hillyard, 1993) subjects needed a cortical representation of the target stimulus (Dalmatian) in order to solve the top-down driven search task. Therefore, it was not surprising, that GBR activity was also present in the no-dog condition. In a subsequent study, Tallon-Baudry and co-workers confronted their subjects with a "delayed-matching-to-sample" task (Tallon-Baudry, Bertrand, Peronnet, & Pernier, 1998). A stimulus was presented followed by a delay and the presentation of a second stimulus. Thus, subjects had to attentively process the shape of the first stimulus in order be able to decide whether or not the second stimulus matches the first. Consequently, the authors found the largest GBR 280 ms after presentation of the first stimulus at occipital electrodes. In the control condition, in which subjects had not to attentively process the stimulus, only a very small GBR with the same latency was observed. This result further supports our findings of an attentional modulation of induced GBRs.

Top-down attentional modulations of GBRs were not only reported in the visual modality but in the auditory and somatosensory modality as well. Tiitinen et al. (1993) reported a significant increase of the evoked auditory GBR when subjects attended to tones presented to one ear to detect target tones, while ignoring the other ear. Tallon-Baudry and Bertrand (1999) showed an increase in induced GBRs in an active listening task as compared to a passive listening task. In the active listening task, in which subjects had to detect rare target tones with a different frequency, induced GBRs occurred with a peak latency of 300 ms and thus in about the same latency range as visually induced GBRs. With respect to the somatosensory modality, Desmedt and Tomberg (1994) reported a phase-locking of 40 Hz activity in prefrontal and parietal human cortex during somatosensory selective attention. Kristeva-Feige, Feige, Makeig, Ross, and Elbert (1993) showed increased gamma-band activity in a sensorimotor integration task over the sensorimotor cortex contralateral to the hand performing the task. This result was interpreted as resembling the findings in monkeys by Murthy and co-workers (Murthy & Fetz, 1992; Murthy et al.,1994).

As in the previous section, most of the studies reported here are related to visual information processing showing a clear relation between attentional processing and increased GBRs. The topographical distribution of gamma power with a centre over posterior areas seems to be in line with the hypothesis that top-down attentional processes are "forcing" synchronization of neurons in lower visual areas by feedback connections from higher visual areas (Milner, 1974; Singer, 1994). Given that top-down attentional processes have also be shown to increase GBRs in other sensory modalities, it is tempting to presume that this mechanism is valid for other sensory modalities as well.

DISCUSSION

Here, we propose that induced GBRs are a signature of attentional information processing. Synchronization of neural activity is hypothesized as a further powerful mechanism to increase the signal-to-noise ratio and thus allows perferential processing of sensory information. Attentive sensory information processing can be divided into two major mechanisms: (1) stimulus-driven bottom-up and (2) task-driven top-down. We suggest that in stimulus-driven bottom-up processing the salience of the stimulus "forces" neurons to synchronize due to their tuning properties. Since many of the animal studies have found such stimulus-driven synchronization in the visual cortex under anaesthesia, it seems to be the case that low-level processing in early visual areas, required in the case of simple bar or grating stimuli, works automatically and pre-attentively. Maybe the well known pop-out effect is a function of stimulus-driven neural synchronization. In the present paper, we have reviewed a number of experiments in humans, which used stimuli based on Gestalt principles. Such stimuli serve as a perfect example of stimulus-driven visual information processing. Based on our hypothesis, one should expect that such stimuli should result in a very early gamma-band increase over occipital areas. However, in the studies, which reported of latencies of induced GBRs, the average latency was well after 200 ms. This seems to be in variance with our proposal. A closer inspection of the reported studies in that section, however, shows that almost all of them were combined with an additional target detection task. Such a task requires attentional object-based top-down processes, which might be reflected in the long latencies. In our study (Gruber et al., 2000) where we used small squares to form objects on the basis of common motion and colour, no task was involved. Our preliminary data analysis shows a much earlier increase in gamma power as compared to other studies. On the other hand, what is largely unknown at the present state is the relation between evoked and induced GBRs. Evoked GBRs occur well before induced activity. It might be the case, that low level processing in early visual areas is reflected by evoked GBRs in the human EEG, which might be complementary to visual evoked potentials (see the results by Herrmann et al., 1999). But these assumptions are highly speculative and should be subject to future studies.

As mentioned earlier, it seems plausible that the later occurrence of induced GBRs is related to object-based top-down attentional processes at later stages where objects are represented and attentional processes select objects by means of these representations (Baylis & Driver, 1993; Duncan, 1984; Hübner & Backer, 1999; Tipper & Weaver, 1998). The detection task introduced in human experiments using stimuli based on Gestalt principles and the latency of induced GBRs in top-down task driven experiments would support such a notion. But the latency of induced GBRs fits equally well with known latencies of feature processing based on visual evoked potentials. When subjects are instructed to selectively attend to a certain feature of a stimulus such as colour, shape, or motion, a broad posterior negativity (selection negativity, SN), which starts between 150 and 200 ms poststimulus and extends for 200 ms or more, can be observed (Anllo-Vento & Hillyard, 1996; Heinze et al., 1994; Hillyard, 1993; Hillyard et al., 1995; Mangun, Hillyard, & Luck, 1993). When subjects are further instructed to respond to targets, which are defined by a certain feature—e.g., colour "red", or being an illusionary square—the SN is assumed to represent the upper time limit with which the visual system can discriminate between target and non-target stimuli, which requires that different features must have been analysed and bound together to a percept. Usually, reaction times lay well beyond the latency of the SN. Based on Treisman's feature integration theory (Treisman, 1993, 1998; Treisman & Gelade, 1980) it is assumed that only features within the spotlight of attention are combined to a coherent representation of the object, which allows for central decision- and motor-related responses (Treisman & Gelade, 1980). Our hypothesis of induced GBRs being related to attentive stimulus processing is in line with this idea.

However, the general hypothesis that GBRs are related to perceptual processes was also questioned. Pulvermüller, Keil, and Elbert (1999) argued that induced GBRs in the human EEG are not a signature of perceptual processes; rather they mirror processes of active memory in Hebbian-like reverberating cell assemblies. They further argued that only stimuli that match a learned representation will induce GBRs. Evidence for their proposal was seen in the finding that (1) stimuli like written words also induce GBRs and (2) our rotating face in horizontal position and the upside-down Mooney faces used by Rodriguez et al. (1999) showed less gamma activity compared with the perception of a face since there is no representation of a no-face. However, written words fulfil an elementary Gestalt principle, namely perceptual grouping. Based on that principle the letter sequence "synchronization" is much easier to identify as opposed to "Sy*n*ChroN**I**Zati**O**N" (Bower, 1972). Unfortunately, Pulvermüller never tested the perceptual impact of his word stimuli. The finding that words as compared to non-words are related to an increase in GBRs was seen as further evidence for the theory of learned representations (see Pulvermüller, 1999). However, it might well be the case that "sun" but not "nus" pops-out and allows further attentive processing. In addition, in Pulvermüller's experiments, subjects were instructed to identify words by a button press, which—similar to the previously mentioned Gestalt experiments—produces a top-down bias of information processing for words. Furthermore, we argue that the pop-out effect of our face as a function of rotation angle and the Mooney faces allowed for further attentive processing, rather than the retrieval of memory processes. We would predict if subjects would have been instructed to identify non-faces, top-down processes would have biased visual information processing—and thus synchronization—in favour of non-faces, resulting in an increase of GBR. This, however should be tested in an experiment. The matching-to-sample experiment by Tallon-Baudry et al. (1998) further argues against Pulvermüller's proposal. When subjects had to attentively process the shapes of the stimuli in order to decide whether they match to a second stimulus, gamma power was significantly higher compared to the control condition in which subjects' attention was not focused on the stimuli. According to Pulvermüller one would expect exactly the opposite. During the first presentation, no gamma-band activity should be present, since no representation of the stimulus is available. In the second run one would expect an increase of GBRs, because now a learned representation of the stimuli should be present, since subjects performed very well in the matching task. However, it was the top-down attentional bias and not the learned representation, that modulated induced GBRs in that experiment.

REFERENCES

Anllo-Vento, L., & Hillyard, S.A. (1996). Selective attention to the color and direction of moving stimuli: Electropysiological correlates of hierarchical feature selection. *Perception and Psychophysics*, *58*, 191–206.

Baylis, G.C., & Driver, J. (1993). Visual attention and objects: Evidence for hierarchical coding. *Journal of Experimental Psychology: Human Perception and Performance*, *19*, 451–470.

Bower, G.H. (1972). Perceptual groups as coding units in immediate memory. *Psychonomic Science*, *27*, 217–219.

Cacioppo, J.T., Tassinary, L.G., & Fridlund, A.J. (1990). The skeletomotor system. In J.T. Cacioppo & J.T. Tassinary (Eds.), *Principles of psychophysiology: Physical, social, and inferential elements* (pp. 325–384). Cambridge, UK: Cambridge University Press.

Castelo-Branco, M., Neuenschwander, S., & Singer, W. (1998). Synchronization of visual responses between the cortex, lateral geniculate nucleus, and retina in the anesthetized cat. *Journal of Neuroscience*, *18*, 6395–6410.

Corbetta, M., Miezin, F.M., Shulman, G.L., & Petersen, S.E. (1993). A PET study of visuospatial attention. *Journal of Neuroscience*, *13*, 1202–1226.

Corbetta, M., Shulman, G.L., Miezin, F.M., & Petersen, S.E. (1995). Superior parietal cortex activation during spatial attention shifts and visual feature conjunction. *Science*, *270*, 802–805.

Desimone, R. (1998). Visual attention mediated by biased competition in extrastriate visual cortex. *Philosophical Transactions of the Royal Society of London, Series B, 353*, 1245–1255.

Desimone, R., & Duncan, J. (1995). Neural mechanisms of selective visual attention. *Annual Review of Neuroscience*, *18*, 193–222.

Desmedt, J.E., & Tomberg, C. (1994). Transient phase-locking of 40-Hz electrical oscillations in prefrontal and parietal human cortex reflects the process of conscious somatic perception. *Neuroscience Letters*, *168*, 126–129.

Duncan, J. (1984). Selective attention and the organization of visual information. *Journal of Experimental Psychology: General*, *113*, 501–517.

Eckhorn, R., Bauer, R., Jordan, W., Brosch, M., Kruse, W., Munk, M., & Reitboeck, H.J. (1988). Coherent oscillations: A mechanism of feature linking in the visual cortex? *Biological Cybernetics*, *60*, 121–130.

Eckhorn, R., Frien, A., Bauer, R., Woelbern, A., & Kehr, H. (1993). High frequency (60–90 Hz) oscillations in primary visual cortex of awake monkey. *NeuroReport*, *4*, 243–246.

Eckhorn, R., Reitboeck, H.J., Arndt, M., & Dicke, P. (1990). Feature linking via synchronization among distributed assemblies: Simulations of results from cat visual cortex. *Neural Computation*, *2*, 293–307.

Engel, A.K., König, P., Gray, C.M., & Singer, W. (1990). Stimulus-dependent neuronal oscillations in cat visual cortex: Inter-columnar interaction as determined by cross-correlation analysis. *European Journal of Neuroscience*, *2*, 588–606.

Felleman, D.J., & van Essen, D.C. (1991). Distributed hierarchical processing in the primate cerebral cortex. *Cerebral Cortex*, *1*, 1–47.

Gray, C.M., Engel, A.K., König, P., & Singer, W. (1990). Stimulus-dependent neuronal oscillations in cat visual cortex: receptive field properties and feature dependence. *European Journal of Neuroscience*, *2*, 607–619.

Gray, C.M., Engel, A.K., König, P., & Singer, W. (1992). Synchronization of oscillatory neuronal responses in cat striate cortex: Temporal properties. *Visual Neuroscience*, *8*, 337–347.

Gray, C.M., König, P., Engel, A.K., & Singer, W. (1992). Oscillatory responses in cat visual cortex exhibit inter-columnar synchronization which reflects global stimulus propeties. *Nature*, *338*, 334–337.

Gray, C.M., & Singer, W. (1987). Stimulus-specific neuronal oscillations in cat visual cortex: A cortical functional unit. *Society of Neuroscience, Abstracts, 13,* 404.3.

Gruber, T., Keil, A., & Müller, M.M. (2000). *Induced gamma-band activity is related to different aspects of Gestalt perception in the human EEG.* Paper presented at the symposium on Neural Binding of Space and Time, University of Leipzig and the Max-Planck Institute of Cognitive Neurosciences.

Gruber, T., Müller, M.M., Keil, A., & Elbert, T. (1999). Selective visual-spatial attention alters induced gamma-band responses in the human EEG. *Clinical Neurophysiology*, *110*, 2074–2085.

Heilman, K.M. (1995). Attentional asymmetries. In R.J. Davidson & K. Hugdhal (Eds.), *Brain asymmetry*. Cambridge, MA: MIT Press.

Heinze, H.J., Mangun, G.R., Burchert, W., Hinrichs, H., Scholz, M., Münte, T.F., Gös, A., Scherg, M., Johannes, S., Hundeshagen, H., Gazzaniga, M.S., & Hillyard, S.A. (1994). Combined spatial and temporal imaging of brain activity during visual selective attention in humans. *Nature*, *372*, 543–546.

Herculano-Houzel, S., Munk, M., Neuenschwander, S., & Singer, W. (1999). Precisely synchronized oscillatory firing patterns require electroencephalographic activiation. *Journal of Neuroscience*, *19*, 3992–4010.

Herrmann, S., Mecklinger, A., & Pfeifer, E. (1999). Gamma responses and ERPs in a visual classification task. *Clinical Neurophysiology*, *110*, 636–642.

Hillyard, S.A. (1993). Electrical and magnetic brain recordings: Contributions to cognitive neuroscience. *Current Opinion in Neurobiology*, *3*, 217–224.

Hillyard, S.A., Mangun, G.R., Woldorff, M.G., & Luck, S.J. (1995). Neural systems mediating selective attention. In M.S. Gazzaniga (Ed.), *The cognitive neurosciences* (pp. 665–681). Cambridge, MA: MIT Press.

Hübner, R., & Backer, G. (1999). Perceiving spatially inseparable objects: Evidence for feature-based object selection not mediated by location. *Journal of Experimental Psychology: Human Perception and Performance*, *25*, 1556–1567.

Kastner, S., & Ungerleider, L.G. (2000). Mechanisms of visual attention in the human cortex. *Annual Review of Neuroscience*, *23*, 315–341.

Keil, A., Müller, M.M., Ray, W.J., Elbert, T., & Gruber, T. (1999). Human gamma-band activity and perception of a gestalt. *Journal of Neuroscience*, *19*, 7152–7161.

Kristeva-Feige, R., Feige, B., Makeig, S., Ross, B., & Elbert, T. (1993). Oscillatory brain activity during a motor task. *NeuroReport*, *4*, 1291–1294.

LaBerge, D. (1995). *Attentional processing*. Cambridge, MA: Harvard University Press.

Luck, S.J., Fan, S., & Hillyard, S.A. (1993). Attention-related modulation of sensory-evoked brain activity in a visual search task. *Journal of Cognitive Neuroscience*, *5*, 188–195.

Lutzenberger, W., Pulvermüller, F., Elbert, T., & Birbaumer, N. (1995). Visual stimulation alters local 40-Hz responses in humans: An EEG-study. *Neuroscience Letters*, *183*, 39–42.

Malsburg, C. von der, & Schneider, W. (1986). A neural cocktail-party processor. *Biological Cybernetics*, *54*, 29–40.

Mangun, G.R., Hillyard, S.A., & Luck, S.J. (1993). Electrocortical substrates of visual selective attention. In D.E. Meyer & S. Kornblum (Eds.), *Attention and performance XIV: Synergies in experimental psychology, artificial intelligence and cognitive neuroscience* (pp. 219–243). Cambridge, MA: MIT Press.

Milner, P.M. (1974). A model for visual shape recognition. *Psychological Review*, *81*, 521–535.

Müller, M.M. (1998). *Oscillatory cortical activities in the human brain*. Habilitation thesis, Universität Konstanz, Germany.

Müller, M.M., Bosch, J., Elbert, T., Kreiter, A., Valdes Sosa, M., Valdes Sosa, P., & Rockstroh, B. (1996). Visually induced gamma-band responses in human electroencephalographic activity—a link to animal studies. *Experimental Brain Research*, *112*, 96–102.

Müller, M.M., Elbert, T., & Rockstroh, B. (1997). Visuell induzierte Gammabandaktivität im menschlichen EEG—Ausdruck corticaler Reizrepräsentation? *Zeitschrift für Experimentelle Psychologie*, *44*, 186–212.

Müller, M.M., Gruber, T., & Keil, A. (2000). Modulation of induced gamma band activity in the human EEG by attention and visual information processing. *International Journal of Psychophysiology*, *38*, 283–300.

Müller, M.M., Junghöfer, M., Elbert, T., & Rockstroh, B. (1997). Visually induced gamma-band responses to coherent and incoherent motion: A replication study. *NeuroReport*, 8, 2575–2579.

Munk, M.H.J., Roelfsema, P.R., König, P., Engel, A.K., & Singer, W. (1996). Role of reticular activation in the modulation of intracortical synchronization. *Science*, *272*, 271–274.

Murthy, V.N., Aoki, F., & Fetz, E.E. (1994). Synchronous oscillations in sensorimotor cortex of awake monkeys and humans. In C. Pantev, T. Elbert, & B. Lutkenhöner (Eds.), *Oscillatory event related brain dynamics*. New York: Plenum Press.

Murthy, V.N., & Fetz, E.E. (1992). Coherent 25- to 35-Hz oscillations in the sensorimotor cortex of awake behaving monkeys. *Proceedings of the National Academy of Science USA*, *89*, 5670–5674.

Neisser, U. (1967). *Cognitive psychology*. New York: Appleton.

Palmer, T., & Tzeng, O.J.L. (1990). Cerebral asymmetry in visual attention. *Brain and Cognition*, *13*, 46–58.

Posner, I.P., & Petersen, S.E. (1990). The attention system of the human brain. *Annual Review of Neuroscience*, *13*, 25–42.

Posner, M.I., & Dehaene, S. (1994). Attentional networks. *Trends in Neuroscience*, *17*, 75–79.

Posner, M.I., Snyder, C.R.R., & Davidson, B.J. (1980). Attention and detection of signals. *Journal of Experimental Psychology: General*, *109*, 160–174.

Pulvermüller, F. (1999). Words in the brain's language. *Behavioural and Brain Sciences*, *22*, 253–336.

Pulvermüller, F., Keil, A., & Elbert, T. (1999). High frequency brain activity: perception or active memory? *TICS*, *3*, 250–252.

Rodriguez, E., George, N., Lachaux, J.P., Martinerie, J., Renault, B., & Varela, F.J. (1999). Perception´s shadow: Long-distance synchronization of human brain activity. *Nature*, *397*, 430–433.

Roelfsema, P.R., Engel, A.K., König, P., & Singer, W. (1997). Visuomotor integration is associated with zero time-lag synchronization among cortical areas. *Nature*, *385*, 157–161.

Rougeul-Buser, A., & Buser, B. (1994). Electrocortical rhythms in the attentive cat: Phenomenological data and theoretical issues. In C. Pantev, T. Elbert, & B. Lutkenhöner (Eds.), *Oscillatory event related brain dynamics*. New York: Plenum Press.

Sem-Jacobsen, C.W., Petersen, M.C., Dodge, H.W., Lazarte, J.A., & Holman, C.B. (1956). Electroencephalographic rhythms from depths of the parietal, occipital and temporal lobes in man. *Electroencephalography and Clinical Neurophysiology*, *8*, 263–278.

Sheer, D.E. (1970). Electrophsiological correlates in memeory consolidation. In G. Ungar (Ed.), *Molecular mechanisms in memory and learning* (pp. 177–211). New York: Plenum Press.

Sheer, D.E. (1989). Sensory and cognitive 40-Hz event-related potentials: Behavioral correlates, brain function, and clinical application. In E. Basar & T.H. Bullock (Eds.), *Brain-dynamics: Progress and perspectives* (pp. 339–374). Berlin: Springer Verlag.

Singer, W. (1994). Putative functions of temporal correlations in neocortical processing. In C. Koch & J.L. Davis (Eds.), *Large-scale neuronal theories of the brain* (pp. 201–237). Cambridge, MA: MIT Press.

Singer, W., Engel, A.K., Kreiter, A.K., Munk, M.H.J., Neunschwander, S., & Roelfsema, P.R. (1997). Neuronal assemblies: Necessity, signature and detectability. *Trends in Cognitive Science*, *1*, 252–261.

Singer, W., & Gray, C.M. (1995). Visual feature integration and the temporal correlation hypothesis. *Annual Review of Neuroscience, 18*, 555–586.
Sokolov, A., Lutzenberger, W., Pavlova, M., Preissl, H., Braun, C., & Birbaumer, N. (1999). Gamma-band MEG activity to coherent motion depends on task-driven attention. *NeuroReport, 10*, 1997–2000.
Spydell, J.D., & Sheer, D.E. (1982). Effect of problem solving on right and left hemisphere 40 Hertz EEG activity. *Psychophysiology, 19*, 420–425.
Steriade, M., Amzica, F., & Contreras, D. (1996). Synchroization of fast (30–40 Hz) spontaneous rhythms during brain activation. *Journal of Neuroscience, 16*, 392–417.
Tallon, C., Bertrand, O., Bouchet, P., & Pernier, J. (1995). Gamma-range activity evoked by coherent visual stimuli in humans. *European Journal of Neuroscience, 7*, 1285–1291.
Tallon-Baudry, C., & Bertrand, O. (1999). Oscillatory gamma activity in humans and its role in object representation. *TICS, 3*, 151–162.
Tallon-Baudry, C., Bertrand, O., Delpuech, C., & Pernier, J. (1996). Stimulus specifity of phase-locked and non-phase-locked 40-Hz visual response in human. *Journal of Neuroscience, 16(13),* 4240–4249.
Tallon-Baudry, C., Bertrand, O., Delpuech, C., & Pernier, J. (1997). Oscillatory gamma-band (30–70 Hz) activity induced by a visual search task in human. *Journal of Neuroscience, 17*, 722–734.
Tallon-Baudry, C., Bertrand, O., Peronnet, F., & Pernier, J. (1998). Induced gamma-band activity during the delay of a visual short-term memory task in humans. *Journal of Neuroscience, 18*, 4244–4254.
Tallon-Baudry, C., Bertrand, O., Wienbruch, C., Ross, B., & Pantev, C. (1997). Combined EEG and MEG recordings of visual 40-Hz responses to illusory triangles in human. *NeuroReport, 8*, 1103–1107.
Tiitinen, H., Sinkkonen, J., Reinikainen, K., Alho, K., Lavikainen, J., & Näätänen, R. (1993). Selective attention enhances the auditory 40-Hz transient response in humans. *Nature, 364*, 59–60.
Tipper, S.P., & Weaver, B. (1998). The medium of attention: Location based, object centered, or scene based. In R.D. Wright (Ed.), *Visual attention* (pp. 77–107). New York: Oxford University Press.
Tootell, R.B.H., Dale, A.M., Sereno, M.I., & Malach, R. (1996). New images from human visual cortex. *Trends in Neuroscience, 19*, 481–489.
Treisman, A. (1993). The perception of features and objects. In A.D. Baddeley & L. Weiskrantz (Eds.), *Attention: Selection, awareness, and control—a tribute to Donald Broadbent* (pp. 5–35). Oxford, UK: Clarendon Press/Oxford University Press.
Treisman, A. (1998). Feature binding, attention and object perception. *Philosophical Transactions of the Royal Society, Series B, 353*, 1295–1306.
Treisman, A., & Gormican, S. (1988). Feature analysis in early vision: Evidence from search asymmetries. *Psychological Review, 95*, 15–48.
Treisman, A.M., & Gelade, G. (1980). A feature-integration theory of attention. *Cognitive Psychology, 12*, 97–136.
Ungerleider, L.G. (1995). Functional brain imaging studies of cortical mechanisms for memory. *Science, 270*, 769–775.
Ungerleider, L.G., & Haxby, J.V. (1994). "What" and "where" in the human brain. *Current Opinion in Neurobiology, 4*, 157–165.
Zeki, S. (1993). *A vision of the brain.* Oxford, UK: Blackwell.

VISUAL COGNITION, 2001, *8* (3/4/5), 593–608

Gamma activity in human EEG is related to high-speed memory comparisons during object selective attention

Christoph S. Herrmann and Axel Mecklinger

Max-Planck Institute of Cognitive Neuroscience, Leipzig, Germany

Among the most important processes of the brain in order to correctly perceive the outside world and act within it are binding, attention, and memory. All three functional mechanisms have been associated with brain activity in the gamma frequency range. It needs to be clarified, however, which subprocesses within the gamma frequency range relate to which perceptual or cognitive functions. In a visual discrimination task, we used Kanizsa figures whose constituent inducer disks need to be bound together to perceive the illusory contours. By a variation of the task requirements we manipulated the allocation of object selective attention as compared to a previous study. One out of four objects had to be detected. This detection process requires the comparison of two object dimensions (form and collinearity) with a working memory template. In order to get behavioural and electrophysiological measures, EEG and reaction times were recorded from 16 and 10 subjects, respectively. We demonstrated that the early evoked gamma activity reflects the process of allocating attention to a selected object as early as 50–150 ms after stimulus onset. We propose that the underlying mechanism is a high-speed memory comparison. In addition, we show that this early gamma activity also determines the reaction times needed to respond to the different stimuli.

INTRODUCTION

Binding and attention are both necessary for the correct function of perceptual processes in the brain. Binding is necessary to link together the different features of single objects that are represented in a distributed fashion in the brain.

Please address all correspondence to C. Herrmann, Max-Planck Institute of Cognitive Neuroscience, PO Box 500 355, 04303 Leipzig, Germany. Email: herrmann@cns.mpg.de

We would like to thank Mark A. Elliott for his editorial work and three anonymous referees for valuable comments on an earlier version of this manuscript. We also express our thanks to Diana Böttger who helped to prepare the experimental set up, to Cornelia Schmidt for collecting the data, and to Andrea Sandmann who helped to design the figures. Diana Böttger was partly supported by DFG grant SCHR 375/8-1.

http://www.tandf.co.uk/journals/pp/13506285.html DOI:10.1080/13506280143000142

The mechanism of attention serves to focus onto a small subset of the vast amount of incoming information. It is still unclear how exactly these two mechanisms operate or interact. Binding is believed to operate at a very early stage in human information processing. According to the temporal correlation hypothesis, the simultaneous firing of neurons indicates that they code features of the same object (Singer & Gray, 1995; von der Malsburg & Schneider, 1986). Electrophysiological studies on humans and animals show strong evidence that brain activity in the gamma frequency range (approximately 30–80 Hz, mostly 40 Hz) could be the correlate of feature binding (Gray, König, Engel, & Singer, 1989; Tallon-Baudry & Bertrand, 1999). Nevertheless, it has been questioned whether gamma activity in the human electroencephalogram (EEG) really reveals processes of feature binding or rather relates to memory access (Pulvermüller, Keil, & Elbert, 1999).

If binding elicits gamma activity in the brain it seems plausible to assume that stimuli which oscillate at a frequency in the gamma range result in enhanced processing by the brain. This lead to an experiment of Elliott and Müller (1998) who demonstrated that stimuli flickering in the gamma range can enhance visual binding. In that study, Kanizsa-like figures had to be detected and reaction time (RT) significantly decreased when target-relevant cues were preattentively flickering at a frequency of 40 Hz prior to the detection period, as compared to other flickering frequencies. Further investigation by Elliott and Müller (2000) with the same paradigm has revealed that an object representation persisted with a 40 Hz oscillatory code for several hundred milliseconds. These findings are in line with previous results about high-speed memory processes in the same frequency range: Jensen and Lisman (1998) demonstrated in simulations that high-speed access to working memory may operate at frequencies in the gamma range, and Burle and Bonnet (2000) performed an auditory interference task suggesting an oscillatory process in working memory. The paradigm of Elliott and Müller also evokes gamma oscillations in the human EEG that determine the enhanced processing when target-relevant cues are presented (Elliott, Herrmann, Mecklinger, & Müller, 2000).

Gamma activity has not only been correlated with binding and memory, but there is also evidence that the same type of activity correlates with attention (Başar-Eroglu, Strüber, Schürmann, Stadler, & Başar, 1996; Müller, Gruber, & Keil, 2000; Tiitinen et al., 1993). In a recent EEG-experiment, Herrmann, Mecklinger, and Pfeiffer (1999) showed that an early gamma response in a visual discrimination task was larger for target stimuli than for non-target stimuli. In that experiment, Kanizsa squares and triangles (Kanizsa, 1976) as well as non-Kanizsa squares and triangles were visually presented to the subjects. The four different stimuli (Figure 1) were comprised of the two features form (3 vs. 4 inducer disks) and collinearity (presence/absence of an illusory Kanizsa figure due to collinear arrangement of the inducer disks). The authors formulated

Figure 1. The four stimulus types used in the experiment: (a) Kanizsa square, (b) Kanizsa triangle, (c) non-Kanizsa square (target), and (d) non-Kanizsa triangle.

the hypothesis that the target effect of the early gamma activity was reflecting an attentional top-down process of stimulus selection.

The objective of the present experiments was to further investigate the possibility of early gamma activity reflecting a process of object-selective attention. Especially, we wanted to investigate how such a process operates and interacts with working memory. In our experiments, we used the identical four stimuli used in the study of Herrmann et al. (1999) but changed the task requirements for the subjects. Whereas Herrmann et al. (1999) used the Kanizsa square as the target, we here defined the non-Kanizsa square as the target that had to be counted. If the assumption is true, that the early gamma activity reflects an attentional process of object selection, it should be largest for the non-Kanizsa square in our new experiment. The amplitude of the visual N170 (negative deflection around 170 ms) was assumed to reflect physical and perceptual properties of the stimuli in the experiment of Herrmann et al. (1999). If this is true, the order of N170 amplitude for the four stimuli should not change in our new experiment. The event-related potential P300 (positive deflection around 300 ms) is known to reflect attentional mechanisms and to be maximal in response to infrequent targets (Donchin & Coles, 1988; Mecklinger & Ullsperger, 1993). Thus, the P300 should also be largest for the non-Kanizsa square. In order to gain additional insights in the attentional mechanism engaged in object selection, we also recorded RTs from another group of subjects performing the same task.

In a previous experiment with the four previously-mentioned stimuli, in which MEG and RTs were recorded simultaneously, Herrmann and Mecklinger (2000) demonstrated that targets (Kanizsa squares) were processed slowest even though they constituted a Kanizsa figure, whereas faster non-targets did not constitute Kanizsa figures. The RT pattern suggested a two-fold mechanism of comparing the two dimensions form and collinearity of an encoded stimulus with a pattern held in working memory. The stimulus which was most dissimilar to the target (non-Kanizsa triangle) was processed fastest in their experiment. In our new experiment, we defined the non-Kanizsa square as the target and expected it to be processed slowest, whereas we expected the most dissimilar stimulus (Kanizsa triangle) to be processed fastest.

METHODS

In our EEG experiment, subjects had to count the occurrence of target stimuli among non-target stimuli. This made the experiment comparable to the one of Herrmann et al. (1999) and keeps EEG responses free from motor artefacts. In order to also acquire behavioural measures of the task, we conducted an additional reaction-time experiment (RT experiment). In the RT experiment subjects had to respond with their right index finger to targets and with their left index finger to non-targets, yielding RTs and error measures under stimulation conditions identical with the EEG experiment.

Subjects

Sixteen subjects with a mean age of 22.6 years (ranging from 18 to 26 years, 7 female) participated in the EEG experiment and ten subjects with a mean age of 23.1 years (ranging from 19 to 31 years, 7 female) participated in the RT experiment. All subjects were right-handed and had normal or corrected-to-normal vision. They showed no signs of neurological or psychiatric disorders and all gave written informed consent to participate in the study.

Stimuli

The stimuli used in this paradigm were composed of three or four inducer disks, which either constitute a Kanizsa figure due to their collinear arrangement (Figure 1a and b) or don't constitute one (Figure 1c and d). The stimuli were identical to those of Herrmann et al. (1999) and varied across two dimensions, which we will refer to as form and collinearity dimension. The dimension "form" determines whether a stimulus is composed of three or four inducer disks, whereas the dimension "collinearity" determines whether a stimulus constitutes a Kanizsa figure due to the collinear arrangement of its inducer disks.

The stimuli were presented for 700 ms with randomized intertrial-intervals ranging from 1000 to 1500 ms. Figures were displayed in black together with a black central fixation cross on white background. Stimuli subtended a visual angle of 4°17' including inducer disks, while the induced illusory figures subtended 2°86' (Figure 2). Thus, the whole stimulus is projected into the field of central vision, i.e., the central 5 degrees of the macular region (Zeki, 1993). Fixation crosses were displayed foveally (0.02°). The ratio of the radius of the inducer disks and the side-length of the illusory figures was 1:4.

Figures were displayed on a computer monitor placed 1 m in front of the subjects. Subjects were instructed to silently count the appearance of the non-Kanizsa square (targets). The experiment was run in four blocks with 100 stimuli per block. The four stimulus types were presented equally probable in a pseudo-randomized order resulting in a target probability of .25.

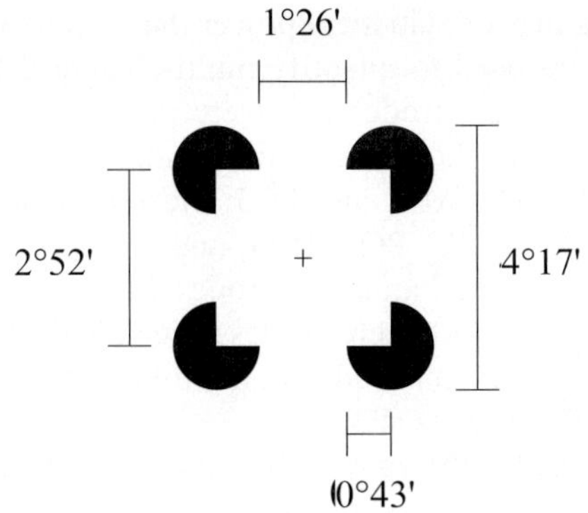

Figure 2. Size of the used stimuli in visual degrees.

Data acquisition

The EEG was recorded with NeuroScan amplifiers using 64 tin electrodes mounted in an elastic cap. Electrodes were placed according to the international 10-10 system. The ground electrode was placed near the left mastoid (M1) and all electrodes were referenced to the left mastoid. Electrode impedance was kept below 5kΩ. Horizontal and vertical electrooculogram (EOG) recordings were registered with four additional electrodes. Data were sampled at 500 Hz and analog-filtered with a 0.05 Hz high-pass and a 100 Hz low-pass filter. An additional, digital 20 Hz low-pass filter was applied before displaying the ERP data.

Averaging epochs lasted from 200 ms before to 900 ms after stimulus onset. All epochs were visually inspected for artefacts and rejected if eye-movement artefacts, muscle artefacts, or electrode drifts were visible. Three subjects had to be excluded from further analysis due to excessive eye-movements. Baselines were computed in the –200–0 ms interval in each single trial and subtracted prior to computing the event-related potential (ERP) averages.

Data analysis

For the interpretation of gamma activity it is assumed to be important that the oscillations occur either phase-locked to a stimulus (evoked activity) or with variable phase relative to a stimulus (induced activity). For the analysis of gamma activity, a wavelet transform based on Morlet wavelets was employed (Herrmann et al., 1999). To differentiate between evoked and induced activity, each subject's ERP is transformed yielding evoked gamma activity and averages of transforms of single epochs are computed yielding induced activity.

In order to avoid a loss of statistical power that is inherent when repeated measures ANOVAs are used to quantify multi-channel EEG data (Oken & Chiappa, 1986), selected electrode sites were pooled to four topographical regions of interest (ROIs). The left anterior region (LAR) was comprised of electrodes FP1, F7, F3, F5, AF7, and FC3; the left posterior region (LPR) included electrodes P7, P5, P3, PO7, PO3, and O1. Regions over the right hemisphere included the homologous electrodes. For statistical analyses, ERP amplitudes were pooled across the electrodes in each of the ROIs. ERP components were defined as mean amplitudes in the following time intervals: 130–180 ms (N170) and 300–500 ms (P300).

EEG data was analysed with two ANOVAs: In one of them, the two stimulus dimensions form and collinearity were used as factors with levels square vs. triangle and collinear vs. non-collinear, respectively. We will refer to this type of ANOVA as stimulus-ANOVA, since it differentiates between the features of a stimulus. In addition, we computed a second type of ANOVA contrasting the target with the mean of the three non-targets. We will refer to this as the response-ANOVA, since it reflects the response requirements. (See Table 1.) ANOVAs conducted for EEG data had an additional factor topography (anterior, posterior).

These repeated-measures ANOVAs were also computed for RTs and error rates of the RT experiment. RTs on trials in which a response error was made, were rejected from the data, as well as trials in which the RT exceeded 2.5 standard deviations of the mean.

Before analysing gamma responses, we evaluated the signal-to-noise ratio (SNR) of the time interval to be analyzed. In order to achieve this, we computed SNR-ANOVAs to determine whether the mean amplitude in specific time intervals (50–150 ms and 200–300 ms) differs significantly from the noise in the baseline (–100–0 ms). Only if this is the case, subsequent ANOVAs which test variations due to experimental conditions make sense.

TABLE 1
Overview of the statistical tests for the experimental variables

Statistical test	*Factors*	*Factor level*
Stimulus-ANOVA	form	(Kan4, Non4) vs. (Kan3, Non3)
	collinearity	(Kan4, Kan3) vs. (Non4, Non3)
Response-ANOVA	targetness	Non4 vs. (Kan4, Kan3, Non3)

The four figural stimuli are abbreviated as Kan (Kanizsa figures) and Non (non-Kanizsa figures) and numbers indicate the number of inducer disks.

RESULTS

Behavioural data

The response-ANOVA for the RTs of the RT experiment yielded a significant main effect, $F(1, 9) = 16.58, p < .005$, demonstrating that targets are processed slower (665 ms) than non-targets (632 ms). The stimulus-ANOVA yielded significant effects of collinearity, $F(1, 9) = 16.27, p < .005$, and form, $F(1, 9) = 42.26, p < .0001$, indicating longer RTs for squares than for triangles as well as longer RTs for non-Kanizsa figures than Kanizsa figures. In addition, the stimulus-ANOVA yielded a significant collinearity × form interaction, $F(1, 9) = 9.96, p = .01$. Post-hoc comparisons revealed that within the triangles there is a significant effect of collinearity, $F(1, 9) = 65.73, p < .0001$, but not within the squares (Figure 3, left).

The response-ANOVA for the error rates yielded a significant main effect of targetness, $F(1, 9) = 15.98, p < .005$, indicating more errors for targets (7.4%) than for non-targets (3.4%). The stimulus-ANOVA of the error rates yielded a significant form effect, $F(1, 9) = 14.70, p < .005$, revealing that error rates are higher for squares than for triangles. Basically, the pattern of the error rates resembles that of the RTs (Figure 3, right). The fact that the pattern of errors is not inverse to that of RTs indicates that we are not dealing with a speed-accuracy trade-off, but an effect of feature processing (Pachella, 1974).

ERP responses

Figure 4 shows the ERPs at selected electrodes over frontal, central, parietal, and occipital areas. In all conditions, there is a prominent N170 peak around 170 ms which is strongest in occipital electrodes. An additional P300 peaks around 400 ms and is strongest for the target condition.

The stimulus-ANOVA for the time interval of the N170 yielded significant effects of collinearity, $F(1, 12) = 39.12, p < .0001$, and form, $F(1, 12) = 13.40, p < .005$. Amplitudes were larger for squares than for triangles and larger for

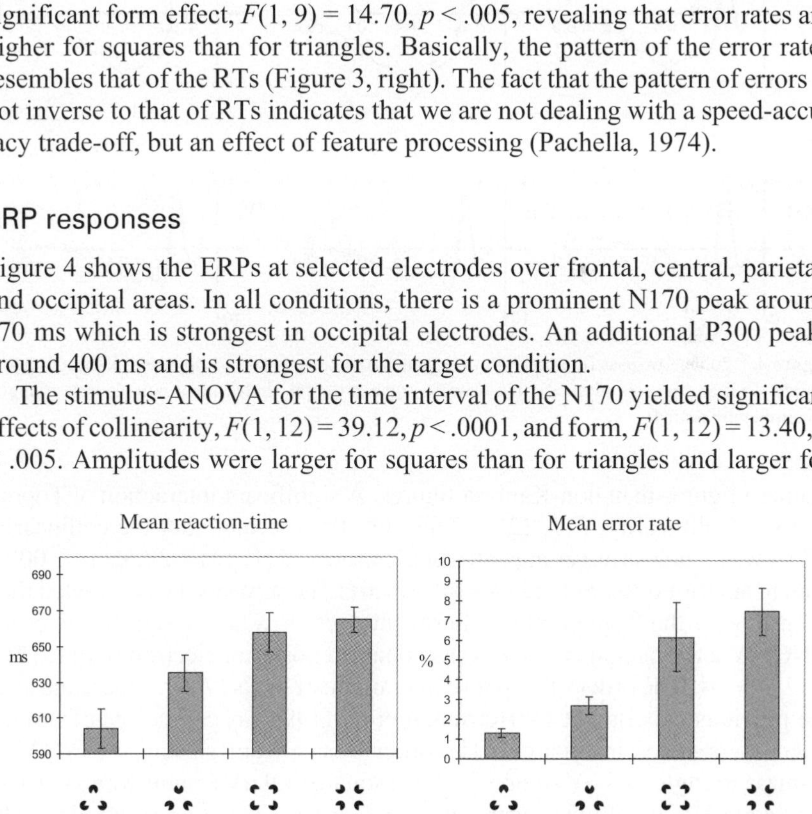

Figure 3. Mean RTs and error rates (means and standard errors of means) for the RT experiment.

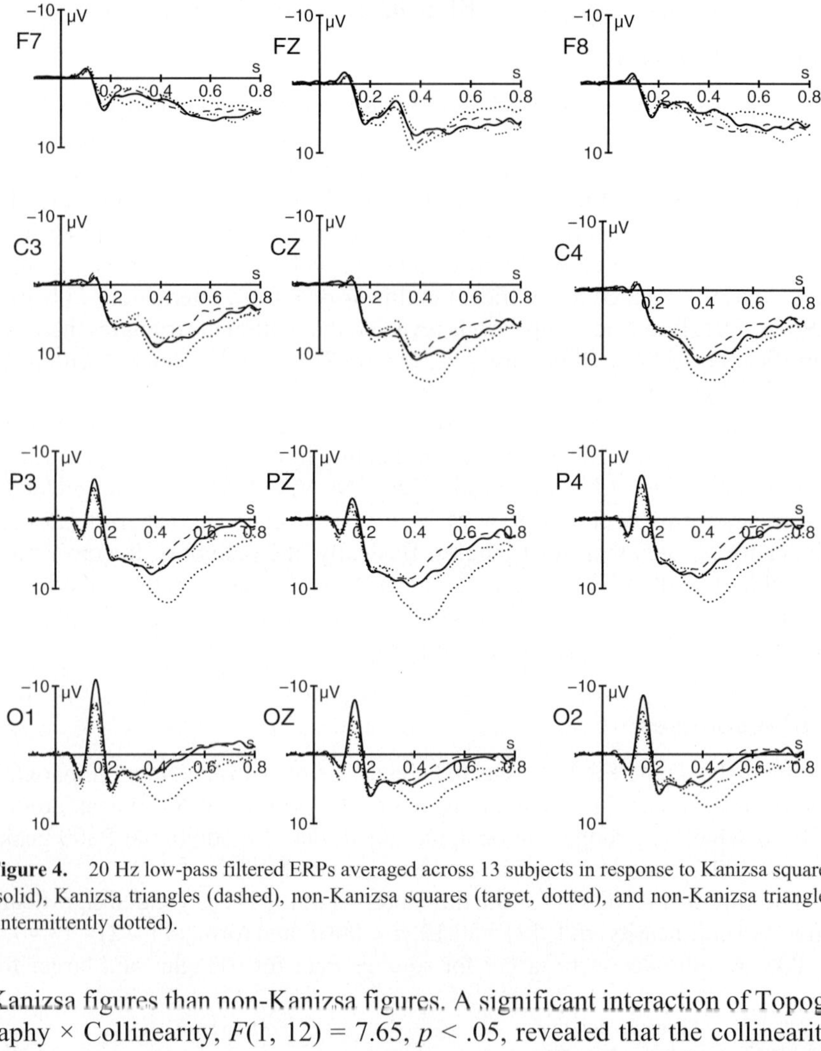

Figure 4. 20 Hz low-pass filtered ERPs averaged across 13 subjects in response to Kanizsa squares (solid), Kanizsa triangles (dashed), non-Kanizsa squares (target, dotted), and non-Kanizsa triangles (intermittently dotted).

Kanizsa figures than non-Kanizsa figures. A significant interaction of Topography × Collinearity, $F(1, 12) = 7.65$, $p < .05$, revealed that the collinearity effect was much stronger at posterior electrodes, $F(1, 12) = 28.02$, $p < .0005$, than in anterior ones, $F(1, 12) = 9.40$, $p < .01$. The post-hoc tests revealed that, even though the Topography × Form interaction was not significant in the ANOVA, a form main effect was significant at posterior electrodes, $F(1, 12) = 9.77$, $p < .01$. The order of response magnitude of the N170 was the same as in the previous experiment by Herrmann et al. (1999) as can be seen from the direct comparison in Figure 5. The order was: > Kanizsa square (7.9 μV) > Kanizsa triangle (6.4 μV) > non-Kanizsa square (5.9 μV) > non-Kanizsa triangle (4.5 μV); amplitudes were averaged across posterior electrodes. The response-ANOVA yielded no significant effect.

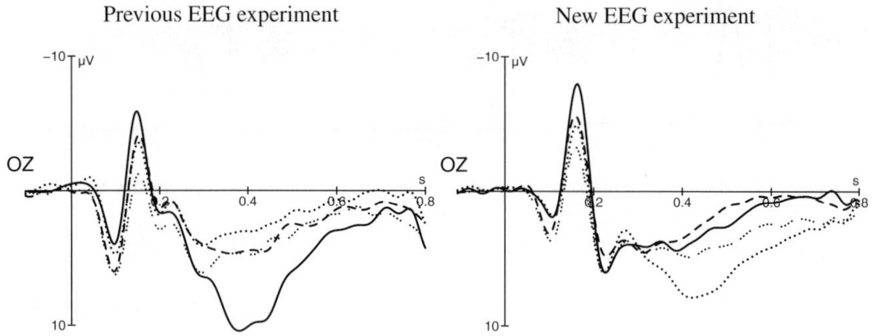

Figure 5. ERPs of electrode OZ for experiments 1 and 2. N170 components are independent of task requirements. The P300 component is affected by the task change between experiments and is delayed in latency and reduced in amplitude.

The response-ANOVA for the time interval of the P300 yielded a significant main effect for targetness, $F(1, 12) = 14.39$, $p < .005$, indicating larger potentials for targets (6.6 µV, amplitudes averaged across all electrodes) than non-targets (5.0 µV). A significant interaction of Topography × Targetness, $F(1, 12) = 7.80$, $p < .05$, justified post-hoc comparisons in the different regions. The target effect was only significant at posterior electrodes, $F(1, 12) = 27.30$, $p < .0005$, but not in anterior ones, $F(1, 12) = 0.12$. The stimulus-ANOVA yielded significant main effects of form, $F(1, 12) = 16.96$, $p < .005$, squares (6.3 µV) being greater than triangles (5.2 µV), and collinearity, $F(1, 12) = 4.75$, $p < .05$, collinear (5.4 µV) figures being greater than non-collinear ones (6.2 µV). Significant interactions were found for Topography × Form, $F(1, 12) = 6.91$, $p < .05$, Topography × Collinearity, $F(1, 12) = 5.36$, $p < .05$, and Form × Collinearity, $F(1, 12) = 5.61$, $p < .05$. Post-hoc comparisons in the individual regions revealed significant effects of form, $F(1, 12) = 20.42$, $p < .001$, squares (6.5 µV) being greater than triangles (4.7 µV) and collinearity, $F(1, 12) = 12.40$, $p < .005$, collinear (4.9 µV) figures being greater than non-collinear ones (6.3 µV) in posterior electrodes but no effects in anterior electrodes.

In the previous EEG experiment by Herrmann et al. (1999), the target-P300 had a latency of 382 ms and an amplitude of 18.1 µV at the PZ recording site. In the present EEG experiment, P300 latency was delayed (444 ms) and its amplitude reduced (14.5 µV).

Gamma responses

The SNR-ANOVA for the evoked gamma activity yielded a significant effect of SNR for the early time interval (50–150 ms), $F(1, 12) = 11.52$, $p < .01$, but not for the late time interval (200–300 ms). This is illustrated for three electrodes (O1, OZ, and O2) in Figure 6. A clear peak can be seen for three of the four

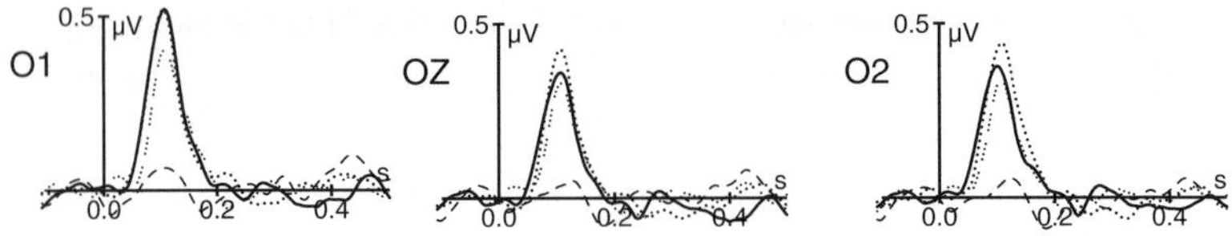

Figure 6. Grand average of the evoked gamma activity across 13 subjects in electrodes, O1, OZ, and O2. A clear peak is visible around 100 ms after stimulus onset.

conditions with a maximum around 100 ms. No difference from baseline is visible after this peak.

The SNR-ANOVA for the induced gamma activity yielded no significant effects. This implies that the SNR of induced gamma activity did not differ from the pre-stimulus baseline period. For this reason we refrained from further analysis of induced gamma activity. The induced gamma activity is illustrated for three electrodes (O1, OZ, and O2) in Figure 7 where no clear peaks can be seen that differ from the baseline activity.

The response-ANOVA for the time interval 50–150 ms of the evoked gamma activity yielded a significant main effect of targetness, $F(1, 12) = 4.93$, $p < .05$, indicating larger gamma activity for the target as compared to the nontargets. The stimulus-ANOVA yielded a significant main effect for form, $F(1, 12) = 5.04$, $p < .05$, indicating larger amplitudes for squares than for triangles. The topographical distribution of the early evoked gamma response is displayed in Figure 8.

Figure 9 shows the total amount of early evoked gamma activity summed across all analysed electrodes for the four conditions. It is obvious that the pattern resembles that of RTs and error rates, i.e., early evoked gamma activity is stronger the more similar a stimulus is to the target. A correlation analysis of the early evoked gamma activity (50–150 ms, averaged across all electrodes and 13 subjects) and the RTs (averaged across 10 subjects) of the four conditions ($n = 4$) revealed a correlation coefficient of 0.9749 ($p < .05$). Notably, the correlation of 0.18 between RT and N170 amplitude was not significant.

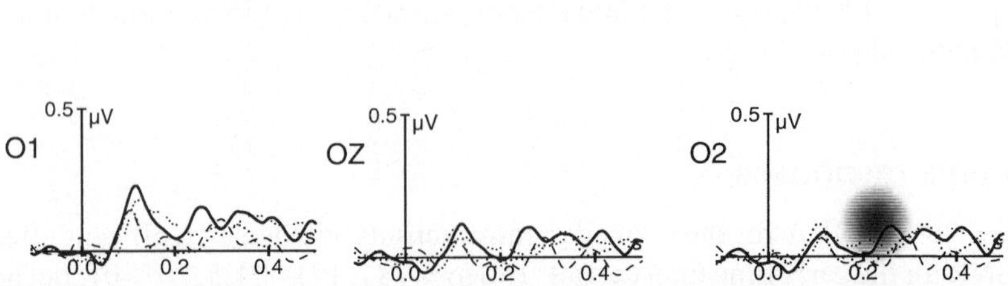

Figure 7. Grand average of the induced gamma activity across 13 subjects in electrodes, O1, OZ, and O2. No clear difference from baseline activity can be observed.

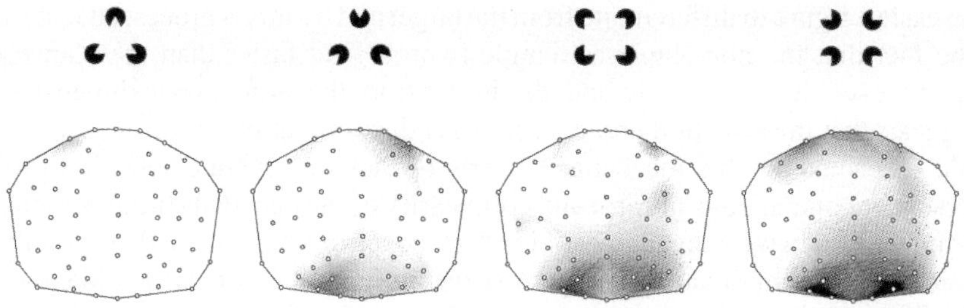

Figure 8. Topography of the early evoked gamma activity for the conditions Kanizsa triangle, non-Kanizsa triangle, Kanizsa square, and non-Kanizsa square (from left to right) in the time interval 50–150 ms averaged over 13 subjects. Gray-scale is from 0 μV (white) to 0.5 μV (black).

DISCUSSION

Behavioural data

From the behavioural data we can see that RTs and error rates show a typical pattern of target discrimination. As expected, the target, which occurs less frequently than the non-targets, is processed slowest (Teichner & Krebs, 1974). In a previous experiment by Herrmann and Mecklinger (2000) this was even the case when the Kanizsa square was the target which would otherwise be expected to be processed faster than a non-Kanizsa square due to its figural features (Pomerantz, 1983). As has been argued by Herrmann and Mecklinger (2000), the pattern of RTs is considered to represent a classification of the targets according to the two dimensions form and collinearity. In our new experiment, the Kanizsa-triangle is dissimilar in both dimensions which define the target: It is composed of three instead of four inducer disks (form) and in contrast to the target constitutes a Kanizsa figure (collinearity). Therefore, it is

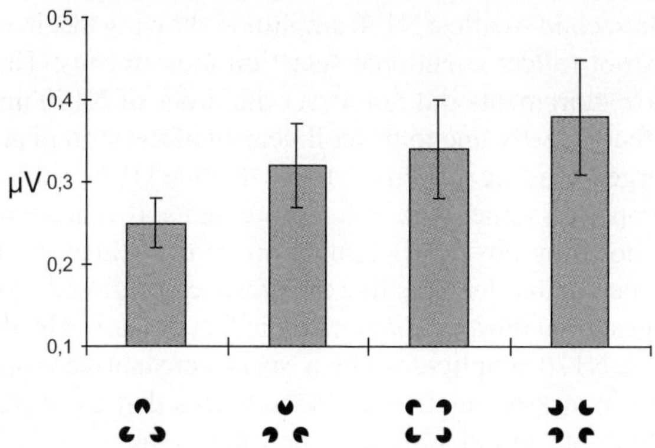

Figure 9. Total amount of early evoked gamma activity (50–150 ms) summed across all analysed electrodes as a function of experimental condition.

the easiest figure to differentiate from the target and by this is processed fastest. The fact that the non-Kanizsa triangle is processed faster than the Kanizsa square, even though they are both dissimilar from the target in one dimension, suggests that the selection process for target discrimination operates as a twofold mechanism. This mechanism seems to include separate selection processes for comparisons of form and collinearity of the encoded stimulus with a template held in working memory. The fact that error rates did not differ significantly when stimuli varied only across the dimension collinearity while they did differ significantly when stimuli varied across the dimension form might be taken to indicate that the dimension form is more salient to the human visual system. This would also explain why the Kanizsa squares are processed slower than the non-Kanizsa triangles that both share one dimension with the target: The Kanizsa square varies across the less salient dimension collinearity, whereas the non-Kanizsa triangle varies across the more salient dimension form.

ERP responses

The order of N170 amplitude is the same as in the previous experiment by Herrmann et al. (1999) as can be seen from the direct comparison in Figure 5 (Kanizsa square > Kanizsa triangle > non-Kanizsa square > non-Kanizsa triangle). From the previous experiment it could have been concluded that the N170 reflects perceptual processes of illusory contour detection, since the N170 was larger for Kanizsa figures as compared to non-Kanizsa figures. But this effect might have been confounded by the Kanizsa square being the target, since attentional selection processes are known to sometimes influence early ERP components (Heinze et al., 1994). In our new experiment, the order of N170 amplitude did not change relative to the former experiment: The target now evoked the second smallest N170 amplitude showing that in our paradigm the N170 does not reflect attentional selection mechanisms. Thus, since the change in task requirements did not affect the order of N170 amplitude, the collinearity effect is really due to the collinearity of the stimuli and not a confound of the target. This nicely demonstrates that the N170 is driven by physical stimulus properties rather than task requirements. It is noteworthy that the N170 reflects not only physical stimulus properties (three vs. four inducer disks) but also perceptual features like the presence of illusory contours. This effect also suggests that illusory contours are in fact processed by the subjects.

The order of N170 amplitude which stays constant across experiments despite changes in task requirements also indicates that the stimuli possess a certain salience to our visual system. According to the order of N170 amplitude, stimuli that are composed of more inducer disks and stimuli which constitute illusory contours appear to be more salient.

The P300 showed a clear target effect in our EEG experiment. But it was delayed in latency and reduced in amplitude as compared to the previous EEG experiment (Herrmann et al., 1999). This suggests that the detection of the non-Kanizsa square is harder than the detection of the Kanizsa square which is more salient according to our above definition.

Gamma responses

It has been previously stated that the early evoked gamma activity is a purely stimulus-driven component, not being sensitive to perceptual/cognitive functions (Karakaş & Başar, 1998). In addition, comparable experiments with Kanizsa and non-Kanizsa figures failed to demonstrate differences between experimental conditions (real triangle, illusory triangle, non-triangle) in the early evoked gamma activity and the effects of targetness were not investigated (Tallon, Bertrand, Bouchet, & Pernier, 1995; Tallon-Baudry, Bertrand, Delpuech, & Pernier, 1996). We were able to show that changing the task across experiments while keeping the perceived stimuli identical changes the early evoked gamma response, whereas other early responses as the N170 were not affected by this attentional variable. Similar changes of early evoked gamma activity with task changes have been found in MEG recordings (Herrmann & Mecklinger, 2000). This indicates that early evoked gamma activity reflects a top-down mechanism involved in selecting the proper response to a stimulus that cannot be purely sensory in origin. In order to differentiate targets from non-targets, both features of a stimulus (form and collinearity) have to be compared to a template in working memory. It has been shown in simulations that high-speed access to working memory may operate at frequencies in the gamma range (Jensen & Lisman, 1998). Furthermore, Burle and Bonnet (2000) showed behavioural data from an auditory interference task, which also suggest an oscillatory process in working memory. Elliott and Müller (2000) showed that the representation of visual objects in working memory is accomplished by gamma oscillations. Therefore, the presence of a template in working memory may be critical for the generation of gamma activity in our task.

A model that accounts for our pattern of results can be sketched as follows: The plain access to working memory itself is probably not a candidate for generating the gamma response, since the amplitude of gamma activity varies for different stimuli and there is no apparent reason why the strength of memory access should vary across stimuli. But the process that compares the perceived stimuli with the template in working memory may well be the generator of the gamma activity. We demonstrated that within the three non-target stimuli the stimulus that is dissimilar to the target stimulus in two features (Kanizsa triangle) is processed faster than those that differ in only one feature. This indicates that the comparison process seems to operate as a two-fold process, separately comparing the two features of which a target is composed. Whenever one of these two comparisons yields a positive result (Kanizsa square and non-Kanizsa triangle), this results in enhanced gamma activity as compared to both comparisons yielding negative results (Kanizsa triangle). When both comparisons yield positive results (non-Kanizsa square), we see the maximal amount of gamma activity. Thus, it seems plausible to assume that a positive comparison with working memory leads to a reinforced feedback of the frequency at which the process operates anyway, i.e., the 40 Hz are amplified more the better a perceived stimulus matches the template. This activity could then propagate to cortical areas that are relevant for correct task performance.

A further interesting result of our EEG and RT experiments was that the early evoked gamma activity correlates significantly with RTs, even though both measures were taken in different experiments. Thus, the gamma activity which peaks around 100 ms is an indicator for the much later motor reaction (approximately 600 ms). It has been reported previously that finger movements are accompanied by 40 Hz activity in the motor cortex (Pfurtscheller, Flotzinger, & Neuper, 1994). Therefore, it seems likely that early evoked gamma activity can be functionally related with motor gamma activity. Due to the additional fact that the evoked gamma activity is highly synchronized to the stimulus (evoked gamma), we think that the process underlying the correlation of early evoked gamma activity and the motor reaction is what Roelfsema, Engel, König, and Singer (1997) have described as visuomotor integration. Roelfsema et al. found highly synchronized gamma activity with zero time-lag between visual and motor areas in cats. If the selection process accessing working memory and the motor process both operate at 40 Hz, this constitutes an ideal mechanism for effective information transmission. Therefore, we render it important for future experiments to investigate the correlation of early evoked gamma activity and later motor gamma activity.

In the results of Herrmann et al. (1999) and Herrmann and Mecklinger (2000) the early evoked gamma activity was distributed more frontally than in this experiment. An unexpected result of this study was the rather occipital topography of the early evoked gamma activity. Further experiments will be needed to investigate the topography of the early evoked gamma activity in detail.

REFERENCES

Başar-Eroglu, C., Strüber, D., Schürmann, M., Stadler, M., & Başar, E. (1996). Gamma-band responses in the brain: A short review of psychophysiological correlates and functional significance. *International Journal of Psychophysiology, 24,* 101–112.

Burle, B., & Bonnet, M. (2000). High-speed memory scanning: A behavioural argument for a serial oscillatory model. *Cognitive Brain Research, 9,* 327–337.

Donchin, E., & Coles, M.G.H. (1988). Is the P300 component a manifestation of context updating? *Behavioural Brain Science, 11,* 357–374.

Elliott, M.A., Herrmann, C.S., Mecklinger, A., & Müller, H.J. (2000). The loci of oscillatory visual-object priming: A combined electroencephalographic and reaction-time study. *International Journal of Psychophysiology, 38*(3), 225–242.

Elliott, M.A., & Müller, H.J. (1998). Synchronous information presented in 40-Hz flicker enhances visual feature binding. *Psychological Science, 9*(4), 277–283.

Elliott, M.A., & Müller, H.J. (2000). Evidence for a 40 Hz oscillatory short-term visual memory revealed by human reaction-time measurements. *Journal of Experimental Psychology Learning, Memory and Cognition, 26*(3), 703–718.

Gray, C.M., König, P., Engel, A.K., & Singer, W. (1989). Oscillatory response in the cat visual cortex exhibit intercolumnar synchronization which reflects global stimulus properties. *Nature, 338*, 334–337.

Heinze, H.J., Mangun, G.R., Burchert, W., Hinrichs, H., Scholz, M., Münte, T.F., Gös, A., Scherg, M., Johannes, S., Hundeshagen, H., Gazzaniga, M.S., & Hillyard, S.A. (1994). Combined spatial and temporal imaging of brain activity during visual selective attention in humans. *Nature, 372,* 543–546.

Herrmann, C.S. & Mecklinger, A. (2000). Magnetoencephalographic responses to illusory figures: Early evoked gamma is affected by processing of stimulus features. *International Journal of Psychophysiology, 38*(3), 265–281.

Herrmann, C.S., Mecklinger, A., & Pfeiffer, E. (1999). Gamma responses and ERPs in a visual classification task. *Clinical Neurophysiology, 110*(4), 636–642.

Jensen, O., & Lisman, J. (1998). An oscillatory short-term memory buffer model can account for data on the Sternberg task. *Journal of Neuroscience, 18*(24), 10688–10699.

Kanizsa, G. (1976). Subjective contours. *Scientific American, 234*(4), 48–52.

Karakaş, S., & Başar, E. (1998). Early gamma response is sensory in origin: A conclusion based on cross-comparison of results from multiple experimental paradigms. *International Journal of Psychophysiology, 31,* 13–31.

Mecklinger, A., & Ullsperger, P. (1993). P3 varies with stimulus categorization rather than probability. *Electroencephalography and Clinical Neurophysiology, 86,* 395–407.

Müller, M.M., Gruber, T., & Keil, A. (2000). Modulation of induced gamma band activity in the human EEG by attention and visual processing. *International Journal of Psychophysiology, 38*(3), 283–300.

Oken, B.S., & Chiappa, K.H. (1986). Statistical issues concerning computerized analysis of brainwave topography. *Annals of Neurology, 19,* 493–494.

Pachella, R.G. (1974). The interpretation of reaction time in information processing research. In B. Kantowitz (Ed.), *Human information processing.* Hillsdale, NJ: Lawrence Erlbaum Associates Inc.

Pfurtscheller, G., Flotzinger, D., & Neuper, C. (1994). Differentiation between finger, toe and tongue movement in man based on 40 Hz EEG. *Electroencephalography and Clinical Neurophysiology, 90,* 456–460.

Pomerantz, J.R. (1983). Global and local precedence: Selective attention in form and motion preception. *Journal of Experimental Psychology: General, 112,* 516–540.

Pulvermüller, F., Keil, A., & Elbert, T. (1999). High-frequency brain activity: Perception or active memory. *Trends in Cognitive Science, 3*(7), 250–252.

Roelfsema, P.R., Engel, A.K., König, P., & Singer, W. (1997). Visuomotor integration is associated with zero time-lag synchronization among cortical areas. *Nature, 385,* 157–161.

Singer, W., & Gray, C.M. (1995). Visual feature integration and the temporal correlation hypothsis. *Annual Reviews in Neuroscience, 18,* 555–586.

Tallon, C., Bertrand, O., Bouchet, P., & Pernier, J. (1995). Gamma-range activity evoked by coherent visual stimuli in humans. *European Journal of Neuroscience, 7,* 1285–1291.

Tallon-Baudry, C., & Bertrand, O. (1999). Oscillatory gamma activity in humans and its role in object representation. *Trends in Cognitive Science, 3*(4), 151–162.

Tallon-Baudry, C., Bertrand, O., Delpuech, C., & Pernier, J. (1996). Stimulus specificity of phase-locked and non-phase-locked 40 Hz visual responses in human. *Journal of Neuroscience, 16*(13), 4240–4249.

Teichner, W.H., & Krebs, M.J. (1974). Laws of visual choice reaction time. *Psychological Reviews, 81*(1), 75–98.

Tiitinen, H., Sinkkonen, J., Reinikainen, K., Alho, K., Lavikainen, J., & Näätänen, R. (1993). Selective attention enhances the auditory 40-Hz transient response in humans. *Nature, 364,* 59–60.

von der Malsburg, C., & Schneider, W. (1986). A neural cocktail-party processor. *Biological Cybernetics, 54,* 29–40.

Zeki, S. (1993). *A vision of the brain.* Oxford, UK: Blackwell Scientific Publications.

VISUAL COGNITION, 2001, *8* (3/4/5), 609–621

EEG gamma-band response during the perception of Necker cube reversals

Daniel Strüber and Canan Başar-Eroglu

Institute of Psychology and Cognition Research & Center for Cognitive Sciences, University of Bremen, Germany

Michael Miener

Institut für Grenzgebiete der Psychologie und Psychohygiene e.V., Freiburg, Germany

Michael Stadler

Institute of Psychology and Cognition Research & Center for Cognitive Sciences, University of Bremen, Germany

In two former studies our research group reported frontal gamma-band enhancement during multistable visual perception and reversal rate dependent differences in the gamma-band. In these studies, a dynamic reversible figure was used which was based on the phenomenon of apparent motion. The aim of this study was to examine whether the results obtained with a dynamic motion paradigm can be replicated with the static Necker cube. The results demonstrate a general frontal gamma-band enhancement and higher induced gamma activity for subjects with a relatively high reversal rate in comparison to subjects with a relatively low reversal rate. This pattern of results fits well to the findings obtained with the dynamic motion paradigm. Therefore, the important role of frontal gamma activity for figure reversals has received further evidence. The results support the involvement of attentional top-down processing of figure reversal that is not directly related to binding processes.

Please address all correspondence to D. Strüber, Institute of Psychology and Cognition Research & Center for Cognitive Sciences, University of Bremen, PO Box 330440, D-28334 Bremen, Germany. Email: strueber@uni-bremen.de

We are thankful to Birgit Mathes for her help in analysing the data.

http://www.tandf.co.uk/journals/pp/13506285.html DOI:10.1080/13506280143000151

INTRODUCTION

Reversible or ambiguous figures like the Necker cube or Rubin's vase/faces make up a well-known class of visual phenomena leading to spontaneous alternations between different stable percepts or interpretations without a physical change of the stimulus (e.g., Attneave, 1971). Since the first "observations on some remarkable phenomenon which occurs on viewing a figure of a crystal or geometrical solid" by Necker (1832), a lot of research has aimed at determining the factors that control the perceptual alternations inherent in the reversal phenomenon. Understanding the processes that underlie perceptual multistability is considered to provide valuable insights into the mechanisms of perceptual organization in general (e.g., Gregory, 1998; Rock, 1983). For a recent review on multistable phenomena see Leopold and Logothetis (1999).

From the neurophysiological point of view, frequencies in the gamma range are associated with processes of perceptual organization, especially with binding together multiple stimulus features to form one coherent object. Binding-related gamma responses have been found in single-cell studies with animals (Gray & Singer, 1987, 1989; Gray, König, Engel, & Singer, 1989; Eckhorn et al., 1988; Engel, König, Kreiter, Schillen, & Singer, 1992; Kreiter & Singer, 1992, 1996), as well as in scalp-recorded EEGs of human subjects (Herrmann, Mecklinger, & Pfeifer, 1999; Lutzenberger, Pulvermüller, Elbert, & Birbaumer, 1995; Müller et al., 1996; Tallon, Bertrand, Bouchet, & Pernier, 1995; Tallon-Baudry, Bertrand, Delpeuch, & Pernier, 1996). Psychophysical experiments provide further evidence for the relevance of gamma activity for binding processes (Elliott & Müller, 1998; Kojo, Liinasuo & Rovamo, 1993). However, the functional correlates of the gamma-band are multifold, ranging from purely sensory origin (Karakaş & Başar, 1998) to short-term memory (Tallon-Baudry, Bertrand, Peronnet, & Pernier, 1998; Tallon-Baudry, Kreiter, & Bertrand, 1999), associative learning (Miltner, Braun, Arnold, Witte, & Taub, 1999), attention (Shibata et al., 1999; Tiitinen et al., 1993), and linguistic processing (Pulvermüller, Lutzenberger, Preissl, & Birbaumer, 1995). For a review of functional correlates of the gamma-band see Başar-Eroglu, Strüber, Schürmann, Stadler, and Başar (1996b).

Our research group reported frontal gamma-band enhancement during multistable visual perception and discussed possible functional correlates of the gamma response related to perceptual multistability (Başar-Eroglu, Strüber, Kruse, Başar, & Stadler, 1996a). In a follow-up study (Strüber, Başar-Eroglu, Hoff, & Stadler, 2000), we analysed the gamma-band separately for subjects with low and high reversal rates since it was assumed that differences in the processing of reversible figures as reflected in the remarkable reversal rate variability among observers correspond to topographical and/or amplitude differences in the gamma-band. The results demonstrated for both the low-rate switchers (LRS) and the high-rate switchers (HRS) the highest gamma activity at frontal locations which was consistent with our earlier study (Başar-Eroglu, Strüber, Kruse et al., 1996a). Differences between the subgroups were found in the overall level of gamma activity such that the HRS showed higher gamma activity than the LRS at all locations. However, in both the previously mentioned studies the same dynamic reversible figure was used, based on the phenomenon of apparent motion. Since it was shown in psychophysical studies (e.g., Long & Olszweski, 1999; Strüber & Stadler, 1999) that the type of reversible figure is an important variable in studying the reversal phenomenon, one should avoid drawing too broad generalizations from findings obtained with only a single reversible figure. For instance, Strüber and Stadler (1999) examined differences in top-down effects on the reversal rate depending on the category of reversible figures (structural perspective reversals like the Necker cube versus meaningful content reversals like the duck/rabbit figure) and found that top-down processes can act more effectively on a change of meaningful images than on a change of a rather abstract geometrical structure. This finding demonstrated a distinct role of top-down mechanisms for the processing of different types of reversible figures. Since the gamma-band results of Strüber et al. (2000) were interpreted to reflect attentional top-down processes, it is an interesting question whether the same pattern of results is maintained with another type of reversible figure or whether the gamma-band results indicate different top-down influences according to the type of reversible figure.

Therefore, the purpose of the present study was to investigate whether the previously described gamma-band results obtained with a dynamic motion paradigm can be replicated with a static reversible figure like the Necker cube.

METHODS

Subjects

The subjects were 20 (12 female, 8 male; aged between 19 and 30 years) healthy, right-handed, neurologically normal students of Psychology at Bremen University, who volunteered to participate. All subjects had normal or corrected-to-normal vision. They were instructed to maintain fixation all the time and to minimize blinking and eye movements.

Electrophysiological recording

The EEG was recorded from Ag-AgCl electrodes at F3, F4, C3, C4, P3, P4, O1, and O2 locations according to the 10–20 system (Jasper, 1958). The electrodes were affixed with Grass electrode paste. Linked earlobe electrodes served as reference. Electrode impedance did not exceed 5 kOhm. EOG (medial upper and lateral orbital rim of the right eye) was also registered. The EEG was amplified by means of a Nihon Kohden (EEG-4421 G) EEG apparatus with band limits 0.1–70 Hz (24 dB/octave). The EEG was digitized on-line with a sampling rate of 250 samples per second and stored on the hard disc of the computer for off-line EEG analysis. An additional notch filter (36 dB/octave) was also applied to remove the mains interference. For the recording of EOG, the time constant 0.3 s with a low pass filter at 70 Hz was used. All channels were displayed on paper and on-line by monitor scope in order to observe both single trials and averaged signals. An additional EMG recording was carried out in order to estimate the contribution of the motor potentials to the main recording.

Stimulus patterns

We used a reversible Necker cube as stimulus with 10 cm line length of the outline cube (Figure 1). At a viewing distance between subject and computer monitor of 150 cm the resulting visual angle for the Necker cube was 3.81°. The stimulus was presented with white lines on a black background. As indicated in Figure 1, one corner of the cube served as fixation point.

Procedure

The subjects sat in a soundproof and echo-free room which was dimly illuminated. After recording of the spontaneous EEG (subjects had to look at a fixation point, no pattern was presented) the Necker cube was presented on a computer screen and the subjects were asked to describe what they perceived. All subjects reported the spontaneous perspective reversals without any further instruction after a few minutes of inspection time. The subjects were instructed

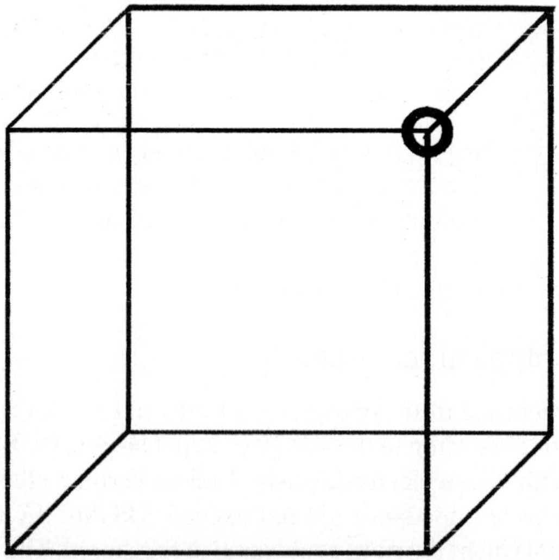

Figure 1. The Necker cube. The circle marks the corner of the cube that served as fixation point. It was not present during the experiment.

to press a button whenever a reversal was perceived, and to look at the fixation point all the time. After a short training session of 2–3 min duration the subjects were asked to suppress eye blinks and saccadic movements, especially during the reversal periods. This training session also served to bring the reversal rate of the subjects into a stable phase that reflects their individual rate, since it is known that the reversal rate increases during the first 2–3 min of observation (Borsellino, De Marco, Allazetta, Rinesi, & Bartolini, 1972; Kruse, Stadler, & Wehner, 1986). Then the Necker cube was presented continuously for 400 s of data collection. The button press served as an indicator for the endogenously induced pattern reversal.

Data analysis

Grouping of the subjects. The subjects were divided into two subgroups according to their reversal rates. Subjects with more than 76 reversals within the 400 s were defined as high-rate switchers (HRS, n = 10, 6 females). The HRS exhibited a mean reversal rate of 113.3 (SD = 36.4) ranging from 87 to 205 reversals. Subjects with a reversal rate below 76 switches were defined as low-rate switchers (LRS, n = 10, 6 females). The LRS produced a mean reversal rate of 51.6 (SD = 23.9) ranging from 17 to 75 reversals. As cut-off point for the separation of the subjects we used the median score.

Selection of time windows. The time window in which the data were recorded had a duration of 2 s and lasted from 1 s before until 1 s after the button press (finger movement-onset = 0). The second before the button press (t = –1000–0 ms) enclosed the reversal phase with the spontaneous switching, the reaction time needed for pressing the button, and the premovement potentials preceding the button press. According to our earlier studies concerning ERPs and multistable visual perception (Başar-Eroglu, Strüber, Stadler, Kruse, & Başar, 1993; Başar-Eroglu, Strüber, Stadler, Kruse, & Greitschus, 1995; Isoglu-Alkac et al., 1998), perceptual switching related ERPs were elicited at approximately 500 ms before the button press. Therefore, the data were analysed in the time window –500–0 ms (button press).

Selective averaging and artefact rejection of data. An automatic on-line artefact rejection procedure was used for the elimination of global artifactual EEG-epochs. These epochs contained movement artefacts, excessive muscle activities, and amplitudes exceeding 50 μV at any electrode. Additionally, in an off-line procedure, the on-line recorded, digitized, and stored single artefact-free EEG-epochs were selected. The EOG-channel was visually inspected for each trial, and trials with eye movement or blink artefact were rejected. The number of artefact-free epochs for the HRS was reduced at random in order to get a corresponding number of epochs to the LRS. The remaining artefact-free epochs were then averaged in two ways. First, for the whole sample (without a distinction between HRS and LRS) in order to demonstrate perceptual switching related ERPs and, second, separately for each subgroup in the gamma range as described in the next section. Additionally, the spontaneous EEG was analysed in the gamma band as a control condition.

Digital filtering and root mean square values. The data were digitally band-pass filtered in the gamma range (28–48 Hz). To measure the amplitudes of the event-related gamma oscillations, root mean square (RMS) values were computed for the time window –500–0 ms on the single trial level. Calculating RMS values from single trials represents the non-phase-locked or induced oscillatory activity (Fell, Hinrichs, & Röschke, 1997). In contrast to phase-locked or evoked activity (RMS values from the time domain averages of the oscillations), the induced oscillatory responses seem to be a more reliable measure in multistable perception, because it is not possible to determine the event (reversal) directly to which the oscillations are phase-locked (Strüber et al., 2000).

RESULTS

Figure 2 shows the ERPs induced by the figure reversals for the frontal electrodes of each hemisphere. As can be seen, a slow positive wave occurred in the time window –500–0 ms. The broadness of this P300-like component is due to an inter- and intra-individual latency jitter according to the variable reaction times of the subjects when indicating a reversal by the button press.

Figure 3 presents the grand averages of the event-related gamma oscillations for each location and the LRS and HRS, respectively. Both subgroups show the highest gamma amplitudes at frontal locations. However, averaging the event-related oscillations in the time domain (as shown in Figure 3) enhances the phase-locked oscillations only, while the non phase-locked or induced oscillations will be diminished. As mentioned earlier, the interpretation of phase-

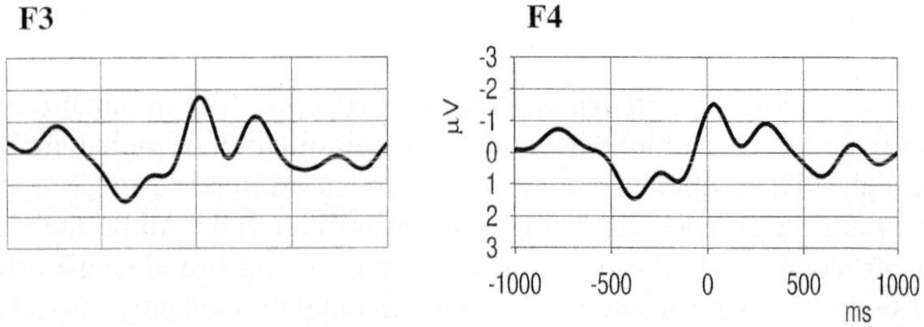

Figure 2. Grand average ERPs induced by the figure reversal for the left and right frontal electrodes ($n = 20$). A slow positive wave occurred in the time window –500 ms to 0 ms ($t = 0$ refers to the button press). The ERPs were band-pass filtered (0.5–4 Hz).

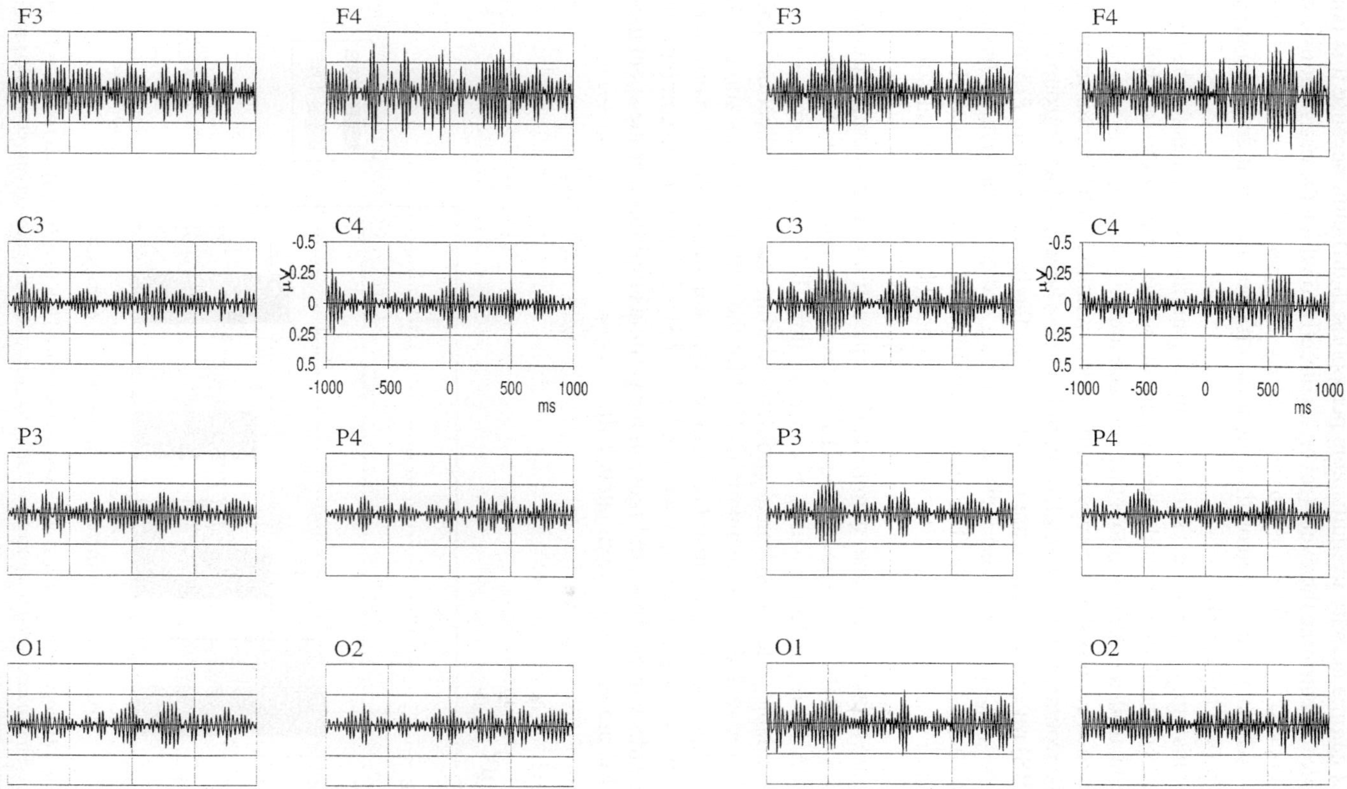

Figure 3. Grand averages of the event-related gamma oscillations for the LRS (left) and the HRS (right). for all locations. x-axis: time in ms ($t = 0$ refers to the button press); y-axis: amplitude in μV.

locked gamma activity in multistable perception is difficult, because it is not possible to determine the event (reversal) directly to which the oscillations are phase-locked. Therefore, for statistical analyses we used the absolute RMS values, which are measured on the single sweep level, i.e., the induced gamma activity (see Figure 4).

The histogram of Figure 4 shows the mean gamma RMS values for the LRS and HRS separately at frontal, central, parietal, and occipital areas (the left and right electrodes were taken together for each area).

A two-way ANOVA for repeated measures with the within-factor location (levels: frontal, central, parietal, occipital) and the between-factor group (LRS vs. HRS) revealed a significant main effect for the factor location, $F(3, 54) = 12.2$, $p < .001$, Greenhouse-Geisser corrected, indicating an overall frontal gamma band enhancement. The main effect for the factor group was also significant, $F(1, 18) = 4.7$, $p < .05$, indicating higher gamma RMS values for the HRS.

Figure 5 shows the mean gamma RMS values of the spontaneous EEG for the LRS and HRS. The spontaneous EEG was analysed in a separate two-way ANOVA for repeated measures, because for three LRS no spontaneous EEG was available due to technical problems during the data collection. The ANOVA revealed a significant main effect for the within-factor location, $F(3, 45) = 5.9$, $p < .01$, Greenhouse-Geisser corrected, but no significant main effect for the between-factor group was found, $F(1, 15) = 2.7$, $p > .05$. In comparison to the RMS values shown in Figure 4, the gamma amplitudes of the spontaneous EEG are less by approximately half.

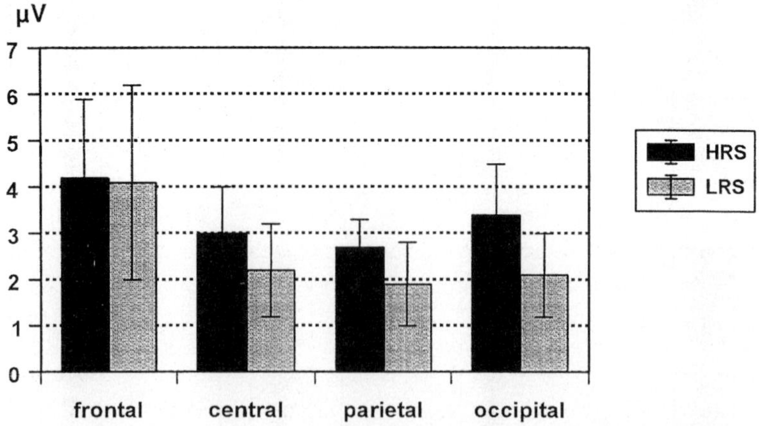

Figure 4. Histogram of grand average RMS values for the HRS ($n = 10$) and the LRS ($n = 10$) at frontal, central, parietal, and occipital areas during the perception of Necker cube reversals. Bars indicate standard deviation.

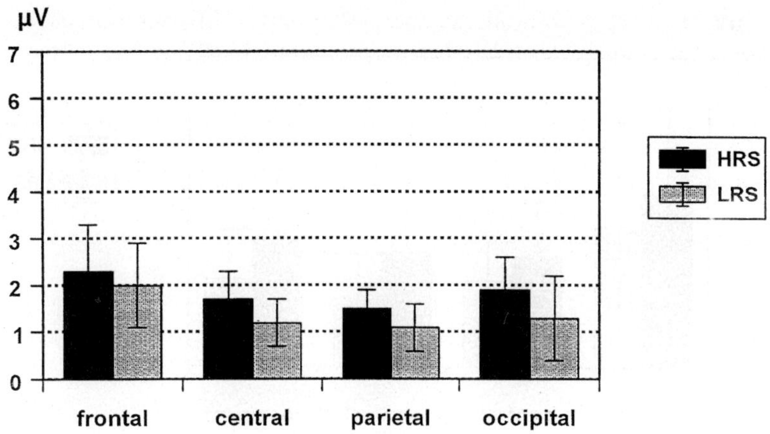

Figure 5. Histogram of grand average RMS values of the spontaneous EEG for the HRS ($n = 10$) and the LRS ($n = 7$) at frontal, central, parietal, and occipital areas. Bars indicate standard deviation.

DISCUSSION

The purpose of this study was to examine whether gamma-band responses during the perception of Necker cube reversals correspond to the results obtained with a dynamic apparent motion paradigm (Başar-Eroglu, Strüber, Kruse et al., 1996a; Strüber et al., 2000). The results of the present study demonstrate a general frontal gamma-band enhancement during Necker cube reversals that is congruent with the findings of Başar-Eroglu, Strüber, Kruse et al. (1996a). The spontaneous gamma activity shows also a frontal topography, but the gamma amplitudes are half as high as during the perception of the Necker cube reversals. The HRS exhibited higher induced gamma activity than the LRS on an overall level when perceiving the Necker cube reversals. This result is nearly identical to the findings of Strüber et al. (2000), which are shown in Figure 6.

Therefore, the important role of frontal gamma activity for figure reversals has received further evidence. According to the interpretation of Strüber et al. (2000), this frontal topography strongly supports the involvement of attentional top-down processing. The relevance of gamma oscillations for attentional mechanisms is also underlined by recent studies concerning the processing of Kanizsa figures (Herrmann & Mecklinger, 2000; Herrmann et al., 1999; Herrmann & Mecklinger, this issue). In these studies, it could be shown that even the early (approximately 100 ms after stimulus onset) evoked gamma is sensitive to attentional top-down processes according to the task demands and not necessarily to bottom-up related binding processes.

In the present study, we cannot give an exact time course of the gamma activity because of the lack of an external stimulus onset in multistable perception. Therefore, it is not yet possible to identify gamma responses which could

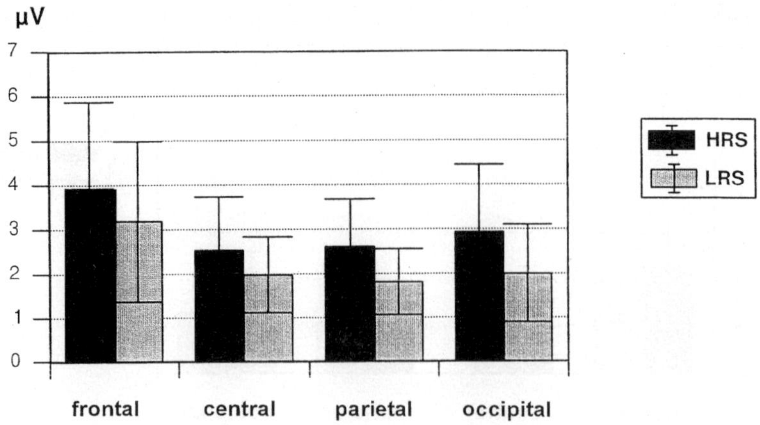

Figure 6. Histogram of grand average RMS values for the HRS and the LRS at frontal, central, parietal, and occipital areas (from Strüber et al., 2000). Bars indicate standard deviation.

be related directly to the de-binding of the actual perceptual alternative until the reversal occurs and the re-binding after the reversal. The occurrence of the slow positive wave may help to define the time of reversal more precisely since this P300-like component reflects the conscious recognition of the reversal and, therefore, indicates the closure of the switching process more directly than the button press. Theoretically, perceptual switching-related gamma activity that reflects binding processes should be stronger in a time interval preceding the positive peak.

However, the gamma amplitude differences between HRS and LRS point to a more general function of the gamma band that could be related to task demands. According to their fast reversal rate, the task of reporting the reversals is probably more demanding for the HRS than for the LRS. Thus, the enhanced gamma activity for the HRS may reflect states of higher arousal, alertness, and/or attention (Desmedt & Tomberg, 1994; Sheer, 1989). This interpretation takes into account that the reversal rate is relatively constant for one individual (e.g., Borsellino et al., 1972; Frederiksen & Guilford, 1934) as long as the subjects are not instructed to control the reversal rate voluntarily (e.g., Strüber & Stadler, 1999). The results of the spontaneous EEG where no task had to be performed are also congruent with this interpretation, because the gamma activity of the HRS and LRS did not differ significantly. However, there is a tendency (although not significant) also for the gamma activity of the spontaneous EEG to be higher for the HRS than for the LRS. From this speculative point of view, gamma-band differences between the subgroups may reflect trait variables that are independent of task demands. As mentioned earlier, the individual reversal rate is known to be relatively constant over time and there are reports in the literature that the reversal rate is correlated with intelligence

(Crain, 1961; Holt & Matson, 1974), personality traits (Frederiksen & Guilford, 1934; Meredith, 1967; Shiomi, 1982), and cognitive flexibility (Klintman, 1984). Combining such correlations with a neurophysiological marker like the gamma activity is a challenge for future research.

In conclusion, the results of the present study replicate the main findings of Başar-Eroglu, Strüber, Kruse et al. (1996a) and Strüber et al. (2000) with another reversible figure. The results, therefore, further support the involvement of top-down processing in figure reversal. To get a more detailed picture of the reversal rate-dependent gamma-band differences between HRS and LRS, further research is needed.

REFERENCES

Attneave, F. (1971). Multistability in perception. *Scientific American, 225,* 62–71.

Başar-Eroglu, C., Strüber, D., Kruse, P., Başar, E., & Stadler, M. (1996a). Frontal gamma-band enhancement during multistable visual perception. *International Journal of Psychophysiology, 24,* 113–125.

Başar-Eroglu, C., Strüber, D., Schürmann, M., Stadler, M., & Başar, E. (1996b). Gamma-band responses in the brain: A short review of psychophysiological correlates and functional significance. *International Journal of Psychophysiology, 24,* 101–112.

Başar-Eroglu, C., Strüber, D., Stadler, M., Kruse, P., & Başar, E. (1993). Multistable visual perception induces a slow positive EEG wave. *International Journal of Neuroscience, 73,* 139–151.

Başar-Eroglu, C., Strüber, D., Stadler, M., Kruse, P., & Greitschus, F. (1995). Slow positive potentials in the EEG during multistable visual perception. In P. Kruse & M. Stadler (Eds.), *Ambiguity in mind and nature: Multistable cognitive phenomena* (pp. 389–405). Springer: Berlin.

Borsellino, A., De Marco, A., Allazetta, A., Rinesi, S., & Bartolini, B. (1972). Reversal time distribution in the perception of visual ambiguous stimuli. *Kybernetik, 10,* 139–144.

Crain, K. (1961). Binocular rivalry: Its relationship to intelligence, and a general theory of its nature and physiological correlates. *Journal of General Psychology, 64,* 259–283.

Desmedt, J.E., & Tomberg, C. (1994). Transient phase-locking of 40 Hz electrical oscillations in prefrontal and parietal human cortex reflects the process of conscious somatic perception. *Neuroscience Letters, 168,* 126–129.

Eckhorn, R., Bauer, R., Jordan, W., Brosch, M., Kruse, W., Munk, M., & Reitboeck, H.J. (1988). Coherent oscillations: A mechanism of feature linking in the visual cortex? *Biological Cybernetics, 60,* 121–130.

Elliott, M.A., & Müller, H.J. (1998). Synchronous information presented in 40 Hz flicker enhances visual feature binding. *Psychological Science, 9,* 277–283.

Engel, A.K., König, P., Kreiter, A.K., Schillen, T.B., & Singer, W. (1992). Temporal coding in the visual cortex: New vistas on integration in the nervous system. *Trends in Neurosciences, 15,* 218–226.

Fell, J., Hinrichs, H., & Röschke, J. (1997). Time course of human 40 Hz EEG activity accompanying P3 response in an auditory oddball paradigm. *Neuroscience Letters, 235,* 121–124.

Frederiksen, N.O., & Guilford, J.P. (1934). Personality traits and fluctuations of the outline cube. *American Journal of Psychology, 46,* 470–474.

Gray, C.M., König, P., Engel, A.K., & Singer, W. (1989). Oscillatory response in the cat visual cortex exhibit intercolumnar synchronization which reflects global stimulus properties. *Nature, 338,* 334–337.

Gray, C.M., & Singer, W. (1987). Stimulus specific neuronal oscillations in the cat visual cortex: A cortical function unit [Abstract]. *Journal of the Society of Neuroscience, 404,* 3.

Gray, C.M., & Singer, W. (1989). Stimulus-specific neuronal oscillations in orientation columns of cat visual cortex. *Proceedings of the National Academy of Sciences, USA, 86, 16*98–1702.

Gregory, R.L. (1998). *Eye and brain: The psychology of seeing* (5th edn., p. 194). Oxford, UK: Oxford University Press.

Herrmann, C.S., & Mecklinger, A. (2000). Magnetoencephalographic responses to illusory figures: Early evoked gamma is affected by processing of stimulus features. *International Journal of Psychophysiology, 38,* 265–281.

Herrmann, C.S., Mecklinger, A., & Pfeifer, E. (1999). Gamma responses and ERPs in a visual classification task. *Clinical Neurophysiology, 110,* 636–642.

Holt, G.L., & Matson, J.L. (1974). Necker cube reversals as a function of age and IQ. *Bulletin of the Psychonomic Society, 4,* 519–521.

Isoglu-Alkac, Ü., Başar-Eroglu, C., Ademoglu, A., Demiralp, T., Miener, M., & Stadler, M. (1998). Analysis of the electroencephalographic activity during the Necker cube reversals by means of the wavelet transform. *Biological Cybernetics, 79,* 437–442.

Jasper, H.H. (1958). The ten twenty electrode system of the International Federation. *Electroencephalography and Clinical Neurophysiology, 10,* 371–375.

Karakaş, S., & Başar, E. (1998). Early gamma responses is sensory in origin: A conclusion based on cross-comparison of results from multiple experimental paradigms. *International Journal of Psychophysiology, 31,* 13–31.

Klintman, H. (1984). Original thinking and ambiguous figure reversal rates. *Bulletin of the Psychonomic Society, 22,* 129–131.

Kojo, I., Liinasuo, M., & Rovamo, J. (1993). Spatial and temporal properties of illusory figures. *Vision Research, 33,* 897–901.

Kreiter, A.K., & Singer, W. (1992). Oscillatory neuronal responses in the visual cortex of the awake macaque monkey. *European Journal of Neuroscience, 4,* 369–375.

Kreiter, A.K., & Singer, W. (1996). Stimulus-dependent synchronization of neuronal responses in the visual cortex of the awake macaque monkey. *The Journal of Neuroscience, 16,* 2381–2396.

Kruse, P., Stadler, M., & Wehner, T. (1986). Direction and frequency specific processing in the perception of long-range apparent movement. *Vision Research, 26,* 327–335.

Leopold, D.A., & Logothetis, N.K. (1999). Multistable phenomena: Changing views in perception. *Trends in Cognitive Sciences, 3,* 254–264.

Long, G.M., & Olszweski, A.D. (1999). To reverse or not to reverse: When is an ambiguous figure not ambiguous? *American Journal of Psychology, 112,* 41–71.

Lutzenberger, W., Pulvermüller, F., Elbert, T., & Birbaumer, N. (1995). Visual stimulation alters local 40-Hz responses in humans: An EEG study. *Neuroscience Letters, 183,*1–4.

Meredith, G.M. (1967). Some attributive dimensions of reversibility phenomena and their relationship to rigidity and anxiety. *Perceptual and Motor Skills, 24,* 843–849.

Miltner, W.H.R., Braun, C., Arnold, M., Witte, H., & Taub, E. (1999). Coherence of gamma-band EEG activity as a basis for associative learning. *Nature, 397,* 434–436.

Müller, M.M., Bosch, J., Elbert, T., Kreiter, A.K., Sosa, M.V., Sosa, P.V., & Rockstroh, B. (1996). Visually induced gamma-based responses in human electroencephalographic activity: A link to animal studies. *Experimental Brain Research, 112,* 96–102.

Necker, L.A. (1832). Observations on some remarkable phenomenon which occurs on viewing a figure of a crystal or geometrical solid. *The London and Edinburgh Philosophical Magazine and Journal of Science, 3,* 329–337.

Pulvermüller, F., Lutzenberger, W., Preissl, H., & Birbaumer, N. (1995). Spectral responses in the gamma band: Physiological signs of higher cognitive processing? *NeuroReport, 6,* 2059–2064.

Rock, I. (1983). *The logic of perception.* Cambridge, MA: MIT Press.

Sheer, D.E. (1989). Sensory and cognitive 40 Hz event–related potentials: Behavioural correlates, brain function, and clinical application. In E. Başar & T.H. Bullock (Eds.), *Brain dynamics* (pp. 339–374). Berlin: Springer.

Shibata, T., Shimoyama, I., Ito, T., Abla, D., Iwasa, H., Koseki, K., Yamanouchi, N., Sato, T., & Nakajima, Y. (1999). Attention changes the peak latency of the visual gamma-band oscillation of the EEG. *NeuroReport, 10,* 1167–1170.

Shiomi, K. (1982). Relationship between reversible-figure latencies and scores on two personality scales. *Perceptual and Motor Skills, 54,* 803–807.

Strüber, D., Başar-Eroglu, C., Hoff, E., & Stadler, M. (2000). Reversal-rate dependent differences in the EEG gamma-band during multistable visual perception. *International Journal of Psychophysiology, 38,* 243–252.

Strüber, D., & Stadler, M. (1999). Differences in top-down influences on the reversal rate of different categories of reversible figures. *Perception, 28,* 1185–1196.

Tallon, C., Bertrand, O., Bouchet, P., & Pernier, J. (1995). Gamma-range activity evoked by coherent visual stimuli in humans. *European Journal of Neuroscience, 7,* 1285–1291.

Tallon-Baudry, C., Bertrand, O., Delpuech, C., & Pernier, J. (1996). Stimulus specificity of phase-locked and non phase-locked 40-Hz visual responses in human. *The Journal of Neuroscience, 16,* 4240–4249.

Tallon-Baudry, C., Bertrand, O., Peronnet, F., & Pernier, J. (1998). Induced γ-band activity during the delay of a visual short-term memory task in humans. *The Journal of Neuroscience, 18,* 4244–4254.

Tallon-Baudry, C., Kreiter, A.K., & Bertrand, O. (1999). Sustained and transient oscillatory responses in the gamma and beta bands in a visual short-term memory task in humans. *Visual Neuroscience, 16,* 449–459.

Tiitinen, H., Sinkkonen, J., Reinikainen, K., Alho, K., Lavikainen, J., & Näätänen, R. (1993). Selective attention enhances the auditory 40-Hz transient response in humans. *Nature, 364,* 59–60.

VISUAL COGNITION, 2001, *8* (3/4/5), 623–636

Switching binding states

Michael H. Herzog

Computation and Neural Systems Program, California Institute of Technology, Pasadena, USA and Human Neurobiology, University of Bremen, Germany

Christof Koch

Computation and Neural Systems Program, California Institute of Technology, Pasadena, USA

Manfred Fahle

Human Neurobiology, University of Bremen, Germany

Recently, we introduced two illusions: Feature inheritance and shine-through (Herzog & Koch, 2001). In both cases, a vernier precedes a grating for a short time. In feature inheritance the grating comprises a small number of elements to which properties of the foregoing vernier are bound. The vernier itself remains invisible. In shine-through, a grating comprising a larger number of elements follows the foregoing vernier. Surprisingly, the vernier becomes visible as an entity in its own right and does not bequeath its features to the grating. Two "objects" are perceived each preserving its properties. Therefore, each of the two illusions represents a different state of feature binding. Our results suggest that feature binding is based on an antecedent segmentation process that might be viewed as a binding process itself.

INTRODUCTION

The binding problem is at the very heart of neural science because it addresses the question of how objects of the external world are coded in the brain. The main question is how features of an object are combined after being analysed in parallel in the various areas of the brain (see Roskies, and related articles, in

---

Please address all correspondence to M. Herzog, Human Neurobiology, University of Bremen, Argonnenstr. 3, 28211 Bremen, Germany. Email: mherzog@uni-bremen.de

Michael Herzog was supported by a fellowship from the Deutsche Forschungsgemeinschaft (Forschungsstipendium) and the SFB 517 "Neurocognition" of the Deutsche Forschungsgemeinschaft. Christof Koch received funding from the Keck Foundation, NIMH, and the NSF-sponsored ERC Center.

http://www.tandf.co.uk/journals/pp/13506285.html DOI:10.1080/13506280143000160

special issue of *Neuron*, 1999). If, for example, motion is represented in one cortical area and colour in another, how is a coloured moving object encoded? And how can such a combination of properties be distinguished from another object with a different combination of features? Many solutions were proposed including binding by attention (e.g., Reynolds & Desimone, 1999; Treisman, 1998), different temporal modes of neural firing (e.g., Gray, 1999; Singer, 1999; von der Malsburg, 1995, 1999), or simply a restricted number of possible representations like grand mother cell coding, i.e., the solution that there is no "real" binding problem (Ghose & Maunsell, 1999; see also Riesenhuber & Poggio, 1999; Shadlen & Movshon, 1999). In most of these approaches the main topic is attributing features, such as colour, to already segmented objects while the preceding segmentation process of the object, also a kind of binding, is usually discussed under different labels such as figure ground segmentation or object recognition.

Under normal circumstances, feature binding is not a problem for the healthy brain. However, Treisman and Schmidt (1982) showed that under heavy attentional load features of one element can be bound to another, i.e., features of different objects are mis-assigned. For example, if various coloured letters are presented centrally and subjects have to simultaneously perform an attention-demanding peripheral task, observers often perceive a feature combination (red H) that was not included in the central letter display. Friedman-Hill, Robertson, and Treisman (1995) presented data from a patient suffering from a lesion in parietal cortex, who had serious problems binding features to objects (like the ones used for illusory conjunctions), even without heavy attentional load, indicating that features might live their own life if not controlled by a strong binding mechanism. Wolford and Shum (1980) showed evidence for feature perturbation and Butler, Mewhort, and Browse (1991) found that features of one element of a display sometimes migrate to other ones. Moreover, texture elements fill in larger regions (e.g., Caputo, 1998) and neon colours can spread (e.g., Bressan, Mingolla, Spillmann, & Watanabe, 1997).

Using a backward masking paradigm we show that features of a perceptually invisible element can be bound to a following grating. As in the previous studies these properties migrate or travel, i.e., they are mislocalized. However, this kind of feature binding depends strongly on the spatio-temporal layout of the grating. Changing the layout of the grating can render the vernier visible, qualitatively change the kind of feature binding, and strongly change performance. Our results suggest that preceding segmentation processes determine the state of feature binding—at least in small spatio-temporal windows. Moreover, the results confine neural mechanisms of temporal coding to a very narrow temporal scale.

We shortly review some of our previous findings, present some new data, and propose a mechanism which might explain the results.

MATERIALS AND METHODS

Apparatus

Stimuli appeared on an analogue monitor controlled by a Macintosh computer via fast 16-bit D/A converters (1 MHz pixel rate). In most conditions an offset vernier stimulus preceded a grating comprising a variable number of aligned verniers.

Stimuli

For trained observers, presentation times of the vernier ranged between 10 and 30 ms in shine-through conditions and between 20 and 50 ms for feature inheritance. Gratings lasted always for 300 ms. Vernier stimuli and grating elements were 10′ (arc min) long and separated by a vertical gap of 60″. Spacing between grating elements was 200–250″ (arc sec). Subjects observed the stimuli from a distance of 1.2 or 2 m in a room illuminated dimly by a background light. The luminance of the stimuli was around 80 cd/m^2. In the experiments we determined thresholds of 75% correct responses with an adaptive staircase method (PEST; Taylor & Creelman, 1967).

Task

In feature inheritance, the task is to discriminate the offset direction induced by the foregoing vernier. Inter-individual differences between observers are quite high. Subjectively, some observers experience very strong effects, whereas those of others are very weak. Sometimes feature inheritance requires substantial training to occur. Quite to the contrary, shine-through occurs for almost all observers almost from the very beginning and reaches asymptotic performance quite quickly. Moreover, performance is much more reliable than in feature inheritance. In shine-through, subjects are asked to judge offset direction of the illusory shine-through element.

BINDING STATES

Feature binding I: One object and feature inheritance

In the feature inheritance illusion, properties of a foregoing element are bound to a subsequently presented grating comprising usually three or five elements. The preceding element remains invisible, i.e., it is *subjectively* not perceived. Therefore, features of two visual "objects" presented within a small spatio-temporal window are bound into *one* single perceptual object. The typical example is a vernier presented for 20–50 ms followed immediately by a grating comprising five elements and lasting for 300 ms. Because of the short presentation time, the vernier remains invisible to the observers. However, the grating appears to be offset in the direction of the preceding vernier. Feature inheritance is not restricted to the offset of a preceding vernier, but also the orientation of a single line can be bequeathed. Lines moving in apparent motion bind their motion to a following grating. Moreover, more than one feature, e.g., vernier offset and motion, can be bequeathed (see Herzog & Koch, 2001). In the following we restrict presentation to the vernier paradigm, showing that feature inheritance of vernier offsets reveals the following characteristics:

1. *Features travel into the focus of attention.* Subjects perceive the offset of the foregoing vernier at *one* of the outer, *attended* (and probably fixated) elements of the grating that is aligned and 400″ apart from the location of presentation (see Figure 1). Features of the grating outside the focus of attention do not play an important role for feature inheritance. Therefore, features have to travel. They are independent of their carrier, i.e., the preceding vernier (see also Herzog & Koch, 2001).

2. *Spread of features.* Feature travel resembles a spread of properties since the closer the vernier is presented to the focus of attention the better is performance (see Herzog & Koch, 2001). For example, if an observer prefers to attend to the left-most element, a preceding vernier presented at the position of

Figure 1. A vernier, offset to the left or right, appeared shortly, followed by a grating comprising five elements. Subjects attended, most times spontaneously, to one of the outer edges. Three conditions were presented in order to show that observers attend to the outer element and perceive an illusory offset at this location. The vernier preceded a grating which did (Pref 2 and Non-Pref) or did not (Pref 1) contain a single offset grating element at one of its edges (in this figure the right-most grating element). Offset direction of this element was always *opposite* to that of the foregoing vernier. The conditions Pref 2 and Non-Pref differed only in the focus of attention. Focusing attention on one edge of the grating did virtually not change performance whether (Pref 1) or not (Pref 2) the grating comprised an element with a real offset—as long as this element was not in the focus of attention. However, focusing on this outer, offset grating element led to a very significant drop in performance (Non-Pref). The strong effect of the focus of attention demonstrates that subjects indeed attend to one of the outer elements—otherwise, there should not be such an effect. Performance was evaluated always according to the offset direction of the foregoing vernier, i.e., performance below 50% correct responses denotes dominance of the grating element with opposite offset (after Herzog & Koch, 2001).

the neighbouring grating element yields many more correct responses than if the vernier appeared at the location of the outer element opposite to the attended edge. Moreover, processing time plays an important role. A grating preceded by the vernier *and* a blank period yields better results than a grating immediately followed by the vernier. Since stimulus energy is identical in both conditions it seems that the additional processing time causes the better performance (see Herzog & Koch, 2001).

3. *Perceptual metamers.* An offset vernier followed by a grating comprising five straight elements yields the same result as the opposite temporal order of straight versus offset features, i.e., a straight vernier followed by an offset grating (offset sizes of vernier and grating are adjusted independently). Therefore, real and illusory, i.e., inherited, features are perceptually equivalent: metamers (see Herzog & Koch, 2001).

4. *Computation of real and illusory features.* In the focus of attention—and only there—offsets of the grating and of the inherited vernier features are computed to produce a coherent percept.

Feature binding II: Two objects and shine-through

If the vernier is followed by a grating comprising more than seven elements the vernier becomes visible as an individual *shine-through* element (see Figure 2). Shine-through is characterized by the following facts:

1. *Shine-through yields much better performance than feature inheritance.* Increasing the number of grating elements increases performance (see Figure 3). This improvement is not caused by additional luminance, i.e., a first-order cue, since it depends on the spatial layout of the grating (see next point).

2. *Shine-through depends on the spatial layout.* For instance, inserting gaps between kernel (see Figure 3) and context renders the vernier almost

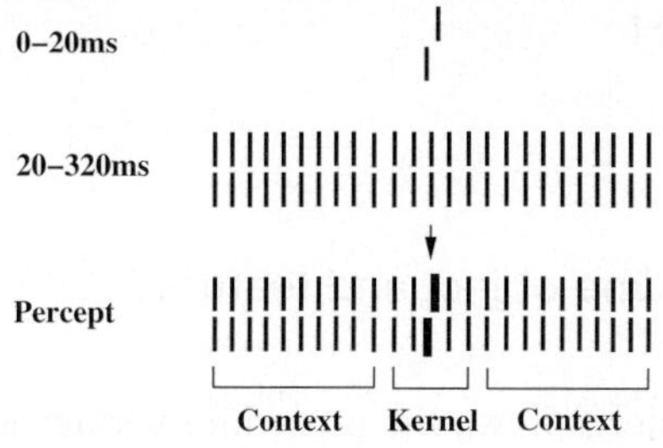

Figure 2. Gratings with more than seven elements render the vernier and its features visible, a phenomenon we label *shine-through* . The shine-through element appears as superimposed on the grating being brighter and wider than the grating elements. We call the central five elements of the grating the kernel and the outer elements the context.

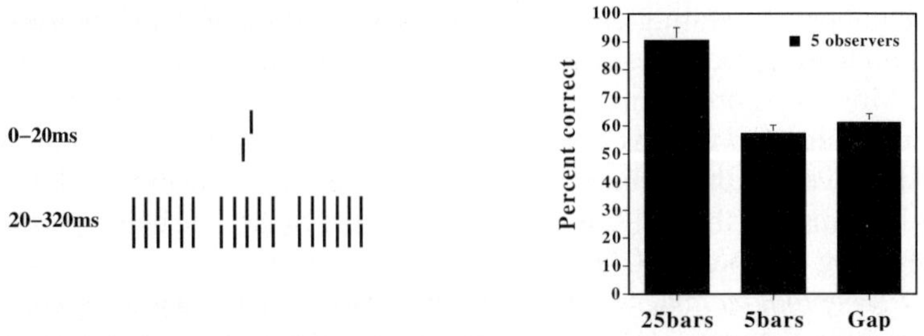

Figure 3. Performance for a grating with 25 elements is far superior to that for a grating with only 5 lines. However, gratings with 25 elements containing gaps yield almost the same performance as 5 element arrays, strongly suggesting a role of spatial layout. Layout represents a higher order cue than luminance, which is a first order cue. Presentation time in shine-through is usually shorter than in feature inheritance (adopted from Herzog & Koch, 2001).

completely invisible. Also several other spatial manipulations, destroying the spatial *homogeneity* of the grating, deteriorate performance and subjective experience of shine-through (see Herzog, Fahle, & Koch, 2001a). For example, a tilted context yields minor performance.

3. *Shine-through depends on the temporal layout.* If the context appears later than the kernel, shine-through is diminished. Already a difference in presentation times of only 10 ms between these grating elements yields a significant deterioration of performance. Almost the same result occurs if only the *two* grating elements between kernel and context are displayed delayed relative to the other elements (see Herzog, Koch, & Fahle, 2001b). These two elements are at the positions corresponding to the gaps in Figure 3.

4. *Shine-through is an illusion.* Shine-through is an illusion in its own right. Specifically, shine-through does not result from perceiving the vernier as an independent event *before* grating onset. In this case, shine-through should also occur with gratings of five elements or those containing gaps. Therefore, the human brain renders the vernier visible in an active and illusory manner (see also experiment 2 below).

Feature binding III: One object and feature integration

If a single straight vernier follows the preceding vernier features of the two elements are integrated—as is often found in the wide realm of feature fusion. For small offsets and presentation times this integration process obeys a Bloch-like law (see Herzog, Parish, Fahle, & Koch, 2001c). We will not discuss this binding state further.

RESULTS

Experiment 1: Shine-through without offset vernier

How much does the percept of shine-through depend on the offset size of the foregoing vernier? The following experiment will answer this question.

Methods. Four observers, familiar with shine-through, perceived either a vernier followed by a grating comprising 25 elements or the same grating not preceded by a vernier. These two conditions were presented randomly interleaved with equal probability. In each trial, the task of subjects was to indicate whether or not a foregoing vernier was present. In the first part of the experiment the preceding vernier (if displayed) was offset as usually, while it was aligned in the second part. Offset size was chosen for each observer to yield *discrimination* performance around 75% correct responses for vernier display time of 10 ms. We used three presentation times.

Results and discussion. The probability of detection is almost identical for offset and straight verniers irrespective of display times (see Figure 4). This result shows that shine-through is not caused by the *offset* of the vernier. Both for offset and straight verniers, detection rate decrease with decreasing presentation time of the vernier. For a display time of 5 ms none of the observers perceived shine-through. Correspondingly, we found performance to be close to 50% chance level. However, an increase of presentation time of only 5 ms yields a much higher detection rate. The longer the vernier is presented the better performance is, indicating that shine-through depends very subtly on vernier energy. Vernier offset *discrimination* tasks yield analogous results (see Herzog, Koch, & Fahle, 2001b).

Experiment 2: Vernier position does not matter

As mentioned previously the position of the vernier, relative to the focus of attention, does strongly affect performance in feature inheritance.

Methods. In this experiment we presented the foregoing vernier in the middle of the screen flanked by the two central elements of a grating comprising 24 elements, i.e., the distance from the virtual centre of the vernier to the centre of the nearest grating elements was 100″ (see Figure 5). Also performance for the standard grating comprising 25 elements was determined (see Figure 2).

Results and discussion. Results are quite similar irrespective of whether the foregoing vernier is presented at the same spatial position as the central grating element or else if there is no overlap between vernier and grating (see

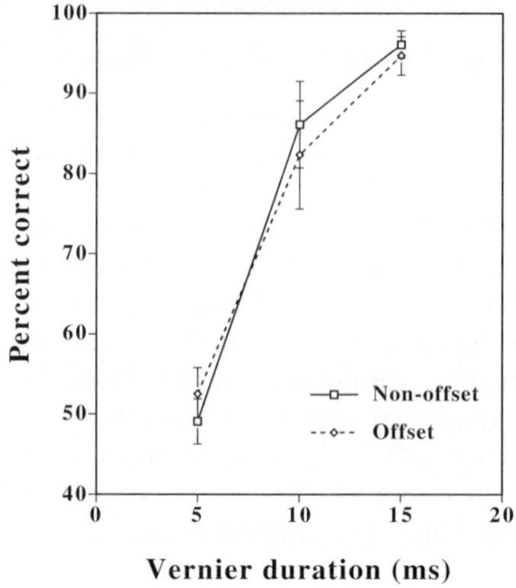

Figure 4. A grating, comprising 25 elements, was presented with or without a preceding vernier. In the first subcondition the vernier, if displayed, was always offset; while it was straight in the second. Vernier offset was chosen to yield *discrimination* performance around 75% correct responses. The observers' task was to determine whether or not a vernier preceded the grating. We used three presentation times. Performance improved almost equally for both conditions, i.e., vernier offset or straight, with increasing display time.

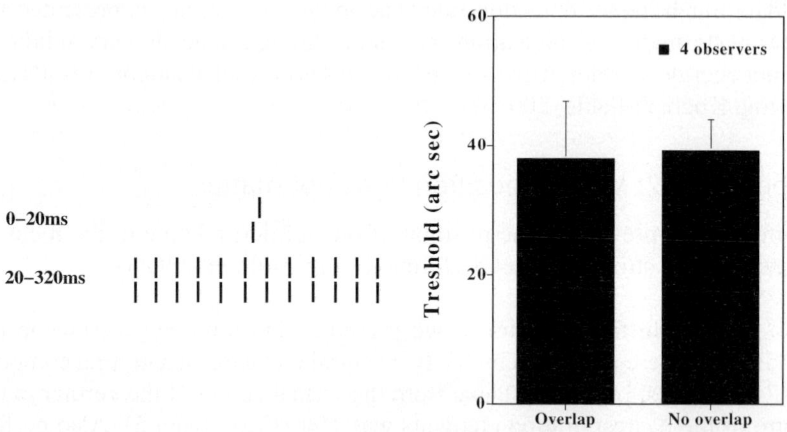

Figure 5. Performance for shine-through with the standard grating comprising 25 elements ("overlap" see Figure 2) and a grating with 24 elements in which the two central elements do not overlap with the preceding vernier (see left part of this figure; in this figure spacing is drawn wider than in Figure 2 and a smaller number of elements is shown for clarity; however, stimulus parameters are identical, except spatial position of the grating). Performance does not differ between the two conditions, indicating that shine-through is not caused by fusion of foregoing vernier and central grating element in the overlap condition.

Figure 5). Please note that at threshold the vernier fits completely in the 200″ wide gap between the two central grating elements (width of vernier and grating elements is smaller than 60″). Therefore, in the common 25 element case, i.e., spatial overlap of vernier and central grating element, shine-through seems not to result from a fusion of these two elements. The grating and the shine-through element are perceived independently.

Moreover, this result shows again that feature inheritance and shine-through are different binding states since in feature inheritance the position of the vernier relative to the focus of attention strongly matters.

MECHANISMS OF FEATURE BINDING IN SMALL SPATIO-TEMPORAL WINDOWS

Our results suggest the following characteristics of feature binding in small spatio-temporal windows.

1. First of all, our results as well as the ones of Butler et al. (1991), Friedman-Hill et al. (1995), Treisman and Schmidt (1982), and Wolford and Shum (1980), show that basic or "low level" features can be freed from their carriers. The offset of the preceding vernier is mis-localized in feature inheritance and the mis-localization process seems to be caused by a spread of features. Therefore, there is a need for a binding mechanism.

2. In our paradigm, the spatio-temporal layout of both grating and preceding vernier determines the state of feature binding. Other aspects including the first order cue luminance seem not to be crucial. It is important to note that binding states can be switched just by changing the spatio-temporal characteristics of the *context*: The kernel of our stimuli is always identical. The prevailing types of feature binding reveal quite different characteristics as well as strong performance differences. Different geometrical layouts of segmented objects entail different binding states (see also Herzog, Fahle, & Koch, 2001a). Therefore, it seems that the state of feature binding is based on the results of segmentation processes.

3. The spatio-temporal homogeneity of the grating seems to play the major role for shine-through to occur. Shine-through does not depend on whether or not the preceding vernier is offset (see Experiment 1). Therefore, it seems that at least two binding processes exist. The first is concerned with finding homogeneous regions, and segmenting objects; its output determines the second process of binding attributes, e.g., vernier offset, to the objects parsed. This process occurs not only in feature inheritance but also in shine-through since the shine-through element is an illusory entity which is rendered visible in an active manner—it does not result from luminance fusion with the central grating element (see Experiment 2).

4. Finding homogeneous regions seems to be a process depending on local coupling between neighbouring elements in space and time. Delaying *two* single contextual elements affects performance and perception almost as much as a delay of the *whole* context. This result moreover implies that finding homogeneous regions is a time-consuming process. Differences in performance caused by different number of grating elements arise with grating durations around 20–60 ms (see Herzog & Fahle, 2001; see also Caputo, 1998; Kurylo, 1997). However, in this study vernier display time was below 20 ms for all observers, i.e., the foregoing vernier had already disappeared. A very short-term memory is needed to explain the results. Rendering features visible seems to be a very active and complex process.

5. If additional features are bound to the segmented objects attention comes into play and reads the product out.

In summary, in small spatio-temporal windows feature binding seems to be a two-stage process where the second step depends on the first one. From a functionalistic point of view, the first process might be interpreted in a speculative manner as a pre-attentive computing of homogeneous regions in order to cope with the curse of dimensionality. Arrays of similar elements may be coded just by some of their "end-points" like edges of a grating. In the second stage, then, additional features are bound to this low level code, e.g., to the "end-points".

What might be the underlying neuronal mechanisms? We would like to suggest a highly speculative scenario in which the spread of neural activity plays a major role as suggested by optical imaging studies and single cell recordings (see Bakin, Kwon, Masino, Weinberger, & Frostig, 1996; Bringuier, Chavane, Glaeser, & Fregnac, 1999). Neuronal activity related to single grating elements spreads within small areas mediated by lateral excitatory connections. Moreover, neighbouring neurons with similar tuning functions are also coupled via inhibitory connections. In shine-through, larger arrays of neurons are activated if grating elements are simultaneously displayed and, therefore, suppress each others due to recurrent inhibition. In this scenario, only activity of neurons associated with inhomogeneities—such as edges or gaps—in their receptive fields survives due to reduced inhibition by missing neighbouring elements. Therefore, activity corresponding to the centre elements of a large homogeneous grating vanishes quickly. Though display time is short, activity of neurons coding the vernier might be enhanced by auto-recurrent connections and thus become prominent, resulting in shine-through. However, in small gratings the winner-take-all activity corresponding to the edges of the grating (display time 300 ms) suppresses this enhancement since edges are closer to the vernier. The same holds for gratings containing gaps: Because of this suppression the foregoing vernier remains invisible. The elements most strongly activated attract attention which itself collects information also from "channels" not used for segmentation. In feature inheritance neural activity regarding vernier offset seem to spread, in an independent "channel" (see Experiment 1), since the preceding vernier has no *offset* neighbours. In the focus of attention these features and features of the grating are bound to a single combined percept (remember that in feature inheritance migrated offsets are traded against real grating offsets). How are these additional features bound? Psychophysical studies do not allow a direct answer. However, if temporal mechanisms are involved they have to operate on a very short-term scale or have to be at least initiated very quickly (see also Herzog, Koch, & Fahle, 2001b). For some subjects, shine-through occurs with presentation times of the vernier shorter than 10 ms. A difference in display time of the *vernier* of only 5 ms can change perception and performance quite strongly (see Experiment 1). On the other hand, delays of *contextual* grating elements in the range of 10 ms can cause strong performance changes. Therefore, neural processes depending on only a very few spikes determine the fate of the preceding features.

It is not clear whether rendering the vernier visible in shine-through also has a functional explanation, e.g., in terms of transparency, or whether it is just an epiphenomenon caused by the current state of the neural machinery. Since spatial parameters in our experiments are very small the hypothetical processes might occur in the primary visual cortex, V1. This scenario is just a speculation. Many other scenarios are conceivable. For example, neurons of the M-system may trigger neurons of the P-system. Also other models might be able to explain the phenomena (for example Grossberg & Mingolla, 1985; Jancke et al., 1999).

GENERAL DISCUSSION

We reviewed basic properties of two recently discovered illusions, feature inheritance and shine-through, which correspond to two different states of feature binding. In feature inheritance only one object is perceived and properties of foregoing elements can be bound to a following grating where they are mislocalized (binding state 1). Changing the spatial layout, e.g., by adding grating elements, can render the foregoing element visible as an illusory entity to which features of the foregoing element are bound (binding state 2). It should be mentioned that in some conditions neither feature inheritance nor shine-through are perceived. For example, if the context is displayed later than the kernel the foregoing vernier and its offset are largely suppressed. It remains to philosophical dispute whether or not suppression reflects an own binding state or is just an instance of "zero" feature inheritance or "zero" shine-through. The changes between binding states occur after manipulations of *context* elements alone, in all experiments the kernel of our stimuli was always identical.

We presented a scenario that models segmentation as the prevalent cue for feature binding. In a first step, prominent features, e.g., verniers *without* offset, are used to determine homogeneous regions. The output of this process determines the state of binding for additional features. A simple model, employing only local excitatory and inhibitory connections is suggested as a coarse model to motivate and direct further research.

Werner (1935) has already shown that features can be separated from their carriers. He showed that a disk with spokes can bequeath these spokes to a surrounding annulus displayed afterwards while the existence of the disk remains invisible to the observer. Suzuki and Cavanagh (1998) introduced a shape contrast effect. For example, if a line is briefly flashed, followed by a circle, an ellipse is perceived, elongated in the direction *opposite* to the axis of the line. Surprisingly, an ellipse is perceived even if line and circle do not spatially overlap (see also Experiment 2). This method of biasing features seems, however, to belong to the category of aftereffects since properties appear to be biased in the opposite direction of the foregoing elements.

Contextual effects on the visibility of a central target occurred in many studies. For example, Banks and White (1984) found that if target letters are masked by flanking nearby letters performance is better if the lateral elements can be grouped. For example, a single letter "T" is more strongly masked by a neighbouring single letter "H" than by many letters "H" of the same size grouped into a vertical column. Other investigations found that detection and discrimination of a target can be enhanced by contextual elements (e.g., Kapadia, Ito, Gilbert, & Westheimer, 1995; Polat & Sagi, 1993, 1994; Verghese & Stone, 1997; Weisstein & Harris, 1974; Yu & Levi, 2000). One difference to these paradigms is that our targets are backward masked (e.g., Bachmann, 1994; Breitmeyer, 1984). From a backward masking point of view the shine-through effect may surprise because more masking energy yields less interference. Breitmeyer (1978) found that flanks can inhibit masking bars in *metacontrast*. These masking bars, when presented alone, inhibit a vernier target. Hence, the flanks are disinhibiting and more energy of the mask leads to less masking as with shine-through, which is, however, backward masking. Ramachandran and Cobb (1995) found that a disc, effectively masked by metacontrast, can become visible if another visible disc is added to the stimulus *and* if attention is paid to both of them. Werner (1935), again, had found similar results.

In summary, the effects of feature inheritance and shine-through together allow investigation of feature binding in small spatio-temporal windows in a qualitative *and* quantitative manner. Binding of elements seems to occur in at least two steps: First, image segmentation via binding of homogeneous features and, second, attributing additional features to the segmented objects. Changing the spatio-temporal layout of preceding element and the following grating allows to switch binding states.

REFERENCES

Bachmann, T. (1994). *Psychophysiology of visual masking.* Commack, NY: Nova Science.

Bakin, J.S., Kwon, M.C., Masino, S.A., Weinberger, N.M., & Frostig, R.D. (1996). Suprathreshold auditory cortex activation visualized by intrinsic signal optical imaging. *Cerebral Cortex, 6,* 120–130.

Banks, W.P., & White, H. (1984). Lateral interference and perceptual grouping in visual detection. *Perception and Psychophysics, 36,* 285–295.

Breitmeyer, B.G. (1978). Disinhibition in metacontrast masking of vernier acuity targets: Sustained channels inhibit transient channels. *Vision Research, 18,* 1401–1405.

Breitmeyer, B.G. (1984). *Visual masking: An integrative approach.* Oxford, UK: Clarendon Press.

Bressan, P., Mingolla, E., Spillmann, L., & Watanabe, T. (1997). Neon color spreading: a review. *Perception, 26*(11), 1353–66.

Bringuier, V., Chavane, F., Glaeser, L., & Fregnac, Y. (1999). Horizontal propagation of visual activity in the synaptic integration field of area 17 neurons. *Science, 283,* 695–699.

Butler, B.E., Mewhort, D.H., & Browse, R.A. (1991). When do letter features migrate? A boundary condition for feature-integration theory. *Perception and Psychophysics, 49,* 91–99.

Caputo, G. (1998). Texture brightness filling-in. *Vision Research, 6,* 841–851.

Friedman-Hill, S.R., Robertson, L.C., & Treisman, A. (1995). Parietal contributions to visual feature binding: Evidence from a patient with bilateral lesions. *Science, 269,* 853–855.

Ghose, G.M., & Maunsell, J. (1999). Specialized representations in visual cortex: A role for binding? *Neuron, 24,* 79–85.

Gray, C.M. (1999). The temporal correlation hypothesis of visual feature integration: Still alive and well. *Neuron, 24,* 31–47.

Grossberg, S., & Mingolla, E. (1985). Neural dynamics of perceptual grouping: Textures, boundaries, and emergent segmentations. *Perception and Psychophysics, 38*(2), 141–171.

Herzog, M.H., & Fahle, M. (2001). *First is best.* Paper presented at the First Visual Sciences Conference.

Herzog, M.H., Fahle, M., & Koch, C. (2001a). Spatial aspects of object formation revealed by a new illusion, shine through. *Manuscript submitted for publication.*

Herzog, M.H., & Koch, C. (2001). Seeing an invisible object: Feature inheritance and shine-through. *Proceedings of the National Academy of Science, USA. 88,* 4271–4275

Herzog, M.H., Koch, C., & Fahle, M. (2001b). Shine-through: temporal aspects. *Manuscript submitted for publication.*

Herzog, M.H., Parish, L., Fahle, M., & Koch, C. (2001c). Competition of features during the first milliseconds of human information processing. *Manuscript submitted for publication.*

Jancke, J., Erlhagen, W., Dinse, H.R., Akhavan, A.C., Giese, M., Steinhage, A., & Schoener, G. (1999). Parametric population representation of retinal location: neuronal interaction dynamics in cat primary visual cortex. *Journal of Neuroscience, 19*(20), 9016–9028.

Kapadia, M.K., Ito, M., Gilbert, C.D., & Westheimer, G. (1995). Improvement in visual sensitivity by changes in local contrast: Parallel studies in human and monkeys. *Neuron, 15,* 843–604.

Kuryl, D.D. (1997). Time course of perceptual grouping. *Perception and Psychophysics, 59*(1), 142–147.

Polat, U., & Sagi, D. (1993). Lateral interactions between spatial channels: Suppression and facilitation revealed by lateral masking experiments. *Vision Research, 33,* 993–999.

Polat, U., & Sagi, D. (1994). Spatial interactions in human vision: From near to far via experience-dependent cascades of connections. *Proceedings of the National Academy of Science, 91,* 1206–1209.

Ramachandran, V.S., & Cobb, S. (1995). Visual attention modulates metacontrast masking. *Nature, 373,* 66–68.

Reynolds, J.H., & Desimone, R. (1999). The role of neural mechanisms of attention in solving the binding problem. *Neuron, 24,* 19–29.

Riesenhuber, M., & Poggio, T. (1999). Are cortical models really bound by the "binding problem"? *Neuron, 24,* 87–93.

Roskies, A.L. (1999). The binding problem. *Neuron, 24,* 7–9.

Shadlen, M.N., & Movshon, J.A. (1999). Synchrony unbound: A critical evaluation of the temporal binding hypothesis. *Neuron, 24,* 67–77.

Singer, W. (1999). Neuronal synchrony: A versatile code for the definition of relations? *Neuron, 24,* 49–65.

Suzuki, S., & Cavanagh, P. (1998). A shape-contrast effect for briefly presented stimuli. *Journal of Experimental Psychology Human Perception and Performance, 24,* 1315–1341.

Taylor, M.M., & Creelman, C.D. (1967). PEST: Efficient estimates on probability functions. *The Journal of the Acoustical Society of America, 41,* 782–787.

Treisman A. (1998). Feature binding, attention and object perception. *Philosophical Transaction of the Royal Society, London B—Biological Science, 29, 353*(1373), 1295–1306.

Treisman, A., & Schmidt, H. (1982). Illusory conjunctions in the perception of objects. *Cognitive Psychology, 14,* 107–141.

Verghese, P., & Stone, L.S. (1997). Spatial layout affects speed discrimination. *Vision Research 37,* 397–406.

von der Malsburg, C. (1995). Binding in models of perception and brain function. *Current Opinion in Neurobiology, 5,* 520–526.

von der Malsburg, C. (1999). The what and why of binding: The modeler's perspective. *Neuron, 24,* 95–104.

Weisstein, N., & Harris, C.S. (1974). Visual detection of lines segments: An object superiority effect. *Science, 186,* 752–755.

Werner, H., (1935). Studies on contour: I. Qualitative analysis. *American Journal of Psychology, 47,* 40–64.

Wolford, G., & Shum, K.H. (1980). Evidence for feature perturbations. *Perception and Psychophysics, 27,* 409–420.

Yu, C., & Levi, D. (2000). Surround modulation in human vision unmasked by masking experiments. *Nature Neuroscience, 3,* 724–728.

VISUAL COGNITION, 2001, *8* (3/4/5), 637–654

The effects of temporal synchrony on the perceived organization of elements in spatially symmetric and asymmetric grids

Andy Parton and Nick Donnelly

Centre for Visual Cognition, Department of Psychology, University of Southampton, UK

Marius Usher

Department of Psychology, Birkbeck College, University of London, UK

Three experiments were conducted to investigate the influence of fast temporally segmented presentations of alternate rows or columns on the perception of grids of either symmetrically or asymmetrically spaced dot-like stimuli. Experiments 1a and 1b demonstrated that observers were able to discriminate between temporally segmented presentations of rows/columns stimuli, but showed a reduced performance in discrimination between non-temporally segmented stimuli and temporally segmented stimuli that were spatially unstructured. Experiment 2 confirmed the influence of temporally segmented presentations of rows and columns using elements whose mean luminance summed to the same as the display background. Experiment 3 demonstrated that the influence of temporal cues reduced when display elements were asymmetrically spaced. The results are discussed in terms of the influence of external spatio-temporal factors on the neural mechanisms of visual grouping.

Please address all correspondence to N. Donnelly, Centre for Visual Cognition, Department of Psychology, University of Southampton, Southampton SO17 1BJ, UK.
Email: n.donnelly@soton.ac.uk

The research was funded by a grant awarded to the second and third authors from the Biotechnology and Biological Sciences Research Council of Great Britain. The results of Experiment 3 were briefly reported at the Association for Research in Vision and Ophthalmology, 1999 (Donnelly & Usher, 1999). For their helpful and stimulating discussions we would also like to thank Y. Bonneh (who suggested Experiment 3), D. Sagi, and E. Neibur.

http://www.tandf.co.uk/journals/pp/13506285.html DOI:10.1080/13506280143000179

INTRODUCTION

Spatially separate visual elements can be perceived as grouped together if, as a set, they conform to one or more of the Gestalt laws of grouping. The Gestalt laws of grouping are known to depend on a variety of spatial and temporal factors. For example, elements are grouped on the basis of spatial properties such as collinearity and on the basis of spatio-temporal properties such as common motion. In addition, it has been proposed recently that rapid temporal modulations, too fast to generate a percept that distinguishes different sets of elements in a display might, nevertheless, influence grouping (Fahle, 1993). According to this proposal, grouping is encoded internally by the synchronous firing of detectors responding to grouped elements (Singer, 1999; von der Malsburg, 1981) and is mediated by lateral/horizontal interactions between detectors with similar visual properties. As a consequence, rapid external temporal modulations of stimuli might, due to the direct effect of retinal stimulation on higher level neural mechanisms, induce a synchronous firing of neurones that is indistinguishable from the internal coding of grouping.

To test the temporal synchrony hypothesis a number of psychophysical studies have examined the effect of fast temporal modulations on perceptual grouping. Typically, these studies have compared the presentation of rapidly alternating stimuli in temporally segmented and temporally non-segmented conditions (Alais, Blake, & Lee, 1998; Usher & Donnelly, 1998; Elliott & Müller, 1998; Fahle, 1993; Fahle & Koch, 1995; Kiper, Gegenfurtner, & Movshon, 1996; Leonards, Singer, & Fahle 1996). In non-temporally segmented conditions, all display elements are presented together in one phase followed by a blank phase when no display elements are presented. In temporally segmented conditions, elements that form part of a target spatial grouping are presented together in a separate temporal phase from the other elements in the display. The number and frequency of the temporal oscillations that define the stimuli are typically varied across conditions. The underlying logic is that the grouping of elements should be stronger in temporally segmented conditions than in non-temporally segmented conditions. This is based on the assumption that external temporal modulations of the display should be reflected in internal modulations of neural firing.

Using this basic paradigm recent studies have reported contradictory results concerning the effectiveness of external temporal modulations on texture discrimination. Leonards et al. (1996; see also Fahle, 1993) demonstrated effects of external temporal modulations on texture discrimination when they asked participants to detect the orientation of a rectangle defined by either temporal and/or spatial (line orientation) cues. They showed that temporal phase alone could define textures so long as the temporal separation between target and background elements was at least 10 ms. In addition, they showed that temporal and spatial cues could compete (when textures defined by temporal phase were different from those defined by spatial cues) or additively facilitate the perception of a texture (when both temporal and spatial defined the same texture). However, when a spatially random temporal pattern is presented alongside a well-defined spatial texture the temporal information has no effect (Kiper et al., 1996; Leonards et al., 1996).

External temporal modulations have also been shown to influence perceptual grouping. Usher and Donnelly (1998) used two different tasks and showed significant effects of 16.7 ms and 13.3 ms stimulus asynchronies on performance in both tasks. In one task, participants had to report the location (one of four quadrants) of a contour defined by quasi-collinear line segments placed within a field of randomly oriented line segments (see Field, Hayes, & Hess, 1993) using a four alternative forced-choice (4AFC) paradigm. When the target contour was presented temporally segmented from distractors, target detection was enhanced by around 20%. They also showed that participants were unable to perform this contour detection task when the target contour was defined only by the temporal segmentation and could not be discriminated from the background on the basis of its spatial characteristics. This control condition indicated that the 16.7 ms and 13.3 ms temporal asynchronies could not be utilized on their own. The results suggested that the use of temporal information in figure grouping is reliant upon the support of spatial factors.

In a second task, Usher and Donnelly (1998) presented participants with a synchronous (non-temporally segmented) and symmetric grid of dots known to be of ambiguous organization in that the dots were perceived as organized in either rows or columns. On different trials they presented either alternate rows or columns in asynchronous frames (i.e., temporally segmented) and asked participants to report whether the display appeared to be organized as either rows or columns. Although the patterns of participants' errors suggested they were unable to discriminate temporally segmented trials from non-temporally segmented trials, choices were made consistent with the temporal manipulation (i.e., rows or columns).

In the present paper we report three further experiments using the symmetric grid stimulus. We begin by testing whether participants are able to detect the existence of the two temporal phases in temporally segmented displays when grouping is minimized. This is important in order to show that the temporal modulations in our previous study had their effect on grouping rather than on a local process of phase discrimination between proximal elements. Both the rows–columns and phase detection stimuli should contain the same number of local phase differences, i.e., any frame contains 50% of the elements that specify a particular stimulus. Therefore, if the rows–columns grouping task is performed on the basis of a local phase difference, observers' performance should not be any more accurate than within the phase discrimination task.

EXPERIMENTS 1a AND 1b

The purpose of the Experiments 1a and 1b was to compare participants' accuracy for phase detection and rows–columns grouping tasks across a range of stimulus sizes, presentation times, and display frequencies. The phase detection task involved distinguishing a non-temporally segmented display, where all elements were present in one phase and absent from the next, from a temporally segmented display, where 50% of randomly selected elements alternated out-of-phase. The grouping task was the standard rows–columns task (see earlier).

The rows–columns task was performed in the same fashion in Experiments 1a and 1b, however, the phase detection aspect of the experiment was performed in two ways. In Experiment 1a, half of the elements were selected independently at random for each trial. In Experiment 1b, the same selection of elements was presented in all trials, and for all participants, in order to minimize the spatial uncertainty for the task making it more similar in this regard to the rows–columns task. The configuration of these elements was chosen to minimize groupings of elements along straight lines.

Method

Participants. In Experiment 1a, eight participants acted as observers and all had normal, or corrected to normal, vision. All participants performed in the rows–columns task. However, one participant was unable to perform the phase detection task (even after extensive training) and so was excluded from this condition. In Experiment 1b, five participants who had taken part in the first experiment took part. Two of the authors participated in all experiments reported in the paper.

Stimuli and apparatus. The experimental stimuli were generated and presented on a Silicon Graphics O_2 workstation with a 21-inch monitor set to either a 60 Hz (Experiments 1a and 1b) or 75 Hz (Experiment 1b) screen refresh rate. Two successive screen frames, specified using the SGI screen buffering facility, defined each of the stimuli with one complete stimulus cycle being at 30 or 37.5 Hz. The stimuli were presented against a grey background (8.66 cd/m^2) and their contrast varied between experimental conditions and amongst participants (from 18.3% to 36.2%).

The experimental stimuli consisted of symmetric grids of evenly spaced circular elements viewed using a chin rest positioned 70 cm from the screen at which distance 1 pixel subtended 1.2 arc min of visual angle. Experiment 1a employed three grid sizes each defined by the number of elements they contained: 4×4, 6×6, and 8×8. The angular sizes of these grids were 3.2°, 5.3°, and 7.3° respectively. Experiment 1b employed two of these grid sizes: 4×4

and 8 × 8. The radius of the circular elements (9.8 arc min) and their separation (61.3 arc min) was held constant across the three grid sizes.

Procedure and design. Both experiments were performed in a darkened room. Experiment 1a comprised two tasks performed in separate blocks. In the rows–columns task, either alternate columns or alternate rows of elements were presented asynchronously, i.e., temporally segmented (see Figure 1). In the phase detection task, either half of the grid elements selected at random alternated out-of-phase (temporally segmented condition) or all the elements alternated in-phase (non-temporally segmented condition: See Figure 2). For both tasks, participants performed a 2AFC discrimination indicating their response by pressing the left (rows/temporally segmented) or right (columns/non-temporally segmented) mouse button. There was no time limit on participants' responses. Both tasks were performed for three exposure durations (33 ms, 99 ms, and 198 ms) and three stimulus sizes (4 × 4, 6 × 6, and 8 × 8). The experiment was blocked by exposure duration and size. There were 80 trials within each block and participants performed one block for each duration/size combination with their order of presentation randomized. Feedback was provided in line with the temporal phase structure of the stimuli. Incorrect responses led to a short beep.

Participants were trained on the 8 × 8 grid in the 192 ms condition until they could reliably perform each task before beginning the experiment. This training was also used to determine the contrast of the stimuli used for each participant during the experiment and was taken as the contrast level at which they could correctly classify 65–75% of the stimuli. Before beginning the experiment proper, participants performed a further two blocks containing a full set of

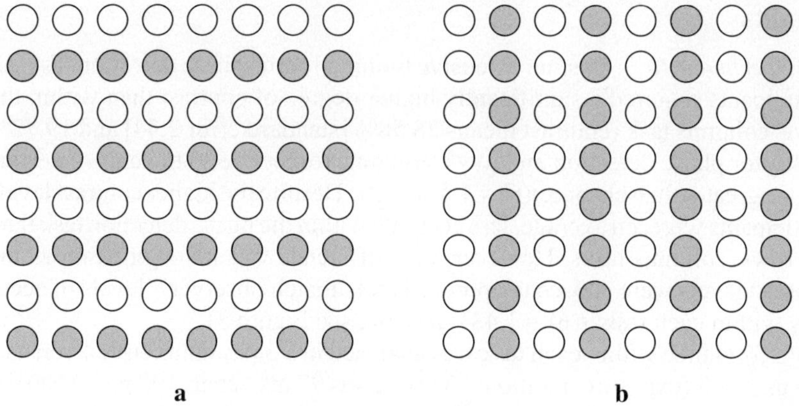

Figure 1. Illustrates the stimuli used in Experiments 1a and 1b for the rows (a) and columns (b) conditions. The temporal structure is indicated by dot colour: White dots were presented in frame 1 and grey dots in frame 2.

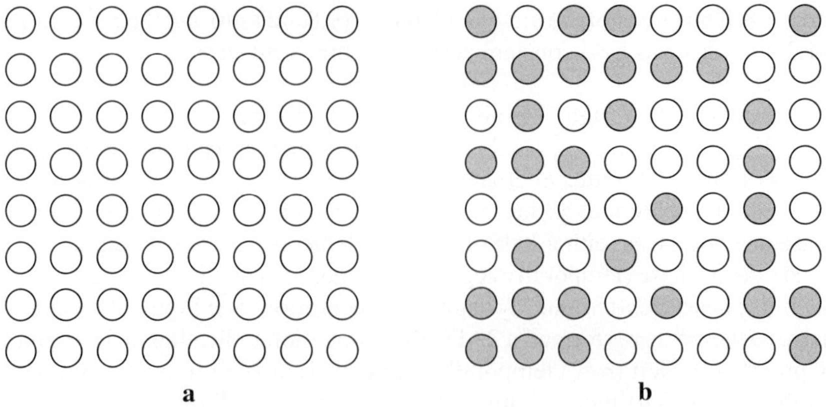

Figure 2. Illustrates the stimuli used in Experiment 1a for the non-temporally segmented (a) and temporally segmented (b) conditions in the phase detection task. The temporal structure is indicated by dot colour: White dots were presented in frame 1 and black dots in frame 2. (Note: In Experiment 1a, a new random stimulus was generated for each temporally segmented trial in the phase task, i.e., b merely depicts a typical example.)

exposure duration and stimulus size manipulations in order to familiarize them with all of the experimental conditions.

The procedure for Experiment 1b was the same as for Experiment 1a with the following exceptions. Stimuli were presented at two temporal oscillation rates (30 and 37.5 Hz), their presentation time was fixed at 132 ms and two sizes were used (4 × 4 and 8 × 8). Additionally, the spatial structure of the phase stimuli was fixed across all trials and participants. In this experiment, participants performed the phase and rows–columns task at the same contrast levels.

Results

Experiment 1a. Despite extensive training for the phase detection task, all participants required a significantly higher degree of contrast than within the rows–columns task (contrast means 28.58% [standard error 2.44] and 19.72% [0.46] for phase detection and rows–columns respectively) to achieve performance greater than chance, $t(6) = 4.4, p < .01$. Despite the higher contrast levels participants were, on average, less accurate within the phase detection task than the rows–columns tasks. However, this difference was not significant as the contrast levels were chosen to approximately match observers' levels of accuracy within each task, $t(6) = 1.431, p > .05$; see Figure 3).

Performance within each task was analysed in a 3 (stimulus size: 4 versus 6 versus 8) × 3 (exposure duration: 33 ms versus 99 ms versus 198 ms) ANOVA repeated over both factors (note that "task" could not be a within-subject variable in the analysis because one participant could not perform the rows–columns task). There was a significant main effect of stimulus size within both

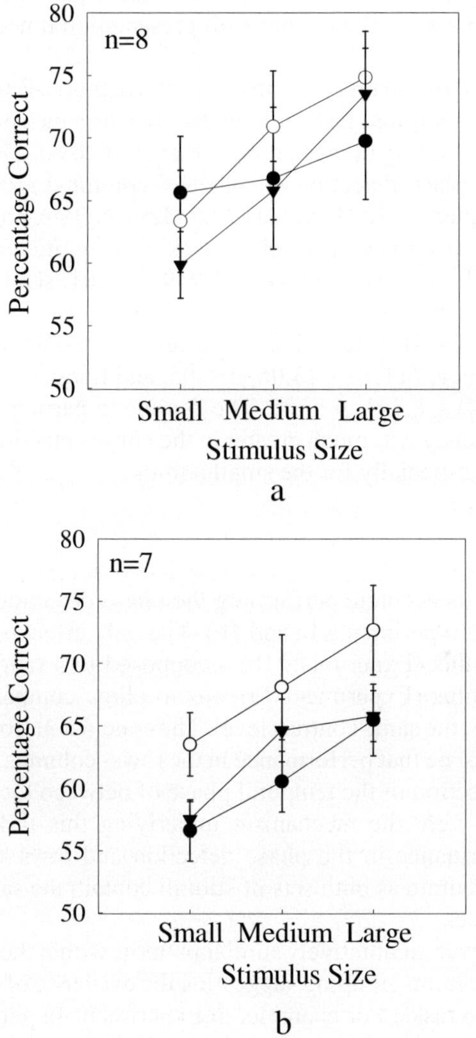

Figure 3. Illustrates the mean percentage rates of correct responses in (a) the rows–columns task and (b) the random phase task for each stimulus size and presentation time. Black circles represent the 33 ms presentation time, white circles the 99 ms time, and black triangles the 198 ms time. Error bars denote ± 1 standard error.

tasks: phase: $F(2, 12) = 7.67$; $p < .01$; rows–columns: $F(2, 14) = 6.44$; $p < .05$. In both cases this was due to the monotonic increase in participants' accuracy with stimulus size. The effect of exposure duration was only significant for the phase task, $F(2, 12) = 4.747$, $p < .05$; however, in both tasks participants' accuracy exhibited a non-monotonic relationship with presentation time.

Experiment 1b. Participants were able to perform this task at the same contrast level as the rows–columns task without their performance in the rows–columns task reaching a ceiling (a mean contrast level of 26%). The results were analysed in a 2 (task: phase detection versus rows–columns) × 2 (stimulus size: 4 versus 8) × 2 (frequency: 30 Hz versus 37.5 Hz) ANOVA repeated over all factors. Participants' accuracy in the phase task was significantly lower than that for the rows–columns task, $F(1,4) = 45.949$, $p < .01$: see Figure 4. Their accuracy decreased with frequency, $F(1, 4) = 130.63$, $p < .01$, and stimulus size, $F(1, 4) = 122.42$, $p < .01$. However, there were significant interactions between task type and frequency, $F(1, 4) = 13.06$, $p < .05$, and frequency, stimulus size and task type, $F(1, 4) = 8.241$, $p < .05$. The decline in participants' accuracy with increased frequency was much greater in the phase detection task than the rows–columns task, especially for the small stimuli.

Discussion

Participants' were less accurate performing the phase detection task than the rows–columns task (Experiments 1a and 1b). The only effect of using a fixed non-structured stimulus (Experiment 1b) as opposed to a randomly varying non-structured stimulus (Experiment 1a) was to allow comparison with the rows–columns task at the same contrast level. The conclusion from both Experiments 1a and 1b must be that performance in the rows–columns task cannot be mediated by the detection of the temporal phase of between local elements of the display. If this were the mechanism underlying this task it would be expected that performance in the phase detection and rows–columns tasks would be equally accurate as both sets of stimuli contain the same number of local phase differences.

There were, however, qualitatively similar patterns within the data for phase detection and row–column grouping suggesting the existence of some relationship between the two tasks. For example, in Experiment 1a participants were similarly affected by increasing stimulus size and lengthening exposure duration. In Experiment 1b, although quantitatively different, the two tasks were similarly affected by increasing the display frequency from 30 to 37.5 Hz and stimulus size from four to eight elements.

Despite the qualitative similarity of performance for the two types of task, the less accurate performance on the phase detection task than rows–columns task suggests localized phase detection does not determine performance in the

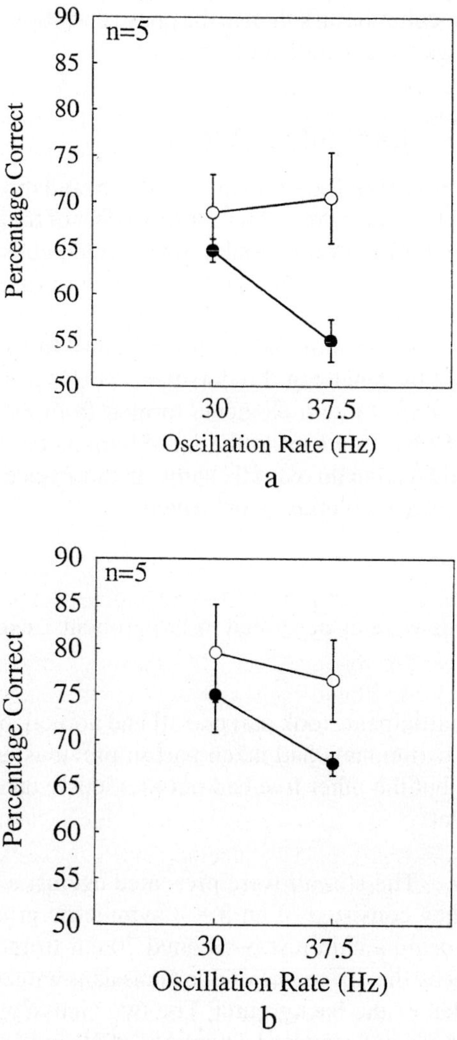

Figure 4. Illustrates for (a) the small and (b) the large stimuli the percentage of correct responses for each task and rate of oscillation. The phase detection task is represented by black circles and the rows–columns tasks by white circles.

rows–columns task. The results are consistent with the suggestion that participants used grouping cues in both the phase detection and rows–columns tasks and that differences in the level of participants' accuracy are due to differences in the relative salience of perceptual groups. The grouping cues are, of course, much stronger in the rows–columns task than in the phase detection task, where any simple linear groupings are dependent on chance.

EXPERIMENT 2

One argument against the results of Experiments 1a and 1b, and those of Usher and Donnelly (1998, Exp. 1), as demonstrating a direct effect of temporal modulations on grouping is that it might be possible for oriented cells with large receptive fields to detect luminance changes during row–column presentations. This would be possible if, within a temporal frame, oriented cells could sum the luminance changes caused by presenting a row (or column). In Experiment 2 this issue was investigated by replacing the dots used in Experiment 1 (and Usher & Donnelly, 1998, Exp. 1) with elements formed from the difference between two Gaussians (DOG) that sum to the same luminance as the background. Such stimuli would lead to no overall change in luminance, relative to the background, when a row (or column) is presented.

Method

The methodological details were as described in Experiment 1 except for the following changes.

Participants. Eight participants took part and all had normal, or corrected to normal, vision. Three participants had taken part in previous experiments using a similar paradigm but the other five had not previously taken part in a psychophysical experiment.

Stimuli and apparatus. The stimuli were presented against a grey background (12.97 cd/m^2). They consisted of an 8 × 8 symmetric grid of evenly spaced elements viewed using a chin rest positioned 70 cm from the screen. Each element was defined by the difference of two Gaussians with a mean spatial luminance equal to that of the background. The two Gaussians had peak contrasts of 27.1% and 15.8% and standard deviations of 10 and 14.7 arc min, respectively. The distance between the centre point of each element was 61.26 arc min. The non-linear relationship between the internal coding of the 256 pixel grey levels and the luminance output of the monitor was corrected using a lookup table. This was produced by measuring the luminance output of the monitor using a LMT L1000 luminance meter and fitting a quadratic expression to the data.

Design and procedure. The participants performed a 3AFC task classifying the stimulus on the basis of its temporal characteristics. The three buttons on the SGI mouse were used to indicate either rows (alternate rows of elements alternated out-of-phase), columns (alternate columns of elements alternated out-of-phase), or non-temporally segmented (all the elements alternated in phase) response. In the event of an incorrect response participants heard a beep. Participants performed four blocks of thirty trials (comprising ten trials for each temporal configuration) at both rates of temporal oscillation (30 and 37.5 Hz).

Results

The results in Table 1 show the proportions of participants' responses that were within each of the three possible categories (rows, columns, and non-temporally segmented) broken down by stimulus type and rate of flicker. The probability of choosing rows, one sample $t(7) = 3.01, p < .05$, or columns, one sample $t(7) = 6.6, p < .01$, consistent with the temporal manipulation was considerably greater than chance. However, the probability of correctly identifying a non-temporally segmented condition was no better than expected on the basis of chance, one sample $t(7) = 1.464, p > .05$. There was no difference in the likelihood of responding correctly between the two rates of flicker, $t(7) = 0.603, p > .05$.

Discussion

The results indicate that participants can perform the discrimination for a stimulus array in which the mean luminance of each element is the same as that of the background. Furthermore, the similarity of the results of Experiment 2 with the rows–columns conditions of Experiments 1a and 1b, and those from Experiment 1 of Usher and Donnelly (1998), suggest that luminance summation

TABLE 1
The stimulus/response matrix (means and associated standard errors for 8 observers) for both rates of flicker

	30 Hz			*37.5 Hz*		
	Response-R	*Response-C*	*Response-S*	*Response-R*	*Response-C*	*Response-S*
Stimulus-R	.44 (.05)	.21 (.05)	.35 (.05)	.48 (.05)	.21 (.05)	.31 (.03)
Stimulus-C	.1 (.02)	.64 (.04)	.25 (.03)	.15 (.02)	.56 (.06)	.28 (.03)
Stimulus-S	.28 (.04)	.30 (.05)	.42 (.03)	.33 (.02)	.32 (.03)	.35 (.04)
Total	.82	1.15	1.02	.96	1.09	.94

The three types of stimuli, R(ows), C(olumns), and S(ynchronous), are shown as rows and the three possible responses as columns. The values are normalized to the fractions of response generated for each stimulus, and the numbers in each row sum to unity.

within cells having elongated receptive fields is unlikely to account for the results of those experiments.

The outer edges of the Gaussian stimuli are closer together than the edges of the circular stimuli used in previous experiments. Therefore, it remains possible that participants performed Experiment 2 by detecting a local motion gradient. Usher and Donnelly argued that if implicit motion were used to perform the rows–columns task then it would affect the distribution of participants' errors. To discriminate between either of the temporally segmented conditions (rows or columns) and the non-temporally segmented condition on the basis of the motion cue merely required the participants to detect the presence or absence of motion. However, to discriminate between the two temporally segmented conditions required participants to distinguish the direction of the perceived motion. Previous studies have demonstrated that thresholds for the detection of motion are lower (e.g., Ball, Sekuler, & Machamer, 1983) or not different from (Levinson & Sekuler, 1975)[1] those for detecting the direction of motion of stimuli moving in orthogonal or opposing directions. Participants were significantly more likely to confuse temporally segmented and non-temporally segmented displays than to confuse the two temporally segmented conditions, $F(1, 6) = 22.5, p < .01$; see Figure 5). Such a pattern of errors runs counter to the pattern expected if the implicit motion argument were true and confirms the results of Experiment 2 to be dependent on temporal alternation affecting perceptual grouping.

EXPERIMENT 3

Experiments 1 and 2 have provided evidence supporting the notion that fast temporal modulations influence perceptual organization. They have done so by investigating whether local discrimination of temporal phase and luminance summation within cells having elongated receptive fields can account for the influence of rapid temporal alternation in perceptual input on the perception of rows–columns in an ambiguous display of dots or dot-like stimuli. In Experiment 3, evidence is sought against the suggestion that participants perform the task by isolating the spatial structure of an individual frame of the stimuli by

[1]The difference in results depends on whether movement in random dots or gratings is being measured. Given that the stimuli used in the present experiments are dots organized like gratings, it is not clear what the appropriate point of comparison should be. On the one hand the regularity makes our stimuli more similar to that of grating stimuli, on the other hand the symmetry between the vertical and horizontal directions makes them more similar to random dot displays. However it is important to note that the threshold for detecting the direction of movement is never lower than that for detecting movement itself. Only if the threshold for detecting direction of movement were lower that that for detecting movement itself would the logic of this experiment be compromized.

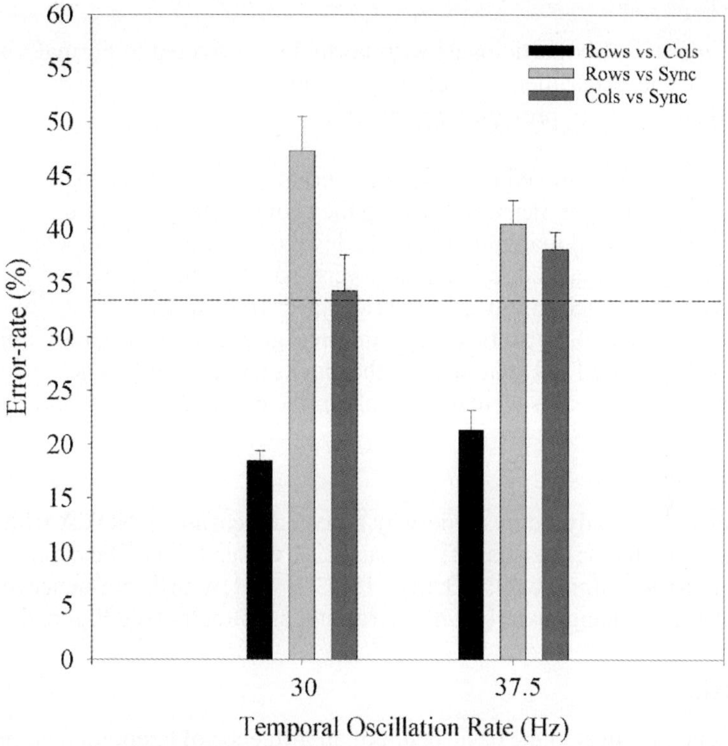

Figure 5. Depicts the mean percentage error rates among rows, columns and non-temporally segmented conditions. Assuming an even distribution of errors within each condition, the probability of making any particular type of error is 33% (denoted by the dotted line).

examining the relationship between spatial and temporal cues. Experiment 3 introduced the same temporal segmentation manipulation as in Experiment 1 but modestly adjusting the spatial arrangement of the grid so that it was no longer symmetrical. If temporal cues are found to influence participants to the same extent as before when the spatial asymmetry increases, then this would suggest they are able to isolate information from individual stimulus frames. This is because the spatial asymmetry within an individual frame (where either alternate columns or rows are omitted generating an asymmetry of 2:1) is of a far greater magnitude than the spatial asymmetry between adjacent elements across frames introduced by the experimental manipulation (that vary between 1.1:1 and 1.3:1). If, however, increasing spatial asymmetry leads to a reduction in the influence of temporal cues on grouping then this would be evidence for an interaction of spatial and temporal cues in the grouping that takes place in the perceptual organisation of the rows–columns ambiguous figure.

Method

Participants. Six participants with normal or corrected to normal vision took part in the experiment. Three participants were naïve observers, while three had taken part in previous experiments.

Procedure. The procedure was as in Experiment 1 except that participants were trained on the symmetrical grid until they could make judgements consistent with the temporal manipulation at the level of 75–80% correct. Once this criterion had been reached, participants were asked to make the same judgement but given 6 blocks of 60 asymmetrical grids (repeating each ratio of spatial asymmetry twice). The ratio of asymmetrical grids presented to participants was 1.1:1, 1.2:1, and 1.3:1. The order of the blocks was counterbalanced using a Latin square. Participants were tested only in the 60 Hz 8 × 8 dot condition.

Results

The results were analysed by a one-way repeated measures ANOVA with the factor (asymmetry: 1:1 versus 1.1:1 versus 1.2:1 versus 1.3:1). The main effect of asymmetry was significant, $F(3,15) = 15.03, p < .01$, with the influence of the temporal cue reducing linearly with increasing asymmetry (see Figure 6).

Discussion

Experiment 3 replicated the basic result of an influence of temporal manipulation on rows–columns decisions when using a symmetrical grid of dots. The asymmetry manipulation has shown, however, that the influence of the temporal cue reduces as the spatial asymmetry increases. This result is important for two reasons. First, it provides further evidence against an account of performance based on the isolation of information from a single stimulus frame. If participants had been isolating different frames within each cycle then the resulting 2:1 asymmetry within each frame would have influenced performance to a greater extent than the 1.1:1 to 1.3:1 asymmetries created by changing the distances of dots in the overall grid.

The second reason why the results of Experiment 3 are of interest is that they demonstrate emergent grouping in the row–column figure to be affected by contributions from both temporal and spatial grouping cues. The influence of the temporal cue over the spatial cue decreases linearly with increasing asymmetry. This effect is most clearly demonstrated in a follow-up experiment in which four participants (two experienced and two naïve observers) were given the same task but performing many more trials per condition. The results for each participant are shown in Figure 7 broken down by whether the temporal and spatial cues are consistent or inconsistent. In each case, spatial cues dominate over temporal cues as spatial asymmetry increases.

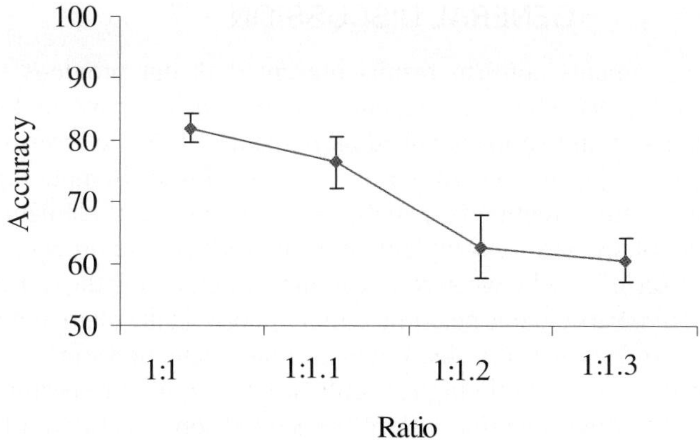

Figure 6. Depicts performance in the rows–columns task as a function of spatial asymmetry.

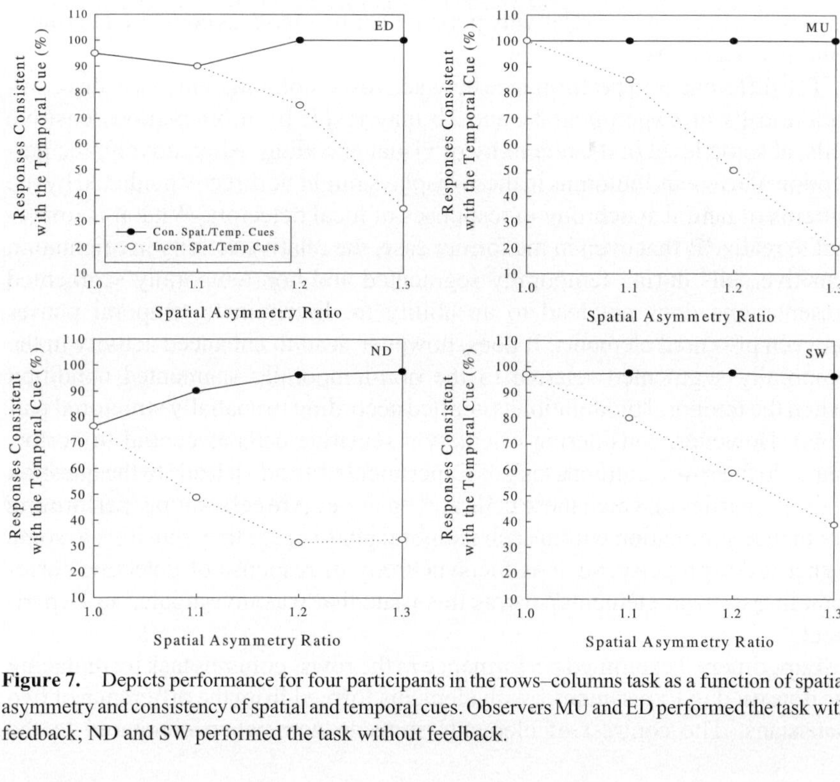

Figure 7. Depicts performance for four participants in the rows–columns task as a function of spatial asymmetry and consistency of spatial and temporal cues. Observers MU and ED performed the task with feedback; ND and SW performed the task without feedback.

GENERAL DISCUSSION

The present experiments confirm results presented in our previous report (Usher & Donnelly, 1998) but extend them in significant and important ways. First, Experiments 1a and 1b investigated participants' ability to discriminate temporally segmented from non-temporally segmented trials (temporal phase detection), when a non-structured (spatially randomized) set of elements was presented in one phase and its complement in the other phase, in contrast to their ability to discriminate between row–column stimuli (using the same temporal modulations). Participants performed more poorly in the phase detection tasks than in the rows–columns tasks. When the phase detection stimuli varied from trial to trial, a significantly higher contrast was required to perform the phase detection than rows–columns task. When a fixed non-structured stimulus was used in the phase detection task, performance in the phase detection was worse with the 13.3 ms than 16.7 ms temporal segmentation interval, whereas performance in the rows–columns task was relatively unaffected by reducing the temporal segmentation interval from 16.7 ms to 13.3 ms. These results demonstrate performance in the rows–columns task cannot be the result of isolating individual frames and making decisions on the basis of spatial asymmetry or a result of a local phase discrimination (between proximal elements). This is because participants are relatively poor at making phase, as compared to rows–columns, decisions.

The differences in performance between rows–columns and phase discrimination tasks in Experiment 1a and 1b may result from orientation sensitive cells, at some level in the hierarchy of visual encoding. Alternatively, the perception of rows and columns in these displays might be directly mediated by the patterns of neural synchrony in responses of local detectors. What it is important to realize is that even in the former case, the relative activity in orientation sensitive cells during temporally segmented and non-temporally segmented presentations does not lead to an ability to discriminate temporal phases between proximal elements. It does, however, lead to enhanced activity in the temporally segmented relative to the non-temporally segmented condition (when the temporal modulation is applied according to spatially structured patterns). However, considering orientation sensitive cells as central to performance in the rows–columns task of Experiments 1a and 1b leads to the question of the properties to which these cells are sensitive? Are cells simply performing luminance summation within each temporal phase or are they sensitive to some higher order property, such as the synchrony of response of detectors corresponding to local elements? It was this issue that was investigated in Experiment 2.

Experiment 2 examined performance in the rows–columns task by replacing the dots used in Experiment 1 with elements formed from the difference of two Gaussians. The contrast of elements sums to zero when compared to the background luminance and so lead to no average change in luminance. The results of Experiment 2 demonstrate that participants were able to perform the rows–columns task as with the dot elements used previously. They showed, therefore, that the orientation sensitive cells are not just performing luminance summation.

Together the results of Experiments 1 and 2 replicate and extend the basic findings of Usher and Donnelly (1998). They are important because they remove grounds for explanations of the effect of temporal modulations on perception of rows and columns based on pair-wise phase discrimination and simple (linear) contrast summation. The effect of temporally segmented presentations of rows and columns on the interpretation of an equidistantly spaced grid of dots suggests that the temporal segmentation had its direct influence on perceptual grouping.

Evidence for how temporal segmentation influences perceptual grouping can be found in Experiment 3. Experiment 3 investigated the effect of introducing spatial asymmetry into the grid of dots. The impact of spatial asymmetry on the perception of rows and columns is well known. The results of Experiment 3 showed that the influence of the temporal cue reduced linearly with spatial asymmetry. These results suggest spatial cues dominated over temporal cues when spatial cues led to an unambiguous interpretation of the display and that both spatial and temporal factors contributed to grouping.

It is important to emphasize that the effect of modulations on grouping were very much reduced when these modulations were applied in relation to non-structured spatial patterns, replicating some of the negative findings reported in previous studies (Kiper et al., 1996; Leonards et al., 1996). These negative findings imply that fast temporal modulations in visual input are able to induce neural synchrony in the responses of visual detectors relevant for task performance only when external modulations are consistent with the internal synchronization patterns supported by lateral connections. Since this is minimized when temporal modulations are applied on non-structured spatial patterns, the reduced effects of temporal modulations in such conditions can be naturally explained. Furthermore, it should be expected that the impact of fast temporal modulations on grouping will be optimal in multi-stable perceptual displays, where the effect of small differences in synchrony can be amplified.

Preliminary computational simulations show that the interaction between spatial and temporal cues in the perceptual organization of the row–column ambiguous figure arise spontaneously in a relatively simple neural network model. The model is composed of clusters of integrate and fire, orientation sensitive, cells whose receptive fields correspond to element locations (Usher, Donnelly, & Parton, 2000). In this model, cells are connected by excitatory lateral connections between isolinear proximal detectors, and via local cross-orientation inhibition. The model shows that for fast temporal modulations the patterns of neural synchrony are dominated by the excitatory lateral connections (which depend on spatial relations) and that externally induced synchrony has its effect only when consistent with the internal synchrony mediated by spatial relations. This makes sense if the visual system is trying to integrate fast temporal modulations in visual input (reducing very significantly their effect in the visual system) while trying to induce its own internal temporal synchrony that plays a role in grouping. The effect of external synchrony (on time scales shorter than the integration of the visual system) can be observed as a small but important effect that provides an opportunity to trick the visual system by tapping in to the coding mechanism for binding.

REFERENCES

Alais, D., Blake, R., & Lee, S.-H. (1998). Visual features that vary together over time group together over space. *Nature Neuroscience*, *1*, 160–164.

Ball, K., Sekuler, R., & Machamer, J. (1983). Detection and identification of moving targets. *Vision Research*, *23*, 229–238.

Donnelly, N., & Usher, M. (1999). The effect of spatial factors on temporal binding in the row/column ambiguous figure. *Investigative Ophthalmology and Visual Science*, *40*, S357.

Elliott, M.A., & Müller, H.J. (1998). Synchronous information presented in 40-Hz flicker enhances visual feature binding. *Psychological Science*, *9*, 277–283.

Fahle, M. (1993). Figure–ground discrimination from temporal information. *Proceedings of the Royal Society of London Series B—Biological Sciences*, *254*, 199–203.

Fahle, M., & Koch, C. (1995). Spatial displacement, but not temporal asynchrony, destroys figural binding. *Vision Research*, *35*, 491–494.

Field, D.J., Hayes, A., & Hess, R.F. (1993). Contour integration by the human visual system: evidence for a local "association field". *Vision Research*, *33*, 173–193.

Kiper, D.S., Gegenfurtner, K.R. & Movshon, J.A. (1996). Cortical oscillatory responses do not affect visual segmentation. *Vision Research*, *36*, 539–544.

Leonards, U., Singer, W., & Fahle, M. (1996). The influence of temporal phase differences on texture segmentation. *Vision Research*, *36*, 2689–2697.

Levinson, E., & Sekuler, R. (1975). The independence of channels in human vision selective for direction of movement. *Journal of Physiology*, *250*, 347–366.

Singer, W. (1999) Time as coding space? *Current Opinion in Neurobiology*, *9*, 189–194.

Usher, M., & Donnelly, N. (1998). Visual synchrony affects binding and segmentation in perception. *Nature*, *394*, 179–182.

Usher, M., Donnelly, N., & Parton, A. (2000, March). *The effect of temporal synchrony and spatial factors on perceptual grouping: Empirical evidence and a theoretical framework.* Paper presented at the Neural Binding of Space and Time symposium, University of Leipzig and Max Planck Institute of Cognitive Neuroscience, Leipzig, Germany.

von der Malsburg, C. (1981). *The correlation theory of brain function* (Internal Rep. 81–2). Department of Neurobiology, Max Planck Institute for Biophysical Chemistry, 3400 Göttingen, Germany.

VISUAL COGNITION, 2001, *8* (3/4/5), 655–677

Effects of stimulus synchrony on mechanisms of perceptual organization

Mark A. Elliott and Hermann J. Müller
Institut für Allgemeine Psychologie, Universität Leipzig, Germany

When neurons adopt a synchronized, oscillatory response to stimulus Gestalten, the phase of those oscillations almost always varies relative to stimulus activity. This has been taken to indicate that form-coding mechanisms are synchronized by internal timing mechanisms, and/or may be sensitive to stimulus activity only via motion detectors. This proposal is problematic for interpreting recent demonstrations of the effects of stimulus synchrony particularly when stimuli are stationary. Here we offer an account of stimulus-driven synchronization supported by evidence that segmentation by stimulus synchrony can be relatively insensitive to explicit motion signals. The argument is made that qualitative similarities between the effects of phase-independent and phase-locked oscillations in the EEG, the effects of phase synchronization at the cellular level and evidence for phase-enhanced stimulus grouping should be considered as functionally equivalent. This argument emphasizes the flexibility of temporal synchrony as a code for perceptual organization.

Visual objects or object groupings may be considered as composites of separable attributes or "features" describing the length, spatial frequency, orientation, colour, motion, etc. of their constituent elements. In order for an object to be perceived, its component features must be "bound" together to form a unified stimulus representation. A candidate process by which feature attributes may become bound is the phase synchronization of neural discharges across the separate mechanisms coding different attributes of the same visual stimulus (e.g., the "temporal-binding" hypothesis of Crick & Koch, 1990; see also

---

Please address all correspondence to M.A. Elliott, Institut für Allgemeine Psychologie, Universität Leipzig, Seeburgstr. 14/20, D-04103 Leipzig, Germany. Email: elliott@uni-leipzig.de

This research was supported by Deutsche Forschungsgemeinschaft project grant SCHR 375/8-1. The authors are grateful to Greg Davis, Anne Giersch, Christoph Herrmann, J. Toby Mordkoff, and two anonymous reviewers for their helpful comments on earlier drafts of this paper. Thanks are extended to Konstantin Meyer and Nils von Daaken for their assistance with data collection and Alex Aksentijević for assistance in manuscript preparation.

http://www.tandf.co.uk/journals/pp/13506285.html DOI:10.1080/13506280143000188

Eckhorn et al., 1988; Gray, König, Engel, & Singer, 1989). Evidence in support of this idea has been provided by physiological studies of phase synchronization in the primary visual cortex (areas 17 and 18) in anaesthetized cat and monkey (see Eckhorn et al., 1988; Engel, König, Kreiter, & Singer, 1991; Gray et al., 1989; Kreiter & Singer, 1992). When visuo-cortical cells with adjacent (but non-overlapping) receptive fields were stimulated by separate bars of light moving in opposite directions, oscillatory neural activity showed low cross-correlation. However, when the bars were passed across the receptive fields in the same direction, a correlative relationship was observed between oscillatory activity within the 20–80-Hz (approximately the gamma) bandwidth. The strongest cross-correlations were obtained when a single, connected, bar stimulated the cells. Thus, cross-correlated neuronal firing was manifest only when cells responded to separate elements of the same "Gestalt" (findings consistent with the temporal correlation hypothesis of von der Malsburg, 1981). These observations have given rise to the idea that oscillatory neural activity and the consequent synchronization of firing patterns represent one important neurophysiological correlate of the "binding" of stimulus feature elements. Occurrences of oscillatory synchronization are not regularly phase-locked to temporal stimulus modulation, that is, even though phase locking can occur, oscillatory synchronization may not be strictly dependent upon the timing of stimulus events. These findings have been taken as evidence for the internal generation of synchrony in primary visual cortex, possibly mediated by mechanisms in higher motion-sensitive areas (Singer, 1996; Singer & Gray, 1995).

These studies have raised a number of important issues concerning the relationship between neural synchronization and perceptual organization. One issue of particular importance is whether or not neural synchronization can be generalized to the coding of "stationary" groupings (i.e., groupings that are regularly presented at the *same place* in visual space). We will review evidence from experimental psychophysics and electroencephalographic (EEG) studies that support this generalization. Some studies have shown that the perceptual organization of stationary forms can be enhanced by rapid, repeated, and synchronized stimulus presentations (Elliott & Müller, 1998; Fahle, 1993; Usher & Donnelly, 1998). This raises the related issue of the extent to which neural synchrony in form-coding mechanisms is *dependent* upon support from motion-sensitive mechanisms coding rapid transient activity in the stimulus. More generally, should synchronization of form-coding mechanisms be considered exclusively in terms of third-party synchronization (e.g., modulated directly or indirectly by motion-sensitive mechanisms)? If not (and we shall argue against the exclusivity of this hypothesis), what assumptions are required in order to account for the various demonstrations of synchronization within a single explanatory framework?

THE EFFECTS OF SYNCHRONIZATION BY TEMPORALLY-MODULATED STATIONARY STIMULUS PRESENTATION

Experimental psychophysics has approached grouping by synchronization from the position that, when two or more stimulus events occur at the same time relative to other stimulus events (i.e., when they are specific to a single phase of multi-phase stimulus activity), the stimuli will be bound together due to common phase angle (Elliott & Müller, 1998; Fahle, 1993; Leonards, Singer, & Fahle, 1996; Usher & Donnelly, 1998) or temporal correlation (Alais, Blake, & Lee, 1998; Lee & Blake, 1999). Underlying this idea is the notion that, when phase-aligned stimuli group according to one or another Gestalt principle, the effects of phase alignment will modulate the temporal structure of neural mechanisms coding the group's elements, making them fire in synchrony. By this logic, the behavioural effects of stimulus synchronization (and its inferred effects upon neural synchronization) could range from the enhancement of groupings that would also be formed in the absence of temporal stimulus modulation, to the induction of groupings that would not be perceived otherwise (henceforth referred to as "enhanced" and "induced" groupings, respectively). Of course, if the individual stimulus events were clearly discernible, the effects of simultaneity would be trivial. Consequently, the to-be-grouped and non-grouping stimuli are presented at phase angles of a common presentation frequency, below the threshold for discriminating their temporal and/or spatial structure (Elliott & Müller, 1998; Parton, Donnelly, & Usher, this issue; Usher & Donnelly, 1998).

The paradigms of Elliott and Müller, Fahle, Leonards et al., and Usher and Donnelly have used stationary stimulus displays consisting of spatial configurations partly or entirely defined by temporal phase relative to background or distractor items. The various findings produced with these paradigms broadly support the idea that stimulus synchronization does influence grouping. The basic paradigm consists of displays composed of subsets of stimulus elements that differ in their presentation phase, with the result that, for certain temporal asynchronies and/or phase angles, either the perceptual saliency of a target subset was enhanced (Fahle; Leonards et al.) or a critical subset primed the detection of a subsequently presented target Gestalt (Elliott & Müller); or observers, presented with lattice displays of potentially bistable (row or column) organization, reported the organization supported by synchronized element presentation (Usher & Donnelly). Although all these studies appeal to synchronizing neural mechanisms to explain their results, the various accounts tend to diverge concerning the functional requirement for the grouping mechanism to respond *directly* to stimulus synchrony. Specifically, there is disagreement as to the extent to which the phase synchrony of repeated stimulus presentations is responsible for generating a matching pattern of phase synchrony in responding neural mechanisms. The basis for disagreement lies in the findings mentioned earlier that, when neurons synchronize with an oscillatory pattern to stimulus activity, the phase of the oscillation varies relative to that of stimulus events.

One possibility examined by Leonards et al. (1996) was that the visual system may operate in different, but interacting modes when segmenting temporal and texture cues. In Leonards et al's study, the observers were presented with a matrix of 7 × 7 equally spaced line segments. This matrix contained vertically or horizontally oriented subsets of 3 × 5 or, respectively, 5 × 3 target line elements ("rectangle"), distinguished from the background elements by either textural or temporal cues or both. Observers had to discriminate the orientation of the target rectangle. There were five experimental conditions: (1) single target rectangle composed of elements that differed slightly in orientation from background elements (textural cues only); (2) single target rectangle with elements presented in frame alternating with frame of background elements (temporal cues only); (3) single target rectangle composed of elements that differed from background elements in both orientation and presentation frame (combined textural and temporal cues); (4) two "superimposed" rectangles, one defined by temporal offset and the other by orientation relative to the background elements; (5) target elements differing from background elements in orientation, but displayed in alternating frames each presenting random constellations of half the target and half the background elements. The results showed that the rectangle could be segregated from the background on the basis of temporal cues alone (given a temporal offset between the target and background elements >10 ms) and textural cues alone, but that figure–ground segregation was enhanced when both types of cue defined the target. When there was competition between the two types of cue, only the more salient figure was reported. Finally, the detection of a figure defined by textural cues was not affected by potentially conflicting temporal cues if these did not themselves define a figure.

Leonards et al. proposed that grouping may be based on two separate systems, the outputs of which might combine in a synergistic fashion[1] the motion-

[1]It is not clear from the psychophysical (% correct) data of Leonards et al. (1996) exactly how the motion and form-based systems interact. Theoretically, both systems could determine the required orientation discrimination separately (assuming that the motion system has independent form representation capability), and there could be a parallel race between both systems to determine the discrimination, without any facultative ("synergistic") interaction between the two systems. Such a parallel race model could equally explain (a) why discrimination performance is superior when both temporal and textural cues are available (because the likelihood that at least one system produces the correct response within the limited exposure time available is increased), (b) why the more salient cues are dominating performance (because these permit orientation to be derived faster), and (c) why texturally-based discrimination is not interfered with by temporal cues that do not themselves define an oriented target form (because the motion-based response does then not conflict with the form-based discrimination). RT methodology designed to test the "race model inequality" (Miller, 1982) is more suited to distinguish between parallel-race and coactivation models.

sensitive system (system A) that processes temporal cues, and the form-based system (system B) that processes textural cues. System A "signal[s] with great precision on- and offset of stimuli, so that the timing of external events is precisely reflected by the time course of neuronal responses. This system could then exploit the synchronicity of responses to simultaneous visual events for binding". In contrast, system B "must allow texture cues to override conflicting temporal cues and should thus be rather insensitive to the temporal structure of stimuli. . . . [system B] responses . . . should be sufficiently sustained to bridge brief temporal interruptions of visual stimuli. . . . the responses to texturally related figure elements conveyed by system B [may] become synchronized and bound together by intracortical interactions and [. . .] *independently of the temporal structure of external stimuli*" (Leonards et al., 1996, p. 2696, emphasis added). Thus, critically, stimulus phase was argued to be neither necessary nor sufficient for neural synchronization to occur in form-based system B. That correlated spatiotemporal changes alone are effective for *motion-based* grouping has recently been demonstrated by Alais et al. (1998; see also Lee & Blake, 1999), who investigated the computation of global motion in a unique direction from local oscillating gratings viewed briefly through four discontinuous, non-overlapping, apertures (arranged in the form of a square). Global motion direction was most reliably derived when the contrast modulations of the four gratings changed in an identical fashion over time (i.e., when they were correlated). Alais et al. restated the "temporal correlation hypothesis" to explain their findings, specifically that "local visual features that vary together over time tend to be grouped together over space" (p. 162)—by synchronization of neural responses to those features, giving rise to the perception of global moving form based "solely" upon correlated (explicit) motion signals. However, as noted by Gegenfurtner (1998), "motion perception is—in the end—nothing but the determination of the spatiotemporal correlational structure of the stimulus. It should therefore not come as a surprise that synchronized contrast changes have a major effect on such correlations" (p. 98).

At issue however, is the extent to which explanations in terms of correlated motion signals might account for synchrony enhanced, or induced *stationary* figure grouping. Usher and Donnelly (1998, p. 179) questioned the idea that the motion-sensitive system is uniquely responsible for mediating the effects of stimulus synchrony. They argued that the orientation discrimination required in the task of Leonards et al. (1996) could be performed "on the basis of local gradients at texture boundaries . . . gradient computations at boundaries [may] generate a (possibly implicit) motion signal that partially mediates the effect". In their own study, Usher and Donnelly attempted to eliminate the potential influence of any such signals, to "demonstrate the existence of a grouping mechanism that is independent of the computation of motion (even if only implicit)" (p. 179). To achieve this, they presented a display matrix composed of identical and equally spaced elements, filled circles, with display frames of alternate rows or, respectively, columns of elements presented successively and repeatedly. The use of identical elements removed the potential for synchrony to be conveyed by implicit motion signals generated at texture boundaries (by orientation displacements of a subset of display elements). In addition, the temporal asynchrony between successive display frames was subthreshold, giving rise to the perception of a "static" matrix with no noticeable motion or flicker. Nevertheless, repeated synchronized presentation of display elements within alternate rows or columns was found to bias observer's reports of the orientation of groupings within the matrix (as rows or columns), without the presentations being experienced in terms of motion. These results would appear to question the proposal of Leonards et al.: How can stimulus-related phase synchronization determine grouping if (1) the motion system (system A) is not engaged by stimulus presentation and (2) grouping within the form system (system B) is unrelated to the regular phase of oscillatory stimulus activity?

Despite the precautions taken by Usher and Donnelly, the possibility remains that their results may still be attributable to motion-sensitive mechanisms engaged by the repeated on- and offsets of the row or, respectively, column stimuli (Gegenfurtner, personal communication). Consistent with this, there is evidence for limited Gestalt representation by the motion system (e.g., Logothetis & Schall, 1989; Yantis, 1992), which, in Yantis' study, was based upon the finding that visual attention was preferentially deployed to sudden-onset stimuli if these formed regular polygons. This would suggest that the deployment of visual attention is important for form to be derived from motion cues (e.g., because visual attention is preferentially allocated in Gestalt configurations).

However, there are several qualifications to this line of argument. Elliott and Müller (1998) found no evidence that localized flickering stimuli summoned visual attention in their paradigm, arguing that the mechanisms involved in Yantis' paradigm are not invoked by all kinds of temporally modulated stimulation, in particular; not by the subthreshold phase modulation of stationary stimulus presentation used in the paradigms of Usher and Donnelly (1998) (and Elliott & Müller, 1998), which rendered the various asynchronized spatial structures within their display matrices non-detectable (i.e., all stimuli were always fully visible within the context of temporally contiguous display matrices). The flickering stimulation used in these paradigms probably generates multiple successive temporal-impulse responses. The partial integration of each response with preceding and subsequent responses would reduce the relative amplitude of any single response. As a result, no single stimulus presentation would generate a response with sufficient relative amplitude to uniquely signal its presence within the flickering display matrices. In other words, unlike a single sudden stimulus onset, an individual stimulus onset within a train of repeated presentations would have insufficient strength to engage the visual attention system (see Elliott & Müller, 2000, for a more detailed development of this argument).

IS PRIMING BY STIMULUS SYNCHRONY DEPENDENT UPON LOCAL MOTION SIGNALS?

Considering all the evidence reviewed thus far, the necessity for facultative interactions between the motion and form systems during stimulus-driven synchrony generation is not generally supported. Instead, synchronized stimulus presentation influences perceptual organization in the absence of implicit or explicit motion cues, and without local transient signals acting in the same fashion as sudden-onset cues. However, these objections simply restate the fundamental question to be answered: How transient signals, although substantially weakened by the relative reduction in response amplitudes following rapid sequential stimulus presentation, become an effective means for synchronization in form coding mechanisms? We considered this question from two alternative perspectives: Either the motion system may not exclusively code stimulus synchrony, or stimulus synchrony is indeed coded as a result of responses within the motion system (despite an absence of implicit or explicit motion signals), though with little or no influence upon mechanisms responsible for the deployment of visual attention. Under these circumstances, the effects of neural synchronization for form coding may be a subtle outcome of coincident neural responses to repeated transient stimuli, which may become available for measurement only under very specific stimulus presentation conditions.

According to the proposals of Leonards et al. (1996), the form-coding system (B) is not capable of responding with the level of temporal precision, and at the temporal frequencies, required for temporal synchrony to be effective. However, this proposal may not be entirely accurate: The local presentation rates at which synchrony priming effects were obtained by Elliott and Müller (1998, 2000) are well within the temporal resolutions of form-coding mechanisms: Elliott and Müller presented premask display matrices (3×3 crosses) composed of four "local" asynchronized subset frames each presented at 10 Hz, for a given presentation time. In Elliott and Müller's paradigm the flickering premask display was followed by a static target display matrix (3×3 90°-corner junctions) that could contain an illusory (Kanizsa-type) target square

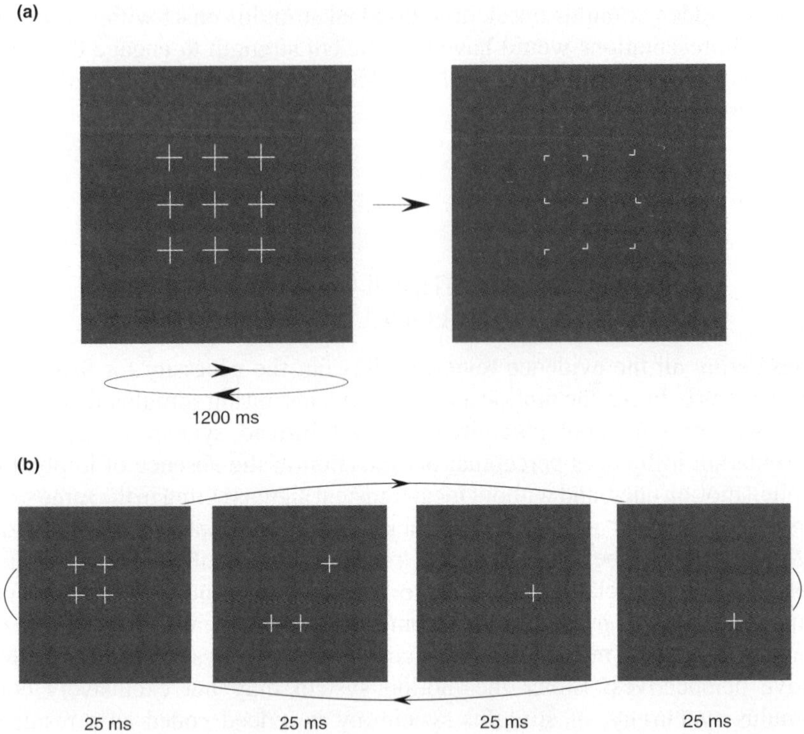

Figure 1. **(a)** Stimuli consisted of a flickering display of nine crosses illustrated on the left-hand side of the figure, followed by the presentation of a target display (right-hand illustration), to which the observers produced their target-present/absent RT response. This illustration shows premask-inducer and target-inducer specifications that are 60% and 20% respectively. In **(b)** an example sequence of the four separate premask-subset frames in the synchronous condition is illustrated (in which the first frame consists of four elements in square arrangement). The 40 Hz premask presentation frequency was defined as the frequency of occurrence of premask subsets per second. In other words, the entire premask matrix was presented as 10 times the 4 premask subsets per 1000 ms, with constant subset exposure duration of 25 ms and < 1ms inter-subset interval. In this way the premask sequence was continually "recycled" during premask presentation.

comprised of grouping corner junctions to be detected amongst the non-grouping distractor junctions (see Figure 1). In one condition, termed the "synchronous-premask" condition, the premask display contained a frame of four crosses in square arrangement presented at the location where the target figure appeared subsequently on target-present trials. This condition was compared to a "random-premask" condition in which the four premask crosses preceding the target figure were distributed across the four separate display frames. The basic finding was a "synchrony priming" effect, such that detection of a target square was expedited when it was presented at the same location as the four premask crosses in the synchronous-premask condition, relative to the random condition.[2] By using a premask display comprised of four different frames each repeating at 10 Hz, Elliott and Müller (1998) found that synchrony priming was specific to conditions under which the *global* rate of premask presentations across the whole display matrix was set at 40 Hz. Elliott and Müller (2000) also found that the prime adopted a 40-Hz structure consistent with the global presentation frequency of the premask frame presentations. Elliott and Müller's proposal that the oscillating prime adopts the precise phase of stimulus presentation has received support from the examination of the matching frequency of neural activity in the EEG (Elliott, Herrmann, Mecklinger, & Müller, 2000). Using the basic paradigm of Elliott and Müller, Elliott et al. recorded a specific pattern of neural activity under priming conditions at the exact frequency and, importantly, locked to the phase of stimulus presentation only at electrodes overlying right posterior cortex (i.e., O2 and T6) which correlated well with more anterior cortical loci (i.e., P3 and T4).

Although little evidence was found by Elliott et al. (2000) to support the idea that priming is generated as a direct response to the local premask-frame repetitions at 10 Hz, generation of the 40-Hz prime is nevertheless related to the presentation of local 10 Hz signals, which could be coded within either magnocellular or parvocellular pathways or both (Lennie, Trevarthan, van Essen, & Wässle, 1990). This means that either, or both the motion and form-coding systems became induced locally by the temporal stimulus modulation. Elliott and Müller (2000) suggested that early mechanisms in the form system might be the principal location for the generation and maintenance of the "synchronous prime". However, there is no a priori reason to suppose that the motion system was not also involved, particularly given the stimulus-locked EEG responses at electrodes over motion sensitive areas (P3 and T6). This raises the question whether the prime becomes (also) active in motion-coding mechanisms. If so, it should be possible to isolate such motion-based effects by varying the structural integrity of the priming (premask) and target stimuli, with the aim of producing synergistic interactions between the form and motion-coding systems along the lines postulated by Leonards et al. (1996). This question was examined in a single experiment described next.

---

[2]The effects of prime synchrony, expedited target detection reaction times (RTs) following synchronized premask presentation, were confined to target-present trials and obtained only when the global frequency of premask presentations was set to 40 Hz. The priming stimuli were non-detectable within the total premask display matrix. Furthermore, the priming effects were spatially specific: Target detection was expedited only when targets were presented in the same matrix location previously occupied by the synchronous premask (while there were neither benefits nor costs associated with synchronous premask presentation at other locations in the matrix relative to the target). This was taken to suggest that priming enhanced target coding in early mechanisms comprising neurons with highly spatially specific receptive fields (see Elliott & Müller, 1998, 2000).

EXPERIMENT

The experiment used a variant of Elliott and Müller's (1998, 2000) synchrony-priming paradigm. Reaction time (RT) measures were taken to the presence or absence of a target Kanizsa-type figures within a static target display matrix of 90°-corner junctions, which was preceded by a temporally modulated premask display matrix of crosses (synchronized and random conditions) (see Figure 1). In their previous studies, Elliott and Müller had used premask and target displays with identical dimensions and upon target display presentation, the premask crosses *reduced* to 90°-corner junctions by "removal" of redundant line segments (although the remaining line segments did not change in size). In the present experiment, the specification of the premask and target display stimuli was systematically varied by independently and factorially varying the length of the line segments making up the crosses (premask display) and corner junctions (target display). With regard to the target display, this effectively produced a variation of the "goodness" of the Kanizsa-type square target, which, according to Shipley and Kelman (1992), is a function of the ratio of the physically specified length of the collinear inducer (junction) segments to the total edge length of the Kanizsa-type square. The ratios introduced in the experiment were 20% ("poor" square), 40%, or 60% ("good" square) (with 20% being the ratio used in previous studies). The same ratios were used for the premask crosses, and premask-cross specification was manipulated independently of target-inducer specification. Thus, it was possible that the target inducers were specified at, say, 60%, whereas the preceding premask crosses were specified at 20%. In such cases of non-identical (i.e., non-covarying) specification, explicit motion cues were produced at target display presentation, for instance, with poorly specified premask crosses "expanding" along their axes into well-specified target inducers, or well-specified premask crosses "contracting" into poorly specified target inducers. In other words, at target display onset, more or less strong motions signals were generated that had the potential to influence target detection. Thus, by introducing these variations, the modified paradigm permitted figural cues (target goodness) to be manipulated independently of motion cues (temporal premask modulation plus any additional motion signals generated by inducer expansions or contractions at target display onset), so that possible interactions between the form and motion-coding systems could be examined.

The predictions were as follows. Target detection RTs, in both synchronous and random-premask conditions, were expected to decrease with increasing target-inducer specification, due to a general increase in target saliency. More important theoretically, based on the assumption of a facultative interaction between the motion and form systems (Leonards et al., 1996), it was also predicted that, as targets became easier to detect with increasing figural specification, the accompanying effects of prime synchrony would decrease significantly in magnitude (i.e., the synchronous and random-condition RTs would converge). Such a pattern would be expected if synchrony priming is generated solely within the motion system, while figural target specification determines the speed of computations within the form system. As these (form-based) computations become faster with increasing target inducer specification, the influence of (motion-based) synchrony priming on detection performance would decrease concomitantly. Such a pattern could be taken to indicate the presence of the prime in motion-coding mechanisms at the time of interaction between the prime and the neural response to target presentation. Conversely, no such interactive pattern of effects is expected if synchrony priming is principally generated and maintained within the form-coding system, consistent with the Elliott and Müller (2000) account. (Since the latter account predicts the null-hypothesis of no interaction, 20 participants were used to increase the power of the experiment to reveal any interaction.)

If the effects of priming become principally active in early mechanisms, as proposed by Elliott and Müller (2000; see also Elliott et al., 2000), local transient stimulus activity might offer a further indication of the relative importance of motion-coding mechanisms for synchrony priming. In conditions in which the premask and target inducer specifications did not covary, there were multiple, sudden local expansions or contractions when the premask elements transformed into those comprising the target display. For each element, expansion or contraction would always occur in two orthogonal directions as the premask crosses simultaneously transformed into corner junctions by removal of two line segments and the increase or decrease in size of the remaining line segments along each element axis. The local expansions or contractions were necessarily correlated between target elements, as the direction of motion was always relative to the center of the Kanizsa-type square but the motion signals induced by local expansions or contractions around the distractor elements were uncorrelated (in contrast with the paradigm of Lee & Blake, 1999). These motion signals are likely to be coded by local neural mechanisms sensitive to direction-specific, transient activity within their receptive fields, leading to the additional hypothesis that matrix expansion or contraction would provide an additional, target-related motion signal. If the motion system was already primed by synchronized premask presentation, this additional signal might serve to increase overall signal-to-noise ratio across spatially localized (i.e., early) synchronized mechanisms, boosting activity across the prime and thereby supporting the interaction of target with prime activity. Conversely, enhanced priming would not be expected under conditions in which the premask and target-inducer specifications covaried.

Method

Observers. Twenty observers (8 male; mean age 27.75 years; all with normal or corrected-to-normal vision), who were naive as to the purpose of the experiment, performed one block of practice trials immediately prior to each of three experimental sessions. Observers were paid at rate of 12.00 Deutschemarks per hour.

Apparatus and stimuli. Event timing, data collection, and stimulus image frame generation were controlled by a PC-compatible computer, which also controlled oscilloscopic image presentation through an Interactive Electronics Systems point plotter buffer with 8 Mb frame store memory (Finley, 1985). Image frames were presented on a 6" Tektronix 608-oscilloscope monitor equipped with a very fast-decay P15 phosphor. The use of a P15 phosphor ensured that on-screen image persistence reduced to 10% of normal image intensity within 2.8 μs of image termination (Bell, 1970). The Interactive Electronic Systems point plotter buffer allowed pixels to be plotted at a rate of one pixel every microsecond. The presentation frequency of frames across the entire premask display was kept constant at 40 Hz, while the entire premask matrix, consisting of a sequence of four separate frames, was recycled at a rate of 10 repeats per second (i.e., each premask frame repeated at 10 Hz). Frames had a constant exposure duration of 25 ms and an inter-frame interval of less than 1 ms. The continual recycling of the premask-frame sequence produced the phenomenal experience of a flickering display of nine crosses, within which observers were unable to discern the structure of a given frame. Both the individual premask frames and the target display frames were presented semi-static at a fixed 1 kHz refresh frequency.

Observers viewed the monitor at a distance of 57 cm (maintained via a chin rest). The experiments were conducted under controlled lighting conditions (mean screen surround luminance 0.078 cd/m^2), with stimulus luminance maintained at 0.3 cd/m^2 upon a background field of 0.075 cd/m^2. Display elements were arranged around the centre of the monitor screen (see Figure 1). Premask crosses (Figure 1b) subtended 51', 1°42', or 2°33' of visual angle and exhibited horizontal and vertical separations of 2°39', 1°48', or 57' for 20%, 40%, or 60% premask inducer specification conditions, respectively. The combination of these display dimensions produced premask displays in which the total 3 × 3 premask display matrix subtended 7°51' × 7°51', 8°42' × 8°42', or 9°33' × 9°33' of visual angle, respectively. For 20% inducer conditions, the premask crosses comprised 21 tightly spaced points, so that their segments appeared as uninterrupted lines, the number of pixels per cross was increased proportionate to the increased inducer specification for 40% and 60% inducer-specification conditions and relative to the 20% condition in order to equalize luminance across inducer-specification conditions. Premask frames could consist of 1, 2, 3, or 4 crosses presented simultaneously (Figure 1b), so that the amount of pixels presented in a given frame for the 20% inducer-specification condition (for example) could be 21, 42, 63, or 84. This would also have resulted in the luminance of premask stimuli varying across frames, with frames comprising fewer elements appearing brighter than those with more elements. Thus in the case of the 20%, inducer-specification condition, an additional 979, 958, 937, and 916 pixels were plotted for one-, two-, three-, and four-element frames (respectively), to an invisible corner of the display (with X,Y coordinates 0,0). Comparable procedures were carried out for the 40% and 60% inducer-specification conditions thereby equalizing the amount of pixels plotted in a single frame and maintaining frame presentations at a constant background frequency of 1 kHz. These procedures ensured that each frame was equiluminant despite changes in the amount of (visible) stimulus information presented. Junction elements in the target display (Figure 1a) subtended 26', 51', and 1°17' of visual angle and were separated horizontally and vertically by between 2°39'–3°30', 1°48'–3°30', or 57'–3°30', for 20%, 40%, and 60% target-inducer specification conditions. These variations produced Kanizsa-type figures representing "square" figures with probabilities of .1, .45, and .71, respectively (see Shipley & Kelman, 1992). The target displays subtended between 6°59'–7°51' × 6°59'–7°51', 6°59'–8°42' × 6°59'–8°42', or 6°59'–9°33' × 6°59'–9°33', respectively. Each target display junction consisted of 11 tightly spaced points. The target display overall consisted of 99 pixels. According to an identical procedure to that used for the premask displays, additional 901 pixels were plotted to an invisible corner of the display (i.e., with 0,0,0, X,Y,Z coordinates).

A trial started with a brief (300 ms) 250 Hz computer-generated tone. Following a delay of 200 ms, observers were presented with the oscillating 3 × 3 matrix of premask crosses, which, after 1200 ms, reduced to simple 90° corner junctions by removal of redundant line segments (see Figure 1a). Observers were told to fixate the centre of the display and avoid eye movements during premask display presentation. Upon removal of the redundant line segments, observers were asked to produce a two-alternative forced-choice RT (keypress) response, as rapidly and accurately as possible, to the presence or absence of a target Kanizsa-type square within the matrix of 90° corner junctions, which remained in view until the response had been made. In the event of an erroneous response, feedback was provided through a (150 ms) 100 Hz computer-generated tone followed by a 500 ms delay.

Design and procedure. Premask and target inducer specifications were varied independently and factorially. Each condition contributed to nine combinations of target-inducer specification (20%, 40%, and 60%) with premask-inducer specification (20%, 40%, and 60%), in addition to the variables target (absent vs. present) and synchrony (synchronous vs. random). Observers performed 1920 trials over three sessions of 640 trials each. All factors were varied randomly within and across blocks.

Results

RT analysis. RTs on trials on which a response error was made (2.6% of all trials) were removed from the data before removing outlier RTs more than 2.5 standard deviations above or below the mean for each observer and experimental condition (2.8% of all trials). Figure 2 presents the correct mean RTs (and associated 95% confidence intervals [CI]) as a function of target-inducer (Figure 2a) and premask-inducer specification (Figure 2b), separately for each target (present, absent) × premask synchrony (synchronous, random) condition.

The data were examined by means of a repeated-measures analysis of variance (ANOVA), with main terms for target (present, absent), synchrony (synchronous, random), premask-inducer specification (20%, 40%, 60%), and target-inducer specification (20%, 40%, 60%). Violations of the homogeneity of variance assumption were corrected by applying either Greenhouse–Geisser or Huynh–Feldt epsilon adjustments (Huynh & Feldt, 1976).

Target-absent RTs were slower than target-present RTs: 588 vs. 527 ms, $F(1,19) = 102.06$, $MS_e = 6675.55$, p .0001. Furthermore, the main effect of synchrony, $F(1, 19) = 29.5$, $MS_e = 483.94$, $p < .0001$, and the synchrony × target

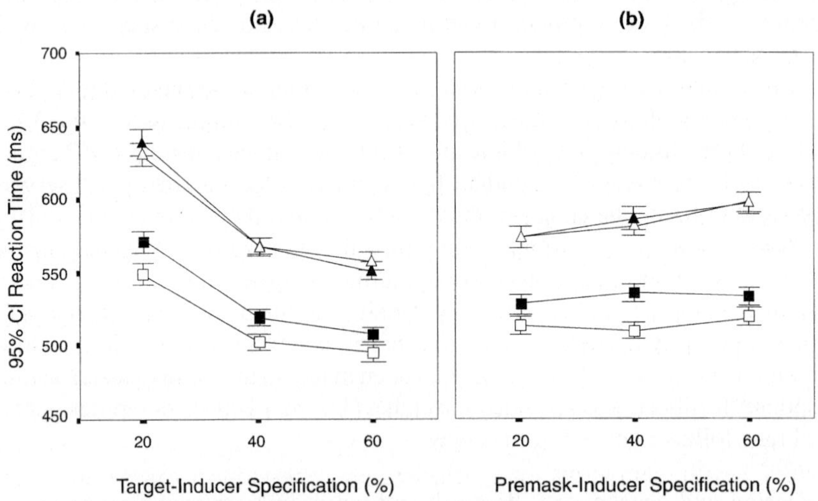

Figure 2. Mean correct target-present and target-absent RTs (±95% confidence interval, in ms) for the synchronous and random conditions as a function of (a) the target-inducer specification and (b) the premask-inducer specification (in percentages). The square symbols represent target-present conditions, the triangle symbols target-absent conditions. The unfilled and filled symbols represent synchronous and random premask presentation conditions respectively.

interaction, $F(1, 19) = 41.126$, $MS_e = 258.36$, $p = .0001$, were significant. This pattern is consistent with previous findings (Elliott & Müller, 1998, 2000), and was due to expedited RTs for synchronous relative to random conditions on target-present trials: 518 vs. 535 ms, simple main effect, $F(1, 19) = 10.65$, $p < .005$; but not target-absent trials: 588 vs. 589 ms; $F(1, 19) = 0.058$, n.s.

As expected, increasing target-inducer specification expedited RT performance (target-inducer-specification main effect, $F(1.054, 20.022) = 47.172$, $MS_e = 13922.172$, $p < .0001$) (see Figure 2a). The main effect of premask-inducer specification was also significant, $F(2, 38) = 7.815$, $MS_e = 1454.227$, $p = .001$, due mainly to an RT increase with 60% premask-inducer specification on target-absent, but not target-present, trials (see Figure 2b): target × premask-inducer specification interaction, $F(1.594, 30.294) = 4.886$, $MS_e = 1201.067$, $p < .025$. This increase reflects a differential influence of premask-inducer specification on processes responsible for target detection as compared to processes responsible for verifying the absence of a target in the display, and, together with the RT decrease with increasing target-inducer specification, accounts for the significant premask-inducer specification × target-inducer specification interaction, $F(4,76) = 2.536$, $MS_e = 428.378$, $p = .047$.

Of greater theoretical importance, there were no significant effects of target-inducer and premask-inducer specification on synchrony priming (see Figures 2a and 2b): The target × synchrony × target-inducer specification, the synchrony × premask-inducer specification × target-inducer specification, and the target × synchrony × target-inducer specification × premask-inducer specification interactions were all non-significant, $F(1.598, 38) = 0.566$, n.s.; $F(3.242, 61.602) = 1.348$, n.s.; and $F(3.98, 75.62) = 2.026$, n.s., respectively. As can be seen from Figures 2a and 2b, the target-specific synchrony effects did not vary substantially with variations in either target-inducer or premask-inducer specification. That is, there is no statistical evidence in support of the (on the Leonards et al., 1996 account) expected interaction between form-based and temporal coding mechanisms.

The target specificity of the synchrony enhancements is consistent with the idea that synchronous-premask presentation primes the subsequent presentation of the target figure (a pattern of interaction that is consistently revealed with the premask paradigm; see Elliott & Müller, 1998, 2000). Consequently, in order to examine the effects of target-inducer expansion or contraction on prime efficiency, further analyses focused upon the pattern of effects revealed for target-present trials only. The target-present RTs were examined using an ANOVA with main terms for synchrony, premask-inducer specification, and target-inducer specification. (Note that no corresponding pattern of effects was revealed from an analogous ANOVA performed on the target-absent RTs.) As expected, the main effects for synchrony and target-inducer specification were significant, while that for premask-inducer specification was non-significant (see the lower two functions in Figure 2b), $F(1, 19) = 49.806$, $MS_e = 497.342$,

$p < .0001$; $F(1.112, 21.131) = 48.016$, $MS_e = 4498.272$, $p < .0001$; and $F(1.798, 34.17) = 2.109$, n.s.

The extent to which synchrony effects were influenced by target-inducer expansion or contraction is illustrated in Figure 3. For larger-range changes in inducer specification (i.e., 20–60% and vice versa), there was a tendency for synchrony effects to be slightly reduced relative to covarying premask-inducer and target-inducer specifications, whereas there was little effect with smaller-range expansions and contractions (20–40% and 40–60%, and vice versa). Statistically, the synchrony × premask-inducer specification and the synchrony × target-inducer specification × premask-inducer specification interactions were only borderline-significant, $F(1.552, 29.489) = 4.346$, $MS_e = 270.446$, $p < .05$; and $F(3.371, 70.898) = 2.891$, $MS_e = 293.938$, $p < .05$, which was mainly due to trend for expedited RTs on random premask trials with the result that the synchronous- and random-trial RTs show a tendency to converge with display expansions (see Figure 3). Further, the possibility that synchrony effects were maintained constant by a trade off between priming impaired by increased figural integrity but enhanced by display expansions or contractions can be ruled out on the basis of synchrony effects under conditions where premask and target specifications covaried. This finding also suggests against Leonards et al.'s (1996) suggestion of facultative interactions between form and motion coding as primarily responsible for mediating the effects of stimulus synchrony.

Error analysis. An ANOVA of arcsine-transformed error data (with the same main terms as the RT data ANOVA) revealed the target miss rates to be slightly higher than the false alarm rates: main effect of target, $F(1, 19) = 8.109$,

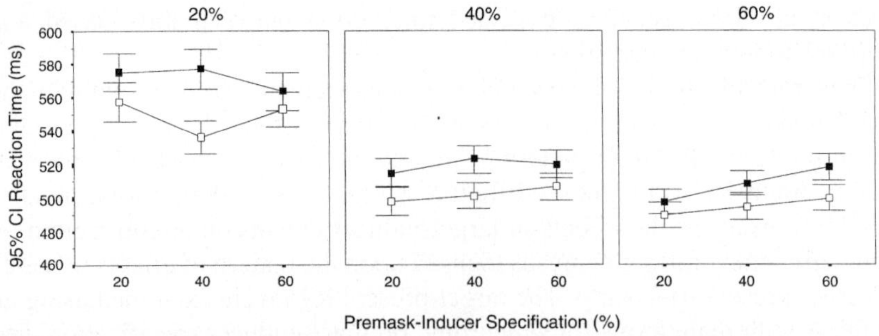

Figure 3. Mean correct target-present and target-absent RTs (±95% confidence interval, in ms) for the synchronous and random conditions as a function of premask-inducer specifications seperately for each target inducer specification condition (inducer specification conditions given in percentages). The square symbols represent target-present conditions, the triangle symbols target-absent conditions. The unfilled and filled symbols represent synchronous and random premask presentation conditions respectively.

MS_e = 0.008, p = .01; 3.1% vs. 2.16%, respectively. Furthermore, trials on which a synchronous premask was presented were found to produce slightly less errors than random-premask trials: main effect of synchrony, $F(1, 19) = 17.428$, MS_e = 0.02, p = .001; 2.27% vs. 2.99%, respectively. Error rates decreased with increasing target-inducer specification, $F(1.185, 22.51) = 45.748$, MS_e = 0.09, $p < .0001$, due to the enhanced salience of the target figure in the 40% and 60% conditions relative to the 20% condition (2.1% and 1.22% vs. 4.58%). There were no effects involving premask-inducer specification, and no other interactions were significant. Thus, the error effects reinforce the RT results.

Discussion

Although target detection RTs did decrease with increasing target-inducer specification, indicating that figure coding was facilitated by a general increase in target saliency, the accompanying effects of prime synchrony remained constant (there was no statistical convergence of the synchronous and random RTs as a function of improving target specification). Consequently, the present results provide no support for the idea, proposed by Leonards et al. (1996), that form-based and temporal information interact facultatively. Instead, the data argue that figure-coding mechanisms are primed by appropriate temporal information, irrespective of variations in the target's figural integrity. Conceivably, the borderline-significant interactions between premask-inducer and target-inducer specification occur due to Gestalt coding across the premask being interrupted by the sudden element expansions or contractions, implying some facultative link between form-coding and motion-coding mechanisms. However, these effects were weak, did not abolish the synchrony effects and were mainly due to faster RTs to targets following random premask presentation. Thus, within the overall pattern of results, they offer little support for the idea that motion-coding mechanisms are the principle mechanisms mediating the generation of priming. Interestingly, one additional implication of these findings is that manipulation of the size of the premask-display crosses does not influence figure–ground segmentation and/or Gestalt coding. This seems somewhat counterintuitive considering other findings (i.e, Shipley & Kelman, 1992) that show the "goodness" of Kanizsa-types figures is largely due to the separation between inducer elements. It may be that, in this instance the collinear line segments do not encourage illusory contour formation (see, e.g., Gurnsey, Poirier, & Gascon, 1996) with the result that activity across the prime, although representing the square-arrangement of the synchronous premask elements, may not be considered in the same terms as the "subjective experience" of an illusory Kanizsa square (which is directly supported by perception of the illusory contours). This is plausible considering that observers do not detect the synchronous-premask frame, rendering tenuous an account of priming according to stimulus properties more commonly associated with subjective experience. An alternative account (earlier stated) is that the prime may simply represent coincidence in the firing of neurons across the elements of the synchronous premask, implying that the effects of stimulus synchrony, although effective in promoting grouping may not be directly responsible for subjective experience of the grouping *per se*. This account would suggest that the neural synchronization responsible for signalling the spatio-temporal structure of the premask display should not be considered directly equivalent to the "perception", or "subjective experience" of grouping or segmentation. Again, this account seems plausible given that the priming stimulus is not detected by observers. Nevertheless, both accounts remain putative, with much more work required to examine these and other possible explanations for this particular pattern of effects.

GENERAL DISCUSSION

Although both parvocellular and magnocellular pathways may respond with zero-phase lag at the frequency of premask presentation, the present results revealed no pattern suggestive of facultative interaction between form and motion-coding systems as a function of the goodness of the target Gestalten. The interaction revealed in the study of Leonards et al. (1996), if they can indeed be interpreted in terms of a facultative interaction (see footnote 1), may be due to the presence of implicit motion signals in their displays (as suggested by Usher & Donnelly, 1998).

These present results, together with those of Usher and Donnelly (1998), suggest an interpretation in terms of the external, stimulus-locked synchronization of form-coding mechanisms independently of the motion system (which does not rule out that effects of synchronizing either system may result in qualitatively similar effects at the level of Gestalt organization). The present results also indicate that the synchronous prime is relatively insensitive to form-based characteristics of either the target stimuli (priming was not significantly influenced by the goodness of the target stimuli) or the premask stimuli (priming was equally effective whatever the premask-cross specification). Consistent with the latter, Müller and Elliott (1999) observed that the grouping effects of stimulus synchrony persisted even when premask circles were displayed instead of cross stimuli (with only the latter, but not the former, sharing figural elements with the subsequently presented target inducers; see also Usher & Donnelly, 1998). These findings support the idea that stimulus-driven synchrony may represent no more than coincidence in the firing pattern of a subset of neurons, although they also suggest that the neural coincidence has the potential to directly influence figure–ground segregation and/or Gestalt coding (see Elliott & Müller, 1998).

Taking previous studies of synchrony priming into consideration, the synchrony effects produced by this priming paradigm appear to differ from physiological recordings of synchronous neural activity in one critical respect: The pattern of synchrony across the prime matches the frequency of premask presentations with zero phase lag (Elliott & Müller, 2000; Elliott et al., 2000). Recall that physiological recordings are usually of synchronization that is not regularly phase locked to stimulus activity. These findings contributed to Leonards et al.'s (1996) suggestion that the external synchronization of form-coding mechanisms could only result from third-party synchronization via motion-coding mechanisms responding to stimulus flicker. However, as will be outlined later, the interpretation of the role of phase-jittered synchronization has been questioned by the results of recent EEG studies that suggest that synchronization between neural assemblies as it relates to coding spatial aspects of the stimulus may be much more sensitive to the timing of stimulus events than previously thought.

Are stimulus-locked and internally timed oscillations functionally similar?

There are two classes of oscillation that are of particular significance for functional accounts of synchronization (for the complete taxonomy of brain rhythms from which these examples are taken, see Başar-Eroglu, Strüber, Schürmann, Stadler, & Başar, 1996, and Galambos, 1992). Stimulus-phase-locked oscillations are generally referred to as "evoked" (i.e., generated directly by the stimulus), and are recorded from human scalp during stimulation with simple stimuli such as auditory clicks or light flashes (see Başar, 1980, and Galambos, 1992, for reviews). Oscillations that show no specific phase locking to stimulus activity are referred to as "induced" and are considered an index of the "cognitive" response to a stimulus (Tallon-Baudry & Bertrand, 1999). For the most part, multi-unit single cell recordings of oscillatory synchronization may be considered as a form of induced activity. Induced oscillations are also revealed in local-field potential (EEG) recordings following presentation of Gestalt groupings (Tallon, Bertrand, Bouchet, & Pernier, 1995; Tallon-Baudry, Bertrand, Delpeuch, & Pernier, 1996, 1997). The stimulus-specific characteristics of induced oscillations contrast with those of evoked activity, recorded in the same EEG, which are relatively insensitive to the type of stimulus presented (Karakaş & Başar, 1998; Tallon et al., 1995; Tallon-Baudry et al., 1997).

Arguably, the effects of stimulus synchrony observed in psychophysical studies with stationary forms should be attributable to evoked, rather than induced, oscillatory synchronization, even though evoked oscillatory activity does not appear to directly influence perceptual organization. However, the claim that induced oscillations are exclusively responsible for stimulus-specific perceptual processing has been challenged by Pulvermüller, Keil, and Elbert (1999), who argue that induced oscillations in the gamma band may be more related to stimulus classification and related memory processes. In addition, recent EEG and magnetoencephalographic (MEG) studies of the neural response to figure presentation have shown that the evoked gamma-band response varies with variations in the spatial configurations of the stimulus (see, Herrmann, Mecklinger, & Pfeifer, 1999; Herrmann & Mecklinger, 2000, this issue). Herrmann et al. replicated the basic paradigm of Tallon et al. (1995) by presenting Kanizsa figures that either grouped or did not group according to the local orientations of inducer pie slices. Contrary to the results of Tallon et al., Herrmann and colleagues reliably observed stimulus-specific variations in oscillatory activity in the evoked, but not the induced, oscillations. Further, employing the same analytical procedure (see Herrmann, Mecklinger, & Pfeifer, 1999, for details), Herrmann, Elliott, Mecklinger, and Müller (1999) first reported that repeated presentation of the premask stimuli of Elliott and Müller (1998) evoked a stimulus phase-locked 40 Hz response over posterior-cortical electrodes (see also Elliott et al., 2000). This response was specific to the synchronous-premask-target condition and might be interpreted as a specific patterning in the EEG that encoded the precise spatial and temporal structure of the priming stimulus. Given the earlier arguments that perceptual effects can arise through variations in spatio-temporal stimulus structure, which may not be specifically attributable to the response of motion-coding mechanisms, these results offer further evidence that the oscillatory neural response to synchronized-stimulus presentation can adopt the phase of stimulus activity with consequent effects on stimulus grouping and segmentation.

Summary and conclusions

We have reviewed investigations of the extent to which external synchrony can encourage or enhance the perception of figural stimuli and presented data, with the aim of resolving some of the issues that have prevented consideration of these effects in similar terms to those of physiological recordings of neural synchrony, with which they are presumed to relate. The principle issue concerns whether or not synchronization could conceivably follow presentation of stationary stimuli. Several studies and paradigms were reviewed in support of this idea, although a further issue arose from their findings: Whether internally generated synchronization, held to be responsible for neural synchronization observed in physiological studies, could be mediated by motion-coding mechanisms responding to rapid repeating stimulus presentation. Experimental evidence was presented consistent with the idea that motion-based responses do not necessarily influence synchrony during form coding. Given the evidence that repeated presentation of synchronized stimuli results in a phase-locked oscillatory response, the distinction between evoked and induced neural oscillations was introduced and their functional correlates in the EEG were reviewed. It was concluded that there is some evidence to consider the effects of evoked oscillatory activity in similar terms to those of induced activity; that is, repeated synchronized stimulus presentations may generate an equivalent, phase-locked pattern of activity in the brain. These considerations might provide the ground for more detailed studies of the timing parameters under which stimulus-evoked synchrony, stimulus-induced synchrony, and the timing of perceptual organization processes, operate.

REFERENCES

Alais, D., Blake, R., & Lee, S.-H. (1998). Visual features that vary together over time group together over space. *Nature Neuroscience*, *1*, 160–164

Başar, E. (1980). *EEG-brain dynamics. Relation between EEG and brain evoked potentials.* Amsterdam: Elsevier.

Başar-Eroglu, C., Strüber, D., Schürmann, M., Stadler, M., & Başar, E. (1996). Gamma band responses in the brain: A short review of psychophysical correlates and functional significance. *International Journal of Psychophysiology*, *24*, 101–112.

Bell, R.A. (1970). *Principles of cathode-ray tubes, phosphors, and high-speed oscillography* (Application note 115). Hewlett Packard Company/Colorado Springs Division, 1900 Garden of the Gods Road, Colorado Springs, Colorado, USA.

Crick, F., & Koch, C. (1990). Towards a neurobiological theory of consciousness. *Seminars in the Neurosciences*, *2*, 263–275.

Eckhorn, R., Bauer, R., Jordan, W., Brosch, M., Kruse, W., Munk, M., & Reitboeck, H.J. (1988). Coherent oscillations: A mechanism for feature linking in the visual cortex. *Biological Cybernetics*, *60*, 121–130.

Elliott, M.A., Herrmann, C.S., Mecklinger, A., & Müller, H.J. (2000). The loci of oscillatory visual-object priming: A combined electroencephalographic and reaction-time study. *International Journal of Psychophysiology*, *38*, 225–241.

Elliott, M.A., & Müller, H.J. (1998). Synchronous information presented in 40-Hz flicker enhances visual feature binding. *Psychological Science*, *9*, 277–283.

Elliott, M.A., & Müller, H.J. (2000). Evidence for a 40-Hz oscillatory short-term visual memory revealed by human reaction-time measurements. *Journal of Experimental Psychology: Learning, Memory and Cognition*, *26*(3), 703–718.

Engel, A.K., König, P., Kreiter, A.K., & Singer, W. (1991). Interhemispheric synchronization of oscillatory neuronal responses in cat visual cortex. *Science*, *252*, 1177–1179.

Fahle, M. (1993). figure–ground discrimination from temporal information. *Proceedings of the Royal Society of London, B*, *254*, 199–203.

Finley, G. (1985). A high-speed point plotter for vision research: Technical note. *Vision Research*, *25*, 1993–1997.

Galambos, R. (1992). A comparison of certain gamma band (40-Hz) brain rhythms in cat and man. In E. Başar & T.M. Bullock (Eds.), *Induced rhythms in the brain* (pp. 201–216). Boston: Birkhäuser.

Gegenfurtner, K. (1998). Visual psychophysics: synchrony in motion. *Nature Neuroscience*, *1*, 96–98.

Gray, C.M., König, P., Engel, A.K., & Singer, W. (1989). Oscillatory responses in cat visual cortex exhibit inter-columnar synchronization which reflects global stimulus properties. *Nature*, *338*, 334–337.

Gurnsey, R., Poirier, F.J.A.M., & Gascon, E. (1996). There is no evidence that Kanizsa-type subjective contours can be detected in parallel. *Perception, 25*(7), 861–874.

Herrmann, C.S., Elliott, M.A., Mecklinger, A., & Müller, H.J. (1999). Electrophysiological correlates of stimulus-entrainment at 40 Hz. *Neuroimage*, *9*(suppl), 867.

Herrmann, C.S., & Mecklinger, A. (2000). Magnetoencephalographic responses to illusory figures: Early evoked gamma is affected by processing of stimulus features. *International Journal of Psychophysiology*, *38*, 265–281.

Herrmann, C.S., Mecklinger, A., & Pfeifer, E. (1999). Gamma responses and ERPs in a visual classification task. *Clinical Neurophysiology*, *110*, 636–642.

Huynh, H., & Feldt, L.S. (1976). Estimation of the box correction for degrees of freedom from sample data in the randomized block and split block designs. *Journal of Educational Statistics*, *1*, 69–82.

Karakaş, S., & Başar, E. (1998). Early gamma response is sensory in origin: A conclusion based on cross-comparison of results from multiple experimental paradigms. *International Journal of Psychophysiology*, *31*, 13–31.

Kreiter, A.K., & Singer, W. (1992). Stimulus-dependent synchronization of neuronal responses in the visual cortex of the awake macaque monkey. *Journal of Neuroscience*, *16*, 2381–2396.

Lee, S.-H., & Blake, R. (1999). Visual form created solely from temporal structure. *Science*, *284*, 1165–1168.

Lennie, P., Trevarthan, C., van Essen, D., & Wässle, H. (1990). Parallel processing of visual information. In L. Spillman & J.S. Werner (Eds.), *Visual perception. The neurophysiological foundations* (pp. 103–128). San Diego: Academic Press.

Leonards, U., Singer, W., & Fahle, M. (1996). The influence of temporal phase differences on texture segmentation. *Vision Research*, *36*, 2689–2697.

Logothetis, N.K., & Schall, J.D. (1989). Neuronal correlates of subjective visual perception. *Science*, *245*, 761–763.

Miller, J. (1982). Divided attention: Evidence for coactivation with redundant signals. *Cognitive Psychology*, *14*, 247–279.

Müller, H.J., & Elliott, M.A. (1999). 40-Hz synchronicity priming of Kanizsa figure detection demonstrated by a novel psychophysical paradigm. In G. Aschersleben, T. Bachmann, & J. Müsseler (Eds.), *Cognitive contributions to the perception of spatial and temporal events* (pp. 323–340). Amsterdam: Elsevier.

Parton, A., Donnelly, N., & Usher, M. (this issue). The effects of temporal synchrony on the perceived organization of elements in spatially symmetric and asymmetric grids. *Visual Cognition*, *8*(3/4/5), 637–654.

Pulvermüller, F., Keil, A., & Elbert, T. (1999). High-frequency brain activity: Perception or active memory? *Trends in Cognitive Sciences*, *3*(7), 250–253.

Shipley, T.F., & Kelman, P.J. (1992). Strength of visual interpolation depends on the ratio of physically specified to total edge length. *Perception and Psychophysics*, *52*, 97–106.

Singer, W. (1996). Neuronal synchronization: A solution to the binding problem? In R.R. Llinás & P.S. Churchland (Eds.), *The mind-brain continuum: Sensory processes* (pp. 101–130). Cambridge, MA: MIT Press.

Singer, W., & Gray, C.M. (1995). Visual feature integration and the temporal correlation hypothesis. *Annual Review of Neuroscience*, *18*, 555–586.

Tallon, C., Bertrand, O., Bouchet, P., & Pernier, J. (1995). Gamma-range activity evoked by coherent visual stimuli in humans. *European Journal of Neuroscience*, *7*, 1285–1291.

Tallon-Baudry, C., & Bertrand, O. (1999). Oscillatory gamma activity in humans and its role in object representation. *Trends in Cognitive Sciences*, *3*(4), 151–162.

Tallon-Baudry, C., Bertrand, O., Delpeuch, C., & Pernier, J. (1996). Stimulus specificity of phase-locked and non-phase-locked 40 Hz visual responses in human. *Journal of Neuroscience*, *16*, 4240–4249.

Tallon-Baudry, C., Bertrand, O., Delpeuch, C., & Pernier, J. (1997). Oscillatory γ-band (30–70 Hz) activity induced by a visual search task in humans. *Journal of Neuroscience*, *17*, 722–734.

Usher, M., & Donnelly, N. (1998). Visual synchrony affects binding and segmentation in perception. *Nature*, *394*, 179–182.

von der Malsburg, C. (1981). *The correlation theory of brain function* (Internal Report 81-2). Department of Neurobiology, Max-Planck-Institute for Biophysical Chemistry, 3400 Göttingen, Germany.

Yantis, S. (1992). Multielement visual tracking: Attention and perceptual organization. *Cognitive Psychology*, *24*, 295–340.

VISUAL COGNITION, 2001, *8* (3/4/5), 679–696

Temporal constraints on binding? Evidence from quantal state transitions in perception

Hans-Georg Geissler and Raul Kompass
Institute of Experimental Psychology, University of Leipzig, Germany

Do behavioural observations on the transitions between alternative perceptual interpretations of stimuli carry information about temporal characteristics of brain activity involved in binding? Promising methods for capturing critical attributes of this activity are the psychophysical methods of parameter adjustment. Of particular value are situations that include an adjustment of periodically repeating components, since the interaction of these with periodic "carrier processes" in the brain may produce informative patterns of interference. Previous evidence reveals that in different paradigms the spectral time signatures of transition tune in to a superordinate structure of quantal time values. In agreement with predictions of the taxonomic "time quantum model" (TQM), quantal time values are organized in groups called ranges which cover intervals of discretely varying sizes. These findings suggest properties characteristic of oscillatory mechanisms which are active in temporal binding. Of critical importance is the extreme precision of timing, agreement of critical periods across individuals, as well as across tasks of varying complexity, and indications of single-shot timing.

Physiological evidence suggests that both the emergence and persistence of percepts depend upon oscillatory processes in the brain. Such processes cause the binding of information that is physically separated in space and time into coherent structures. Psychology, as it relates percepts to physical stimulus conditions does not provide methods for direct determination of temporal characteristics of these processes. Yet, time is an integral part of the physical stimulus conditions, and perceptual events can be related to physical time, thus, psychologists can ask whether the unfolding of perception in time contains important

Please address all correspondence to H.-G. Geissler, Institut für Allgemeine Psychologie, Universität Leipzig, Seeburgstr. 14–20, D-04103 Leipzig, Germany. Email: geissler@rz.uni-leipzig.de

This work was supported by the German Research Council (DFG) grant GE 678/12-1 to H.-G. Geissler and H. Müller. The authors wish to thank Stephen W. Link and Mark A. Elliott for their helpful comments on an earlier version of this paper.

http://www.tandf.co.uk/journals/pp/13506285.html DOI:10.1080/13506280143000197

constraining information about temporal-binding mechanisms that physiologists are searching for.

The simplest approach to address this question are experimental paradigms in which percepts undergo abrupt, noticeable change while there is only a small change, or no change at all, in the stimuli. Such conditions exist in most of the classical investigations of psychological science, for example, in discrimination performance at threshold, or perceptual rivalry in bistable figures. However, most of the experimental methods traditionally employed in these examples do not take into consideration temporal dynamics of psychophysical relations while questions of temporal binding explicitly aim at dynamic aspects of perception. Specifically, and this is our central claim throughout this paper, perception seems to be bound to drifting sequences of temporal frames of reference with anchor points of most precise timing at moments of perceptual change.

There are alternative methods focused on regularities of rapid change, which are derivatives of the classical psychophysical method of limits. By these methods of "adjustment", perceptual change can be induced within a well-defined temporal context. Of special interest are applications to stimuli composed of regularly repeating components, in the simplest case to periodic stimuli.

In this paper, we briefly review evidence indicating that, under these circumstances, the temporal structures of stimuli and of carrier processes in the brain may interact, producing patterns of interference that may be considered diagnostic of the temporal organization of brain activity. As will be shown, there exists evidence to indicate the influence of general quantal laws within the organizational dynamics of temporal brain activity. These laws are restricted neither to adjustment procedures nor to rapid perceptual change, but seem to apply to a broad range of cognitive phenomena and to various conditions of their study. Some possible consequences for binding will be discussed in the concluding section.

PERCEPTION OF PERIODICITY AND DURATION

Indications of temporal quantization in changes produced during near-periodic stimulation exist in simple psychophysical tasks. Evidence dates back to the 1930s. Brecher (1932), using an ascending method of limits, found in 14 subjects that the fusion thresholds in vibration perception occur, on the average, at a critical period of 55.3 ms or, in terms of frequency, 18 Hz. What is most striking about his result is the low standard deviation across individuals of 1.2 ms for the critical period duration. Also, the variation in the value of the critical period measured at different sites on the skin (SD = 2.3 ms) is extremely small when compared with the variation of receptor density. Both of these findings suggest a central, cortical origin of the period.

With a different paradigm von Békésy (1936) went a step further by demonstrating a series of 11 local invariances in the absolute intensity threshold of sound perception measured as a function of frequency in a range from 2 to 100 Hz (see Figure 1). In his experiment, frequency was increased continuously from below threshold until the stimulus became noticeable while intensity was kept constant. This procedure was repeatedly applied at step-wise decremented levels of intensity. Local invariances were defined as those points where the stimulus became noticeable at the same critical frequency for more than one adjacent intensity. The inset figure of Figure 1 illustrates this for a level found at 18 Hz where the same point of transition was observed on six levels of intensity, while intensity was being step-wise diminished up to half its original value. As von Békésy noted, the corresponding critical duration of 55.6 ms agrees not only numerically very well with Brecher's fusion period, but it is also comparable to this period in so far as it demarcates a boundary at which perceived quality changes suddenly, in this case from a pulsing signal to that of a pure tone.

The observation of multiple distinct periods permits the extraction of further regularities that provide a basis for the comparison of findings from different experimental paradigms. Of most importance are regularities of temporal spacing among critical periods. What springs directly from von Békésy's data is that, with one exception, the series of levels falls into three sub-series of approximate harmonic doubling: 4.5, 9, 18, and 38 Hz; 6, 11, and 22 Hz; 7.5, 14, and 28 Hz.

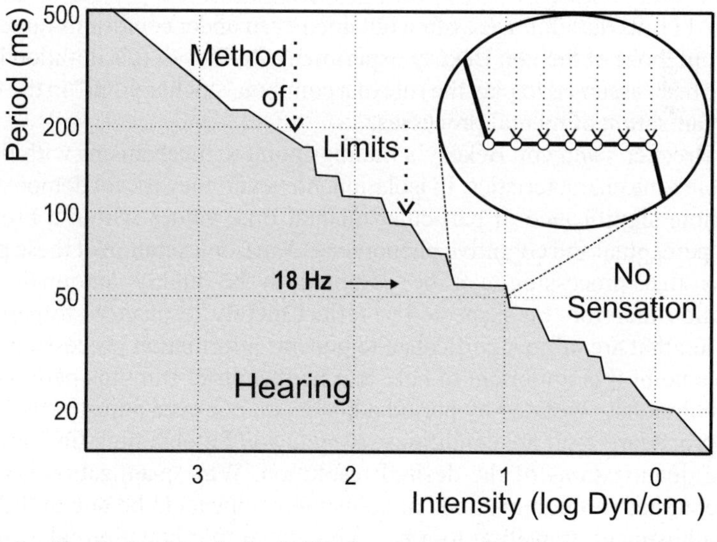

Figure 1. The absolute intensity threshold in the perception of low-frequency sound as a function of frequency exhibits intervals of local invariance. Arrows denote trajectories of adjustment. Results for 18 Hz after von Békésy (1936).

Important for the generalization of these findings to other experimental paradigms is the additional observation that critical periods come close to integer multiples of a smallest epoch of 4.5–4.6 ms. This property became a central postulate in a taxonomy of quantal structures (Geissler, 1987). In von Békésy's case, converting the durations into multiples of 4.6 gives the integer values of $N = 6, 7, 8, 10, 12, 16, 20, 24, 28, 36, 48$. These include a level at 32 Hz ($N = 7$) that does not fit in with the previous three doubling schemes in the frequency domain. Note that the differences between neighbouring N values can be considered as a measure of temporal resolution. However, for durations >110 ms ($N > 24$), assignment to integer multiples becomes subject to increasing uncertainty because of flatness of levels and rounding of measurements to 0.5 Hz. Therefore, for interpretation, we confine ourselves to the sufficiently exactly identifiable values of $N \leq 24$. The corresponding differences between neighbouring values are 1, 1, 2, 2, 4, 4, and 4, yielding a sequence which again exhibits a striking regularity of doubling.

A second group of attributes of relevance for the identification of regularities in temporal dynamics are indications of relative strength in which critical periods may markedly diverge. In von Békésy's paradigm, the height of a given discontinuity which corresponds to the number of interspersed measurements can be considered as a measure of strength. In other cases the relevant measure may be just relative frequency of occurrence. In von Békésy's experiment the local invariances at 9 and 18 Hz were measured five and six times, respectively, whereas other periods occurred only two to four times. A reanalysis of several paradigms (see Geissler, 1987, 1990, 1992) has shown that periods of around 1000/9 = 111 ms duration were often obtained even under conditions quite different from those of the von Békésy experiment. Periods of this duration have therefore been assumed to play the role of a common "anchor point" in the temporal organization of mental processes.

Both Brecher's and von Békésy's findings point to mechanisms with fixed, very stable time characteristics. In isolation, however, they do not demonstrate the possible significance of particular quantal time values within a broader range of perceptual and cognitive phenomena. A major limitation of these paradigms is that processing can be assumed to be highly automatic and quantization therefore be suspected to reflect merely resonances to periodic stimulation that are of no significance to general information processing.

At this point it is important to note that neither strict stimulus periodicity, which is obviously violated by period adjustment, nor even adjustment as the applied procedure itself are conditions *sine qua non* for obtaining fine-grained temporal quantizations of the desired resolution. Why quantization is most readily obtained through methods of adjustment appears to be due to the fact that, in adjustment, transition to a new perceptual interpretation takes place within a given trial on a background of preceding states that are preserved and updated during adjustment and thus provide coherent reference frames for transitions in the temporal neighborhood of the moments of change. The experiments in time perception by Kristofferson and co-workers indicate that this condition of temporal coherence can also be attained by other means, on a trial-by-trial basis. The method of single stimuli is such an example, drawn from Kristofferson's (1980) studies of duration discrimination. In this procedure, one time interval is presented on a trial. Subjects, judging the intervals either "long" or "short", during extensive practice create internal referents that can be retrieved quickly enough to become integrated in the evaluation of the currently presented brief stimulus interval. Coherent access to stimulus information can also be provided by the specific temporal patterning of stimuli as in "pulse-train" experiments where signals of equal temporal distance in a row are directly followed by a deviant (see Kristofferson, 1990).

In these paradigms, the computation of quantal periods is dependent on specific assumptions about distributions and thus does not yield a precision that can be obtained with adjustment methods. Still fundamental regularities of temporal quantization can be established relying on these paradigms. Kristofferson's studies in successiveness discrimination (see Kristofferson, 1967) demonstrated that a quantal period of some 50 ms is involved in the perception of successiveness. This is the order of Brecher's period. In addition, individual durations turned out to come close to half of the subject's dominant alpha periods. This finding substantiates the view that critical period durations of around 50 and 110 ms obtained in various paradigms are related to alpha activity. Later experiments of Kristofferson revealed a multiplicity of interrelated critical periods including those of much longer durations. The most informative results in duration discrimination (Kristofferson, 1980, 1984, 1990) are schematically summarized in Figure 2. These data reveal a doubling law like that found in von Békésy's paradigm outlined earlier.

Unlike von Békésy's findings, doubling applies on both axes, yielding two coordinated rows of quantal values, one of step-wise increasing quantal thresholds Δ_i ($i = 1, 2, 3, \ldots$), which are shown as standard deviations in the figure, and one of intervals of base durations, to which they belong. This rule was found to extend up to 1.6 s, which is far beyond any durations relevant in auditory or tactile perception.

There is one more novel characteristic of these data. The horizontal segments of the function in Figure 2 develop during practice. At the start of training, the corresponding parts of the function are not horizontal but tend to follow the upper dashed line representing Weber's law. The horizontal segments in Figure 2, corresponding to the function after prolonged practice, connect this upper dashed line with a lower dashed line. Because of the doubling relation inherent in the depicted function, the slope of the latter is half of that of the former. The quantal threshold values and the upper bounds of the corresponding intervals of base durations are therefore interrelated by Weber's Law. More specifically, in the adopted idealization, the intervals of constant

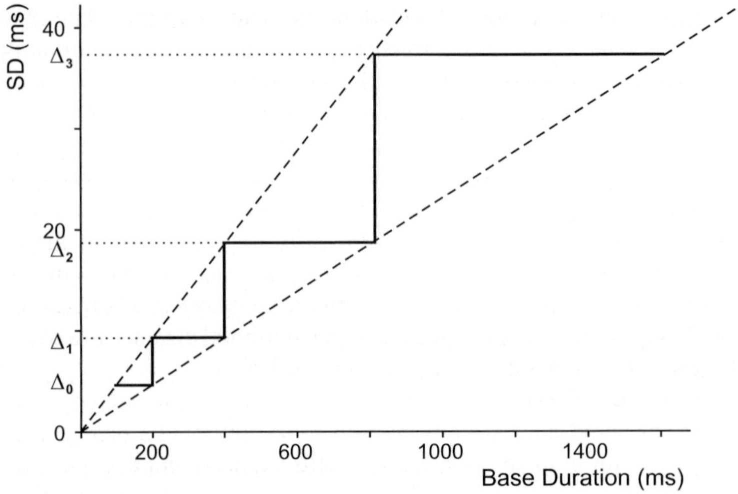

Figure 2. Duration discriminability in a single-stimulus method after prolonged training. Idealized schematic representation after Kristofferson (1980, 1984, 1990). Discrimination errors (standard deviations) and corresponding intervals exhibit doubling relations: $\Delta_{k+1} = 2\Delta_k$.

discriminability form ranges with upper bounds at $T_i = 2\Delta_i/k$, where k denotes Weber's constant.

TAXONOMIC RULES

The results of Kristofferson indicate that quantal regularities, which imply integer relations between critical time values, occur in paradigms not involving near-periodic repetitive stimuli. Beyond this, there are two major findings that provide new perspectives: First, the staircase-like doubling of Δ as a function of base duration in Kristofferson (1980) suggests that quantal time architectures on different scales are self-similar. Second, the relatedness of this function to Weber's law suggests the existence of very general principles of temporal organization. Neural mechanisms operating on quite different time scales from a few milliseconds to, at least, seconds appear to be integral parts of a general timing system. The functional significance of this integration can be seen in a "regime" of temporally coordinated activities within which the composite mechanisms work with maximum possible precision.

The taxonomic time quantum model TQM (Geissler, 1987, 1992) captures important characteristics of such a system by using a small set of rules. A key idea in the formulation of these rules is that critical periods of different magnitudes form analogously structured time ranges. This structure is characterized by three properties. First, range-specific resolution gives the smallest unit within a given range, of which any critical periods belonging to this range are integer multiples. Second, there is a largest possible multiple of this unit belonging to a given range defined as range length. Third, the smallest units of any range are supposed to be integer multiples of an absolutely smallest period of 4.5 to 4.6 ms duration, called the "time quantum" TQ_0. Evidence from various sources suggests that the upper limit of any range is to be found at the multiple $N = 30$ of the smallest unit characterising that range. A value of around this figure was, for example, found for the upper end of the horizontal segment of Δ as a function of base duration in the "pulse-train" paradigm of duration discrimination (Kristofferson, 1990). Most recently, nearly exactly this value was found for the maximum operation time in an item-recognition paradigm employing complex verbal material (Petzold, Edeler, & Geissler, 1999).

The basic rules of quantal structuring formulated so far do not account for the property of relative strength of discrete values introduced via the previous example in which the intervals of local invariance of critical periods greatly diverged. The rules can, however, be easily extended by assumptions that open a door to understanding this property. For this we have to realize that empirical measures of strength are to be represented by an appropriate property of the constrained sets of integers which are the constituents of these rules. The simplest of these properties is the number of possible decompositions into integer factors (see Geissler, 1985). A duration of six elementary units, for example, can be decomposed into six one-unit segments, into three segments of two units, or into two segments of three units, and, in a hierarchy, the period can be simultaneously related to other durations (in terms of elementary units) 3 and 1, and 2 and 1. This gives a number of five possibilities as an estimator of strength. This calculation can be applied to the problem raised above of why critical period durations of about 110 and 55 ms are empirically so frequent. In terms of multiples these durations correspond to $N = 24$ and $N = 12$, respectively. Applying the decomposition idea to them yields 16 and 12 possible hierarchies as respective theoretical estimates of strength. Thus, it turns out that, within a range of multiples as high as 30, these figures are indeed the highest.

Temporal ranges in the sense defined earlier operate as frames in which specific spectral quantum signatures emerge as a function of specific conditions. As suggested previously, these signatures within the confines determined by temporal stimulus structuring are shaped by autonomous constraints such as relative strength. The strongest determinant, however, is certainly task-related selectivity whose specification is not part of TQM itself. In the Kristofferson (1980) experiment, for example, task constraints should enforce representation of base durations and of smallest possible differences between those and representations of test durations.

Under the conditions of von Békésy's experiment, the specific constraints should act somewhat differently. Here it appears sensible to assume that during stimulus adjustment the range structures get adjusted so as to grant maximum resolution at the intensity threshold for any given frequency. In other situations, task-specific selectivity may act in a still different way. In memory search, for instance, ranges and segmentation may be adjusted to facilitate the scanning of specific item-set representations (see, e.g., Geissler, 1997).

A REAL-TIME IMPLEMENTATION OF TQM

TQM as outlined provides for a hypothetical system of admissible quantum values. Yet, it remains an open issue how more dynamic properties could account for the Weber-law-like increase of variability with period duration or the strength of a given period as introduced above. This problem is addressed by a real-time implementation of TQM (Geissler, 1991, 1997; see also Geissler, Scheber, & Kompass, 1999). In this implementation oscillatory or, more generally, cyclic carrier processes are the correlates of quantal timing. The fundamental assumptions are:

(1) *Limited coherence*: Quantal timing is based upon neural carrier processes which can be represented as groups of near-synchronous cyclic processes. Near synchronicity expires after the "coherence length" of $M = 30$ group periods as a consequence of slight incommensurable differences in period durations (cf. Geissler, 1985).

(2) *Cross-coupling*: Carriers of globally different group periods are coupled by phase-locking. Assumption (2) provides for carrier processes to form hierarchically and/or heterarchically ordered clusters, consisting of mutually locked near-synchronous cyclic processes of globally differing group periods. Assumptions (2) and (1) together suggest that such clusters in relation to an included carrier of shortest period duration form transient time-frequency windows of limited depth (see Geissler, Kompass, & Lachmann, 1998). Figure 3

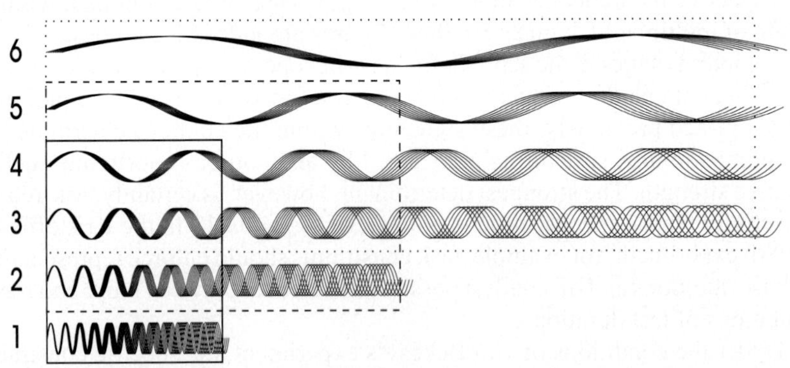

Figure 3. Hierarchies of cross-coupled cyclic carrier processes are supposed to form transient time-frequency windows. Schematic illustration of the principle, with coherence length M arbitrarily set at 12.

illustrates this notion for the example of three hierarchies, setting, for convenience, M arbitrarily to 12. Hierarchy depth four follows then on the assumption that a minimum of one period of the longest cycle should be traversed before near-periodicity on the level of the shortest cycle duration expires.

Time-frequency windows of the described type are the real-time equivalents of temporal ranges (as already defined). Beyond this, as theoretical constructs, they may be considered as tools for a better understanding of how specific quantum signatures emerge depending on task and stimulus conditions. Reiterating the previous examples, in duration discrimination a carrier will probably be selected from a memory-stabilized hierarchy of period durations appropriate for representing a given set of base durations. The quantal discriminability approached during training can be taken to reflect the smallest difference discernable within this framework. The extension of the branches of the discrimination function at which discriminability is constant should thus map directly the operative ranges of base durations.

Correspondingly, to account for the breaks in von Békésy's paradigm, it appears natural to assume that the breaks represent points of optimal tuning to particular cycles within hierarchies that are generated for every frequency separately. As a consequence, the varying ranges corresponding to the activated hierarchies of oscillations will be reflected only indirectly through the varying distance between the observed breaks.

Although a more comprehensive discussion of the time-frequency scheme is beyond the scope of this paper, it should be emphasized that the scheme is incomplete and needs specification in several respects in order to enable an account of temporal dynamics in perception and cognition. This holds already true for accounts of variability in elementary tasks as considered earlier. For example, according to assumption (1) the dispersion of phase differences in agreement with Weber's law increases with time from zero (or a very small value) to its maximum value. The variability of judgements observed after training in duration discrimination, however, is nearly constant. To model this property requires a detailed consideration of phase read-out processes in addition to the oscillatory carrier processes. These read-out processes within the limits of coherence recover nearly the exact phase information of the cyclic group processes both for the of inner standards and for the test stimuli, whereas the phase differences between their representations cannot be forced down below the limit given by the smallest quantal unit. Similarly, in tasks implying multiple use of the assumed frequency clusters of a given window, the relevant dispersion depends on the frequency of the cyclic group processes to which the particular information processing is tuned.

The need of completion is even more imperative if the natural continuous flow of information and multi-stage processing are at issue. To attain an appropriate description of continuing information inflow, one will have to account for the encoding of temporal relations and for the fact that, although new information is represented in small windows of maximum resolution, other information detached of its sensory origin persists in more expanded temporal horizons. Also, transitions between time-frequency windows occurring during processing are certainly not completely predetermined, but are in their actual course shaped by many factors, among them by action of attentional mechanisms. In perception (in the narrow sense of immediate input-supported world representation), the integration of information is to be expected to proceed within a framework of windows that make up shifting sequences of increasing temporal uncertainty alternating with resets to maximum resolution at moments of change. All what in the view of TQM can be presently said about these issues, which represent future directions of research, is that we expect that constants such as TQ_0 should prove to be invariants of valid models however complex the portrayed processes might be. The general claim of TQM is that it should be useful to know such invariants before entering into specific modelling.

EVIDENCE FROM LONG-RANGE APPARENT MOVEMENT

It may appear questionable that temporal discrimination of simple dimensionally ordered near-periodic stimuli has anything to do with binding considered as the neural integration of information separated in space and time. We therefore examine some findings in apparent motion induced by spatio-temporal configurations which meet this definition and to which the idea of binding by neural synchrony can be applied.

Figure 4 provides a sketch of stimulus displays and resulting percepts. On the left hand this is done for periodic beta movement. When the two circular patches of light are presented at appropriate time intervals at different spatial positions, *one* circle appears to move smoothly forth and back. To study gamma movement, that is, the apparent expansion and shrinking of a perceived object at a single location, periodic presentation of a rectangular patch of light as shown in Figure 4 on the right was employed. In both cases of seen motion, for a given exposure duration (ED) there is at low ISIs a point where apparent motion suddenly gives way to the impression of stimulus flicker. This "simultaneity threshold" was determined by adjusting ISI from a start value continuously to shorter values.

Two experiments were carried out with 46 subjects. A factorial design, with one replication of each condition, included twelve levels of ED (3, 20, 40, . . . , 200, 250 ms), three angular separations (3°, 6°, and 12°) in beta movement and two vertical extensions (3° and 6°) in gamma movement. Subjects reported verbally that the apparent motion changed qualitatively from a smooth movement to flickering. The ISI at this point was considered a critical ISI.

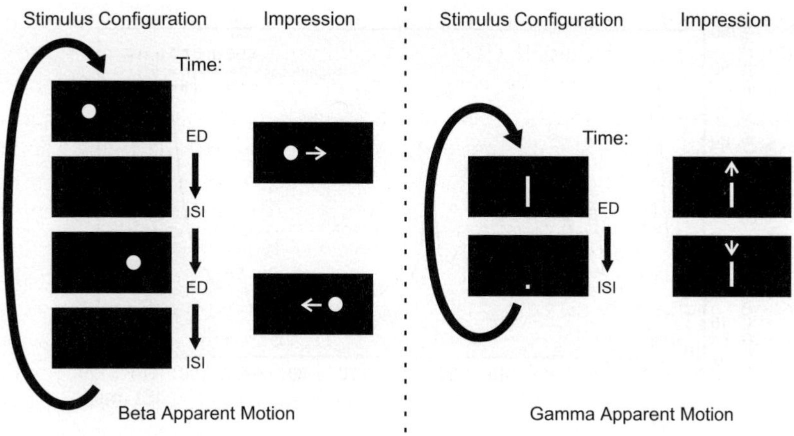

Figure 4. Stimulus displays of apparent movement experiments.

For beta movement, the quantal properties revealed in the experiment of Geissler et al. (1999) can, in relation to TQM hypotheses, be summarized by the following statements:

(1) An overall distribution of critical ISIs (cISIs) reaching from a few milliseconds to about 140 ms suggests timing in agreement with the smallest predicted range (R_1) which, adopting for the "time quantum" $TQ_0 = 4.5$ ms, is expected to expand from 4.5 ms as the smallest period to a period of $30 \times 4.5 = 135$ ms. The overall cISI distribution shows several strong peaks. Significant or near-significant peaks were found at 5, 9, 22, 27, 43, 55, and 107 ms cISIs in close agreement with quantal values which are for $TQ_0 = 4.5$ ms predicted at 4.5, 9, 22.5, 27, 45, 54, and 108 ms. From regression follows that the positions of the modes can be optimally represented by a largest common divisor of 4.49 ms. Figure 5 (topmost diagram) shows the cISI distribution smoothened with an Epanechnikov kernel (Silverman, 1986). The lower diagram in Figure 5 exhibits as measures of strength the combinatorial frequencies of occurrence within possible hierarchies of the multiples N from $N = 1$ to $N = 28$ for which equal a priori frequencies are assumed. Both diagrams show a good visual correspondence as to the U-shaped overall trend and to the most pronounced peaks at $N = 2$, 6, 12, and 24. This suggests that the equal a priori frequency assumption holds to some approximation for the cISI distributions pertaining to the particular EDs from which by variation of ED across its entire range, an overall distribution is pieced together that strongly resembles the predicted distribution.

(2) Further evidence for a quantal microperiod of about 4.5 ms comes from small local fluctuations that appear as periodicities in the distributions of differences between cISIs of first trials and replications and between cISIs obtained

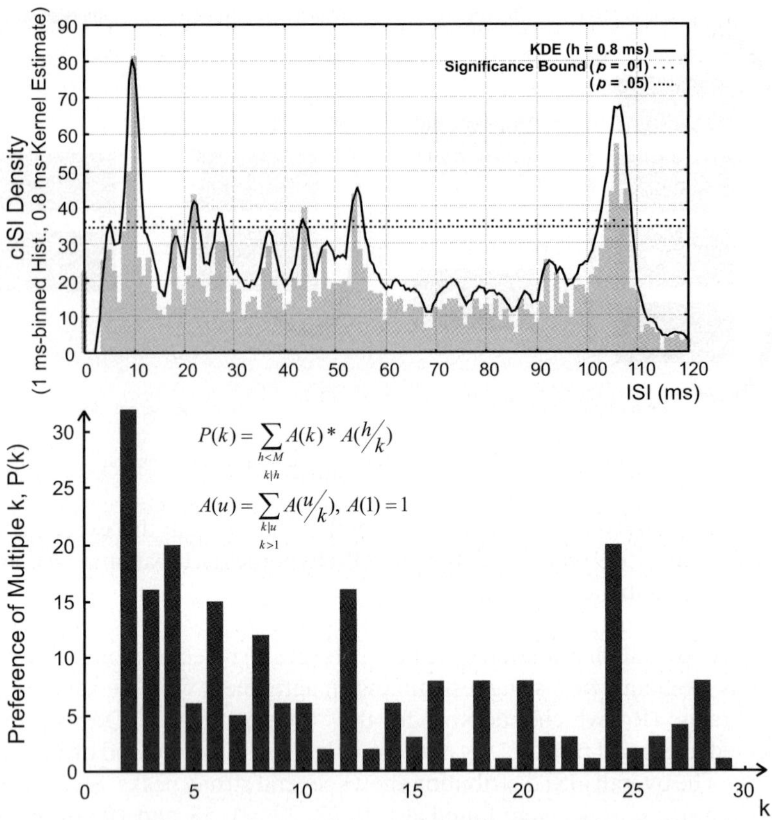

Figure 5. cISI distribution collapsed across subjects, exposure duration and angular separation (top) and theoretical frequencies of occurrence of multiples of TQ_0 in possible hierarchies (bottom). Note the overall agreement and fairly good correspondences for major peaks at 9, 54, and 107 ms. No counterpart was found for a preference predicted at 13.5 ms.

for neighbouring ED values. This denotes that small variations of cISI accord with the quantum assumption. The respective estimates of 4.50 and 4.56 ms deviate from the largest common divisor of the peak positions by less than 2%.

(3) Local variability is found to increase in accordance with Weber's law, with the exception of periods in the vicinity of 107 ms (corresponding to the most prominent peak) where absolute differences drop down to values comparable to those for very small ISIs.

The evidence for quantal structures in gamma movement can be summarized as follows (for an extensive discussion, see Kompass, Geissler, & Schebera, 2001): The empirical range doubles nearly exactly that observed in beta movement. According to TQM, this suggests that the next larger range R_2

is implied. The simple combinatorial rule for predicting strength of critical periods does not seem to hold any longer as an approximation. The reason may be that the overlap with R_1 violates independence of events across ED-specific sections. Despite this, fundamental range properties are maintained. Moreover, 16 observed maxima of cISI-density are located significantly close to a lattice of 9 ms distances, which supports the assumption that timing is related to R_2 wherein this is the smallest possible distance. Four of these peaks are statistically significant as single values and exhibit the integer ratios of 3:4:6:8 (see Kompass et al., 2001).

CONSIDERATIONS AND CONCLUSIONS OF POSSIBLE SIGNIFICANCE TO BINDING

These results strongly suggest that basic temporal regularities of perceptual transition in simple psychophysical tasks, and those obtained for the more complex spatio-temporal configurations in apparent motion, are not different in principle. Because perceptual change in the case of apparent motion corresponds to transitions between different perceptual interpretations of the same physical spatio-temporal configurations, relatedness to the binding problem seems obvious. This motivates a more detailed analysis of the possible role that the identified critical periods may play in the maintenance and disintegration of motion percepts although the involved mechanisms are likely to be highly specialized.

Physiological approaches emphasize oscillations as possible address mechanisms for flexible access to information to be processed jointly (Singer, 1999). Do our findings tell us something about such relationships?

In a restricted sense, the answer is Yes. In beta movement, for fixed ED, stimulus induced timing can be represented by sequences ISI_1 ED, ISI_2 ED, ISI_3 ED, ISI_4 ED, ... , ISI_N ED with $ISI_1 > ISI_2 > ISI_3 > ISI_4 > ISI_N$,where the index value N is to denote the break-down of apparent motion. As results indicate, ISI_N is quantized in a majority of instances. But the experimenter-defined ED values are not. Consequently, the full period $ISI_N + ED$ does not show a regular quantum structure. Therefore, if the observed quantal periods have anything to do with binding, this cannot mean maintenance of the cycling percept by a periodic carrier process of period duration ISI + ED or fractions of it. Rather, ISI must be timed by entrained “single-shot” activity in each half cycle of motion anew. Correspondingly, integration by temporal binding is to be understood as a repeating local process. As a general consequence, the demonstration of aperiodic quantal timing suggests that synchronous oscillations in the brain persisting over more than a brief period of a few milliseconds may not be a necessary condition for temporal binding to occur.

These conclusions are based upon the supposition that the break-down of beta movement at quantal cISI values is indicative of the role of ISI as a constituent of the integration process yielding the percept. In general, however, it will not be possible to decide which of two alternating percepts a quantal break-down is related to, or whether it is characteristic only of the transition between them. That a decision seems possible for beta movement is due to the fact that the transition between the alternating percepts corresponds to a spatial redistribution in perceptual appearance which has no counterpart in gamma movement. To see this, one has to express the inter-stimulus interval of flickering defined by ISI_F in terms of the inter-stimulus interval of beta movement defined by ISI_M. This relation is $ISI_F = 2ISI_M + ED$. Therefore, quantal levels of ISI_M translate into functions that increase with ED, that is, in a way unrelated to quantal regularities. This strongly suggests that the process critical for transition relates to the motion percept rather than to flickering.

In conjunction with the "single-shot" argument, it follows that the point of break-down should have the character of a threshold below which the perceptual system is incapable of connecting the sensory signals of sequential stimuli in order to produce the percept of one moving object. Change to flickering below threshold thus appears not as a transition to a competing alternative state of binding. Rather, it presents itself as the automatic consequence of lost access to momentary temporal integration which through repetition constitutes perceived periodic movement.

These conclusions do, of course, not exclude the existence of more global oscillation-based neural processes corresponding to seen forth-and-back motion as a continuing event or to single-trial apparent motion (e.g., Neuhaus, 1930). However, the empirical cISIs of break-down of apparent motion at simultaneity threshold do not permit inferences as to the existence of such global processes.

A convincing argument for a relation to cyclic processes in the brain, which are present not only at the very moment of change but function as neural carriers of constituent processes, comes from investigations with a different paradigm by Elliott and Müller (e.g., 2000; also this issue). Elliott and Müller demonstrated that detection of a target configuration requiring stimulus disambiguation is modulated by premasks repeating at defined frequencies, if the premasks include a temporally separated and figurally relevant configuration. By our interpretation, the rapid transitions between interpretations in this task is part of the processing of test stimuli. The crucial point is that the inducing periodic activity persists for a certain period of time after premask offset as a free oscillation and that facilitation varies as a function of phase. Times of persistence, as far as investigated, agree with limits of temporal coherence predicted by TQM. A maximum of enhancement was observed at inducing frequencies of around 40 Hz. Most recent findings within the same paradigm (Elliott & Müller, 1999), however, suggest even finer temporal structures which closely agree with those reviewed in this paper. Specifically, Elliott and Müller report that the RT-priming effects occurred at approximately 6 Hz intervals. In the time domain, these separations translate into intervals of 4.28–4.51 ms, that is, periods fairly close to the assumed time quantum of the order of 4.5 ms. Whatever the final exact interpretation of this finding may be, it ensures involvement of fine-tuned oscillatory processes in the perception of ambiguous figures never previously reported in the binding literature. As these processes are not produced by inducing oscillations at the moments of presentation of test stimuli, they are likely to emerge as part of the constituent perceptual process itself.

The precision of timing in our and in Elliott and Müller's paradigms is not easily reconciled with physiological measurements concerning synchronous activity involved in binding which show much higher variability (e.g., see Eckhorn et al., this issue). This is, however, not a question of principle. Since fine-grained temporal quantization in several paradigms is a psychologically well-established fact, sooner or later physiological correlates of it will be found. Currently, two reasons can be seen, which, in isolation or together, may be responsible for obscuring quantal relations in physiological records: First, in the view of the-winner-takes-all principle, directly effect-related quantized activity necessarily makes up but small fractions of co-occurring "envelope activity" representing neuronal processes that participate in the race, but are only indirectly related to the ultimate effect. Second, according to TQM, the fractions of directly effect-related activity are to be considered as composites of non-stationary components whose relevance for information processing expresses itself in their mutual tuning. In addition, these components will normally differ in their topographical distribution. Their detection on the background of other activity requires therefore refined techniques taking into regard just these properties which are still in an early stage of development (see Schack, Vath, Petsche, Geissler, & Möller, 2001).

In any case, the extreme precision and individual agreement of quantal periods in apparent motion which keep within the limits of ±1 ms are rather challenging for physiological research. Interestingly, a precision as high as this has already been shown for neural signal generation and propagation on the level of single-cell analysis by Abeles and co-workers (e.g., Abeles, Vaadia, Bergman, Prut, Haalman, & Slovin, 1994). By single-cell recordings from the forebrain of monkeys, these authors demonstrated inter-spike interval durations to reoccur with a precision of ±1 ms many times during information processing within and between cells for periods of up to 200 ms durations. At first glance, it appears puzzling that up to these durations there were no indications of a Weber-law-type increase in variance. This can, however, be explained, when assuming that this extreme precision is bound to activity reverberating between fixed groups of identical neurons, whereas the global result of information processing refers to ever changing subgroups of neurons. This account is compatible with our own finding that dispersions increasing with durations are mainly concentrated in the non-quantized fraction of data. It could also explain the drop of variability around the most prominent quantal period at 110 ms, which may be based on activity attracting much larger neuronal masses than cyclic activity of other periods.

A theoretically profound question concerns the general relations between binding on the one hand and rules of discrete timing as stated by TQM on the other. To provide a tentative answer, we have to go beyond the description of temporally quantal effects. Indeed, it would be extremely surprising if quantum regularities arising under special conditions would have nothing to do with the laws according to which phenomena develop that under most circumstances show no obvious signs of temporal quantization. The view of TQM is different. States of quantal temporal structuring are considered as convenient starting points for the formulation of invariants which apply to other cases as well, including chaotic states (e.g., see Geissler et al., 1999; Geissler & Kompass, 1999). Furthermore, complete initial synchronization or formation of complete oscillation hierarchies as postulated in the oscillatory implementation of TQM are merely easily tractable idealizations. To account for concrete conditions, they have in many cases to be replaced by partial synchronization or formation of incomplete hierarchies of varying depths. Generally, the rules formulated by TQM are seen to represent hypothetical elements of a temporal coding system ensuring precise communication among neural units that, depending on their function and phylogenetic origin, may differ widely in their temporal characteristics (Geissler et al., 1999, p. 708).

As a consequence of this view, we hypothesize that oscillatory processes involved in binding are generally subject to same rules acting as non-specific temporal constraints. The foregoing deliberations on apparent motion and target disambiguation can be considered as first examples indicating that these constraints provide new tools of phenomenological analysis. Beyond this, however, quantal constraints will yield strict quantitative criteria for deciding among otherwise equivalent microtheories.

REFERENCES

Abeles, M., Vaadia, E., Bergman, H., Prut, Y., Haalman, I., & Slovin, H. (1993). Dynamics of neural interactions in the frontal cortex of behaving monkeys. *Concepts in Neuroscience, 4*(2), 131–158.

Brecher, G.A. (1932). Die Entstehung und biologische Bedeutung der subjektiven Zeiteinheit—des Moments [Emergence and biological significance of the subjective time unit—the moment]. *Zeitschrift für vergleichende Physiologie, 18*, 204–243.

Elliott, M.A., & Müller, H.J. (1999). *On the role of 40-Hz, and evidence of faster frequency oscillations during visual-object perception.* Paper presented at the 15th annual meeting of the International Society for Psychophysics, Tempe, Arizona, USA.

Elliott, M.A., & Müller, H.J. (2000). Evidence for a 40-Hz oscillatory short-term visual memory revealed by human reaction-time measurements. *Journal of Experimental Psychology: Learning, Memory and Cognition, 26*(3), 703–718.

Geissler, H.-G. (1985). Sources of seeming redundancy in temporally quantized information processing. In G. d'Ydewalle (Ed.), *Cognitive information processing and motivation: Selected/revised papers of the 23rd International Congress of Psychology* (Vol. 3, pp. 119–128). Amsterdam: North-Holland.

Geissler, H.-G. (1987). The temporal architecture of central information processing: Evidence for a tentative time-quantum model. *Psychological Research*, *49*, 99–106.

Geissler, H.-G. (1990). Foundations of quantized processing. In H.-G. Geissler (Ed.), *Psychophysical explorations of mental structures* (pp. 193–210). Göttingen/Toronto: Hogrefe & Huber.

Geissler, H.-G. (1991). Zeitcodekonstanten—ein Bindeglied zwischen Psychologie und Physiologie bei der Erforschung kognitiver Prozesse? Hypothesen und Überlegungen zu Quantenstrukturen in der Alphaaktivität des Gehirns [Time code constants—a link between psychology and physiology in the investigation of cognitive processes? Hypotheses and deliberations on quantal structures in the alpha activity of the brain]. *Zeitschrift für Psychologie, 199*, 121–143.

Geissler, H.-G. (1992). New magic numbers in mental activity: On a taxonomic system for critical time periods. In H.-G. Geissler, S.W. Link, & J.T. Townsend (Eds.), *Cognition, information processing and psychophysics* (pp. 293–321). Hillsdale, NJ: Lawrence Erlbaum Associates Inc.

Geissler, H.-G. (1997). From behavior to nonlinear brain dynamics. *International Journal of Psychophysiology*, *26*, 381–393.

Geissler, H.-G., & Kompass, R. (1999). *Psychophysical time units and the band structure of brain oscillations*. Paper presented at the 15th annual meeting of the International Society for Psychophysics, Tempe, Arizona, USA.

Geissler, H.-G., Kompass, R., & Lachmann, T. (1998). *Ultra-precise pacemaker mechanisms: On converging evidence from movement perception and reaction time paradigms*. Paper presented at the 14th annual meeting of the International Society of Psychophysics, École de Psychologie, Université Laval, Quebec City, Canada.

Geissler, H.-G., Schebera, F.-U., & Kompass, R. (1999). Ultra-precise quantal timing: Evidence from simultaneity thresholds in long-range apparent movement *Perception & Psychophysics*, *61*, 707–726.

Kompass, R., Geissler, H.-G., & Schebera, F.-U. (2001). Temporal range formation: The case of gamma movement. *Manuscript submitted for publication.*

Kristofferson, A.B. (1967). Successiveness discrimination as a two-state quantal process. *Science*, *158*, 1337–1339.

Kristofferson, A.B. (1980). A quantal step function in duration discrimination. *Perception and Psychophysics, 27*, 300–306.

Kristofferson, A.B. (1984). Quantal and deterministic timing in human duration discrimination. In J. Gibbon & L. Allan (Eds.), *Annals of the New York Academy of Sciences*: Vol. 423. *Timing and time perception* (pp. 3–15). New York: New York Academy of Sciences.

Kristofferson, A.B. (1990). Timing mechanisms and the threshold for duration. In H.-G. Geissler, (Ed.), *Psychophysical explorations of mental structures* (pp. 269–277). Göttingen/Toronto: Hogrefe & Huber.

Neuhaus, W. (1930). Experimentelle Untersuchungen der Scheinbewegungen. *Archiv für die gesamte Psychologie, 75*, 11–18.

Petzold, P., Edeler, B., & Geissler, H.-G. (1999). *Discrete clusters of reaction time in a verbal recognition task*. Paper presented at the 15th annual meeting of the International Society for Psychophysics, Tempe, Arizona, 25–30.

Schack, B., Vath, N., Petsche, H., Geissler, H.-G., & Möller, E. (2001). Phase coupling of the theta-gamma EEG rhythms during short-term memory processing. *Manuscript submitted for publication.*

Silverman, B.W. (1986). *Density estimation for statistics and data analysis*. London: Chapman & Hall.
Singer, W. (1999). Neuronal synchrony: A versatile code for the definition of relations? *Neuron*, *24*(1), 49–65.
von Békésy, G. (1936). Über die Hörschwelle und Fühlgrenze langsamer sinusförmiger Luftdruckschwankungen [On thresholds for hearing and feeling of sinusoidal low-frequency air pressure oscillations]. *Annalen der Physik*, *26*(5), 554–556.

VISUAL COGNITION, 2001, *8* (4), 697–704

Subject index

http://www.tandf.co.uk/journals/pp/13506285.html